EDWARD HARRIS.
Woonsocket, R.I.

SAMUEL BATCHELDER.
Boston

JAMES Y. SMITH.
Providence R.I.

REPRESENTATIVE

MANUFACTURERS,

OF NEW ENGLAND.

RICHARD BORDEN.
Fall River Mass.

JEFFERSON BORDEN.
Fall River Mass.

LEMUEL POMEROY.
Pittsfield Mass.

A HISTORY

OF

American Manufactures

FROM

1608 TO 1860:

EXHIBITING

THE ORIGIN AND GROWTH OF THE PRINCIPAL MECHANIC ARTS AND MANUFACTURES, FROM THE EARLIEST COLONIAL PERIOD TO THE ADOPTION OF THE CONSTITUTION;

AND COMPRISING

ANNALS OF THE INDUSTRY OF THE UNITED STATES IN MACHINERY, MANUFACTURES AND USEFUL ARTS,

WITH A NOTICE OF

The Important Inventions, Tariffs, and the Results of each Decennial Census.

BY J. LEANDER BISHOP, A.M., M.D.

WITH AN APPENDIX, CONTAINING

STATISTICS OF THE PRINCIPAL MANUFACTURING CENTRES, AND DESCRIPTIONS OF REMARKABLE MANUFACTORIES AT THE PRESENT TIME.

IN THREE VOLUMES:
VOL. II.

PHILADELPHIA:
EDWARD YOUNG & CO.,
NO. 441 CHESTNUT STREET.
LONDON:
SAMPSON LOW, SON & CO., 47 LUDGATE HILL.
1866.

S. A. GEORGE,
STEREOTYPER, ELECTROTYPER, AND PRINTER,
124 N. SEVENTH ST., PHILADELPHIA.

A HISTORY

OF

MANUFACTURES IN THE UNITED STATES.

CHAPTER I.

A REVIEW OF THE STATE AND CONDITION OF MANUFACTURES IN THE FIRST TEN YEARS SUCCEEDING THE ADOPTION OF THE CONSTITUTION.

DURING the twenty-five years that elapsed between the peace of Paris, which established the supremacy of Great Britain upon this continent, and the commencement of the present government of the United States, American industry received its first considerable impulse in the direction of Manufactures. The various non-intercourse measures and the war with the parent state promoted a steady growth of the domestic manufactures, which it had been the policy of Great Britain to discourage, particularly those of the household kind. Although by no means emancipated from dependence upon the workshops of Europe, a broad and permanent foundation for their future growth had been laid in the industrious, prudent and enterprising character of the early population of the country. Gathered from the productive ranks of the most active and ingenious nations of Europe, with a preponderance of the Anglo-Saxon element, their colonial training was well fitted to develope habits of patient toil, self-reliance, ready invention, and fertility in the use of resources. These qualities, so necessary to success in all the practical arts, were conspicuous in the American character. A varied and dexterous mechanical industry was all but universal. Upon this basis had been long growing up a comprehensive scene of domestic household manufacture from native materials of great aggregate value, which had materially lessened the annual balance against the Colonies, and had promoted the comfort of all classes. Notwithstanding parliamentary restraints, a long and impoverishing war—exhaustive as well of men as of means,—the high price of labor, onerous public debts, and a worthless paper currency, several important branches of Manufactures had already obtained a permanent foothold and respectable magnitude. Some of these had long furnished a surplus for exportation, others only required the security arising from an efficient central authority, a restoration of public and private confidence and a reasonable protection against foreign competition, to become well established industries. Many new establishments and some entire branches of manufacture had been entirely ruined by the enormous importations which followed the peace and by the financial distress which overtook all classes, in consequence of the heavy drains of specie thereby occasioned, at a time when money and credit were at the lowest ebb. Against this state of things, the old Confederation, which had no power of commercial legislation or to enforce treaties, could provide no remedy, while the inharmonious and often conflicting laws of the several States could give but partial relief within their own jurisdictions.

Hence the general enthusiasm with which the adoption of the new Constitution was hailed in the principal centres of mechanical industry and trade as the palladium of the future industrial interests of the nation. The new form of government organized under it, was regarded by the agricultural, manufacturing and commercial classes with no vain confidence as securing to their investments and labors those immunities and rewards which they had sought in vain under the old Confederation. A more efficient administration of affairs now took the place of the wretched system of distrust, jealousy and weakness which had paralysed all enterprise, and new energy was infused into all departments of business. Agriculture improved rapidly; Commerce expanded; and Manufactures, which were still subordinate in importance to the former, put forth bolder efforts. American labor began steadily to change its form from a general system of isolated and fireside manual operations, though these continued for some time longer its chief characteristic,—to the more organized efforts of regular establishments with associated capital and corporate privileges, employing more or less of the new machinery which was then coming into use in Europe. To trace consecutively the leading facts in the progress, during our constitutional history, of one branch of the national industry, is our province, and derives additional importance from the fact that at this time an assault upon the political life of the Republic has, for a time at least, utterly paralyzed every peaceful pursuit, and threatens to roll back the tide of general prosperity at the period of its unexampled fullness.

The first formidable or protracted resistance to lawful authority in this country, since it became self-governing, occurred soon after the war of

Independence, in consequence of those very evils for which in the ensuing year a remedy was so happily found in that Constitution, whose guaranties ambition or misguided judgment would now set aside. That the productive classes regarded the Constitution of 1787 as conferring the power and right of protection to the infant manufactures of the country and thus of seconding the general zeal for their increase, is manifest from the jubilant feeling excited in numerous quarters upon the public ratification of that instrument. Their confidence in the ability and disposition of the new government formed under it to aid them, as well as the extreme peril in which their interests were then placed, are also apparent from the fact that the first petition presented to Congress after its first assembling in March, 1789, emanated from upward of seven hundred of the mechanics, tradesmen and others of the town of Baltimore, lamenting the decline of manufactures and trade since the Revolution, and praying that the efficient government with which they were then blessed for the first time, would render the country "independent in fact as well as in name," by an early attention to the encouragement and protection of American Manufactures, by imposing on "all foreign articles which could be made in America, such duties as would give a decided preference to their labors."

This was followed by memorials from the manufacturers and mechanics of the City of New York, who recognized in the government then established, the power for which they had long looked "to extend a protecting hand to the interests of commerce and the arts," and discovered in the principles of the Constitution, "the remedy which they had so long and so earnestly desired." A petition of the tradesmen and manufacturers of the town of Boston, presented soon after, asking the attention of Congress to the encouragement of manufactures and the increase of American shipping, declares that "on the revival of our mechanical arts and manufactures, depend the wealth and prosperity of the Northern States," and that "the object of their independence was but half obtained till these national purposes are established on a permanent and extensive basis by the legislative acts of the Federal government." Similar memorials from the shipbuilders of Philadelphia and Charleston, from citizens of New Jersey and others, were also received, asking protection and encouragement to their respective branches. Congress, as the guardian of the interests of all classes, appears to have entertained no doubt of its duty and privilege to extend at least an incidental support to the feeble manufactures of the States, as was manifested in the fiscal measures so promptly adopted to discharge the public debts and meet the future wants of the government. In virtue of its constitutional authority "to lay and collect taxes, duties, imposts and excises;" and in response to numerous petitions, Congress enacted as the first act of the consolidated government, after that regulating the administration of oaths to support the Constitution, a statute framed for the joint purposes of revenue and protection, and which declared in its preamble that it was "necessary for the support of government, for the discharge of the debts of the United States, and the encouragement and protection of Manufactures that duties be laid on goods, wares and merchandise imported." This measure, which was brought forward by Mr. Madison, within two days after counting the presidential vote, before the routine of business had been settled, and before the inauguration of Washington, who signed the bill on the national anniversary, after it had received a full and lengthy discussion, passed the house by a vote of forty-one to eight. Thus, in the first Revenue bill, which became the basis of subsequent Tariff acts, the principle of legislative protection to American industry, was recognized by a nearly unanimous vote of many who had been active in framing the Constitution and in urging its adoption in the legislatures and conventions of their respective States. The debate brought into view all the principal questions which have entered into later discussions upon the subject, save that of its constitutionality. This does not appear to have been at all questioned by men who may be supposed to have understood and respected the spirit and letter of the instrument framed by themselves for their guidance and that of posterity. The act of the first Congress, composed as it was, is chiefly important, as an answer to the charge that the progress of manufactures in this country, so far as it has depended upon statutes framed in a similar spirit, has been made in violation of the fundamental law of the government, and proves that the founders of our Government felt themselves competent to afford legislative encouragement at a time when all branches of industry were imperilled by adverse foreign policy and financial disorder at home. It was indeed fitly urged by Madison, who favored a free system of commerce generally, that those States which in regard to population were most ripe for Manufactures, were entitled to have their interests considered, inasmuch as they had yielded up, under the Constitution, the authority to regulate trade, and with it the power of protection, in evident expectation that such power would be exercised by Congress.

It appears that then, as now, members differed in opinion as to the amount of duty to be levied on different articles, as to the duration of
the Act, which was finally limited to June 1, 1796; and in respect
1789 to the question of discrimination in regard to foreign powers.
Madison's original resolution proposed temporary specific duties upon rum, and other spirituous liquors, wines, tea, coffee, sugar, molasses and

pepper, and blank ad valorem duties on all other imports, and a tonnage duty on all vessels, with discriminations in favor of those owned wholly in the United States, or in countries with which we had treaties. On motion of Mr. Fitzsimmons, of Pennsylvania, who advocated an effective system of permanent protection to the infant Manufactures of the country, the following articles were added to the list for specific duties with that object in view, viz: beer, ale, porter, cider, beef, pork, butter, cheese, candles, soap, cables, cordage, leather, hats, slit and rolled iron, iron castings, nails, unwrought steel, paper, cabinet-ware and carriages. Anchors, wool-cards, and tin-ware were added at Mr. Goodhue's suggestion as also deserving of protection. In the Senate, where considerable reductions were made in the specific duties and the discriminations in tonnage stricken out, cotton and indigo were added to the list for protection. The duties on rum, molasses, cordage, hemp, steel, spikes, nails and brads, salt, tobacco, paper, teas and tonnage, elicited considerable discussion, the southern members generally favoring low duties, except on rum, which all concurred in regarding as too extensively used. A capital of half a million of dollars was supposed to be employed in the business of distilling, which had suffered greatly during the Revolution, and was at one time nearly destroyed. The exportation of rum to Africa had been resumed, and new markets opened in the north of Europe. A western member stated, that hemp could be plentifully grown on the Ohio, and they were already able "to construct boats of great dimensions capable of floating down many tons," to the mouth of the Mississippi. Mr. Burke, of South Carolina, said the cultivation of cotton was contemplated in the South, and if good seed could be obtained, he hoped it would succeed. At the instance of the Virginia members, who stated that coal mines had been opened in that State, capable of supplying the whole United States with this important mineral, a duty of two cents per bushel was laid on imported coal. The tonnage employed in the conveyance of American products was estimated at about 600,000 tons, only two-thirds being American, and the interests of navigation were favored by allowing a discount of ten per cent. on goods imported in American vessels, and by a discrimination of about fifty-six per cent. on teas imported directly from beyond the Cape of Good Hope in foreign vessels. The China trade, thus secured to American merchants, already employed more than forty vessels from Massachusetts, principally from Salem, with some from New York and Philadelphia. The cargoes were chiefly paid for in ginseng and other domestic produce exchanged on the outward voyage.

The fisheries, as another branch of the national industry, also obtained a share of legislative regard by the Act of July 4. The cod fishery was stated to have been nearly destroyed during the War, but had so far recovered as to employ 480 vessels, amounting to 27,000 tons, and half as much more in transporting the fish to market. The fishermen asked a remission of the duty on salt imported and used for their business, in lieu of which a bounty was given of five cents on every quintal of dried or barrel of pickled fish exported to foreign countries.

During the session, Congress also passed acts providing for the collection of duties, for the registration and enrollment of vessels, and the establishment of the executive departments, including the Treasury. For this last most responsible office, the highest financial ability was secured by the appointment of Alexander Hamilton, as the first Secretary, who in May following, took as his assistant, according to the provisions of the act, Mr. Tench Coxe, an ardent and able advocate of American industry.

Nearly contemporaneous with the organization of the new government, was the settlement of the great States of Ohio and Kentucky. In the beginning of the year, a new town to be called Losantiville, afterward changed to Cincinnati, was laid out on the site of the commercial and manufacturing Capital of the West. The first log-cabin was built there, in the midst of the forest, in the previous December, eight months after the "Ohio Company" had made the first settlement at Marietta. During the summer of this year, the Company erected the first saw-mill in the State at Wolf Creek, and granted donations of land to those who would make similar improvements. The act, organizing a new Government for the Northwest Territory, was passed August 7, 1789.

Limiting our view to what appear to be the most important events in the manufacturing history of the year, we note the following:

It was hailed as an indication of progress in manufactures, that early in the year, John Brown of Providence, one of the wealthiest merchants and manufacturers of New England, appeared dressed in cloth made from the fleeces of his own flock. The yarn, it is added, was spun by a woman eighty-eight years of age.[1]

During the year, the mechanics and manufacturers of Providence, formed an Association for mutual aid, and obtained a charter of incorporation. The institution proved highly serviceable to the mechanics and the community generally.[2]

The builders of a bridge over the Charles River at Boston, were at this time engaged in building one or more upon the same plan in Ireland, the wood for which was all carried from Massachusetts.

At the opening of the year, the manufacturing committee of the Pennsylvania Society, for the encouragement of manufactures and the

(1) Staples's Annals of Providence, 352. (2) Ibid, 626.

useful arts, offered for sale their first printed cottons, with corduroys, federal ribs, jeans, flax, and tow linen, etc. Under an act to assist the cotton manufactures of the State, passed soon after, the Assembly authorized a subscription of one thousand pounds for one hundred shares in the stock of the Company, and the day following, made a loan of two hundred pounds to John Hewson, calico-printer to the Society.

Another act favorable to the industry of the State, enabled aliens to buy, hold, sell, or bequeath real estate, without relinquishing their former allegiance. It was renewed at its expiration in 1792.

Burrell Carnes, under the firm of Le Collay & Chardon, established a manufactory of Paper Hangings in Philadelphia, which in the next nine months made ten thousand pieces.[1]

The Philosophical Society was presented with a model of a silk reel, by Edward Pole of Philadelphia; also, with a printed book, the leaves of which were made of the roots and bark of different trees and plants, being the first essay in that kind of manufacture. A specimen of petroleum, found in considerable quantity in Oil Creek, a branch of the Allegheny, was presented by Wm. Trumbull.[2]

A Company was formed in Baltimore, by Messrs. Caton Vanbibber, A. McKim, Townsend, and others, to manufacture cotton on a small scale, using the new (stock) carding machinery and small hand jennies. They made some jeans and velvets, but did not ultimately succeed.

In the autumn of this year (November 17), Samuel Slater, the father of American Cotton Manufactures, arrived at New York from England, and entered into the employ of the New York Manufacturing Company, where he remained until the close of the year; after which he removed to Providence by invitation of Moses Brown.

President Washington, during his tour to the Eastern States in the autumn, visited several of the young manufactories in Philadelphia and New England, manifesting an interest in their prosperity.

The first successful crop of Sea island cotton, was raised on Hilton Head, near Beaufort, South Carolina. It was also raised on Sapelo Island, Georgia, from seed of the Pernambuco variety, sent three years before, by Mr. Patrick Walsh of Jamaica to Frank Levett of that place, and both previously of Bahama. In some other parts of the Southern States, cotton began to be a frequent crop from this period onward..

During this year also, the first steam-engine for cotton-spinning was erected at Manchester, England.

(1) Communicated by T. Westcott, Esq. (2) Transactions, vol. iii.

The President's first Annual Message to Congress, at its second session in the following year, was delivered in a full suit of broadcloth, ordered at the woolen factory of Colonel Wadsworth, at New
1790 Haven, Connecticut. The Message, among other objects recommended, says, "That of providing for the common defence will merit particular regard. To be prepared for war is one of the most effectual means of preserving peace." It continues, "a free people ought not only to be armed, but disciplined; to which end, a uniform and well-digested plan is requisite: and their safety and interest require that they should promote such manufactures, as tend to render them independent of others for essential, particularly for military supplies.

"The advancement of Agriculture, Commerce, and Manufactures, by all proper means, will not, I trust, need recommendation. But I cannot forbear intimating to you the expediency of giving effectual encouragement, as well to the introduction of new and useful inventions from abroad, as to the exertions of skill and genius in producing them at home, and of facilitating the intercourse between the distant parts of our country, by a due attention to the post office and post roads.

"Nor am I less persuaded, that you will agree with me in opinion that there is nothing which can better deserve your patronage than the promotion of science and literature. Knowledge is in every country the surest basis of public happiness."

Acting upon these enlightened suggestions, Congress ordered "that it be referred to the Secretary of the Treasury to prepare and report to this House, a proper plan or plans, conformably to the recommendation of the President in his speech to both Houses of Congress, for the encouragement and promoting of such manufactories as will tend to render the United States independent of other nations, for essential, particularly for military supplies." The report was made toward the end of the ensuing year.

In conformity with another resolution of the previous session the Secretary reported to Congress a plan for the support of the national credit, by a faithful discharge of the principal and interest of the public debt, estimated in the aggregate at $79,124,464. The result was an Act providing for the prompt and regular payment of the interest and overdue instalments of the foreign debt and its final liquidation; for the assumption by the General Government of the several State debts, and the conversion of the whole domestic debt into a voluntary loan, subscriptions to which were payable in certificates of such debt at par value, and in continental bills of credit at one hundred for one—the duties on tonnage and imports under new acts, and the faith of the Government, being pledged for the interest.

To provide additional revenue for these objects, the tariff underwent a revision, whereby the duties the House proposed to levy were in the Senate, with a few exceptions, augmented twenty-five, fifty, and in some cases one hundred per cent. above the former rates. The free list was somewhat extended, and an increase of ten per cent. on goods imported in foreign vessels, substituted for the discount previously allowed to that amount on importations made in American ships. The Tonnage Act was remodelled, but without any change in the rates of duty or further discrimination between foreign vessels.

The obvious justice to the public creditors, of the Funding Act, and its advantages, so ably set forth by Mr. Hamilton, soon became apparent. A new impulse was given to industry, and confidence in the stability of the Union was evinced by an immediate rise in the current value of the continental certificates, which had already advanced since the passage of the first revenue bill. A rapid augmentation of the tonnage of the United States, which followed, has been ascribed by many to the discriminating duties on tonnage and imports made in the acts above referred to.

As required by the Constitution of the United States, which was first to ordain the systematic enumeration at regular intervals of the population, as a basis of representation and taxation, Congress passed its first act for a census of the inhabitants of the whole Union. The schedules prepared under this law did not embrace any account of the occupations, wealth, or industry of the people, which have since become universally regarded as an equally important index of the progress and prosperity of nations. The population on the first of August, was found to be 3,921,326, including 697,697 slaves, and exclusive of Indians not taxed.

By virtue of the eighth section of the first article of the Constitution, three other laws, having important relations to the progress of industry and knowledge, were enacted by Congress. One established a uniform rule of naturalization.

Another, designed to promote the progress of useful arts, secured to citizens of the United States, the inventors of new machines or processes, or improvements upon old ones, the right to enjoy under letters patent, to be issued by a Board, consisting of the Secretaries of State and War, and the Attorney General, the sole and exclusive use of their inventions, for a period of fourteen years. The first patent under this law was issued by the Secretary of State on the 31st July, and two others during the year.

An act for the encouragement of learning by securing the copies of maps, charts, and books, to the authors and proprietors of such copies, authorized like the foregoing by the Constitution, and recommended to the especial attention and encouragement of Congress in the presidential speech, granted to authors, citizens, or residents of the United States, the copyright of their works for fourteen years, with the privilege, at the end of that time, of renewing it for a like term.

A memorial to Congress in March, from the manufacturers of snuff, and other manufactured tobacco in Philadelphia, deprecating a proposed tax upon those articles, represents that since the commencement of the Revolution, the importation of snuff and prepared tobacco had almost entirely ceased. There were in the city of Philadelphia, at least thirty manufactories, in which not less than three hundred men and boys were employed. Nearly every inland town in the state contained one or more factories. Snuff mills, recently invented in the city, and driven by water, were in use. Steam was soon after employed. At Albany, New York, was a very complete set of mills for manufacturing tobacco, snuff, mustard, etc., recently erected by Mr. James Caldwell, an enterprising merchant of the city. They were regarded as the most extensive and perfect of the kind in the country. The snuff mill was considered capable of making, in nine months of the year, sufficient snuff for the whole northern part of America. The works, which were destroyed by fire in 1794, at a loss of £13,000, and immediately rebuilt, contained patent machinery of Mr. Caldwell's designing.[1]

March 16th.—The Manufacturing Society of New York city was incorporated.

In April, William Almy, Smith Brown, and Samuel Slater of Providence, Rhode Island, entered into articles of copartnership, under the name of Almy, Brown & Slater, to carry on the spinning of cotton by water power, in which the last mentioned was to bear one half the expense, and be entitled to one half the profits.

(1) The manufacture of snuff and of tobacco for chewing and smoking, was quite extensively carried on in several States, having been early introduced. Tobacco was grown in New Netherlands by the Dutch, from nearly the first settlement, and sold there, in 1646, at forty cents a pound. The extensive and widely known house of Lorillard, is probably the oldest now in America, Pierre Lorillard having commenced the manufacture in 1760. By his widow, and subsequently by his sons, it has been continued to the present time. Gilbert Stuart, the father of the celebrated painter, emigrated from Scotland to Kingston, R. I., (where the artist was born, in 1756), for the purpose of engaging in the snuff manufacture. He was not successful, however, and during the Revolution found shelter for his loyalty in Nova Scotia. A snuff-mill was started in East Hartford, Conn., in 1784, by Wm. Pitkin. Tobacco farms were not uncommon in the neighborhood of Philadelphia in 1790, and Connecticut has long raised excellent tobacco. A duty of six cents a pound, intended to be prohibitory, was laid on manufactured tobacco by the first tariff, and ten cents a pound on snuff this year, 1790. From August, 1789, to September 30th, 1790, 15,350 pounds of snuff were exported.

It was ascertained that the number of gunpowder works in Pennsylvania was twenty-one, in which were annually made 625 tons of powder. Four others were in course of erection. A company was formed in Baltimore, to erect an extensive gunpowder factory in that city. It was built the next year on Gwinn's Falls, and was in operation until September, 1812, when it blew up, and was never rebuilt.[1]

(1) Annals of Baltimore.—The earliest reference to the manufacture of gunpowder in this country, is found in an order of the General Court of Massachusetts, of June 6, 1639, when Edward Rawson was granted 500 acres of land at Pecoit, "so as he goes on with the powder, if the saltpeter comes." In June, 1642, to promote the public safety, "by raising and producing such materials amongst us as will perfect the making of gunpowder, the instrumental meanes that all nations lay hould on for their preservation, &c., do order that every plantation within this Colony shall erect a house in length about 20 or 30 foote, and twenty foote wide within one half year next coming, &c., to make saltpetre from urine of men, beasts, goates, henns, hogs, and horses' dung, &c." *Records*, i. 263; ii. 17. This injunction to preserve organic matters for the formation of nitre beds, was conformable to the practice required of the citizens of London and Westminster, by royal proclamation in 1626, and with that of Sweden, in the present day, where every peasant is required by law to have his compost shed or *nitriary*, and to furnish the State a certain quantity of saltpetre, yearly. It was enforced by subsequent orders, and by considerable fines. In May, 1666, Richard Wooddey and Henry Russell, of Boston, having made preparations for saltpetre and powder works, were granted certain privileges by way of encouragement. A powder mill was built at Dorchester, previous to 1680. A law of the General Court, enacted previous to 1704, prohibited the exportation of gunpowder, and authorized "the undertakers of the powder mill," to impress workmen by a warrant from the magistrate, as in the case of a public work. The numerous French and Indian wars, and the nature of colonial life and trade, created a vast demand in England for gunpowder for America. During Frontenœ's expedition, in 1696, it sold for a pistole the pound. In 1761, the London Society of Arts, to stimulate its production, offered a premium for nitre imported from America. Four years after, expectation was a good deal raised in England, by news that a "sulphur mine" had been discovered near Albany, and some powder manufactories, it was said, were about to be erected in the province. A mill at Rhinebeck, in September, 1775, supplied powder at £20 per cwt. We have met with no account of more than one powder mill built before the Revolution, which found the Colonies quite unprovided with this "instrumental meanes." As the exportation of powder and its materials from England, was prohibited by an order in Council, of October 19, 1774, the utmost encouragement was given to their manufacture by the Continental Congress and the several State Conventions, assemblies, and Committees of Safety. A resolution of the Provincial Congress of Massachusetts, December 8, 1774, states, that the ruins of several powder mills existed there, and many persons understood the business. It recommended the restoration of one or more of the mills, or the erection of others. Hence, the manufacture of powder appears to have been attempted, at least in that Colony, previous to the erection, in 1775, of a powder mill at East Hartford, Connecticut, which has since been spoken of as the first in this country. This was built by William and George Pitkin, under an Act of the Assembly regulating their erection, and giving a bounty of £30 each for the first two powder mills erected, and £10 for every cwt. of saltpetre made during the next year. Liberty was at the same time given to Jedediah Elderkin and Nathaniel Wales, to set up a powder mill at Windham.

About the same time a powder mill was erected at much expense at South Andover,

Considerable quantities of Epsom Salts were manufactured in the town of Bridport, Addison County, Vermont, from mineral springs, which were found, by the Rev. Sylvanus Chapin, to be strongly impregnated with sulphate of magnesia. In the clay soil of a well in the same county similar springs exist, from which those salts have been made.

Massachusetts, by Hon. Samuel Phillips, who the same year founded the Academy at Andover, which bears the name, and has repeatedly received the benefactions of the family. This mill, and another at Stoughton, supplied large quantities of powder to the army. The former blew up in 1778, and the proprietor, ten years after, erected a paper mill at the place, conducted by Phillips and Hughes. One or more powder mills were built in Pennsylvania, before that of Col. Pitkins. The committee of the City and Liberties, in 1775, established a large saltpetre works on Market street, Philadelphia, under the superintendance of Messrs. Biddle, Clymer, Allen, Mease, L. Cadwallader and Dr. Rush, to which the local committees were requested to send persons to be instructed. Congress, the same year, published a manual giving several methods of making saltpetre, in which experiments were made by Thomas Payne and Captain Pryor. Saltpetre works were set up in Boston, by Dr. Whitaker, and by others, in different places. The Council of Safety caused the erection of several saltpetre and gunpowder factories in Pennsylvania, including the Continental Powder Mill, at French Creek, which exploded in March, 1777. They allowed $8 per cwt. for gunpowder.—*Pennsylvania Archives.*

A powder mill was built early in the war at Morristown, New Jersey, by Col. Ford, and being amply supplied with saltpetre by the inhabitants, afforded considerable supplies when they were most needed. The Provincial Congress of New York, in 1776, offered premiums of £100, £75, and £50, for the first three powder mills, capable of making 1000 lbs. per week, erected in the State. Henry Wisner built a powder mill and published a method of making it. Maryland, in 1775, authorized a loan of £1000 toward the erection of one or more saltpetre works, and half a dollar per pound for the product. A like sum was voted to build a provincial powder mill. Saltpetre works were the next year in operation in Cecil County, under John Mingle, and in Hartford County, under Amos Garrett. The tobacco houses in Maryland and Virginia, were also dug up, and the earth lixiviated for nitre. It yielded about an ounce to the quart, and produced much enthusiasm for a time. The discovery of a "sulphur mine" in Virginia, was announced to Congress in 1775, and a messenger was dispatched for samples of the mineral. Many similar discoveries were made elsewhere. Nitre was manufactured in April, 1776, at Warwick and Petersburg, and the Provincial Congress resolved to set up a third factory in Halifax County, under Commissioners, who were to receive 1*s.* a pound. It appropriated £500 for a powder mill in the same county. A Virginian, also, published directions for making gunpowder. North Carolina offered £25 per cwt. for saltpetre, and £200 for the first 500 weight of gunpowder equal to English powder of 85*s.* the cwt.; also, £100 for the first 1000 lbs. weight of refined sulphur. As early as 1707, South Carolina passed a law to encourage the manufacture of saltpetre and potash; and in November, 1775, voted premiums of £200, £150, £100, and £50, respectively, for the first works that produced each 50 lbs. of good merchantable saltpetre. Sums of £200, £100, and £50, were offered for the first sulphur works, producing 100 lbs. of refined sulphur, which the State agreed to take at 5*s.* per lb. over and above the premium. Georgia, also, encouraged the manufacture of saltpetre, sulphur and gunpowder.

These efforts, made under the pressure of a stern necessity, resulted in the permanent establishment of the manufacture of powder in several States, of which a striking example is stated in the text. They were, however, inadequate to the immediate necessities of the war, and considerable sup-

The Messrs. Christopher and Charles Marshall, chemists, commenced the manufacture of Sal Ammoniac and Glauber Salts, on a large scale in Philadelphia. Specimens of these salts had been presented to the American Philosophical Society, as early as 1786, by the manufacturers, who were among the earliest technical chemists in the country.

Clarified or Dutch Quills, are noticed as a new article of domestic manufacture in Boston.

A committee of Congress recommended a loan of $8,000 to John F. Amelung, the proprietor of an extensive glass manufactory in Frederick, Maryland.

June 5.—The steamboat built by John Fitch, propelled by twelve oars, made her first trip on the Delaware, as a passenger and freight boat, between Philadelphia and Trenton, performing eighty miles between four o'clock A. M., and five P. M., against a strong wind, all the way back, and sixteen miles of the distance against the current and tide. She thus accomplished the most successful experiment in steam navigation as yet made in Europe or America. During four months she continued to perform regularly advertised trips, between Philadelphia, Trenton, Burlington, Bristol, Chester, Wilmington, and Gray's Ferry, running about 3,000 miles in the season.

July 17.—Upward of half a ton of maple sugar was brought to Philadelphia, from Stockport, on the Delaware. A sloop also arrived, September 3, from Albany, with forty hogsheads of maple sugar, the property of Judge William Cooper, of Cooperstown, Otsego County, N. Y., the whole of it made on the waters of the Susquehanna. These samples were pronounced equal or superior in quality to the best Muscovado. Loaf sugar, made from the product of the maple tree, by Messrs. Edward and Isaac Pennington, sugar refiners, formerly of the West Indies, was also offered for sale, and considered equal to any made from cane sugar. Otsego County, though thinly inhabited, produced this year 300 chests of 400 pounds each. These and similar evidences of a rapid increase and improvement in an art, which, originally learned of the Indians, had throughout the Northern Colonies for many years yielded the families of farmers occasionally from one or two hundred to a thousand pounds

plies were procured from the West Indies and elsewhere, to which end the commercial restrictions were somewhat relaxed. Much gunpowder was also obtained opportunely by capture. The first tariff laid a duty of ten per cent. on gunpowper, but admitted saltpetre and sulphur free. The price within a year or two fell to £3.12, or $16 per cwt. for powder, for which merchants paid in England, after deducting the drawback, *75s.* or *76s.* Some sulphur was obtained from the interior of Virginia, but chiefly by importation; and in 1791, saltpetre was cheaper in Philadelphia than in London. In 1793, the gunpowder magazine in Philadelphia, which then received none but American powder, contained nearly 50,000 quarter casks, manufactured in that State.

of sugar for a few weeks' labor, during the months of February, March and April, and had been greatly extended by the forced economy of the Revolution, were regarded, particularly by the friends of African emancipation, as pointing to a domestic source for ample supplies of sugar for the whole Union. Estimates based upon information given by Mr. Cooper and others, as to the average yield of each tree, the number per acre, and the extent of Sugar Maple lands in New York and Pennsylvania, went to show that 263,000 acres of such lands would supply, by the ordinary family labor, the whole demand of the Union for sugar and molasses, computed at about 42,000,000 lbs. annually. Each of the counties of Albany, Montgomery, Otsego, Tioga and Ontario, in New York, or of Northampton, Luzerne and Northumberland, in Pennsylvania, were supposed to contain more than that number of acres of sugar maple trees, to say nothing of the large number of sugar trees in other parts of these and in sister States. The subject was recommended by Mr. Henry Drinker, who made the previous year sixty barrels on his own estate, on the Delaware; by Dr. Rush, in a letter to the Secretary of State, published in the American Philosophical Transactions, and by Mr. Tench Coxe, who jointly published a pamphlet, detailing the utensils, materials and process, employed in the manufacture. Large quantities of maple sugar were also made in Vermont, New Hampshire, and other parts of New England.

The ship Columbia, of Boston, Captain Gray, having sailed, September 30th, 1787, with the sloop Washington, of ninety tons, for the northwest coast of America, and thence with furs to China, returned home by Cape of Good Hope, completing the first American voyage around the world.'

Samuel Slater, having completed, under many difficulties, and chiefly with his own hands since the 18th of January, the entire series of Arkwright machines, at Pawtucket, R. I., started at that place, the first complete and successful water-spinning mill for cotton in the United States. The machinery, operated by the water-wheel of an old fulling-mill, embraced three carding, one drawing and roving-machine, and seventy-two spindles. The skill and energy which thus introduced THE ERA OF THE COTTON MANUFACTURE, deserve to be commemorated in some lasting memorial by the American people. By the time list, he appears to have commenced with four carders and spinners, whose names were Torpen and Charles Arnold, Smith Wilkinson, and Jabez Jenks, to whom were soon after added Eunice and Ann Arnold, John and Varnus Jenks, and Otis Borrows.

Carolina planters about this time began generally to clothe their slaves in homespun, from the produce of their cotton fields. The material was usually prepared for the spindle by the field hands, who picked the seed from the wool, at the rate of four pounds per week; and having been spun in the family, it was sent to the nearest weaver. A manufacturing establishment of Irish settlers, near Murray's Ferry, in Williamsburg district, supplied the adjacent country.

A small cotton mill with eighty-four spindles, driven by water, was in operation near Statesburgh, and a woolen mill on Fishing Creek, near the Catawba River.

An unsuccessful attempt was this year made to introduce power-looms into Manchester, England.

The publication in Philadelphia, by Thomas Dobson, of the first half volume of the Encyclopedia Britannica, to be completed in fifteen volumes, quarto, with much original matter, at fifteen guineas, or seventy dollars, the subscription price of the English edition, was the commencement of an increased amount of enterprise in the printing business in the United States.[1] An edition of the Catholic Bible was also printed this year by M. Carey.

Benjamin Franklin and James Bowdoin, late Governor of Massachusetts, both distinguished friends and proprietors of American Manufactures died, the former in the eighty-fifth, and the latter in the sixty-fourth year of his age.

1791 The Committee of the Lords of Trade, to whom was referred in September, 1789, the Acts of Congress, imposing discriminating tonnage and other duties, with instructions to consider and report what proposals of a commercial nature were proper to be made to the Government of the United States, presented a report drawn up by Lord Liverpool. They recommended negotiation on the subject of duties; and while they admit the full right of the United States to impose duties "either for the purpose of revenue or of encouraging the produce or manufactures of their territories," by way of preventing such an increase of those duties as would exclude British manufactures, they suggest two provisions in the proposed treaty. First, "that the duties on British manufactures imported into the United States, shall not be raised above what they are at present." "It may be of use," they say, "to bind the United States not to raise those duties above what they are at present,

(1) The publisher then had but 246 subscribers, and could procure only two or three engravers. One thousand copies of the first volume were printed; two thousand of the second; and when he had completed the eighth, the subscription extended so far as to render it necessary to reprint the first. He then found no difficulty in procuring printers for the work. In 1786, four booksellers thought an edition of the New Testament for schools a work of risk, requiring much consultation, previously to the determination of the measure.—*Hopkins's Oration before the Academy of Fine Arts.*

by obtaining an express stipulation for this purpose ; but, if this concession cannot be obtained, it may be sufficient perhaps to stipulate that the duties on British manufactures should not at any time be raised above the duties *now* payable on the like manufactures imported from Great Britain into France and Holland, according to the commercial treaties with those powers."

The second proposition was, "that the duties on all other merchandise, whether British or foreign, imported from Great Britain into the United States, shall not be raised higher at any time than on the like merchandise, imported from any other European nation." As the basis of a commercial treaty, they offered the single proposition, that British ships should be treated in United States ports in like manner as American ships shall be treated in the ports of Great Britain. It could not, however, be admitted, *even as a subject of negotiation*, that this principle of equality should be extended to the Colonies and Islands of Great Britain; or, that United States ships should there be treated as British. The profitable circuitous trade by which ships from Great Britain, carrying British manufactures to the United States, there load with lumber and provisions for the West Indies, and thence return with the produce of the Island to Great Britain, they say, was wholly a new acquisition, created by his Majesty's order in Council (of 1783), which had operated to the increase of British navigation, compared with that of the United States, in a double ratio, "but it has taken from the United States more than it has added to that of Great Britain." The retention of the American market, and the carrying trade, was thus an object of especial desire,[1] but the urging of it was postponed by the revolution in France, which operated to the increase of American manufactures and navigation.

In conformity with a plan suggested by the Secretary of the Treasury, for providing a circulating medium for the requirements of government and trade, Congress established at Philadelphia (February 25), the United States Bank, with a charter for twenty years, and a capital of $10,000,000, divided into 25,000 shares, one-fifth of which were held by the government. In conjunction with the funding system, the active

(1) Pitkins's Statistics.—Mr. Pitt's bill for a temporary regulation of communication between the two countries, proposed in March, 1783, failed through the violent opposition of the navigation interests, headed by Lord Sheffield, and the death of the Chancellor. The orders of the King in Council, in whom the authority was subsequently lodged, wholly excluded American vessels from ports in the British West Indies; and several staple American productions, as fish, beef, pork, butter, lard, etc., when carried in British ships. The mercantile interests, also, procured the rejection of a plan for a commercial treaty on principles of reciprocity, proposed by Mr. Adams, the American Minister in London, who thereupon strongly recommended the States to pass Navigation Acts, which was done by several of them.

capital thereby created was deemed favorable to the restoration of public credit, and the progress of commerce and the arts. It was the fourth institution of the kind in the country, banks already existing at Philadelphia, Boston and New York; and others went into operation this year at Baltimore and Providence.

On March 2, a slight amendment was made in the last Tariff Act, by which the duty of one cent per pound on bar and other lead was extended to all manufactures, wholly or chiefly of lead; and that of seven and a half per cent. on chintzes and calicoes was made to include all printed, stained and colored manufactures of cotton or linen.

At the call of Secretary Hamilton, an act was also passed (March 3), laying, on spirits imported after 30th June, a considerably higher duty, varying from twenty to forty cents a gallon, according to strength, and an excise duty of eleven to thirty cents, upon domestic spirits, distilled from molasses, sugar, or other foreign materials; and of nine to twenty-five cents per gallon on that made from materials the growth or produce of the United States. For the collection of these duties, each State was made a collection district, with as many supervisors as were necessary, whose duty it was in the case of home-distilled spirits, to appoint officers each to have charge of one or more distilleries, to gauge, prove and brand every cask, according to its contents; and having collected the excise in cash, or by bond, to give a certificate, without which it could not be removed, on pain of forfeiture. On private stills, in country places, using domestic materials, a yearly duty of sixty cents per gallon on the contents of the still was imposed. Every distiller was required to place upon his buildings, and the doors of his vaults, the words "Distiller of Spirits," and before commencing the business, was to enter in writing, at the nearest inspection office, a particular description of his buildings and apartments; when they were subject to the inspection of the officers, who were also to furnish, and from time to time inspect books, in which the distiller was required to make a daily entry of the quantity and quality of spirits distilled, sold, or delivered, according to the marks; and to verify the same by his oath, or affirmation. An allowance equal to the duty in each case, less half a cent per gallon was allowed, by way of drawback upon spirits exported; and upon spirits distilled from molasses in the United States, an additional allowance of three cents per gallon, equivalent to the duty laid upon molasses. The net product of the duties was pledged for the payment of interest on loans, and the surplus, if any, to the reduction of the public debt; and the act was to cease when these objects had been attained.

The discrimination co-operated with the duty of three cents upon molasses to favor the grain distillers of the United States. Notwithstanding considerable opposition, strengthened by a resolution of the Pennsylvania Assembly, then in session, against it, the act passed by a vote of thirty-five to twenty-one. The large number of private distilleries affected by this important act (amounting it is said to at least five thousand in the State of Pennsylvania alone), caused strong remonstrances to be also made in that State, and in North Carolina, Virginia and Maryland, where stills were likewise numerous. The legislative dissent thus expressed, doubtless encouraged the active resistance made during the next three years to the enforcement of the act, particularly in the four western counties of Pennsylvania. Commencing in North Carolina, the whisky rebellion assumed its most formidable proportions in Westmoreland, Washington, Fayette and Alleghany counties, where a large body of Scotch and Irish distillers and farmers questioned the power of the new government to impose so heavy a tax upon the only staple which would bear the cost of transportation, by the means then in use, to the eastern or other distant markets.

Opposition to the excise commenced in a public meeting, held July 27, at Redstone Old Fort, (Brownsville, to which the Legislature has recently restored the old name), on the Monongahela. It was more fully organized by a Convention held at Pittsburg, later in the year, embracing some of the most wealthy and influential citizens of those counties, and was countenanced by the western members, Smiley and Findley, who had opposed the law in Congress, and denounced it among their constituents. Mr. Gallatin, afterward the able Secretary of the Treasury, also opposed the law, without sanctioning unconstitutional modes of resistance. Many outrages were committed upon the officers of the excise, or their supporters. The collection was only enforced after some modifications of the law had been made, and a vigorous exercise of authority by the Federal Executive had suppressed an insurrection of alarming extent.

The distillation of molasses was chiefly carried on in the seaport towns, particularly in New England. In this business, Massachusetts exceeded all the other States together, and had, in 1783, no less than sixty distilleries. The extent of the business is indicated by the quantity of molasses imported into the United States, which amounted for the fiscal year to the unusual number of 7,194,606 gallons. The total exports of American spirits in the same time were 513,234 gallons.

President Washington, having made a tour to the Southern States after the adjournment of Congress, thus recorded his impressions of the favorable influence of the measures of Government upon the credit and industry of the country. "In my tour, I confirmed by observation the accounts which we had all along received of the happy effects of the General

Government upon Agriculture, Commerce and Industry. The same effects pervade the Middle and Eastern States, with the addition of vast progress in the most useful manufactures."

The evidences of progress are also referred to in his speech to the second Congress, at its first assembling, and proof of public confidence in the strength and resources of the Government, was found in the fact that the whole subscription to the Bank of the United States was filled in a single day.

Samples of the first yarn, and of the first cotton cloth made in America, from the same warp, were presented, October 15th, to the Secretary of the Treasury. A portion of it in the possession of Mr. Clay, in 1836, was as fine as No. 40.[1]

A manufactory of Turkey and Axminister carpets was in operation in the Northern Liberties, Philadelphia, conducted by William Peter Sprague, who about this time wove a national pattern, with a device representing the crest and armorial achievements pertaining to the United States.

A "Society for the Promotion of Agriculture, Arts, and Manufactures," was formed in New York, under the presidency of Hon. Robert R. Livingston, whose name also appears among the patentees this year, for a mechanical improvement in spindles.

Through the exertions of Alexander Hamilton, an association of individuals in New York, New Jersey, and Pennsylvania, was also formed for establishing useful manufactures, by the subscription of 5000 shares, of $100 each (of which only 2267 were fully paid up). With a view to the establishment of a great emporium of manufactures, and as a primary object the manufacture of cotton cloth, the company selected the Falls of the Passaic as the seat of their operations, the Great Falls having been ascertained to have an elevation of 104 feet, and to be capable of driving 247 undershot water-wheels, and the Little Falls four miles above, a fall of 36 feet, sufficient to drive 78 water-wheels. The Society was fully organized at New Brunswick, under the following directors: William Duer, John Dewhurst, Benjamin Walker, Nicholas Low, Royal Flint, Elias Boudinot, John Bayard, John Neilson, Archibald Mercer, Thomas Lowring, George Lewis, More Furman, and Alexander McComb. Mr. Duer was chosen the first governor. The company was incorporated by the Legislature of New Jersey under the name of "The Society for the Establishment of Useful Manufactures," with extensive privileges, including a city charter, over a district six miles square, then containing about ten houses, which they named

(1) Memoirs of Slater, 89.

PATTERSON, in honor of Judge William Patterson, the Governor of the State. They invited and encouraged artizans and manufacturers to settle there, by leasing water privileges and by aiding them with capital. Though not at first successful in their immediate purpose, they became the founders of that flourishing centre of industry, by attracting thither artizans and manufacturers of different kinds, even from England and Scotland, many of them having been engaged by Mr. Hamilton, at the request of the company, before the act of incorporation. (*Vide* A. D. 1794.)[1]

At least 32,000 tons of shipping were built in the United States this year. The largest amount built in any one year, before the war, was 26,544 tons.

The cotton crop of the United States was set down at about two millions of pounds, of which one and a half millions were grown in South Carolina, and half a million in Georgia. The total export of American cotton was 189,316 lbs., the average price of which, at the place of exportation, was 26 cents per lb.[2]

The quantity of potash and pearlash manufactured this year in Vermont, was estimated at one thousand tons.[3] This was about one-sixth of the whole amount exported from the United States.

The first patents for machines for threshing grain and corn, were this year granted (March 11) to Samuel Mulliken of Philadelphia, who took out four other patents at the same time, and (Aug. 2) to William Thompson of Richmond, Virginia. Patents were issued (Aug. 26) to Messrs. James Rumsey, John Fitch, Nathan Read, John Stevens, and Englehart Cruse, severally for various modifications of steam apparatus, and for the application of steam as a motive power to navigation, and other economical uses, for which it began about this time to be employed in this country. Several of the patentees had previously obtained exclusive privileges from some of the State Legislatures. A machine for spinning cotton by water power was patented (Dec. 31) by William Pollard of Philadelphia, who put it in operation in that city, but did not succeed.

Mr. Jefferson, Secretary of State, to whom was referred the petition of Samuel Breck and others, proprietors of a sail-cloth manufactory in Boston, asking the exclusive privilege of using particular marks to designate their manufactures, reported that it would conduce to fidelity in manufactures to grant to each establishment the exclusive right to some mark on its wares proper to itself. He recommended a general law on

(1) Barber & Howe's Hist. Coll. of N. J. —White's Memoir of Slater.

(2) Woodbury's Treasury Rep. 1835-6.—Pitkins' Statistics.

(3) Williams' Hist. Vermont.

the subject, so far as it related to goods intended for exportation, over which alone Congress had jurisdiction.

In obedience to the resolution of the first Congress of January 15, 1790, Mr. Hamilton, Secretary of the Treasury, laid before the House of Representatives his able and voluminous report on the subject of Manufactures.

In collecting and analyzing the materials for that elaborate document, the Secretary employed a great amount of industry, and all the energies of an acute, comprehensive, and powerful mind. His labors resulted in presenting to the nation such a broad yet circumstantial view of the importance of this branch of the national industry in all its relations, its resources, prospects, and claims on the patronage of Congress, and in shaping such a system for its encouragement in harmony with all the great interests of the country, as has seldom been furnished to any government. His able refutation of the current objections to the encouragement of manufactures, his vindication of their importance as a source of public wealth and happiness, of the necessity of countervailing commercial regulations, and his suggestions as to the best means of promoting manufactures, all evince the clearest comprehension of the whole subject, and an intimate knowledge of their existing condition. The paper is replete with calm and forcible reasoning, practical views, and the soundest maxims of political economy, while it preserves a dignified abstinence from those acrimonious and invidious references to the policy of rival nations, which were sometimes heard from prominent members in the national councils.

The Report was a noble appeal to the nation in behalf of a branch of the public economy, which had a limited though increasing number of ardent supporters, but of which the importance was not generally apprehended, and was even the subject of considerable misapprehension. It well nigh exhausted the arguments in defence of manufactures, and its principles and logic have formed a common resource for later reasoning on the same subject. The remarkable forecast, and appreciation of the merits of the subject displayed in guiding the legislative patronage into the channel of manufactures, at a time when public occurrences in Europe were about to lead enterprise and capital strongly in the direction of commerce, is the more conspicuous, inasmuch as the Secretary's previous associations had been rather with the commercial than with the manufacturing classes. We regret that our limits do not permit us to present in full, this first Official Report on Manufactures, made to our government—a State paper in many respects one of the ablest in the national archives, and we are unwilling to mar its general excellence, by lengthy extracts, or any attempt at abridgment.

Many of the arguments, moreover, in favor of manufactures, which were novel then are axioms now. We must, however, advert to the fact, that he scouts as mischievous and erroneous the idea of conflicting interests between the Northern and Southern States. He says, "Ideas of a contrariety of interests between the Northern and Southern regions of the Union, are, in the main, as unfounded as they are mischievous. The diversity of circumstances, on which such contrariety is usually predicated, authorizes a directly contrary conclusion. Mutual wants constitute one of the strongest links of political connexion; and the extent of these bears a natural proportion to the diversity in the means of mutual supply. Suggestions of an opposite complexion are ever to be deplored as unfriendly to the steady pursuit of one great common cause, and to the perfect harmony of all the parts." The unity of interest is shown by reference to the demand which would be created in the North for raw materials, among which, cotton, indigo, lead, coal, hemp, flax, and wool, were either peculiar to the South, or produced there in greater abundance and of better quality. "The extensive cultivation of cotton," it is observed, "can, perhaps, hardly be expected, but from the previous establishment of domestic manufactures of the article."

Referring the reader to the Report in full as given in Hamilton's works, we shall limit our extracts mainly to the facts which show the progress which had been made in manufactures up to this period.

1. Iron.—Peculiar advantages and inducements for the prosecution of the Iron manufacture, existed in the abundance and quality of nearly every quality, and the plenty and cheapness of fuel, particularly charcoal. Productive coal mines were already worked, and there were indications of an abundance of coal in many other places. Proofs had been received that manufactories of Iron, though generally understood to be extensive, were much more so than commonly supposed. Several trades, of which Iron was the basis, required but small capital. Iron works were carried on more numerously, and more advantageously, than formerly, and the price of Iron had risen, chiefly on that account, from about $64, the average before the Revolution, to about $80.

In the manufacture of *steel* considerable progress had been made, and some new enterprises on a more extensive scale had been lately set on foot. There was no doubt it could be made to supply all internal demands and a considerable surplus for exportation.

The United States already in a great measure supplied themselves with nails and spikes. They were able and ought to do it entirely. The first and most laborious operation was performed by water-mills, in which boys were chiefly employed, who thus acquired early habits of industry. It was not less curious than true that in certain parts of the country, the making of nails was an occasional family manufacture. The expediency of an additional duty on these articles, was indicated by the fact that in the course of the year ending September 30, 1790, about 1,800,000 lbs. of them were imported into the United States. A duty of two cents per pound would probably put an end to such an importation, a thing in every way proper to be done. An inspection of the articles intended for exportation might be desirable to secure more care and honesty than was observed in this and some other branches. Implements of husbandry were made in several States, and could be made to supply the whole country. Edge tools of different kinds were also made, and much hollowware. Although the business of casting was less perfect than might be wished, it was improving, and as respectable capitals were engaged in this and other infant branches of the Iron manufacture, they might all be soon acquired.

Manufactories of fire arms and other military weapons already existed, which only required a certain demand in order to supply the whole United States. It would aid them, and be a means of public safety, if a certain quantity were purchased annually, to form arsenals, in which a competent supply should always be kept. It might become desirable to establish manufactories of all necessary weapons on government account, according to the reasonable practice of other nations. It appeared improvident to leave the instruments of national defence to the casual enterprise of individuals. It seemed one of the few exceptions to the general rule that government manufactures were to be avoided.

2. Copper.—Manufactures of this article (including those of brass) were also of great extent and utility. The material was a natural production of the country, and mines of it had been profitably wrought. It could be obtained easily and cheaply from Ohio. Coppersmiths and brass-founders, particularly the former, were numerous, and some of them carried on extensively.

3. Lead—Abounded in the United States, and could be made to more than supply the domestic demand. A prolific mine of it had long been wrought in southwestern Virginia, and under public administration, yielded considerable supplies during the late war. It was now in the hands of individuals, who not only carried it on with spirit, but had established manufactories of it at Richmond.

3. Fossil Coal—Was important as an instrument of manufactures, for household fuel, and as an article of freight coastwise, as signally exemplified in Great Britain. Several coal mines were worked in Virginia, and there were appearances of deposits in many places. A bounty on coal of home production, and premiums for opening new mines, if

thought necessary or useful, were warranted by the importance of the article.

4. WOOD.—Several manufactories of this article flourished in the United States. Ships were nowhere built in greater perfection, and cabinet-wares, generally, were made little, if at all inferior, to those of Europe. Their extent was such as to have admitted of considerable exportation. An exemption from duty of all woods used in manufactures, seemed to be all that was required, and was the policy of other nations. An early and systematic preservation of the stock of timber and magazines of ship-timber were desirable.

5. SKINS.—Few manufactories were of greater importance. They were recommended by their influence on agriculture in promoting the raising of cattle. In the principal branches, the progress was such as nearly to defy foreign competition. Tanneries were carried on, both as a regular business, and as an incidental family manufacture. Farther encouragement, by an increased duty on manufactories of leather, and by prohibiting the exportation of bark, which, in consequence of exportation, it was alleged, had risen in price within a few years from three to four and a half dollars per cord, seemed to be expedient, although it was not certainly so. The rise in price of bark was more probably due to increased home demand and diminished supply, than to exportation. One species of bark being in some sort peculiar to the United States, and the material a valuable dye in some manufactures in which the United States had begun a competition, was made an additional reason for a prohibition, and the importance of the leather branch might justify increased duties. Glue, which was rated at five per cent., might be subjected to an excluding duty, with benefit to this branch. It was made in great quantities, and like paper, was an entire economy of materials, otherwise useless.

6. GRAIN.—Manufactures of several kinds of grain were entitled to peculiar favor, both as being connected with subsistence and the support of agriculture. A general system of inspection for flour in all domestic ports, would improve its quality and reputation; but difficulties stood in the way of it. Next to flour, ardent spirits and malt liquors, of which the former were made extensively, and the latter to a considerable extent, were the principal manufactures of grain, and the exclusive home market for both should be secured as fast as possible. Existing laws had done much toward this, but additional duties on foreign distilled spirits and malt liquors, and perhaps an abatement of those on domestic spirits, would more effectually secure it. An increased duty would benefit the distillers of molasses as well. The price of molasses had been for some years successively rising in the West Indies, owing partly to fresh competition, partly to increased demand in this country; and the late dis-

turbances in the islands would enhance it still more. This high price, and the duty of three cents per gallon, rendered it difficult for the distillers to compete with West India rum, which was of superior quality. Hence, a greater difference in the duties on foreign and domestic spirits was deemed proper even by the most candid distillers. Geneva, or gin, was extensively consumed in this country, and distilleries of it, though but recently grown to any importance, were becoming of consequence, and required protection. The smaller cost of some materials, and of labor, in Holland; the large capital employed in the business there, and other circumstances, rendered it difficult for distillers, under the present duty, to compete with the foreign article. An addition of two cents per gallon on foreign spirits of the first class of proof, and a proportionate increase in those of higher proof, was therefore recommended, and a deduction of one cent per gallon on domestic spirits of the first proof, and a proportionable deduction in the higher classes of proof.

By far the greater part of malt liquors consumed in the United States was the produce of domestic breweries. The whole should, and probably could be supplied by them. In quality, though inferior to the best, they were equal to the greater part of those usually imported. A growing competition, increased by whatever would attract capital into that channel, would still improve them. A duty of eight cents per gallon generally, in lieu of the existing duty, would be a decisive encouragement, and probably banish the inferior qualities; and with a prohibition of all importation, except in casks of considerable capacity, would ultimately supplant all foreign malt liquors.

7. Flax and Hemp.—The importance of the linen branch to agriculture; its effects in promoting household industry; the ease with which the materials could be produced at home, and the great advances made in the coarser fabrics, especially in families, constituted claims of peculiar force to the patronage of Government. This patronage could be rendered by promoting the growth of materials, by restraining foreign competition and by direct bounties or premiums upon the home manufactures.

As to hemp, something had been done in the first mode, by a high duty on foreign hemp, and on the whole, was not perhaps exceptionable. Bounties or premiums seemed either too expensive, or too unequal toward different parts of the Union, and were otherwise attended with practical difficulties. With regard to foreign competition, duties on imports were the most obvious expedients. Sail cloth already employed a flourishing factory at Boston, and several promising ones in other places.

8. Cotton.—There was something in the texture of this material which adapted it in a peculiar degree to the application of machinery.

The signal utility of the lately invented cotton-mill had been noticed, but other machines of scarcely less utility were employed on it with exclusive, or more than ordinary effect. This circumstance particularly recommended cotton fabrics, to a country deficient in hands. The variety and extent to which the manufactures of this article are applicable still farther recommended them.

A vigorous pursuit of the cotton branch in its several subdivisions was still farther recommended by the faculty of the United States to produce the raw material of a quality which, though alleged to be inferior to some, was capable of being used in many fabrics, and would probably by more experienced culture be carried to much greater perfection.

In addition to what had been previously stated, it was announced that a Society was forming with a capital, which it was expected would be extended to half a million of dollars, and measures were in train for prosecuting, on a large scale, the making and printing of cotton goods.[1] These circumstances indicated the propriety of removing obstacles, and adding such encouragements as might appear proper and necessary to the successful prosecution of the manufactories in question. The present duty of three cents on cotton was a serious obstacle. The injurious tendency of duties on raw material, as regards manufactures, and their inutility in preventing the growth of the material, were before adverted to. Cotton had not the same claims as hemp, because not generally grown throughout the country, and on account of its shorter and weaker fibre, doubts were entertained of the quality of the national cotton for manufacturing. It would be wise to let the infant manufactories have the full benefit of the best materials, which was the more necessary, as workmen were more unskilled and inexperienced. Inexpert workmen made great waste of indifferent materials. A repeal of the duty on cotton was therefore recommended. A more encouraging substitute would be a bounty on the national cotton when wrought at home, and an additional bounty on exportation. The British bounty on coarse linens applied also to certain kinds of cotton goods of similar value. One cent per yard, of a given width, on all goods of cotton, or cotton and linen, made in the United States, with one cent additional per pound on the material, when of domestic growth, would be a considerable aid both to the production and manufacture. The magnitude of the object would justify the expense. The printing and staining of cottons was a distinct business. It was easily accomplished, and added much to the value of white goods, and deserved to be encouraged. A drawback of the whole

(1) The Society referred to was that incorporated by the Legislature of New Jersey, and which commenced operations at the Falls of the Passaic, near Patterson.

or part of the duty on imported white cottons, would be a powerful encouragement until such time as there was a domestic supply. The duty of seven and a half per cent. on certain kinds of cottons, if extended to all goods of cotton, or principally cotton, would probably counterbalance the effect of the proposed drawback on the fabrication.

"Manufactures of cotton goods not long since established at Beverly, in Massachusetts, and at Providence, in the State of Rhode Island, and conducted with a perseverance corresponding with the patriotic motives which began them, seem to have overcome the first obstacles to success; producing corduroys, velverets, fustians and jeans, and other similar articles, of a quality which would bear a comparison with the like articles brought from Manchester. The one at Providence had the merit of being the first to introduce into the United States the celebrated cotton-mill, which not only furnishes materials for that manufactory itself, but for the supply of private families for household manufacture."

Other manufactures of the same material, as regular businesses, had also been begun at different places in the State of Connecticut, but all upon a smaller scale than those above mentioned. Some essays were also making in the printing and staining of cotton goods. There were several small establishments of this kind already on foot.

9. Wool.—In a climate like ours, the woolen branch could not be regarded as inferior to any which relates to the clothing of the inhabitants. Household manufactures of this material were carried on to a very interesting extent. But the only branch which could be said to have acquired maturity, was the making of hats. Hats of wool, and of wool and fur, were made in large quantities in different States, and materials only were wanting to render the manufacture equal to the demand.

"A promising essay toward the fabrication of cloths, cassimeres, and other woolen goods, is likewise going on at Hartford, in Connecticut. Specimens of the different kinds which are made, in the possession of the Secretary, evince that these fabrics have attained a very considerable degree of perfection. Their quality certainly surpasses any thing that could have been looked for in so short a time, and under so great disadvantages; and conspires with the scantiness of the means which have been at the commamd of the directors, to form the eulogium of that public spirit, perseverance and judgment, which have been able to accomplish so much."

To promote an abundant supply of wool, would probably best serve to cherish and promote this precious embryo. To encourage the raising and improving the breed of sheep for this end would be the most desirable expedient, but might not be sufficient, as it was yet doubtful whether our wool was capable of being rendered fit for the finer fabrics. Premiums would best promote the domestic, and bounties the foreign supply. The first might be accomplished by an institution to be hereafter submitted. The last required specific legislation. A fund for the purpose of duties could be derived from an addition of two and a half per cent. to the present rate of duty on carpets and carpeting, which might encourage some beginnings already made toward their manufacture at home.

10. Silk—Is produced with great facility in the United States. Some pleasing essays were made in Connecticut. Stockings, handkerchiefs, ribbons and buttons were made, though as yet in small quantities. A manufactory of lace on a scale not very extensive, had been long memorable at Ipswich, in Massachusetts. An exception of the materials from the present duty on importation, and premiums upon the production, to be dispensed under the direction of the institution before alluded to, seem to be the only encouragement advisable at so early a stage.

11. Glass.—The materials of glass are everywhere found. In the United States, there was no deficiency. The sands and stones called *tarso*, which include flinty and crystalline substances generally, and the salts of various plants, particularly of the sea-weed Kali, or Kelp, were the essential ingredients. Fuel was abundant for such manufactures. They however required large capitals and much manual labor. Different manufactures of glass were on foot in the United States, and received considerable encouragement in the duty of two and a half per cent. If more was given, a bounty on window-glass and black bottles would be the most proper. Bottles were an important item in breweries, and a deficiency was complained of.

12. Gunpowder.—No small progress had been made of late in the manufacture of this important article. It ought to be considered as already established, but its high importance renders its extension desirable. Its present encouragement was a duty of ten per cent. on the rival article, and the free admission of saltpetre. It would be proper also to exempt sulphur from duty, as little had been as yet produced from internal sources. Its use in finishing the bottoms of ships was a farther reason. To regulate its inspection would also have a favorable tendency.

13. Paper.—Manufactures of paper were among those which had arrived at the greatest maturity and were most adequate to national supply. Profitable progress had been made in Paper hangings. This branch was adequately protected by the duty on imported articles, in the list of which shooting and cartridge paper were however omitted, and being simple manufactures necessary to military supply, and in ship-building, were equally entitled to encouragement with other kinds.

14. Printed Books.—The great number of presses in the United States, was sufficient to render us independent of foreign countries for

the printing of the books used in the country. The business would be aided by a duty of ten per cent. instead of five, as now charged. The difference, it was conceived, would have no unfavorable tendency upon the supply of books to families, schools, and other seminaries of learning. With the wealthier classes of professional men, the difference of price would be little felt; but books imported for the use of particular seminaries and public libraries, should be totally exempted. A constant and universal demand for books in general family use, would stimulate to an adequate domestic supply, for which the means were ample, and ultimately would probably cheapen them. To encourage the printing of books would also encourage the manufacture of paper.

15. REFINED SUGAR AND CHOCOLATE—Were among the extensive and prosperous domestic manufactures. Drawbacks of the materials used in cases of exportation, would benefit the manufacturer and conform to the precedent, in the case of molasses, and distilled spirits. Cocoa paid a duty of one cent per pound, while chocolate, which was a prevailing and very simple manufacture, was rated at only five per cent. Two cents per pound on chocolate it was presumed would not be inconvenient.

In regard to the measures thus proposed, it was suggested that although bounties were difficult to manage and liable to frauds, these objections were more than countervailed by their advantages when rightly applied. They had been shown to be indispensable in some cases, particularly in the infancy of new enterprises. They should however be dispensed with great circumspection. They should be confined to regular manufactories and not to incidental or family manufactures. A diminution of revenue might be feared by the arrangements submitted. "But there is no truth which may be more firmly relied upon, than that the interests of the revenue are promoted by whatever promotes an increase of national industry and wealth." The measures proposed would probably for some time to come, rather augment than reduce the public revenue.

The additional duties to be laid, should be appropriated in the first instance to replace all defalcations arising from an abolition or diminution of duties pledged for the public debt. The surplus would serve:

First. To constitute a fund for paying the bounties which shall have been decreed. Secondly. To constitute a fund for the operations of a board, to be established for promoting arts, agriculture, manufactures and commerce.

An outline of the plan of this institution, of which different intimations were given in the Report, was briefly as follows—

To set apart an annual sum under the management of three or more commissioners, composed of certain officers of government and their successors.

The commissioners were to apply the fund to defray the expenses of the emigration of artists and manufacturers in particular branches of extraordinary importance; to promote by rewards the prosecution and introduction of useful discoveries, inventions, and improvements; to encourage by honorary and lucrative premiums, the exertions of individuals and classes in relation to objects they were charged with promoting; and to afford such other aids to those objects as may generally be designated by law.

The commissioners to render an annual account of transactions and disbursements. Monies unapplied at the end of three years, to revert to the treasury. They might be authorised to receive voluntary contributions for specific objects.

The government, it was conceived, might thus aid in supplying skillful workmen, the want of which, there was reason to believe, had retarded particular manufactures, and in importing and stimulating useful improvements, among which machinery was an important item.

The operation of premiums had been favorably illustrated in the case of certain public and private societies, of which the Pennsylvania Society for the promotion of manufactures and useful arts was an example, although its funds were too limited to produce more than a very small portion of the good to which its principles would have led.[1] "It may be confidently affirmed, that there is scarcely any thing which has been devised, better calculated to excite a general spirit of improvement than institutions of this nature. They are truly invaluable."

"In countries where there is great private wealth, much may be effected by the voluntary contributions of patriotic individuals; but in a community situated like that of the United States, the public purse must supply the deficiency of private resources. In what can it be so useful as in promoting and improving the efforts of industry?"

The Report of the Secretary, so unequivocal in its principles, and so lucid and ample in its reasoning, created very general satisfaction among the friends of American industry. It infused new energy into many branches of manufactures, and induced the mechanical classes to enlarge and diversify their operations. A disposition too generally prevailed at the time, to ascribe undue influence to the measures of government in

(1) In our first volume we have several times adverted to the influence of this Society, as well as to that of one or two of a kindred character in this country. The premiums, honorary rewards, and other efforts of the London Society, are also frequently referred to, and unquestionably exerted much influence upon the progress of Agriculture, Chemistry, Mechanics, and other departments of the useful and fine arts in England and her colonies.

determining the success of manufactures, which in general is far more dependent upon the aggregate of individual enterprise and skill. The proposition embodied in the Report to give direct encouragement to manufacturing enterprises, and especially the plan to which he was believed to be zealously devoted, to establish under a charter from the State of New Jersey, a large manufacturing corporation, was regarded with jealousy by some manufacturers. The special privileges and aid to be accorded such societies, were complained of as subversive of private interests, by securing to large monied and privileged monopolies an unjust advantage in regard to raw materials, and profits in certain branches of business. The project of a joint stock company, to be incorporated for manufacturing purposes by the State of Maryland, was opposed for the same reason.

The publication of the Report in England, early in the following year, also created much alarm in the manufacturing districts. Meetings were called in many of the towns, and fifty thousand pounds are said to have been subscribed at a single meeting in Manchester, to be invested in English goods, for the purpose of overstocking the American market, and thereby discouraging the newly excited hopes of manufacturers.[1]

In lieu of the drawback on salt intended for the fisheries allowed by the act of 20th July, 1789, Congress authorized the payment, during

1792 seven years, of one dollar per ton, to fishing boats under twenty tons; one dollar and fifty cents per ton, on vessels of twenty to thirty tons; and two dollars and fifty cents per ton, on vessels above thirty tons; the allowance to each not to exceed one hundred and seventy dollars. Toward the close of the session an additional bounty of twenty per cent. was allowed on vessels engaged in the Bank or other cod-fishery.[2] By these acts, navigation and ship-building were greatly promoted.

Petitions were received and read in Congress, from the tanners of New York, New Jersey, and Pennsylvania, praying relief from the inconveniences suffered by the erection of mills to grind tanners' bark for exportation, representing that a patent had recently been granted to an individual in England, for the importation of oak bark for dyeing and tanning, whose agents in the different States were paying on an average for shaved bark, from ten to thirteen dollars per cord, and that this increase in the price of bark, from three to four dollars and a half per

(1) Address of American Society, for encouragement of Domestic Manufactures, to the people of the United States, Dec. 31, 1816.

(2) Laws of United States.

cord, which it had been for several years previously, must injure or prevent the manufacture of leather, which, in the United States, was an important branch. A committee, in consequence, recommended an increase of the duties on leather and shoes.[1] The export of ground oak bark for the year ending Sept. 30, was two thousand nine hundred and twenty-one hogsheads, against one thousand and forty the previous year.

Some preliminary steps having been authorized by the first Congress, a code of laws was adopted (April 2), for the establishment of a Mint, at the seat of government, (Philadelphia), and the regulation of the coins of the United States. The officers were to be a Director, Assayer, Chief Coiner, Engraver, and Treasurer. Bullion brought to the mint, was to be assayed and coined free of expense, or exchanged on the spot for coin with a deduction of one half per cent. Dr. David Rittenhouse was the first Director. The Mint was established in Seventh street above Market, where a portion of the building still remains, in which it was conducted for about forty years. The power first used in the coining department, was that of four or five horses, which gave place to a steam engine after the partial destruction of the building by fire in 1815.

As the most feasible mode of meeting the expenses of the Army, which, since the defeat of St. Clair, had been augmented for the defence of the frontier, the Secretary of the Treasury made a report recommending a temporary increase of the duties on imports, by an addition of two and a half per cent. to manufactured articles which then paid five per cent. This measure, however much to be regretted as an increased burthen upon commerce, and on account of the disadvantages of frequent change, Mr. Hamilton hoped might succor and aid the manufacturing spirit, already more extensively prevalent than ever before, and thus "serve to promote essentially the industry, the wealth, the strength, the independence and the substantial prosperity of the country."

In near conformity with his recommendations, additional duties were granted by a new act, May 2, raising the average rate of duties to about thirteen and a half per cent. In apportioning the rates, regard appears to have been had to the spirit of the Secretary's Report on Manufactures. Mr. Madison and some others, who had formerly opposed the duty on hemp and cordage, as injurious to the navigation interests, now supported an increase, as at once a protection to Manufactures and Agriculture. Copper in pigs and bars, *lapis caliminaris*, unmanufactured wool, wood and sulphur, were to the same end added to the free list. Cotton was originally added to the same list, and some Massachusetts and Pennsylvania members desired to retain it there, as an article

(1) American State Papers.

needful to their manufactures, and only to be obtained from abroad. The old duty of three cents per pound, was allowed to remain upon the assurances of Southern members, that it was raised in South Carolina in abundance and of good quality, and that there was no market for it.

To render the excise law more acceptable, a reduction was also made by a new act, of from one to seven cents per gallon, according to proof and material used, upon spirits distilled within the United States. The highest rate was fixed at twenty-five cents, and the lowest at seven cents per gallon. The owners of small country stills of less capacity singly or together than four hundred gallons, were to pay fifty-four cents per gallon yearly on the capacity of their stills, or if they preferred it, seven cents per gallon on the product, or ten cents monthly upon the capacity of the still, with the privilege of taking out a license for one month instead of a year; a provision which greatly alleviated their burthens.

Among the most useful of the numerous societies organized toward the close of the last century for the advancement of Agriculture and the Useful Arts, was the "Massachusetts Society for promoting Agriculture," incorporated March 7, of this year. By a judicious use of its funds in holding public exhibitions, offering rewards for the encouragement of agriculture and the arts, in importing improved agricultural implements and breeds of stock, and machinery to serve as models for manufacturers, and in collecting and disseminating information through its agents and publications, it has been alike servicable to agriculture and many branches of manufactures. A "Chemical Society" was formed in Philadelphia, to analyze minerals, give an account of them, and encourage the manufacture of chemicals. It was under the patronage of Drs. Seybert and Woodhouse.

By a British order in council of April 1, American manufactures were first admitted into that kingdom.

A turnpike road from Philadelphia to Lancaster, a distance of sixty-two miles,—the first improvement of this kind in the United States—was commenced in June by a private company. Two thousand two hundred and seventy-six shares were sold, and thirty dollars paid on each share in about twelve hours. The shares being limited by law to six hundred dollars, a lottery was instituted to reduce the subscriptions to the legal number. The work was completed in 1794, at a cost of $465,000, and the road was afterward paved with stone and subsequently Macadamized.

The Rev. Dr. Stiles, of Connecticut, was shown a silk gown belonging to Rev. Mr. Atwater of Branford, manufactured throughout in his own family from material raised by him, being the first article of the kind of purely domestic production in the United States. In January of the previous year, he saw a pair of white silk stockings weighing four ounces, woven at Norwich in that state, in a loom made in the town; also a handkerchief made at Northfield, which weighed two and a half ounces—both made of silk raised in New Haven and Northfield. Several dresses of beautiful changeable silk, of even and lustrous fabric and bright and fast colors, were the same year spun and woven from native cocoons in the family of Mr. Brandagee of Berlin. One of these, of red and black, was intended for the lady of General Washington, but for some reason was not presented.[1]

The manufacture of Linseed oil was commenced at Easton, Mass., and for a number of years, from an annual stock of three thousand bushels of seed, produced as many gallons of oil.[2] Its price in Philadelphia at this time was 2s.1d., and in London 2s.3d. to 2s.4d.

The Patent Law of 1790 was repealed, and a new act passed, (Feb. 21,) prescribing the formalities to be observed in obtaining letters patent, the rights of inventors and the fees to be paid, which were fixed at thirty dollars, exclusive of charges for copies of papers or drawings.

1793

In March, the Society for the promotion of Useful Arts of the State of New York was incorporated, and had its charter renewed 2d April, 1804. Early in the same year "The Lehigh Coal Mine Company" was formed to work the anthracite coal, recently found at Mauch Chunk, Pa.

About this time Almy, Brown & Slater, of Providence, built at Pawtucket a small cotton mill, (the first built by them, and long known as the Old Factory,) in which seventy-two spindles were employed, which were gradually increased as prospects became more encouraging. Into this mill Slater introduced such regulations as his experience in England taught him would most conduce to the comfort and efficiency of the operatives, and the success of the establishment. Among these was the system of Sabbath-school instruction, which had been twelve years or more in use in England, and for some years in the mills of Messrs.

(1) Holmes' Annals; Blydenburg's Silk-worm, vol. 7.

(2) The attention given to the raising of flax seed for exportation in colonial times, caused the early erection of oil mills, which in some states and particularly in interior towns, remote from market, became quite numerous. The exportation of seed and also its manufacture into oil, was encouraged by various measures of the local legislatures. Oil making was at this time on the increase. It was commenced as early as 1715 in New York, and in 1718 oil was produced in Connecticut by John Prout, Jr. The Moravians, Tunkers, and others in Pennsylvania also, erected oil mills at an early date, and in 1786 there were four within a few miles of Lancaster. Several in Winchester, Virginia, at the same date, paid 2s. and 2s.6d. a bushel for flax seed. A writer in 1789 suggested its use for making soap, as it sold in Philadelphia for 4d. the pound, and for much less in the interior towns.

Strutt and Arkwright, in Derbyshire. These, which were the first of the kind in New England, as well as public worship and day schools, often supported at his own expense, were encouraged in connection with all the mills in which he was subsequently interested. This exerted a favorable influence upon the moral and intellectual character of the work-people, which in New England factories has ever since been well sustained.[1]

Conducive to the same end, was the establishment this year of a Mechanics' Library, in New Haven, Conn.; one of the earliest of these useful institutions.

A subscription to the amount of $25,000 was about this time made in the territory south of the Ohio, for the purpose of carrying on the cotton manufacture. The population of the territory was only 30,000 whites and 5,000 blacks.

The caterpillar, (*noctua xylina,*) cotton moth or chenille insect, which in 1788 destroyed 280 tons of cotton in the Bahamas, and afterward caused the culture of the gossypium to be abandoned in several of the West India Islands, first made its appearance this year in Georgia. It caused nearly a total destruction of the crop. From one field of 400 acres only eighteen bags were made.[2]

Committees of Congress to whom were referred petitions of the manufacturers of cordage, twines, lines, and pack-thread, in Philadelphia and Providence, and of printers and booksellers in Philadelphia, reported that the former branch was a most important manufacture in the United States, whether considered in reference to commerce and navigation, or the number of persons it employed. The exports of cordage were considerable and would probably increase. They recommended an allowance to exporters of domestic cordage equivalent to the duty on hemp, and an increased duty on cod or other lines. In addition to many paper mills then running, several large ones were building, and in preference to a reduction of duty on printers' paper, which the petitioners said was inconveniently scarce, they recommended that rags be exempted from duty on importation.

The political revolution in France having brought on a declaration of war against England and Holland, was followed during the early

(1) White's Mem. of Slater.—The general introduction of Sabbath-schools is believed to have done much to prepare the way for Mechanics' Institutions. Those established by Slater have been spoken of as the first in America. But a Sunday-school, probably the first in the world, was opened some years before the Revolution at Ephrata, in Lancaster Co., Pennsylvania, by Ludwig Hoecker and others of the German Seventh Day Baptists, whose school-house was used as a hospital after the battle of Brandywine. A Sunday-school Society, under the presidency of Bishop White, was instituted in Philadelphia in 1791, and incorporated in 1796.

(2) Seabrook's Memoir of the Cotton Plant.

part of the year, by treaties between Great Britain, Russia, Spain, Prussia, and Germany, prohibiting the exportation of military and naval stores, grain and other provisions, from their ports to those of France. The proclamation by General Washington of strict neutrality in the contest, and the opening of the French colonial ports, enabled the United States to engross nearly the whole of the carrying trade of Europe, and gave an immense impulse to the foreign commerce and agriculture of the United States. The increased demand and high price during the next twenty years, of agricultural productions and shipping, attracted an unusual amount of capital into these branches, and in the same proportion withdrew it from manufacturing enterprises, with the exception of ship-building, which was increased to a degree unparalleled in any age or country. The tonnage of the United States at the close of this year, exceeded that of any other nation except Great Britain; and the increase alone of registered shipping, during the next fifteen years, amounted to 480,572 tons. In proportion to population, the United States had already taken rank as the most commercial nation. Its trade, in point of value, was only second to that of Great Britain. The exports were estimated at $33,026,233, an increase of more than one fourth over those of 1792, and they continued to increase during the war.

Peter Legaux, a Frenchman, having in 1787 commenced a vineyard with 150 plants from Burgundy and Champagne, at Spring Mill on the Schuylkill, in Montgomery county, had at this date 18,000 foreign and native vines growing. In consequence of his success, and upon his representations, the Legislature of Pennsylvania passed an act, to continue in force twenty years, authorizing the Governor to incorporate "The President, Managers, and Company, for promoting the cultivation of vines" in the state, so soon as 500 shares of twenty dollars each had been subscribed. Commissioners were appointed to open subscriptions, but failing to obtain the full amount, the time was extended by subsequent acts until 1802, when the company was organized with Mr. Legaux as chief vintner.[1]

Eli Whitney having, in November of the last year, turned his attention to the construction of a machine for cleaning cotton, completed his first working model of the saw gin. The cylinder was only two feet two inches in length and six in diameter. It was turned by hand by one person, and was capable of cleaning fifty pounds (after separation) of green seed cotton in a day. Mrs. Greene, the generous patron of the invention and the first instigator of the contrivance, eager to communicate the knowledge of an invention so important to the state, of which

(1) Laws of Pennsylvania, chaps. 1,653, 1,694, 2,110, 2,160.

the markets were then glutted with all the ordinary staples, and the negroes without employment, invited to her house gentlemen from different parts of the state. The day after their arrival she conducted them to a temporary building erected for the machine, and they saw, with delight and astonishment, that more cotton could be separated in one day by a single hand, than could be done by the ordinary mode in many months. Its success being no longer doubtful, Mr. Phineas Miller, the husband of Mrs. Greene, (also of Connecticut, and a graduate of Yale College,) and the friend and patron of Whitney, entered into co-partnership with him for the purpose of maturing and patenting the machine at the expense of Mr. Miller. The articles provided "that the profits and emoluments to be derived from patenting, making, vending, and working the same, should be mutually and equally shared between them." They immediately after commenced business; Mr. Whitney having repaired at once to Connecticut to complete the machine, obtain a patent, and manufacture and ship to Georgia, as many machines as would supply the demand. Application for a patent was made to Mr. Jefferson, then Secretary of State, who promised to grant it so soon as the model was lodged in the patent office. An affidavit of the invention was also filed, with the notary public of the city of New Haven. But the patent was not issued until the following March. Before this, however, and ere the inventor had reached Connecticut, in consequence of the imprudent exhibition of the machine above referred to, and the intense excitement created, encroachments upon the rights of the proprietors had already commenced. Intelligence of the invention had spread far and wide throughout the state, and multitudes came from all parts to see it. This privilege being properly denied them until a patent could be secured, some of the populace, unrestrained by law or justice, broke into the building by night and carried off the machine. A number of gins, with slight evasive deviations from the original, were constructed and put in operation before the patent was obtained. A series of wholesale depredations upon the rights of the inventor, of which there are few such examples on record, was now commenced, and received little check either from the gratitude or the moral sense of the community. The unfortunate arrangement of Whitney and Miller, toward the close of the year, to erect gins throughout the cotton district, and engross the business of ginning for a toll of one third, instead of selling the machines and patent rights, stimulated the spirit of infringement. The operation was too extensive and complicated for the means of the proprietors, and was unsatisfactory to the planters. As a monopoly, it furnished a pretext and a market for an illegal manufacturer of the machines, which ultimately involved the patentees in more than sixty expensive and annoying lawsuits; and compelled Whitney, early to abandon all hopes of compensation for his invaluable discovery, especially in Georgia, and to find a more profitable exercise of his talents in another field. He afterward met, however, a more generous appreciation of the value of his invention in other states.[1]

Previous to this time, as appears from a letter of Moses Brown of Providence, to J. S. Dexter, Nov. 1791, American cotton had been so badly cleaned, that Samuel Slater could not be induced to use it, and obtained his supply under the charge of the impost from the West Indies. Mr. Brown suggested that some encouragement be given to the raising and cleaning of cotton fit for the manufacturer.

The manufacture of combs was carried on to considerable perfection and profit, at Leominster, Mass. Two or three manufacturers together employed constantly ten and occasionally twenty hands, who made about 6,000 dozens annually. One manufacturer, Jonathan Johnson, employed five men, who made yearly 2,500 dozens. Ivory combs of excellent quality were made by one person. At West Newbury, where

(1) Memoir by Professor Olmstead, in Amer. Jour. of Science for 1832. The importance of this truly *revolutionary* instrument, in its relations to the political, social, and industrial interests, not only of the United States but of the world, may justify a farther reference to the peculiar circumstances of its origin. Whitney, who was born in Westboro, Worcester Co., Mass., in Dec. 1765, exhibited very early evidence of energy and remarkable mechanical ability, as well before as during his residence at Yale College, where he graduated in 1792. On his way to Georgia to fulfill an engagement as a teacher in a private family, he made the acquaintance of Mrs. Greene; and on his arrival, finding another teacher employed, he was invited to make his home in her family while he pursued the study of the law. Having displayed his inventive talent in the construction of a tambour embroidery frame on a new plan, Mrs. Greene recommended him to a company of revolutionary officers assembled at her house, who were regretting the want of a means of cleaning their green seed cotton, with the remark, "Gentlemen, apply to my young friend, Whitney, he can make any thing." Having never seen cotton or cotton seed, he went to Savannah, (it being out of season for cotton in the seed,) and searching the ware-houses and boats, found a small parcel of it. Encouraged by Mr. Miller, he secluded himself in a basement room, and with such rude implements and materials as were at hand, he made tools better suited to his purpose, and drew his own wire, (of which the teeth of his earlier gins were made,) an article not then to be found in the market of Savannah. He is said to have obtained his first clue to the invention and the use of metallic points, by the accidental use of a toothpick to try the tenacity of the seed, while reflecting upon the subject during a walk (De Bow's Rev. xv. 473). Within ten days after his plan was conceived he had constructed a small model; and encouraged by the result, proceeded to make a larger one, which was completed and exhibited as above stated, in April. Although it has undergone some modifications, the principle has entered into all the most efficient ginning machines since employed. Thus was opened to the southern agriculturist an unbounded source of wealth in a new staple, without which his prospects were poor indeed. The exports of cotton in 1793, were 187,600 lbs., in 1794, 1,601,760, and in 1795, 6,276,300 lbs.

the business first commenced, large quantities of horn combs were also made; and the two towns here mentioned, have ever since been the principal seats of the business. At Graham's comb factory on Charter St., Boston, combs of good workmanship were also made at this time, and probably in some other places. The importation of combs had greatly decreased since the peace in 1783.[1]

Among the patents granted this year, the most important were a machine for manufacturing tobacco, by James Caldwell and C. Batterman, Jan. 26, which was employed in an extensive factory owned by Mr. Caldwell, near Albany, N. Y. (see A. D. 1794); an improvement in windmills, by Joseph Pope; and in the manufacture of bricks, by Christopher Colles (Jan. 26); both among the most skillful mechanics and engineers in the country; double pendulums and clock pendulums, by Robert Leslie of Phila. (Jan. 30); the manufacture of oiled silk and linen, by Ralph Hodgson (Feb. 1); an improvement in paper moulds, by John Carnes of Del. (April 11); manufacturing rhus or sumach, by R. Rosewall Saltenstall (May 1).

A line of packet boats, two in number, commenced running between Cincinnati and Pittsburg, and were advertised to perform the voyage,
1794 each, once in every four weeks; passengers would be made safe under cover, proof against rifle or musket balls, with convenient port holes for firing out of. Each boat was armed with six pieces, carrying a pound ball, and a number of good muskets and plenty of ammunition.

During the past and present years several new branches of manufacture were attempted in Philadelphia. A number of carding machines for cotton and wool were constructed, eight spinning frames on the Arkwright principle, and several mules of one hundred and twenty spindles were erected at the Globe mill in Northern Liberties. James Davenport was granted letters patent, Feb. 24, for weaving and beating sail duck,

(1) Whitney's Hist. Worcester Co., 198, Mass. Hist. Coll. 3,277. The first manufacture of horn combs in America, appears to have been about the year 1759. In that year Mr. Enoch Noyes, a self-taught mechanic of West Newbury, commenced, without previous instruction, the making of horn buttons and coarse combs of various kinds. He continued the business until 1778, when he employed William Cleland, a deserter from Burgoyne's army, a comb-maker by profession, and a skillful workman. That town has ever since held a leading place in the business. Combs were made in Philadelphia, as appears by the card of Christopher Anger, combmaker, in Oct. 1759, informing the public that he continued to supply, wholesale or retail, all sorts of combs, and also powder horns and punch-spoons. The Provincial Congress of Mass. in Dec. 1774, recommended to the people, among other things of public utility, the encouragement of horn-smiths in all their various branches. Isaac Tryon of Conn., a soldier of the Revolution, made combs by a machine of his invention, patented in 1798.

and soon after proceeded to erect at the same establishment an ingenious set of machinery for spinning and weaving flax and hemp by water power. Ten good English stocking frames were imported, and several new ones were made by Messrs. Hadderly & Ouram, who came from England expressly to carry on the business, to which they had been regularly bred. Two Europeans also brought out with them the machinery for spinning and drawing gold and silver wire, and the manufacture of thread lace and embroidery, articles of large consumption for a young country. The manufacture of straw and chip hats was about this time introduced, and was for a time carried on with success and profit; twenty dollars' worth of raw materials being converted into $2000 worth of hats. Wrought mohair and silk buttons had also been made for a year or two at Germantown, by a native of Germany. His patterns were much approved, and were fast getting into fashion when an English imitation of them is said to have been sent in such quantities as to compel him to give up the business, as also happened afterward in the case of straw hats. Two or three experienced potters from England set up their business, but soon abandoned it for want of encouragement. Nearly all these, and several other attempts made about the same time, contended for a number of years with foreign competition, but most of them were ultimately abandoned or changed hands, the projectors going into other business.[1]

On March 26, an embargo was laid for thirty days, and at its expiration was renewed for thirty days longer.

In accordance with a resolution of 2d January, Congress passed, March 27, an act, authorizing the President to provide and equip a naval armament against the Algerine cruisers, to consist of four ships of forty-four guns and two of thirty-six guns each. Six frigates, the Constitution, President, and United States, each of forty-four guns, and the Chesapeake, Constellation, and Congress, of thirty-six guns each, were immediately put on the stocks at the following ports respectively, viz. : Boston, New York, Philadelphia, Portsmouth, Va., Baltimore and Portsmouth, N. H. This formed an initial step toward a national navy.

In May a patent was granted by the British government to Robert Fulton, a native of Little Britain, Pennsylvania, for a "double inclined plane" to be used in transportation. The Society of Arts in London, also granted him the silver medal for the invention of a mill for sawing marble and other stone, which was then at work near Torbay in Devon. A model of it was presented to the Repository of the Society.[2] A machine for spinning flax and another for making ropes, afterward pat-

(1) Essay on the Manufacturing interests of the United States by a member of the Society of Arts, Philadelphia, 1804.

(2) Repertory of Arts, vol. 17. Trans. of Society of Arts, v. 12, p. 329.

ented in England by Fulton, it is supposed were invented about this time.

In June Congress passed acts to lay a duty upon carriages, which from October 1st were to pay, whether public or private, an annual rate of one to ten dollars each; a duty on licenses for retailing wines and liquors; to make all stills not entered liable to forfeiture and limiting the privilege of drawback on exportation to quantities of one hundred and fifty gallons or upward; and duties of eight cents per pound on snuff and two cents per pound on refined sugar manufactured in the United States.

The manufacturers of snuff and refiners of sugar were required, twenty days before commencing business, to render an exact account in writing of every house or building, snuff mill and mortar, or sugar pan and boiler employed by them, and give bonds in $5000 each to keep and render quarterly—on pain of forfeiting all such mills and utensils and the sum of $500—an exact account of all snuff or refined sugar made and sent out by them, of which they were to make oath annually. The duties on manufactured tobacco and refined sugar were increased to four cents a pound each and on snuff to twelve cents when imported from abroad. No refined or lump sugar was to be imported after 31st of December in vessels under one hundred and twenty tons, or packages or casks of less than six hundred pounds, and no drawback was to be allowed on manufactured tobacco, snuff or refined sugar exported, except that made in the United States, which in quantities of twelve dollars' worth, was allowed a drawback equal to the duty, with an additional drawback on sugar of the three cents duty chargeable on raw sugar used by them.[1]

These laws were followed by a general modification of the tariff, increasing the duties to an average rate of about fourteen per cent., and two days after, by a duty of one quarter to one half per cent. on the purchase money of all sales at auction. The internal duties were limited to two years.

A number of petitions relative to import and excise duties, were presented to Congress from manufacturers and others, in different parts of the country. The manufacturers of paint, and dealers in oil and painters' colors, in Baltimore and Alexandria, petitioned (Jan. 22), that the duties on dry paint might be taken off and an equivalent duty be laid on paints ground in oil, or be so regulated as to encourage the grinding of them in the United States. Samuel Swann and others of Richmond, asked (Feb. 10) for an additional duty on imported coals,

(1) Laws United States.

or other encouragement for opening coal mines in the United States. Messrs. Walley, Tudor, Payne, and McLean, of Boston, prayed (Feb. 13) for additional duties on window-glass.[1] The merchants and manufacturers of iron, and ship-builders, in and near Philadelphia (Nov. 3), desired a repeal of the import on bar iron, and were followed (18th) by a counter petition, from Levi Hollingsworth and other proprietors of iron works in the state, asking a continuance of the duty on bar and cast iron, or other encouragement for the erection of furnaces and forges in the United States.[2] Mr. Trappal, of Newark, asked for encouragement to the stocking manufacture by increased duties on hosiery. The manufacturers of tobacco in Philadelphia, petitioned (May 2) against the proposed excise on snuff and tobacco.[3] Memorials were also received from the manufacturers of hats in New York, Pennsylvania, Delaware, and Virginia, and from other classes in the country.

The act which was approved on 7th June, laid on coffee and clayed or lump sugar, one cent per pound, on cocoa two cents, cheese three cents, shoes five cents a pair, boots twenty-five cents, coal half a cent per bushel; on carriages, four and a half per cent., and two and a half to five per cent. on most of the articles paying *ad valorem* duties, in addition to the rates already payable. Ten per cent. was added on goods brought in foreign vessels. By this act, cotton and linen goods (plain excepted) paid twelve and a half per cent., and iron, brass, copper, and tin wares, leather, hats, window-glass, etc., paid fifteen per cent. *ad valorem*, the highest rate, except on wines, spirits, teas, coaches, certain kinds of glass, and a few others. The act was to have force until Jan. 1, 1797.

The first incorporated woolen company in Massachusetts, erected a factory at the Falls of Parker River, in Byfield Parish, Newbury. The machinery was made in Newburyport, by Messrs. Strandring, Armstrong, and Guppy. The stockholders were Wm. Bartlett, principal, afterward sole owner, Wm. Johnson, Nicholas Johnson, Michael Hodge, Joseph

(1) A Glass Company in Boston, incorporated in 1787, commenced the manufacture of window glass in a new factory, of large size and improved construction, on 11th Nov., 1793.

(2) Pennsylvania was the largest producer of pig and bar iron at this time, and considering the number and extent of the furnaces and forges, it was estimated that the new iron works erected in the state since 1787, were equal to one half of all those built before and during that year.

(3) In the debate on the resolution for a tax on snuff, May 1, Mr. Murray of Maryland stated that snuff was then made and sold in the country for twenty-five cents a pound, equal in quality to what was formerly imported and sold for seventy-five cents. His colleague, Mr. Smith, considered the tax would tend to destroy the staple of three or four states; others regarded it as one of the best on the list.

Stanwood, Mark Fitz, Mr. Currier of Amesbury, Mr. Parsons (late Chief Justice), Jonathan Greenleaf, James Prince, Abraham Wheelwright, Philip Coombs, and others. The English operatives by whom it was started, were Arthur, John and James Scholfield, John Lee, Mr. Aspinwall, Abraham and John Taylor, John Shaw, and James Hall, principally from Oldham and Saddleworth, England.[1]

Among the manufactures of Boston at this date, were soap, candles, rum, loaf-sugar, cordage, duck twines and lines, cards, fish-hooks, combs, stained paper, stone ware, glass, etc. Great improvements had been made in some of these since the Revolution, as well in the quality as in the process of manufacture. Soap and tallow candles had been long manufactured. By newly invented American machines, great expedition and saving of cotton had been effected in the business of candle making. Spermaceti candles of superior quality, were made and exported in large quantities, by four different factories. The privilege of making sperm candles, was granted Benjamin Croft, as early as 1751.[2]

There were thirty distilleries and seven sugar refineries, the latter capable of making yearly 100,000 lbs. each, on an average. A large incorporated sail duck factory, made sail cloth which was in high repute. There were several manufactories of cloth and wool cards, one of fish-hooks, Graham's comb factory on Charter St., which, with similar works in other parts of the country, had greatly diminished the importation of combs. Paper hangings were made in sufficiency for the supply of the state, and also for exportation to other states. Mr. Fenton, from New Haven, had recently erected a stone pottery on Lynn St., where Liverpool ware was made and sold lower than the imported. The clay was obtained from Perth Amboy. Iron and brass cannons, balls, stoves, and hollow-ware, were made at the foundry of Paul Revere. Chocolate had been long made from the large quantities of cocoa obtained in the West India trade, and had been greatly expedited by recent inventions. The chocolate mill of Mr. Welsh, at the north end, could turn out twenty-five hundred weight daily. Calico printing was carried on with considerable skill, and the general use of calico since the peace, rendered it increasingly profitable. Plain India cottons were imported for that purpose; but the importation of printed calicoes was large. Pot and pearlash, which had been made there for forty or fifty years, had then ceased, on account of the scarcity of wood. Considerable quantities made in inland

(1) Stryker's Amer. Register, vol. 2, p. 388.

(2) In 1760, Newport, R. I., had seventeen sperm candle and oil works. Lord Sheffield (1783) states, that the spermaceti candles manufactured in the colonies, exceeded in value the oil sent to Europe. The duty on spermaceti in England, was £18 per ton, or nearly prohibitory, and the manufacture of candles for the West India market was consequently great.

towns, were inspected in Boston and shipped abroad. Mr. Wm. Frobisher, of the town, had contributed to the reputation and manufacture of American potash, by investigating the principles of the process, and by demonstrating its superiority for soap-making. Dr. Townsend, the inspector at that time, had also published a pamphlet on the manufacture and inspection of pot and pearl ashes.[1] Glass works, as

(1) Potash was an important product of the American forests, and in later colonial times was exported in considerable quantities. Its production was strongly recommended to the first settlers of Virginia, and was even enjoined by the terms of some of the patents of land. In 1619 and 1620, men were sent thither, in part, for that business. Its manufacture was limited in England, where ashes cost 12*d.* a bushel, in addition to the cost of collecting them from culinary fires. In 1623 a patent was granted to Sir Wm. Russell and others, for a method of making hard soap "with a material called Barilla," without the aid of fire; and also for making potash from the stalks of peas, beans, kelp, fern, and other herbaceous plants, which are richer in alkaline salts than wood. It was renewed in a subsequent reign, and yielded the exchequer, it is said, £10,000. The increasing use however, of those carbonates in the arts, and the interruption of trade with Russia, whence the chief supply was obtained, caused the price of potash to advance from £12 a ton in 1620, to £40 or £50 in 1650. This made it an object to encourage its production in America, where forests were an incumbrance; and potash could be economically made as a collateral process in the act of clearing the lands. The manufacture was early attempted in several colonies. As early as 1707, a law was enacted in South Carolina, "for encouraging the making of Potash and Saltpetre." In New York, where several potasheries, one of them at much cost, were set up under the Dutch dynasty, the business was renewed by a London gentleman about 1709, but without success. About twenty-five years after it was attempted in New Jersey, and again a few years later, in New York, by Mr. Hasenclaver. Experiments were made by John Penn in 1735, and in 1741 a factory was set up in Connecticut, by Samuel Willard and others. About the middle of the last century Parliament remitted the duties on potash, and encouraged its importation from the colonies. Under its patronage Mr. Thomas Stephens, in 1756, published in London, "A method and plain process of making potash," and the same year came to America, (where his book with the proof bottles were offered for sale,) in order to advance the business. With letters from members of Parliament and Gov. Belcher of Mass., he purchased in Philadelphia, in connection with the Messrs. Franklin and others, the potash works of "the Liverpool Company," which had suspended business. They erected a large furnace and additional buildings, and in one month put the new process in operation, in the presence of Governor Denny and other gratified spectators. Thence he proceeded to the Rappahannock in Virginia, for the purpose of starting another factory of the Liverpool Company, which had been given up, and from that to Georgia.

The increased consumption of potash in bleaching, calico-printing, glass, soap, and other manufactures; and its decreasing production in the north of Europe, induced the Society of Arts in London, about 1761, to offer a premium of £4 for every ton of merchantable pearlash imported into London from the colonies, and large premiums also for the cultivation of Kali or glass-wort for Barilla, in the colonies south of the Delaware. Between that time and 1782, the Society paid nearly £900 in pecuniary rewards, and distributed fourteen honorary gold medals to promote the manufacture in America, in which they were quite successful. Among other persons of capital who embarked in the business, was Mr. Edward Quincy, a merchant of Boston, who was encouraged thereto by a personal visit to the

already mentioned, were in operation; hats formed a considerable branch of manufacture, the fine beaver hats being considered preferable to the English.

Considerable quantities of various household manufactures found a

Society in 1760, and six years after wrote to Mr. Hollis, a member, that the business was then so firmly established, that it needed no further assistance from them, than how to assay it, and detect frauds, and maintain its credit. (He states by the way, that he had also encouraged the silk culture to his utmost.) Among the medals awarded by the London Society, was one in 1767 to Dr. Wm. Lewis, and one in 1768 to Robert Dossie, Esq., for practical essays describing the process pursued in America where the best potash was made, the latter also prescribing the management of glass-wort. These treatises, which were circulated with the list of premiums in the colonies, and some American essays on the same subject, gave quite an impulse to the business before the Revolution. Of the American essays, one was a quarto pamphlet published in 1757, in Boston; and another, in 1765, described the process of calcining pearlash as practiced in Hungary, with a cut of the furnace. A Society in New York, on the plan of the London Society, of which Mr. Hasenclaver, before mentioned, was a member, also, in 1764, offered premiums of £30 for the greatest quantity of potash, not less than five tons, made in the province; and smaller sums for less quantities. Premiums were also offered by the Society for the Encouragement of Arts in Pennsylvania, and works were, in 1772, erected in Philadelphia by Wm. Henderson, and in 1787 by John Rhea and probably others. Many persons in England and America, in the hope of large profits, engaged in the business on too large a scale, and as in other branches were ruined. New England, Massachusetts particularly, and New York were the largest producers. The number of potash works in Massachusetts in 1788, was nearly 250. The first in the state is said to have been erected on a very large scale, near Belchertown, Hampshire Co. An immense building was put up and lined with iron bound vats and tubs, and in the centre were built four large furnaces, the fires of which met in a common flue where the intense heat was intended to evaporate the lye, conducted to it in a small stream while the dry salt fell into a pan beneath. After a great outlay for apparatus, ashes, etc., the fire was urged upon a stream of lye, when the chimney suddenly blew up and the proprietor was obliged to boil the lixivium in pans and finally to abandon an impracticable plan. Potash works of large extent were afterward erected at Suffield, Conn., by a Scotch company, who brought every portion of the apparatus with them, and by prudent management and business tact succeeded better. From that time potasheries were built on a more inexpensive plan and were more remunerative. In 1789 some of the most profitable works were set up at a cost of less than twenty dollars, exclusive of iron kettles, which were the chief item of expense. At the date in our text, the business was a large and increasing one in Vermont, nearly every town having one or more potasheries. The business was well understood and much effort was made to improve it. The product was equal to any in America. In Lancaster county, Mass., there were many pot and pearlash works. The first complete *ton* of potash sent to market is said to have been from Ashburotiam, in that county, where it was made almost from the first settlement in 1735. The first introduction of iron kettles in the business has also been ascribed to Colonel Caleb Wilder of Lancaster, in the same county (*Whitney's Worcester*). By the laws of Massachusetts (Nov. 1784), Pennsylvania (1790), and other exporting states, pot and pearlash intended for exportation were subject to a careful assay or inspection as to quality and packing before shipment, which contributed to the reputation of American alkalies. The manufacture and exportation increased rapidly after the peace, and were encouraged by the bounties of different Societies and Legislatures.

market in Boston, and paper was made at twelve mills in the state. Powder was made at Andover and Stoughton. Cannon and iron tools, and implements, as axes, hoes, shovels, scythes, etc., and nails of all kinds in different places. Slitting mills were erected at Stoughton, a cotton mill at Beverley; women's shoes, to the number of 170,000 pair, were annually made at Lynn, and snuff in large quantities in several towns. Within a few miles of Boston the following and some other articles were made, viz.: tow cloth, cotton and linen sheeting, thread, checks, bedticks, striped flannels, thread cloth and worsted hose, gloves and mitts, diapers, cotton and woolen coverlets.[1]

In July of this year the extensive tobacco manufactory belonging to Mr. James Caldwell near Albany, was consumed by fire, with a stock valued at $37,500. A loan of $20,000 was immediately opened by his friends at the bank; the Legislature of the state resolved to assist him with a like sum, and the work people of the city volunteered their labor to assist in its reconstruction. Extensive works for the manufacture of roll and cut tobacco, Scotch and rappee snuff, mustard, chocolate, starch, hair-powder, split peas and hulled barley, were commenced and put in operation within eleven months. The works were decidedly superior to any of the kind in America. All the operations, even to the spinning of tobacco, were performed by water power. The most important machinery was the tobacco mill, patented by Mr. Caldwell and Christopher Batterman, Jan. 26, 1793, which manufactured about 100,000 lbs. annually. The operations employed the next year about fifty men and children.

In the same month, a fire also broke out in the large ropewalk of Edward Howe, near Gray's wharf in Boston, destroying that and six other factories, one-half the whole number in the town, in addition to about ninety-six other buildings, including forty-three dwellings. The largest, being at the west end of the town, were not damaged; one of the latter was one hundred and sixty fathoms long and could turn out a cable of about one hundred and forty fathoms. The selectmen requested that no more ropewalks should be built in the heart of the city, and tendered the sufferers the use of the west side of the Common, where they built six, which were burned down February 18, 1806. Five were rebuilt and again burnt in 1819. The first patent for manufacturing cordage was granted this year, June 16, to George Parkinson, who in 1791, had patented a machine for spinning flax and hemp. But the hemp and yarns used by the Boston ropemakers were mostly imported. There was also a company that manufactured twines and lines of every size,

(1) Dr. Thacher in Mass. Hist. Coll. for 1794, vol. 3.

employing in 1792 over fifty hands. Their cod lines were considered equal to the noted Bridport lines from England.[1]

The discontents among the whisky distillers and others in Western Pennsylvania, on account of the revenue laws, aggravated by a scarcity of specie, now assumed the character of an open insurrection. By the temperate but vigorous action of the President, who issued two proclamations and a call for fifteen thousand militia, order and obedience to the laws were restored without bloodshed.

Aug. 20.—The victory of Gen. Anthony Wayne over the Ohio Indians near the rapids of the Miami of the Lakes, restored tranquillity to the north-western territory, and was followed by a rapid influx of population and the establishment of the industrial arts, to which security was given by the treaty of Greenville in the following year.

Nov. 19.—A treaty of commerce and navigation was negotiated between the United States and Great Britain. By the 2d section of the 15th article, Great Britain reserved the right of laying duties to countervail those payable on goods imported into the United States in British and American vessels. In relation to the West India trade, Mr. Jay on the part of the United States recommended the right of transporting sugar, molasses, coffee, cocoa, and cotton to Europe, neither he nor Mr. Greenville being aware, apparently, that the last named had become an article of export from the Southern States. The ratification of the treaty was therefore strongly opposed and for some time postponed.

The first calico-printing in Providence, R. I., was about this time commenced by Messrs. Schaub, Tissot, and Dubosque, in a chocolate mill on the present site of the Franklin foundry. Mr. Dubosque, who had

(1) Ropemaking had been carried on in Boston and vicinity for more than a century and a half, having been commenced there in 1641, and in Charleston in 1663. In that as in several of the commercial cities, it had become an important branch of industry. The fatal Boston massacre of 5th March, 1776, which precipitated the Revolution, commenced in a skirmish with the workmen in John Grey's ropewalk near the site of the fire above mentioned, some of whom were the first victims. In the Federal procession in Boston, in Feb. 1788, the ropemakers, preceded by Mr. William McNeil, outnumbered any other class of mechanics, being seventy-five in number. The first ropewalk in New York city was built about 1718 along Broadway, between Barclay Street and Park Place. In 1755 several ropewalks extended in the direction of East Broadway from the Bowery. They became numerous and profitable in the city. Several ropemakers, having "large and curious ropewalks, especially Joseph Wilcox," are spoken of in Philadelphia in 1698. They had about sixty representatives in the Federal celebration in 1788, who bore the motto "May the production of *our* trade be the neckcloth of him who attempts to untwist the political rope of our Union." Ropemaking was an extensive business in later years. The first ropewalk in Baltimore was early erected by Mr. Lux, and Wm. Smith built one near Bond Street about 1771. In 1792–3 there were more manufactories in Maryland and Virginia, according to Coxe, than in any two of the states of New York, New Jersey, Connecticut, and New Hampshire. American cordage was preferred by our merchants, even in Colonial times, to the foreign.

been attached to the French navy, and married in Rhode Island, had learned the art in early life, as it was practiced in Alsace in France. The cloth printed was imported from Calcutta. The printing was done with wooden blocks, and the calendering by friction on a hard substance with flint stone—metal rollers being then unknown. A calendering machine was introduced there in 1790, and about the same time Herman Vandusen commenced calico printing in the same manner at East Greenwich, cutting his own blocks, but the business in Providence was the first of any extent in the state. Three years after calico printing was also carried on in Providence by Peter Schaub and Robert Newell.

The first sewing-thread ever made of cotton was this year produced by Samuel Slater of Pawtucket, who commenced its manufacture in Rhode Island, whence it extended into Europe. The idea is said to have suggested itself to Mrs. Slater, whose attention was attracted by the evenness and beauty of the yarn while spinning a quantity of Sea Island cotton. Some of it having been doubled and twisted, a sheet was made, half with cotton and half with linen thread, and the linen was the first to give way. The introduction of cotton stocking yarn in America is also ascribed to Slater. The prices of cotton twist yarn at this time were, for No. 12, 88 cents; No. 16, 104 cents; No. 20, 121 cents.[1]

The first cotton factory of Patterson, N. J., 90 feet by 40, and four stories high, began in 1792, was completed under the superintendence of Peter Colt of Hartford, who, in January 1793, had succeeded Major l'Enfant, a Frenchman, as engineer. Cotton yarn was spun in the mill, the first having been made the previous year with machinery moved by oxen. Calico shawls and other cotton goods were also printed, the bleached and unbleached muslins being purchased in New York. The Society likewise turned its attention to the culture of the silk-worm and directed the superintendent to plant mulberry trees.[2]

A steamboat with a stern wheel was navigated from Hartford, Conn., to New York city, by Samuel Morey of Connecticut, the builder.

The Massachusetts Charitable Fire Society was instituted to relieve sufferers by fire and to stimulate genius to useful discoveries for the preservation of life and property from destruction by that element.

An agent, Joseph Stacy Sampson, was about this time sent to England by Oliver Evans, with drawings and specifications of his steam engine, for the purpose of taking out a patent in connection with the English engineers. He published the next year the "Miller and Millwright's Guide," a very useful work to young mechanics and about the earliest systematic treatise on the subject by an American.

(1) Memoir of Slater, 262, 293, 382. (2) Ibid. 383.

The Legislature of New York granted £1500, to enable a Mr. Boyd to re-establish at New Windsor, in Orange County, a valuable set of works for the manufacture of scythes.

The most important patents issued this year were one to James Davenport (Feb. 24) for weaving and beating sail duck, which was put in operation at the Globe Factory in Philadelphia;[1] the cotton gin by Eli Whitney (March 14); a circular saw by Zechariah Cox (March 14); an improvement in manufacturing paper, etc., by John Biddle (March 31). This process for making paper was afterward put in operation by the patentee at New Milford, which town in its present shape was laid out by him, and a mill for making paper and pasteboard of nearly every kind, composed principally of saw-dust, was erected before the close of the century. An improvement in the steam still was patented (Sept. 2) by Alexander Anderson of Philadelphia, which by means of a condensing tub saved fuel and labor and was generally adopted. A threshing machine, patented (Nov. 5) by James Wardrop of Virginia, was the next year introduced in England.

1795 A supplementary tariff act, substituted after the first of March the following duties, viz.: on printing types ten per cent., and on girandoles twenty per cent. *ad volorem;* on white clayed or pure dried sugars three cents, and on all other clayed or powdered sugars one and a half cents per pound; on Malaga wine twenty cents and Burgundy and Champagne forty cents per gallon; imperial or gunpowder tea to pay the same as hyson.[2]

Memorials and remonstrances were received from the manufacturers of tobacco in Philadelphia, and the refiners of sugar in that city and Baltimore, praying for a revision or a repeal of the act of last session (June 5th), laying excise duties on snuff and refined sugar, and that a tax be laid on the pan or boiler, in lieu of two cents per pound on sugar refined in the United States.

The law was amended by repealing the eight cents duty on snuff and laying instead thereof, the following annual rates of duty on snuff mills after April 1st, viz.: upon every mortar contained in any mill worked by water, and upon every pair of millstones employed in the manufacture of snuff, $560; upon every pestle in any other than hand mills $140; upon every pestle in any mill worked by hand $112; and upon every mill in which snuff was manufactured by stampers and grinders $2240. Entries of the mills, buildings, and apparatus, to be made, and a license obtained before commencing business, and annually

(1) See page 71. (2) Laws of the United States.

thereafter. A drawback of six cents per pound was allowed on snuff exported in quantities of not less than 300 pounds at one time by the same person.

The shoe business of Lynn at this time employed about two hundred master workmen and six hundred apprentices, who made annually about 300,000 pairs of shoes, exported chiefly to the Southern States.

In March a number of public spirited individuals of the most industrious and and respectable of the mechanical classes in Boston formed the "Boston Association of Mechanics," for the promotion and regulation of the arts and the interests of their class. Having in a few months increased in numbers, resources and usefulness, in order to extend the benefits of the Society and meet the general desire to elevate the mechanic interests, they assumed the title of "The Association of Mechanics of the Commonwealth of Massachusetts," and were subsequently incorporated (May 1806) as the "Massachusetts Charitable Mechanics' Association," which became eminently useful in promoting ingenuity and good workmanship in the mechanical branches.

In July 14, the Spanish government made a grant to Senor Marquis de Maison Rouge, a French knight, of thirty superficial leagues of land in the rich alluvial bottoms of the Wachita river in Louisiana, on condition that he introduced a colony of thirty families by way of the Ohio, for the purpose of cultivating wheat, erecting mills, and establishing other useful arts. The Spanish governor was to pay $100 to each useful laborer or artificer, assist in their transportation thither and make a grant to each family of four arpents of land. The conditions were fulfilled by the Marquis according to agreement.

At North Providence, R. I., on the Pawtucket, were at this time three anchor forges, one slitting mill, two nail cutting machines, one tanning mill, one oil mill, three snuff mills, one grist mill, one cotton factory, one clothier's works, and three fulling mills, all carried by water.

A cotton mill of considerable extent, with Arkwright's water spring machines, was established at Warwick, Kent county, in the same state, and answered the highest expectations of the proprietors. It was followed in the next fifteen years by one cotton mill annually on an average, beside two woolen mills, twelve grist mills, an anchor forge, and a gin distillery.

William Almy of Providence wrote to his partner (Sept. 18), Samuel Slater, that Georgia cotton was growing more plentiful. He had received several invitations from New York to purchase a quantity there which was represented to be good and cheap. They then paid one shilling six pence per pound for cotton.

Considerable quantities of cotton were at this time still imported from the West Indies. The total importation of that article for the fiscal year was 4,106,793 pounds, and the exports 6,276,300 pounds.

The first cotton mill in Delaware was about this time put in operation by Jacob Broome at Wilmington, in the Old Academy on Market street. It was afterward removed to the Brandywine to be driven by water, but was soon after burned down.

Paper had been extensively manufactured for several years about one mile from the town, on the Brandywine, by Messrs. Joshua and Thomas Gilpin, and Myers Fisher, merchants of Philadelphia and proprietors of large flour mills at the same place. Their paper manufacture was about this time greatly extended on account of the interruption to the neutral trade with Europe.

December.—The Alleghany lumber trade, a valuable branch of the business of Pittsburg, was commenced by Mayor Craig, who purchased a large quantity of boards for the public service from Cornplanter, the Seneca chief, who had a saw mill at Genesadaga, on the right bank of the Alleghany, four miles below the State line, upon a portion of the Alleghany reservation of the Senecas.

The fourth Congress, soon after assembling, instituted for the first time a Standing Committee of Commerce and Manufactures. It had charge of those subjects during the next twenty-four years, when the duties were consigned to separate committees.

The Act of Parliament of 1786, prohibiting the exportation of tools and machinery used in the iron and steel manufactures, was made perpetual by the statute 35 Geo. 3 c. 38. It recapitulates the several descriptions of machines, engines, implements, utensils, and models, or parts thereof, employed in rolling, slitting, pressing, casting, boring, stamping, piercing, scoring, shading or chasing, and die-sinking iron and other metals. It included machines used in the button, glass, pottery, saddle and harness, and other manufactures, wire moulds for paper, etc. It proved afterward, as it had before, extremely embarrassing to new branches of manufactures in the United States.[1]

Among other patents issued this year was the first one to Jacob Perkins for cutting nails (Jan. 16), and one to Josiah G. Pierson of New York (March 23), for the same purpose, which was soon after put in operation at the Ramapo works of the patentee in Rockland county. Nautical ventilators for ventilating the holds of ships, patented (June 19) by Benjamin Wyncoop, were approved of by a number of leading ship-masters in Philadelphia, as a very useful invention.

(1) Pope's Laws of the Customs and Excise.

Philadelphia held communication with neighboring cities and towns by the following modes of transportation, viz.: with New York by four daily stages, at the hours of four, five, six, and eight o'clock,
1796 A. M., and a line of packet boats to Burlington or Bordentown, thence by stage to Amboy and by packet to New York: with Baltimore by daily stage and a mail carriage tri-weekly, and by packet and land carriage combined (occupying two days in the route) six times in the week; with Lancaster and Burlington by stage twice a week; and with Bethlehem, Wilmington, Dover, Harrisburg, Reading, and Easton, each, once a week by stage.[1]

A census of Pittsburg, giving the first authentic statement of its population, made it 1395. It was incorporated as a borough in 1794.

The excise duty on snuff manufactured in the United States continued to give dissatisfaction, and petitions were sent into Congress from many of the manufacturers, complaining of the inequality of its operation since the transfer of the duty to the mortar and mill without reference to the quantity made. Difficulty was found in dealing with the question consistently with the interests of the public and the manufacturer. The drawback of six cents a pound enabled some large manufacturers to realize fortunes, and more was paid in that way than was received for duties. The gross amount of duties was about $20,000 in the last year, and the drawback allowed was $25,000. Frauds were practiced by the use of hand mills which made no noise and escaped the tax. The amount exported in a year before the tax was estimated at 100,000 pounds. To tax this amount without allowing a drawback was unjust and impolitic. It was stated that one mill near Newcastle, Del., belonging to Mr. Jones of Philadelphia, made 11,000 pounds of Scotch snuff a month, or 500,000 pounds yearly, which, supposing his tax to be 2,240 dollars, reduced the duty to one cent a pound. Another had drawn large sums from the treasury in drawbacks. These large concerns, which had been built up in dependence on the continuance of the drawback, would be ruined by withholding it. To lay a duty of three cents a pound on Scotch snuff and allow an equal amount to be drawn back on exportation, still allowed too much to those who paid no duty. Many small manufacturers had given up the business because they could not obtain licenses for less time than one year. An act was finally passed suspending the act of March 3, 1795, until the next session of Congress. It was again suspended by later acts until April 24, 1800, when it was repealed.[2]

By an act of the same date distillers who were unavoidably prevented from

(1) Philadelphia Directory, 1796.

(2) Laws United States. American State Papers.—Seybert, 469.

working their stills throughout the year, were permitted to pay a monthly duty of ten cents a gallon on the capacity of their stills in lieu of fifty-four cents yearly.

In the year ending 30th June, 1,475,509 gallons of spirits were distilled in Massachusetts from foreign, and 11,490 gallons from domestic materials, yielding a revenue of $148,769.36. The sum paid from the United States treasury for drawbacks on spirits exported this year amounted to $117,014.98.

In June, Philip Henri Neri de Tot Bastrop, a Dutch nobleman residing in Louisiana, was granted by the governor-general, the Baron de Carondelet, a tract of land twelve leagues square for an extensive agricultural colony, on similar terms with the grant to M. de Maison Rouge in the last year. He was required to introduce not less than 250 families, allot 400 acres of land to each, and erect upon the bayous, mills for the manufacture of flour for exportation. The grant was laid out on the bayous Siard Berthelemi and the Wachita, including the rich elevated prairie and the sugar and cotton lands of the garden of the Wachita. Bastrop fulfilled his contract so far as he was able, but the failure of the government to complete its engagement caused the abandonment of the enterprise after the transfer of the province to the United States on 30th April, 1803.

In August another grant of 458,963 acres on the western bank of the Mississippi, now partly in Missouri and partly in Arkansas, was also made by the Spanish government to James Clamorgan, a merchant of St. Louis, for the purpose of establishing a rope manufactory to supply the Spanish navy and the Havanna with cordage. Cultivators of hemp were to be introduced from Canada and instructed in the manufacture. This enterprise was not carried out until the transfer of the province.

The first successful attempt to manufacture sugar from the cane in Louisiana was this year made by M. Etienne Boré, at his plantation, a few miles above New Orleans, where Carrollton now stands. On the failure of his indigo crop in 1792 he had turned his attention to the sugar cane. He bought canes of a man named Mendez, who had made a few barrels the previous year, and contrary to the strong advice of his friends laid out a considerable plantation. He employed, at a salary of $1500 a year, a practical sugar maker named Morin, who had learned the business in St. Domingo and had superintended Mendez's operations, to build and put in operation sugar mills similar to those in the island. He was partially successful in 1795, and completely so in the present year, having sold his crop for $12,000, then considered a large sum. A large and curious but doubting assemblage collected on the day appointed for the experiment. The announcement made to them on the second strike, "Gentlemen, it

5

grains, it grains!" was enthusiastically repeated, and proved not only a gratifying triumph to the persevering planter, but an important epoch in the industrial history of the state. The business of sugar making may be considered as established from that date, though not much progress was made for some years.

One or two varieties of cane only were cultivated at that time: the common Creole or Bengal cane, introduced in 1751 from Hispaniola, and the Otaheite, naturalized in this or the following year. Both of these afterward gave place, in a measure, to the Bourbon and red or purple ribbon cane, a native of Java.[1]

The Chinese sugar cane was this year introduced into British India by Earl Cornwallis.

During this summer a company of fifty shareholders was formed to erect a furnace, and manufacture salt on a small scale on the Muskingum, about seven miles above Duncan's Falls, where salt springs were found the year before. Kettles were bought at Pittsburg and carried by water to the Falls, thence by pack-horses to the licks. A well was dug, in which

(1) De Bow's Industrial Resources, vol. 3, p. 275; Commercial Review, vol. 22, p. 618; Gayarre's History of Louisiana. Father Hennepin, in the seventeeth century, saw an indigenous sugar-cane growing near the Mississippi. The Malabar, crystalline or Creole variety above mentioned was sent in April, 1751, in a transport from St. Domingo, by the Jesuit fathers of Port au Prince, to their fraternity in New Orleans, along with a few negroes acquainted with its cultivation and the manufacture of sugar. As early as 1518 there were twenty-eight *ingenios* or sugar mills in that island. The reverend Fathers planted the canes in their spacious gardens above the town, near Canal street, now in the first district of the city. In 1754 they made an unsuccessful attempt to produce sugar. In 1758 a wealthy and enterprising planter built the first sugar house and mill in the colony, below the town now in the Faubourg Marigny, and attempted the business on a larger scale, but not very successfully. In 1764 the Chevalier de Mazan sent to Spain, from his plantation on the opposite side of the Mississippi, some sugar, pronounced by courtesy equal to the Muscovado of St. Domingo. The yield was said to be three thousand pounds to the acre. The next year the French Colonial Treasurer Destrehan and others, erected works like those of Dubreuil, and the first by the Spaniards on the left bank of the river. But in 1769 all attempts were abandoned. The exports of the city at this time were lumber, indigo, peltries, tobacco, tar, rice, corn and cotton. Dubreuil had some years before invented a machine for cleaning cotton (see vol. 1, p. 351), and was now the richest planter in the colony. He had five hundred slaves, a brickyard, an indigo plantation, a nursery for silkworms, and gathered annually eight to ten thousand pounds of vegetable or myrtle wax from the *Myrica Cerifera*, of which he had several nurseries. No other attempts were made with sugar for nearly twenty-five years. In 1790 M. Solis, a Spaniard, at Terre Boeuf, cultivated the cane for making *tafia* or rum from the juice, which sold readily. But he had failed in making sugar. In 1791 he sold his lands and apparatus to A. Mendez, who employed Morin, as stated in the text, to make and even refine sugar. He presented some diminutive loaves, one of which would sweeten two cups of coffee, to the Spanish intendant. Vines were purchased of him by M. Boré, who made the next and most successful experiment.

was inserted a hollow tree to exclude fresh water, and the brine was raised by a sweep and pole, worked day and night by successive relays of men. About one hundred pounds of salt were made every twenty-four hours, at a cost of at least three dollars per bushel. It was very dark and inferior in quality, being much impregnated with chloride of lime. Every fifty pounds required eight hundred gallons of water to be evaporated. This was the first salt made in the Muskingum valley. The furnace consisted of two ranges of twelve kettles each. The saline was forty miles from Waterford, from which, during the winter, provisions were packed on horses, and salt sent to the settlements in the same way. After three or four years the springs passed into other hands and finally to the state, which leased them at a fixed rate.[1]

During this year also the Ohio valley first began to be supplied with salt from the Onondaga salines through the enterprise of General O'Hara, who, in connection with Major Craig, also made arrangements for the erection of the first permanent glass works in Pittsburg.[2]

The first paper mill west of the Alleghanies was put in operation four miles east of Brownsville, Fayette County, Pennsylvania. It was the "Red Stone Paper Mill," and was erected by Samuel Jackson and Jonathan Sharpless, two ingenious mechanics of the Society of Friends, who had been raised near the extensive paper mill of the Gilpins on the Brandywine. Brownsville (Red Stone Old Fort) then contained twenty-four grist, saw, oil, and fulling mills. A profitable business was done in building Kentucky boats, which were constructed annually to the number of one hundred of twenty tons each, for the transportation of emigrants to Maysville and other points in Kentucky.

Discrimination was first made at the Treasury Department in the value of domestic and foreign merchandise exported. The total value of exports reached the sum of $67,064,097, an increase in five years of $48,052,056. Of the total, $40,764,097 was from domestic produce and manufacture. The imports amounted to $81,436,164.[3]

Gaslights were made and exhibited by Peter Ambrose & Co., manufacturers of fire-works, at their amphitheatre in Arch street above Eighth, Philadelphia. The inflammable air issued from orifices in bent tubes in figures of an Italian parterre, masonic emblems, etc.

John Fitch navigated a yawl by steam, with a screw propeller, on the Collect or Fresh Water Pond, north of the present City Hall in New York.

Robert Fulton, residing in England as an engineer, published in

(1) Hildreth's Pioneer History of the Ohio Valley, p. 476.

(2) See vol. 1, pp. 243. 293.

(3) Seybert, p. 466.

London a Treatise on the Improvement of Canal Navigation, quarto, illustrated by seventeen plates and a portrait. His plans were strongly recommended by the British Board of Agriculture, under the presidency of Sir John Sinclair. On this subject, which chiefly engaged his attention at this time, he contributed some essays in 1795 to the London Morning Star, and sent copies of his writings to the United States, setting forth the advantages of canals. He obtained a patent from the British government for canal improvements and soon after went to France to introduce them there.

The manufacture of printing types was about this time permanently established in Philadelphia by Messrs. Archibald Binney and James Ronaldson, who soon after introduced the hand mould, since known in Europe as the American, the greatest improvement made since the invention of the art. It enabled a man to cast six thousand types in a day, instead of four thousand as by the old process. The success of the proprietors was decisive.

Eleven patents, out of the total number of forty-three, were this year granted for improvements in the manufacture of nails and brads, the greater part of them relating to the cutting and heading of nails by machinery. The first patent recorded for a machine combining those operations, was taken out by Isaac Garretson of Pennyslvania (Nov. 16); and was followed by another for the same process, to George Chandler of Maryland (Dec. 12). Daniel French, of Conn., patented (Dec. 23) improvements in the manufacture both of cut and wrought nails. Oliver Evans patented (May 28) an improvement in burr millstones, of which he was one of the earliest manufacturers in the country. Four patents related to the manufacture of leather, including one for making sumach, and one to James Stansfield (Nov 16), for an improvement in splitting sheep skins, the first of that kind on the records. Of the same date, was a patent to the English engineer, Mark Isamlard Brunel, for a method of ruling books and paper; and one to Apollos Kinsley of Conn., for an improvement in the printing press, which has since been the subject of over 100 patents in America.

Samuel Lee, Jr., of Conn., also received (April 30) a patent for the "Composition of bilious pills," the first of that class of inventions. Lee's Windham pills, and Lee's New London pills, the subject of three or four patents by him and his son S. H. P. Lee, were highly popular for a long period.

Another invention of the empirical class, which created much sensation for several years, was a method of "removing pains, etc., by metallic points," commonly known as the "*metallic tractors;*" patented by Elisha Perkins of Connecticut, Feb. 19th. It was a kind of galvanic application, for curing disease by the use of steel and brass points. The delusion of Perkinism extended even to Europe; but the author of it, who also invented an antiseptic medicine, fell a victim to misplaced confidence in his own nostrums, while combating the yellow fever in New York, in 1799. But his son established, in London, a Perkinean institution for the benefit of the poor, under the presidency of Lord Rivers. The tractors soon fell into neglect, but were the occasion of a very clever satire entitled "Terrible Tractoration, a Poem by Christopher Caustic," published in London in 1803, and written by an American.[1]

The impulse given to agriculture at this time, attracted much attention to labor-saving machines, applicable to the principal staples of the country. Several machines for threshing and cleaning wheat, rice, and other grains, and inventions connected with flour-mills, had already been patented. The success of Whitney had given a prominence to the cotton crop, and this year, three patents were granted for improvements in ginning cotton. The most important of these, was one issued May 12, to Hogden Holmes, who, early in the last year, appeared as a formidable contestant of Whitney's invention, which, until then, had only to contend with the *roller* gin. Holmes' machine was the same in principle as Whitney's, but had the teeth cut in circular runs of iron, instead of being made of wires, as was the case in the earlier forms of Whitney's gin. From this circumstance it was called the *saw* gin. It was the occasion of his principal law-suits afterward.[2] While embarrassed with

(1) Cases of cures to the number of five thousand were published in England, with certificates from eight professors, forty physicians and surgeons, and thirty clergymen. The tractors were much ridiculed by the medical profession, and their popularity was short lived. In 1801, Thomas Green Fessenden, of N. Hampshire, the author of the poem referred to, visited London to introduce a new hydraulic machine. Not succeeding in his object, he produced, under circumstances of much pecuniary distress, the "Terrible Tractoration," in relation to Perkins's tractors, and its success was so complete as to relieve its author, and give occasion for several editions in England. It was enlarged and reprinted in this country, in 1806, as "The Modern Philosopher," and in another edition before his death in 1837.

(2) Whitney afterward proved, that the idea of teeth instead of wires had early occurred to him. That the principle was the same in both, was ingeniously demonstrated by Whitney at one of the trials, by sinking the plate below the surface of the cylinder, so as to make the saw teeth look like *wires;* and preparing another cylinder, in which the wire teeth were made to look like *saw teeth.* When produced in court, the witnesses swore the *saw* teeth upon Whitney, and the wire teeth upon Holmes; upon which the judge declared it was unnecessary to proceed any farther, the principle in both being manifestly the same. So inveterate was the purpose to defraud him, that, on a similar occasion, he had the greatest difficulty to prove in court, that the machine had even been used in Georgia, although at the same moment, three separate sets of the machinery were in motion, within fifty yards of the building in which the court sat; and so near, that the rattling of the wheels could be distinctly heard on the steps of the Court House. Few men in Georgia, at one time, dare testify to the

this new rival, and an evident general intention to invade his patent, and burthened with debt, Whitney arrived in New Haven about April 1795, to find himself reduced to bankruptcy, by the destruction of his shop and all his machines and papers, by fire only the day before his arrival. At the time the rival gin of Holmes was patented, Miller and Whitney had thirty gins in operation, at eight different places in Georgia; some carried by oxen or horses, and some by water; and about $10,000 invested in real estate connected therewith. While endeavoring to borrow money at twelve per cent. their operations were nearly brought to a stand, by reports from London, that the staple was greatly injured by the machine, a judgment which was soon reversed. Through these and similar difficulties, the energy and confidence of Whitney enabled him to persevere.

Three patents were taken out by the ingenious Amos Whittemore, of Cambridge Mass., one of them for an improved self-acting loom for weaving duck, believed to be similar in principle to the power loom now in use.

President Washington, on meeting Congress for the last time, called their attention to the necessity of a naval force, to insure respect to a neutral commerce, and the desirableness of beginning, without delay, to provide and lay up materials for the building and equipping ships of war, in which the nation might proceed by degrees, as its resources rendered it practicable and convenient. "Congress," he observes, "have repeatedly and not without success, directed their attention to the encouragement of manufactures. The object is of too much consequence not to insure a continuance of their efforts, in every way which shall appear eligible. As a general rule, manufactures on public account are inexpedient. . . But to the extent of the ordinary demand for the public service, were they not recommended by strong considerations of natural policy, as an exception to the general rule? Ought our country to remain in such cases dependent on foreign supply; precarious, because liable to be interrupted? If the necessary articles should, in this mode, cost more in time of peace, will not the security and independence thence arising, prove an ample compensation?"

The President, in the same speech, again called the attention of Congress to the subject of a national university and of a military academy; and was the first to suggest, on that occasion, the importance of a

simple facts within their knowledge, in reference to the machine. The issue of the first trial they were able to obtain early in the next year, contrary to the pointed charge of the judge and the expectation of the defendant, was given against them. A second trial could not be obtained, until their business had been nearly destroyed by surreptitious gins.—*Olmsted's Memoir.*

national Board of Agriculture, "charged with collecting and diffusing information, and enabled by premiums and small pecuniary aids, to encourage and assist a spirit of discovery and improvement." Societies of that kind, he observed, had been found to be "very cheap instruments of immense national benefits." He had, nearly three years before, communicated to Sir John Sinclair, the eminent agriculturist, the outlines of such an organization for the state of Pennsylvania, but feared the country was not yet prepared to sustain one with Congressional aid. A national Agricultural Society was not formed until 1809.

The Andersonian University at Glasgow, was this year incorporated, by the magistrates and council of that city. The bequest of Dr. Anderson provided for colleges of Medicine, Law, Theology, and the Arts. The last of these, under Dr. George Birkbeck—who, in 1799, was appointed to the chair of Natural Philosophy, and instituted a course of lectures to mechanics, on elementary science and philosophy—became the first practical school for the operative classes, and the parent of Mechanics' Institutes throughout the world.

Benjamin (Thompson) Count Rumford of Munich, a native of New England, presented $5,000 to the American Acadamy of Arts and Sciences, as a fund, the interest of which was to be given once in two years, as a premium to the author of the most important discovery or improvement in heat and light, in any part of America or its islands.[1]

Col. Matthew Lyon, who, in 1783, commenced the erection of mills at Fair Haven, Vt., had in operation, previous to this year, one furnace and two forges, one slitting mill, one printing office, one paper mill, (built in 1794,) one saw mill, and one grist mill. His printing was done on paper manufactured by himself, from the bark of basswood. He had emigrated from Ireland at the age of sixteen, and was sold in Connecticut for his passage.[2]

One of the earliest manufactories in the United States, of any extent, for spinning and weaving flax, hemp, and tow, by water power, was that of James Davenport, put in operation with patent machinery

1797 within the last twelve months, at the Globe Mills, at the north end of Second Street, Philadelphia. It was visited, at the beginning of the year, by Washington and several members of Congress, who were highly pleased with the ingenuity and novelty of the machinery. The President in particular expressed a high opinion of the merits of the patentee, Mr. Davenport, and an earnest wish that a work so honorable to the infant manufactories of the Union, might be extended to different

(1) Holmes's Annals. (2) Hayward's Gazetteer of Vermont.

parts of the country. The labor was chiefly performed by boys; one of whom was able to spin, in a day of ten hours, 292,000 feet of flax or hempen thread, using twenty to forty pounds of flax or hemp, according to its fineness. One boy could also weave, on the machinery, fifteen to twenty yards of sail cloth in a day. Specimens of the spinning and weaving were deposited in Peale's Museum for public inspection. It was the purpose of the proprietor to manufacture the machinery for sale. But he died soon after, and the machinery of the Globe factory was sold in April, 1798, and the business broken up.

On the failure of a bill introduced in Congress, in accordance with the recommendation of the Secretary of the Treasury and a resolution of the House, and favored by the mercantile classes, to lay a direct tax on lands, houses, and slaves, in order to meet the demands upon the Treasury, the following additions were made (March 3) to the existing duties upon imports, viz.: On brown sugar, one half cent per pound; Bohea tea, two cents; molasses, one cent per gallon; on velvets and velverets, and muslins and muslinets, and other cotton goods not printed, stained, or colored, two and a half per centum *ad valorem*. The duty on the above descriptions of woven fabrics, was thereby made twelve and a half per cent. on the value, or the same as on printed and stained goods.[1]

By an act of the same date, option granted to the distiller by the law of 8th June, 1792, either to pay an annual duty of fifty-four cents per gallon on the capacity of the still, or at the rate of seven cents a gallon upon the quantity of spirits distilled, was withdrawn after 30th June. In lieu of the duty, he was thenceforth to pay for a license to use any such still for two weeks, six cents per gallon upon its capacity, including the head; for one month ten cents per gallon; for two months eighteen cents; and six cents per gallon additional for every additional month up to six months.[2]

On Jan. 14, Congress prohibited, until the end of the next session, the exportation of arms and ammunition, and allowed them to be imported duty free for two years. The prohibition was renewed at the expiration of the act, for another year.[3]

In July, duties were laid by Congress on stamped vellum, parchment, and paper, to commence 1st July, 1798, and continue until 4th March, 1803.[4]

An additional duty of eight cents per bushel (making it twenty cents) was imposed on salt imported in United States vessels, with an

(1) Laws U. S., vol. 3, ch. 64.
(2) Ibid. vol. 3, ch. 65.
(3) Ibid. vol. 4, ch. 2.
(4) Ibid. vol. 4, ch. 11.

additional ten per cent. when brought in foreign vessels. An allowance of twelve cents per barrel on pickled fish exported, and an addition of thirty-three and one third per cent. to the allowance before granted to vessels in the bank or other cod fisheries, were also authorized. This law continued in force until April 12th, 1800, when the act of 1792 was revived for ten years, and the additional allowances authorized by it and by the above act, were continued only so long as the correspondent duties on salt, respectively for which they were granted, were paid.[1]

On June 20, the first laws were enacted in New York respecting salt works, and the first leases of lots at the Onondaga Salt Springs were made by the state, to manufacturers under a commissioner, who required them to make contracts at not above sixty cents a bushel, and to pay a duty to the state of four cents per bushel.

The city and suburbs of Philadelphia contained at this time, ten rope-walks, which manufactured about 800 tons of hemp annually; thirteen breweries, said to consume 50,000 bushels of barley yearly; six sugar houses; seven hair powder manufactories; two rum distilleries and one rectifying distillery; three card manufactories; fifteen manufactories for earthenware, six for chocolate, and four for mustard; three for cut nails and one for patent nails; one for steel; one for aquafortis; onef or sal-ammoniac and Glauber's salt (which supplied the whole Union with the latter article); one for oil colors; eleven for brushes; two for buttons; one for morocco leather, and one for parchment; besides gunmakers, copper-smiths, hatters (of which there were 300 in the state, who made 54,000 fur, and 161,000 wool hats annually); tin-plate workers, type-founders, coach makers, cabinet makers, ship-builders, and a variety of others. The city contained thirty-one printing offices, four of which issued daily gazettes, and two others semi-weekly gazettes, one of them in the French language; besides two weekly journals, one of them in German. The other offices were engaged in printing books, pamphlets, etc. The catalogue of books for sale in the city, contained upwards of 300 sets of Philadelphia editions, besides a greater variety of maps and charts, than was to be found any where else in America.[2]

The United Brethren at Nazareth, Pennsylvania, had in operation a factory for spinning and twisting cotton, and had recently begun to draw wax tapers.

In the spring of this year, the "Hamilton Manufacturing Society," the proprietors of extensive glass works with hydraulic appurtenances, ten miles west of Albany on the great Schoharie Road, was incorporated by the state. The business was commenced about nine years before,

(1) Ibid. vol. 4, ch. 15. (2) Morse's Gazetteer, vol. 1.

and, under the patronage of the Legislature, at this time presented one of the most conspicuous examples of private manufacturing enterprise in the country.[1]

Robert Fulton, in company with Joel Barlow of Connecticut, then residing in Paris as a merchant, made experiments upon the Seine with a submarine vessel.

The first steamboat on the Hudson was this year built by Chancellor Livingston. A steamboat with paddle wheels at the sides, built at Bordentown, N. J., by Samuel Morey and Burgess Allison, was navigated to Philadelphia and back.

The first American vessel on Lake Erie, was the schooner *Washington*, built this year at Four Mile Creek, Erie, Pa. She was lost soon after, and the enterprise was not repeated for some time.

Three of the six frigates authorized by Congress, in 1794, were launched, and ordered to be manned and put in service. They were the Constitution, built at Boston, the United States at Philadelphia, each of forty-four guns, and the Constellation of thirty-eight guns, constructed at Baltimore. They were the first commissioned and afterwards the most conspicuous for their success of any in the naval serviee, and were the only naval force upon which the United States relied, in the unpleasant relations it then held with France, growing out of the numerous hostile decrees and predatory acts affecting the neutral commerce of the Union, which compelled the government to annul the infracted treaty with that power.

The emigration this year to western New York from Pennsylvania, Maryland, New Jersey and New England, exceeded that of any previous year. The Genesee country was already so far improved that the inhabitants lived in comfort and even luxury. When Messrs. Gorham & Phelps, in 1789, opened the first land office in the state, there was not a white inhabitant upon the tract. In 1793 there were at least six thousand, and it contained several grist and saw mills, flying stores, churches, and chapels. An academy for youth at Canandaigua was proposed within two years after the settlement. About three thousand emigrants arrived yearly, and the improvements were rapid, especially in regard to saw, grist, and merchant flouring mills, potash works, roads and bridges, etc. "The Bath Gazette" newspaper was started in 1796, and a sloop of forty tons was built about the same time to run as a packet between Geneva and Catharines Town on Seneca Lake. Her launching drew together for the first time the inhabitants of the country to the number of several thousand, who were mutually astonished at their own numbers. A press

(1) See vol. 1, p. 240.

and weekly paper were the same year started at Geneva with eight hundred subscribers, who before six months increased to one thousand. Flax and hemp were cultivated on the Genesee Flats. Wheat and Indian corn were abundantly grown, and flour equal to any on the continent was made at numerous mills. From the apple and peach orchards of the Mohawk, fruit was supplied in great plenty. One farmer made in a season one hundred barrels of cider, another furnished a distillery with one hundred bushels of peaches, and a third sold cider to the value of twelve hundred dollars. A very considerable brewery was this year set up by a Scotchman at Geneva. Whisky, previously brought four hundred miles from Northumberland, Penn., and sold at one dollar and fifty cents per gallon, was now made in considerable quantity. Fifteen familes in No. 4, seventh range, made two tons of maple sugar in a season. During the following year a respectable mercantile house in Baltimore, built merchant mills at Tioga Point and established an extensive manufactory of cordage for ships from the hemp of the Geneva Flats. Arks for the transportation of lumber, flour, and other produce, were introduced about the same time. Few sections of the country have made more rapid progress in population and industry.[1]

Among the patents, about fifty in number, granted this year, the most important were those to Amos Whittemore (June 5), for an improvement in the manufacture of wool cards, and Benjamin Seymour (June 26), for rollers for slitting and other mills for rolling iron, both of which have been in extensive use to the present time. Eli Terry of Connecticut, the first extensive clock manufacturer in that state, received (Nov. 27) letters patent for an improvement in clocks, time-keepers, and watches. Several were granted for nailmaking, and for threshing, and other agricultural machines, and six for improvements in stoves, chimneys, and fireplaces. The last was by Charles Wilson Peale, the portrait-painter. He also patented an improvement in bridges, which were the subject of three other patents beside. One of these last was given to Timothy Palmer of Newburyport, Mass., who had previously constructed bridges over the Merrimack and other New England rivers, and afterward built one at Easton, Pa., and the Schuylkill Permanent Bridge at Philadelphia, which were all regarded as triumphs of engineering skill, and led to the general approval and adoption of his architectural principles.

Eli Whitney, having abandoned all hopes of pecuniary advantage from the cotton gin, entered into contract with the United States
1798 government to make ten thousand stand of muskets at the price

(1) Doc. Hist. N. Y., by O'Callaghan, vol. 2.

of $13.40 each; four thousand to be delivered on or before Sept. 30, 1799, and the remainder in one year from that time. He proceeded to erect a complete and extensive gun factory in the town of Hamden, a few miles from New Haven, where the village of Whitneyville now stands. In consequence of the works having to be constructed, machinery and tools made, and much of it invented, raw materials collected, etc., the contract was not finally closed until January, 1809, during which time his genius was so impressed upon every part of the works as to render it a model establishment for the whole country.[1]

A Society for the Promotion of Agriculture, Manufactures, and Arts, was established by the Legislature of New York.

The dismissal of American envoys from France, and other hostile decrees, produced great indignation and a disposition to vote "millions for defence, not one cent for tribute." For the protection of commerce, Congress authorized the President to cause to be built, purchased, or hired, not exceeding twelve vessels of twenty-two guns each. To carry the intentions of government into effect, with greater system, a new Executive Department, that of the navy, was established. Ten small vessels were authorized to be built, purchased, and fitted out as galleys. Armed vessels, offered by private persons on favorable terms, were to be accepted. A marine corps, consisting of the several grades of officers and privates, was established. Three additional ships of thirty-two guns each, were authorized to be built, for which $600,000 were appropriated.[2]

The manufacture of corn brooms, on a small scale, for the New York market, was commenced by the United Society of Shakers in Watervliet, N. Y., who began in 1791 to raise broom corn on the alluvial lands of the Mohawk. The handles were made of soft maple turned in a foot lathe, and the twine was wound upon the husk by means of a cylinder turned by a crank, while the handle was held in one hand and the brush in the other. This simple mechanism was afterward improved by adding a bench to the roller fitted to a frame in the bench, and a rag wheel to hold the cord when wound by a short crank as before. The brooms sold for fifty cents each, and two dozen a day was an achievement equal to seven or eight dozen at present. The original society at the Shaker settlement still carry on the business somewhat extensively, and all other societies of Shakers throughout the Union to a greater or less extent.[3]

(1) See vol. 1, p. 516.—Olmsted's Memoir.

(2) Laws United States, vol. 4, chaps. 48, 52, 56, 81, 89, 99.

(3) Benjamin Atkinson, of Byberry township, now a part of the consolidated city of Philadelphia, about 1790, commenced the first domestic manufacture of brooms, from the pannicles of broom corn (Sorghum saccharatum), a plant said to have been first raised in this country by Dr. Franklin,

The President was empowered to purchase cannon, arms and ammunition, for which $800,000 were appropriated, or if more practicable he might lease for a term of years, or purchase in fee simple for the United States, one or more suitable places, and establish founderies and armories for the casting and manufacture of cannon and small arms, for which he was authorized to employ artificers and laborers under proper superintendents. An annual account of expenditures was to be laid before Congress. The armory at Harper's Ferry was established under this act, and the first muskets, to the number of 293, were made there in 1801.[1]

At the Springfield armory 1044 muskets were made this year. The number made in the three previous years were 245, 838, and 1028, respectively.[2]

To meet these expenditures a direct tax was for the first time laid by Congress (July 14), to the amount of $200,000, to be assessed upon dwelling houses, lands, and slaves, according to a valuation, ordered by a previous act. Dwellings were to pay from two-tenths to one per cent. on the valuation, and slaves fifty cents each, the balance to be assessed upon lands.[3]

On May 19, the armed national galley, President Adams, was launched at Pittsburg. The galley Senator Ross was then on the stocks, and the two were among the earliest sea-going vessels constructed on the Ohio. A brig of 120 tons, called the Arthur St. Clair, then building at Marietta by Commodore Preble, and launched the next year, is said to have been the first sea-rigged vessel from that river.[4] After going to Havana, she was sold in Philadelphia. The ship John Adams, of thirty-two guns, was built this year, at Cochran's ship-yard in Charleston, S. C., by Paul Pritchard.

The first American vessel built on Lake Ontario, the "Jemima," of thirty tons, was also launched from Hanford's Landing, three miles below Rochester.

The manufacturing town of Steubenville, on the Ohio, was laid out this year, by James Ross, Esq., of Pittsburg.

from a single seed taken from an imported whisk, and planted in his garden. Mr. Atkinson raised the corn and made the brooms himself for four years, when he associated with Bezaleel Croasdale. They jointly supplied Philadelphia and neighboring towns, Baltimore, and occasionally New York, until 1815 or 1816, when others engaged in the business, in consequence of the high price of brooms during the war, when they sold for $4.50 per dozen. Their first manufacture were round, and secured at the neck by horn instead of twine, retained in its place by a wooden peg. The handles were of oak, rough shaved with a drawing knife. The business is still continued in the neighborhood.

(1) Ibid., vol. 4, chap. 55.

(2) Seybert, 627.

(3) Laws U. S., vol. 4, chap. 92.

(4) Craig's Hist. Pittsburg. — Brown's Western Gazette, 309.

The manufacture of straw plait or braid for hats and bonnets, was originated at this time, in Providence, R. I. Miss Betsy Metcalf, afterward Mrs. Baker, at the age of twelve years, without previous instructions, succeeded in making from oat straw, smoothed with her scissors and split with her thumb-nail, a bonnet of seven braids with bobbin inserted like open work, and lined with pink, in imitation of the English straw bonnets, then fashionable, and of high price. It was bleached by holding it in the vapor of burning sulphur. The article was much admired, and many came from neighboring towns to see it, and to order bonnets for themselves, at half the price of the imported. Young women were gratuitously instructed in the art by the inventor, and this laid the foundation of an extensive branch of business in Providence, Dedham, Wrentham, and other towns in New England and throughout the country.[1]

In June, 1798, Matthew Carey issued the thirteenth volume of the American Museum, a periodical which contributed much to the advancement of literature and manufactures in the United States. Twelve consecutive volumes were published between the years 1787 and 1792, but inadequate means compelled the editor, long a disinterested benefactor of the manufacturing classes, to discontinue it.

The Cyclopedia, in 18 volumes quarto, with numerous plates, the first of its kind in the United States, was also issued by Thomas Dobson of Philadelphia. Three additional volumes were afterward published.

The manufacture of dye stuffs was commenced in New York by the founder of the respectable house of William Partridge & Son, still engaged in the same business. Among the articles first introduced in this country by them, were lac dye, bichromate of potash, argal, peach and Nicaragua wood.

Mr. Tennant, of Glasgow, this year patented an improved method of preparing chloride of lime for bleaching, which had an important influence upon the cotton and linen manufacture.

Long cotton began first to be generally grown as a crop in South Carolina about this time.

Samuel Slater entered into copartnership with Oziel Wilkinson, whose

(1) This traditional account of the humble but independent origin in the United States, of an art long practiced in Tuscany and other Italian states—but then of recent introduction in England, where it was the subject of a patent, in May, of this year, by Peter Boileau—was the subject of a confirmatory memoir, read by Judge Staples, author of the Annals of Providence, before the Rhode Island Society for the encouragement of Domestic Manufactures, Sept. 29, 1858, and published in the Society's Transactions. It is also authenticated by a letter written a few years ago by Mrs. Baker, who made a fac simile of the first bonnet braided by her, which was deposited in the Society's collections.

daughter he had married, and Timothy Green and William Wilkinson, also sons-in-law of the latter, under the firm name Samuel Slater & Co., Mr. Slater owning one half the stock. They erected on the east side of the Pawtucket river, a cotton mill, afterward known as the *New Mill*, which was the second built by Slater, and the first upon the Arkwright principle in Massachusetts. Both the old and new mills were superintended by Slater, who received a compensation of $1.50 per diem from each, and by his laborious and constant personal attention, overcame the numerous difficulties attending first enterprises.

The hands in this mill soon after revolted, and five or six of them went to Cumberland and erected a small mill, owned by Elisha Waters and other persons, named Walcot. By these men and their connections several factories were commenced in various parts of the country; most of the establishments erected from 1790 to 1809 having, in fact, been built by men who had directly or indirectly derived the knowledge of the business from Pawtucket, the cradle of the cotton manufacture. Slater's patterns and models were stolen by his servants; his improvements thus became extended over the country, and the business was rapidly introduced in other places.[1]

The large Ramapo or Pierson's Iron works on the Ramapo river in Hampsted, Rockland Co., New York, were put in operation this year by J. G. Pierson & Brothers. They consisted of a forge, rolling and slitting mills, works for cutting and heading nails by water, saw and grist mills, etc.[2] The nail machine was patented by J. G. Pierson in March 1795.

John Fitch navigated a model steamboat at Bardstown, Kentucky. The Legislature of New York had repealed, in March, the law granting special privileges to Fitch, and transferred them to Robert R. Livingston for twenty years, on condition that he should within twelve months build such a boat to go four miles an hour. The unfortunate inventor of the steamboat, having previously tried his fortunes unsuccessfully in Europe, died in the course of the year at Bardstown, while prosecuting his claims to lands purchased in Kentucky, many years before, and just as a brighter prospect was dawning upon him. In conformity to his wishes he was buried on the shores of the Ohio, that he might repose "where the song of the boatman would enliven the stillness of his resting place, and the music of the steam engine soothe his spirit."

Experiments in steam navigation, with a boat of thirty tons, were made near New York by Nicholas I. Rooseveldt and Robert R. Livingston, soon after the partner of Robert Fulton, who during the year pro-

(1) Memoir of Slater. (2) Spafford's Gazetteer of N. Y.

posed to the Legislature of the state to propel a vessel by steam on new principles, if assured of its exclusive advantages when successful.

Rooseveldt, in connection with James Sullivan, took out a United States patent (May 31) for a double steam engine, and soon after constructed probably the first effective steam engine, after those of Fitch, ever built in America. He completed one in 1800, with a wooden boiler, through which long cylindrical flues or heaters wound several times before entering the chimney. It was for the use of the Philadelphia water works, for which he constructed two double engines, and contracted to supply three millions of gallons of water daily if required, with the privilege of using the surplus power of the lower engine on the river Schuylkill for various manufacturing purposes.

A steam saw mill, the first recorded, was patented by Robert McKean (March 24). David Wilkinson, an ingenious and enterprising machinist of Pawtucket, who rendered Slater and the early cotton manfacturers much service, patented a screw cutting machine, afterward operated by water power at Pawtucket Falls.

Seven or eight patents were given for hydraulic machinery of different kinds, for which the demand was becoming extensive, including a machine for raising water by M. I. Brunel.

In December, Hon. Hugh Orr, for over half a century an ingenious and enterprising mechanician of Bridgewater, Mass., who made the first muskets, and bored cannon, and the first cotton machinery in this country, died at the age of eighty-two.

Amos Whittemore visited England, for the purpose of securing
a patent for his card machinery. On his return the same year, he
1799 formed a partnership with his brother and Robert Williams of
Boston, under the firm style of Williams, Whittemore & Co.,
and commenced the manufacture at West Cambridge, where the business
has been carried on by the family of the inventor, nearly or quite to the
present time. They were soon able to finish 200 dozen pair per week.

The sales of cotton yarn had at this time become sufficiently promising to induce another company to set up a cotton mill in Rhode Island; and Messrs. Almy, Brown & Slater, made considerable addition to their "old mill." Their investments during the next seven years, were more particularly in the business of spinning, and it was thenceforth continually on the increase.

Robert Fulton this year introduced into Paris the first panoramic painting, aided by optical illusions, ever exhibited in that city.[1]

(1) See vol. 1, 289-90.

The patents issued this year, included one to Mark Isambard Brunel, for a machine for writing with two pens (Jan. 17); to John Sears, for a machine for manufacturing salt (Jan. 24). The patentee was an enterprising salt manufacturer of Cape Cod, Mass. One to Benjamin Dearborn, for his celebrated steelyards or Patent Balance (Feb. 14); to Jacob Perkins, for an improvement in making nails (Feb. 14); and one to the same, for a check to detect counterfeits (March 19). Both of these last were valuable inventions; to Benjamin Tyler for a flax and hemp mill (Feb. 26); to Charles Whiting of Mass., for extracting oil from cotton seed (Mar. 2);[1] and to Robert R. Livingston of New York, for manufacturing paper.

As this year closes the century, it may be proper to give a brief summary of the state of commerce in the country.

The total value of the exports of the United States for the year, was $78,665,522, of which $33,142,522 was the growth, produce, or manufacture of the Union. The total value of the imports was estimated at $79,069,148.

New York this year, first took the lead of other states in the amount of its exports, which were $18,719,527. The other states ranked in the following order, as to the value of their exports; Maryland, Pennsylvania, Massachusetts, South Carolina, Virginia, Georgia, Connecticut, Rhode Island, North Carolina, New Hampshire, Delaware, Vermont,

(1) In 1769-70, Dr. Otis, of Bethlehem, Pa., presented to the Am. Philosoph. Society, through Dr. Bond, a sample of oil made from hulled cotton seed. It was made,—as were specimens of the oil of sunflower seed exhibited at the same time,—by the Moravians at that place, and in much the same way as linseed oil, at the rate of nine pints of oil to a bushel and a half of seed. It was said to be used medicinally in the West Indies.—*Phil. Trans.* vol. 1. The London Society of Arts, in 1783, having learned that cotton seed yielded oil seed cake as food for cattle, in order to encourage the cultivation of cotton, offered a gold medal as a premium for oil expressed from cotton seed, and oil cake from the remaining seed, made by planters in the British West India Islands, in quantities of not less than one ton of oil and five hundred weight of cake. A silver medal was offered for smaller quantities, and the premiums were annually renewed for six years. But the large quantity required appears to have defeated the object. A medal was offered by the S. C. Agricultural Society soon after its organization in 1785, for oil from cotton seed and other oleaginous seed. Patents were taken out in 1819, by Daniel Gillett of Springfield, Mass., for preparing food from cotton seed, and the next year by Geo. P. Digges of Virginia, for extracting oil from the seed. But it is only within a few years that a new source of profit to the Southern cotton planter, has been found in the manufacture of oil and seed cake, from the thousands of tons of seed which annually encumbered the estates, or was used on the poorer soils as manure. The saving to be thus effected has been differently estimated at from twenty to thirty millions of dollars annually. Some sixteen or more patents have been taken out, for machines for hulling the seed for that purpose.

New Jersey. The exports from Vermont were $20,480, and were the first from that state of which returns were made.

The average annual exports of flour from the United States during the last five years, were 596,140 barrels; of potash 4,627 tons; of pearl-ash 2,024 tons; of tobacco 74,100 hogsheads; of tar 52,712 barrels; of pitch 7,145 barrels; of rosin 9,802, and of turpentine 43,696 barrels. The average yearly value of all domestic articles exported in the same period, was $32,822,965.

The exports from the United States to Louisiana and the Floridas, were $3,504,092, of which $447,824 were domestic articles. The imports from the same were $507,132. St. Genevieve and New Bourbon, in Upper Louisiana (now Missouri), produced 170,000 pounds of lead, of which 36,000 pounds were sent to New Orleans. The population of St. Louis was 925.

The total tonnage of every description belonging to the Union, was 946,408 tons, of which 669,197 was registered tonnage engaged in the foreign trade, 220,904 enrolled in the coasting trade, and the balance was enrolled and licensed tonnage employed in the coasting trade and fisheries.

CHAPTER II.

ANNALS OF MANUFACTURES.

1800—1810.

DIRECTING our attention, first to those acts of legislation, which may be said to have had a direct or indirect bearing upon manufacturing industry, we note, that on Feb. 28, Congress passed an act, pro-
1800 viding for the second census of the inhabitants of the United States, to commence on the first Monday in August. The returns gave the total population of twenty-one states and territories, as 5,319,762, of which number, 896,849 were slaves.

In April, the law relating to Patent Rights, was modified so as to restore to aliens, who had resided two years within the United States, all the rights and privileges enjoyed by citizens, under the act of 21 Feb., 1793. The legal representatives of a deceased inventor, were empowered to receive a patent. The violation of the rights of patentees was made punishable, by a forfeiture of three times the amount of the damages.

The quantity of spirits distilled in the United States from foreign materials (chiefly in the Eastern States), during the year, was 1,290,476 gallons, and from domestic materials 51,625 gallons, on which the gross amount of duties was $142,779. The aggregate capacity of all the stills employed, was 2,084,212 gallons; upon which the aggregate duty was $372,561. The total quantity of spirits distilled from molasses since Jan. 1, 1790, was 23,148,404 gallons, of which 6,322,640 gallons were exported.[1]

The quantity of refined sugar sent out of the refineries during the year, was 3,349,896 pounds, and the gross amount of duties thereon, was $66,998.[2]

The quantity of cotton grown in the United States this year, was about 35,000,000 of pounds, of which 17,800,000 were exported. Of this, about 16,000,000 of pounds went to England, constituting over one-fourth of the total importation of cotton into that country. The quan-

(1) Seybert, 261, 461. (2) Ibid, 470.

tity manufactured in the United States, was upward of 8,000,000 pounds, of which, only about 500 bales were consumed in regular establishments.[1]

The caterpillar or cotton-worm, first commenced its devastations in South Carolina.

The first cotton-spinning machine in France, was this year introduced from England, through Ghent, and was presented to the first consul. It was, about the same time, introduced for the first time into Switzerland, in the canton of St. Gall, where it was followed the next year by the power loom, recently brought into general use in England. Machine spinning was introduced into Saxony the year previous.

The price of cotton twist in Rhode Island, was as follows: for number 12, 103 cents; number 16, 119 cents; number 20, 136 cents; an increase of fifteen cents on the prices of 1794.

The manufacture of morocco leather was about this time commenced, at Lynn, Mass., by William Rose, an Englishman, who had been regularly bred to the business in London. His dwelling and manufactory, occupied the present site of the grounds and residence of Stephen Oliver, Jr. His success was great, but through imprudence he became bankrupt in about eight years; and in 1809, resumed the business in Charlestown, where it had been previously revived since the Revolution,—about the year 1796,—by Elisha Mead. In the following year he removed to Northampton, Connecticut, which he left in 1814, and four years after, died in poverty, at Sterling, Mass. The morocco business in Lynn, was successively prosecuted by Joshua R. Gore, Francis Moore & Henry Healy, Wm. B. & Joshua Whitney, Carter & Tarbell, Samuel Mulliken, Daniel R. Witt & Joseph Mansfield; who were the principal manufacturers during the ten years after Rose left. The apprentices of the latter introduced the business in several other towns.

The Salem Iron Manufacturing Company, in Mass., was incorporated with power to hold real and personal estate, to the value of $330,000. A rapid increase in the production of iron commenced about this time in England, which this year made 180,000 tons.

The building of vessels was commenced at Elizabeth, on the Monongahela river, sixteen miles above Pittsburg, by Col. Stephen Bayard, who laid out the town in 1787; and at this time took out a company of ship carpenters from Philadelphia, and established a ship-yard. The first vessel built was the ship Monongahela Farmer.

(1) Claiborne's Report to Commissioners of Patents, 1857.

Patents were this year granted to Oliver Evans (Jan. 16), for an improvement in stoves and grates. This was for the luminous stove, with doors or lights of talc, and designed for burning the recently discovered hard Lehigh or stone coal, which could not be burned in common stoves. His grate stoves are believed to have been the first to come into general use, and were the first in which talc was used. John G. Gebhard, of N. Y., received a patent (Feb. 4) for extracting oil from Palma Christi.[1] John J. Hawkins, of Philadelphia, patented (Feb. 12) an improvement in the piano-forte, which he manufactured and sold, at fifteen South Second st., under the name of Patent Portable Grand Piano, as his card states, at little more than half the price of imported grand or square pianos. He also manufactured a patent ruling machine; and later in the year, took out another patent, for an improvement in musical instruments. John Biddis, who had before received two patents for improvements of a chemical nature, was granted one (May 6) for an engine for reducing silk, cotton, worsted, cloth, etc., to their original state, to be manufactured. This was a very early attempt to utilize such refuse materials, which, by the aid of modern machinery, now form the basis of an extensive manufacture of *shoddy* in England, and to some extent in this country, and which has materially affected the production of woolen goods in the United States. Peter Lorillard, of New York, patented (June 28) a machine for cutting tobacco, of which he was an extensive manufacturer. Jonathan Grant, Jr., of Belchertown, Mass., filed (Oct. 4) the description of an improved telegraph. This invention, made two years before, was put in operation between Boston and Martha's Vineyard, a distance of ninety miles, and a question was transmitted and answered in less than ten minutes.[2]

In February, Henry Wiswell, Zenas Crane, and John Willard, of

(1) The manufacture of castor-oil, from the castor-oil bean or palma christi, the *Ricinus Communis* of Linnæus—which is now extensively prosecuted in several parts of the Union, particularly in the Western States—employed one or two mills in New York, as early as 1789. The Agricultural Society of South Carolina, soon after its incorporation in 1785, offered among other premiums, medals, for the largest quantities of oils from the olive—cuttings of which they distributed—from ground nuts, sesamum or bene seed, cotton and sunflower seeds, and for castor oil. The palma christi or castor nut, grew abundantly in the state, and yielded from 100 to 150 gallons of oil to the acre. A Mr. Rudolph, of Camden, a few years after the date in our text, had fifty or sixty acres under cultivation with the plant, from which he had produced large quantities of cold drawn oil by expression. It was first extensively manufactured in the United States, some years later, at New-bern, in North Carolina. In quality, American castor oil is equal to the best East Indian.

(2) Holmes's Annals.

Dalton, Mass., proposing to erect a paper mill at that place, issued an earnest appeal to the ladies of Berkshire, to save their rags.
1801 They built the first paper mill in the county, which went into operation the next year, and is now known as the "Old Berkshire" mill. They made about twenty tons of paper annually, until 1807, when Wiswell and Carson became the managers until 1810, since which time, it has been run by David Carson and his sons. In 1855, this mill made 180 tons of paper yearly, worth twenty cents a pound. It employed sixty hands, having been much enlarged by its present owners.[1]

A blast furnace, erected about 1786, near the Chicopee Falls, by James Byers and William Smith, this year passed into the hands of Benjamin Belcher, of Easton, and Abijah and Wm. Witherill, who built a foundry and enlarged the business. In 1805, Mr. Belcher purchased the right to the whole, and continued the business until 1822, when he sold the land and water privilege, on which the extensive manufacturing village of Chicopee Falls now stands, the iron business having been still conducted by his sons until 1846. Some castings are yet made there.[2]

Robert Fulton, having for several years pursued his experiments with a submarine boat, and had his plans twice rejected by the French Directory, and also by the British Government, descended in the presence of commissioners appointed by Bonaparte, with three men, in a plunging boat in the harbor of Brest, to the depth of twenty-five feet, and remained one hour. His vessel was capable of sailing like a common boat on the surface, and, after striking her mast, could be made to dive and be moved in any direction under water at the rate of about three miles an hour. He also blew up a small vessel in the harbor with a submarine bomb containing twenty pounds of powder, and made various other experiments at Brest and Havre with diving boats, with a view to having them employed by the government against the enemy's shipping. He was unsuccessful, and in 1804 repeated his experiments in England, where on the 15th Oct., 1805, he blew up a strong Dutch brig of 200 tons, in Walmar Roads, but fortunately did not succeed in introducing into the naval appointments of the nation so destructive an agency. In December of the following year he returned to America, where his genius found its greatest triumph in the achievement of steam navigation.

The ship Benjamin Franklin arrived at Philadelphia bringing Don Pedro, the first full-blooded Merino buck imported into the United States. He was one of four lambs, shipped in the same vessel, the others having perished during a boisterous passage. They were selected at the request

(1) Holland's Western Mass. (2) Ibid.

of M. Dupont De Nemours, who accompanied them, by M. Delessert, a banker of Paris, who was at the head of a commission to select in Spain on behalf of the French government, a flock of 4000 merino sheep out of the number of 6000, which Spain had stipulated by the treaty of Basle to present to France. Two of the sheep were intended for Rosendale, the farm of M. Delessert at Kingston, on the Hudson, one for M. Dupont's place near New York, and one as a present to Mr. Jefferson at Monticello. Don Pedro was kept as a stock ram, first by Mr. Dupont and afterward at Rosendale, when he was sold, with the rest of Mr. Delessert's flock, at public auction, in 1805. He was purchased by Mr. Dupont for sixty dollars and transferred to the farm of E. I. Dupont, near Wilmington, Delaware, where the farmers were offered the use of him gratis. Fine wool sheep were thus multiplied in the neighborhood by Mr. Dupont and others, and soon after Dupont & Co. erected works for manufacturing fine wool. His progeny in New York were scattered among the farmers, who knew little of their value until Chancellor Livingston, who purchased many of the ewes to cross with his Rambouillet stock, imported in the mean time, taught them how to appreciate the breed.

Dr. James Mease, of Philadelphia, in 1796–7 sent two orders for merino sheep, and had one shipped to him which was washed overboard, in a storm at the capes of Delaware, and this year sent another order to Yznardi, the son of the American Consul at Cadiz, by whom two rams and two ewes were shipped, which arrived in Dec. 1803.[1]

Arthur Scholfield, of Pittsfield, Mass., who accompanied Samuel Slater from England, and, in 1793, was concerned in starting the first incorporated woolen factory in the United States, at Byfield, in Newbury, completed the first improved carding engine in New England. The machine was constructed without the aid of patterns or drawings, which the laws of England did not suffer him to bring away. During its construction the builder is said to have been obliged to make one or two voyages to England, to refresh his memory of the parts, and to have smuggled portions of the machine, or models and plans, concealed in his

(1) Mease's Archives of Useful Knowledge, vol. 1, p. 103. This appears to have been the first introduction of Spanish sheep, attended with any practical result. In a letter of Robert Morris, dated Oct. 30, 1789, reference is said to be made to two sheep, sent by M. Le Conteulx de Coumant, to this country, presumed to have been of the Spanish breed. In 1793, the Hon. Wm. Foster, of Boston, while a young man, traveling in Spain, smuggled, on account of their exportation being prohibited, two ewes and a ram on the ship Bald Eagle, to Boston; which he gave to his friend, Andrew Cragie, Esq., of Cambridge, who seems not to have been aware of their value, or to have found no market for the wool. Mr. Foster, after an absence of some years, is said to have met him at a sale where he was paying $1000 for a merino ram, and inquiring what became of those he gave him, Mr. Cragie replied, "I simply ate them."

bedding. On its completion he announced that he was prepared to card wool into rolls, at twelve and a half cents the pound; mixed, fifteen and a half cents; or if previously picked, mixed, and greased, ten cents and twelve and a half cents per pound. He soon after commenced the manufacture of carding machines.

The dressing of cloth had been recently commenced in Dalton, by Ezra Maynard.

About this time the first carding machines in Chelmsford (Lowell) were run by Moses Hale.

Miller and Whitney, proprietors of the saw gin, having submitted to the Legislature of South Carolina proposals to sell to the state, for the sum of $100,000, so much of the patent right as appertained to that state, where its use had become very extensive, and petitions having been presented from the planters, urging the transfer, the Assembly voted the sum of $50,000 for that purpose. Although the price was deemed a great sacrifice, the patentees accepted it as a certainty, and present relief from their embarrassment.

President Jefferson, in his first annual message to Congress, adverted to the success which had attended the continued efforts to introduce, among the Indians, the implements and practice of husbandry, and the household arts. A spirit of peace and friendship generally, prevailed among them, and some had begun to increase in population, instead of diminishing as heretofore. A letter from the Indian agent, Benjamin Hawkins, accompanying the message, states that one nation had just been supplied with 100 pairs of cards, and eighty spinning wheels; there were eight looms in the nation, four of them wrought by Indian women, and the remainder by white women. A young Englishman who could make looms and spinning wheels, and understood weaving, was appointed a temporary assistant. One of the looms and two spinning wheels, were made by an Indian for his own family.

The quantity of cotton grown this year, in all countries, was estimated at 520,000,000 pounds. Of the whole amount, 48,000,000 pounds, worth $8,000,000, were the product of the United States.

The capital employed in growing it was about $80,000,000, and the number of persons employed in growing and otherwise dependant upon it, was 100,000. The American states produced cotton in the following proportions, viz: South Carolina, 20,000,000 pounds; Georgia, 10,000,000; Virginia, 5,000,000; North Carolina, 4,000,000; and Tennessee, 1,000,000 pounds. The quantity exported from the United States, was 20,100,000, viz: South Carolina, 10,000,000, Virginia and North Carolina, 5,000,000, and Georgia, 3,000,000 pounds. The average price, during this year, of all kinds of American cotton, at the place of exportation, was forty-four cents, and the price in England was from seventeen to thirty-eight pence sterling.[1]

The quantity manufactured in the United States was 500 bales.

Buffalo, at the outlet of Lake Erie into Niagara river, at the mouth of Buffalo creek, was this year laid out by the Holland Land Company. In 1798 there were five dwellings, one tavern, and one store, all of logs, on the site.

A company of French merchants, under the name of Tarascon, Berthoud & Co., from Philadelphia, with twenty ship carpenters, joiners, and other mechanics, commenced this year the building of vessels and keel boats, to navigate the Ohio, being the first to engage in that business. This undertaking was originated by Louis Anastasius Tarascon, a wealthy and enterprising Frenchman, who, in 1794, established himself in Philadelphia as an importer of silks and French goods, and in 1799 sent two of his clerks, Charles Brugiere and James Berthoud, to examine the Ohio and Mississippi from Pittsburg to New Orleans, and ascertain the practicability of clearing ships, ready rigged, from Pittsburg to the West Indies and Europe. Their report being favorable, he immediately, with his brother and others, commenced a large establishment at Pittsburg, consisting of wholesale and retail store, warehouse, ship-yard, rigging and sail-loft, anchor shop, block manufactory, and every thing necessary to complete a vessel for sea. He built, during the summer of this year, the schooner Amity, of 120 tons, and the ship Pittsburg, of 250 tons. In the following spring they sent the schooner to St. Thomas, and the ship to Philadelphia, laden with flour, and thence to Bordeaux, and brought back a cargo of wine, brandy, and other French goods, part of which was sent to Philadelphia, at a cost of six to eight cents per pound for transportation. They built, the next year, the brig Nanino, of 200 tons, and in 1803, the ship Louisiana, of 350 tons, which they sent ballasted with "Stone Coal" and other articles, to Philadelphia, where the coal sold for thirty-seven and a half cents per bushel. In the ensuing year the ship Western Trader was built by the same firm.[2]

(1) Secretary Woodbury's Report, 1835–36.

(2) Harris's Pittsburg Directory, for 1837. Simpson's Lives of eminent Philadelphians. Previous to this time travel and traffic upon the western rivers, was carried on almost exclusively in flat-boats, occupying several months of toilsome labor with sweeps, in the upward passage from New Orleans, and requiring the transhipment of goods at the Falls. Louis Philip, afterward king of the French, who spent some time at Pittsburg, in 1796, and other distinguished travelers, had no better conveyance. Pittsburg now has a continuous river communication with at least sixteen states and territories, nearly 400 counties, and five or six millions of population, over about 11,212 miles of navigation, with three avenues by water to the ocean. This, with its immense system of railway communication, renders it truly "the gateway of the west." Its vast river trade, now conducted like its land traffic, with the utmost speed and regularity by

Mr. John Irwin about the same time established a ropewalk in Allegheny, which he carried on extensively with his son, thirty-five years after.

The American Company of Booksellers, doing business in New York, Philadelphia, and Boston, was formed. It regulated the sale of books by Fairs, the first of which was held in the ensuing year, and prohibited auction sales by any of its members on pain of expulsion. A system of exchanges was also arranged between these cities, and large and expensive editions were published at the joint expense of the company, each dealer subscribing for a certain number of copies; these were called Trade Books, and were delivered in sheets, folded and collated, in which form these and other new books were at first chiefly offered at the Trade Sales.

The Philadelphia Premium Society was instituted for the purpose of fostering American industry by giving premiums for improvements in arts and manufactures.

The compound or oxyhydrogen blow pipe was this year invented by the late Prof. Robert Hare, of Philadelphia. By its aid many substances before deemed infusible were readily melted in a burning jet of the mixed gases. Profesor Silliman, a few years later, succeeded in melting lime and magnesia with it, and burned all the well-known metals, gun flint and corundum gems, producing, during the operation, light brighter than that of the sun. The hydrostatic blow pipe or bellows, invented by Dr. Hare soon after, was also capable of melting strontia and other refractory substances.[1]

Flax was this year first grown on the Genesee Flats, in Ontario Co., New York, where it has since been extensively cultivated.

The Connecticut Academy of Arts and Sciences, instituted at New Haven in 1799, was this year incorporated "for the purpose of encouraging literary and philosophical researches in general, and particularly for investigating the natural history of the state."[2]

The President sent a fleet into the Mediterranean to protect American shipping. The government purchased twelve acres of land at Philadelphia, for a Navy Yard, at a cost of $37,500.

means of steam, was first commenced in 1756, by the ascent from the Mississippi of about thirty batteaux and 150 men, laden with supplies for Fort Duquesne. On the 23d Feb., 1777, fourteen carpenters and sawyers arrived from Philadelphia, and were set to work near a saw mill on the Monongahela, fourteen miles above Fort Pitt, where they built thirty batteaux, forty feet long by nine feet wide, and thirty-two inches deep, to serve as transports. This was the beginning of the boat building business there. The building of Kentucky flat and keel-boats, became a large business on the several tributaries of the Ohio.

(1) Silliman's Jour., vol. 1, p. 98. Reg. of Arts, vol. 1, p. 362.

(2) Miller's Retrospect of 18th Century, vol. 2, p. 259.

The manufacture of straw bonnets was this year commenced at Wrentham, Mass., which soon became a principal seat of that business.

The extensive establishment of Oliver Ames & Sons, for the manufacture of spades and shovels, was commenced at Easton, Mass.

Oliver Evans, of Philadelphia, this year completed, at his own expense, a small steam engine, with a six inch cylinder and eighteen inch stroke, at a cost of $3,700, which he applied to grind plaster of Paris, recently introduced as a fertilizer, from Nova Scotia, chiefly through the efforts of Judge Peters, of Philadelphia, who published a treatise on the subject in 1797. The success of the little engine, with which he was able to break 300 bushels, or twelve tons, of plaster in twenty-four hours, excited much attention. It was soon after employed to drive twelve saws, in sawing stone at the rate of 100 feet of marble in twelve hours. This engine was upon the high pressure system, since so extensively employed on railways, steamboats, and in factories, and which was this year patented by the Cornish engineer Trevethick, in England, whither Evans had sent drawings and specifications of his engine, several times during the last twelve or fifteen years, during the whole of which time the inventor had continually urged its importance for the propulsion of carriages, and of steamboats on the western rivers, by the aid of paddle wheels. It was commenced in the last year, his original purpose being to construct a locomotive steam carriage, as a debt of honor to the state of Maryland, which, in 1786, granted him exclusive privileges for the use of his improvements in flour mills and steam carriages, after his own state had rejected the latter as visionary. He had been unable to find any person to risk the expense, but was encouraged by Professor Robert Patterson, of the University of Pa., and Mr. Charles Taylor, a steam engineer from England, to whom he explained the principles of his engine, which they pronounced new to them. The Philosophical Society also, so far countenanced it as to reject that portion of a report on steam engines, by B. F. Latrobe, Esq., a scientific engineer of the city, in which he ridiculed the "Steam Mania" of Evans and others. The Society, however, retained a part of the report, in which Mr. Latrobe labored to show the impossibility of propelling boats economically by steam, on account of the engine, a scheme nearer realization in America than steam propulsion by land.[1] The locomotive was not completed until 1804.

(1) The first legislative act ever made authorizing a public railroad, was this year granted by Parliament, for the Surry iron tramroad in England, nine miles long, on which horse-power was employed, although private tramways of wood had been long in use. A locomotive, built by Trevethick & Vivian, was employed for the first time on the Merthyr Tydvit road, in South Wales, in 1804; and the first public railroad on which steam was applied, was the Stockton and Darlington, twenty-five miles long, opened Sept. 26, 1825, and worked by locomotive and stationary engines, and horses.

Among the patents issued this year, was one to Col. Alexander Anderson, of Philadelphia (Jan. 26), for brewing with Indian corn, and one to the same (Jan. 28), for a condenser for heating the wash in distilling. This process, by which the whole heat of steam is communicated to the wash without danger of burning it, effected a great saving in fuel and labor, and was one of the most important improvements as yet introduced in distilling. Messrs. Anderson and Hall, the former of whom had also patented a steam still in 1796, had the improvements in operation soon after in their stills at Lamberton, N. J., and they were also adopted by others. Two patents for improved evaporating processes in distilling, were also patented (Feb. 12 and March 2) by Benjamin Henfrey. Jesse Reed, of Mass., took a patent (June 9) for nails milled out of heated rods, and Wm. Leslie one for cutting and heading nails (Nov. 5).

Richard Robotham, of Hudson, N. Y., received letters patent (Oct. 10) for an air pump ventilator for ships, mines, etc., and one of the same date for a machine for ruling paper, etc. Making paper from curriers' shavings was the subject of a patent (Dec. 28) by Joseph Condit, Jr., of New Jersey.

A memorial presented to Congress, March 30, from citizens of Morris, Sussex, and Bergen counties, in New Jersey, concerned in the manufacture of bar, cast, and rolled iron, nail rods, and nails, asking an
1802 increase of duties on imported iron, was accompanied by the following statement of the number of furnaces, forges, etc., in the state. The number of forges then actually carried on was over 150, which at a moderate calculation, would produce twenty tons of bar iron each, annually amounting to 3000 tons. Seven blast furnaces in operation would yield on an average 500 tons each, amounting to 3500 tons annually. There were six blast furnaces not then in operation, and many unimproved sites equal to any in the state, besides many forges and sites for forges in the same condition. Of the forges above mentioned, about 120 were in the counties of Morris, Sussex, and Bergen, besides three blast furnaces all actually going. The state was capable of furnishing at least 5000 tons of bar iron annually, and 7000 tons of cast iron. There were four rolling and slitting mills, which rolled and slit on an average 200 tons, one half of which was manufactured into nails. The memorial was adopted at a public meeting and is signed by John Cobb, chairman.

By a resolution of the house these reports and memorials, with others from sundry calico printers, cordwainers, and shoemakers, were laid over to the next session.

The internal revenue duties on licences for the sale of wines and liquors, on refined sugar, sales at auction, and on carriages, which by an act of the last session had been continued without limitation, were repealed along with those on distilled liquors and stills, and on stamps, all of which ceased after 30th June.

April 29th.—A supplementary copyright act, required the notice of such right having been secured to be inserted in the title page or the following, instead of being published in the newspapers. It extended the privileges of copyright to embrace designs, etchings, or engravings of historical or other prints.

A proposition was made to light the neighborhood of Central Square, in Philadelphia, with gas. Benjamin Henfrey, an Englishman, who in 1797 endeavored to form a mining company, and during the last year had explored for coal near Baltimore, and also experimented with gas from wood in that city, and Richmond, which he actually succeeded in lighting with it, was proposed as a proper person to accomplish it. He proposed to light it with gas from coal, and was also an applicant to light the United States light-houses on the sea-coast in the same manner. He received letters patent from the United States government (April 16) for an "improvement, being a cheap mode of obtaining light from fuel."

In the spring of this year, the first application of gas which attracted any attention, was made by Mr. William Murdoch, the engineer of Messrs. Bolton and Watt, who, on the occasion of the national illumination at the peace of Amiens, lighted up the front of the Soho manufactory of his employers, with a public display of gas lights. The first application of coal gas for illumination, was made by Mr. Murdoch in 1792, when he lighted his own dwelling-house and offices at Redruth, in Cornwall, and in 1797, erected gas apparatus in Ayrshire, and the next year fitted up the gas work at Soho, near Birmingham. In 1804–5, the extensive cotton mills of the Messrs. Philips and Lee, at Manchester, were fitted up with 900 burners, giving a light equal to 2,500 candles, under the superintendence of Mr. Murdoch, who has been considered the parent of this mode of illumination. Its use from that time became general, and London was lighted with gas in 1807.[1]

(1) The earliest distinct mention of an inflammable product from coal, is contained in a "Letter from Mr. John Clayton, Rector of Crofton, at Wakefield, in Yorkshire, to the Royal Society, May 12, 1688, giving an account of several observations in Virginia, and in his voyage thither, more particularly concerning the Air." The author, whose remarks on the natural history of Virginia we have before cited, in speaking of the meteorology of the country, compares the sulphurous smell, sometimes observed during heavy thunder storms, to "some sulphureous spirits I have drawn from coals, that I could no way condense, yet were inflammable, nay, would burn after they passed through water, and seemingly fiercer if they were not overpowered therewith. I have kept of this spirit a considerable time in bladders, and though it appeared as if it was only blown with air, yet if I let it forth and fired it with a match

The first considerable importation of Spanish merino sheep yet made into the United States, arrived in May, in the ship Perseverance of 250 tons, Capt. Caleb Coggeshall master, about fifty days from Lisbon, where they were shipped on the 10th April, by the Hon. David Humphreys, United States Ambassador at the court of Madrid. They were landed at Derby, Conn., having been transferred to a sloop in the harbor of New York. They consisted of twenty-one rams and seventy ewes, from one to two years old, out of a flock of 100, four rams and five ewes having died on the passage. They had been purchased for Col. Humphreys in Spain, by a reputable person, and driven across the country of Portugal by three Spanish shepherds, escorted by a guard of Portuguese soldiers. The Trustees of the Massachusetts Society for Promoting Agriculture, at a meeting held on 28th August, when a letter on the subject from Mr. Humphreys to Aaron Dexter was read, voted the thanks of the meeting for the communication, and on 29th Oct., voted to present him with the gold medal of the Society, "for his patriotic exertions in importing into New England 100 of the merino breed of sheep, from Spain, to improve the breed of that useful animal in his own country."

On the 14th April, Mr. Humphreys dedicated to the Prince Regent of Portugal a poem "on the Industry of the United States of America," written at Lisbon, and designed "to show the prodigious influence of national industry in producing public and private riches and enjoyment."[1]

About the same time that Mr. Humphreys' flock arrived from Spain, the Hon. Robert R. Livingston, the American minister resident at Paris, sent, for his farm at Clermont, in New York, some half-a-dozen or more selected from the national stock at Rambouillet, near Paris.

The introduction of these two lots of pure merinos, and the exertions of their respective owners, within a few years, much improved the breeds of the country, and several manufactories of fine woolens, with appropriate machinery, were established, which afforded a market for the wool, and induced others to import fine wooled sheep, while it stimulated improvements in sheep husbandry generally. The price of Spanish merino bucks, at this time, was about $300.

In June, a literary Fair or Trade Sale of books was held in New York for the first time in the United States, which was attended by a large number of booksellers. It was held under the auspices of the American

or candle, it would continue to burn until all were spent." In a letter written about the same time, to the Hon. Robert Boyle, published in the Philosophical Transactions for 1739, he details more fully his experiments, in the distillation of the "*Spirit of Coals*," and appears to have made a near approach to a practical discovery.

(1) Miscel. Works of D. Humphreys, 4th ed., N. Y., 1804, pp. 225, 346.

Company of Booksellers, among whom was Mr. Carey of Philadelphia, a leading publisher, and who was one of the first to suggest it, and most energetic in its support. It was proposed to hold them statedly, and alternately at New York and Philadelphia. The publishing business was, through their agency, rapidly increased in all the principal cities.[1]

On July 31, two weekly journals were published in Ohio; the "Western Spy," at Cincinnati, and the "Sciota Gazette," at Chilicothe, the first inland town in the north-western territory which had a press. They were printed on paper of inferior quality, brought from Georgetown, Kentucky, on horseback, and their united circulation did not exceed 600 copies. The latest news in the Spy of this date, from France, was dated May 17; from London, May 10; from New York, July 9; and from Washington, July 25.[2]

The white population of Ohio was 76,000. A state constitution was framed at Chilicothe, by virtue of which Congress authorized its admission as a state of the Union.

The first press and newspaper in Mississippi, "The Natchez Gazette," was this year established by Col. Andrew Marschalk, who continued it under different names for about forty years. Natchez was a large village, consisting chiefly of small wooden buildings scattered irregularly over considerable space. The currency of the territory consisted at this time in part of "Cotton Receipts," negotiable by law as bills of exchange or money. They represented so much cotton deposited in public gins, for cleaning, the farmers being in general too poor to have private gins.[3] The first exports from the territory, of which there is any account, were made the last year to the value of $1,095,412, and this year $526,016.

The first official return of the exports from Kentucky and Tennessee, was this year made, and amounted in the former to $626,673, and in the latter to $443,955. The first exports of Indiana were made the year before, to the amount of $29,430.

The Legislature of North Carolina agreed to purchase, of Miller and Whitney, the patent right of the saw gin for that state, and laid a yearly tax of two shillings and six pence upon every saw (amounting in some gins to forty), employed in ginning cotton, during the next five years, which contract was faithfully performed. About the same time negotiations were entered into between the patentees and the state of Tennessee, which in the following year laid a tax of thirty-seven and a half cents per annum, on each saw used in that state within the next four years.

The second annual message of President Jefferson, recommended to

(1) Miller's Retrospect, vol. 2, p. 387.
(2) Histor. Mag., vol. 3, p. 127.
(3) Monatte's Valley of the Mississippi, vol. 2.

Congress, among the landmarks and rules of action by which they were to be guided for the public good, "to cultivate peace, and maintain commerce and navigation in all their lawful enterprises; to foster our fisheries as nurseries of navigation and for the nurture of man, and *protect the manufactures* adapted to our circumstances, etc.," as also "to cherish the Federal Union as the rock of safety."

A Mechanics' Association, of about 100 members, was formed at Portsmouth, New Hampshire, for the purpose of encouraging and promoting industry, good habits, and an increase of knowledge in the mechanic arts, and for the mutual benefit of its members. It is still in existence.

The Danvers & Beverly Iron Company was incorporated with a capital of $330,000.

The only manufactory of sheet copper in the country was that of the Messrs. Revere, at Boston, Massachusetts.

Additional glass works were built in Pittsburg by General O'Hara, who made preparations to manufacture white and flint glass, and sent an agent to England to obtain workmen, in which he was unsuccessful.

The Legislature of Pennsylvania having, on the 7th March, 1800, revised the act incorporating a company for promoting the cultivation of the vine, under new commissioners, and in the January following, by a supplementary act removed the chief obstacle to obtaining subscriptions, the organization of the company was this year completed, with Dr. Benj. Say as president, Isaac W. Morris, treasurer, and Jared Ingersoll, John Vaughan, Dr. Jas. Mease, Fred. Heiss, and Elisha Fisher, as managers.

The company had 30,000 vines growing at Spring Mill, under the care of Mr. Legaux, whose disagreement with the company soon after, led to the establishment of separate vineyards at that place.

In addition to the vine company's, there were several private vineyards in the city and county at this time, viz: Montmollin's, Ridge Road four miles from the city, consisting of 4,000 plants; Peter Kuhn's, one mile from the last, consisting of Lisbon, Malaga, and Madeira grapes; Dr. James Mease's "in the line of Cherry street," with 3,000 plants; Paul Labrouse's, about one mile from the city, between Second and Third streets, Southwark; Crownsillat's, four miles from Philadelphia, on the banks of the Schuylkill, 1,500 plants; Thunn's, south of the last named, and Stephen Girard's, near the same place, with forty or fifty plants only. The grape was at this time cultivated successfully by Mr. Autill in New Jersey, and by Mr. Notnagel near Bristol, and others in these and neighboring states.

The Catawba grape was this year first discovered by Mr. Murray, an emigrant from Pennsylvania, on the Block Ridge mountain, in Buncombe county, North Carolina, about ten miles S. E. of Ashville.

They were named the Catawba by Senator Davy, who transplanted some of them to his residence at Rocky Mount, on the Catawba river. whence he introduced them, a few years after, under that name, among his friends in Washington and Maryland. Major Adams, of Georgetown, first discovered its value as a wine grape about 1822, and two or three years after, sent slips of it to Nicholas Longworth of Cincinnati, who established its reputation, as well as the wine manufacture in the west.

It was estimated that $130,000 was invested in the manufacture of salt, in Barnstable Co., Mass., which yielded a net profit of twenty-five per cent. on the investment. The process had been much improved within a few years, and several patents had been obtained by individuals on the cape. The salt was very pure and white, and the glaubers salt produced in the process was of the best quality. The number of works in the county was 136. The number of feet of surface was 121,313, and the capacity equal to the manufacture of 40,438 bushels of common salt, and 181,969 lbs. of glaubers salt, worth together $40,700. The works were to be increased the next year, by the addition of 27,578 feet. Capt. John Sears was the only successful manufacturer, by solar evaporation alone, for which he had extensive works in Dennis, having triumphed over numerous difficulties. Salt was also made at Martha's Vineyard, Nantucket, Plymouth, Kingston, Rochester, Hingham, and Dorchester; in nearly all of which it had been commenced within two or three years. The works in Dorchester were erected this year, at Preston's Point, by Capt. Deane, and consisted of a series of vats 200 feet in length, by twenty feet wide, or 4,000 superficial feet of evaporating surface; and were soon after followed by others on an improved plan. Two patents were taken out in this branch, one by Benjamin Ellicott, of Maryland (May 12), for a machine for manufacturing salt; and the other by Valentine Peers (Dec. 18).

The manufacture of clocks by water power, for a wholesale trade, was this year commenced at Plymouth, Conn., by Eli Terry; an enterprise regarded by many, as a rash adventure. Simon Willard, of Mass., patented (Feb. 8), his celebrated time-piece.

Among the patents (sixty-five in number), insued this year, the following, in addition to those mentioned, were the most important. Manufacturing starch from potatoes, by John Biddis (March 22). Improvement in a saw mill, which returns the log after each cut, by Moses Coates (April 1). This contrivance, which was not appreciated at the time, performed automatically, by very simple mechanism, several operations which successive improvements were only able to attain thirty years after.[1] Edward West patented (July 6) a machine for cutting, and another for heading and cutting nails; an improvement in the gun lock, and another in the steamboat. It has been claimed for him, that he made the first working model of a steamboat in this country, which he is said to have run upon a river in Kentucky. Several other patents were granted for nail-making. An improved boiling cistern, by Timothy Kirk, of Yorktown, Pa. (Dec. 28), was considered a novel and useful invention.[2] Burgiss Allison and John Hawkins, received letters patent (Dec. 30), for manufacturing paper from corn husks.

A memorial to Congress, from the gun manufacturers of the borough of Lancaster, Pa., against the remission of duties upon arms manufactured in foreign countries, states that manufactories of arms
1803 had been established there, and in other parts of the state, at much expense, and 20,000 stand were nearly completed for the Commonwealth of Pennsylvania. Mills for boring gun barrels had been erected, and the locks, and every other part, were made in the best manner. They were confident 20,000 stand of arms could be annually made in the state, and in five years, with continued protection, the business would be fully established.

The committee of commerce and manufactures, reported, on the subject of petitions from the Franklin Association and other journeymen printers, calico printers, cordwainers, paper makers, letter founders, makers of umbrellas, brushes, glass, stoneware, gunpowder, hats, and starch, in favor of protecting duties. The committee considered it justice to the petitioners, and sound policy, to extend protection to such manufacturers, as were obviously capable of affording to the United States an adequate supply of their respective products, either by a free admission of raw material, or by higher duties on manufactures. The existing rates, being nearly equal on most articles, they considered rather a burthen to the workingman, than a protection to the manufacturer. They recommended the Secretary of the Treasury to prepare, against the next session, a plan for new and more specific duties, which should leave the amount of revenue the same at it then was.

A very complete and curious set of merchant flouring mills, capable of manufacturing from five to six hundred bushels of wheat into flour daily, went into operation at the village of Madison, four miles from the mouth of Catskill Creek, in Greene Co., New York. They were built by Ira Day & Co., and contained two water-wheels and four pairs of stones with elevators, fanning mills, smut machines, cooling apparatus,

(1) Pat. Off. Rep. 1843, p. 299. (2) Dom. Encyclop. vol. 5, p. 357.

weighing hoppers, packing screws, and other machinery, moved by the water wheels; each of which was turned with about one half the quantity of water required for a common grist mill. Catskill contained seven grist mills, and about as many saw mills.

In April, the New York Legislature passed an act, extending to Messrs. Livingston and Fulton, for the term of twenty years from this date, the rights and exclusive privileges granted to Mr. Livingston in 1798, of navigating all the waters of that state, by vessels propelled by fire or steam. It also extended for two years,—and by a later law, to 1807,—the time in which to make proof of the practicability of propelling a boat of twenty tons, at the rate of four miles an hour, against the current of the Hudson.

Messrs. Livingston and Fulton, after several trials with models, in the last year, at Plombieres, in France, having adopted paddle wheels, completed, about this time, an experimental boat which, meeting with an accident, was nearly altogether rebuilt, sixty-six feet long by eight feet wide, and finished in July. The first trial of a steamboat on the Seine, was made by them early in August, in presence of the French National Institute, and a great concourse of Parisians. Encouraged by their success, and to attain greater speed by improved machinery, an engine was immediately ordered from Messrs. Watt & Bolton, of Birmingham, to be sent to the United States, whither Fulton proceeded to construct and operate, under the foregoing act, his first steamboat in America. Miller and Symington, in March, 1802, navigated the Forth and Clyde canal, with the side-wheel steamer Charlotte Dundas, in which Fulton was a passenger.

During this year, John Stevens, of Hoboken, is said to have made an experiment on the Passaic river, with a boat propelled by forcing water through an aperture in the stern, by means of a pump.[1]

In consequence of letters written in the last year, to a gentleman in Kentucky, by Oliver Evans, stating that he had his steam engine in operation, Capt. James McKeever, of the U. S. Navy, and M. Louis Valcour, united to build a steamboat of eighty feet keel and eighteen feet beam, to ply between New Orleans and Natchez. The boat was built this year in Kentucky, and floated to New Orleans, to be supplied with an engine, by Evans. The subsidence of the river, which was not expected to rise again for six months, having left the boat on dry land, and the capital of the owners having been exhausted, they allowed Mr. William Donaldson to put up the engine in a saw mill, and were astonished to learn that it was sawing 3,000 feet of boards every twelve

(1) Renwick on the Steam Engine.

hours, when boards were selling at $60 per thousand. They were now confident of succeeding with the steamboat, but were disappointed and ruined by the burning of the mill, after two previous incendiary attempts of hand sawyers, whereby they lost $15,000. The engine consumed one and a half cords of wood daily, and ran over twelve months without getting once out of order, and in 1810 was set to pressing cotton.

Cotton machinery was manufactured in Philadelphia at this time, by Mr. Eltonhead.

Calico printing was carried on by the following persons in Philadelphia and vicinity, viz.: John Hewson, at the Globe Mills, in the city, Mr. Stewart, at Germantown, and Mr. Thorburn, at Darby. The three were expected to turn out, during the year, 300,000 yards of goods.[1]

Manufactures were this year first regularly distinguished, as to quantity and value, from other articles, in the returns of exports. The total value of exports was $55,800,033. The value of domestic articles exported, was $42,205,961, in the following proportions, viz.: products of the sea $2,635,000, of the forest $4,850,000, of agriculture $32,995,000, and of manufactures $1,355,000. Of agricultural products, vegetable food constituted a value of $14,080,000. Cotton of domestic and foreign growth was exported to the value of $7,920,000. The exports of Michigan were for the first time embraced in the returns, and amounted to $210,392.

In December, the ship Eliza, Captain Bissel, sixty days from Cadiz, arrived, with two merino rams and two ewes, for Dr. James Mease, of Philadelphia, who had ordered one pair, two years before. To his great disappointment, they all proved to be black, though fine wooled, a circumstance which he could only attribute to a desire to increase the profits, black sheep being little valued in Spain, and their wool chiefly used for the clothing of shepherds and the poor peasantry. Their price to him was sixty dollars and the freight twenty dollars.

The total tonnage of new vessels built in the United States during the year, was 88,448 tons.

The "Miami Exporting Company," of Cincinnati, was incorporated for forty years, with a capital of $450,000 for banking purposes, being the first in that city. Its dividends, for a number of years, were ten to fifteen per cent.

The brig Ann Jane, of 450 tons, was built at Elizabeth on the Monongahela, sixteen miles above Pittsburg, for the Messrs. McFarlane,

(1) Communicated by Thompson Westcott, Esq.

merchants. She was one of the fastest sailers of her day, and ran for some time as a packet to New Orleans.

The brig Marietta of 130 tons, another of 150 tons, and the schooner Indiana of 100 tons, were built in Ohio in the spring of this year.

The "flax rust," the most destructive disease to which the flax crop in New York is subject, first made its appearance at Bridgehampton, near the east end of Long Island. This parasite appeared in Berkshire county, Massachusetts, three years after.

The manufacture of dressed deer skins for gloves, money belts, under clothing, etc., was this year commenced as an independent business at the village of Gloversville, New York, by Ezekiel Case, who had learned the art at Cincinnati. From him and Talmadge Edwards, the business was learned by W. T. Mills and James Burr, who became noted manufacturers, and improvers of the art. The business extended thence to Johnstown, the county seat.

The manufacture of cotton and wool cards was established in New York, under the management of Samuel Whittemore, a younger brother and partner of Amos and William Whittemore, of Cambridge, Mass.

A large plaster mill, seventy-five feet by forty-five, now a part of the Auverge or "New Mills," at Newburg, New York, was erected this year, by a Mr. Belknap. The use of plaster of Paris, as a fertilizer, was much promoted by the exertions of Chancellor Livingston.

The Legislature of South Carolina annulled the contract made last year with Miller and Whitney, proprietors of the saw gin; suspended payment of the balance due them ($30,000), and instituted a suit, to recover what had been already paid them, alleging as the reasons, a want of validity in the patent, and the non-performance of certain conditions of the contract by the patentees. In Georgia, the most persistent efforts were made to invalidate the patent. Prior claims to the invention were preferred on behalf of Hogden Holmes and Edward Lyon, of that state, and of a Swiss machine of earlier date. The Governor, in his annual message, advised that compensation be withheld, and a committee reported in favor of instructing their representatives to procure a modification of the patent act, so as to get rid of the monopoly, and if that failed, to endeavor to induce Congress to purchase the patent right, and release the Southern States from so burthensome a grievance. The states of South and North Carolina and Tennessee were invited to cooperate with Georgia. Popular feeling, stimulated by the most sordid motives, was so far awakened in the cotton states, that Tennessee suspended the payment of a tax laid earlier in the year, upon cotton gins, for the benefit of the patentees. A similar attempt, afterward made in the Legislature of North Carolina, wholly failed, and both branches declared by resolution, that "the contract ought to be fulfilled with punctuality and good faith." Honorable men in other states, were indignant at the measures of the Legislatures, and South Carolina, the next year, rescinded the resolution of the previous house, and testified its respect for Mr. Whitney by marked commendation, expressions grateful to those whose sense of justice was not obscured by interest or prejudice.

Mr. Whitney's partner died on 7th December of this year, weighed down with repeated disappointments in his business transactions.[1]

The first cotton manufactory in New Hampshire was built at New Ipswich.

The second cotton factory in Massachusetts, and the third in the vicinity of Providence, was erected this year, and was followed by a fourth the next year. The whole number of mills in operation in the United States, at this time, was but four. They were rapidly multiplied in Rhode Island from this time.

The price of cotton yarn at Providence, was, for number 12, 94 cents, for number 16, 110 cents, for number 50, 126 cents per lb.

At Queretaro, near the city of Mexico, at this time, were cotton factories as large as any in France, as well as large woolen manufactories, which, during the year, worked up about two million dollars' worth of woolen cloths, bay, druggets, serges, and cotton stuffs. The establishment consisted of factories and workshops, in the latter of which, more than 300 in number, the operators worked at the cost of their employers.

Levi Thurston commenced the manufacture of scythes in Orange, Connecticut, with the first trip hammer in the town.

The manufacture of blacking was, about this time, commenced by Lee & Thompson, who long supplied the public with "Lee's Improved Steam Blacking," at No. 1 John St., New York, and acted as agents of the celebrated Day and Martin's liquid blacking, first introduced, only two years before, in England.

The practice of treading out wheat, barley, and other grain, by oxen and horses, upon open, circular threshing floors, of hard rolled earth, was extensively practiced, at this time, in Rhode Island and portions of the Middle States, as the most expeditious and economical method, notwithstanding the introduction of several patent horse power threshing machines.

Among the patents issued this year, were several for improvements, by citizens of different states, in machines for ginning cotton; an apple paring machine, the first of its kind, by Moses Coats, an ingenious mechanic of Downingtown, Pa. (Feb. 14); a machine for cleaning clover

(1) Olmstead's Memoirs.

seed, long exhibited in the model room of Peale's Museum, (March 21); an improvement for cutting grain and grass, by Richard French and John T. Hawkins of N. J. (May 17), which was the first mowing or reaping machine recorded. Several other patents were taken out for agricultural machinery, a number connected with distilling, for ruling paper, making wrought and cut nails, and for extracting the coloring matter of vegetables, and preparing dyers', painters', and printers' colors, etc.

Feb. 7.—The Board of Managers of the Pennsylvania Society for the Encouragement of Manufactures and the Useful Arts, organized in August, 1787, addressed a circular communication, with a plan of
1804 their constitution, to all societies for the promotion of useful knowledge, and to the people of the United States generally, for the purpose of exciting a renewed interest and activity in the advancement of the *manufacturing interest* of the country, an object which the Society was established to promote, and in which it had recently experienced increased energy. The "Manufacturing Committee" of the Society, a body distinct from the Board, had, for several years, suspended the business of their department, in consequence of the destruction, by fire, of a large part of its stock in furniture, raw materials, manufactured goods, and some valuable cotton machinery, but were now resuming operations.[1] The community was cautioned in a particular manner against similar dangers in labor-saving manufactories. The Society invited communications from associations engaged in promoting either science or manufactures. In view of the great influence which the progress in chemistry, natural history, mechanics, and the doctrine of fluids, had exerted within fifty years, in elevating the character and increasing the profits of the manufacturing classes, they suggested to all scientific institutions the formation of a standing committee of arts and manufactures, and to societies, kindred to their own, a particular examination of all matters relating to manufactures within their sphere, and the publication of the results, with a detail of the facts. The circular, which was impressed with the ardent mind of the president of the Board, Mr. Tench Cox, was accompanied by a "Report on the state of manufactures in the United States generally, and particularly in the State of Pennsylvania, at the time of the establishment of this Society, and of their progressive increase and improvement, to the present time."

The first machine for cleaning docks by steam, ever constructed, was about this time completed by Oliver Evans, at the Mars Works, Philadelphia, by order of the Board of Health. It was called the *Eruktor*

(1) See vol. 1, p. 409.

Amphibolis, and consisted of a large flat or scow, with an engine of five horse power for working machinery. Having been fitted with temporary wheels on wooden axles, the machine, of a weight equal to 200 barrels of flour, was driven through the street to the river Schuylkill, where it was launched, and with paddle-wheels at the stern, was propelled a distance of sixteen miles into the Delaware. Later in the year, Evans submitted to the Lancaster Turnpike Company an estimate of the profits of a steam carriage, to carry 100 barrels of flour fifty miles in twenty-four hours, and offered to build such a locomotive carriage. He published, the next year, "The Young Engineer's Guide," descriptive of the principles and manner of working the steam engine for propelling boats or land carriages.

The Province of Louisiana, having, by the treaty of April 3, 1803, been transferred by France to the United States, for the sum of $15,000,000, Upper Louisiana was, in conformity with the act of 20th October of the same year, surrendered (March 10) to the agent of the United States, Capt. Amos Stoddard. That portion of the colony south of the thirty-third parallel, now the State of Louisiana, previously taken possession of, was called the Territory of Orleans, and all lying north of it, and west of the Mississippi, the District of Louisiana, attached to the Territory of Indiana. The village of St. Louis contained but two American families, and its population was less than 1,000 souls. The fur trade constituted its chief business interest, and amounted, during the next fifteen years, to $203,750 annually. *Peltry-bonds*, or bills, payable in peltries, was its principal currency. The first returns of exports, from the Territory of Orleans, this year, amounted to $1,600,362.

Many of the petitions, presented in the last session of Congress, from manufacturers and tradesmen, were renewed, and others from the manufacturers of plated trappings for carriages and horses, the stainers of cotton goods, cork-cutters, and artizans of nearly all kinds, asked protection and encouragement of their several branches, and were the subject of a report by the Committee of commerce and manufactures.

Congress, by a unanimous vote, increased the duties upon imports by about two and a half per cent., the proceeds to constitute a "Mediterranean Fund," for defraying the increased expense of naval operations to suppress the piracies of the Barbary powers.

A duty of fifty cents per ton, as light money, was imposed on all foreign vessels, entering the United States ports. Additional specific duties were laid on certain articles. It was also enacted that a registered vessel lost its American character, if its owner, being a naturalized citizen, resided for more than one year in his native country, or more than two years in a foreign country, except as a consul or public agent.

The charter of the Society of Agriculture, Arts, and Manufactures, in New York, granted in 1791, having expired, it was re-incorporated, as the "Society for the Promotion of the Useful Arts." It published, previous to 1815, nine volumes of Transactions.

The Middlesex County Agricultural Society, in Massachusetts, formed in 1794, and probably the first county association of the kind in the United States, was also incorporated this year.

In May, John Cox Stevens, and his son, Robt. L. Stevens, crossed from Hoboken, N. J., to New York, in a boat propelled by *steam.*

The village of Harmony, in Butler Co., Pa., was settled by about twenty families of "The Harmony Society," from Wirtemberg, in Swabia, under Mr. George Rapp, who preceded them about a year, and purchased 4,700 acres of land. During the next six years the Society was increased to 140 families, and cleared 1,600 acres of land, erected frame and brick dwellings, barns, and warehouses, laid out a vineyard, built grist, sawing, corn, oil, and hemp mills, a tannery, brewery, distillery, dye-house, potash, soap boilers and candle works, etc. They also erected a large factory, and commenced successfully the manufacture of broadcloth, from the wool of merino sheep raised by them. Their vines and merino sheep, which were special objects of attention, not succeeding so well as they wished, the Society sought a more favorable climate in Indiana, and renewed their enterprises at New Harmony, on the Wabash, whence they returned in about ten years, and settled at Economy, in Beaver Co., Pa.

The tonnage of new vessels registered and enrolled this year, was 103,753 tons. The total tonnage of the Union, of every description, was 1,042,404. The average tonnage of vessels annually built and registered in the British Empire, in the last twelve years, was 100,487 tons.

The first iron foundry in Pittsburg was established by Joseph McClurg.

Cotton was carded and spun in Pittsburg, by the carding machine and spinning jenny, to the amount of $1,000, being the first manufacture of the kind in the place.[1]

The first ark load of bituminous coal was sent down the Susquehanna, 260 miles, to tide water at Columbia, by Mr. W. Boyd. It was from the vicinity of Oldtown, now Clearfield, and was a curiosity to the inhabitants of Lancaster Co.[2] The existence of brown coal, or lignite, in Missouri, was this year noticed by Lewis and Clarke, who traced it from about twenty miles above the Mandan villages, on the Missouri,

(1) Cramer's Almanac for 1804. (2) Taylor's Statistics of Coal, Am. ed. p. 330.

2,454 miles up the river, and nearly to the base of the Rocky Mountains, as well as upon the Yellowstone, and other tributaries of that river.[1]

The improvement of the texture of the cotton fibre was, about this time, made the subject of successful experiments, by Kinsey Burden, Sen., of St. John's, Colleton, in South Carolina, who, in this or the following year, produced from carefully selected seed, specimens of cotton worth, in the English market, twenty-five cents per pound more than any other. The secret of his success was long unknown. The crops in that state were this year destroyed by the hurricane. The cotton fields of Iberville, in Louisiana, were about this time first devastated by the Chenille or cotton insect.[2]

The first regular cotton factory in the State of New York, was erected in Union Village, Washington Co., by William Mowry, who had acquired a knowledge of the business in the pioneer establishment of Samuel Slater, at Pawtucket. It continued in almost constant operation until 1849, when it was still the largest in the country—a large and flourishing village having grown up around it.

The cotton manufacture was about this time commenced also in Connecticut.

The first broadcloth from merino wool, was made at Pittsfield, Mass., by Arthur Scholfield. It was gray-mixed cloth, and all the merchants in town declined purchasing it when finished, although Josiah Bissel, a principal dealer, is said to have made a journey to New York a few weeks after, and brought home two pieces of the same goods, bought as foreign cloth. Mr. Scholfield at this time also carried on the manufacture of single and double carding machines of improved pattern, and the carding of wool, at eight cents per pound for white, and twelve and a half cents for mixed wool. Carding machines and various manufacturing operations, were from this period rapidly introduced into Pittsfield, Lenox, Lanesborough, Dalton, and neighboring towns. Cards made by the Shakers were in use at this time.

The manufacture of gunpowder was carried on upon the Brandywine, in Delaware, by Mr. E. Irene Dupont de Nemours, whose powder, in packages impressed with the figure of an eagle, was already celebrated for its excellence.[3] The proprietor patented a machine for granulating gunpowder, early in this year.

(1) Taylor's Stat. of Coal, Am. ed. pp. 490, 491.

(2) Cotton Plant. De Bow's Industrial Resources, vol. 1, pp. 172, 173.

(3) Wilson, the American Ornithologist, in his poem, "The Foresters," speaks of the woodman in the wilds of Pennsylvania, admiring his powder during his pedestrian tour in 1804. He says it left no stain on paper when burned:

The first quarto Bible, from movable types, ever set up in the United States, was printed in Philadelphia, by Mathew Carey, at a first cost of $15,000. The type was furnished by James Ronaldson, in South street above Ninth, the only type founder, at that time, in the country. The type was kept standing until 200,000 impressions were printed.[1]

The American Company of Booksellers offered a gold medal of the value of fifty dollars, for the greatest quantity, and best quality of printing paper, not less than fifty reams, made from other materials than linen, cotton, or woolen rags; and a silver medal worth twenty dollars, for the greatest quantity, not less than forty reams, of wrapping paper, from new materials. The Messrs. H. and S. Fourdrinier, wealthy stationers and paper manufacturers of London, this year purchased, of Didot & Gamble, the patents in Robert's machine, and commenced at Boxmoor a series of costly experiments and improvements in the machine which bears their name. Its success was greatly promoted by the skill of Mr. Donkin, the eminent manufacturer of paper machinery, who this year erected, at Two Waters, his second machine, which proved the practicability of making paper in continuous sheets.[2]

The American Philosophical Society about this time, offered an extra Magellanic premium—a gold medal, worth from twenty to forty dollars, or its equivalent in money—for an essay upon the subject of American permanent dyes, or pigments, illustrated by experiments, and accompanied by specimens of the materials and of the articles colored.[3]

Surgeons' instruments were made in Philadelphia, by R. B. Bishop. The Axle Tourniquet, patented in 1801, by Dr. Joseph Strong, of Pa., was described, in the London Medical and Physical Journal for Oct., as the invention of a Mr. Blake, in England.[4]

A patent was issued (Jan. 25) to Thomas Benger, for an improvement in preparing quercitron or black oak bark, for exportation or home consumption, for dyeing and other uses. O. Evans patented (Feb. 14) a screw mill for breaking and grinding hard substances, and also an improvement upon the steam engine, "by the application of a new principle, by means of strong boilers to retain and confine the steam; thereby increasing the heat in the water, which increases the elastic power of the steam to a greater degree." A spinning and twisting mill, for making cordage, was patented (Feb. 27) by Wm. B. Dyer; and a

"From foaming Brandywine's rough shores
it came,
To sportsmen dear its merits and its name;
Dupont's best Eagle, matchless for its power,
Strong, swift and fatal as the bird it bore."

(1) Philadelphia and its Manufactures, by Edwin T. Freedley.

(2) Munsell's Chronology of Paper.

(3) Philad. Med. Museum, vol. 1, p. 449.

(4) See Coxe's Phila. Med. Museum, vol. 1, pp. 186, 311.

machine "for preparing what is commonly called top or swingled tow, for paper" (March 19), by Abraham Frost; and an improvement in manufacturing coat and waistcoat buttons, by Geo. W. Robinson (March 24) The patentee became, at Attleboro, Mass., the most extensive manufacturer of metal buttons in the United States. A straw and hay cutter, patented (April 30) by Moses Coates, of Downingtown, Pa., was considered more simple and cheap than any in use, and was generally adopted in the neighboring counties. An improved lantern, a composition for drawing or writing tablets, and a machine to cut strips or chips of wood, for hats, bonnets, etc., were the subjects of patents, by Amos D. Allen (May 10). Burgiss Allison and Richard French, patented (June 8) a machine for making nails and spikes, which was successfully put in operation this year or earlier; Asa Spencer, an improvement in making thimbles (June 8). Another machine for cutting chips or strips of wood to make chip hats and bonnets, brooms, baskets, sieves, matting, and for various other uses, by John Roberts, Amos D. Allen, and Ezekiel Kelsey (Sep. 5), was in aid of a business, which was soon after prosecuted in several parts of the country. E. I. Dupont de Nemours, patented (Nov. 23) a machine for granulating gunpowder, which was brought into use in his extensive powder mills, on the Brandywine. A machine for boring gun barrels, by Nathan Fobes (Dec. 31). The whole number of patents issued was eighty-three, a greater number than in any previous year.

The Middlesex canal, connecting Boston harbor with Concord river, a branch of the Merrimac, above Lowell, through Medford, Woburn, and Wilmington, was completed by a company, incorporated in 1789. It was the first great work of the kind finished in the United States. The distance was about twenty-seven miles, and the cost upwards of $550,000. The summit level was 107 feet above tide-water, and thirty-two above the Merrimac, at Lowell, and the whole descent was effected by twenty-two locks, ninety feet long by twelve feet wide, of solid masonry. The water power and communication thus obtained, prepared the way for the manufacturing operations of the neighborhood.

The manufacture of printing presses, copperplate, and book binder's presses, and printing-house furniture of all kinds, was carried on at this time, in Carter's alley, Philadelphia, by Adam Ramage.

The first *busts* ever executed in American marble, were carved for James Traquair, stone cutter, Tenth and Market sts., Philada., by Jos. Jurdella, an Italian, who had been employed, ten or twelve years before, by the celebrated Italian sculptor, Cerracchi, in making, in this country, under his direction, busts of Washington, Jefferson, Hamilton, and Rittenhouse. Busts of Washington, in Carrara marble, from a cast by Uden, also of Hamilton—from whose bust by Cerracchi casts in plaster were this year struck in New York, by John Dixey—were made at $100 each, and half size likenesses of Penn, Washington, and Franklin, both in Italian and Pennsylvania marble. Busts of Penn and Washington were presented to the Pennsylvania Hospital, which was about this time also presented with a leaden statue of the founder, by his grandson, the Hon. John Penn, of Stoke, England.

In March, a company was incorporated in Pennsylvania, for obtaining slate, from quarries in the county of Northampton, suitable for roofing, and other purposes.

1805 The cloth manufacturers and dressers, in Pittsfield, Mass., had become so numerous, that, in April, a public proposal was made for their combination into a society, for the purpose of investigating the natural qualities of chemical liquids, and improving the making and dressing of cloth. Arthur Scholfield made and sold double carding machines for $400, or $253 without the cards, and picking machines, for thirty dollars each. The first machines made by him, about four years before, are said to have sold for $1,300 each.[1]

Mr. John Lee, who had become the proprietor of the woolen mill in Byfield, succeeded, about this time, in shipping clandestinely, from England, in large casks labelled as "hardware," in charge of his brother-in-law, James Mallalow, a quantity of cotton machinery, consisting of drawing, and spinning frames, or mule throstles, which, to avoid suspicion, he followed in another vessel. The machinery was erected in the factory building, where it was at first employed in spinning wick yarn, and warp, which were in much demand for household manufactures. Bed ticking, coarse gingham, and sheeting, and other heavy articles, all woven by hand, were soon after added. The last article then sold at fifty cents a yard, and gingham for about seventy cents.

This factory is said to have been one of the first to produce that class of goods.

The Kings County Society of Mechanics and Tradesmen, in New York, was incorporated.

In the spring of this year, a settlement, called New Switzerland, was made on the Ohio river, in Indiana, by emigrants from the Pays de Vaud, in Switzerland, under grants made by Congress to John J. Dufour, and his associates, for the purpose of encouraging the cultivation of the vine, and the making of wine. The grape culture was successfully carried on by them for a number of years, first, with Madeira, and other foreign vines, but to better advantage with the native Cape or Schuylkill grape,

(1) Holland's Western Massachusetts.

the superiority of which to all others, as a wine grape, was long maintained by the founder of the colony.

The returns of exports, for this year, discriminated, for the first time, between Sea Island and other cotton. The amount of the former exported, was 8,787,659 lbs., and of other kinds, 29,602,428 lbs. The total value of this staple exported, was $9,445,000. The value of domestic manufactures exported, was $2,300,000.[1]

The total value of the real and personal property of the United States, exclusive of Louisiana, according to an estimate made by Mr. Gallatin, Secretary of the Treasury, for this year, was $2,505,500,000. The estimate included 1,000,000 slaves, valued at $200 each, and 10,000 flour, grist, saw, iron, and other mills, valued at not less than $400 each.[2] A tabular estimate, and classification of the whole population, for the same year, by Mr. Blodgett,[3] made the whole number of persons, in the Union, to be 6,180,000, of whom 1,866,000 were classed as active, or productive persons, and the aggregate money value of the whole people, $2,822,000,000. The entire number classed as mechanical artizans, was 500,000, of whom one fifth were active persons, and the estimated value of each of the class was $500, or $250,000,000 for the whole. The other classes were estimated as follows: slaves on plantations, 800,000, worth $200 each; slaves otherwise employed, 200,000, at $300 each; free planters, and agriculturists, 4,800,000, at $400 each; fishermen, 30,000, at $900 each; seamen, etc., 400,000, at $700 each; professional, and all other classes not enumerated, 250,000, at $500 each.

The annual consumption of British, and other dry goods, by the 6,000,000 of inhabitants, on an average of three years, was $35,000,000, and of all other foreign articles, $52,000,000, or, altogether, $87,000,000 in value of foreign articles. The produce of the sea and rivers consumed, was valued at $5,000,000, annually; of agricultural food, etc., $85,000,000; of domestic manufactures, $30,000,000; of all other produce, of the forest, etc., $12,000,000, making the total domestic consumption, annually, $219,000,000.[4]

The quantity of cotton manufactured in the United States, this year, was 1,000 bales, or double the amount consumed in the year 1800.

The cotton manufactory, established at Beverly, Mass., in 1787, about this time suspended operations, after having struggled with many difficulties, and sunk more than half its capital.

(1) Seybert, 147; Pitkin, 116. Mr. Blodgett (Statistical Manual, p. 111), and the American Register (vol. 3, for 1808, p. 459), set down the value of manufactures exported this year, at $2,525,000. In Vethake's Ed. of McCulloch's Com'l. Dict. vol. 2, p. 42, it is placed at $2,445,000.

(2) Blodgett, p. 196.

(3) Ibid. p. 89.

(4) Ibid. p. 90.

The price for numbers twelve, sixteen, and twenty, of cotton twist yarn, at Pawtucket, R. I., was respectively, ninety-nine, 115, and 131 cents. The number of spindles in Slater's cotton mill was increased to 900.

The first agency in the United States, for the sale of American manufactures, was about this time established in Philadelphia, by Elijah Waring. He was the agent of Almy & Brown, of Providence, R. I. who consigned to him, for sale, cotton yarns and threads, in great variety. To these were added, as their manufactures improved, plaids, stripes, checks, denims, chambrays, tickings, etc. The depot for those articles was, for many years, a very small store, at No. 152 Market street. In 1812, Jeremiah Brown opened a second agency in the city, for Samuel Slater.

During the last four years the following vessels were built at Pittsburg, viz.: the ships Pittsburg, Louisiana, General Butler, and Western Trader; and the schooners Amity, Alleghany, and Conquest. The ships Monongahela Farmer, and Ann Jean,—the last, of 450 tons, in 1803,—were built at Elizabethtown, on the Monongahela.[1]

The number of iron furnaces in Pennsylvania, at this date, was sixteen; and the forges, thirty-seven. The slitting and rolling mills cut and rolled 1,500 tons of iron per annum. On the west side of the Alleghany mountains were eleven forges, estimated to make about 400 tons annually. There were about the same number of furnaces, some of which had failed for want of ore. About 2,000 tons of iron were annually made in Pennsylvania, and about the same quantity in Massachusetts.[2] Two charcoal furnaces, three forges, and a bloomery, were this year erected in Pennsylvania.

The Amesbury Nail Factory Company, in Massachusetts, was incorporated, with a capital of $450,000.

The New Hampshire Iron Manufacturing Company, at Franconia, was chartered in New Hampshire.

About this time, a gunpowder mill was established at Southwick, Mass., which is still in operation, and makes about 200,000 lbs. of powder annnally.

The first carriage built in the United States, is said to have been made this year in Dorchester, Mass., by a man named White, for a private gentleman in Boston. It was an imitation of an English chariot,

(1) Lyford's Western Directory for 1837. It is related that a Pittsburg ship, about this time, visited an East Indian port, and was about to be confiscated, because no such clearing port was known to the custom house officials. The captain, having traced out upon the map his circuitous route, backward to the head waters of the Ohio, obtained the release of his vessel.

(2) Morse's Geog., fifth ed. 1805.

but much lighter. Though creditable to the manufacturer, it was found difficult to compete with English and French carriages.[1]

The manufacture of silver-ware, which had been commenced in Providence, R. I., soon after the Revolution, by Messrs. Sanders, Pitman and Cyril Dodge, now employed four establishments in that town. These belonged to Nehemiah Dodge, Ezekiel Burr, John C. Jenckes, and Pitman & Dorrance, who were chiefly engaged in the manufacture, on a limited scale, of silver spoons, gold beads and finger rings. About this time they commenced the manufacture of cheap gold jewelry,—at the present time so extensively carried on there. They employed about thirty workmen in making breast-pins, ear-rings, watch keys, and other articles.[2] Mr. N. Dodge claims to have been the first in this branch, as early as 1794, and that the business was afterward started in Attleboro, by persons who purloined the secret from him.

The first settlement was made in Howard county, Missouri, at Booneslick or Mackay's Saline, near the mouth of the Great Osage river, by Major Nathan, son of Col. Daniel Boone, for the purpose of making salt, which has long been carried on there. Salt springs abound in the country, which also contains iron in abundance, lead, copper, zinc, sulphur, alum, copperas, saltpetre, and traces of silver, etc.

Patents were this year issued, among others, for the following objects, viz.: to Robert Crane, Jr., Waterbury, Conn. (May 4), for iron wheels; Isaac Baker, Amherst, Mass. (May 8), sawing shingles; Asahel A. Kersey, Hartford, Conn. (Oct. 9), for a shingle machine; John Bennock, Boston, Mass. (June 1), for a planing machine, the first recorded;

(1) Although this is claimed to have been the first carriage built in America, the business in all its branches, appears to have been commenced in New York, as early as 1768, by two persons named Deane from Dublin (see vol. 1, p. 538). It was also carried on previous to 1790, in Philadelphia, on Arch st. between Fourth and Fifth, by George Bringhurst, coach and harness maker, who manufactured "all kinds of coaches, chariots, post chaises, phætons, coachees, waggons, curricles, chaises, kitteræns, chairs, and whiskeys of the newest fashion, for home or abroad." Massachusetts, in 1754, was assessed on 1,355 carriages, including six coaches, and eighteen chariots toward a manufacturing fund. Virginia, in 1788, had 360 coaches, chariots, and phætons, and 1,549 one-horse chairs, besides waggons, etc. Philadelphia, in 1796, owned 307 four-wheeled carriages, of which thirty-three were coaches, and thirty-five chariots, in addition to 553 two-wheeled carriages. Yet in the year following, August, 1789, only $5,000 worth of carriages were imported. In 1801, the last year of the excise first laid on carriages by Congress, taxes were paid on 21,721 carriages. Indeed, the importation of carriages as stated in the Report of the Pennsylvania Society of Arts, before cited, had, at this date, nearly ceased. The duty on imported carriages, by the act of 3d March, 1797, was twenty-one per cent. *ad valorem.* In 1810, Virginia and a part of Massachusetts, returned 2,413 carriages, built in the year; from other states, there was no return of the number, but the value of the manufacture in seven states, was $1,449,849.

(2) Census of Providence, by E. M. Stone., M.D., 2d ed., 1856.

Alexander McNitt, Geneva, N. Y. (June 15), for separating and collecting sulphate of potash; Wm. Wing, Hartford, Conn. (August 28), casting types; Wm. King, and H. Salisbury, Hartford, Conn. (August 29), for carriage springs.

A company was formed for the manufacture of cotton, on a large scale, in the town of Pomfret, on the west side of the Quinnebaug river, in
1806 Conn. It consisted of James, Christie, and William Rhodes, brothers, of Pawtucket; Oziel Wilkinson, and his four sons, Abraham, Isaac, Daniel, and Smith Wilkinson, of North Providence, with his two sons-in-law, Timothy Green and William Wilkinson, of Providence. One thousand acres of land, lying partly in the three towns of Pomfret, Thompson, and Killingly, were purchased, for the double purpose of excluding taverns and the sale of liquors from the vicinity of their works, and to give employment to the parents of children employed in the factory. By these measures, and the early establishment of schools and Sabbath worship, for which purposes they erected a brick building in 1812, the demoralizing influences exerted by European factories were not experienced. Many of the operatives were able to lay up from $200 to $800, in three or four years. The establishment was known as Conger's Mills in Pomfret county. The capital invested by the company, from April 1, of this year, to October, 1808, was $60,000, of which five twelfths was in real estate.[1]

Samuel Slater, having, on account of the prosperity of his business, about this time invited his brother to come to this country, the village of Slatersville, in Smithfield, R. I., was projected by Almy, Brown & Slaters, with all the recent improvements in machinery, which Mr. John Slater was able to bring with him. In June, the latter removed to Smithfield as superintendent of the concern, which commenced spinning in the following spring, and was managed by him for upwards of fifty years, with uninterrupted improvement and profit, contributing to the large estate accumulated by Samuel Slater, in the cotton, iron, and nail business, in all of which he was engaged. The establishment at Slatersville, originally owned by the four partners in equal proportion, eventually became the sole property of John Slater, and the heirs of his brother. Within twelve years after the commencement of this factory, nine cotton mills, with 11,000 spindles, half of them in the factory of Almy, Brown & Slaters, a paper mill, two distilleries, two scythe factories, and manufactories of lime, whetstones, etc., rendered Smithfield a place of considerable importance; and the power loom,

(1) White's Memoirs of Slater, 2d ed., 127.

dressing machine, and hydrostatic press, were there introduced in the cloth business, by Mr. Gilmore, a few years after.

The Rensselaer Glass Factory, and the Hudson Mechanical Association, were incorporated in New York, March 21.

The Legislature of Pennsylvania passed an act of the same date, to raise $7,000 by lottery, to enable the Vine Company to pay its debts, and accomplish the object of the Association.

Congress, April 18, in resentment of the frequent aggressions upon its neutral commerce, by the belligerent powers of England and France, and the impressment of its seamen by the former, and in vindication of the principle that free ships make free goods, prohibited the importation, after 15th November, from Great Britain, and its dependencies, or any foreign port, of all British manufactures, composed wholly or principally of leather, silk, hemp or flax, tin or brass; all woolen cloths invoiced above five shillings sterling per square yard; woolen hosiery; window glass; silver, and plated wares; paper of every description; nails and spikes; hats; ready-made clothing; millinery of all kinds; playing cards; beer, ale, and porter; and pictures and prints. On the 19th December following, the act was suspended until the 1st July, 1807, and the President was empowered to continue the suspension if he saw fit, until the second Monday in December of the same year.

Congress made additional appropriations of $150,000, for the fortification of the ports and harbors of the United States, and $250,000, for fifty additional gun boats for the protection of the harbors, coasts, and commerce.

The first official returns of exports from Ohio, were made this year, to the amount of $62,318.

The total value of domestic manufactures exported was $2,707,000.

Nov. 21.—Napoleon issued his Berlin decree, declaring the British islands in a state of blockade, and prohibiting all commerce, and communication with them. This, and the various other decrees, orders in council, and retaliatory acts, and instructions, by which the contending parties sought to cripple each other's power, together with the acts of non-intercourse and embargo, to which the United States were forced in self-defence, nearly destroyed the prosperous commerce of the Union, which reached its maximum the next year; but the interruption of its foreign commerce was attended by a corresponding increase in domestic manufactures.

The annual message of President Jefferson to Congress, stated that the revenue for the fiscal year amounted to nearly $15,000,000, and that during this, and the four and a half years preceding, upwards of $23,000,000, of the principal of the funded debt, had been discharged.

It recommended the continuation of the duties constituting the Mediterranean fund, about to cease by law, in lieu of the existing impost on salt. In view of a probable surplus in the treasury, after paying the regular instalments of public debt, the inquiry was made "to what other objects shall these surpluses be appropriated, and the whole surplus of impost, after the entire discharge of the public debt, and during those intervals when war shall not call for them? Shall we suppress the impost, and give that advantage to foreign over domestic manufactures?" On most articles it was believed the patriotism of the people would "prefer its continuance, and application to the great purposes of public education, roads, rivers, canals, and such other objects of public improvement as it may be thought proper to add to the constitutional enumeration of federal powers."

Three ships, the Rufus King, of 300 tons; the John Atchison and Tuscarora, each of 320 tons; the brig Sophia Green, of 100 tons, and two gun boats of seventy-five tons, were built this year at Marietta, Ohio.

Mr. Blodgett estimated the profit of capital invested in farm lands, at their current low prices, and in the necessary stock and labor—the latter being worth more than a bushel of corn per diem—to be more than double, with less labor, than that of the best mechanical employment suited to the country and the present habits of the people. The profits of the fishery and of agriculture were the principal causes heretofore, of a neglect of manufactures.

In Louisiana, near New Orleans, the lands were said to produce twenty bushels of corn per acre, worth about sixteen dollars. The same labor would give 250 lbs. of cotton, worth fifty dollars, and 1,000 lbs. of sugar, worth eighty dollars, with about seven dollars' worth of molasses.[1] The "Mexican" variety of cotton seed, the one chiefly cultivated there, at present, is said to have been, about this time, introduced in Mississippi, by Walter Burling, of Natchez, from Mexico, whither he was sent, this year, by General Wilkinson, on a mission connected with the western boundary question. It superseded the "upland" or black seed, first cultivated, and the "Tennessee" cotton.[2] It was no uncommon thing for a planter, in the year 1800, to sell his cotton crop for $10,000.

(1) Statistical Manual, p. 91.

(2) Cotton was cultivated in Louisiana and the Illinois country, by the French, as early as 1722, in which year Charlevoix saw it growing in the garden of Sieur Le Noir, the company's clerk at Natchez, and it was sent down the river in boats, to New Orleans, in 1746, some years before its cultivation in Georgia. It is related that Mr. Burling, while dining with the Spanish Viceroy, in Mexico, requested leave to import some of the cotton seed of the country, which was refused, because forbidden by the Spanish government, but over his wine, the

The price of upland cotton in England, this year, was fifteen to twenty-one and a half pence sterling; of New Orleans, seventeen to twenty-four; Sea Island, thirty to thirty-seven; Pernambuco, twenty-three and a half to twenty-nine; Maranham, twenty-one and a half to twenty-six; Surat, seventeen; Demerara, twenty-two to twenty-six and a half pence.

The cotton manufactory at Pittsburg, in Pennsylvania, at this time, spun 120 threads at a time, with the assistance of a man and boy. The large cylinder of the carding machine had ninety-two pairs of cards, attended by a boy; the reeling was done by a girl. A wool carding machine was about to be erected there.[1]

The first paper mill in Ohio, was built this year, by John Beaver, Jacob Bowman, and John Coulter, on Little Beaver creek, just within the Ohio line. It was called "the Ohio Paper Mill," and was the third west of the mountains, the Redstone mill, and Cramer's, at Pittsburg, having preceded it.

The erection of the first paper mill in South Lee, was commenced by Samuel Church, on the present site of Owen & Hurlbut's mill. Lee is now the largest paper manufacturing town in the Union.

The water privilege on the north side of Chicopee river, was this year sold by Oliver Chapin, the first settler, to Wm. Bowman, Benjamin and Lemuel Cox, who erected a paper mill, in which paper-making was carried on by hand for fifteen or sixteen years, when they sold out to Chauncey Brewer and Joshua Frost, who continued the business five or six years longer. It then passed into the hands of David Ames, who introduced machinery, and became, in 1825, the most extensive paper manufacturer in the United States. His sons, David and John Ames, conducted the business until 1853, when the Lenox Chicopee Manufacturing Company became the proprietors.[2]

The first cargo of ice shipped from Massachusetts, was this year loaded at Gray's wharf, in Charlestown, on board the brig Favorite, purchased expressly for that purpose, by Mr. Frederic Tudor. The cargo, consisting of 130 tons from a pond in Saugus (Lynn), belonging to Mr. Tudor's father, was sent to St. Pierre, in Martinique, and was attended by considerable loss. Another shipment of 250 tons was made the following year, per brig Trident, to Havana. It was resumed after the war, and, in 1816, six cargoes of 12,000 tons were shipped, and in

governor sportively accorded him permission to take home as many *Mexican Dolls* as he pleased, and the favor being well understood, was freely accepted. They are presumed to have been stuffed with cotton seed.

(1) Cramer's Almanac.

(2) Holland's Western Massachusetts.

1856 the trade had increased to 363 cargoes of 146,000 tons, from Boston to domestic and foreign ports.[1]

The first ark load of anthracite coal from Mauch Chunk Mountain, on the Lehigh river, in Pennsylvania, where it had been used for about fifteen years in blacksmiths' forges, was this year sent to Philadelphia, by William Turnbull, who had an ark constructed at Lausanne, which brought down two or three hundred bushels. It was sold to the Centre Square Water Works, but being found unmanageable, the experiment was not repeated for several years.

Two cotton mills were this year established at Cumberland, R. I., and two at North Providence.

Among the patents issued, were the following: Philip Bennet, Rochester, N. Y. (Feb. 8), a loom for weaving chips; Geo. Richards, Stonington, Ct. (Feb. 14), a dough machine; Israel Newton, Norwich, Vt. (Feb. 28), essence of tansy; Daniel Pettibone, Roxbury, Conn. (March 22), welding steel to iron; Abner Guild, Dedham, Mass. (March 31), carding wool hats: Richard Tripe, Dover, N. H. (April 1), a diving machine; Ephraim Hubble, Middlebury, Vt. (May 1), a water wheel, being the first of about 306 patents granted up to 1857, for water wheels, a greater number than for any other article; Standfast Smith, Suffolk, Mass. (June 12), three patents for extracting salt from sea water and for facilitating the process; Thos. Woodward (Aug. 7), manufacturing slates; B. A. De Carrendeffez, New York (Sept. 2), yellow paint.

Congress prohibited, under heavy forfeitures and penalties, the importation of slaves into the United States, after the first of January,

1807 1808, the earliest period at which such a law could take effect under the Constitution.[2] The near approach of the period in which Congress could constitutionally terminate all participation of American citizens in wrongs, "which the morality, the reputation, and the best interests of our country have long been eager to proscribe," was made the subject of congratulatory reference by President Jefferson, at the opening of the session. This inhuman traffic, which had never been legalized in some of the states, and had been discouraged or prohibited by several state and federal laws of earlier date,[3] was about the same time (March 25), formally abolished by act of Parliament, in England.

The duty on salt imported into the United States, raised by act of

(1) See Report of Boston Board Trade, 1857, p. 79.

(2) Laws U. S., vol. 8, chap. 67. See acts of 22d March, 1794; 7th April, 1798; 10th May, 1800, and 28th Feb., 1803.

(3) See Tucker's Blackstone, Bk. 2, sec. 1. Walsh's Appeal, sec. 9.

July 8, 1797, to twenty cents per bushel, was repealed after 31st December, though several petitions were presented against its repeal The bounties granted by the same act, on salt provisions and pickled fish, were also taken off. The duties constituting the Mediterranean Fund, were continued until 1st Jan., following, and by subsequent acts to 1816. The product of the Onondaga Salt Springs this year, was 165,448 bushels.

The "American Botanical Society, held at Philadelphia," established in June, 1806, resolved to extend its inquiries to natural history in general, and took the name of the "Philadelphia Linnean Society," under the presidency of Professor Benjamin Smith Barton, whose "Elements of Botany," published in 1803, was the first elementary work on Botany, by an American. The Society, through separate committees on Mineralogy, Botany, and Zoology, was useful in acquiring and disseminating information respecting the natural productions of the country, and their uses in the arts and manufactures. (See A. D. 1810.)

The Philadelphia Society, for the encouragement of Domestic Manufactures, instituted in 1805, was incorporated (March 11), under the name of the "Philadelphia Domestic Society," with a capital stock of $10,000 in shares of fifty dollars each, with power to increase the stock to $100,000. The directors were empowered to make advances either in cash or raw materials, as might suit the applicants, upon all American manufactures, particularly those of wool, cotton, or linen, to the amount of one half the value affixed to the articles when deposited in the warehouse of the Society, and pay the residue when sold, deducting legal interest upon the money advanced, and a commission of five per cent. for selling. Money was lent to manufacturers upon good notes, at legal interest, and in that way the Society was believed to have accomplished much good. At the time of its establishment, it was ascertained that 500 weavers were out of employment, and were forced into other occupations. By the aid of the Society all found employment. During the first six years, the dividends—which were a secondary consideration with the stockholders—were six and sometimes eight per cent. The president of the Society was Paul Cox, and the warehouse was at No. 11 South Third street.[1]

The Hon. Robert R. Livingston communicated to the Agricultural Society of Dutchess Co., New York, a statement of the profits upon a flock of pure and mixed merino sheep, wintered at Clermont, in Columbia Co. The flock comprised five full blood merinos of the Rambouillet stock, imported by him, from which 28¾ pounds of wool were shorn, and sold to Mr. Booth for ten shillings per pound; twenty-four

(1) Laws of Pa., vol. 8, chap. 1770.—Mease's Pict. of Phila., in 1811, p. 264.

three-quarter bred, which yielded 106 pounds of wool, sold at five shillings a pound (but worth eight shillings); and thirty half bred sheep which gave 139½ pounds of wool, sold for five shillings a pound. This was the first wool sold by him, and one of the first sales of that article in the United States. The net profit for the year, upon the sixty-four sheep, exclusive of the value of forty-three lambs, was £137 18s. Full blood ram lambs brought $100. Seven-eighth ewes were valued at $40, and rams at $50. A lot of seventeen common sheep, in the same flock, yielded 62½ pounds of unwashed wool, at 2*s.* 6*d.* a pound. Their keeping was attended with a loss, excluding the value of fifteen lambs. The quality of his merino sheep was found by Mr. Livingston, to have improved since their importation. During the next three years his stock was increased to the number of 645 sheep, from full to half blood, and 310 of the best American ewes, and half or three-fourth wethers. His example and counsel did much to turn the attention of farmers to the improvement of their breeds of sheep, and to prepare the way for an improvement in the woolen manufacture.

Sheep of the English breed, called the Bakewell, and mixed English and merino, had been recently introduced into Cheshire, Mass., notwithstanding the exportation of sheep from Great Britain had been made a penal offence, by act of Parliament (28 Geo. 3, Cap. 38). In the autumn of this year, Mr. John Hart, of Cheshire, offered half blood ram lambs, at thirty dollars per head.

About this time the Clermont, the first steamboat built by Messrs. Fulton and Livingston, which had been launched in the spring of this year, from the shipyard of Charles Brown, on the East river, was completed. Having been supplied with a steam engine built by Watt and Bolton, of Birmingham, England, she was moved across the stream to the Jersey shore, and soon after made her first trip to Albany, in thirty-two hours, returning in thirty hours, a distance of 150 miles. This interesting event, which demonstrated the practicability of stemming the current of the largest rivers by steam vessels, was witnessed by many astonished spectators, many of whom had, from the commencement of the enterprise, constantly predicted its utter failure, and treated the enterprising projector with open ridicule or the coldest reserve. The boat was soon after advertised, and established as a regular passage boat between New York and Albany; and by her success permanently introduced the era of navigation by steam. The state Legislature at its ensuing session, prolonged for the term of thirty years, the exclusive privileges previously granted the proprietors, and declared all attempts to injure or destroy the boat—of which some had already been made—to be public offences, punishable by fine and imprisonment.

About this time, an attempt was made by Jonathan Nichols and David Grieve, two ingenious mechanics of Providence, R. I., to propel a vessel by means of screws moved by horse power. A three mast vessel, called the "Experiment," about 100 feet in length and twenty feet beam, of light draught, built by Mr. John S. Eddy, by subscriptions in shares of fifty dollars each, and filled with machinery, constructed by Ephraim Southworth, was navigated from Eddy's Point to Pawtucket Village. The power was supplied by eight horses, and the boat made an average of four knots an hour with wind and tide, but without sails. She was stranded in returning, and there seized and sold by the sheriff to pay her cost, to Mr. John Peck, of Boston, the eminent naval architect, who designed to carry out the plan of the projectors. While being towed to Boston, this early "screw boat" was lost in a gale; but was considered to have proved the feasibility of navigating by propellers in the manner since so successfully carried out by Ericsson and others.[1]

A manufactory of a new article of patent floor cloth or summer carpet, was in operation in Philadelphia. Specimens of the manufacture were deposited in the wareroom of the Domestic Society, in Third street. It is described as strongly woven, for the purpose of the best floor, on a seven yard loom, without seam, of any peculiar size or shape. The carpets were furnished plain or in colors, with borders to match, at from $1.25 to $2.00 per square yard, according to the number of colors: and when partly worn, could be *recoated*, painted or ornamented, and with appropriate borders. By the same process, old woolen or worsted carpets could be coated on one side at half price, and baize or coverings for trunks and baggage, made water-proof. The manufacture appears to have been that at present known as Floor Oil cloth.

Blodgett's canal, around the Amoskeag Falls of the Merrimac, in New Hampshire, was, about this time, completed. It was one mile in length, and was commenced about the year 1794, through the enterprise of the Hon. Samuel Blodgett, who foresaw the immense value for manufacturing purposes, afforded by a fall of forty-five to fifty feet at that place, and expended a large fortune in the construction of locks, but died just before its completion. The manufacturing town of Manchester has grown up in consequence of the ample power obtained at this place, afterward rendered more available by the Amoskeag canal and other improvements.

The export trade of the United States, this year, reached a higher value than in any other year previous to 1838. It amounted to $108,343,150 in value, an increase, in sixteen years, of $89,331,109. The domestic exports amounted to $48,699,592, and the foreign, to

(1) Hazard's U. S. Register, vol. 4, p. 293.

$59,643,558. Assuming the population to have been 6,300,000 persons, the domestic exports were in the proportion of $7.73; the foreign, $9.46, and the total, $17.19 for each individual. The total value per capita, of exports in 1790, was $4.84.

The domestic exports embraced manufactures, to the value of $2,309,000, cotton, about 66,200,000 lbs., worth twenty-one cents on an average, and valued at $14,232,000; and flour to the value of $10,753,000. The value of cotton exported was nearly $6,000,000 in excess of the previous year, and nearly $8,000,000 above the average of the previous ten years.

The total value of the imports was $138,500,000, exceeding that of any year previous to 1834, with the exception of 1816.

Between one and two thirds of all the exports of British produce and manufactures, during this and the preceding year, or £11,417,334 on an average of the two years, were believed to have been made to the United States. The value of cotton goods exported to the United States, from Great Britain (exclusive of Scotland), on an average of the same two years, was £4,393,449, or $19,000,000; and of woolen goods £4,591,487, or $20,000,000.[1]

This prosperous condition of the foreign commerce, attained, in a great measure, through the neutral position of the United States, in relation to the wars in Europe, had raised the whole tonnage of the Union to 1,176,198 tons.[2] The American tonnage employed in the foreign trade, as compared with that of all other powers so employed, was in the proportion of more than twelve to one.

The revenue, this year, reached nearly $16,000,000, and a surplus remained in the Treasury of $8,500,000, after paying, during this and the previous five and a half years, $25,500,000 of the funded debt, in addition to the current expenses and interest.[3]

But the foreign trade of the Union was about to be suddenly reduced to less than one third the present amount, through the measures of the foreign belligerent powers, among the most important of which, were the king's proclamation recalling all British seamen from abroad, and the British order in council, of November, restricting all direct trade with France and her allies, and declaring their ports (including all European ports but those of Sweden) to be in a state of blockade, to be visited only under certain restrictions, by vessels licensed to do so; and the French Milan rejoinder, declaring all ships, of tever nation, which

(1) Report of Com. of Commerce and Manufactures, Feb. 13, 1816.

(2) Seybert. The actual tonnage of the Union on 31st Dec., 1807, including sea-letter, and all other vessels, as returned to Congress by the Secretary of the Treasury, was 1,268,548½ tons; and the total tonnage on which duties were paid during the year, was 1,450,585¼ tons.

(3) President's Message, Oct. 27, 1807.

submitted to the British orders in council, to be denationalized, and liable to capture as lawful prizes. These were followed by other decrees and orders, affecting neutral vessels.

For the protection of the ports of the United States, the president was authorized by Congress, to cause one hundred and eighty-eight additional gunboats to be built, or purchased.

As the safer, and more peaceful mode of inducing the belligerent powers to withdraw the orders and decrees, affecting the neutral maratime trade of the United States, and of protecting its seamen and ships from their operation, Congress laid a general embargo upon all vessels within the jurisdiction of the United States, cleared or not cleared, bound to any foreign place. All registered, or licensed coasting vessels, bound from one port of the United States to another, were required to give bond in double the value of vessel and cargo, and fishing vessels, in four times the value, to reland their cargoes in the United States. This act continued in force until January 1st, 1809, and in conjunction with the non-importation act assisted to complete the overthrow of the foreign commerce of the Union, during that time.

The new tonnage built this year, was 99,784 tons, from which amount it fell off to less than one-third in the following year.

At a session of the United States court, held in Georgia, in December, the first important decision was rendered by Judge Johnson, in the case of Whitney *vs.* Arthur Fort, for trespass upon the patent right of Miller and Whitney in the saw gin. A decree for a perpetual injunction was ordered against the defendant, but the decision did not terminate the aggressions. More than sixty suits had been brought in that state, before a single decision on the *merits* of Whitney's claim was obtained, and thirteen years of the patent had expired.[1]

(1) Olmstead's Memoir, p. 46. The memorable decision of Justice Johnson, rendered on this occasion, contains the following remarks upon its utility. "The whole interior of the Southern States was languishing, and its inhabitants emigrating for want of some object to gain their attention, and employ their industry, when the invention of this machine at once opened views to them, which set the whole country in active motion. From childhood to age it has presented to us a lucrative employment. Individuals who were depressed with poverty, and sunk in idleness, have suddenly risen in wealth and respectibility. Our debts have been paid off, our capitals have been increased, and our lands trebled themselves in value. We cannot express the weight of the obligation which the country owes to this invention. *The extent of it cannot now be seen.* Some faint presentiment may be formed from the reflection that cotton is rapidly supplanting wool, flax, silk, and even furs, in manufactures, and may one day profitably supply the use of specie in our East India trade.

"Our sister States, also, participate in the benefits of this invention; for, besides affording the raw material for their manufactures, the bulkiness and quantity of the article afford a valuable employment for their shipping."

During the last three years, ten cotton factories were erected, or commenced in the state of Rhode Island,—five of them this year,—and one in Connecticut, making fifteen in all, erected in the United States up to the close of this year. About 8,000 spindles were employed in them, and about 300,000 pounds of yarn were produced in a year.[1]

By the interruption of the foreign trade, and the suspension of imports, labor and capital began, from this time, to be more than ever directed to manufactures, and small manufactories of cotton were rapidly multiplied, particularly in New England, and near the original seat of the business. Efforts were also made to improve the machinery, and Hines, Dexter & Co., of Rhode Island, introduced an improved cotton picker, which was, however, superseded by a picker made by a Scotchman.

The Maine Cotton and Woolen Manufacturing Company was, this year, incorporated in Massachusetts, with a capital of about $100,000, and erected works at Brunswick, in Maine, where, in 1822, it employed 1,800 spindles, and thirty-two power looms, in the manufacture of sheetings.

In Pittsburg, Pa., which had rapidly advanced in manufactures and the mechanical arts since 1793, was, at this time, a cotton factory, belonging to Kirwin and Scott, which employed a mule of 120 threads, a jenny of forty threads, four looms, and a wool carding machine, under the same roof.

Among the other manufacturing establishments of that borough, were O'Hara's white glass works, producing to the value of $18,000 annually, and one green glass factory, upon the opposite side of the Monongahela; McClurg's air furnace; four nail factories, one of which made 100 tons of cut and hammered nails annually; two extensive breweries (O'Hara's and Lewis's), making beer and porter, which had already much of the repute which has ever since appertained to Pittsburg ale; two rope-walks (Irwin's and Davis's); three copper and tin factories; one wire weaving and riddle factory; one brass foundry; two earthenware potteries and a factory for clay smoking pipes; six brickyards; four printing offices and one copperplate printer. The following additional master workmen were enumerated in various branches: house carpenters and joiners, thirty-two; boot and shoemakers, twenty-one; blacksmiths, seventeen; weavers and tailors, of each, thirteen; mantua-makers, twelve; blue dyers, ten; butchers, eight; coppersmiths, cabinet-makers, tanners, seven of each; saddlers, milliners, bakers, hatters, six each; watch and clockmakers, and silversmiths, five; Windsor chair makers,

Such a view of the benefits already conferred, and in prospect, from this great invention, should have been a sufficient rebuke to the sordid injustice inflicted by the people of that state upon the inventor.

(1) Gallatin's Report on Manufactures, April 17, 1810.

coopers, boat-builders, bricklayers, plasterers, five each; plane makers, house painters, four each; wagon makers, spinning wheel, spindle, and crank makers, stone cutters, stone masons, three each; gunsmiths, tobacconists, soap-boilers, book-binders, tinners, mattress makers, barbers, straw bonnet makers, ship-builders, looking-glass makers, booksellers, two each; of manufacturers of the following articles, one each; viz.: bells, scythes and sickles (five miles up the Alleghany), brushes, wool and cotton cards, wove stockings, cut glass, sails, upholstery, machinery and whitesmithing, cutlery and tools, ladies' shoes, split bottom chairs, leather breeches, gloves, trunks, horn combs, turnery, reeds, saddle-trees, flutes and jewsharps, pumps, ladies' lace, locks, harness and saddlery, starch. There were sixteen school teachers, four physicians, one gardener and seedsman, fifty store-keepers, and thirty-three tavern-keepers.[1]

An order was this year received from merchants in Calcutta, for sixty hogsheads of Philadelphia porter, some of which had been previously taken out and brought back uninjured. Among the principal manufacturers of porter, brown stout, and ale, were Robert Hare and son, the former of whom, in connection with J. Warren, both previously of London, was the first to introduce the manufacture of porter at Philadelphia, just previous to the Revolution.

The article was regarded as in all respects superior to English malt liquor, as it contained no other ingredients than malt, hops, and pure water, while the English article, on account of the exorbitant duty upon hops and malt, was extensively sophisticated with tobacco, aloes, liquorice, quassia root, and green vitriol.[2]

The manufacture of artificial Carbonated Mineral Waters, was, about this time, first introduced in this country, at Philadelphia, by Mr. Joseph Hawkins. With patent machinery of his own invention, and an improvement upon the process employed abroad,[3] the business was first commenced by Cohen & Hawkins, at 38 Chestnut st., and soon after, more extensively by Shaw & Hawkins, at 98 Chestnut st., the latter furnishing capital for the business. Abraham H. Cohen established a separate business at

(1) Cramer's Almanac; Lyford's Western Directory.

(2) Mease's Pict. of Philadelphia.

(3) Acidulous waters of this kind are believed to have been first artificially compounded by M. Venel, though in ignorance of their nature. This was first demonstrated, about the year 1767, by Dr. Priestly, to be due to the absorption of carbonic acid, or forced air, as it was called, and he contrived an easy method of effecting the impregnation. About the same time an unsuccessful attempt was made, by a person named Owen, to manufacture mineral waters as a commercial article. The manufacture was successfully undertaken in London, in 1792, by J. Schweppe, previously of Geneva, encouraged by Dr. Pearson and others, and Mr. Hawkins made some improvement upon his process. Appropriate apparatus was invented by Dr. North, and improved by others at an early period.

31 South Second st. These parties obtained testimonials from the most respectable physicians and chemists of the city, as to the purity and healthfulness of the waters made by them, which contained three and a half times the quantity of carbonic acid gas found in any natural springs. Artificial Seltzer, Soda, Pyrmont, and Ballstown waters were supplied by them at six cents the glass, and from one to two dollars per dozen bottles, according to size, and from the fountain, to subscribers, at $1.50 per month, or four dollars per quarter, for one glass daily.

Manufactories of shot had been lately established or revived in Philadelphia, with a fair prospect of superseding the importation of foreign shot. Lead found in Louisiana, and shipped from New Orleans, was chiefly employed. The patent shot tower of Paul Beck, on the Schuylkill, one of the earliest, was upon a large scale, being over 170 feet high, and very complete in its machinery.

An improvement in printing, the invention of Mr. Hugh Maxwell, was in use in three or more printing offices in Philadelphia. It consisted in the use of a roller, in place of balls, for inking type, and was estimated to save to each press, six dollars per week, in addition to the gain in time, and superiority of workmanship. The cost of the machine, complete, was $100.

Patent iron-bound boots and shoes were manufactured in Philadelphia, by Mr. John Bedford, by a process claimed to be a saving of three-fourths the labor, and by greater durability, of one half the leather required by the common method. Mr. Bedford offered patent rights for the county at $100 each, and for states, districts, and towns, in proportion. He continued the manufacture many years, and subsequently patented a process of nailing on the soles of boots and shoes. A patent was also granted this year (Feb. 10), to Samuel Milliken, of Lexington, Mass., for manufacturing boots and shoes with metallic bottoms.

A manufactory of carpeting, considered equal to the best imported, was established in Philadelphia, about this time, by Mr. John Dorsey.

The General Society of Mechanics of New Haven, was formed and incorporated (in October), to regulate and promote the mechanical arts, and to assist young mechanics by loans, etc.

A manufactory of hard metal buttons, recently established in Waterbury, Conn., by Abel Porter & Co, produced triple, double, and single gilt coat and vest buttons, in every variety of shapes, forms, and colors, and military and naval buttons, according to sample. The gilding of buttons, sword hilts, etc., was done by a workman from London.

Several patents were granted for making cut and other nails, brads, and tacks, of which the most important was the machine for cutting and heading nails by one operation, issued (Feb. 22) to Jesse Reed, of

Boston, who took one patent previously, and several afterward. His machine came into extensive use.[1] Samuel Milliken, of Lexington, Mass., a large morocco manufacturer, patented (Feb. 10) boots and shoes with metallic bottoms; Charles Fales, Worcester, Mass. (Feb. 11), manufacturing charcoal from peat; Sylvester G. Whipple, Hallowell, Mass. (April 17), bark for hats and bonnets; Ebenezer Jenks, Canaan, Conn. (April 18), fire brick machine; Jonathan Mix, New Haven, Conn. (Feb. 18), main spring for carriages. This was a spring of elliptical form, placed parallel to the axle, to which it was screwed in the centre, and was considered a great improvement in cheapness and convenience, over the ordinary imported high steel springs. Cornelius Toby, Hudson, New York, (May 7), a bark mill of iron; this was the first to supersede the old stone crushers, and, with few improvements, is the one still in use among tanners; Wm. Young, Philadelphia (May 20), manufacturing lasts; Simeon Glover and D. Parmelee, Newtown, Conn. (June 8), a mortising machine; Isaiah Jennings, New York (Nov. 20), thimbles for sail-makers, being the first of about thirty-five different patents received during the next thirty years, by the inventor of the patent burning-fluid.

Petitions were laid before Congress by the Messrs. Paul and J. W. Revere, of Boston, melters and refiners of copper, and manufacturers of copper in sheets, bolts, nails, etc., for fastening ships, praying for
1808 a duty of seventeen and a half per cent. on copper in sheets,—in which they professed to be able to supply the United States,—and the free importation of old copper. Counter memorials from the merchants, copper smiths, and braziers, of New York and Philadelphia, representing that under the existing duty on manufactured copper, and the free admission of unwrought copper, foreign wares were seldom imported, but considerable quantities of domestic wares were yearly exported to the West Indies, and asking a repeal of the duty on spelter, old copper, brass, and pewter. Congress therefore enacted (March 4), that after 1st April, old copper, saltpetre, and sulphur, imported as raw materials, should be admitted duty free.

An act of Parliament (March 28), laid certain duties upon all mer-

(1) Previous to Sept. 25, 1809, twenty-two of Reed's patent machines were put in operation at Malden, five miles from Boston, by Thomas Odiorne and associates, who purchased the patent. They were also concerned in two establishments in Pa., one on Chester creek, with ten machines, and the other on French creek (Phœnixville), where they were preparing to erect twenty machines. The three works, including buildings, machinery, etc., and two rolling and slitting mills, cost $90,000, and required an active capital of $75,000. The fifty-two machines, with sixty men and boys, were capable of making from the nail plates 1,500 tons per annum.

The machine was afterward adapted to cutting tacks, by Mr. Odiorne.

chandize exported from Great Britain under the regulations established by the orders in council of Nov. 11, 1807. Cotton wool was to pay a duty of ninety-nine pence sterling per pound; cotton yarn, two shillings; India cottons and muslins, twenty-five per cent.; bar iron, three pounds per ton; saltpetre, one pound and eight shillings per cwt.

Orders were published, in April, encouraging American citizens to violate the embargo.

April 14.—Parliament prohibited the exportation of cotton wool from the United Kingdom, until the end of the next session.

The importation of merchandise of American growth and manufacture, was, by act of Parliament (June 23), permitted to be made directly from the United States into Great Britain, in British or American vessels, subject to such duties only, as were payable on the like commodities imported from other countries.

April 8.—Mr. Gallatin, Secretary of the Treasury, in pursuance of a resolution of the United States Senate, of March 2, 1807, made an elaborate report on the subject of Public Roads and Canals.

It stated that a great number of artificial roads had been completed in the Eastern and Middle States, at a cost varying from less than $1,000 to $14,000 a mile. In the state of Connecticut alone, fifty turnpike companies had been incorporated since the year 1803. All the roads undertaken by them were turnpikes, of which thirty-nine, extending 770 miles, were completed. The most expensive, that from New Haven to Hartford, cost at the rate of $2,280 per mile. Its net income from tolls, was only $3,000. Thirty-two others, extending 615 miles, cost but $550 a mile, and gave a net income of $38,000, or about eleven per cent. Of six others, reaching 120 miles, no account was received. In Massachusetts, besides some turnpikes, several roads of a more expensive kind, costing from $3,000 to $14,000 per mile, had been built, but were less remunerative than those of Connecticut. The Salem road yielded six per cent., and another eight, but the others did not average over three per cent. The largest amount of capital invested in turnpikes, was in New York, where in less than seven years, sixty-seven companies had been incorporated with a nominal capital of nearly $5,000,000, for the construction of more than 3,000 miles of artificial roads. Twenty-one other companies, with a capital of $400,000, had been incorporated for the erection of twenty-one toll bridges. Twenty-eight turnpike companies, with a capital of $1,800,000, were known to have completed 900 miles of road, and had 200 more to finish. The cost varied from $1,250 to $10,000 a mile. In Pennsylvania, which was the first to build a turnpike road, many roads were completed or in progress, at a high cost, and two companies had been chartered to extend them to Pittsburg on the

Ohio, 300 miles from Philadelphia. Others were in progress toward the Genesee, and Lake Erie. Several had been undertaken at considerable cost, in New Jersey and Maryland, besides the United States turnpike, from Cumberland, in Maryland, to Brownsville. There were few south of the Potomac.

In regard to bridges the same difference was observed in favor of the more populous northern states, and, south of Pennsylvania, their want was much felt, even on the main post roads. In New England, and especially in Massachusetts, wooden bridges, uniting boldness and elegance, were erected over the broadest and deepest rivers. In Pennsylvania, and in some places more eastwardly, bridges with stone piers, and abutments, and wooden superstructure, were common, of which the Schuylkill Permanent bridge, erected by a company at a cost of $300,000, might be considered the first and most expensive example in the United States. A bridge had been recently thrown across the Potomac, three miles above Washington, wholly suspended on iron chains, without intervening piers, and was deserving of notice on account of its boldness, and comparative cheapness.

The report recommended the appropriation, from the public revenues, of $2,000,000 annually, for ten years, for the following objects of national importance, as perfecting the communication between different parts of the Union, viz.:

1. For canals across the several headlands on the Atlantic coast, except Cape Fear, and for a great turnpike road from Maine to Georgia.

2. To improve the navigation of the four great Atlantic rivers; for four first-rate turnpike roads across the mountains to the western rivers; for a canal around the falls of the Ohio; and the improvement of roads to Detroit, St. Louis, and New Orleans.

3. For inland navigation from the North river to Lake Champlain, and also to Lake Ontario; and for a canal around the Falls of Niagara. The aggregate expense of these works was estimated at $16,600,000, and $3,400,000 was proposed for various subsidiary improvements, to equalize to the several sections of country the advantages of the grand improvements proposed.

The report was accompanied by communications from Messrs. B. H. Latrobe and Robert Fulton, upon the relative cost and advantages of canals, turnpikes, and railroads. In reference to the latter, Mr. Latrobe observed, "Railroads leading from the coal mines (of Virginia), to the margin of James river, might answer the expense, or others from the marble quarries near Philadelphia, to the Schuylkill. But these are the only instances within my knowledge, in which they at present might be employed."

Much interest on the subject of internal improvements, was excited by the able report of the Secretary, and, about this time, the first distinct motion was made in the New York Legislature, by Joshua Forman, for the survey of a canal route between the Hudson and Lake Erie.

April 23.—Congress authorized the President to purchase sites for, and erect such additional armories, and manufactories of arms, as he might deem expedient, under the limitations and restrictions provided by law. The limitation of workmen to the number of 100 was repealed.

An appropriation was also made, of $20,000 annually, to provide arms and military equipments for the whole militia of the United States, in proportion to the number in each. Under these acts the public factories were enlarged, and supplied with additional machinery, and contracts were made with private manufacturers of arms. During the next eight years, 62,606 arms were delivered to the executives of the several states.[1]

Mr. Bibb, of Georgia, introduced in the House of Representatives, the following resolution; "That the members of the House of Representatives will appear at their next meeting clothed in the manufactures of their own country." Not meeting with general approval, it was withdrawn.[2]

Samuel Slater & Co., cotton spinners, of North Providence, announced for sale, by Samuel Haydock, 38 South Second st., Philadelphia, cotton twist and filling, brown and bleached, three-threaded bleached yarn, numbers eight to forty, and bleached cotton sewing thread, numbers twenty to forty, also checks and stripes, and tickings of superfine and middling qualities.

The steamboat Phœnix, built by John Stevens, was navigated from Hoboken, N. J., to Philadelphia, by Robt. L. Stevens, being, probably, the first steam vessel that ever navigated the ocean.

The Clermont, having been enlarged, resumed her trips as a passage boat between New York and Albany. Other boats were soon after built for the Hudson, and for steamboat companies formed in different parts of the Union. The New York Legislature this year extended the exclusive privileges of Fulton and Livingston to thirty years.

The total exports of the United States, for the year, were reduced to $22,430,960, of which $9,433,546 were of domestic productions, including manufactures to the value of $411,000, and cotton worth $2,221,000. The exportations were principally made in the last three months of the previous year, having been subsequently suspended by the embargo.

The manufactures of South Carolina were, at this time, very inconsiderable; but, while the privations created by the embargo were severely felt, Dr. Shecut, by a series of warm addresses published in the Charleston City

(1) Seybert, 609, 610, 626. (2) Benton's Debates of Cong., vol. 3, p. 710.

Gazette, succeeded in arousing a spirit favorable to domestic industry. After several public meetings, an association, called the South Carolina Homespun Company, was formed, and soon after incorporated with a capital of about $30,000, to promote the manufacture of common domestic fabrics. A lot of ground was purchased, and a procession of 4,000 persons, and a still larger assemblage, attended the laying of the corner stone of the first edifice on a large scale, in that part of the Union, devoted to domestic manufactures. A congratulatory address was delivered by Wm. Loughton Smith, Esq., and approval and support of the measure was regarded as a test of patriotism.

Increased value had been given to the rice crop, within a few years, by the general use of mills for threshing and cleaning it, introduced and improved by the Messrs. Lucas, by Mr. C. Kinlock, of Georgetown, and Mr. Deneale, of Virginia. The Agricultural Society also offered gold and silver medals for various hydraulic machines, for agricultural purposes.

About this time also, the subject was pressed upon the people of Virginia, in an address issued at Richmond, signed by Messrs. W. H. Cabell, Wm. Wirt, Wm. Foushee, Sen., Peyton Randolph, and Thomas Ritchie, advocating such a system of domestic manufactures, as would render them independent of foreign nations. The address stated that it was possible, "even if the present attacks on our trade should blow over, Congress may adopt the policy of encouraging our own manufactures, by rather higher duties on the imported articles of Europe, if they should discover, from the experience of the intermediate time, that we have really the inclination and the spirit to clothe ourselves."

The President, in opening the second session of the tenth Congress, adverted to the fact, that the suspension of foreign commerce had impelled the country to apply a portion of its industry and capital to internal manufactures and improvements, to a daily increasing extent, and that "little doubt remains, that the establishments formed, and forming, would, under the auspices of cheaper materials and subsistence, the freedom from labor and taxation with us, and of protecting duties and prohibitions, become permanent."

A memorial to Congress, presented early in the session by ten manufacturers of twines and lines, in Boston, Charlestown, Plymouth, Salem, and Beverly, Mass., asking an increased duty upon these articles, with which they claimed to be able to supply the United States, as cheaply as they could be imported, but for the extended credit given the importers, states that they manufactured annually, from hemp, 46,000 dozen of lines, and from flax, 27,500 lbs. of twine.

The total tonnage of new vessels built this year, was only 31,755 tons, or about one-third that of the previous year. Ship-building was given up on the Ohio, in consequence of the embargo, only one schooner, of 100 tons, having been constructed at Marietta. Of the gunboats authorized by Congress, in December last, 103 were built during this year.

The first flint glass manufactory was established in Pittsburg, by Messrs. Bakewells & Co., who met with many difficulties in discovering the proper materials, seeking and training workmen, etc., but succeeded in establishing an extensive business.

A steam flouring mill, calculated to run three pairs of stones, was also erected in the borough, by Oliver and Owen Evans, at a cost of $14,000.

The valuable water power of French creek, in Chester Co., Pa., was, at this time, appropriated by the erection of a large cut nail factory, and rolling and slitting mill, where the manufacturing borough of Phœnixville now stands. The works were principally owned by Mr. Longstreth, who, in connection with Thomas Odiorne, of Malden, Mass., erected twenty of Jesse Reed's machines for cutting and heading nails at one operation. Ten of these machines were previously put in operation, by Mr. Odiorne, on Chester creek. The French creek works were subsequently owned, among others, by Lewis Wernwag, the distinguished architect of the Fairmount wooden bridge; by Messrs. Jonah and George Thompson, by whom new works were erected in 1822; and by Reeves & Whittaker, of whom Reeves, Buck & Co., the present owners, are the successors. This was the commencement of an extensive nailing and iron business in the valley of the Schuylkill.

A series of articles were published in the Aurora newspaper, at Philadelphia, upon "the applications of chemistry in the arts and manufactures," by Dr. James Cutbush, afterward acting professor of chemistry in the United States Military Academy, and the author of a posthumous "System of Pyrotechny," and other works.

The Union Manufacturing Company, of Maryland, was incorporated with a capital of $1,000,000, in 20,000 shares, of fifty dollars each, owned by over 300 persons, including the state, which owned 200 shares, to carry on the manufacture of coarse cotton goods, on a large scale.

A site was selected upon the Patapsco river, ten miles from Baltimore, adjoining the lower mills and works of the Messrs. Ellicott. A dam was built of timber, 170 feet wide, and a canal 514 rods in length, affording water power for eight mills of the largest class. Two mills were erected 110 by forty-four feet, five stories high, and adapted for 10,000 spindles, with the requisite water looms. The first mill commenced running in May, 1810, and continued until Dec., 1815, when its machinery, consisting of 6,000 spindles and their appendages, was destroyed by fire. The second mill was started in July, 1814.

The Washington Cotton Manufacturing Company, with a capital of

$100,000, in shares of fifty dollars each, was incorporated about one year after the Union, and erected works on James Falls, five miles from Baltimore. It was confined to spinning cotton by water power.

The manufacture of cotton was rapidly increasing in Rhode Island, and the adjoining states. The following mills were this year established in Rhode Island: the Potowomut company, at Warwich, one at South Kingston, and one at Coventry; one at Rehoboth, Mass., and one at Sterling, Conn. The Pawtucket mill of S. Slater was still the largest in the Union.

Shoes began this year to be manufactured in Georgetown, Mass., where the business has since become extensive.

The high price of potash in Canada, where it is said to have risen, in consequence of the embarrassments of commerce, from $100 or $120 per ton, to $300, gave a great impulse to its manufacture in northern New York. Nearly the whole population of Essex Co. engaged in the manufacture and transportation of the article to Montreal, which was continued until the declaration of war, in 1812.[1]

The Laws of Louisiana (Territory), the first book printed west of the Mississippi, was published this year.

The manufacture of hats began at Plainfield, N. J., where it is still actively carried on.

The Emperor Napoleon, in order to create in France a rival industry to the cotton manufacture of England, which enabled her to carry on the war successfully, offered a premium of 1,000,000 francs, to any person, of any nation, who would invent a machine for spinning flax with the same facility that cotton was spun by machinery. The award was never made. John Dumbell took out a patent in England, in August, for flax spinning.

Barlow's Columbiad was issued in a style making it the most magnificent volume which had yet appeared in America. It was in quarto form, and was illustrated by engravings executed in London, several of which were designed by Robert Fulton, the friend of the author. The sale was quite limited on account of the high price, and was followed by a cheaper edition in the next year.

Among the patents issued this year, was one to Oliver Evans (Jan. 22), renewing by special act of Congress, for fourteen years, his patent of Dec. 18, 1790, for manufacturing flour and meal. An alleged informality in the old patent had caused a suit, in the courts of Pennsylvania, to be given against him, and otherwise deprived him of its benefits. Under the new patent, he claimed not only the exclusive use of the ma-

(1) Watson's Ag. Sur. of Essex Co.

chinery specified, but also to prohibit the use of any other invention that should accomplish the same effect, however different in principle. He also advanced his charges for the use of his machinery, to many times the former rate, viz. : for the right to use it with a pair of stones four and a half feet in diameter, from thirty dollars to $300 ; and for a mill to run five pair of stones seven feet in diameter, $3,675, for which his former demand was only $200. Memorials were afterward presented to Congress for an amendment or repeal of the act, in which testimony was adduced that Evans was not the original inventor of any portion of the machinery.[1] Wm. B. Dyer, Baltimore (Feb. 27), a cordage spinning wheel; Reuben Ainsworth (May 14), making pearlash without ovens; Wm. Rhodes, New York (May 16), a floating dry dock; Caleb Johnston, New Glasgow, Va. (June 3), a double lever tobacco press; James Armour, Jr., Baltimore (June 27), spiral folding carriage springs; Abel Brewster, Hartford, Conn. (July 11), vitriolic test for bankbills; Stephen W. Dana, Rutland, Vt. (August 30), an improvement in carriages. This consisted in attaching a separate axle of iron to each wheel, and making it revolve with the wheel. It was supported near the wheel, by a metal box causing little friction, the other end resting also in a strong metal box under the body. A committee of the most respectable mechanics of neighboring towns, after fully testing it, bore public testimony to its value as an improvement. Elisha Callender, Boston (Oct. 3), lightning rods, the first for that object; Daniel Pettibone, Philadelphia (Oct. 28), stoves for rarifying air for warming houses by pure heated air. This improvement was soon after put in use in the Almshouse, and House of Employment, in Philadelphia, and Drs. T. C. James, Chapman, several members of Congress, and others, gave testimonials of its utility for general use, particularly for warming and ventilating churches, courts of justice, hospitals, manufactories, etc., of which it appears to have been the earliest attempt in this country.

The first meeting in Pittsfield, Mass., to form a company to manufacture fine cloth and stockings, was held in January, when it was *resolved*, "that the introduction of spinning jennies, as is practiced in

1809 England, into private families is strongly recommended, since one person can manage by hand, by the operation of a crank, twenty-four spindles." Fine broadcloth had been made in the place for four or five years, by Arthur Scholfield, from the wool of merino sheep, recently introduced, for weaving which he received forty to sixty cents per yard.

The quantity of salt made at the Onondaga Salines, was about 300,000

(1) Benton's Debates of Congress.

bushels annually. The domestic manufacture of salt in the United States had not, for several years, kept pace with the increase of population. At the Indiana or Wabash Saline, where the cost of manufacture did not exceed seventy-five cents per bushel, the market price of salt had not been less than two dollars a bushel, the quantity being short of the demand. The average annual importation of foreign salt,—much of it in ballast,—during the six years ending Dec. 31, 1807, was about 3,000,000 bushels of fifty-six lbs. each, exclusive of the quantities used in the cod fishery, and for pickled and salted provisions exported. The quantity in the country was considered very inadequate to the supply of the year, and the most eligible modes of meeting the deficiency were the relaxation of the commercial restrictions, or an increase of the Onondaga and sea shore manufactures, either by a bounty on the product, or by a renewal of the duty on foreign salt. The whole sea coast, from Maine to Georgia, afforded opportunity for the profitable employment of capital, with suitable protection. Extensive works were erected, during the next ten years, along the coast, particularly of North Carolina.

The manufacturers of salt in Massachusetts petitioned Congress for a duty on salt imported from abroad.

A report of the first Geological Survey of the United States, by William Maclure, dated January 20th, and published in the sixth volume of the Transactions of the American Philosophical Society, was the first work on the subject. It has been followed by those of Professor Cleveland, in 1816; C. Lyell, in 1845; and E. de Verneuil, in 1847.

Mining operations, which had been suspended by the Revolution, were resumed in the lead mines at Southampton, Mass., by Perkins Nichols, Esq., of Boston. They were continued by him and others, especially David Hinckley, until the death of the latter, about 1828, when they ceased until 1852, at which time they were reopened by Stearns and Sturgess. The neighboring mines of Northampton were, about the same time, reopened.

The scarcity and high price of woolen goods created by the restrictions upon trade, at this time turned public attention strongly to sheep husbandry, and the domestic manufacture of wool. The few full blood Spanish merino sheep in the country, derived from the importations of Messrs. Humphreys and Livingston, speedily rose in price to $500 and even $1500 each, and fine merino wool from seventy-five cents to two dollars per pound. In the course of this year Wm. Jarvis, Esq., of Weathersfield, Vermont, the American consul at Lisbon, purchased 1,400 of the crown flocks of the Escuriel, sold by order of the French government,—which he shipped to this country. During this and the following year, he sent upward of 2,000 more pure merinos. These, with some importations by other parties, to the number in all of about 5,000 imported up to this time, soon reduced the price, and introduced the breeds widely throughout the country. A few of the full blood Paular stock of Mr. Humphreys, and their half blood descendants, had been introduced into Bennington Co., Vt., by Mr. Stoddard, of Rupert, soon after their arrival. A half blood buck from his flock had also been taken into Washington Co., N. Y., by Aaron Cleaveland, and this year the first full blooded buck was hired from Mr. Stoddard for fifty dollars, by Hon. N. Wilson, of Salem, for which he received the bounty of fifty dollars, offered by the state to the person who should introduce the first merino buck into each county,—a measure also recommended by the governor of New Hampshire, at the next session of its Legislature. The New York Assembly also further encouraged the woolen branch by offering premiums of silver plate, worth eighty, 100, and 160 dollars respectively, in addition to bounties from each county, for the three best specimens of narrow cloth, woven in families, and like premiums for the best samples, of 200 yards each, of cloth made by professed manufacturers.

The prize was awarded through the Society of Arts, and last year, was given to domestic cloth made from Mr. Livingston's three-quarter bred sheep. In 1810, the county premium was given to that from Mr. Cleaveland's quarter bred lambs. About this time also, Robt. Prince, a merchant of New York, purchased some of the Jarvis importation at $600 each, which were placed in charge of A. McNish, of Salem, and the half blood lambs were annually sold to neighboring parts. These were the first merinos in Washington Co. and the neighboring towns of Vermont, which are now among the most extensive wool growing districts in the Union, and still furnish specimens of unmixed merino stock. Select specimens of the Escuriel flock of Mr. Jarvis, were also introduced into Queens Co., Long Island, by Judge Lawrence and his Quaker neighbors, which were in high repute, and also furnished pure and grade bucks during the next ten years, to large sections of the Northern and Middle States.[1]

The efforts of agriculturists were not confined to merinos. Other improved breeds were obtained and propagated through individual enterprise, and the exertions of various local societies. Among these the Cattle Society of Philadelphia, instituted this year, and the Berkshire Agricultural Society, in Massachusetts, by establishing periodical exhibitions of farm stock, became prominent. A Merino Society was soon after formed in the Middle States.[2]

(1) Fitch's Agricultural Survey of Washington County.

(2) At the first semi-annual shows of the Cattle Society, held in July and October, sheep of the Merino, Irish, Tunis or Barbary, New Leicester or Bakewell, and Southdown

The possession of an improved quality of wool and the scarcity of woolens, also called into existence a number of small manufactories of various kinds of woolen goods, and notwithstanding the high price of material, many of them were profitably conducted until after the war. Several companies were this year formed in the interior of Massachusetts for this purpose, although one only, that at Byefield, the oldest in the state, was named in the report of Mr. Gallatin, presented to Congress early in the ensuing year, and containing particulars respecting fifteen woolen mills in the different states. The Northampton Woolen Manufacturing Company of James Shepherd & Co., was extensively engaged, from about this time, in manufacturing broadcloths and cassimeres. A mill started at Danville, Pa., about this time, is said to have yielded a net profit of forty per cent. on the capital stock. President Madison was this year inducted into office, in the first inaugural suit of American broadcloth.[1] Mr. Jefferson, who ordered sheep from Spain this year, in a letter to Col. Humphreys, likewise acknowledges the receipt of a piece of cloth from his manufactory "as good as any one would wish to wear in any country," presented, doubtless, like the former, in admiration of the foreign commercial policy of the distinguished recipient. That policy, however promotive of this and several other branches of domestic manufacture, was the subject of much complaint among the commercial classes, particularly of Massachusetts, and produced considerable jealousy and even hostility toward the manufacturing industry of the country.

The superior regard at this time generally bestowed upon the commer-

breeds, were exhibited. A premium of fifty dollars was offered for the introduction into Philadelphia or Delaware counties of a full blood ram of the last named stock, and $100 to any person who would originate, by selection and admixture from native stock, a new breed that would fatten easily, and produce the most and finest wool. In October, a large sale of ninety-eight sheep and lambs, crosses between the Dishley or Leicester and common sheep, were sold at Flemington, N. J., by Mr Joseph Capner, for $927. Full blood bucks of that breed, valued for its fattening qualities, and the wool, which was esteemed for combing and the manufacture of worsted, let for $150 to $200 the season. Among the improvers of sheep in the Middle States beside Mr. Capner, were Miles Smith and Mr. Farmer, near New Brunswick, Mr. Caldwell of Haddonfield N. J., Dr. Mease and Mr. Thomas Bulkley, near Philadelphia, Mr. Dupont in Delaware, and others. Geo. Washington Custis, Esq., long a distinguished stock grower, had recently called public attention to a remarkable breed of wild sheep on Smith's Island, off the coast of Virginia, which were shorn twice a year, and yielded wool, when full grown, five to nine inches long, and superior in fineness to any in the world. Maryland, Virginia, and other states, were also improving their stock of sheep.

(1) The coat is said to have been made at the extensive factory of Col. David Humphreys, on the Naugatuck, at Humphreysville, in the town of Derby, Conn., from the wool of his merino flock, and the waistcoat and small clothes from fleeces of the Livingston flock in New York, presents from these gentlemen respectively. The manufacture of the material has, however, been also ascribed to Arthur Scholfield of Pittsfield, Mass., the pioneer in this branch of manufacture.

cial interests of the nation, which, with the agriculture of the country, had been greatly augmented and enriched during the long period of war in Europe, rendered it for some time difficult for the manufacturers to obtain that command of capital and aid from the monied institutions of the country, that was necessary to place their new enterprises at once upon a successful footing. The encouragement afforded by the tariff had been in general inadequate to the efficient protection of the home manufacturer against the products of the capital, skill, and cheap labor of Europe, brought to his doors by a plethoric commerce, and aided by long standing prejudice in favor of foreign manufactures. A change was, however, about to take place, both in the general appreciation of domestic manufactures, and in the disposition to encourage and promote them by individual example and effort. The household manufactures consequently were extended even more rapidly than those of regular factories, and the disposition to use them, which had become in part a necessity, was rapidly growing into a fashion. In the woolen and linen branches, particularly, the great mass of production was still of this character, evidence of which is furnished in the official report on the subject by the Secretary of the Treasury.

The letter of Mr. Jefferson, above referred to, and other correspondence of this date, are supposed to indicate a considerable change in his views regarding the measure of encouragement to be given to domestic manufactures, and the weight of his opinions went far to influence the general sentiment. The spirit everywhere aroused by the circumstances which had produced his favorite measure of the embargo, he supposed to be unchangeably in favor of the future independence of the country, in respect to the products of manufactures. About this time he wrote to Thomas Leiper, of Philadelphia: "I have lately inculcated the encouragement of manufactures to the extent of our own consumption, at least in all articles of which we raise the raw material. On this, the federal papers and meetings have sounded the alarm of Chinese policy, destruction of commerce, etc. . . . . This absurd hue and cry has contributed much to federalize New England; their doctrine goes to the sacrificing agriculture and manufactures to commerce; to the calling all our people from the interior country to a sea-shore to turn merchants; and to convert this great agricultural country into a city of Amsterdam. But I trust the good sense of our country will see that its greatest prosperity depends on a due balance between agriculture, manufactures, and commerce, and not in this protuberant navigation which has kept us in hot water from the commencement of our government, and is now engaging us in a war. That this may be avoided, if it can be done without a surrender of rights, is my sincere prayer."

To Governor Jay, a little later, he wrote: "An equilibrium of agriculture, manufactures and commerce, is certainly become essential to our independence. Manufactures sufficient for our own consumption of what we raise, the raw material—and no more. Commerce sufficient to carry the surplus produce of agriculture beyond our own consumption, to a market for exchanging it for articles we cannot raise—and no more. These are the true limits of manufactures and commerce. To go beyond them, is to increase our dependence on foreign nations and our liability to war."

On March 1st the embargo was repealed, and an act was passed interdicting all commercial intercourse between the United States and Great Britain, France and their dependencies, after 20th May. In case either belligerent should revoke or modify its offensive orders or decrees, the President was empowered to re-open, by proclamation, the trade with that country.

On assurances received from the resident British Minister, Mr. Erskine, that the British orders in council would be withdrawn after 10th June, the President (April 19) issued a proclamation suspending the non-intercourse act after that time, in so far as it related to Great Britain. Unusual joy and activity immediately took possession of all our seaports, preparatory to the resumption of trade between the two countries. But the British government having disavowed the act of its envoy, who was recalled, a second proclamation (Aug. 9) re-established the interdict, and diplomatic intercourse between the two countries soon after ceased.

On June 7th the House of Representatives adopted the following resolution:—

Resolved, That the Secretary of the Treasury be directed to prepare and report to this house at their next session, a plan for the application of such means as are within the power of Congress, for the purpose of protecting and fostering the manufactures of the United States, together with a statement of the several manufacturing establishments which have been commenced, the progress which has been made in them and the success with which they have been attended; and such other information as, in the opinion of the Secretary, may be material in exhibiting a general view of the manufactures of the United States."

Circulars calling for information on the subject, were issued from the Treasury Department on the 28th July, and the report was made in the following April.

The House also ordered the reprinting of Secretary Hamilton's Report on Manufactures, presented in 1791.

A petition from John Allen and other manufacturers of hemp into linen, asking, in view of a renewal of foreign importations, the interposition of Congress in behalf of manufactories created by the embargo, states that Kentucky already manufactured sufficient baling linen for the greater part of the cotton country; other factories were in course of erection, and several persons were extending their views to finer linen and sail cloth. The state could produce hemp for the whole Union, although much was imported.

The Committee of Commerce and Manufactures, to which was referred so much of the message of the President as related to the revision of the commercial laws for the purpose of protecting and fostering the manufactures of the United States, and also the petitions and memorials of sundry manufacturers of hats, of cotton goods, of hemp into linen, of shot, of woolen cloths and of salt, made a report to the House (June 21). They say that in giving "manufactures the support necessary to withstand foreign competition, skill, and capital, the committee had on all occasions endeavored to avoid the danger of fastening on the community oppressive monopolies;" and that, "A nation erects a solid basis for the support and maintenance of its independence and prosperity, whose policy is to draw from its native sources all articles of the first necessity." The committee recommended additional duties on the following articles: on ready made clothing and millinery, on cotton manufactures from beyond the Cape of Good Hope, on bed ticking, and on corduroys and fustians, two and one half per cent. ad valorem; on shot and other manufactures of lead, one and a half cents per pound; on salt eight cents per bushel.

The Hon. Richard Peters of Philadelphia, a zealous promoter of agriculture and the useful arts, communicated to the Philadelphia Society for promoting Agriculture a plan for the establishment, under the patronage of the Society, of a manufactory, warehouse, and repository of agricultural instruments and models—of which no general manufactory as yet existed. He argued that it would be a means of improving the manufacture and would at once satisfy and increase the already prodigious demand for such implements.

Sales were about this time made in Boston of the first Cotton Duck made in New England, if not in the world. Sail duck of flax and cotton, and cotton bagging, were already extensively made in Philadelphia and in Kentucky. The cotton sail cloth was made by Seth Bemis, Esq., an enterprising manufacturer of Watertown, and a pioneer in several branches of manufacture, who in March employed a Mr. Douglass to construct for him a twisting machine of forty-eight spindles, and, in October, had six English weavers employed at fourteen cents per yard. His first sales were at sixty-five cents per yard for number one, and fifty-eight cents for number two. Encouraged by his success, he increased the business during the next two years, employing as his selling agent Capt. Winslow Lewis, who, by his energy, and the use of the new article upon his own ships, contributed to bring it into notice.

The "Columbian Agricultural Society for the Encouragement of Rural and Domestic Economy," was organized (November 28), at Union Tavern, Georgetown, D. C., for the purpose of encouraging home manufactures and the rearing of domestic animals. The names of seventy gentlemen of high respectability were reported as subscribers, and Osborne Sprigg, Esq., of Prince Georges' county, Maryland, was chosen president. In December following, the standing committee appointed three premiums of $100, $80, and $60, respectively, for the best "two toothed ram lambs," and premiums of ten to thirty dollars for the best pieces of cotton fabrics suitable for men's coats or women's dresses, fancy patterns for vests, pantaloons or small clothes, for cotton counterpanes and stockings, and for hempen or flaxen sheetings, shirtings, table linen, stockings, and twilled bagging of hemp, flax, or cotton.[1]

The Athenian Society of Baltimore was formed during this year, and incorporated the next, for the establishment of a warehouse for the deposit and sale of domestic manufactures. The stock was $20,000, in shares of twenty dollars each. Goods were received for sale on commission, from individuals or large manufactories, and advances were made upon the deposits of small manufacturers. The goods were disposed of on liberal terms, in a manner and with an object similar to those of the Domestic Society of Philadelphia. The sales this year amounted to $17,608, and were much increased in the following years.[2]

In Washington county, Maryland, about eighteen small vineyards were under cultivation with American grapes, from cuttings obtained from Mr. Legaux at Spring Mill, near Philadelphia, and elsewhere. Each had produced several barrels of wine, and the cultivation was prosecuted with spirit, aided by several Swiss, Austrian, and other European vine-dressers.

The influence of the embargo in developing the internal resources and manufactures of the Union, was adverted to in the President's message, as well as in those of several of the governors to their respective Legislatures. President Madison observed, "In the cultivation of the materials and the extension of useful manufactures, more especially in the general application to household fabrics, we behold a rapid diminution of our dependence on foreign supplies. Nor is it unworthy of reflection that this revolution in our pursuits and habits is in no slight degree a

(1) Amer. Register, ch. 7, p. 171. (2) Niles' Register, vol. 1, p. 461, vol. 2, p. 325.

consequence of those impolitic and arbitrary edicts by which the contending nations, in endeavoring each of them to obstruct our trade with the other, have so far abridged our means of procuring the productions and manufactures of which our own are now taking the place."

The Governor of Pennsylvania says, "In proportion to the difficulty of access, to and commerce with, foreign nations, is the zeal and exertion to supply our wants by home manufactures. Our mills and furnaces are greatly multiplied; new beds of ore have been discovered, and the industry and enterprise of our citizens are turning them to the most useful purposes. Many new and highly valuable manufactories have been established, and we make in Pennsylvania various articles of domestic use, for which, two years since, we were wholly dependent upon foreign nations. We have lately had established in Philadelphia large shot manufactories, floor cloth manufactories, and a queen's ware pottery upon an extensive scale. These are all in successful operation, independently of immense quantities of cotton, wool, hemp, flax, leather, and iron, which are manufactured in our state, and which save our country the annual export of millions of dollars."

Governor Stone, of North Carolina, observes, "If therefore the native ingenuity and enterprise of our citizens can be properly aided, there can exist no doubt but they will, by the manufacture of our own materials into articles of necessity and convenience, soon render the state completely independent of supplies derived from foreign countries. The advances already made, and hourly making in this respect, afford a consoling presage of relief from the violence and injustice of the enemies of our government. We were content, if permitted to do so, to advance in the business of manufacture by the slow movements indicated and made necessary by the ordinary increase of our numbers, and the protection afforded by the duties necessary for the support of government. But the injustice of the warring nations of the world has driven us from this course, and our people find themselves now compelled to purchase foreign manufactures, and to sell our own surplus produce at prices induced by an unjustly and unreasonably restricted commerce, or to make such of these articles as their occasions require, for themselves. It therefore becomes one means of national defence, that the Legislature of our improving state should foster her infant manufactures, and to this end nothing can more favorably conduce than to facilitate the transportation of our products by opening and improving our roads, removing obstructions to the navigation of our rivers, cutting canals, etc."

Governor Irwin, of Georgia, says, "While articles of foreign manufacture, in consequeuce of their commotions, continue to rise in value and demand in proportion to the great scarcity among us of circulating specie, does it not behoove us to encourage and cherish every institution for the promotion of agriculture and domestic manufactures. Already, a spirit of patriotism and enterprise has manifested itself generally, and our citizens, foreseeing the evils which must result from too great a reliance on articles of foreign manufacture, are shaking off those fashionable fetters which held them in a state of servile dependence upon other nations, and making every exertion to clothe themselves in fabrics of their own. Will you not second their efforts, and, by rendering all the aid in your power, give a spur to their laudable pursuits?"

The general statistics of the Cherokee nation in Tennesee, communicated to the Secretary of War by the Indian Agent, Return J. Meigs, showed them to consist of 12,359 persons, exclusive of slaves owned by the chiefs, and of white people. Since the year 1796, they had acquired, under the fostering care of government, property, exclusive of land, valued at $571,500, including live stock to the value of $390,530, and 583 negro slaves, worth $174,900. Their progress in improvements and useful arts was indicated by the construction, since 1803, of upward of 300 miles of wagon road, and the possession of thirteen grist mills, valued at $260 each; three saw mills, at $500 each; thirty wagons, at forty dollars each; 1572 spinning wheels, 429 looms, 567 plows, two saltpetre works (one of which, carried on at Nickajack by Col. Ore, made in five years over 60,000 lbs. of saltpetre, most of which was used in making powder); one powder mill, forty-nine silversmiths, five schools, and ninety-four children at school. They raised their own cotton and indigo, and made their own looms.

The Harmony Society, under Mr. Rapp, in Butler Co., Pa., this year built a fulling mill, which did much business for the adjacent country; also a hemp mill, an oil mill, a grist mill, a brick warehouse forty-six by thirty-six feet, another brick building of same size, with an arched cellar under the whole for a wine vault. A considerable quantity of land was cleared, and in addition to many thousand bushels each of corn, wheat, oats, rye, and potatoes raised, 4,000 lbs. of hemp and flax, fifty gallons of sweet oil from white poppy, beer from 100 bushels of barley, and spirits from 1,200 bushels of rye, were produced and much of the product sold.

The subject of a railroad was this year agitated by Oliver Evans, who endeavored to form a company, and proposed to invest his whole fortune in the enterprise. Col. John Stevens, in New York, also proposed it in the place of a canal, which at this time engaged public attention in that state. Henry Meigs also advocated a railroad, but all were considered visionary speculatists.

The number of turnpike companies in New York was sixty-seven, with a capital stock of over $5,000,000, and the miles of road built were 3,071. The toll bridge companies were twenty-one, capital $415,000.

The number of cotton mills erected before the close of this year was at least eighty-seven, sixty-two of which (forty-eight water and fourteen horse mills) were in operation, and worked 31,000 spindles. The other twenty-five would go into operation during the ensuing year, and with the increased machinery of the old ones, it was estimated would work 80,000 spindles at the commencement of 1811.

The mills were thus distributed, viz.: in Maine, one at Waldoborough; in New Hampshire, two at New Ipswich, and four erecting in other towns; in Massachusetts, one at Dedham, one near Newburyport, and eight in towns adjoining Rhode Island, in which five others were erecting; in Rhode Island, seventeen in Providence and vicinity, with seven more erecting—and one in operation at East Greenwich; in Connecticut, one each at Pomfret, Stirling, New Haven, and Derby, and two erecting at Killingly and Plainfield; in Vermont, two, and two more building; in New York, one in Washington Co., one at Hudson, one at Whitestown, and one erecting in Washington Co., and two in Dutchess Co.; in New Jersey, one at Patterson, one at Belleville; in Pennsylvania, two near Philadelphia, one at Shippensburg, one at Pittsburg, the last two horse mills; in Delaware, one water and one horse mill near Wilmington; in Maryland, two near Baltimore, and a horse mill in Washington Co., and water mills erecting, one near Baltimore, and one at Pawtuxent; in Virginia, one at Petersburg. The following horse mills were in operation; one at Charleston, S. C.; one at Louisville, Geo.; one at Cincinnati, Ohio; six at different places in Kentucky, and one at Nashville, Tenn.

The seventeen mills in Providence and its vicinity, working 14,196 spindles, were estimated to have consumed, during this year, 640,000 lbs. of cotton, and to have made 510,000 lbs. of yarn, which was sold as thread, consumed in the manufactories, or used as wick, and in family manufactures, or was exported. Eleven hundred looms were employed in weaving the yarn into goods, principally ticking at fifty-five to ninety cents per yard; stripes and checks at thirty to forty-two cents; ginghams at forty to fifty cents; shirtings and sheetings at thirty-five to seventy-five cents, and counterpanes at eight dollars each. The articles were equal in appearance and superior in durability to English goods of the same description.

The principal establishment in that vicinity, erected in 1806, employed about $56,000 in capital, and consumed about 40,000 lbs. of cotton yearly.

Among the new mills established this year, fourteen were within thirty miles of Providence, with a capacity for 23,600 spindles, the largest of which was that of Butler and Wheaton at Meriden, Massachusetts, to commence with 10,000 spindles. The others were at Attleborough, Northbridge, Meriden, and Swansea, Massachusetts, total capacity, including the first named, 13,000 spindles; two at Cranston, two at Smithfield, one at Scituate (2,500 spindles), one at Johnston, and one at Coventry, R. I., with an aggregate of 7,600 spindles, and one at Killingly and one at Plainfield, Connecticut, each 1,500 spindles. The whole number of spindles in operation in this region was 20,406, of which 14,196 were in Rhode Island, 4,820 in Massachusetts, and 1,390 in Connecticut.[1]

The cotton manufacture of Great Britain was estimated to employ 800,000 persons, and its annual value to amount to £30,000,000 sterling. Of this product the United States had for a number of years taken a greater value than the whole of continental Europe together. Parliament this year granted Dr. Cartwright £10,000 for his power loom, invented in 1787.

A power loom was about this time projected by Dr. Josiah Richards, while a student of medicine at Claremont, New Hampshire. He attempted to put it in operation by water power at the Byfield cotton factory in Massachusetts, but failed, through some defect in the machinery.

A manufactury of cotton and woolen machinery was established in Cincinnati about this time.

Two companies were incorporated in Massachusetts for the manufacture of glass, one of which—the Boston Crown Glass Company—commenced in 1789. In New York the Madison and Woodstock Glass Manufacturing Associations were also chartered. Two companies were incorporated in New York for manufacturing paints and other articles, one of them on a large scale at West Farms, twelve miles from New York. Charters were also granted in New York to the Union Cotton factory at Greenwich, Washington Co., and to the Pleasant Valley Manufacturing Company, whose factory had a capacity for 2,500 spindles.

A large manufactory of gunpowder was about this time established near Richmond, Va., by Brown, Page & Co. A suit was afterward brought against the superintendent of the works by Dupont de Nemours & Co., for purloining from their powder works, on the Brandywine, certain machinery, valued by them at $10,000, on which the superiority of their gunpowder was supposed in a great measure to depend. One powder mill in that county (Henrico), according to the marshal's returns the next year, made 60,000 pounds, or about one half of all that was made in Virginia by fifty-three mills. James Tweddel had also a powder manufactory on the Brandywine at this time, and Schott & Mandeville were manufacturers, near Frankford, Pa.

(1) Gallatin's Report on Manufactures in 1810, see *post.*

The Hampshire Leather Manufacturing Company was incorporated in Massachusetts, with a capital of $100,000, chiefly owned by merchants of Boston, who purchased the extensive tanneries of Col. William Edwards and his associates, at Northampton, Cunnington, and Chester. These works had a capacity for 16,000 full grown hides, and employed three bark mills (with stones), three hide mills, and three rolling machines, all carried by water, and copper cylinders for applying heat in the extraction of the tannin. Most of the improvements were introduced by Mr. Edwards, who still continued to conduct the operations, receiving hides of the company on contract, at six cents per pound, and paying them one half the profits for the use of the establishment.

Letters patent were this year granted to four different persons for the manufacture of combs, viz. : to Moses Moss of Farmington, Conn. (Jan. 10), and to Timothy Stanley of Southington (July 6), for manufacturing hair combs; to Nat. Jones of Southington (May 9), for making wooden combs, and to Robert Gedney of New York (June 26), for manufacturing combs from the hoofs of cattle; Samuel Green, New London, Conn. (Feb. 15), making paper from seaweed, and Francis Bailey, Salisbury, Pa. (July 31), for hot-pressing paper; Amos and William Whittemore, Cambridge, Mass. (March 3), a renewal of patent for making cotton and wool cards; Jesse Reed, Massachusetts (April 19), a wheel for cutting and heading nails; Mary Kies, Killingly, Conn. (May 5), weaving straw with silk or thread; Ira Ives, Bristol, Conn. (June 24), the striking part of a clock; Thomas Newell, Sheffield, Mass. (July 7), astronomical clocks; Samuel Goodwin (July 7), balance pendulum clocks; Lemuel J. Kilborn, Pennsylvania (Oct. 12 and 13), the striking part of a clock, and casting wheels for clocks; Oliver Ames, Plymouth, Mass. (June 24), tuyere and water back; N. Foster, Flemingsburg, Ky. (June 28), spinning hemp and flax, and Jacob Alricks, Wilmington, Del. (Oct. 11), a spinning machine; Jacob Perkins, Boston (June 26), polishing and graining morocco; Burgiss Allison, Pennsylvania (July 6), distilling spirits from corn stalks; Simeon Jocelyn, New Haven, Conn. (July 13), pruning shears—this was for the useful article still employed for lopping the outer and upper branches of trees by means of a pole and cord, &c., which, however, is said to have been previously in use in Germany; Abel Stowell, Worcester, Mass. (July 19), cutting wood screws; Ezra L'Hommedieu, Saybrook, Conn. (July 31), double-podded screw auger. The patentee informed the Secretary of the Treasury in November, that he made his own wire, from which a man and two boys could make per day three hundred weight of assorted screws superior to the imported, and it was thought the United States would soon be supplied by his cheap and simple process. Daniel French, New York (Oct. 12), patented a steam engine for boats, mills, &c., with vibrating cylinder. Under this patent several of the first boats on the Ohio were built and supplied with engines by the patentee. Joseph Coppinger, Beaufort, S. C., received (Nov. 21) a patent for distilling in cast-iron stills; Peregrine Williamson, Baltimore, Md. (Nov. 22), metallic writing pens, the earliest mention we have seen of such pens; Samuel Ellis, New Bedford, Mass. (Nov. 29), geometrical writing plates; George Huling, Shaftesbury, Vt. (Nov. 24), circular saw mill; William Russell, New Bedford (Dec. 1), mariners' compass.

During this year, also, nineteen patents were taken out for washing machines, simple and combined, for which during the previous two years about the same number were received. Between 1797, when the first one was issued, and 1857, about three hundred and thirty were obtained.

Congress appropriated $5,000 for the purpose of testing the practical value of torpedoes or submarine explosives, proposed by Robert Fulton, as a means of harbor defence. The Commissioners appointed for that purpose did not agree in their reports of the experiments.

In obedience to the resolution of the House, of 7th June, 1809, Mr. Gallatin, Secretary of the Treasury, submitted to the house a report in part on the subject of Manufactures. The report, though ad-
1810 mitted to be in general incomplete and defective, contained much important information, which the approaching census, it was suggested, might afford an opportunity to render more detailed and accurate.

The following manufactures were ascertained to be carried on to an extent which might be considered adequate to the consumption of the United States, as the value of their products, annually exported, exceeded that of the foreign articles of the same general class annually imported, viz.: Manufactures of wood, or of which wood is the principal material, leather, and manufactures of leather, soap and tallow candles, spermaceti oil and candles, flaxseed oil, refined sugar, coarse earthenware, snuff, chocolate, hair powder, and mustard.

The following branches were firmly established, supplying in several instances the greater, and in all, a considerable part of the consumption of the United States, viz.: Iron, and manufactures of iron; manufactures of cotton, wool, and flax; hats; paper, printing types, printed books, and playing cards; spirituous and malt liquors; several manufactures of hemp; gunpowder; window glass; jewelry and clocks; several manufactures of lead; straw bonnets and hats; wax candles.

Progress had also been made in the following branches, viz.: Paints and colors; several preparations and medicinal drugs; salt; manufactures of copper and brass, japanned and plated ware; calico printing; queens, and other earthen and glass wares, &c.

Many articles, respecting which no information had been received, were undoubtedly omitted, and the substance of the information obtained on the most important branches, was comprehended under the following heads:

WOOD AND MANUFACTURES OF WOOD were all carried to a high degree of perfection, and supplied the whole demand of the United States. They consisted principally of cabinet ware and other household furniture, coaches and carriages, and ship building, of which last the average annual tonnage of vessels above twenty tons, built from 1801 to 1807, was 110,000. The annual exportation of furniture and carriages was $170,000. The value of the whole, including ship building, could not be less than $20,000,000 a year. Of pot and pearl ashes, 7,400 tons were exported annually.

LEATHER AND MANUFACTURES OF LEATHER.—Tanneries everywhere existed, some of them on a large scale; one establishment employing a capital of $100,000. One third of the hides used in the great tanneries of the Atlantic states were imported from South America, and cost five-and-a-half cents a pound, while in England they cost seven cents. The bark to tan them cost in England nearly as much as the hides, but in America not one tenth as much. Some superior, or particular kinds of English leather and morocco, were imported, but 350,000 pounds of American leather were annually exported. Some of the American leather was of inferior quality, but it was generally better made in the Middle than in the Northern or Southern States. The tanneries of Delaware employed a capital of $120,000 and ninety workmen, and made annually $100,000 worth of leather. Those of Baltimore numbered twenty-two, of which seventeen had together a capital of $187,000, and tanned annually 19,000 hides, and 25,000 calf skins. Morocco leather was made in several places from sheep and imported goat skins, and deer skins—an article of export—were dressed and manufactured in sufficient quantity for the country.

The manufactures of leather were boots and shoes, harness and saddlery. The average importation of boots was 3,250 pairs, and of shoes 59,000 pairs, principally kid and morocco; and the exports of American boots 8,500, and of shoes 127,000 pairs. The shoe manufactures of New Jersey were extensive. Those of Lynn, Mass., produced 100,000 pairs of women's shoes annually. The value of all articles of leather was estimated at $20,000,000 annually.

SOAP AND TALLOW CANDLES were principally a family manufacture. There were also several extensive manufactories in all the large cities, and in other places. Those of Roxbury, near Boston, alone employed a capital of $100,000, and made annually 370,000 lbs. of candles, and 380,000 lbs. of brown soap, and 50,000 lbs. of windsor and fancy soap, with a profit, it was said, of fifteen per cent. on the capital. The importations were 158,000 lbs. of candles and 470,000 lbs. of soap, and the exports of domestic candles 1,795,000 lbs., and of soap 2,220,000 lbs. The total value of the manufacture, including the household, was at least $8,000,000.

Spermaceti Oil and Candles.—Establishments existed at Nantucket and New Bedford, Mass., and Hudson, N. Y., which furnished for exportation a surplus of 230,000 lbs. candles, and 44,000 gallons of oil. Value of the manufacture about $300,000, but the exclusion from foreign markets had lately affected it unfavorably.

Refined Sugar.—The quantity annually made was estimated at 5,000,000 lbs., worth $1,000,000—the capital at $3,500,000. Some establishments had declined in business with the increase in their number. A renewal of the drawback of the duty on brown sugar was desirable, and had been the subject of a special report to the Committee of Commerce and Manufactures.

Cotton, Wool, and Flax.—I. *Spinning Mills and Manufacturing establishments.*—Fifteen cotton mills were erected (in New England) before the year 1808, working at that time almost 8,000 spindles, and producing about 300,000 lbs. of yarn a year. Returns had been received of eighty-seven mills, erected at the end of the year 1809, sixty-two of which were in operation and worked 31,000 spindles.[1] The capital required to carry them on, to the best advantage, was estimated at the rate of $100 for each spindle, including fixed capital, expenses, and all contingencies. Only about $60 per spindle was actually employed. The average consumption of cotton was about forty-five pounds, worth twenty cents per pound per spindle, and the produce about thirty-six pounds of yarn of different qualities, worth on an average $1.12½ per pound. Eight hundred spindles employed forty persons, viz. : five men, and thirty-five women and children. On these data it was estimated that the eighty-seven mills, including the twenty-five new ones to go into operation this year, and the increased machinery of the old ones, would, in 1811, produce the following results, viz. : eighty-seven mills would employ a capital of $4,800,000, and use 3,600,000 lbs. of cotton, worth $720,000. They would spin 2,880,000 lbs. of yarn, worth $3,240,000, and employ 500 men and 3,500 women and children, or 4,000 hands.

(1) See the details under this head, A. D., 1809.

The increase of carding and spinning of cotton in regular establishments had therefore been fourfold in two years, and would be tenfold in three years. The principal establishments were in Rhode Island, and within thirty miles of Providence,[1] and their manufactures were chiefly bed-ticking, stripes and checks, ginghams, cloth for shirts and sheeting, and counterpanes. The same articles were manufactured in several other places, particularly at Philadelphia, where were also made, from the same material, webbing and coach laces (which had excluded, or would soon exclude the foreign articles), table, and other diaper cloth, jeans, vest patterns, cotton kerseymeres, and blankets. The manufacture of fustians, cords, and velvets, had also been commenced in the interior and western parts of Pennsylvania and Kentucky.

Some of the mills also carded and spun wool to a small extent, but that was chiefly done in private families and woolen factories.

Some information had been received respecting fourteen of these,[2] manufacturing each on the average, ten thousand yards of cloth yearly, worth from one to ten dollars a yard. Others were believed to exist, and it was known that there were several on a smaller scale in Philadelphia, Baltimore, and some other places. All their cloths, as well as those made in families, were generally superior in quality, though somewhat inferior in appearance, to imported cloths of the same price. The principal obstacle to the extension of the woolen branch was the want of wool, which was still deficient in quantity and quality, though daily improving through the introduction and general attention to merino and other superior breeds of sheep occasioned by the great demand for Wool.

Establishments for spinning and weaving Flax were few. One in the State of New York employed a capital of $18,000 and twenty-six persons, and spun and wove annually about 90,000 lbs. of flax into canvas and other coarse linen. Information had been received of two in the vicinity of Philadelphia, of which one produced annually 72,000 yards of canvas made of flax and cotton; in the other the flax was both hackled

(1) See the details under this head, A. D., 1809,

(2) A woolen mill was established at each of the following places: New Ipswich, N. H.; Byefield, Mass.; Warwick and Portsmouth, R. I.; Humphreysville, Conn.; Poughkeepsie, N. Y.; two on the Brandywine, Del.; two at Baltimore and Elkton, and one at Frederick, Md.; three (and sundry smaller ones) at Philadelphia, and one at Germantown, Pa. The capital (when stated) was from three to twenty thousand dollars each; the number of hands from eight to twenty-nine, and the product from 5,000 to 27,000 yards annually. Those at Humphreysville, Poughkepsie, and one on the Brandywine, used merino wool, and made broadcloth chiefly, and some broadcloth was made at Baltimore. Cassinet (wool and cotton) was made in Philadelphia.

and spun by machinery; thirty looms were employed, and it was said 500,000 yards of cotton bagging, sail-cloth and coarse linen might be made annually.

Hosiery was almost exclusively a household manufacture. That of Germantown had declined, and it had not been elsewhere attempted on a large scale. There were some exceptions; Martha's Vineyard exported annually 9,000 pairs of stockings.

II. *Household Manufactures.*—By far the greater part of the cotton, flax and wool was manufactured in private families for their own use and for sale. The articles were principally coarse cloth flannel, cotton stuffs and stripes of every description, linen and mixtures of wool and cotton. Information from every state, and more than sixty different places, showed an extraordinary increase in the last two years and rendered it probable that about two thirds of the cloth, including hosiery, house and table linen, used by the inhabitants outside of the cities, was the product of family manufactures. In the Eastern and Middle States, carding machines carried by water were every where established and others were extended southwardly and westwardly. Jennies and other spinning machines, and flying shuttles, were introduced in many places, and fulling mills sufficient for furnishing all the family manufactures.[1]

(1) In Delaware 150,000 lbs. of wool were annually spun and wove in private families. Large exportations of linen were made from the western counties of Pennsylvania, and some from Kentucky and several places in the Eastern and Middle States. In 1809, eighty thousand yards were brought to Pittsburg alone, for sale, and the looms in that town had increased since 1807 from seventeen to forty-four. In the lower counties of Virginia, North Carolina generally, and the upper counties of South Carolina and Georgia, almost the whole summer-clothing of all classes was of household manufacture, and the slaves were entirely clothed in that manner. The scarcity of wool alone prevented the winter clothing being made in the same way. Stores for the sale of foreign goods in Matthews County, Va., had decreased since 1802, from fifteen to one. And of 1500 persons attending a militia review in North Carolina, less than forty wore any thing but *homespun*.

In New Hampshire nearly every township of 200 or 300 families had a carding and fulling mill. The former cost about $500 each, and carded for seven cents per pound. Every farm house had one or more wheels, and every second house at least a loom for weaving linen, cotton and coarse woolen cloths, which was done by the women. From 100 to 600 yards of cloth were thus made yearly on an average in each family, without an hour's loss of farm labor. Flaxen cloth worth fifteen to twenty cents a yard, was sold to country traders, who sent it to the Southern States at a profit. There were about 140 fulling mills in New Hampshire, of which the average cost was $1,500. They received, for dressing about 6,700 yards each, on an average, $1,225, of which $600 was for labor and materials. The cost of manufacturing eighteen pounds of wool into twenty yards of cloth, was about $21.24 (or 106 cents per yard of three-quarters wide). It was finer than English cloth of six-quarters, which sold in the stores for $3.50 per yard, and was more durable. In Vermont were 163 fulling mills, and 1,040,000 yards of cloth and flannel, and 1,315,000 yards of cotton and flax were woven in families.

The value of all the goods made annually of cotton, wool and flax, was estimated to exceed forty millions of dollars.

Connected with this subject was the manufacture of cards and wire. Whittemore's card machine had completely excluded foreign cards. The capital employed in that branch was estimated at $200,000, and the annual consumption amounted, until lately, to 20,000 dozen pairs of hand cards and 20,000 square feet of cards for machines, worth together about $200,000. The demand in 1809 was double that of 1808, and was still increasing. The wire was imported, and serious inconvenience would attend a stoppage of the supply, although the manufacture might and would be immediately established to supply all demands if the same duty were laid on wire, now free, as on other articles of the same material. The annual consumption of wire for cards did not exceed twenty-five tons, worth $40,000.[1]

Hats.—The annual importations were $350,000, the exportation of domestic hats $100,000, and the manufacture therefore nearly equal to the consumption. The hat company of Boston estimated the manufacture in Massachusetts at four times the number required for the state. It otherwise appeared that a capital of near three millions was applied to the business in that state and the number of hats made was 1,550,000, of which 1,150,000 were fine hats, worth four dollars each, and 400,000 felt hats worth one dollar each. That it was profitable appeared from a late establishment on Charles river calculated to make annually 35,000 hats, at five dollars apiece, and to employ 150 men. In Rhode Island 50,000 hats, worth five dollars each, were made, exclusive of felts. New York and Connecticut manufactured more than they consumed, the largest factory being at Danbury, where 200 persons were employed, making hats to the value of $130,000. Vermont supplied its own consumption, and in Philadelphia 92,000 hats, worth five dollars, were annually made, in addition to 50,000 *country* hats, worth three dollars

(1) Commmunications from Wm. Whittemore of Cambridge, and Abel Stowell of Worcester, accompanied the report. A. and W. Whittemore had fifty-five of their patent card making machines (the patent for which had been recently renewed for fourteen years). Of those thirty-seven were in use, and, with the apparatus to carry on the business, cost them about $40,000. The only imported article used was the wire, and that could be made as good and nearly as cheap here as in England. The Lake Champlain iron was found equal or superior for wire to any imported. The manufacture of iron and brass wire had been frequently attempted with success, but had been abandoned on account of the free admission of foreign wire. A duty on wire as on other manufactures of iron would cause, it was believed, a considerable investment in its manufacture, and produce an adequate supply for cards, screws, and other uses.—See Patents 1809.

each. In many places wool for coarse hats was scarce. The annual value of hats made was near ten millions of dollars.[1]

Paper and Printing.—Some foreign paper was still imported, but the consumption was chiefly of an American manufacture, which, if proper attention was paid to the preservation of rags, would supply the demand. Paper mills were erected in every part of the Union. There were twenty-one in the States of New Hampshire, Vermont, Rhode Island, and Delaware alone, and ten in only five counties of New York and Maryland. Eleven of the mills had a capital of $200,000 and 180 workmen, and made annually $150,000 worth of paper.

Printing was done equal to the demand. In addition to newspapers, a large item, all books for which there were sufficient purchasers, were printed in the United States. The manufacture of hanging papers and playing cards was also extensive, and that of printing types, of which there were two establishments, the principal one at Philadelphia, was equal to the demand, but had lately been affected by the want of regulus of antimony.

Manufactures of Hemp.—Annual importation of foreign hemp, 6,200 tons. In Massachusetts, New York, Kentucky, and several other places, its cultivation had been greatly promoted by the interruption of commerce, and would soon, it was believed, produce a sufficiency.

The manufacture of ropes, cables and cordage was equal to the demand. Exclusive of those in the seaports, the ropewalks in Kentucky alone were fifteen, consuming about 1,000 tons of hemp annually, and six new works were prepared for operation the present year. Manufactures of sail-duck, formerly established in Rhode Island and Connecticut, and at Salem, were abandoned or suspended by the high price of hemp and want of capital. Some was still made, and the species of canvas called cotton-bagging was manufactured in several places extensively. An establishment at Philadelphia employed eight looms and could make annually 7,000 yards of duck or 45,000 of cotton bagging. There were thirteen manufactories in Kentucky and two in West Tennessee. The five at or near Lexington made annually 250,000 yards of duck and cotton bagging.

Spirituous and Malt Liquors.—The spirits distilled in 1801 from

(1) A manufactory of hats at Albany employed a capital of $8,000, and twenty hands, and made 1,600 hats worth seven dollars each, 1800 worth three dollars, and 3,000 worth one dollar each: total, 6,400 worth $19,600, at a profit of fifteen to twenty per cent. The net profit on fine hats at seven dollars was $1.06½, on napped hats of first quality at five dollars $1.93, and of second quality at four dollars $1.16, and on felts sixty cents each. The materials were raccoon, beaver, muskrat and wool. The making and finishing cost $1.25 to $1.50.

grain and fruit (exclusive of the large gin distilleries in cities), was estimated at nine millions of gallons, and at this time at twelve millions, to which were to be added about three millions of gallons of gin and rum distilled in cities, making an aggregate of fifteen millions of gallons. Foreign spirits were however largely imported, and in 1806 and 1807 amounted to $9,750,000 a year, yielding a revenue of $2,865,000.

The annual importation of foreign malt liquors amounted to 185,000 gallons, and the exportations of American beer and cider to 187,000. The amount actually made could not be stated, but the breweries of Philadelphia were said to consume annually 150,000 bushels of malt, exclusive of numerous small establishments throughout the city. Extensive breweries existed in New York and Baltimore. The aggregate value of spirituous and malt liquors made could not be set down at less than ten millions.

Iron and Manufactures of Iron.—The information received in this branch was imperfect. Iron ore was abundant, and numerous furnaces and forges supplied a sufficient quantity of hollow-ware and castings; but about 4,500 tons of bar iron were annually imported from Russia, and probably as much from Sweden and England together. The amount of bar iron used in the United States was vaguely stated at 500,000 tons, which would leave about 40,000 as American manufacture. Although the ore of Vermont, Pennsylvania, Maryland and Virginia, was of superior quality, and much of the iron made there equal to any imported, yet on account of the demand and want of attention, much inferior iron came to market, which made the want of Russia iron to be felt in some of the slitting and rolling mills. A reduction of the duty on Russia iron was asked for by several, but generally a high and prohibitory duty on English bar, slit, rolled, and sheet iron, was considered beneficial, that usually imported on account of its cheapness being made with pit coal and of an inferior quality. The manufacture of sheet, slit and hoop iron amounted to 565 tons annually, and the quantity rolled and slit in the United States was estimated at 7,000 tons. In Massachusetts alone, were thirteen rolling and slitting mills, in which about 3,500 tons of bar iron, chiefly Russian, were rolled or slit. A portion was for sheet iron and rods for wrought nails, but two-thirds of the whole quantity flattened by machinery in the United States was used in the manufacture of *cut nails*, which had extended throughout the whole country, and being altogether an American invention, substituting machinery to manual labor, deserved particular notice.[1]

(1) The details on this subject were embraced in supplemental communications and the historical facts have been sufficiently stated in previous pages, under the head of

The annual product of that branch alone might be estimated at $1,200,000, and the expense of cut nails, exclusive of the saving of fuel, was not one third that of forging wrought nails. About 280 tons were already annually exported, but the United States still imported more than 1,500 tons of wrought nails and spikes, on which an increase of duty, with a drawback on cut nails exported, was generally asked.

Considerable blistered and some refined steel was made, but 11,000 cwt. were annually imported. The manufactures of iron were principally agricultural implements and the usual blacksmiths work. To these were to be added anchors, shovels and spades, axes, scythes and other edge tools, saws, bits and stirrups, and a great variety of coarser ironmongery; but cutlery and all the finer hardware and steel work, were almost entirely imported from Great Britain. Balls, shells, and cannon of small calibre, were cast in several places, and three foundries for casting solid those of largest calibre, with the proper machinery for boring and finishing them, were established at Cecil County, Md., near the city of Washington, and at Richmond, Va.; each of the two last could cast 300 pieces of artillery a year, and a great number of iron and brass cannon were made at the one near Washington. Those of Philadelphia and near the Hudson were not then employed. Several iron foundries made every kind of machine castings. The one at Philadelphia manufactured steam engines.

At the public armories of Springfield and Harper's Ferry, 19,000

patents, and elsewhere. The quality of cut nails was stated to have so much improved within a few years, and was so far superior to any English nails except fine drawn wrought nails, that the protection and patronage of government against the foreign article thrown upon the market at cost and charges, was alone wanting to its complete success. The quantity of nails and brads made in Massachusetts was estimated by a principal manufacturer to have averaged during the last three years 2,000 tons, of which 1,700 tons were cut and the residue hammered. The perfection attained in nail-cutting machinery at this time had by no means been reached without many signal failures; and the cost of bringing it to this state, when a machine would cut about 100 nails per minute, has been computed at more than one million of dollars. The report of Mr. Gallatin was instrumental in making its value better known to the public. During this year a patent was taken out in England by Joseph C. Dyer of Boston, then resident as a merchant in London, for the nail-cutting machinery invented in Massachusetts. The card-making machinery of that state was patented in England by the same person the next year.

The principal business of the rolling and slitting mills was the making of nail plates and rods for wrought nails, hoops, tires, sheet iron and sheet copper. The mills in Massachusetts were situated as follows: one at Dover owned by the Boston Iron and Nail Factory, composed of J. and S. Welles and R. Whiting; one at Plymouth by S. Spear, W. Davis, and N. Russell; one each at Dover, Beverly, and Amesbury, all incorporated, and owned in part by Wm. and S. Gray, and Osgood; one at Newton, by R. Ellis and Gen. Elliot and others; one at Norton; three at Taunton, by Leonard & Crocker and others; and two at Bridgewater. They rolled about 3,500 tons annually, but could make 7,000 tons.

muskets were made annually, and about 20,000 more at several factories, of which the most perfect was that near New Haven, all private establishments, except that at Richmond erected by the State of Virginia. These did not include gunsmiths employed in making rifles and other arms. Swords and pistols were made in several places.

The value of iron and the manufactures of iron produced, was believed to be from twelve to fifteen millions of dollars yearly. The importations, including bar iron and all manufactures of iron and steel, were estimated at near four millions.

Copper and Brass.—Rich copper mines were found in New Jersey, in Virginia, and near Lake Superior, but were not wrought. The principal manufactures of copper were stills and other vessels, but copper in sheets and bolts was almost wholly imported, the only manufactory for that object, which was at Boston, not receiving sufficient encouragement, although $25,000 had been invested in a rolling mill and other apparatus. The reason was that these articles were imported free of duty, and the owners were principally employed in casting bells and other articles. Zinc had lately been discovered in Pennsylvania, and there were a few manufacturers of metal buttons and brass wares.

Manufactures of Lead.—Lead was found in Virginia and some other places, but the richest mines were in Upper Louisiana, and also, it was said, in the adjacent country east of the Mississippi. They did not yet furnish, after supplying the western country, over 200 tons annually to the Atlantic states.

The importations of red and white lead were 1,150 tons annually; of lead itself and other manufactures, 1,225 tons. The principal American manufactures were those of shot and colors of lead. Of the first, two establishments on a large scale existed at Philadelphia, and another in Louisiana, which were more than sufficient to supply the whole demand, stated at 600 tons a year. Of red and white lead, litharge, and some other preparations of that metal, 560 tons were made in Philadelphia alone. The manufacturers asked a repeal of the duty of one cent per pound on lead, and an equalization of that on its manufactures, by charging all with the two cents per pound laid on white and red lead. Various other paints and colors were made in Philadelphia and elsewhere.

Tin, Japanned, and Plated Wares.—Tin-ware was extensively made, and Connecticut supplied nearly the whole United States with it, but the sheets were always imported. Plated-ware, principally for coachmakers and saddlers, employed seventy-three workmen at Philadelphia, where over $100,000 worth was made annually. Similar establishments existed at New York, Baltimore, Boston, and Charleston.

Gunpowder.—Saltpetre was found in Virginia and Kentucky, and some other of the Western States and Territories, but principally came from the East Indies. The manufacture of gunpowder was nearly, and could at any time be made quite equal to the consumption; the importation of foreign powder being only 200,000 lbs., and the exportation of American powder 100,000 lbs. annually. The manufactory on the Brandywine, which employed a capital of $73,000 and thirty-six work men, and was considered the most perfect, made alone 225,000 lbs. annually, and might make 600,000 lbs. if there were a demand for it. Two others near Baltimore had a capital of $100,000, and made 450,000 lbs., of a quality said to be equal to any imported. There were several other powder mills in Pennsylvania and other places, but the total amount manufactured was not ascertained.

Earthen and Glasssware.—Sufficient pottery of the coarser kinds was made everywhere, and information had been received of four manufactories of a finer kind lately established. One in Philadelphia, with a capital of $11,000, manufactured a species similar to that made in Staffordshire, England, and the others in Chester Co., Pa., in New Jersey, and on the Ohio, made various kinds of queensware.

Information had been received of ten glass manufactories, which employed about 140 glass blowers, and made annually 27,000 boxes of window glass of 100 square feet each; that of Boston made crown glass equal to any imported, all the others green or German glass, worth fifteen per cent. less; that of Pittsburg used coal, and the others wood for fuel.

The importations of window glass were 27,000 boxes, the extension of the domestic manufacture, which supplied precisely one half the consumption, being prevented by want of workmen. Some green bottles and other ware were made, and two works, employing together six glass blowers, had lately been erected at Pittsburg, and made decanters, tumblers, and every other description of flint glass of a superior quality.

Chemical Preparations.—Copper was extracted in large quantities from pyrites in Vermont, New Jersey, and Tennessee. About 200,000 lbs. of oil of vitriol and acids were annually manufactured in a single establishment at Philadelphia. Various descriptions of drugs were also made there, and in some other places; and the annual amount exported exceeded $30,000 in value.

Salt.—The salt springs in Onondaga and Cayuga, in New York, furnished about 300,000 bushels a year, and it could be increased with the demand. Those of the Western States and Territories supplied about an equal quantity—the Wabash Saline, belonging to the United States, making about 130,000 bushels. Valuable discoveries had also been made on the banks of the Kanahwa. But the annual importation of foreign salt was more than 3,000,000 bushels, and could not be superseded by American salt, unless it were made along the sea coast. The works of Massachusetts were declining, and could not proceed unless the duty on foreign salt was again laid. It was necessary to shelter the works from the heavy summer rains by light roofs, moving on rollers, which considerably increased the expense. The erection of 10,000 superficial square feet cost $1,000, and produced only 200 bushels a year. A more favorable result was expected on the coast of North Carolina, on account of the climate, and works, covering 275,000 square feet, had lately been erected.

MISCELLANEOUS.—Of the other manufactures previously enumerated, information had been received of two only.

Straw bonnets and hats were made with great success. A small district in Rhode Island and Massachusetts exported to other parts of the Union to the amount of $250,000.[1]

Several attempts had been made to print calicoes, but the manufacturers did not seem able, without additional duties, to withstand foreign competition. Their difficulties were stated in the petition of the calico printers of Philadelphia, to Congress. Considerable capital was invested in an establishment near Baltimore, which could print 12,000 yards a week, and might considerably extend it if the profits and demand afforded sufficient encouragement.

From the information received, the Secretary was able with certainty to infer that the annual product of American manufactures exceeded $120,000,000. The raw materials, provisions, and other articles consumed by the manufacturers, probably created a home market for agricultural products, not very inferior to that which arose from foreign demand, a result more favorable than might have been expected from a view of the natural causes which impeded the introduction and progress of manufactures in the United States.

The most prominent of those causes were the abundance of land compared with population, the high price of labor, and the want of sufficient capital. The superior attractions of agricultural pursuits, the great extension of American commerce during the late European war, and the continuance of habits after the causes which produced them had ceased to exist, might also be enumerated. Several of these obstacles had,

(1) This business was commenced in 1801 at Wrentham, Mass., (where it amounted to $100,000 at least), and other towns in Norfolk county were estimated to make an equal amount. Wrentham, Franklin, Medway, Medfield, Billingham, Walpole, Sharon, and Foxburg, were the principal places where it was carried on, but some towns in Bristol and Worcester counties also made considerable, and it had been commenced in other parts of the State. They were exported to all the principal cities, and to the West Indies.

however, been removed or lessened. The cheapness of provisions had always, to a certain extent, counterbalanced the high price of manual labor, and that was now in many important branches nearly superseded by the introduction of machinery.[1] A great American capital had been acquired during the last twenty years, and the injurious violations of the neutral commerce of the United States by forcing industry and capital into other channels, had broken inveterate habits and given that general impulse, to which must be ascribed the great increase of manufactures during the last two years.

The incidental support derived from duties on importations, the exemption from oppressive taxes, and from those systems of internal restrictions and monopolies, which impeded the freedom of labor in other countries, had also promoted the general prosperity of the United States, its agriculture, commerce, and manufactures, and must give them a decided superiority over those less favored in that respect. The only powerful obstacle to the success of American manufactures was the vastly superior capital of the first manufacturing nation of Europe, which enabled her merchants to give long credits, to sell on small profits, and to make occasional sacrifices. The information obtained was not sufficient to enable the Secretary to submit, in conformity with the resolution of the House, a plan best calculated to protect and promote American manufactures. The most obvious means were bounties, increased duties on importations, and loans by government.

Occasional premiums might be beneficial, but a general system of bounties was more applicable to articles exported than to those manufactured for home consumption. The system of duties might be equalized, and imposed to protect some species of manufactures, without affecting the revenue. Prohibitory duties destroyed competition, taxed the consumer, and diverted capital and industry into channels less profitable to the nation than those which individual interest could seek. A moderate increase was less dangerous, and if adopted, should be continued during a certain period; for the repeal of a duty once laid, materially injured those who relied on its permanency, as had been exemplified in the salt manufacture. As capital was the chief need, which bank extension only partially supplied, and for short periods, the United States might create a circulating stock, bearing a low rate of interest, and lend it at par to manufacturers, on principles similar to that formerly

(1) The diminution of manual labor in the cotton manufacture of Great Britain, by means of machinery, was about this time estimated as two hundred to one. The jealousy of spinners, weavers, and other operatives, was frequently manifested by riot and destruction of machinery.

adopted by New York and Pennsylvania in their *loan offices*. Five to twenty millions might be thus lent without material risk, and without injury to any part of the community.

In conformity with the recommendation contained in the foregoing report, Congress passed, May 1, an amendment to the act providing for the taking of the third Census, making it the duty of the marshals, secretaries, and their assistants, to take also, under the directions and instructions of the Secretary of the Treasury, an account of the several manufacturing establishments and manufactures within their several districts, territories, and divisions, and to return the same to the Secretary of the Treasury. It authorised him to appropriate for this service $30,000, out of the sum of $150,000 set apart by the previous act for taking the census, a sum understood to have been more than adequate to the expenses.

The entire popuiation of the Union, by this enumeration, was 7,239,903.

The returns made upon the subject of manufactures, on account of the limited time allowed for taking the census, the absence of any formula or instruction to secure uniformity and completeness, and the reluctance or inability of many persons to give correct information, were necessarily irregular and discordant, as well as in many respects extremely deficient. The accounts from the different states and territories, and even from divisions of the same state, varied with the different views of the agents, their intelligence, industry and other qualifications, which rendered a comparison of the general results quite difficult. The returns fall far short of a full and reliable statement of the actual number and condition of the manufactures of the country. Those from Pennsylvania, Connecticut, Massachusetts, New York and Virginia, were the most complete, those from South Carolina the least so, but great deficiencies were apparent in all of them. A few examples out of many, which might be cited, will illustrate the nature and extent of some of those deficiencies, which have been since obviated, in a measure, by providing the agents of government with proper schedules for their guidance. No attempt was made, in general, to take an account of the capital, or raw material, the number of hands, or the cost of labor employed. The number of manufacturing establishments, or manufacturers, the machinery, and the quantity and value of the product of the regular and household kind alone were given, and these were frequently defective in one or all of the items. Thus the number of printing offices—stated by Mr. Thomas, a competent authority, at more than 400 in 1810—was returned by the marshals as 110. Bookbinders, calico-printers, and dyeing establishments were returned only for one state. No glass works were returned for Massachusetts, which had long made and exported glass of superior quality to other states. Bark mills were given for only one state; carriage-makers for three; blacksmith's shops for five; hatters for four; tin and copperware shops for two—and these the least considerable in that branch. The number of tallow candle factories in Massachusetts was not given, although that state was credited with nearly one-half the product in that branch, and the same was the case with morocco factories.

Notwithstanding their defects, however, the returns contained a vast amount of valuable information, which will be interesting in all future time, as the first systematic statement of American Manufactures in detail. The results were looked for with considerable interest, and the Committee of Commerce and Manufactures in the House proposed, so soon as they were in possession of them, to make them the basis of some measures for the benefit of the manufacturing interests. The returns were sent into the Treasury Department in November, 1811, and at the request of the above committee, one of its members, Mr. S. L. Mitchell of New York, examined them, and in a letter to the chairman, dated January 7, 1812, professed his inability, after several attempts, to arrange the materials in a compendious or useful form, on account of their heterogeneous character. He presented, however, some general facts, which were published subsequently,[1] and showed the value of the information embodied, and also expressed a wish to see them in the hands of some one who would extract it more fully. On the 21st February, Mr. Seybert, of Pennsylvania, moved in the House, that a person be employed to prepare and report at the next session a digest of the census returns of Manufactures, and in obedience to a joint resolution of both Houses, approved 19th of March, the Secretary of the Treasury, Mr. Gallatin, committed the documents for that purpose to the charge of Mr. Tench Coxe, of Philadelphia. From his valuable and well digested tables, completed in May, 1813, and published by Congress, we extract the following particulars of the leading branches of industry and general summaries of the entire product of manufactures in the Union and in the several states, territories and districts.

The marshals reported 21,211,262 yards of flaxen, 16,581,299 of cotton, and 9,528,266 of woolen goods made in families. The total amount of all kinds of cloths exceeded 75,000,000 yards. There were 1776 carding machines, by which 7,417,216 lbs. of materials had been

(1) Amer. Med. and Philosoph. Register, vol. 2, p. 405. Emporium of Arts and Sciences, vol. 1, p. 68.

carded; 1682 fulling mills, by which 5,452,960 yards of cloth had been fulled; 372,743 spinning wheels; 122,647 spindles; 325,392 looms; one silk manufactory which made 1800 yards of silk, worth $1800; 842 hatteries; 153 iron furnaces, which manufactured 53,908 tons of iron; 330 forges, which made 24,541 tons of bar iron; 135 bloomeries; 316 trip hammers; thirty-four rolling and slitting mills which rolled and slit 9,280 tons of iron; four steel furnaces, which made 917 tons of steel; 410 naileries, making 15,727,914 lbs. of nails; 117 gun manufactories; 111 cutlery shops; 4,316 tanneries, producing 2,608,240 lbs. of leather in addition to morocco manufactories, making 44,053 dozen skins, and other dressed skins and leather, making a total value of $8,388,250; 383 flax-seed mills, making 770,583 gallons of oil; 14,191 distilleries, producing 22,977,167 gallons from fruit and grain, and 2,827,625 gallons from molasses; 132 breweries, making 182,690 barrels or 5,750,000 gallons; 11,755 gallons of grape and currant wine; eighty-nine carriage-makers, who made 2,413 carriages; 14,569 wooden clocks; thirty-three sugar refineries, in which 7,867,211 lbs. of refined sugar had been manufactured; 179 paper mills, producing 425,521 reams and 22,500 rolls of paper; four paper stainers which stained and stamped 148,000 pieces of paper-hangings; twenty-two glass works, which produced 4,967,000 square feet of window-glass and 14,600 bottles; 194 potteries; eighty-two snuff-mills; eight drug manufactories; 173 ropewalks, which made 10,843 tons of cables and cordage; 208 gunpowder mills, producing 1,397,111 lbs. of powder; eight print works, employing 122 hands; sixty-two salt works, making 1,238,365 bushels of salt; straw bonnets to the value of $606,058.

Among the establishments and products classed as of a doubtful nature were 2,917 wheat mills, 350 grist mills; 2,526 common saw mills, making 94,000,000 feet of lumber; ninety-one cane-sugar works, producing 9,671 hogsheads of sugar; 9,665,108 lbs. of maple sugar; 94,371,646 bricks (in three states); saltpetre, including the product of twenty-two caves in West Tennessee, 429,607 lbs.; forty indigo works (in Orleans Territory), making 45,800 lbs; and 489 lime kilns (in Pennsylvania and Rhode Island).

A Summary of the Total Value of the Several Branches of Manufactures in the United States, Exclusive of Doubtful Articles, According to the Census of 1810.

1. Goods manufactured *by the loom*, of cotton, wool, flax, hemp, and silk, with stockings..$39,497,057
2. Other goods of these five materials, spun 2,052,120

3.	Instruments and machinery manufactured—value $186,650, carding, fulling, and floor cloth stamping by machinery—value $5,957,816	6,144,466
4.	Hats of wool, fur, etc., and of mixtures of them	4,323,744
5.	Manufactures of iron	14,364,526
6.	Manufactures of gold, silver, set work, mixed metals, etc.	2,483,912
7.	Manufactures of lead	325,560
8.	Soap, tallow candles, wax, and spermaceti, spring oil and whale oil	1,766,292
9.	Manufactures of hides and skins.	17,935,477
10.	Manufactures from seeds	858,509
11.	Grain, fruit, and case liquors, distilled and fermented	16,528,207
12.	Dry manufactures from grain, exclusively of flour, meal, etc.	75,766
13.	Manufactures of wood	5,554,708
14.	Manufactures of essences and oils, of and from wood	179,150
15.	Refined or manufactured sugars	1,415,724
16.	Manufactures of paper, pasteboard, cards, etc.	1,939,285
17.	Manufactures of marble, stone, and slate	462,115
18.	Glass manufactures	1,047,004
19.	Earthen manufactures	259,720
20.	Manufactures of tobacco	1,260,378
21.	Drugs, dyestuffs, paints, etc., and dyeing	500,382
22.	Cables and cordage	4,243,168
23.	Manufactures of hair	129,731
24.	Various and miscellaneous manufactures	4,347,601
		$127,694,602

From a consideration of all the reported details, and a valuation of the manufactures which were omitted or imperfectly returned, the foregoing amount of $127,694,602 was by Mr. Coxe extended to $172,762,676, exclusive of doubtful articles. These last embraced such manufactures as from their nature were nearly allied to agriculture, including cotton pressing, flour and meal, grain and saw mills, horse mills, barrels for packing, malt, pot and pearl ashes, maple and cane sugar, molasses, rosin, pitch, slates, bricks, tiles, saltpetre, indigo, red and yellow ochre, hemp and hemp mills, fisheries, wine, ground plaster, etc., altogether estimated at $25,850,795, making the aggregate value of the manufactures of every description in the United States in 1810, equal to $198,613,474.

The returned and estimated values of the manufactures proper were assigned to the different states and territories according to the following table.

SUMMARY OF THE RESPECTIVE VALUES OF MANUFACTURES IN EACH OF THE STATES AND TERRITORIES OF THE UNITED STATES IN 1810, ACCORDING TO THE RETURNS OF THE MARSHALS, AND ALSO AS ESTIMATED BY MR. TENCH COXE, EXCLUSIVE OF DOUBTFUL ARTICLES.

	Value as Returned.	Value as Estimated.
Maine (District)	$2,137,781	$3,741,116
Massachusetts	17,516,423	21,895,528
New Hampshire	3,135,027	5,225,045
Vermont	4,325,824	5,407,280
Rhode Island	3,079,556	4,106,074
Connecticut	5,900,560	7,771,928
New York	14,569,136	25,370,289
New Jersey	4,703,063	7,054,594
Pennsylvania	32,089,130	33,691,111
Delaware	990,711	1,733,744
Maryland	6,553,597	11,468,794
Virginia	11,447,605	15,263,473
Ohio	1,987,370	2,894,290
Kentucky	4,120,683	6,181,024
North Carolina	5,323,322	6,653,152
East Tennessee	1,156,049	3,611,029 (East and West Tennessee)
West Tennessee	1,552,225	
South Carolina	2,174,157	3,623,595
Georgia	2,743,863	3,658,481
Orleans Territory	814,905	1,222,357
Mississippi Territory	314,305	419,073
Louisiana Territory	34,657	200,000
Indiana Territory	196,532	300,000
Illinois Territory	71,703	120,000
Michigan Territory	37,018	50,000
Columbia (District)	719,400	1,100,000
	$127,694,602 [1]	$172,762,676

Among the important publications issued at Philadelphia in the last and present year was the second volume of Wilson's American Ornithology, a work in seven volumes folio with colored plates. The number of volumes annually printed in the city was estimated at half a million. The printing offices numbered fifty-one, and the presses 153. There were upward

(1) The marshals of several of the states represented the amount of manufactures to be much greater than was returned by their assistants; those of Rhode Island twenty-five to thirty-five per cent; those of Connecticut considerably greater; those of New York were *inofficially* estimated, and given to the Treasury in December 1811, at $33,387,566, including some articles of a doubtful class; the iron manufactured in Kentucky, and generally throughout the Union, was considered greater than reported; the various cloths and distilled spirits in South Carolina was thought to be double the value reported, and the manufactures generally as greater. Those of Georgia were considered decidedly too low.

of sixty engravers and employment for twenty more. The art of engraving had been much improved within a few years.

The number of newspapers printed in the United States was estimated at upward of twenty-two millions annually. The paper mills were estimated, by Thomas, at 185, viz.: New Hampshire, seven; Massachusetts, thirty-eight; Rhode Island, four; Connecticut, seven; Vermont, nine; New York, twelve; Pennsylvania, sixty; Delaware, four; Maryland, three; Virginia, four; South Carolina, one; Kentucky, six; Tennessee, four. Rags began about this time to be imported largely for the use of paper makers.

The repeal of the embargo was followed by considerable activity in ship building in Maine, New Hampshire, and Massachusetts, and about one hundred new vessels, chiefly ships, were launched within a few months in the two states.

The value of exports for the fiscal year rose to $66,757,944, whereof over fifteen millions were in cotton, upward of five in tobacco and nearly seven in flour.

The first lot of cotton goods printed in the United States, by engraved rollers and machinery driven by water power, reached Philadelphia, October 6th, from the Bleach and Print works of Thorp, Siddall & Co., about six miles from Philadelphia. The cylinder machine was brought from England during the last year by Mr. Siddall, and was the first to supersede the tedious process of block printing previously in use. One man and two boys were able to print ten thousand yards of cloth or fifty thousand children's handkerchiefs in a single day. Cotton and linen goods were stained and dyed of one color for various uses, by similar means, within the next two years. The manufacture of every description of cotton machinery was commenced about the same time at Holmesburg, near Philadelphia, by Alfred Jenks, a pupil and colaborer with Samuel Slater. He contributed many improvements during subsequent years, and the business is still extensively conducted by his successors.

Mutual Benefit Societies, or associations of the various classes of mechanics and tradesmen for mutual assistance, by the appropriation of small sums from their earnings to a common fund, for the support of the sick or needy, were a prominent feature in the social organizations of this period. Of these provident associations there were in Philadelphia, in addition to numerous societies for general and special charities, national and patriotic associations, the following, the most of them incorporated: The Carpenters' Society, the oldest, instituted in 1724; the Shipmasters', Pilots', and Mariners' Societies; Stonecutters' Company; Master Bricklayers' Society; Hair Dressers' and Surgeon Barbers' Society; Typographical Society; Master Tailors' Society; Provident

Society of House Carpenters; Master Mechanics' Benevolent Society; and similar societies of the Cordwainers, Journeymen Blacksmiths, Journeymen Tailors—who had two, the Hatters, Bricklayers, Master Coopers, and Journeymen Coopers. Similar societies existed in most of the principal cities and were annually increasing.

Public attention was also at this time invited, through a paper by Dr. Mease, in the "Archives of Useful Knowledge," to the importance of establishing a Bank of Industry, for the benefit of the laboring classes, similar to those known in Europe as "Banks of Savings." This appears to have been the earliest proposition in the United States to found a savings institution. They had existed for some years in France, and since 1804 in England, where Mrs. Priscilla Wakefield that year established the first at Tottenham, in Middiesex, and conferred an immense benefit upon the classes for whose use it was designed.

Philadelphia was at this date supplied with water through about thirty-five miles of pipe, made of wood of three or four inch bore, connected by cylinders of cast iron. The whole expense of the works to November 1, had been $500,000. The number of manufacturers supplied was 1922, being an increase during the year of 332.

The extension of useful manufactures and the substitution of domestic for foreign supplies, was mentioned in the presidential message, Dec. 5., as a subject of satisfaction, and "in a national view the change was justly regarded as of itself more than a recompense for their privations and losses resulting from foreign injustice, which furnished the general impulse required for its accomplishment. How far it might be expedient to guard the infancy of this improvement in the distribution of labor by regulation of the commercial tariff, was a subject which could not fail to suggest itself to the patriotic reflections of Congress."

The jewelry manufacture of Providence, R. I., employed about 100 workmen, and the product amounted to $100,000 annually.

Lapidary work and glass cutting were carried on by two or three persons in Philadelphia, one of whom, John Benson, from Europe, claimed to be the only regular bred lapidary in America.

A German named Eichbaum "Formerly glass cutter to Louis XVI., late king of France," is stated to have recently established his business in Pittsburg, where a six light chandelier, with prisms of his cutting, suspended in the house of Mr. Kerr, innkeeper, was supposed to have been the first ever cut in the United States. Three glass works in that town produced flint glass to the value of $30,000, and bottle and window glass worth $40,000. Among the manufactures of Pittsburg were the following articles of ironmongery: chisels, claw hammers, steelyards, shingling hatchets, drawing knives, cutting knives, shovels, tongs, buckles, gimlets, augers, squares, door handles, jack screws, files, stock locks, spinning wheel irons, axes, hoes, chains, kitchenware, &c., to the amount of $15,000. About 200 tons of cut and wrought nails of all sizes were made annually, and a manufactory of bridle bits and stirrups had been recently established. Six manufactories of tin, copper, and japanned ware, manufactured to the value of $30,000.

The Swiss colony at Vevay, Indiana, had eight acres of vineyard under cultivation, from which they made 2,400 gallons of wine, partly from the Madeira grape.

The manufacture of drugs and chemicals, such as aqua ammonia, sulphuric ether, sweet spirits of nitre, salt of tartar, benzoic acid, and refined saltpetre, was about this time commenced at Elizabethtown, N. J., by Innes & Robertson, who, three or four years after, began to make calomel and other drugs.

An extensive bed of Kaolin, or decomposed felspar, was found at Monkton, Addison Co., Vt., and a company was chartered for the manufacture of fine porcelain from it. The same mineral exists at Brookline, Windham Co.

Among other establishments incorporated this year was the Humphreysville Manufacturing Company, at Derby, Ct., having a capital of $500,000. The extensive broadcloth works of Genl. Humphreys, in whose honor the village and company were named, and a cotton manufactory at the same place belonged to the company. The Munson & Brimfield Manufacturing Company, on the Chicopee, in Hampdown county, Mass; and the following in New York: The Mount Vernon, Oneida (cotton), Ontario, Lenox, Utica and Geneva Glass, and the Oneida Iron and Glass Manufacturing Companies or Associations; the Galen Salt Company; the Manlins (cotton and woolen); the Oneida; the New Hartford (capital $200,000); and the Milton Manufacturing Associations. The last named was a large woolen manufacturing company, whose cloths soon acquired a high reputation. One of the first steam cotton mills in the United States was established within a few years after at Ballston, in the same town. The Home Manufacturing Company, in Rensselaer county; the Rensselaer Woolen and Cotton Factory; the Schoharie Paper Manufactory (Wood & Reddington), the New York State Company; and the New York Economical School.[1] The Powhatan Cotton Works, on Gwinn's Falls, six miles from Baltimore, were erected at this time, and incorporated in 1815.

The following were some of the patents issued this year: to John P. Spies, Baltimore, Md. (Jan. 8), for manufacturing horn combs and plating

(1) Laws of New York.

with tortoise shell; David Williams 3d, Hartford, Ct. (May 28), ivory combs; and Eli Parsons, Bristol, Ct. (Aug. 16), socket hair combs; John B. Lawin and T. B. Wait, Boston (Feb. 1), circular printing press;[1] George Murray, Philadelphia (Feb. 15), a mode of engraving to prevent counterfeiting; and also to Jacob Perkins, Boston (June 16), for a mode of preventing counterfeiting. The forging of bank bills, which these inventions were designed to counteract, was very rife at this time, and was rendered easy by the rudeness of the art. The stereotype check plate, first patented by Perkins, in 1799, was thought to render it nearly impossible, and the Legislature of Massachusetts required all bank notes to be impressed by his process. His mode of transferring engravings from one plate to another, by means of steel roller dies, upon which he and Murray soon after conjointly patented an improvement, was, in 1808, applied to calico printing by Mr. Locket, of Manchester, England; and about the year 1820, after having been long in use in this country, his method of engraving bank notes was extensively introduced in England, by Perkins, Fairman, and Heath. Perkins's steam gun, tested in England near the same time, was invented about this date, but not patented. George Easterly, Richmond, Va., received a patent (Feb. 5) for making barilla from tobacco stems; Robert Lloyd, Philadelphia (Feb. 8), loom for weaving girth cloth; Mellen Battle, N. Y. (April 2), wheelwright's labor-saving machine; Amos Miner Marcellus, N. Y. (April 11), spinning wheel heads. This invention, first patented Nov. 16, 1803, and embracing a double geared great wheel and a horizontal little wheel, did not attract attention until 1804, when a partnership was formed, and a small manufactory, highly original and ingenious in its plan, was erected by Miner, Demming, Pierce & Co., who the present year, employed twenty hands, and made weekly from six to nine thousand of the patent accelerating wheel heads. The gain of velocity, in the spindle, by the accelerating wheel, was said to be as nineteen to nine, or more than double, and the saving of labor in spinning wool to be one third, in worsted one half, and for merino wool it was indispensable. It was also much employed for cotton and tow, and the wheel heads were extensively counterfeited in New England. Peter Lorillard, N. Y. (April 25), received a patent for manufacturing tobacco; John Nicholson (April 28), for casting metal screws; James Davis, Philadelphia (May 15), manufacturing suspenders; Henry Burke, Philadelphia (June 18), winding and spinning wire; Winslow Lewis, Boston (June 8), reflecting and magnify-

(1) In July of this year a printing press on a new plan, more simple than any in use, and designed to secure, by means of a lever without a screw, greater power and speed, was completed, but not patented, by Benjamin Dearborn, of Boston, who had invented a wheel press about twenty-five years before.

ing lantern. This lantern was adapted for lighthouses, and Congress, two years after, authorized the purchase of the patent right, for the use of the United States, and a contract with the inventor, if it proved to be original, to erect them in all the lighthouses of the states and territories, for which purpose $60,000 were appropriated. Phineas Dow, Boston (July 12), patented a leather splitting machine; Elisha Winter, New Orleans (Sept. 4), double screw press; Elisha Perkins, Shrewsbury, N. J. (Sept. 16), elastic clear starch from wheat; Oliver Stetson and William Sebree, Georgetown, Ky. (Dec. 11), a screw auger; Leonard Beatty, Wilkesbarre, Pa. (Dec. 28), printing calico and paper.

CHAPTER III.

ANNALS OF MANUFACTURES.

1810—1820.

THE interruption of Commerce with the Baltic, by enhancing the price, had given a great impulse to the cultivation of hemp, and a considerable

1811 increase to its manufacture, which in Kentucky alone was this year valued at $500,000. Early in the third session, the House of Representatives, by resolution, instructed the Committee of Commerce and Manufactures to inquire into the expediency of encouraging the culture of hemp by protective impost duties or by prohibiting its importation, on which occasion Mr. Mitchell, of New York, stated his conviction that enough could be raised on the Genesee Flats and the Wallkill river, in that state, to supply the North, and in Kentucky for the South. In discharge of this duty, Mr. Newton, for the above committee, laid before the House (Jan. 21) a letter from the Secretary of the Navy on the subject. The discouragements arising from early inexperience, errors, and doubts of the fitness of the soil and climate, were stated to have been in a great measure overcome, and the quantity raised was yearly increasing. The crop was a very certain one, and yielded from $100 to $200 worth of dressed hemp per acre, with less labor and expense than tobacco and several other crops. The practice of "dew rotting" was strongly condemned as expensive and injurious to the fibre. The process and advantages of "water rotting," as practiced in Russia, were described and recommended, as all that was necessary to make American hemp equal to foreign, and probably secure its adoption for the use of the navy, in which dew-rotted American hemp was already used for running and standing rigging. The Secretary recommended an annual appropriation to enable him to contract for American watered hemp for the naval service. During the year large importations of hemp, amounting to 228,390 cwt., or nearly four times the amount of the previous year, were made, chiefly for Russia.

Extensive manufactories of cordage, bale rope, bagging, etc., had been established in Louisville, Lexington, Shelbyville, and Frankfort, Ky., and the following quantities of raw material and manufacture had been sent down the Ohio in two months following Nov. 24, 1810, viz.: hemp, 400 lbs.; tarred rope, 479 lbs.; bale rope, 20,784 lbs.; rope yarn, 154,000 lbs.; thread, 1,484 lbs.; bagging, 27,700 yards; tow cloth, 4,619 yards. During the year 1810, 1,378,944 lbs. of hemp and spun yarn, worth, at fifteen cents per pound, over $206,000, passed through Pittsburg to the Baltimore and Philadelphia markets.

A lengthy and earnest memorial was at this time presented to Congress, from Lewis Sanders and one hundred and twelve other citizens of Lexington, Ky., praying for some more decisive encouragement to the internal industry of the country. The protection and support of government appeared to them to have been almost exclusively given to commerce and the fisheries by the immense sums expended in fortifications of the seaports, the establishment of a navy, expenditures occasioned by foreign intercourse, tonnage duties, bounties to fishermen, credits at the custom house, etc. To these they did not object; but while commerce had received an unnatural extension, manufactures had been left to struggle almost unaided with obstacles unknown to their foreign competitors. In the event of a peace, it would be wise, by a little judicious encouragement, to create a domestic market for the labor, capital, and produce, which would thereby be compelled to seek other channels. Petitions were also presented from the manufacturers of morocco leather in Charlestown and Lynn, Mass., for additional duties on the foreign article, or its prohibition. The former stated that 800,000 skins were annually manufactured in the United States, equal or superior to the best foreign, of which number 150,000 were made in Charlestown.

The Legislature of New York, in February, enacted a general law for the incorporation of manufacturing companies, under which most associations for that purpose were organized, until 1848.

On motion of Mr. Clinton, the Senate of New York passed a resolution, in which the House concurred, recommending all members of the Legislature to appear at the next session in cloth of American manufacture. In March of this year, the Emperor Napoleon established in France several depots of merino sheep, in order to encourage their increase, and during the same month a numerous meeting of noblemen and gentlemen was held in London, when it was resolved to establish a society to improve and extend the merino breed of sheep throughout the United Kingdom. Sir Joseph Banks was chosen president. These examples were speedily followed in the United States, where the supply of woolens, more than most other articles, was affected by the restrictive measures of the government, and the undeveloped state of the woolen manufacture, chiefly on account of the scarcity of wool. As an evidence of this inadequacy of domestic supply, it is said, the Secretary of War, during this year, being in need of only about $6,000 worth of blankets for the Indian department, was compelled to ask of Congress a suspension of the non-intercourse act to enable him to obtain them from England. The recent renewal of that act and the great demand for wool and woolens, led to the formation, during the summer, of the "Merino Society of the Middle States," which, on the 5th of October, held its first stated meeting, after its organization, at the farm of Mr. Caldwell, the president, near Haddonfield, N. J. Several hundred full-blood merinos were exhibited and the society soon after arranged and published a list of premiums, of from twenty to fifty dollars, to be adjudged in July following, for essays on subjects connected with sheep husbandry and for the best merino stock. Sheep of that breed sold at public auction, in Philadelphia, during the previous year, from $230 to $250 each, a lot of twenty-five having sold for $5900, and another lot of thirty-three ewes for $250 each, and bucks for $350 each. In the State of New York, where greater zeal was shown for their propagation, sums of $500, $1,000, and even $1500, were repeatedly paid during the same year. A translation of a complete treatise on Merino and other sheep, with plates, recently published at Paris by M. Tessier, inspector of the Rambouillet and other establishments in France, was this year printed at the Economical School Office in New York and published. A translation of another French work on the subject, by M. Daubenton, was published in Boston. These efforts manifested the strong interest taken in the subject at this time, and seemed to warrant the extensive preparations, completed this year, by the Messrs. Dupont & Bauduy, on the Brandywine, for the manufacture of superfine broadcloth, on a large scale.[1]

The United States this year exported 1,445,612 barrels of flour, worth $14,662,000, being more than double the value of the same article exported the last year. The total value of domestic exports amounted to $45,294,041, including manufactures to the value of $3,039,000.

The total importation from Great Britain was only £1,874,917 sterling, against £11,217,685 the previous year. Of the aggregate value of British produce and manufactures exported to all parts of the world during the seven years, from 1805 to 1811, the United States had received annually 20.11 per cent.[2] The substitution of the non-importation act for the embargo, caused exchange on England, which under the latter act had risen to nine per cent. above par—payable in English currency, which was ten per cent. below metallic money—to fall in the United States this year to twenty per cent. below par. A large influx of specie took place and a new impulse was given to improvements in agriculture, manufactures, and real estate.

(1) Archives Useful Knowledge, vol. 1, p. 207; vol. 3, p. 193. (2) Seybert.

The quantity of Cotton produced throughout the world was estimated at 555,000,000 of pounds, of which 80,000,000 were the growth of the United States and valued at $12,500,000. Of the domestic product, 62,000,000 of pounds, valued at $9,000,000, were exported, being 31,000,000 of pounds and 6,000,000 in value below the exports of the last year. The cotton states produced as follows: South Carolina, forty; Georgia, twenty; Tennessee, eight; North Carolina, three; Louisiana, seven; and Alabama, two millions of pounds. The average price of all kinds in the United States was fifteen and one-half cents per pound. The best was raised in the valley of the Red river in Louisiana. The crops of blackseed cotton, in this and two following years, were nearly cut off by the "rot," in consequence of which, and of the low price of cotton, the attention of many was turned to sugar. In Georgia, sugar, wine, and oil, were attempted. Two pipes of excellent red wine were produced by Mr. John Cooper of St. Simons, and much sweet and castor oil was made on the sea-coast of that state. Samples of good Muscovedo sugar were made by Mr. Cooper and Mr. Thomas Spalding, on Sapelo Island, and by Mr. Grant.

Several attempts had also been made within the last few years to produce Opium from the white poppy. In Georgia, and some of the Northern States, good samples of the drug—which in 1808 rose to fourteen dollars per pound—were made, as well as oil from the seed.

The manufacture of Isinglass which also rose in price during the embargo to ten dollars a pound—was about this time recommended as profitable. Several samples had been sent to England before the Revolution, in consequence of premiums offered there for its manufacture in the colonies. Caviar made from the roes of different species of sturgeon—from the sounds or air-bladders of which, in common with those of other fish, the Icthyocolla or pure animal gelatin called isinglass is made—had long been an article of domestic manufacture and export.

The following summary was published of the principal manufacturing establishments in the city and county of Philadelphia, which contained at this period a greater number and variety of manufactures than any city in the Union. The population in 1810 was 111,210, that of New York being at the same time 96,372.

Looms, 273; spinning wheels, 3,648; oil mills, three; carriage shops, seventeen (value of work in 1810 $498,500); soap and candle works, twenty-eight; glue manufacturers, fourteen; distilleries, eighteen (gallons distilled in 1810, 1,283,818); sugar refineries, ten; ropewalks, fifteen; potteries, sixteen; tobacco and snuff mills, twenty-seven; copper, brass, and tin factories, forty-four; hatters' shops, 102; paper mills, seven; printing offices, fifty-one; cutlers' shops, twenty-eight; gun factories, ten; glass works, three.[1] To these may be added, from the official digest of the marshals' returns afterward published: looms with fly shuttles, 186; spindles in factories, 4,423; stocking looms and factories, 105; print works, eight; print cutting establishments, four; naileries, twenty; saw factories, two; bell founderies, ten; shot factories, three; morocco factories, seven; breweries, seventeen; blacksmith shops, 201; cooper shops, 124; drug mills, six; brush factories, twenty-four; drum makers, five; engraving establishments, sixteen; book binders, eighty-six; printing press factories, two; Spanish segar factories, nine (making 3,900,000 Spanish segars in addition to 26,900,000 American segars made); wheat mills, thirty-three; saw mills, seventeen; mahogany saw mills, twenty-one; brick-kilns, thirty; etc., etc.[2]

The total value of manufactures within the above limits was $16,103,869, and those of the whole state $44,194,740.

In Delaware and Pennsylvania, there were at this time seventy-six paper mills, with ninety-three vats.

An era in the commercial history of the Western States, was the construction at Pittsburg this year of the steamboat "New Orleans," the first that ran on the western waters. The boat was built partly by subscriptions in New York and Pittsburg, but chiefly by Messrs. Livingston & Fulton, and Nicholas I. Roosevelt; Mr. Roosevelt, in 1809, made a tour of exploration, to ascertain the practicability of navigating the Mississippi by steam, and superintended the building of the boat, aided by Mr. Stowdinger, engineer in chief of the North river boats. She was 138 feet long by thirty feet beam, and between 300 and 400 tons burthen. Her cost was $40,000, one-half of which was reimbursed by the *net* profits of her first year's business. She was wholly constructed at Pittsburg, engine, boiler, and machinery, and was launched in March. On the 29th October she left Pittsburg for New Orleans, and arrived at Louisville, upward of 700 miles below, in seventy hours. She was detained at the falls by low water for several weeks, during which she made several trips to Cincinnati, and in December proceeded on her voyage, arriving in New Orleans on the 24th, having received her first freight and passengers at Natchez. She continued to ply between New Orleans and Natchez, for which trade she was built, making the round trip in about seventeen days, until 1814, when she was wrecked, upon a snag at Baton Rouge.

In July of this year there were five steamboats running from New York to Albany, and one to New Brunswick, one on the Delaware, one on Lake Champlain, one on the Ohio (the Orleans), and one on the St.

(1) Mease's Picture of Philadelphia. (2) Coxe's Census Digest.

Lawrence. There were also building, on the St. Lawrence one, on the Hudson river as a ferry boat one, and two others for the associates of the Jersey Company, to run, according to contract with the city of New York, every half hour between that city and Paulus Hook. In these last the ingenious Fulton carried out the arrangements still observed in the ferry boats, including side cabin, rudder at each end to avoid turning, the floating bridge or coffer to facilitate landing, and contrivances to guide the boat into the dock, and to break the shock on reaching the bridge.

About this time also, Mr. Bell produced his steamboat, "Comet," on the Clyde, the only one at this time on the British waters.

The number of cotton factories in Rhode Island on 31st October, was thirty-seven, the number of spindles 32,786, with a capacity for running 56,257.[1]

Mr. Madison, in his first speech to the Twelfth Congress (Nov. 5), while recommending continued military and naval preparations, suggested that, "Although other subjects will press upon your deliberations, a portion of them cannot but be well bestowed on the just and sound policy of securing to our manufactures the success they have attained, and are still attaining, under the impulse of causes not permanent; and to our navigation the fair extent of which it is at present abridged by the unequal regulations of foreign governments. Besides, the reasonableness of saving our manufacturers from sacrifices a change of circumstances might bring on them, the national interest requires that, with respect to such articles as belong to our defence and our primary wants, we should not be left in unnecessary dependence on foreign supplies."

It was recorded as an instance of extraordinary dispatch that the message above referred to was received in Philadelphia on the 5th, by express, in nine and a half hours from Washington, and in Boston in sixty-four hours.

The tonnage of new vessels built during the year exceeded that of any previous one, and amounted to 146,691 tons of enrolled and registered vessels. In February, 9,145 tons were on the stocks at Philadelphia, and over 3,000 tons, including five ship-rigged vessels of 300 tons each, were built at Rochester, Mass.

About 500,000 pounds of lead were this year made and sold to traders by the Sac and Fox Indians, from the mines of Prairie du Chien, on the Mississippi, eighty miles above those of Dubuque, then owned by the natives. The ore was rudely smelted on piles of wood.

Some valuable salt works were already established at Mine river, on the Upper Missouri, under the management of Mr. Braxton Cooper.[2] The Columbian Chemical Society was formed in Philadelphia.

(1) Stone's Census of Providence, etc. (2) Breckenridge's View of Louisiana.

In New York, sixty-six acts of incorporation were granted for manufacturing and industrial purposes, of which forty-seven represented a capital of nine millions of dollars. The following were chartered under the general act of the previous year, certificates of which were to be deposited with the Secretary of State, viz: the Manlius Cotton and Woolen Manufacturing; the Stanford Manufacturing; the Whitesboro Cloth Manufacturing (for weaving, dyeing, and finishing cloth); the Farmers' Woolen and Cotton Factory; the Manlius Glass and Iron; the Geneva Glass; the Elba Iron and Steel Manufacturing (capital $100,000, with extensive works on the Au Sable, in North Elba [Keene], Essex county, built by A. McIntyre and associates); the Mohawk Factory; the Ontario Manufacturing; the Rutland Woolen Manufacturing; the Newport Cotton Manufactory; and the Schenectady Manufacturing Companies and Associations. The following were incorporated by special acts of the Legislature: The Oriskany (woolen, at Whitesboro, Oneida co.); the Clinton Woolen; the Somerstown and the West Chester County Manufacturing; the Bristol Glass, Cotton, and Clay; the Jamesville Iron and Woolen Factory; the New York Sugar Refinery; the Chenango Manufacturing; the Columbia Lead Mine; the Cornwall Cotton Manufactory; the Montgomery and the Oldenbarueveld Manufacturing; and the Susquehanna Coal Companies, Associations, and Societies.

In conformity with resolutions of the House, in December, 1810, with a view to a revision of the patent laws, the Secretary of State, in January of this year, laid before the House a list of the patentees and their inventions, and a special committee reported a bill for a revision of all the acts upon the subject. The Massachusetts Association, for the encouragement of useful inventions, presented a petition in February, signed by its president and secretary, Benjamin Dearborn and John Fairbanks, praying for such a revision of the laws as should secure inventors more fully against infractions of their patent rights, and the wrongs to which they were subject by the exportation of copies of specifications, drawings, and models, surreptitiously obtained at the patent office for the purpose of securing patents in foreign countries.

From information afterward communicated by the Secretary of State, it appeared that the number of patents issued, from 31st July 1790 to 31st December 1811, was 1,613 (an average of seventy-seven annually during the twenty-one years), and the gross amount of fees received was $49,110. The sums received for patents had annually increased, and amounted in the present year to $6,810. The secretary was directed to make an annual report of the patents issued. Patents were granted this year to Archibald Binney of Philadelphia (Jan. 29), for a type mould for printers, which greatly expedited the manufacture of types, and was adopted in

Europe; and another (Feb. 4) to the same, for a process of smoothing or rubbing types; to Robert Fulton, New York (Feb 9), for improvements in the steam engine for boats and vessels; and to John Stevens of New York (May 21), for constructing steam engines for propelling boats; William Pond, Wrentham, Mass. (Feb. 28), for wove straw plait; Robert Hancock, and Edw. W. Carr, Philadelphia (March 1), a machine for cutting wood screws, which was put in operation in Philadelphia; Thomas Massey, Philadelphia (March 4), a water loom; Barzillai Russell, Hartford, Ct. (March 4), an improvement in warming rooms; Lyman Cook, Whitestown, N. Y. (March 28), four wheeled manual carriages; Cyrus Alger, Boston (March 30), a mode of casting large iron rollers for rolling iron; William Baley, Nelson county, Ky. (April 10), a stave and shingle machine. This machine, by which a man and boy could dress and joint the staves for 100 barrels, hogsheads, or casks, in twelve hours, was driven by one or two horses, and in 1815 was in full operation in Cincinnati, when the proprietors were preparing to export staves to New Orleans. It was equally adapted to shingles.[1] Barnabas Langdon and William Mowry, Washington Co., N. Y., patented a machine for shaving, jointing, and forming the staves and heads of barrels, which was put in operation in Whitehall, N. Y.; Eleazer Hovey, Canaan, N. Y. (May 20), a shearing machine, which sheared perfectly a yard of cloth per minute. It was manufactured at New Lebanon, N. Y.; Perkins Nichols, Boston (May 18), a rimming auger; Edward Ramsey, Christian co., Ky. (April 16), and five other persons severally during the year, took patents for machines for breaking and dressing hemp and flax; Josiah Noyes, Herkimer co., N. Y. (June 21), a steam stove for cooking; Samuel B. Hitchcock and John Bement, of Homer, N. Y. (July 30), manufacturing boots and shoes. This was a patent for pegging boots and shoes, which was thus early practiced in New York, and very generally in Connecticut, with much relief to the workmen, and with increased dispatch, durability, and neatness in the work.[2] It was probably the origin of that description of manufacture; Robert Hare, Philadelphia (Aug. 22), a mode of ripening and keeping malt liquor and cider—consisting of air-tight casks, fitted with a pneumatic cock, with two orifices, etc., and in general use in Philadelphia at the time; Charles Reynolds, East Windsor, Ct. (Aug. 21), propelling carriages by steam; Jacob Pierson, Knoxville,

(1) A machine patented in 1807 by J. McIlvain, of Chester, Pa., for dressing shingles, by means of knives fixed in a wheel connected with a shaft, and turned by horse power, was in operation in West Philadelphia at this time. A man and boy could dress and pile away two thousand in a day, and by water power three thousand.—*Mease's Philadelphia.*

(2) Archives of Useful Knowledge, 3. 192.

Tenn. (Oct. 17), wooden screw press for cotton; Samuel Wetherell, Jr., Philadelphia (Oct. 29), for a mode of washing white lead, and another for setting the beds or stocks in making white lead; and to the same (Nov. 1), for screening and separating white lead, and also for separating oxidized from metallic lead, in the process of making red lead, and using a machine for that purpose;[1] Benjamin Bell, Boston (Nov. 6), sulphuric acid; Benjamin King, Washington, D. C. (Nov. 15), for welding steel, etc., by means of pit coal.

Early in the first session of the twelfth Congress, the Committee on Commerce and Manufactures were instructed to inquire into the **1812** expediency of encouraging the manufacture of iron, either by protecting impost duties, or by the prohibition of manufactures of that material. Petitions in favor of the measure were presented from the iron manufacturers of New Jersey, Pennsylvania, and New Hampshire, representing their inability to contend with the recent low price, induced by heavy importations from Russia. The directors of the New Hampshire Iron Factory Company stated that they had not realized one dollar upon a capital of upwards of $300,000 invested in their works at Franconia, which had been in operation over three years. Samuel Headley & Co., and Wadsworth, Allyn & Bostwick, in counter petitions against the free importation of iron wire, stated that since 1st August, 1811, they had erected in Simsbury and Winchester, Ct., two manufactories, where, without previous knowledge, they had succeeded in making from native ore the various kinds of iron wire, of the best quality, and at moderate price.

On the 3d March a resolution of the Legislature of Massachusetts was submitted to the Senate of the United States, offering to contract with the government to supply all the blankets and clothing it might need in

(1) The white lead made at the extensive manufactory of the patentee, established several years before in Philadelphia, was at that time considered by painters equal to the imported. Red lead was made by several, and to the amount of over $13,000 annually, by three small factories in Pittsburg. Paints of over twenty-two different colors, of bright and durable quality, were made in Philadelphia. One of these, the brilliant Chromate of lead (chromic yellow), was first made in this country, a few years before, by Mr. Godon, who supplied several cabinets with samples, and the process was perfected by Mr. Hembel, of Philadelphia, who published an account of his methods in Cooper's Emporium of Arts and Sciences, in June 1814 (N. S. vol. 3, 305). The material, chromic iron, was found abundantly near the city, in Chester county, embedded in steatite, or soap rock, lying above the primitive limestone, and in similar position at the Bare Hills, near Baltimore, where it was used as a material for turnpikes. The manufacture, on a commercial scale, was first undertaken by Mr. George Chilton, who was followed by Clinton and Jarvis, of New York, in 1812, and by others. It first sold for $3 per pound. All the mineral acids and chemical drugs were made by several in Philadelphia at this date.

12

any contingency, and representing that commonwealth as able to supply such articles, principally from its own manufactures.

An act of Congress authorized (March 12) the enrolling and licensing of steamboats, employed on the bays and rivers of the United States, and owned wholly or in part by resident aliens.

An act laying a temporary embargo on all ships and vessels in the ports and harbors of the United States, for ninety days, was, by recommendation of the President, passed and approved April 4. It was followed, on the 14th, by an act prohibiting the exportation during the same period, of any specie, or any goods, wares, or merchandise, under penalty of forfeiture and a fine of ten thousand dollars.

A declaration of war against Great Britain, of which the foregoing acts were the precursors, was made by Congress, and approved 18th June, and proclaimed on the following day. On the 5th of the same month, and before a knowledge of this act had reached England, the British orders in council were repealed.

The commencement of hostilities called for appropriate fiscal measures to sustain it, and after authorizing the issue of five millions of dollars in treasury notes, a law was approved on the 1st July; adding one hundred per centum to the permanent duties then levied upon imports, with an additional ten per centum on goods imported in foreign vessels, and $1.50 per ton additional on vessels owned wholly or in part by foreigners. This act, which passed by a vote of seventy-eight to forty-six, was to continue in force until the expiration of one year after the conclusion of peace, but was continued until June, 1816.

Through the combined effects of double duties, the obstruction and spoliation of commerce, the prices of nearly all articles of prime necessity immediately advanced. Between the 9th June and 13th July, hyson tea rose from 96 cents to $1.35 per lb.; white Havana sugar from $14.75 to $18.50 per cwt.; Russia hemp advanced from $242.50 per ton, on 9th June, to $300 on 10th August; and salt, between 1st May and 1st August, from 55 to 85 cents per bushel, and continued to rise to $3 per bushel in October 1814. Tin advanced from $25 per bar, on 1st May, to $32 on 1st August, and rose to $50 in 1814. Merino wool rose in price, between May and October, from 75 cents to $1.50 per pound, and at the end of 1814 sold from $3 to $4 per pound. Cloth advanced from $8 per yard in May 1812, to $14 in May 1814, and during the war to $18 a yard.

Under the stimulus of high prices and a steady demand, capital and enterprise were again turned more powerfully than ever to the increase of manufactures, especially to those branches which were immediately subservient to the war, or of which the want was most pressing. The woolen and cotton manufactures in particular received a remarkable extension. Many joint stock companies were formed, and in common with those which had been established a few years past, enjoyed, so long as the war operated as a protection, an ample remuneration for their expenditures, notwithstanding a rise of twenty to fifty per cent. in the wages of operatives, two to three hundred per cent. in mill seats, and of many raw materials in the same proportion. Great losses were incurred in many instances through the incapacity and sometimes the dishonesty of mechanists and operatives.

The annual value of domestic exports of the United States, calculated on an average of ten years, ending 30th September, amounted to $37,454,583, and of foreign merchandise re-exported $30,563,563. The average annual value of domestic manufactures exported in the same period was $2,096,000, or 5.51 per centum of all domestic exports. The produce of agriculture exported in the same time was $27,875,026, or 73.36 per cent. of the whole; of the sea $2,124,242, or 5.59 per cent., and of the present $4,404,946, or 11.59 per cent. The total value of exports this year was $38,527,236.

The average annual value of domestic produce exported to Great Britain and her dominions in the last ten years was $16,853,102, or 44.99 per centum of the whole, and the value so exported to France and her dominions was $3,118,217, or 8.32 per cent. of the whole. The total value of all articles of domestic and foreign origin exported to the two countries in the same period were respectively 27.44 and 13.9 per cent. of the whole value of exports.

The advantages and profits of this vastly more important trade with Great Britain, was now placed in jeopardy by a war waged upon pretexts, which would have been equally valid against France, and in support of claims which were finally abandoned, so soon as Napoleon, whose intrigues had involved the two countries in hostilities, had been humbled by Great Britain. The war was in consequence extremely unpopular with a large and influential class, who believed the difficulties might have been adjusted without a resort to arms.

At the fair and cattle show of the Berkshire Agricultural Society, held at Pittsfield, Mass., the prize of $50 was awarded to the president, Elkanah Watson, Esq., for the best piece of broadcloth exhibited. It was believed to be superior in all respects to any cloth ever made in America, and probably any ever imported. One-half the piece was left for inspection at the warehouse for American goods in Albany. The first cloth mill of any size in Berkshire was this year erected by Mr. L. Pomeroy, at Pittsfield, which was itself small, for several years employing but one set of machines, and five or six hand looms, and consuming about 1,200 lbs. of wool in the manufacture of broadcloth. The first power loom was not introduced there until 1825 or 1826.

The largest manufactory of fine cloths and cassimeres in operation in New England, if not in the country, at this date, was that of the Middletown Woolen Manufacturing Company—Isaac Sanford and others—in Connecticut. It was wholly employed on fine Spanish wool, which yielded the best profits and the steadiest sales. It made daily from thirty to forty yards of broadcloth, which sold at nine and ten dollars a yard by the piece. The mill employed one of Evans's steam engines, of twenty-four horse power, which drove all the machinery for carding, spinning, reeling, weaving, washing, fulling, dyeing, and finishing with the aid of a brushing machine, as well as for warming the building, etc.[1] The dyeing department was under the management of a Mr. Partridge, previously of Philadelphia, a superior dyer from the west of England. The cloths were finished without the disagreeable gloss, until recently, nearly universal with English cloths, which were finished by hot pressing. Superfine cloths, made from the first imported merino wool, and thought to compare favorably with any imported, were exposed for sale at the warehouse of the Domestic Society in Philadelphia. The product of the factory was about to be doubled. It was no longer found difficult to obtain good workmen in every branch, from among their own apprentices or other Americans. Gig-mills, for teasling and napping cloth, were erected to some extent in New England and New York, and were driven by steam or water; but hand cards were still used exclusively in Pennsylvania. Some sixteen or eighteen patents had been granted in the country for shearing cloth by steam or water power, several of which were in use. Hand shears had also been operated by water power. Blankets were at this time made in considerable quantity in that state, as well as in Massachusetts. The manufacture of blankets was greatly expedited by a machine invented and patented in April of this year, by Elkanah Cobb, a native of Vermont, belonging to the United States army, which enabled a single workman to make twelve blankets in a day.

(1) Oliver Evans, the first steam engine builder in the United States, had in operation, in February of this year, ten of his high pressure engines, considered by many more economical and convenient for manufactories than Bolton & Watts. They were from ten to twenty-five horse power, and were employed, one in Florida, two in Louisiana, one at Lexington, Ky., one at Natchez, Miss., one at Marietta, Ohio, two at Pittsburg, one at Middletown, Ct., and one at the Mars Iron Works of the builder, in Philadelphia. They performed the various operations of sawing timber, grinding grain, drawing wire, grinding glass, turning wood and metals, etc., manufacturing cloth, and building steam engines and machinery. Ten others, most of them of greater powers, were building, or ordered, for saw and grain mills, paper mills, rolling mills, steamboats, etc. Stackhouse & Rogers built engines at Pittsburg, under Evans's patent.

Numerous small factories for coarse woolen cloths were going into operation in New England, and generally throughout all the northern sections of the Union; unusual activity and preparation was apparent in the woolen branch. The first steam engine in Providence, R. I., one of thirty horse power, built by Evans, was also put in operation this year in the mill of the "Providence Woolen Manufacturing Company," consisting of S. G. Arnold, S. Dorr, J. S. Martin, and David Lyman, whose factory occupied the present site of P. Allen & Co.'s Print Works. The new woolen mill of E. I. Dupont & Co., near Wilmington, Del., was said to be making woolens to the value of between $150,000 and $200,000 annually. The quantity of wool sheared in the United States, estimated, from the imperfect returns in 1810, at thirteen to fourteen millions of lbs., was this year computed by Mr. Coxe to be twenty to twenty-two millions, and by some still higher. The proportion of fine wool was rapidly increasing, and no country probably ever witnessed so rapid a change in the extent and quality of its flocks, as a few years effected in the United States.

As on former occasions when the United States had felt compelled to refuse the manufactures of the principal producing nation of Europe, and to draw upon its own resources for supplies, the efforts of the cotton and woolen manufacturers were aided by a general disposition of the people of all classes to dress in homespun fabrics; and the chief magistrate is said to have set the example of wearing cloth made exclusively of domestic wool in New England factories.

The cotton manufactures of Rhode Island and adjoining states, in common with the woolen branch also, received at this time its great impulse as a result of the war. The village of Pawtucket already contained twenty-four cotton factories, and upward of twenty thousand spindles. An instance of the commendable regard for the moral interests of the operatives, and their consequent efficiency, first introduced by Mr. Slater, and at this time conspicuously exhibited by the Humphreysville Woolen Company, in Connecticut, was also shown this year by the Messrs. Wilkinson and others, proprietors of the Pomfret Cotton Factory, in the erection of a convenient brick edifice, as a school-house and place of worship for the employees and their families.

Public attention was about this time first called by Mr. Charles Whitlow, a nurseryman and florist, of New York, to a native filiaceous plant, believed to be an undescribed species of nettle, and therefore named, in his honor, *Urtica Whitlowi*, the fibres of which were thought to be superior to either flax or hemp as a material for manufacture. The plant, a hardy perennial, found in the low grounds of Orange co., N. Y., and Sussex co., N. J., where it had been for some time occasionally used in making thread, was described in the Baltimore Medical and Philosophical Lyceum (vol. 1, No. 4). Mr. Whitlow, who claimed to have first discovered its useful properties, proposed, in a petition to Congress in December 1811, to disclose to it the important discovery, in consideration of being allowed to import by special license all such seeds, grains, and plants as he might desire. A special committee was appointed to consider it, but was discharged without reporting. The subject was also before the New York Legislature, and experiments were instituted by the Mayor and corporation of New York. In January of this year Mr. Whitlow was granted a patent by the United States, and sold the privilege of using it to the Agricultural Society of South Carolina for $300. Similar offers were made to the trustees of the Massachusetts Society for Promoting Agriculture, and probably others. A company was the next year incorporated in New York, to manufacture the fibre, which had been previously spun into six hank yarn, valued at $11 a pound, with a yield of fifty per cent. An acre was estimated to produce 1,000 lbs. (in its native soil), and 500 lbs. of dressed fibre suitable for six hank yarn. A certificate from several manufacturers of flax, hemp, and cotton, represented it as superior in quality and productiveness to any flax or hemp they had ever seen. A tract of meadow twenty miles wide, throughout the western counties of New York, known as the "Holland Purchase," abounded in this species of Urtica, which had also been found in Maine. It has never yet superseded the annuals hemp and flax, but attention has been again directed to it recently, as worthy of cultivation, for properties which it possesses in common with other species of nettle, hops, etc.[1]

Francis Guy, of Baltimore, introduced this year a new kind of carpet, made of common paper hangings, which, it was thought, would prove as durable as canvas floor cloth, and be much more beautiful, and fifty per cent. cheaper. It was patented in 1819, but a specification of the

(1) As early as 1760 the Society of Arts in London offered a premium for cloth made from hop stalks or bines, which was attempted the next year by a Mr. Cooksey. In 1785 the Society renewed the offer of a gold medal or twenty pounds for such cloth, which was then made in Sweden. In 1803 the Society of Economy at Haarlaem offered prizes for the best memoir on the use of nettles for cloth, etc., and in 1809 Mr. Edward Smith, of Brentwood, in Essex, made two communications to the London Society on the use of the stinging nettle (U. Dioicous), for such purposes, having given his attention to it since 1793. He was the next year awarded by the Society a silver medal for specimens of yarn, paper, etc., from the nettle, and in 1811, having much extended his experiments, was awarded the silver Isis medal of the Society for samples of cloth and cordage made from the same plant. The same society, in 1816, voted Mr. Whitlow its silver medal for a method of preserving potatoes for sea stores or for transportation, by packing them in barrels with dry sand.—*Transactions Soc. Arts*, vols. 3, pp. 68, 141; 28, p. 109; 29, p. 81; 33, p. 196.

invention was filed as early as 1806, since which time he had been engaged in perfecting and testing the value of the article. It was intended principally for summer use.

A communication addressed by Mr. Coxe to the Secretary of the Treasury, on 8th December 1812, and printed with the digest, contained some interesting facts and statements based upon the census and other official returns and documents. These sources of information enabled him to state with confidence that American manufacturers in their demand for raw material had greatly surpassed the abilities of the planter, farmer, landholder, and miner, to supply wool, flax, hemp, hides, and skins of domestic animals, and the various metals, and the same was true of the crude sugars and molasses of Louisiana, considered as a raw material for refiners and distillers. From forty to fifty millions of pounds of the first five articles had for several years been annually imported from abroad as raw materials. Hemp to a considerable amount was regularly imported, notwithstanding an extraordinary duty upon it, and the great and sudden increase in the growth and manufacture of cotton. It was "an impressive fact that manufactures in America outrun agriculture in most instances;" cotton was the only redundant material. The number of American articles on the regular lists of exports from the United States, was about one hundred and ten, of which about seventy were manufactures of the country.

Gold and silver wares were made sufficient for every demand, and the present workmen could make for foreign sales a quantity equal to that exported by any nation of Europe. The manufacture of gold and silver leaf had been recently introduced, and flourished particularly in New York. Rollers and other machinery were used in that, and the button and other manufactures of the finer metals.

The most weighty fact respecting the iron manufactures was, that instead of exporting iron as they had formerly done, they could not obtain enough of pig metal and brass to satisfy the great and increasing demand of labor-saving mills and machines, and of the numerous handicraft workmen. They had raised the price of bar iron, since the Revolution, from sixty to one hundred and ten dollars the ton. The manufacture of common steel, iron wire, and edged tools, had greatly advanced since 1810. Edged tools were then made from rolled steel by a recent improved process. But greater attention was desirable to fine manufactures, such as cutlery, fine tools, watch springs, etc. Pharmaceutical preparations were made to the number of seventy. The recent employment of children and females in manufacturing operations, the improved means of communication and correspondence, the extension of sound bank facilities to manufactures, the introduction of new and exotic raw materials, of laborers, artizans, and manufacturers, and of new processes in every branch, were among the evidences of progress.

The first Artificial Globes manufactured in the United States were made about this time at Bradford, Orange co., Vt., by James Wilson.

At Strafford, in the same county, 8000 lbs. of copperas were made in 1810 by the Vermont Mineral Factory Company, which early in this year petitioned Congress for a duty on the foreign article, under the belief that they could supply the whole Union, from inexhaustible beds of pyritius iron, in that town and Shrewsbury. The manufacture of copperas was also commenced this year on the Mogothy river, in Maryland, by Richard Colton, Esq., and others. About three years after, the manufacture of alum was added at this place, by a Society incorporated in 1818, with whom was associated the eminent mineralogist and crystallographer, Dr. Girard Troost, who about this time superintended the chemical laboratory of Mr. Wetherell, and was a principal agent in founding the Acadamy of Natural Sciences in Philadelphia. Copperas was also made during the war at Pequannock, Morris co., N. J., from the sulphurets of Copperas Mountain. But the principal domestic supply, for the states east of the Alleghanies, was for many years derived from the Vermont Works, which have since produced as much as one thousand tons a year of copperas, preferred by the dyers to any other.

The manufacture of Emery, an article of much value in cotton, woolen, glass, steel, and lapidary works, was also commenced at this time, when about to become scarce and dear. It was first attempted by Pliny Earle & Brothers, card makers, of Leicester, Mass. The business was also about to be commenced by Gilbert J. Hunt, of New York. The material, corundum, and similar minerals, was thought to be abundant in granite and other primitive rocks, particularly near Haddam, Ct., Chestnut Hill, Pa., Baltimore, Md., and Lake George, N. Y.

In consequence of the scarcity of Pins, which this year rose in price to one dollar per paper by the package, the manufacture of them was commenced by some English pin-makers, who brought the necessary implements, and established themselves at the State Prison, in Greenwich, N. Y., under the management of a person named Haynes. He occupied a part of the Almshouse, at Belleville, and contracted for pauper labor; but the business was abandoned on the return of peace. It was resumed about 1820, with the use of the same tools, by Richard Furman, who carried it on at considerable loss for a year or two, when he died, and the manufacture was given up.

The first Flint Glass works on a large scale were this year established at Pittsburg. Preparations were also made for the same business at

Boston, where a large factory went into operation about four years later. Mr. Carnes, who is still engaged in the business in South Boston, commenced the manufacture this year.

A domestic supply of "Burr" millstones, for the western country, was found in an extensive quarry of cellular and amorphous quartz, opened near the head of Raccoon creek, Athens co., Ohio. It was considered identical in composition with the French curb stone.[1] The first pair were put in the steam flour mill of the Marietta Mill Company, started in January by Messrs. Gilman, Barber, Skinner, Fearing & Putnam, who afterward added woolen machinery. Large steam saw and flour mills were also erected this year at Cincinnati and Louisville. The first iron castings were made at the latter place this year by Paul Skidmore, whose successors, Prentiss & Bakewell, in 1816, added the manufacture of steam engines for steamboats and factories.

Louisiana was this year admitted into the Union. It produced 10,000,000 lbs. of sugar, and 20,000 bales of cotton were shipped from New Orleans.

The scarcity of Virginia coal, which up to this time had been the principal source of domestic supply, led to renewed experiments with the Pennsylvania anthracite, which had lately been analyzed, and was employed in the rolling mill of Mr. Joshua Malin, near Philadelphia, as well as in some private houses. The first anthracite from Pottsville reached the city this year, from the Centreville mines, and was sold for the cost of transportation. The first coal stove in the borough of Reading was introduced by Wm. Stahle, stone coal having been brought to that place about the same time by Marks John Biddle. The availability of anthracite for manufacturing purposes was more fully established about this time by Messrs. White & Hazard, wire drawers, at the Falls of Schuylkill. A memorial which they and others presented to the Legislature to obtain a law for the improvement of the Schuylkill river, and urging, among the inducements, the coal deposits at its head waters, is said to have drawn from the senator from Schuylkill county a declaration that there was no coal there, only a "black stone" called coal, which would not burn.[2] So little was then known of this vast mineral resource and manufacturing agent.

The now flourishing city of Rochester, N. Y., dates its existence from

(1) Burr millstones had been made of Georgia stone, in Philadelphia, by Oliver Evans for some years. There was also, in 1810, a manufactory in Baltimore. The Esopus millstones of New York were also in use.

(2) During the year 1860, seventy-eight operators, owning one hundred and thirteen collieries, mined 3,276,879 tons in Schuylkill county.

this year, in which it was first laid out, and the first framed house, bridge, merchant's store, and post-office, were set up in it, and a mill lot on west side of the Genesee, purchased ten years before by Nathaniel Rochester, was first occupied. The village had no place in the State Directory, published the next year, and was not incorporated as such until 1817.

The minds and the pens of many mechanicians and men of science were considerably exercised about this time by the pretended solution of the great problem of perpetual motion. A man in Pennsylvania named Redheffer, exhibited in different parts of the Union an ingenious contrivance, which, by a system of weights and wheels, and ostensibly self-winding, appeared, to the unwary, really to perpetuate its own motion, and brought the inventor a rich harvest at one dollar a head. The momentum was, however, derived from another source, and the art lay in effectually concealing its origin from the incredulous, while the multitude were put on the wrong pursuit by the visible mechanism. The celebrated Jacob Perkins, at this time engaged in constructing machinery for boring cannon and other improvements in artillery, and in pyrotechny, etc., at once detected the inadequacy of the visible mechanism, and ordered a saw passed through a certain part which is supposed to have concealed a secret cord. But the exhibitor refused the test. Robert Fulton also consented to visit the machine in New York, and by his ear soon discovered the agency of a crank, by the unequal motion produced. He charged the showman with imposture, and proceeded to demonstrate it by demolishing a portion of the wall of the room, through which a catgut string, leading from the machine, was traced to a remote cock-loft, where an aged man sat unconsciously turning a crank. The deluded crowd demolished the apparatus, and the proprietor soon disappeared.

In the early part of this year Col. John Stevens, of Hoboken, N. J., published a memoir entitled "Documents tending to prove the Superior Advantages of Railways and Steam Carriages over Canal Navigation." The use of a steam carriage to transport one hundred tons of produce from Lake Erie to Albany, a distance of one hundred miles, at a cost of fifty cents per ton (the expense by canal being estimated at $3 per ton), was described in the pamphlet seventeen years before Mr. Stephenson built the first effective locomotive in England. The advantages of railways had been previously urged by Stevens, upon both the canal commissioners of New York, and the United States government.

The first cotton mill at Fall River, Mass., then called Troy, was this year erected by a company incorporated by the name of the Fall River Company. The Troy Manufacturing Company was also chartered, and proceeded to erect another factory at the same place. A third factory was built there in 1821, and two more the following year. The James River Cotton Manufacturing Company, at Kingston, was incorporated.

The "Waltham Cotton and Woolen Manufacturing Company," with a capital of $450,000, was also incorporated. This, and the "Boston Manufacturing Company," chartered the next year, with large factories on the Charles river, at Waltham, were among the most extensive and prosperous in the country at the close of the war, and for many years after. The Monson Woolen Manufacturing Company, in Hampden county, was also incorporated.

The unexampled increase of cotton and woolen factories, and the consequent demand for cards,[1] led to the establishment of the New York Manufacturing Company, incorporated in June of this year, with a capital of $800,000, of which $300,000 was to be employed in manufacturing cotton and wool cards and erecting the necessary buildings, and the remainder in banking. The patent right and machinery of the Messrs. Whittemore was purchased on 20th July, for $120,000, and buildings were commenced with formal ceremonies, on New York Island. The new impulse given to manufactures by the war, gave the company active and profitable employment, until the large importations, which followed the peace, compelled the factories to stop, and with them the demand for cards. In 1818 the entire manufacturing property was sold to Messrs. S. & T. Whittemore, brother and son of the inventor, the former of whom carried it on many years, while the original company, with increased capital, assumed the name of the "Phoenix Bank," which still survives. On the expiration of the patent, in 1825, the machinery, built in part by the inventor, returned, after an absence of twenty-five years, to the possession of his son in West Cambridge, where the elder Whitney died, in 1828, and where the business is still conducted by the family.

The following companies and associations were also incorporated in New York the present year, under the general act:—The Steuben Woolen, the Nassau, the Verbank, the Walloomsock, the Farmers and Mechanics, and the Broadalbin Woolen Manufacturing, the Troy Wool and Cotton Factory,[2] and the Orange Factory. Special charters were

(1) The celebrated William Cobbett, in his Essay on the Regency, stated that he had been credibly informed that the value of cotton and wool cards shipped from Liverpool to America, in 1810, to supply the new manufactures created by the embargo and non-intercourse acts, exceeded the annual value of cloths exported thence from the counties of Somerset and Gloucester.

(2) The village of Troy already possessed considerable manufacturing industry, attracted by its fine water power. It contained a rolling mill, fire-arms manufactory, spade and shovel factory, several nail works, a large cotton and woolen factory (above mentioned), carding machine, fulling mill, paper mill, a large ropewalk, a distillery, several grain and saw mills, etc., and two banks.—*Spafford's Gazetteer.*

granted to the Butternuts Woolen and Cotton Factory, the New York Marble, the United States Lead Mining and Manufacturing, the Dutchess County Slate, the Clason Woolen, the Onondoga Manufacturing, and the Cambridge Farmers' Woolen, Companies and Associations.

Two hundred and thirty-seven patents were issued this year, a considerable number of which were for apparatus for spinning, weaving, and other processes in the manufacture of wool, cotton, flax, and hemp. Upward of a dozen were for spinning machinery, among which was a portable or family spinning machine, of very simple construction, invented and patented (April 27) by Rev. Burgiss Allison, of Philadelphia.[1] It drove ten to fifteen spindles, and occupied very little more space than the common spinning wheel. It spun wool to any fineness required, and could be used for cotton if previously carded into rolls. Improvements in the loom also engaged much attention, at this time, on account of the great impulse given to manufactures in England by the power loom, the construction of which was still a secret, and its exportation, as well as of all models, drawings, etc., forbidden. Among those who labored to produce a power-loom were Judge Daniel Lyman, of Providence, and Mr. F. C. Lowell, of Mass. Mr. Lowell had just returned from a residence in Europe, where he had conceived the idea of an extensive prosecution of the cotton manufacture in the United States, such as he had witnessed abroad, with all the recent appliances, including the power loom. Having, in connection with his brother-in-law, Mr. Patrick T. Jackson, set himself to the invention of such an engine, he produced, in the autumn of this year, after many failures and experiments, a working model of a power loom. They secured the services of an able mechanician, Mr. Paul

(1) Portable spinning jennies and billies of six to twenty-four spindles, for family use, were at this time in quite extensive use, particularly in country parts remote from the larger factories, and in the Southern States. Billies carrying twelve spindles, to spin fourteen cuts to the pound, or by spinning a second time, twenty cuts, were made and sold in Philadelphia for $48 each, by Joseph Bamford, 5 Filbert st., who also manufactured machinery for large establishments. Nearly every second farm house had also its hand-loom. We learn from letters written this year by Mr. Jefferson to Genl. Kosciusko, and to Mr. Melish, whose "Travels" showed the same system of household industry to pervade the Western States, that he employed a carding machine costing $60, and worked by a girl twelve years old, a spinning machine, for wool, of six spindles, which cost $10, another spinning machine of twelve spindles, costing about $25, for cotton, and a loom with flying shuttle, weaving its twenty yards a day. This machinery, which cost him $150, worked by two women and two girls, was more than sufficient to make the necessary coarse fabrics for his farms, some 2000 yards annually. Many private families did much more than he in that way, and he soon after doubled the number of his spindles. The British Parliament this year rewarded with grants of five thousand pounds each, Mr. Samuel Crompton, the inventor of the mule spinner, and Mr. Wright, the inventor of the double mule. The spindles in Great Britain at this time were between four and five millions.

Moody, of Amesbury, to build the machine (which they patented in 1815), and with the first efficient American power loom proceeded to carry out their project, at Waltham, where they erected a cotton mill the ensuing year.

Some eight or ten patents were issued this year for looms of various kinds, including one to John Thorp, of Providence (March 28), for a hand and power loom; to Cyrus Shepherd, Philadelphia (April 27), for a water loom; and one to J. and Rozanna Sizer, New London, Ct. (Oct. 21), for a loom for weaving feathered cloth. Patents were also granted to Enoch Leonard, of Canton, Mass. (Jan. 6), for making steel from pig-iron; two to Morris B. Belknap, Greenfield, Mass. (Jan. 16 and June 13), for a machine for cutting files and sickles, which cut from five to six dozen twelve inch files daily; also to Charles Hesser and Amos Paxson, of Philadelphia (April 11), and to William T. James, of Greenwich, Washington co., N. Y. (Nov. 19), for file cutting. The latter was put in operation at Union village, where an ingenious manufactory of files and of cast steel existed at this time. Files were also extensively made in Philadelphia. Charles Whitlow, New York (Jan. 11), for a plant applicable to various uses; Uri K. Hill, New York (Feb. 7), types for music; Daniel Waldron, New York (March 4), manufacturing fish glue (icthyocolla); Mellen Battle, Herkimer, N. Y. (March 27), a rotary steam engine; William Dunn, Boston (April 1), preparing magnesia; Elkanah Cobb, Georgetown, D. C. (April 29), making blankets; Robert U. Richards, Norfolk, Ct. (May 23), manufacturing boots and shoes with wooden pegs, screws, etc.; E. Hazzard and Joseph White, Philadelphia (May 25), cutting screws; James Howell, Philadelphia (June 11), rolling wire; also to J. T. & Thomas Walden, New York (Oct. 6), and to John J. Staples, Flushing, N. Y. (Oct. 31), for drawing wire; E. Gordon, Philadelphia (June 26), a rolling press for edge tools; Richard Marden, New York (Aug. 21), manufacturing oil of vitriol; William Edwards, Northampton, Mass., three patents, viz. (Oct. 19), one for tanning, and one for the roller for preparing leather, and (Dec. 30) one for tanning sole leather. These were all capital improvements of Mr. Edwards. The rolling machine, particularly, is still in use in nearly its original form, and gives to leather the finishing process, by which it acquires that smoothness of surface and solidity of texture peculiar to hammered leather.

1813 Congress authorized, January 2d, four ships of war, of seventy-four guns each, six of forty-four guns, and six sloops of war, to be built, equipped, and commissioned, and as many sloops or armed vessels as the public service might require on the lakes, to be procured, equipped, and commissioned. An appropriation of $100,000 was made for the erection of a public dockyard for the repair of public vessels. The President was also empowered, July 5th, to cause to be built as many barges, not less than forty-seven feet long, capable of carrying heavy guns, as the service might require.

A second series of the "Emporium of Arts and Sciences," commenced in May of the last year, under the conduct of Dr. John Redman Coxe, Professor of Chemistry in the University of Pennsylvania, was begun, in February, to be managed by Dr. Thomas Cooper, Professor of Chemistry, Natural Philosophy, and Mineralogy, in Dickinson College, Pennsylvania. It was devoted to the publication of practical papers on manufactures and the arts from the more scarce and voluminous among foreign publications, and of original essays, many of them by the editor. It was the means of diffusing much scientific and practical information, particularly in relation to the chemical and metallurgic arts, at a time when it was needed to enable American manufactures to participate in the progress of science, then becoming a powerful auxiliary to practical knowledge in other countries. The prospectus of Professor Cooper advanced a number of strong arguments in favor of the encouragement of manufactures, as a means of supplying a home market for agriculture, and of lessening the dependence upon, and indebtedness to foreign manufactures. Protecting duties, to aid their introduction, and afford a reasonable safety to capital and industry, he regarded as expedient, a position which he appears afterward to have abandoned, when, as President of Columbia College, South Carolina, he became one of the ablest champions of a free trade system.

The Archives of Useful Knowledge, edited by Dr. James Mease, of Philadelphia, which completed its third volume this year, also performed a useful service as an instructor in science and the practical arts.

There were at this date, as appears by petitions and communications addressed to Congress by Joseph Revere, of Boston, and Levi Hollingsworth, of Maryland, asking for a duty on copper imported in sheets and bolts, three manufactories of sheet copper, bolts, rods, spikes, etc.; those of the Messrs. Revere, which made about three tons per week, the Gunpowder Copper Works of Mr. Hollingsworth, ten miles from Baltimore, and that of Mr. Livingston, in New York. The last two were capable of making each about 100 tons per annum. They could each double the amount of their product if it were warranted. The quantity of crude copper annually imported was about four hundred tons, chiefly from the western coast of South America, Buenos Ayres, Caraccas, Mexico, and the Levant.

An act was passed, February 25, imposing a duty on iron wire imported equal to that on iron, steel, or brass, and other manufactures of iron.

Mr. Tench Coxe completed, May 1, by order of the Secretary of the Treasury, and conformably to a resolution of Congress, a digest of the census returns on the subject of manufactures in 1810. A careful estimate of all the facts within his knowledge, convinced him that, notwithstanding an interrupted importation of certain raw materials, the several branches of manufactures had advanced, since the autumn of 1810, at the full rate of twenty per cent. The whole population, taken at 8,000,000 of persons, he estimated would produce in the current year an aggregate value of manufactures, exclusive of doubtful articles, of $200,000,000, or £45,000,000 sterling. The State of New York had partaken most largely in the increase, especially by her joint stock companies, and by reason of emigration from the Eastern States. The general result furnished a gratifying comparison with the product of English manufactures, which, in 1787, when the population of England alone was about the same as that of the United States at this time, or 8,500,000, were computed at $266,000,000. This state of manufactures had been in a great measure attained by the United States in the thirty years since the completion of its independence, and with only an incidental support from government, while England had been hundreds of years progressing under many forms of governmental aid.

A sample of sugar, made from the butternut or white walnut tree, by Jonathan Pearson and Moses P. Gray, of Epsom, N. H., was presented to the Massachusetts Agricultural Society. The yield was at the rate of one and a quarter pounds from nine quarts of sap, or greater than that of the sugar maple. The trustees recommended a critical test of the sugar-producing qualities of the white walnut, sugar having become scarce and dear.

Congress imposed, July 24, the following internal duties to be paid during the war, and until the expiration of one year thereafter, viz: on all public and private carriages, annual rates varying from two to twenty dollars each, on all sugars refined in the United States, four cents a pound, with the privilege of drawbacks on exportation to the amount of $12; on sales at auction, one per cent., except on sales of ships or vessels, which was one quarter of one per cent.; on stills or other implements employed in distilling domestic materials, a change from nine cents per gallon on the capacity of the still, for every two weeks, to one hundred and eight cents a year—half these rates when employed in distilling roots; upon stills employed on foreign materials, the rate was from twenty-five cents per month to one hundred and thirty-five cents per annum for each gallon of the capacity. In all cases in which steam was employed, the rates were double. Duties were also laid, August 2, on all bank and promissory notes, bills of exchange, etc.

An impost duty of twenty cents on the bushel of fifty-six lbs. was laid, July 27, on all foreign salt imported during the same period, and a bounty of twenty cents a barrel on pickled fish exported, together with an allowance of $2.40 to $4 per ton, according to size, to vessels engaged in the bank or cod fisheries. This act was continued indefinitely in 1816, and while in force greatly promoted the manufacture of salt, which, since the duty was taken off, in 1807, had sold in New York from fifty cents to one dollar a bushel for Turks island. The manufacture was much extended in Massachusetts, which state, after the repeal of the former duty, had exempted its salt works from taxation. The increased price of salt, occasioned by the war, and the inability to obtain it from the New York salines, led this year to the first manufacture of salt on the Conemaugh and Kiskiminetas, in Western Pennsylvania. Mr. William Johnston succeeded in penetrating the solid rock, on the bank of the Conemaugh, near the mouth of the Loyalhanna, where numerous salt springs indicated a supply, and at the depth of four hundred and fifty feet, struck an abundant fountain. Having erected furnaces, pans, and other apparatus, he was soon able to make about thirty bushels daily, which sold at a high price, and induced many others to engage in the business. The pumps were at first worked by horse power, and afterward by small steam engines. The salt works of Onondaga, N. Y., in 1810, consisted of 125 blocks, with 1,010 kettles, and produced 435,840 bushels of salt. The state was this year estimated to yield 700,000 bushels. Salina village contained eighty salt works or houses, and Liverpool, three miles below, thirty-five salt works, in addition to the middle works, and some detached ones.

Pittsburg, in addition to large quantities of ironmongery and coarse hardware, japanned and tinwares, white metal buttons, etc., made for the western country, contained at this time five glass factories in the town, producing flint and green glass to the amount of $160,000; two large iron foundries (McClurg's & Beelen's), which cast about six hundred tons a year, worth $54,000, and a small one for casting butt-hinges, carried on by Mr. Price; an extensive edge tool and cutlery manufactory, by Brown, Barker & Butler; a steam manufactory of shovels, spades, scythes, etc., by Foster & Murray; one rolling mill, by C. Cowan, erected this year, with a capital of $100,000; a lock and coffee mill factory, commenced the last year by James Patterson, an Englishman; a factory for files and door handles, etc., by Updegraff; two steam engine works, Stockhouse's and Rogers & Tustin's; one steel furnace, by Tuper & McKowan; a wool carding machine factory, by James Cummins; one woolen factory, by James

Arthurs; one flannel and blanket factory, by George Cochrane; one cloth steam machine factory, by Isaac Wickersham; two manufactories of stirrup irons and bridle bits; one wheel iron factory, by Stevenson & Youard; one wire mill, by Eichbaum & Sons; one button factory, by Reuben Neal; one knitting needle factory, by Frithy & Pratt; two silver platers, B. Kindrichs and Mr. Ayers; a morocco factory, by Scully & Graham; one white lead factory, by Beelen; a suspender factory, by Wm. Gore; one brass foundry; three coopers; a trunk factory, by I. M. Stevens; a brush factory, Blair's; six saddle factories; two breweries; a steam flax mill; a ropewalk, by John Irwin & Co.; eleven copper factories; and three plane factories. The curriers' knives, made in Philadelphia, were declared by the curriers to be equal to the best imported.

The first Stereotyping in America was done this year in New York, by D. & G. Bruce, at their foundry, William street, near Exchange Place, and also by John Watts, who issued the Assembly of Divines' Catechism, believed to have been the first issue of the American press from stereotype plates. The Messrs. Bruce, in 1815, stereotyped the first Bible in America.

A manufactory of blacklead Pencils, of excellent quality, was in operation at Granville, Washington co., N. Y. The manufacture was commenced in New York city, within four or five years after, at which date graphite, or Plumbago, was stated, by Professor Cleveland, to exist in Maine, New Hampshire, Massachusetts, Rhode Island, Connecticut, New York, New Jersey, Pennsylvania, and North Carolina. The mountains of Essex and Clinton co., N. Y., were known to have nearly inexhaustible quantities, and Ticonderoga now makes many tons of black lead yearly.

Essex county at this time had fifteen bloomeries for making bar iron, besides several anchor shops, trip hammers, etc. Extensive iron works and a woolen factory were this year erected on the Au Sable, at Keeseville, four miles west of Lake Champlain, by Richard and Oliver Keese and John W. Anderson. These and neighboring works in the Adirondac region, have produced iron of a superior quality, much of which has been made into nails, horse-shoes, edge-tools, machinery, and merchant iron direct from the ore. Ticonderoga at this time contained a broom manufactory, carried by water, by which one man made one hundred brooms daily.

The town of Scipio, Cayuga county, produced about 2,500 skeins of sewing silk. The white mulberry was introduced there, by Samuel Chidsey, at its first settlement. During the war, about this time, he sold sewing silk to the amount of $600 in a year.

The charter of the East India Company having expired, the trade with

British India was thrown open to the public under certain restrictions. The cultivation of cotton in that country, for exportation, had for many years been encouraged by the British public. In view of a rupture with the United States, in 1809, these efforts were renewed by the Society of Arts and other agencies, with such energy as to produce an exportation of thirty millions of pounds to England, but were again relaxed on the resumption of commerce with the United States. During the present year, American cleaning machines were introduced at Tinnivally, in the Carnotic, where a Mr. Hughes had succeeded in producing Bourbon cotton, with more success than in Bengal. Experimental farms, established five years after by the government of Madras, demonstrated the possibility of raising cotton of fair quality on the Coromandel coast, over one hundred and fifty miles from the sea.

The average price of cotton at its place of exportation in the United States was this year twelve cents per pound, including all kinds, and the quantity exported was about 19,400,000 lbs. The low price of material, and the high price of manufactured cotton, was favorable to the increase and profits of manufacturers.

The manufacture of woolen cloths continued to engage a large share of attention. Many factories were employed upon army and navy cloths, blankets, negro cloths, and other coarse fabrics, but the manufacture of broadcloths received an increased amount of attention. Mr. Rapp's colony, at Harmony, Pa., had, two years before, a flock of one thousand sheep, one-third of them merinos, and manufactured broad and narrow cloths, considered as good as any made in England. They could sell their best broadcloths, as fast as made, at ten dollars a yard. The Society then consisted of eight hundred persons, and had increased, by extraordinary industry, its original stock, since 1804, from $20,000 to $220,000.

An extensive broadcloth factory was this year erected at Walcottville, Ct., in which Governor Walcott of that state was a principal owner. Another manufactory of woolen cloths was established at Goshen, in the same county, by Louis M. Norton, and two associates, with a capital of $6,000, of which upward of one half was expended in its erection. They purchased wool at $1.50 per pound, and sold broadcloths, which, at the present day, would probably not bring over one dollar per yard, for eight to twelve dollars, one invoice of 178½ yards, having sold for the sum of $1,769.33, and another, of 255 yards, for $2,551.15, or upwards of ten dollars a yard. Notwithstanding the high prices obtained for their cloth, this little factory did not long survive the peace, and in common with many others, succumbed to the immense influx of English cloths which followed. It settled up, with the loss of its capital and three times as much more. Indeed, the charge of extortion, afterward advanced against the manufacturers of this period, on account of the prices obtained for their manufactures, had probably little foundation in fact, the advance in the price of raw materials, labor and expenses, having been greater than in the price of cloth. Broadcloths rose the next year to fourteen dollars per yard, and during the war were as high as eighteen dollars a yard, but wool also advanced in the next year to three and four dollars a pound, and indigo to four dollars a pound. As the labor of mechanics was scarce, because everywhere employed to the utmost, there is reason to believe that the percentage of profits was not increased in a ratio with the price of cloths, and that manufacturers generally, throughout the war, did not make greater profits than the mercantile and agricultural classes, by whom the charge was preferred. But the profits of all were large, and the general prosperity great.

Another woolen factory was built in Goshen, during the war, and the cloths made by the two factories, though greatly inferior to those of the present day, obtained considerable local reputation for durability, fineness, and elegance of style. The county (Litchfield), in 1819, contained eight woolen and four cotton factories, fifty carding machines, and forty-six cloth dressing establishments. It was also the seat of an extensive iron manufacture, having thirty-nine forges, many of them large, beside various minor branches of industry.

One of the earliest broadcloth mills in Massachusetts was about this time erected by E. H. Derby, of Salem, who, two years before, shipped at Lisbon a flock of eleven hundred merino sheep, of the Montarco breed, of which two-thirds reached New York, and were sent to his farm at Ten Hills, near Boston. A company was incorporated for the manufacture of woolens, at Billingham, Mass., with a capital of $400,000. The woolen manufactures of the country were still insufficient to meet the sudden demand for articles suitable for the army and navy, and the government was compelled, in the course of the year, to purchase of foreign manufacturers, chiefly British, at the current high prices, naval and army cloths, blankets, etc., to the value of $593,076. Large quantities also found entrance into the country through clandestine channels.

Cotton was this year manufactured by Phineas Whiting and Josiah Fletcher, in Chelmsford, Mass., the eastern part of which is now the city of Lowell. They erected, at a cost of about $3,000, a large wooden factory, on the Concord river, at Wamesit Falls, and five years after transferred the building and water privilege to Thomas Hurd, who erected a brick edifice, and converted both into a woolen factory, which run fifty power looms, and in 1826 was burned and rebuilt on a larger scale. In 1828 it became the property of the Middlesex Company, and Fletcher, Whiting & Co. transferred their business to Northbridge, Worcester county.

The most interesting event of this year was the incorporation, in February, of the Boston Manufacturing Company, and the completion, late in the year, of a cotton manufactory at Waltham, Mass., with about seventeen hundred spindles, in which the successful use of the power loom and all the operations for converting raw cotton into finished cloth, were for the first time introduced in this country, and probably in the world. Cotton mills in the United States up to this time had been principally for spinning, the weaving being done elsewhere, in hand looms, and in England the power looms were used in separate establishments. This enterprise, from which the cotton manufacture on a large scale in the United States dates its origin, was mainly due, as we learn from a pamphlet sent us by its author, the late Hon. Nathan Appleton, to the genius and and energy of Francis C. Lowell, Esq.[1] To that portion of Chelmsford, whither his associates afterward transferred their operations, the name of Lowell was given by them after his death, as a fitting acknowledgement of his agency in the undertaking. Mr. Appleton, whose long connexion with the cotton manufacture began here, was associated with the enterprise from the first, and was an original stockholder to the amount of $5,000. The stock of $400,000, only one-fourth of which was designed for immediate use, was principally taken by Mr. Lowell, Patrick Tracy Jackson, of Boston, an enterprising merchant, who relinquished trade to take the management of the concern, and the brothers of Mr. Jackson. The company purchased the water power of Bemis's paper mill at Waltham, and built the factory originally for the purpose of weaving cotton fabrics by the power loom. It was, however, deemed more profitable to do their own spinning, and the mill was started for that purpose. The power loom, already referred to as the invention of Mr. Lowell, was added in the following year, and worked quite successfully from the first. The engineer department was entrusted to Mr. Paul Moody, a machinist of acknowledged skill. The loom, which was the principal feature of this establishment, was found to differ considerably from English power looms. "The principal movement was by a cam, revolving with an eccentric motion, which has since given place to the crank motion, now universally used; some other minor improvements have since been introduced, mostly tending to give it increased speed." The patent dressing machine of Horrocks, of Stockport, England, of which Mr. Lowell had procured a drawing, was added

(1) Introduction of the Power Loom and Origin of Lowell, by Nathan Appleton.—*Lowell*, 1858.

G. P. A. Healy. S. A. Schoff

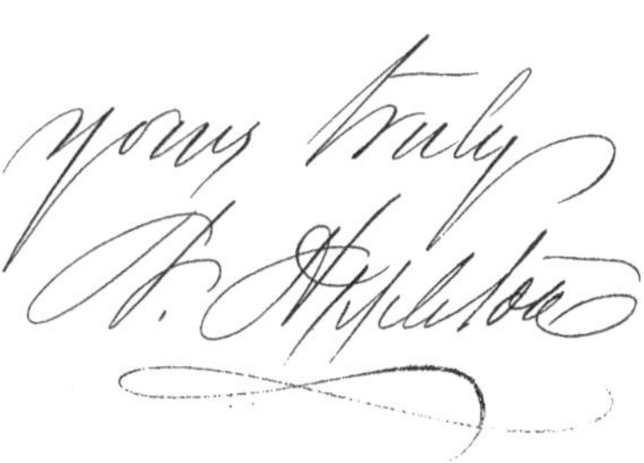

as a necessary accompaniment of the power loom, and received essential improvements, which more than doubled its efficiency. It is still in use. The stop motion for winding on the beams for dressing, also originated with this company. Other valuable improvements were made in the machinery, of which the most important was the double speeder, to regulate the movements of the fly-frame in filling the spool, for which Mr. Lowell performed the nicest mathematical calculations. This, with other improved mechanism, was constructed by Mr. Moody, and patented in 1819, and the two following years. It gave rise to several suits at law for infringement of the patent.

The description of goods first made by this company, at Waltham, was heavy unbleached sheetings of No. 14 yarn, thirty-seven inches wide, forty-four picks to the inch, and in weight something less than three yards to the pound. They were of the kind which has since formed the staple of American cotton manufactures for domestic use and exportation. They were offered at the only shop for the sale of domestic goods, then kept in Boston, that of Mr. Isaac Bowers, on Cornhill, but though praised, they found no purchasers.[1] They were then sent to the store of B. C. Ward & Co., importers of British goods, of which Mr. Appleton was the capitalist, and by them were offered at auction, through a Mr. Forsaith, who sold them rapidly for something over thirty cents, at which they long continued to be sold. B. C. Ward & Co. became the selling agents of the Company at the low commission of one per cent., which continued to be the established rate when large sales had made it highly profitable. Mr. Lowell died in 1817, at the age of forty-two, after having introduced into the Waltham factory, of which he was the informing soul, all the arrangements for the complete manufacture of cotton cloth in the same building. The system introduced by him, including careful provision for the moral character of the operatives, is still preserved in many of its details. His partners and associates were also men of great talent and energy.

A cotton mill was built this year at Plympton, Mass., and another at Enfield, which was sold, in 1821, to D. & A. Smith, and having been burned in 1836, and rebuilt, became, in 1852, the property of the Swift River Company, for the manufacture of woolen goods. The manufacture of cotton and wool cards was also commenced at Enfield, and continued until 1851, when it was removed to Holyoke. "Quobbin Whetstones" had been a principal article of export since 1790. The Franklin

(1) In the New York Exhibition of 1853–4, Mr. Hagerson exhibited a specimen of British calico, purchased in Boston by him, in 1813, at eighty-five cents a yard. It was thirty-three and a half inches wide, and the same quality could be bought, in 1854, for three and a half cents a yard, such had been the progress in manufacturing skill.

Manufacturing Company, at Franklin, Mass., was also incorporated—capital $200,000.

The cotton mills of Providence and its vicinity were at this time running about 120,000 spindles, and made about 11,000 lbs. of yarn weekly. They consumed 6,000,000 lbs. of cotton in a year.

In Baltimore and vicinity, where the marshals reported eleven cotton mills, with 9,000 spindles, in 1810, preparations were making to run 1,500 to 2,000 more, before 1st January. Messrs. Worthington, Jessop, Cheston, and others, took up water rights on Gwinn's Falls, for the erection of the Calverton mills, four miles west of the city. A large woolen factory was about this time erected at the same place by the Franklin Company. A paper mill had been in operation there since 1802. The Athenian Society of Baltimore sold, the last year, American goods to the value of $80,893.

In the State of New York, a large amount of capital had, for a number of years past, been annually invested in turnpike roads, toll-bridges, water companies, banks, etc., through the medium of joint stock companies. About one hundred and eighty turnpike companies, exclusive of several whose charters had expired, had been incorporated previous to the middle of April of this year. This business having been found to be somewhat overdone, the circumstances of the country directed enterprise as strongly toward corporate associations for manufacturing purposes. Among the objects, the manufacture of cotton and wool greatly predominated. The following charters were granted this year, under the general manufacturing law of 1811. To the Manlius Cotton and Woolen, Litchfield Iron, Ulster, Stamford, Fishkill Woolen, Pine Grove Woolen, Whitestown Cotton and Woolen, Western Woolen and Linen, Paris Friendly Woolen and Cotton, Broome Glass, Schenando Cotton, Paris Farmer's Woolen, Broome County, New York Eagle, Verbank Woolen, Homer Cotton, Beekman Cotton, Hanover Cotton, Salisbury, Susquehanna Cotton and Woolen, Otsego Cotton, Glen's Falls, Burlington, Eagle Cotton, Elm Grove Woolen and Cotton, Ticonderoga Iron, and Wharton Creek Manufacturing Companies, Societies, and Associations. Special charters were also given to the Flushing Manufacturing, the Urtica Whittlowi, the Otsego Card and Wire,[1] the Lake

(1) A manufactory of wood screws went into operation this year near the Cohoes Bridge, in Watervliet, Albany county, and opposite Lansingburg. A set of machinery, invented by a self-taught mechanic, Wm. C. Penniman, and driven by water power, was erected to draw the wire, which had been previously imported, and thus to furnish the screws from iron in the bar. The company was incorporated with adequate capital. A bell foundry and brass works in the town made brass cannon on contract for the State of Connecticut, and a considerable variety of other works, as plated wares, surveyor's compasses, etc., of superior quality.—*Spafford's Gazetteer.*

Champlain Steamboat, the Dutchess County Marble, the Canandaigua Mechanics', the New York Commission, and the Alleghany Coal Companies.

The following were included in a list of a hundred and seventy-nine patents issued this year. To Stephen Dempsey, New York (Feb. 4), for acetate of copper; Geo. W. Robinson, Attleboro, Mass. (March 17), for brass, copper, and composition nails; Jacob Perkins, Newburyport, Mass. (March 23), two patents, one for bank vault locks, and one for manufacturing the shanks of screws. Five other patents were given for cutting and making screws, two of them to Abel Stowell, Worcester, Mass. (Feb. 4 and July 15), for making and finishing the heads of screws. The others were to Jacob Sloat, of Ramapo Cove, N. Y.[1] (May 4); John Hames, Richmond, Va. (Dec. 30); and A. Burnham and T. S. Barnum, Sharon, Ct. (Dec. 31). J. Perkins received, in connection with G. Murray, of Philadelphia, another patent (June 25), for an improvement on Perkins' dies; and another (June 29), for a copper and steel plate printing press. Three other patents for printing presses were taken by William Elliot, New York (Feb. 17); printing press and ink distributor, Zach. Mills, Hartford, Ct. (Feb. 26), and Daniel Pierson, Newburyport, Mass. (July 16); Daniel Pettebone, Philadelphia (May 6), plane irons and scythes; T. Norton and G. Biddis, Milford, Pa. (April 15), carding, spinning, and roping. This machine carded and spun wool at one operation, without making it into rolls, and at the rate of a pound in twenty-five minutes, with seventeen flyers, in its imperfect state, before it was patented. Thomas Blanchard, Sutton, Mass. (May 4), horizontal shearing machine; William Shotwell and Arthur Kinder, of New York (July 23 and Nov. 4), for hair cloth, spun from the hair of neat cattle. The patentees had in operation at Rahway, N. J., early in the ensuing year, a large factory for making coarse fabrics called *Taurino* cloth and carpets, from the hair of cows and oxen, with a small admixture of sheep's wool. They had a capital of $400,000, and in the infancy of the business were capable of making five hundred yards of cloth daily. It was continued a number of years. Hez. Steele, Hudson, N. Y. (Sept. 8), paper hangings with satin ground; John Warely, Albany, N. Y.

(1) Ramapo, or Pierson's Works, in Hampstead, on the road from New York to Albany, consisted at this time of a forge or bloomery (of which there were five in the town and and twelve in the county), a rolling and slitting mill, and an extensive nail works, which, in 1810, made one million pounds of nails. They belonged to J. G. Pierson & Brothers, and employed one hundred and fifty men, and gave support directly and indirectly to nearly eight hundred persons. Dater's Works, two miles above, with six forge fires, employed one hundred and forty men. Nearly twenty-five years after, patents were again taken out for screws by Mr. Sloat, and by J. H. Pierson of these works, established in 1798 by J. G. Pierson, one of the first patentees of nail machinery on the records.

(Oct. 13), forming wool and rorum hats; Eb. Harrick, Stockbridge, Mass. (Oct. 22), a stocking loom, the first we believe recorded; Eb. Jenks, Colebook, Ct. (Nov. 13), elastic steel card teeth, fish hooks, etc.; Thomas Ewell, Georgetown, D. C. (Dec. 7), manufacturing gunpowder. The patentee claimed three important improvements, by which the risk, waste, and expense were diminished one half. They consisted principally in boiling the ingredients by steam, in the use of a wheel for incorporating them, and in a mode of granulating the powder. He offered to manufacturers the right of using the first two, and to furnish the wheel for $1,000 for every one hundred pounds made in a day, none less than three hundred pounds. For the use of the granulating machine, which he also put up, he demanded, for the first year the whole saving made by discontinuing the sifter, one half the saving for the second year, and one fourth for the third and fourth years.

The American naval force on the Atlantic stations consisted, on 4th March, of thirty-three vessels, independent of gunboats, only twenty-seven of which were in actual service. The whole coast, from the
1814 Mississippi to Long Island, being in a state of rigorous blockade, according to the proclamation of Admiral Warren, at Halifax, in 16th November, 1813. The attention of the Coast and Harbor Committee of New York, and of the President of the United States, was drawn by Robert Fulton to a model plan and specifications for the construction and armament of a floating steam battery or frigate of war, for harbor defence, in favor of which he obtained the certificates of many prominent naval commanders. This destructive engine, to be called the Demologas, in addition to a powerful battery, and the means of discharging a vast column of hot water upon the decks of an enemy's vessel, was fitted with furnaces for heating, red hot, shot or balls of one hundred lbs., to be thrown by submarine guns into her hull, below the water line. On the 9th March, Congress appropriated $320,000 for building one or more such batteries, under the superintendance of a sub-committee of five, with Mr. Fulton as engineer. The keel was laid 20th June, and on 29th October the first steam vessel of war ever built, named Fulton the First, was safely launched from the shipyard of the contractors, Adam & Noah Brown, in New York. Her keel was one hundred and fifty-six feet, breadth of beam fifty-six feet, depth twenty, diameter of wheel sixteen feet, and capacity 2,473 tons. The bulwarks of her main deck were fourteen feet ten inches thick, of solid timber, and pierced with thirty-two port-holes, for thirty-two pound guns. Her engine, of forty-eight inch bore, and sixty inch stroke, was put on board on the following May, previous to which time her ingenious projector had ceased to exist (Feb. 24), leaving

also, unfinished on the stocks, an improved submarine vessel, which he was building under executive authority, and which none of the mechanics were able to complete according to his plans. The steam frigate Fulton gave complete satisfaction, and on her trial trip in July made six and a quarter miles an hour, and afterward, in November, with her full armament, five and a half miles, drawing eleven feet of water. The peace having been ratified in the mean time, she was made a receiving ship until June 4, 1829, when she unaccountably blew up, killing and wounding a number of persons.

Congress, on 20th November, ordered twenty additional vessels, of eight to sixteen guns, to be built or purchased. Of those ordered in the last year, three were built during this year, at Vergennes, Vt., whence the lake fleet of McDonough was fitted, and sailed in September. Of one of these ships, the Saratoga, one hundred and sixty feet long, twenty-eight guns, and five hundred tons, the timber was all standing in the forest on 2d March, the keel was laid on the 6th, and the vessel was launched on 11th April.

The more peaceful fruits of the genius of Fulton and of our naval architects were witnessed this year, in the first passage of a steam ferry boat between New York and Long Island, that of the Nassau, which cost $33,000 and commenced running on the first of May. Fulton also built at Pittsburg, for a company at New York, Philadelphia, and New Orleans, the steamboat Vesuvius, of 340 tons. She was intended for the Louisville and New Orleans trade, and sailed in the spring from Pittsburg, being the third boat built in the west. In July, with a cargo, she made one half the distance from New Orleans to Louisville in ten days, which was regarded as nearly a demonstration of the ability of loaded boats to stem the current of the largest rivers by steam. The Enterprise, of seventy-five tons, also built this year at Brownsville, Pa., with an engine made at Bridgeton, under D. French's patent, took a load of ordnance to New Orleans, in December, and afterward made six hundred and twenty-four miles in six and a half days. This vessel was the first that ever ascended from New Orleans as far as Louisville, which she reached, in May 1816, in twenty-five days. She was commanded by Captain Henry M. Shreve, the inventor of the steam snag boat, to whom the citizens of Louisville gave a public dinner on the occasion. To Captain Shreve the western people considered themselves most indebted, next to Fulton, for the early establishment of steam navigation on their rivers, for having, in December of this year, on the first visit of the Enterprise to New Orleans, and subsequently with the Washington brought to a legal test, the claim of Fulton and his partners to a monopoly of the use of steam propulsion. Both boats were seized, as the captain desired, and the trial having been carried up to the supreme bench, resulted in the overthrow of the exclusive pretensions of the prosecutors. There was at this time but one steamboat in Great Britain, the Clyde. The new vessels built this year amounted to only 29,039 tons. The Embargo Act of December 1813 was repealed by Congress on 14th April.

The high prices of manufactures, raw materials, labor, and real estate, at this time, were the result in part of the war, and the suspension of foreign trade. They were, however, still more a consequence of the speculative disposition which had prevailed for several years in the Middle States, and were stimulated at this time by the fiscal measures resorted to by the government to carry on the war, by means of heavy loans, and an immense use of treasury and bank issues, which became rapidly depreciated in value. After the failure of the United States Bank to obtain a renewal of its charter, public and private banking institutions, and even manufacturing and bridge building associations had been rapidly organized, in the expectation of creating wealth by the facile process of emitting paper notes, rather than from the slow proceeds of industry and labor. So rife had this spirit become, that in Pennsylvania a law was enacted, in March 1810, restraining incorporated associations from the issue of notes, or performing other functions of a bank, but without effectually checking the evil. The only corrective to over-issues of paper money by the banks, the return of the notes for payment, was in a great measure removed by the war, which put a stop to the annual exportation of specie for the China and India trade. The banks then entered upon a system of wholesale issues of worthless paper, and of credits to the government, and to individuals, far beyond the limited requirements of the foreign trade. In New England, which was exempt from the rigors of the blockade, and carried on considerable foreign trade in neutral vessels, more stringent laws existed on the subject of banks, which preserved its currency from depreciation, and caused a continual drain of specie from the Middle States, and from the South and West, which also participated in the prevalent infatuation. In Pennsylvania a bill passed both Houses, in the Session of 1812–13, for the incorporation of twenty-five banking institutions, with capitals amounting to over $9,500,000, and having been returned by the Governor, was reconsidered and lost. The application was renewed in this year, and forty-one banks, representing $11,500,000 of capital, were authorized by a large majority in the Legislature, and after having been also returned by the Governor, was finally passed by a two-third vote, on 19th March. Of these thirty-seven went into operation. On the 29th August, at which time specie bore a premium of fourteen to twenty per cent., and a principal bank in Philadelphia found its specie reduced, since the 4th January, from $1,201,831 to $144,640, a general suspension of specie payments was declared by the banks of that city, in which they were followed, on 1st September, by those of New York and Maryland. This suspension continued nearly three years, during which the currency suffered still further discredit to a vast amount, with a corresponding drain of specie, a general inflation of prices, the utter derangement of business, and much eventual loss to the community. The commissioners, which met at Ghent, in August, signed a treaty of peace and amity between England and America, on 24th December, which was ratified by the President in February following.

The total value of domestic exports this year was only $6,782,000, and of articles of foreign origin $145,169. Of the former, manufactures constituted a value of only $411,000. The average annual value of domestic exports for the last five years was $30,618,196, or more than twelve per cent. below that of the preceding five, and a sixteenth below that of the five years from 1795 to 1799.

On the 9th of August the first ark load of twenty-four tons of Lehigh coal, from the Summit mines of Mauch Chunk, was shipped by Messrs. Miner, Cist, and others, and reached Philadelphia on the 15th, at a cost of fourteen dollars per ton. With much difficulty families and smiths were prevailed upon to make the experiment of using it. Several persons bore public testimony this year to its superiority for welding gun barrels, etc.

A duty of twenty cents a gallon on all spirits distilled within the United States, whether from domestic or foreign materials, in stills or boilers, was imposed on 21st December, in addition to those laid by the act of 24th July 1813. Additions were also made to the licenses payable by the former act.

The quantity of saltpetre made annually in Kentucky during the war, was upward of 400,000 lbs., and of gunpowder about 300,000 lbs. Saltpetre was obtained from the numerous limestone caves, in which the earth was so strongly impregnated as to yield often fifty pounds of nitre to every one hundred pounds of earth, and the latter, if returned after leeching, in a few years regained its former strength. The counties most productive in this article were Barren, Rockcastle, Montgomery, Knox, Estle, Warren, Cumberland, and Wayne, of which the last produced from 50,000 to 70,000 lbs. a year. A contract was made this year to supply $20,000 worth from the Mammoth Cave in Edmonson county. The state produced, in 1810, 201,937 lbs. of saltpetre, and Tennessee 162,426 lbs., Virginia 59,175, and Massachusetts 23,600, making nearly half a million pounds of home-made saltpetre, which, with the capacity for increasing the product, and the number of powder mills, were supposed to be adequate sources of supply.

A settlement, called New Harmony, was this year made on the Wabash, fifty-four miles below Vincennes, by George Rapp, and the community of Harmonists, who sold out their land and improvements in Butler county, Pa., for $100,000, with the view of cultivating the vine and raising merino sheep, under more favorable circumstances. Upon their new purchase, held, like all their property, in common, and in the name of Mr. Rapp, they erected a beautiful village, an extensive cotton and woolen manufactory, a brew house, distillery, steam mill, etc., and cultivated the vine with considerable success. Their cloth, made of merino wool, was considered equal to any made in the country. The unhealthfulness of the climate, however, compelled them, at the expiration of ten years, to remove, and they purchased another large tract of land on the Ohio, at Economy, in Beaver county, Pa., where they once more renewed the scenes of industry and skill, which everywhere attended their labors. The property in Indiana was sold for $190,000, to Robert Owen, the socialist.

The Zanesville Canal and Manufacturing Company, was this year incorporated—with banking privileges—for the construction of a canal and locks around the falls of the Muskingum, at an estimated cost of $70,000 to $100,000, and for the manufacture of iron in all its branches, cotton, wool, hemp, flax, paper, etc., by the water power of the rapids at Zanesville. Four miles above the town, on the Licking river, were a furnace and forge, carried on pretty largely by Dillon & Son, which were probably the earliest in the state. The census of 1810 returned three furnaces, one in Columbiana, one in Muskingum, and a furnace and forge in Trumbull, which together made 1,187 tons of pig, and fifty tons of bar iron. There were also twenty-four naileries. Coal was found abundantly in several parts of the state. Large quantities of maple sugar were made in the state, amounting, in 1810, to over three millions of pounds. The town of Aurora made, in the spring of this year, seventeen tons.

A cannon foundry, the beginning of the Fort Pitt Iron Works, was this year established at Pittsburg, Pa., by Joseph McClurg, at which the first cannon were made on contract for the fleet on Lake Erie, and for the defence of New Orleans. The first guns were cast at the old Pittsburg foundry, corner Fifth and Smithfield streets, commenced ten years before by McClurg, and they were finished at the new foundry, at the corner of Etna and O'Hara streets, where for several years the boring machinery was driven by horse power. There were then but three or four steam engines in the city or neighborhood. The works have continued the manufacture of cannon to the present time, and have produced many of the heaviest columbiads in the world.

Iron works were this year erected on French street, Baltimore, by Robert and Alexander McKim, to be driven by steam power. The price of solid castings at this time was about five cents a pound, and of hollow ware sixty dollars a ton. Bar iron cost as high as $150 the ton.

A petition presented to Congress in March, by Elijah Waters & Co. and others, inhabitants of Sutton, Millbury, Oxford, and Dudley, in Worcester county, Mass., praying for a duty on imported scythes and mill saws, stated that the manufacture of scythes was a flourishing and increasing business in those towns, which, in 1810, had eleven shops in which they were made, nine of them in Sutton, and two in Oxford. Seven others had been erected since, some of which could make one thousand dozens of scythes annually. The business had increased in nearly an equal degree throughout the state, and probably through the Northern States generally. Mill saws were also made to a considerable extent in that vicinity, and in other parts of the Union, and they believed the Union could be supplied with the domestic article, if the protection extended by the war was continued after its termination. Mill saws, mill irons, and scythes, were made at this time, somewhat extensively, by S. & A. Waters, at Amsterdam, in Montgomery county, N. Y. The works were erected at a cost of $6,000, and the sales amounted annually to $8,000 or $10,000, including about 6,000 grass scythes, all of which bore a high reputation.

The manufacture of steel, edge-tools, castings, iron ware, and sundry articles of hardware, had been already greatly extended and improved, by the suspension of foreign trade. That of wire making was considered well established.

The price of hemp increased from $210 per ton, in the last year, to $250, and $275 in the present. The high price of all materials, except cotton, which was not above thirteen cents per pound during this year, led to an extended cultivation of flax in Washington county, N. Y., in which James Whiteside, of Cambridge, led the way, and was soon followed by others. Its culture was found profitable at the current price of eighteen and three-quarter cents per pound. Washington and Rensselaer counties, particularly the valley of the Hoosic, have ever since been the principal flax region of the state, which in 1845 had 46,000 acres in flax, and produced 2,897,062 lbs. The culture was much promoted by the number of oil mills in the district, and the profitable exportation of flax-seed to the linen districts of Ireland, whence the first cultivators in Cambridge were derived.[1] An incorporated linen factory was in operation at Schaghticoke.

(1) Fitch's Survey of Washington County.

The manufacture of carriages was commenced during the last or present year, in Albany, by Mr. James Gould, who soon after added that of stage coaches. The business was also begun this year at New Haven, Ct., by Mr. Brewster, whose efforts to promote the moral and intellectual character of his workmen, by lectures delivered to them by himself and by Professors Olmsted, Silliman, and Shepherd, on scientific and mechanical subjects, at his expense, deserve mention no less than his eminence as a manufacturer. The business in all its branches has been ever since extensively conducted by these men or their representatives, and both the cities named, and their neighborhood, have long been principal seats of that business.

Chemical manufactures, which received their first prominent establishment in the United States, during the political troubles of this period, received considerable aid from the chemical and metallurgic skill of Dr. Erick Bollman, a scientific Dane, resident in Philadelphia, who introduced Wollaston's method of working crude platinum into bars, sheets, and other forms, serviceable in the arts. He succeeded in plating iron and copper with that metal, of which there chanced to be in the county a considerable and cheap supply, for which there was no demand. He also prepared the silver-colored metallic lustre or glaze for porcelain, with the oxide, and about this time made, for Mr. John Harrison, an enterprising manufacturer of oil of vitriol, the first platinum still used in the country for concentrating the acid. This use of the metal had been only recently introduced in Europe. The still weighed seven hundred ounces, and contained twenty-five gallons, and was in use about fifteen years. We believe he afterward applied it to the manufacture of crucibles and plates, or slabs, for glass-workers. A glass manufactory was this year incorporated in Keene, N. H., where it is still a principal business. The chief materials were abundant in the town.

The manufacturing business of Paterson, N. J., where little had been done, although several water privileges had been leased, since the failure of the first Company, and the destruction of their factory, in 1807, was about this time permanently revived by Mr. Roswell L. Colt, of Hartford, a son of the former superintendent of the Company's affairs. He purchased this year, at a reduced price, the principal shares, and reanimated the association. The admirable water power of the Passaic Falls at this place, was improved with much judgment by a dam, basin, guard-gates, and canals, supplying, on three separate planes of different elevation, the whole head and fall of twenty-two feet to mills on each side, without any inconvenience of back water. The expense of the improvements, amounting to $40,000, and of keeping them in repair, was borne by the Company, and Paterson became, in a few years, one of the principal manufacturing towns of the Union. With a short intermission after the peace, its progress has been uniform since that time.

The county of Essex, N. J., contained, in May of this year, twenty cotton mills, and it was expected that before the first of September there would be 32,500 spindles in use, making 30,000 lbs. of yarn, which, converted into cloth, would sell at forty cents a yard, giving a yearly value of $1,672,000. Within four years after, the county had in operation ten woolen factories, making cloth to the value of $650,000 per annum. Paterson, at the same time, had five cotton factories, mounting 20,000 spindles.

Mr. William Gilmour arrived in the United States about this time from Glasgow, bringing with him patterns of the power loom and dressing machine, in use in that country. He was invited to Smithfield, R. I., by Mr. John Slater, who wished to have these valuable machines constructed, but was unable to obtain the consent of all his partners. He remained two or three years engaged in mechanical labors for the Company, during which time he introduced, to the great advantage of the business, the hydrostatic press of Bramah, for pressing cloth. At the invitation of Judge Lyman, of Providence, he subsequently removed to that place, where the machines were constructed for him and others, and from whom he received a compensation of fifteen hundred dollars.

The price of cotton yarn, which, in 1810, was worth, on an average, one dollar and twelve and a half cents per pound, was this year worth less than one dollar, partly in consequence of improvments in machinery.

The second steam engine in Providence, one of twenty-four horse power, by Evans, was this year erected by Messrs. Whitney & Hoppin, in one of the buildings recently standing, of the Providence Dyeing, Bleaching, and Callendering Company. It cost $17,000, a large part of which was for transportation from Philadelphia.

The ardor with which manufacturing was engaged in at this time was manifested by the incorporation this year, by the General Court of Massachusetts, of thirty companies, for the manufacture of cottons, woolens, glass, files, wire, and other articles. About fifty companies had been incorporated in that state since 1806, principally for making cotton and woolen goods. Among those chartered this year was the Bellingham Cotton and Woolen Factory, on Charles river, with a capital of $15,000, and the Hampden Cotton Manufacturing Company, and one consisting of B. & W. Jenks, Joseph Bucklin, and others, who established at Jenksville, in Ludlow, Hampden county, a manufactory of cotton warps, to be woven in families, with woolen filling, according to the frequent practice of that day. The Company was not regularly organized according to its charter until December, 1831, when, by the name of the Springfield Manufacturing Company, it commenced an extensive manufacture of cotton, but failed, in July 1848, for a large amount. The first cotton mill in Franklin county was this year put in operation at Coleraine, by W. P. Wing. A woolen mill was built at Middlefield, Hampshire county, by William D. Blush, which was destroyed by fire in 1850. At Plympton, Plymouth county, a cotton and woolen factory was established, which manufactured this year about 15,000 pounds of wool.[1]

At Fishkill, Dutchess county, N. Y., where a woolen company had been previously incorporated, the first cotton mill was this year erected by Peter A. Schenck, Peter H. Schenck, and Henry Dowling. It was the foundation of the Matteawan Manufacturing Company, for many years the largest in the state. It was the only factory in the place until 1822, when the Messrs. Schenck, who had become sole owners, united with William B. Leonard, long favorably known as the agent of the Company, and erected another large manufactory, to which was added, in 1832, an extensive machine shop, etc.

The Literary and Philosophical Society of New York, established to promote the useful arts, diffuse knowledge, and enlighten the human mind, commenced its proceedings at this time.

The Manufacturing Company of Lancaster, Pa., went into operation this year, with a paid-up capital of $128,000, which was expended in buildings and machinery, and the manufacture of cotton yarn and cloth, until 1818, when its affairs were closed by the transfer of the whole to some of the parties interested, on payment of $34,000 of borrowed notes. It had thus sunk the whole capital, and was a striking example of the disasters which overtook many, in consequence of the flood of foreign goods which came in after the peace.

A large woolen manufactory, one hundred and twenty by forty feet, and five stories high, was built at Lexington, Ky., by James Prentiss & Co. It went into operation in 1816, and employed one hundred and fifty persons, but stopped during the financial troubles, about six years after. At the same place, which grew most rapidly at this time, a company was incorporated, in the winter of this year, with a capital of $50,000, afterward increased to $75,000, for the manufacture of white lead. It was owned by Messrs. Samuel Trotter, Levy, and others, and made annually from 80,000 to 120,000 lbs., with facilities for making 200,000 lbs.

Two hundred and seven patents, for new inventions, were issued this

(1) Holland's Western Massachusetts.

year, among which were the following: to Daniel Pettibone, Philadelphia (Feb. 1), for twisted screw auger for boring guns; Charles Osgood, Salem, Mass. (Feb. 26), composition for black lead pencils; John McThorndike (March 7), making paper from pelts; Eb. Ford, Baltimore (April 14), a torpedo; Archibald Binney, Philadelphia (May 17), moulds for casting printers' types. This lever hand mould was in general use in the United States until superseded by power machines, and enabled a workman to cast six thousand in ten hours, or two thousand more than with the ring-tailed mould in use in Europe (see A. D. 1811). Benjamin Porter, Salem, Mass. (May 18), a brick press, the first recorded; Joseph H. Derby, Leominster, Mass. (May 26), cutting combs at a single operation, and to several others for comb-making; James Harrison, Boston (Aug. 22), time part of wooden clocks, and patents the same day to five others for different parts of clocks; Moses L. Morse, Boston (Aug. 22), for manufacturing pins of wire at one operation. This machine is said to have shown much mechanical genius, and was used to some extent, but being too intricate or delicate, and remaining unimproved in other hands, it fell into disuse, or was superseded by other machines. Wm. F. Hill, New York (Oct. 15), a needle and pin machine; Samuel Browning, Franconia, N. H. (Nov. 25), a magnetic cylinder (or separating machine). This machine, for separating granular magnetic iron ore, and titaniferous iron sand from its gangue, by magnetic attraction, was first patented, October 13,1810, and was renewed by act of Congress, March 3, 1831, having proved highly useful to iron manufacturers. Aug. Boulia, Philadelphia (Dec. 21), a permanent color for calicos.

For the support of government, and the discharge of the public debt, Congress, on 18th January, enacted, that after 15th April, the following

1815 internal duties should be levied on articles manufactured in the United States for sale, viz: upon pig, bar, rolled, and slit iron, one dollar per ton, on castings one dollar and fifty cents; nails, brads, and sprigs, other than wrought, one cent per pound; wax candles, five cents; mould candles of tallow, etc., three cents; hats, caps, and bonnets, and umbrellas and parasols, above two dollars in value, eight per cent. ad valorem; paper, three per cent.; playing and visiting cards, fifty per cent.; saddles and bridles, six per cent.; boots and bootees, exceeding five dollars per pair in value, five per cent.; beer, ale, and porter, six per cent.; tobacco manufactured, cigars, and snuff, twenty per cent.; leather, five per cent. The duties which accrued from this source, during the current year, amounted to $793,625, and the amount received up to 22d February following, when the act was repealed, was $951,769. Duties were at the same time laid upon household furniture, gold and silver watches, and (July 27th), on gold, silver, and plated wares, jewelry and pastework, all of which were repealed the next year.

On the 10th February, the President, by special message, laid before Congress a copy of the treaty of peace and amity, between the United States and Great Britain, signed at Ghent, on 24th December, and since ratified by both parties. On this occasion Mr. Madison remarked, "The most liberal policy toward other nations, if met by corresponding dispositions, will, in this respect (in relation to commerce), be found the most beneficial policy toward ourselves. But there is no subject that can enter with greater force and merit into the deliberations of Congress than a consideration of the means to preserve and promote the manufactures which have sprung into existence, and attained an unparalleled maturity throughout the United States, during the period of the European wars. This source of national independence and wealth I anxiously recommend therefore to the prompt and constant guardianship of Congress."

In conformity with this recommendation, Congress, on 3d March, repealed the discriminating tonnage and other duties, in favor of such foreign nations as should abolish their countervailing duties, in favor of the United States.

On the 3d July, a convention was held at London, by the terms of which it was agreed to equalize the duties on tonnage and imports, so that the produce or manufactures of the one country could be imported into the other, in the ships of either, upon equal terms, and the same as those of the most favored nation. This treaty was reciprocal only so far as it related to the British territories in Europe, and the East Indies, and did not secure to the United States equal privileges in the British colonial trade in America. Congress, on the 1st March following, repealed all such parts of existing laws, laying duties on tonnage and imports, as were inconsistent with the provisions of the convention. The treaty was renewed for ten years, on 20th October 1818, and again indefinitely on 6th August 1827.

The earnest appeal of the executive, in behalf of manufactures, was soon after importunately urged by the manufacturers, who saw the temporary protection they had enjoyed during the war suddenly withdrawn, and their heavy investments about to be engulphed in a common ruin, by the renewal of foreign trade, under enlarged privileges. Congress at length responded to the call by a more decided measure of encouragement than had yet been accorded to this branch of the national interests.

The privations experienced during the war had convinced many American statesmen of the impolicy of withholding adequate protection to the manufacturing classes. The remarkable spring given to manufacturers during the few years of non-intercourse and war, had clearly shown the capacity of the country for their most profitable extension. The development they had already received in various new branches, and in the aggregate was quite remarkable, and their almost total subversion, as in former periods, through passive neglect, became a subject of just apprehension.

From the peace of Paris, in 1763, to the adoption of the Constitution, was a period of twenty-six years, characterized by the Stamp Act, and various laws prohibitive of manufactures, a seven-years' war, countervailing commercial regulations, debt and embarrassed credits, during which the country laid the foundations of a diversified national industry, and considerably relaxed its dependence on foreign countries. From the organization of the new government to the second peace with England, was a like period of twenty-six years, in which occurred the several embargos and orders in council, twenty years of European and two and a half of American war, an enormous accumulation of debt and a reckless abuse of public and private credit, notwithstanding which, domestic manufactures had grown in a manner quite unexampled in the previous history of any country. They had at length taken a position as one of the principal sources of national prosperity. The great body of manufacturers, who had transferred millions of capital from other pursuits to manufacturing establishments, had already become alarmed at the effects upon their interests of the revival of manufactures abroad, which would follow the general pacification of Europe, and of the unrestrained influx of British goods upon a peace with England.

Immense cargoes of foreign manufactures were already crowding the portals of the nation before peace had thrown open the gates of commerce, and several petitions had gone up to Congress to avert the danger which was impending. Many branches of the domestic industry were yet new and imperfectly established, and few of the more recent enterprises had yet reimbursed the heavy expenses incidental to first undertakings on a large scale. Among the petitions presented to Congress early in the present year, was one from Thomas Gilpin and others, manufacturers of Philadelphia, on 25th July, against the introduction of goods subject to ad valorem duties, at one-fourth to one-half their real value, and asking a revision of the revenue laws, which they suggested might be found either in the substitution of specific for ad valorem duties, or in the establishment of a Board of Appraisers at each custom house, with power to decide on the value of merchandise entered.

So great were the importations of foreign goods which immediately followed the peace, that during the first three quarters of the present year, their value amounted to upwards of eighty-three millions of dollars, and for the fiscal year next ensuing, amounted to one hundred and fifty-five and a quarter of millions, of which value, over one hundred millions' worth paid ad valorem duties, about seven-tenths of the last named sums being in woolens and cottons. The duties that accrued during the present year from imports, notwithstanding the under-valuation, amounted to $36,306,022, a sum nearly equal to the total average value of domestic produce, annually exported during the twelve years immediately preceding the war, which was $38,500,000.

It was supposed to be an object worth large sacrifices on the part of English manufacturers to break down the formidable rivalship of growing but immature manufactures in America, by means of heavy consignments of goods to be disposed of at auction, and upon the most liberal credits, to the merchants. That this policy had, also, the approval of eminent British statesmen, was inferred from the remarkable language of Mr. Brougham in Parliament, soon after the peace, when he declared in reference to the losses sustained by English manufacturers in these transactions, that "it was even worth while to incur a loss upon the first exportations, in order by the glut to stifle in the cradle these rising manufactures in the United States, which the war had forced into existence, contrary to the natural course of things."

American merchants were in no wise averse to the encouragement of these excessive importations, and were lured by the large profits and ample fortunes realized by the first cargoes—some of which were at once sold entire for clear profits of fifteen, twenty, and twenty-five per cent., and in some cases as high as forty and fifty per cent. on large sales—to engage in extensive transactions. The greatest life and activity were at once given to all the avenues of trade, the shipyards were set at work, the banks, already relieved from the payment of specie, discounted most unsparingly, and thereby stimulated all classes to seek their fortunes in mercantile operations and the largest ventures.[1] The increased revenues from imports, and the activity imparted to commerce, appeared to furnish evidence of unusual prosperity, but were soon followed by a reversal of the flattering prospects. To a very large number of manufacturers, however, the enormous importations which burthened the warehouses of the merchants, and soon after fell greatly in price, were fraught with the most

(1) Three package sales, which took place in June, July and August, 1815, on account of one merchant, amounted to $1,515,174. A single cargo was purchased for $300,000, divided into four notes each $75,000, all of which were discounted in different banks. The purchaser lost $80,000 by the speculation. The notes issued by one auctioneer, and those received by him for goods sold, extant at one time, and discounted at the different banks, amounted to $1,200,000. These facts exhibit a state of things portentous of an approaching hurricane, which soon burst with violence. As early as the close of 1815 a lamentable change took place, and goods experienced a ruinous fall. Goods at Passmore and Birkhead's auction store, which sold in August and September at the enormous advance of 200 to 230 per cent., sunk, in December, down to 90, 100 and 125.—*The Crisis, by M. Carey*, p. 34.

disastrous consequences. Many were compelled to close their factories, in which their whole capitals were invested. Many others who ventured to continue, became in the end hopelessly bankrupt. Large numbers of workmen were compelled to seek support in other pursuits, to which they were unaccustomed. The revival of the foreign demand for raw cotton raised the price of uplands from thirteen cents in 1814 to twenty cents in the present, and twenty-seven cents in the following year, and thereby still further reduced the profits of that branch, already nearly overwhelmed with British and India cottons, sold at or below cost in their own markets. Peculiar circumstances alone postponed for a time the more severe distresses which ultimately overtook nearly all classes.

One of the principal agencies by which our manufactures—that of cotton in particular—were enabled to survive the total ruin with which they were threatened, and eventually become thoroughly established, was the introduction of the power loom. Aided by that and other improved machines, the cotton manufacture of Great Britain had enabled her triumphantly to defend the liberties of Europe under the most onerous taxes throughout an exhausting war. Thus the mechanical combinations of a few ingenious minds became, in their results, more potent than the most powerful armies guided by consummate skill, and enabled a people, without utter ruin to important interests, to contravene the plainest maxims of political economy.

A power loom invented by F. C. Lowell, which cost about $300, was already in operation at Waltham, by the aid of which the proprietors stated to Congress, in the following year, that they were making a profit of twenty-five per cent., and stood in no need of further protection. The Scotch loom, of which patterns were brought to this country during the last year by Gilmour, was about this time constructed, at a cost of only $70, for several of the manufacturers of Rhode Island, who made a liberal subscription to Gilmour for the use of his drawings and instructions. This engine, which was considered superior to the Waltham loom, was constructed in about sixty days, at Pawtucket, by David Wilkinson, who added some improvements of his own, and commenced making them for sale. It was put in the Lyman Factory at North Providence. Its comparative cheapness enabled the small as well as large manufacturers to dispense with the hand looms, which were soon after superseded entirely for factory use, with a consequent increase of the cotton business, which without its aid would probably have been abandoned.

The extent and value of some of the interests which were imperilled at this time, is derived from two reports of the Committee of Commerce and Manufactures made to Congress in 1816.

The cotton manufacture of the United States employed this year

(1815) a capital of $40,000,000; males employed from the age of seventeen and upward, 10,000; women and female children, 66,000; boys under seventeen years of age, 24,000; wages of 100,000 persons averaging $1.50 each, $15,000,000; cotton wool manufactured, 90,000 bales, or 27,000,000 lbs.; yards of cotton of various kinds, 81,000,000; cost, at an average of thirty cents per yard, $24,300,000.

The woolen manufacture was supposed to have invested in buildings, machinery, etc., $12,000,000; value of raw material consumed, $7,000,000; increase of value by manufacturing, $12,000,000; making the value of woolen goods manufactured annually, $19,000,000; number of persons employed constantly, 50,000, occasionally, 50,000; total 100,000.

A memorial to Congress represented the cotton manufacture, within thirty miles of Providence, to employ, at the same time (Nov. 8), one hundred and forty manufactories, containing in actual operation 130,000 spindles; bales of cotton used annually, 29,000; yards of cotton goods of the kinds usually made, 27,840,000; the weaving of which, at eight cents per yard, amounted to $2,227,200; total value of the cloth, $6,000,000; persons steadily employed, 26,000.[1]

In the city and neighborhood of Philadelphia, there were employed at this time, in the cotton branch, 2,325 persons; in the woolen, 1,226 do.; in iron castings, 1,152 do.; in paper making, 950; in smithery, 750 do. The manufactures of Pittsburg employed 1,960 persons, and amounted to the value of $2,617,833. Nearly every part of the country exhibited a corresponding degree of prosperity at the return of peace.

In his annual message to Congress, on 5th December of this year, President Madison again urged the propriety of encouraging manufacturing in the following terms. "In adjusting the duties on imports, to the object of revenue, the influence of the tariff on manufactures will necessarily present itself for consideration. However wise the theory may be, which leaves to the sagacity and interest of individuals the application of their industry and resources, there are in this, as in other cases, exceptions to the general rule. Besides the condition which the

(1) A meeting of stockholders and representatives of cotton establishments, was held in Providence, on 6th November, and a committee was appointed to assess the several factories one cent on each spindle, "for the payment of the expenses of an agent to proceed to the city of Washington, to enforce the memorial or petition of the cotton manufacturers." The Hon. James Burrill was employed as the agent; and Mr. John Waterman, in collecting the assessment and statistics, found the number of cotton mills, "in and near Providence," to be as follows: In Rhode Island, ninty-nine mills, with 75,678 spindles; in Massachusetts, fifty-seven mills, 45,650 spindles; in Connecticut, fourteen mills, 12,886 spindles; total, one hundred and seventy cotton mills, and 134,214 spindles.—*Dr. Stone's Census of Providence.*

theory itself implies, of a reciprocal adoption by other nations, experience teaches that so many circumstances must concur in introducing and maturing manufacturing establishments, especially of the more complicated kinds, that a country may remain long without them, although sufficiently advanced, and in some respects even peculiarly fitted for carrying them on with success. Under circumstances giving a powerful impulse to manufacturing industry, it has made among us a progress, and exhibited an efficiency which justify the belief, that with a protection not more than is due to the enterprising citizens, whose interests are now at stake, it will become, at an early day, not only safe against occasional competitions from abroad, but a source of domestic wealth, and even of external commerce. In selecting the branches, more especially entitled to the public patronage, a preference is obviously claimed by such as will relieve the United States from a dependence on foreign supplies, ever subject to casual failures, for articles necessary for the public defence, or connected with the primary wants of individuals. It will be an additional recommendation of particular manufactures, where the materials for them are extensively drawn from our agriculture, and consequently impart and insure to that great fund of national prosperity and independence, an encouragement which cannot fail to be rewarded."

The petitions which were presented early in the session, from the cotton manufacturers of Massachusetts and Rhode Island, asking a prohibition of coarse cotton fabrics, especially those from beyond the Cape of Good Hope, and increased duties on others, represented the trade as particularly embarrassed by the quantities of low priced India cottons, made of inferior stock, and badly manufactured, introduced by the revival of the carrying trade, and by the further abstraction of specie, already at a premium of fifteen per cent. It was stated that a single ship, the Princess Charlotte, arrived at New York on 15th June, from Calcutta, with nine hundred bags of sugar, indigo, spices, saltpetre, etc., and nearly six hundred tons of piece goods, selected for the American market. This quantity, at the large allowance of four ounces to the yard, and the average price of twenty-five cents a yard, would make about five millions of yards, worth $1,200,000, brought by a single foreign ship. The duty being ad valorem, yielded little revenue on the coarser fabrics in the largest quantities. The Massachusetts memorial, presented December 13, contained the first suggestion of a mininum duty on cotton, which was granted during the session. The Assembly of New Jersey was about the first legislative body which came to the relief of the manufacturers at this time. On the 15th October, acting upon the report of Mr. Dayton, from the committee to which was referred the petition of Charles Kinsey, and other cotton and woolen manufacturers, it resolved to abolish the tax upon spindles employed in the cotton manufactories.

At Newark, in that state, a manufacturer of coach lace employed at this time about twenty hands. His supply of "floss silk" (raw silk freed from the natural gum), was obtained from Connecticut, and was found to be both in strength and lustre "much superior to the best imported silk." The silk of Connecticut had been previously made chiefly into sewings, and the raw silk used for coach lace, tassels, and fringe, had been principally imported at an average cost of six dollars per pound, which was increased by the war to thirty dollars per pound. From this time forward, large quantities of raw silk were also required for the manufacture of Tuscan braid for hats.

The revival of commerce at this time caused unusual activity in shipbuilding, which had been remarkably depressed throughout the war. The number of vessels, of all classes, constructed during the year, was 1,314, and their united tonnage was 154,624, a greater amount than was built in any previous year, and more than five times that of the last year.

The jewelry manufacture of Providence, R. I., employed at this time about one hundred and seventy-five workmen, and the value of its products for the year was $300,000. It was nearly abandoned during the next two years, but was revived in 1818.

The extensive Orange Powder Works of Daniel Rogers, near Newburg, New York, went into operation about this date, and afterward became capable of making two hundred and fifty to five hundred thousand pounds of gunpowder annually. It occupied twenty-seven buildings in the various operations.

The law of New York, relative to the incorporation of manufacturing companies, enacted in 1811 (and continued by successive acts), was amended to include companies for manufacturing clay or earth for any uses whatever. It was extended the next year to include *pins*, and in the following, *leather*.

At least one hundred and fifty millions of card tacks were made this year, at Abington, Mass., and sold in Boston, New York, Philadelphia, and Baltimore, and some in more distant places. An extensive iron factory, at the Saco Falls, in Maine, was considered one of the most complete in the country. It included a rolling mill, and five superior nail machines, one of which, with the help of a boy of twelve or fifteen years of age, would make one hundred and fifty shingle nails, and a stronger one, one hundred of the largest nails in a minute. At the same place, in addition to a fulling mill and three grist mills, was a saw mill, with eighteen saws, which cut 36,000 feet of boards every twenty-four hours. The water power was thought sufficient for 2,000 mills and factories throughout the year, and its subsequent manufacturing importance was confidently predicted.[1]

At Haverhill, Mass., considerable manufacturing was done. It contained two cotton and two woolen factories, and produced large quantities of shoes and hats for exportation, horn combs, leather gloves, leather, etc., and employed constantly thirty men in the manufacture of plated ware for saddles and harness, previous to the tax upon that article.[2]

At Cincinnati, Ohio, which, in June of this year, contained about 6,000 inhabitants, and 1,100 public buildings and dwellings, were four cotton spinning establishments, most of them small, containing 1,200 spindles, moved by horse power. A large woolen manufactory, owned by the Cincinnati Manufacturing Company, and calculated to make sixty yards of broadcloth daily, went into operation in the winter of this year. It employed a steam engine of twenty horse-power. The town had produced handsome pieces of carpeting, diaper, plaid, denim, and other cotton fabrics. Two extensive ropewalks made small cordage and spun yarn. The latter had been exported for several years, as had also fur hats. No wool hats were made there. There were six tanneries, and a considerable manufacture of shoes, boots, and saddlery. Many deer skins were dressed in alum, and leather gloves and brushes were made. A manufactory of cotton and woolen machinery, established in 1809, had since made twenty-three cotton spinning mules and throstles, carrying 3,300 spindles, seventy-one roving and drawing heads, fourteen cotton, and ninety-one wool-carding machines, besides wool-spinning machinery to the amount of one hundred and thirty spindles, twisting machines, and cotton gins. Plated saddlery ware and carriage mountings of all kinds, every description of fashionable enchased jewelry and silver ware, swords, and dirks, mounted in any form, fluted or gilt, and clocks of every kind, were among its manufactures. Stone and marble work, pottery, household furniture, carriages, plane stocks, weaver's reeds, turned and other wood work, were made. A manufactory of green and window glass, and hollow glassware, was about to go into operation, and to be followed in the ensuing summer by another for white flint glass. Clean white sand for glass-making abounded at the mouth of the Scioto, but clay for crucibles was obtained from Delaware. An extensive steam flour mill, with four pairs of six feet burr stones, and an engine of seventy horse-power, capable of manufacturing seven hundred barrels of superior flour weekly, and a steam saw mill of the newest construction, with four saws in separate gates, each capable of sawing two hundred feet of board

(1) Second Massachusetts Historical Collection, vol. 4, p. 184.

(2) Ibid., vol. 4, p. 121.

in an hour, were among the recent enterprises of this rising town. The Cincinnati Manufacturing Company had in operation a white lead factory, the third west of the mountains, the product of which was claimed to be superior to the imported, being free from whiting. The Company was about to add the manufacture of red lead. A sugar refinery was in course of erection, and there were several distilleries. Two breweries consumed 80,000 bushels of barley in the manufacture of beer, ale, and porter. Tobacco and snuff, pot and pearl ashes, soap of several kinds, and candles, were made and exported. A mustard manufactory, and a mineral water factory, were in operation. Two newspaper offices had an extra press each, for book printing, and had issued, since 1811, twelve different volumes of bound books, averaging two hundred pages each, in addition to pamphlets. The paper had been formerly obtained from Kentucky, but was now supplied by mills in the state.[1]

The lands, lots and dwelling houses in Ohio, were valued at $61,347,215. A manufactory of white, flint, hollow and other glassware, red lead and pearlash, was commenced at Wellsburg, in Western Virginia, and produced glass of superior quality.

In consequence of the high price of all imported drugs and dyestuffs, the trustees of the Massachusetts Society for Promoting Agriculture, offered premiums of $100 each for the greatest quantities, not less than three hundred, and one thousand pounds respectively, of woad and madder raised in the commonwealth, within two years, from 14th June 1814. The same sum was offered to the inventor of the most approved machine for threshing or separating grain (suitable for a medium farm), before June 1816, and seventy-five dollars for the best and cheapest machine for cutting straw or cornstalks, by horse-power, for fodder.

Trials made in England, in August and November, of American, and the most approved English ploughs, proved the latter to be superior in simplicity, and equally effective with the best in use then. The American ploughs were made under the directions of Judge Peters, President of the Philadelphia Society for Promoting Agriculture, and combined the best principles and powers of those in use in America, with especial regard to simplicity of construction, and were sent to Robert Barclay, Esq., of Bury Hill, near Dorking, where one of the trials took place. An American scythe and cradle, sent at the same time, proved superior in every respect, in the hands of an American cradler, to the Hainault scythe, used by an expert hand.[2]

The number of patents issued this year was one hundred and sixty-six, among which were nine to citizens of Connecticut, for button making,

(1) Drake's Picture of Cincinnati.

(2) Memoirs of Philadelphia Society for promoting Agriculture, vol. 4, pp. 13, 160, 163.

viz: L. Merien, New Haven (Jan. 4), for turning and polishing; William Lawrence, Meriden (April 12), a lathe pin for turning wire-eyed buttons; John B. Collins, Meriden (April 12), single jointed pewter moulds for wire-eyed buttons; Anson Matthews, Southington (April 26), wooden moulds; Ira Ives, Bristol (Aug. 7), three patents, viz: for a holdfast while polishing, for setting eyes of metal in the moulds, and for smoothing and rending the eye of metal; Heman Matthews, Southington (Sept. 12), two patents for a machine for finishing, and for a machine for making wire neck buttons; Jacob Perkins, Newburyport (Jan. 16), cutting cylindrical nails, and another (Nov. 1), for an improvement on the foregoing; Sylvanus Tousley, Manlius, N. Y. (Feb. 7), cast iron sleigh shoes on wrought iron rods; Oliver Evans, Philadelphia (Feb. 7), by special act of Congress, a renewal of his patent for steam engines, granted February 14, 1804; S. Blydenburgh, and Hez. Healy, Worcester, Mass. (Feb. 20), a loom to go by water, steam, etc.; F. C. Lowell, and P. T. Jackson, Boston (Feb. 23), a loom (power), see page 213; Thomas Bakewell, Pittsburg (March 3), manufacturing glass; George Stiles, Baltimore (April 4), a floating battery steam ship; Cadwallader D. Colden, N. Y. (May 19 and again June 2), hydrostatic paradox, applied to move machinery; Henry Tanner, Philadelphia (July 1), etching end pieces of bank notes; John Eberts, Philadelphia (Sept. 8), fall-top gig; Lewis Euters and W. Zigler, Georgetown, D. C. (Sept. 28), light from stone coal gas; James Hale (Nov. 22), ardent spirits obtained from lime; L. Merritt and S. Rogers, New York (Dec. 27), relieving toothache by steam; Jesse Sprague, Cape May, N. J. (Dec. 27), a wind saw mill.

In consequence of the low price of cotton, and the high price of sugar, during the war, increased attention had been given by the planters in Georgia and Louisiana to the cultivation of the sugar cane. The
1816 success of the business in the latter state was no longer regarded as doubtful. Several improvements in the process of manufacture had been introduced, by which the quantity and the quality of the product had been increased. Mr. Dorosne, in France, had taught, in 1811, the use of animal charcoal, or bone dust, for discharging the color and impurities, in the place of vegetable carbon, used since 1805; and in 1812 Mr. Howard, in England, afterward the inventor of the vacuum-pan, had introduced, as a superior defecating agent, a preparation of alumina, known as Howard's finings. The ribbon cane, an earlier and hardier species than the Creole and Otaheite, previously cultivated, was also introduced about this time, from Georgia, and became thenceforward the favorite plant. The sugar lands of Louisiana yielded from one to two hogsheads, of one thousand weight each, to the acre, which sold

for about $100 per hogshead. The crop, though uncertain, was on the whole considered more profitable than any other. A farm of one hundred and fifty acres employed about fifty hands, and produced 150,000 lbs. of sugar, worth, at eight cents per pound, $12,000, an average of $240 for each hand. One hundred acres of rice, with the same labor, only yielded $4,000, and two hundred and fifty acres of cotton produced about 6,000 lbs., worth, at fifteen cents per pound, $9,000. Indigo had been nearly abandoned for many years, and yielded, with the same labor, at one dollar per pound, about $7,000, and tobacco only $5,400. Cattle mills were exclusively used at this time. The cost of a mill, capable of grinding three hundred gallons per hour, and delivering two tons, or more, of sugar daily, was about $1,000, and the pestles, buildings, draft beasts, etc., for an establishment to make two hundred hogsheads, was at least as much more. The total crop of Louisiana, at this time, was about 1,500 hogsheads, which was increased in the next two years to 25,000 hogsheads.

This industry had become sufficiently important to claim the patronage of government, and on 5th January, a memorial was communicated to Congress, from Bernard Merigny, and other sugar planters of Louisiana, setting forth the importance of the business to the Union, the great expense and hazards attending it, and praying that "the same sound policy which has hitherto invariably excited the General Government to protect the growing manufactures of our country, and consequently made us, in many branches, completely independent of foreign nations, may be extended to the cultivation of the cane, and that the duties laid during the war on foreign sugar, rum, and molasses, be made permanent by law." By the tariff subsequently enacted, they were left in the enjoyment of three cents duty on sugar, a reduction of two cents from the double war duties.

The manufacture of Refined Sugar in the Eastern and Middle States, kept pace with the increase of population, and Congress, on the 1st February, continued, without limitation, the act of 20th July, 1813, imposing an internal duty of four cents on all sugars refined, and allowing a drawback of the duty, upon its exportation to a foreign country, in quantities of not less than five dollars' worth. In addition to the drawback, an allowance of four cents was allowed, April 30th, on every pound of sugar refined from foreign sugars, when exported as above. The quantity refined this year amounted to about 5,000,000 lbs., worth $1,000,000, and duties accrued thereon to the amount of $141,335, being nearly double the amount of duties in the previous year.

A large number of memorials and petitions were presented, early in the first session of the fourteenth Congress, by those interested in the manufacture, especially of cotton and wool, and also of glass, white lead, copperas, and chemicals of different kinds, olive oil and indigo, sugar, candles, etc., and the breeders of merino sheep, praying for the prohibition of, or increased duties on, foreign manufactures, whereby their own might be protected from the ruinous competition to which they were then subject.

The general interest awakened at this time, on the subject of legislative protection to manufactures, caused the opinions of public men, and particularly of Mr. Jefferson, as the head of a large political party, to be much canvassed. His views, as expressed in the Notes on Virginia, in 1785, were employed with effect, by the opponents of protection. In answer to a letter from Benjamin Austin, of Boston, on the subject, he stated in his reply, dated Jan. 9, that his opinions in view of the altered circumstances of the country and the policy of foreign nations, were as follows:

"We have experienced what we did not then believe, that there exists both profligacy and power enough to exclude us from the field of interchange with other nations; that to be independent for the comforts of life, we must fabricate them ourselves. *We must now place the manufacturer by the side of the agriculturist.* The former question is suppressed or rather assumes a new form. The grand inquiry now is, shall we make our own comforts, or go without them at the will of a foreign nation? He, therefore, who is now against domestic manufactures, must be for reducing us, either to a dependence on that nation, or to be clothed in skins, and live like wild beasts in dens and caverns;—I am proud to say I am not one of these. Experience has taught me, that manufactures are now as necessary to our independence as to our comfort; and if those who quote me as of a different opinion, will keep pace with me, in purchasing nothing foreign, when an equivalent of domestic fabric can be obtained without regard to price, it will not be our fault if we do not have a supply at home equal to our demand, and wrest that weapon of distress from the hand which has so long wantonly wielded it."

The public debt of the United States, contracted chiefly by loans for the support of the war, having increased since the 1st January 1812, from $45,855,070 to $123,016,375, additional measures became necessary to support the public credit. On the 5th February, the act laying double duties on imports during the war, was continued in force until 30th June; after which time an addition of forty-two per cent. to the duties then existing, was to be levied until a new tariff of duties should be established by law.

On the 13th February, Mr. Dallas, Secretary of the Treasury, in obedience to a resolution of the House, of 23d February 1815, transmitted to Congress an elaborate report, on the subject of a general tariff of duties, comprehending a view of its incidents upon the peace establishment, a statement of the general principles for reforming it, including the means of enforcement and a schedule of articles, with the rates of duty proposed for the consideration of Congress.

The annual revenue demanded for the service of government, was stated to be, in round numbers, about twenty-four millions, of which the Committee of Ways and Means proposed to raise by direct taxes upon lands, houses, and slaves, and by internal duties upon stills, stamps, refined sugar, carriages, licenses, sales at auction, and from sales of public lands, the sum of $6,925,000, leaving $17,075,000 to be raised by custom duties. This it was proposed to raise, by an addition of about forty-two per cent. upon the product of the single duties, in force on 1st July 1812, estimated at about $12,000,000.

The Secretary set forth the claims to protection of American Manufactures, which owed their existence, particularly those which had been introduced during the restrictive system and the war, exclusively to the capital, skill, enterprise and industry of private citizens. Their preservation from the ruin to which they would be exposed by foreign competition, became "a consideration of general policy, to be resolved by a recollection of past embarrassments, by the certainty of an increased difficulty of reinstating, upon any emergency, the manufactures which should be allowed to perish and pass away, and by a just sense of the influence of domestic manufactures upon the wealth, power, and independence of the government."

From the imperfect information he was able to obtain, the Secretary made the following classification of American Manufactures.

First.—Those which were firmly and permanently established, and which wholly or almost wholly supplied the demand for domestic use and consumption. They embraced the following articles—cabinet-ware and all manufactures of wood; carriages of all descriptions; cables and cordage; hats of wool, fur, leather, chip or straw, and straw bonnets; iron castings, fire and side arms, cannon, muskets, pistols; window glass; leather and all manufactures of leather, including saddles, bridles, and harness; paper of every description, blank books; printing types.

Second.—Manufactures which, being recently or partially established, do not at present supply the demand for domestic use and consumption; but which, with proper cultivation, are capable of being matured to the whole extent of the demand. These embraced cotton goods of the coarser kinds; woolen goods of the coarser kinds generally, and some of the finer kinds; metal buttons, plated wares, iron manufactures of the larger kinds, shovels, spades, axes, hoes, scythes, etc., nails large and small; pewter, tin, copper and brass manufactures; alum, copperas; spirits, beer, ale, and porter.

Third.—Manufactures which were so slightly cultivated, as to leave the demand of the country wholly, or almost wholly, dependent upon foreign sources for a supply. These comprised cotton manufactures of the finer kinds, muslins, nankeens, chintzes, stained and printed cottons of all descriptions; linen of all descriptions, linen cambrics, lawns; hempen cloths, sail cloth, Russian and German linens; silk goods of all descriptions; woolen goods of many descriptions, worsted goods of all kinds, stuffs, camblets, blankets, carpets, and carpeting; hosiery of all descriptions, including knit or woven gloves; hardware and iron-mongery, excepting the large articles, cutlery, pins and needles; china ware, earthenware, porcelain; glass of all descriptions except window glass and phials.

Duties amounting, wholly or nearly, to a prohibition of similar articles imported, it was conceived might be laid upon the first class, and a well directed legislative patronage would not only preserve the second class, but speedily raise them to the condition of the first class. The cost to the consumer would, in the first case, be kept down by competition, and in the second would not be necessarily increased. The inconvenience would be but temporary, while the future advantages to the nation would be great, and particularly to the agriculturist, who would thereby find a ready market in his own neighborhood for his cotton, wool, and produce.

Upon the third class, the rate of duty could be adjusted simply with reference to revenue.

The tariff of duties proposed by Mr. Dallas, in accordance with these general principles, was from ten to thirty-three and one-third, and in one case forty per cent. higher on all the principal articles of manufacture, forty-four in number, than the rates finally adopted. On cotton goods, which by the old tariff paid twelve and a half per cent., Mr. Dallas proposed thirty-three and a half, which was reduced to twenty-five per cent. On china, pottery, glass (other than window), it was reduced from thirty to twenty per cent., and hammered bar and bolt iron from seventy-five cents to forty-five cents per hundredweight.

On the same day that the Secretary's report was sent in, Mr. Newton, of Virginia, from the Committee of Commerce and Manufactures, to whom had been referred the memorials of the manufacturers of cotton wool, also made a report, from which we have presented, on a previous page, some statistics of that industry.

It stated the consumption of cotton to have increased from five hundred bales, in the year 1800, to ninety thousand bales in 1815, the capital employed to amount to forty millions of dollars, and the value of the product to be twenty-four millions.[1] An increase of the duties on imports was urged in a lengthy and forcible argument, in favor of the general policy of protection to manufactures.

"The American manufacturers," say the committee, "have good reasons for their apprehensions—they have much at stake. They have a large capital employed and are feelingly alive for its fate. Should the National Government not afford them protection, the dangers which invest and threaten them will destroy all their hopes, and will close their prospects of utility to their country. A reasonable encouragement will sustain and keep them erect; but, if they fall, they fall never to rise again.

"The foreign manufacturers and merchants know this; and will redouble with renovated zeal the stroke to prostrate them. They also know, that should the American manufacturing establishments fall, their mouldering piles—the visible ruins of a legislative breath—will warm all who shall tread in the same footsteps of their doom, the inevitable destiny of their establishments. . . . Do not the suggestions of wisdom plainly show, that the security, the peace, and the happiness of the nation, depend on opening and enlarging all our resources, and drawing from them whatever shall be required for public use or private accomodation? The Committee, from the views which they have taken, consider the situation of manufacturing establishments to be perilous. Some have deceased and others have suspended business. A liberal encouragement will put them again into operation with increased powers; but should it be withheld they will be prostrated. Thousands will be reduced to want and wretchedness. A capital of near sixty millions of dollars will become inactive, the greater part of which will be a dead loss to the manufacturers. Our improvi-

(1) In reference to the remarkable growth of the cotton manufacture as developed in this report, a very intelligent writer in Edinburg, is said to have used the following language: "The great extent of the cotton manufacture in the United States, stated in the preceding report, is more like what the sanguine views of the parties had contemplated than what had been actually achieved. Indeed it would have been impossible, even in a country with an extensive population and established manufacturing habits, to have reared, in the time, a manufacture of the magnitude they mention. But whatever prosperity it had attained, was put an end to by the restoration of peace with England, and this notwithstanding the heavy tax levied on foreign cotton goods. That the failure of those attempts, however, was not occasioned by any defect in the plan or general conduct of the establishments, we know from a gentleman who visited the principal cotton works in America, in 1816. He found the machinery in many of them of excellent construction, and those who had the charge of them were men who had been bred in this country, and who were possessed of both skill and judgment. But the circumstances in the state of America which we have mentioned, were so adverse to the nature of the undertaking as to render success in the opinion of those persons impossible."

dence may lead to fatal consequences. The Powers jealous of our growth and prosperity will acquire the resources and strength which this Government neglects to improve."

A duty of at least ten cents on the square yard, was considered by the Committee necessary to protect the American cotton manufacture, and an ad valorem duty of even forty or fifty per cent. on India goods, on account of the lowness of their first cost, would not give the requisite encouragement.

With the machinery already erected, including at least 500,000 spindles, the cotton manufacturers could supply the United States with about ninety million yards of cloth annually. These consisted chiefly of ginghams, plaids, bed-ticks, stripes, checks, sheetings, shirtings, and in part of canvas and velvets, and other cut stuffs. The shirtings made from yarn No. 12 would then bring twenty-three cents in New York, at which price they could not be afforded; the same article had been sold for thirty-three to thirty-five cents. Of the spindles then in operation, very few were effectually at work before the war. Such establishments had as yet reaped no profit whatever. There was one manufactory of cut fustians and velvets at Hudson, and one about to begin at Frankfort, and these goods required a duty higher than was proposed for other goods. They cost more—say from fourteen pence to thirty pence per yard, of eighteen inches width—and therefore required a duty of thirty cents per square yard, for such as cost twenty-three pence and under, and thirty-six cents for such as cost more.

The same Committee, on 6th March, reported on the memorials and petitions of the woolen manufacturers. This branch employed a capital of twelve millions of dollars, and one hundred thousand hands, producing goods to the value of nineteen millions of dollars. Every reason urged in the foregoing report, for sustaining the cotton manufacture, applied with equal force to this, and the Committee felt bound to accord the same justice to the manufacturers of wool.[1]

With these principles and objects before it, and at the earnest solicitation of numerous memorialists, Congress, on the 20th February, for the first time addressed itself to the consideration of a tariff bill, reported by

(1) Messrs. Arthur W. Magill and Wm. Young, whose estimates were accepted by the Committee, stated, in a letter to the chairman, that the manufacture of woolen cloths, in Connecticut alone, then employed twenty-five establishments, and 1,200 persons, besides as many more hands indirectly. Their capital was $450,000, and they probably made 75,000 yards of narrow, and 25,000 yards of broadcloths. As many as 500,000 yards were supposed to be made annually in families. The manufacture was capable of an increase, throughout the Union, of twenty-five to thirty per cent. per annum.

15

Mr. Lowndes, of South Carolina, Chairman of the Committee of Ways and Means, with a primary view to the encouragement of domestic manufactures, those of cotton and wool being prominent objects of regard.

In this bill, embracing the schedule reported by Mr. Dallas, the *minimum* principle, as applied to certain foreign goods, was first adopted in connection with low-priced cottons. Its object was virtually to exclude the coarse, low-priced India cottons, then imported in large quantities, alike to the prejudice of the American manufacturer and cotton grower. The introduction of the minimum valuation has been ascribed to Mr. F. C. Lowell, of Massachusetts, who secured for it the advocacy of Messrs. Lowndes and J. C. Calhoun; and those gentlemen, with other representatives from South Carolina and the Southern States, were, during the discussion of the bill, among the ablest supporters of the principle of protection, apparently without any suspicion of the unconstitutionality of the measure, which was afterward discovered in that quarter. There was a difference of opinion as to the degree of protection required, or that was proper to be granted through the tariff; but a general concurrence in the propriety and necessity of the measure at that particular crisis. Many regarded the faith of the Government as involved in the support of manufactures, created by its restrictive measures and the war, and which had, to so great an extent, been the dependence of the country during that period. A portion of the commercial and landed interests, which had suffered from the causes that created and sustained manufactures, now felt themselves entitled to be relieved from all unnecessary burthens in support of an industry which had thriven during their embarrassments. They were disposed to limit the duties to such rates and duration as was compatible with the object which all were disposed to cherish. Mr. Clay, to try the sense of the House as to the extent to which it was willing to go in protecting domestic manufactures, moved to amend the bill by increasing the duty on imported cottons from twenty-five to thirty-three and one-third per cent.—afterward reduced to thirty—and advocated a thorough and decided protection by ample duties, as did also Mr. Ingham, of Pennsylvania, who stated that not less than one hundred millions were believed to have been invested in manufactures within the last eight or ten years; all of which was endangered by the accumulated amount, cheapened cost, and improved quality of foreign manufactures. The commercial interests were well defended by Mr. Smith, of Maryland, and Daniel Webster, then a representative from New Hampshire, both of whom favored moderate protection. Mr. Webster, who considered permanency, rather than a high duty, desirable, proposed a maximum duty on cottons of thirty per cent., to be reduced after two years to twenty-five, and in two more to twenty per cent. He endeavored to avert the sudden destruction of the India trade, which was stated to employ forty ships, capable of carrying one thousand bales, of eighteen hundred yards each, or a total of seventy-two million yards of cloth, worth nearly six and a half millions of dollars, which value, with the eighteen million pounds of cotton consumed in its manufacture, was so much taken from the industry of the United States. Under the minimum provision of the bill, by which cotton cloths (except nankeens from China), the original cost of which, at the place whence imported, was less than twenty-five cents the square yard, were to be deemed to have cost twenty-five cents, and to pay duty accordingly, the trade in India cottons was intended to be arrested. Mr. Pickering, of Massachusetts, who did not believe the existing manufactures required a duty of twenty-five per cent., for two years, moved in Committee of the Whole to strike out that clause, but found few supporters. Afterward, before the House, he moved to amend it by a return to the old double duties, and during the discussion, Mr. Randolph, who was disposed to encourage none but household or family manufactures, again moved to strike out the minimum proviso. This drew from Mr. Calhoun an earnest defence of the principle of protection, upon grounds of prudence and national policy, as well as of justice to manufacturers, which had originated in the public necessity of the times. The bill was then carried by a vote of eighty-eight to fifty-four, and was approved on the 27th. Mr. Wright, of Maryland, proposed to exclude the votes of members interested in cotton manufactures. The duty on woolen manufactures, except blankets, rugs, and worsted or stuff goods, was fixed at twenty-five per cent. ad valorem for three years, from 30th June, and on cotton cloths, twist yarn, or thread, at twenty-five per cent., for the same time, after which, cottons were to pay twenty per cent. ad valorem. The minimum valuation of cotton cloths was, in effect, a specific duty of six and a quarter cents a yard, and was also applied to unbleached and uncolored cotton, twist yarn or thread, costing less than sixty cents a pound, and to bleached or colored yarn, costing less than seventy-five cents per pound.

By this act a discrimination was first made between hammered and rolled bar iron, which, under the permanent duties, had paid alike fifteen per cent., and double rates during the war. On hammered iron, chiefly made in Russia and Sweden, a duty of seventy-five cents per cwt. was proposed, but was reduced, on motion of Mr. Webster, to forty-five cents, or nine dollars per ton, equivalent to about thirteen per cent. upon its first cost.[1] On rolled iron, which was made in England, by the new and cheaper process, at about half the price of the former, the duty was one dollar and fifty cents per cwt., or thirty dollars per ton, equal to about eighty-five per cent. on its cost. This difference was the subject of remonstrance by Great Britain, as a departure from the provisions of the Convention of July 3, 1815.

The principal foreign manufactures and products were admitted at the following ad valorem rates, calculated on the net cost at the place whence imported, exclusive of packages, commissions, and exchanges, with the usual twenty and ten per cent. additional, viz:

At seven and a half per cent., ad valorem, saltpetre, jewelry, watches, gold and silver wares, laces, etc.; at fifteen per cent., gold leaf, and articles otherwise free; at twenty per cent., hempen, or sail cloth (except Russia, German, and Holland linen and duck), cotton and wool stockings, types, brass, copper, iron, steel, pewter, lead and tin wares, brass wire, cutlery, pins, needles, buttons and moulds, buckles, gilt, plated and japanned wares, cannon, muskets, fire and side arms, Prussian blue, china, earthen, stone and porcelain wares, glass, other than window, and black quart bottles; at twenty-five per cent., cotton and woolen goods; at thirty per cent., umbrellas, parasols, and parts thereof, bonnets and caps, artificial flowers and millinery, hats and caps of all kinds, painted floor cloths, mats, salad oil, mustard, pickles, sweetmeats, wafers, cabinet wares, and all manufactures of wood, carriages and parts thereof, leather and manufactures of leather, paper, pasteboard, paper hangings, blank books, parchment vellum, brushes, canes, whips, and ready made clothing.

The following specific duties were laid, viz: on ale, beer, and porter bottled, fifteen cents, unbottled, ten cents a gallon; alum and copperas, one dollar a cwt.; black glass bottles, one dollar and forty-four cents per gross; window glass from eight by ten and under to ten by twelve in size, one dollar and fifty cents to three dollars and twenty-five cents per hundred square feet; boots, one dollar and fifty cents; shoes and slippers of silk, thirty cents, of leather, twenty-five cents, childrens', fifteen cents per pair; tallow, whiting, and Paris white, ochre dry (in oil one and a half cents); lead in pigs, bars, or sheets, one cent; spikes, shot of lead, two cents; bristles, tarred cordage and cables, tallow candles, cotton, chocolate, red and white lead, nails, soap, brown sugar, etc., three

(1) The excise collected upon iron made in all the states, between 18th April, 1815, and the 22d February, 1816, amounted to $61,903, of which Pennsylvania paid $27,941, showing that state to have made nearly as much iron as all the others. Yet two representatives from that state voted for a reduction of the duty, while Messrs. Calhoun and Maynard, from South Carolina, voted for the higher rate.

cents; white clayed or powdered sugar, untarred cordage, yarns, twines, packthread and sieves, copper and composition rods, bolts, spikes or nails, four cents; coffee, glue, iron or steel wire, not exceeding No. 18, five cents; wire over No. 18, nine cents; wax and spermaceti candles, six cents; gunpowder, eight cents; cheese, nine cents; lump sugar and manufactured tobacco, ten cents; loaf sugar, sugar candy, and snuff, twelve cents; indigo, fifteen cents a pound; coal, five cents the heaped bushel; salt, twenty cents a bushel; spirits from grain, forty-two to seventy-five cents, and from other materials, thirty-eight to seventy cents, according to proof; molasses, five cents; wines twenty-five cents to one dollar a gallon; anchors, rolled bar, and bolt iron, one dollar and fifty cents, hammered iron, forty-five cents, iron in sheets, rods, and hoops, two dollars and fifty cents per cwt.; Russian duck, two dollars, ravens, one dollar and twenty-five cents, Holland, two dollars and fifty cents per piece; segars, two dollars and fifty cents per thousand; teas, twelve to sixty-eight cents per pound; olive and spermaceti oils, twenty-five cents, whale and other fish oils, fifteen cents a gallon.

This tariff, though falling far short of the measure of protection, which the more ardent friends of manufactures felt themselves entitled to, was accepted as an advance upon the permanent duties to which they were about to return. Although, upon the whole, as much calculated to benefit the farming and planting interests, which had opposed it, as the manufacturing, it doubtless averted the speedy ruin, which would otherwise have overtaken several branches, and probably destroyed the cotton manufacture altogether. The benefits expected from it increased very greatly, however, the competition in manufactures, and with the decline in prices that soon followed, as a result of improved machinery, and increased enterprise abroad, and the resumption of specie payments, brought the severest distress upon the manufacturing classes.

The immediate effect of its operation upon the accumulated supplies of foreign manufactures, which began to flood the country after the peace, was to replenish the public treasury, of which the receipts from customs during the year amounted to $36,306,874, or seventy-three per cent. above the estimate, and more than double the maximum before the embargo, when it reached $16,363,550, in 1807. The total amount of ad valorem duties, at twenty-five per cent., chiefly on cottons and woolens, paid in 1815 and 1816, was $28,826,419. The foreign imports retained for consumption were double the value of domestic exports, which were greater than that of any previous year, by nearly fifty per cent. The total imports exceeded one hundred and forty-seven millions in value.

Financial embarrassment to importers and manufacturers was the inevitable consequence, and was only partially alleviated by the operations of the new United States Bank, created with a view to restore the currency. That institution was chartered on the 10th April, for twenty years, and was opened early in the ensuing year, with a capital of thirty-five millions (of which seven millions were held by the United States), in shares of one hundred dollars, bearing five per cent. interest, with twenty-five branches in the different states. The resumption of specie payments was thereby forced upon the other banks, and a general improvement of the currency resulted, although the sudden curtailment of their heavy issues produced much commercial distress during a few subsequent years. The Bank of England, which had not paid specie since 1797, also partially resumed, in December, by paying specie for one and two pound notes. The greatest distress, however, prevailed in England as a consequence of the general peace in Europe, which was more immediately disastrous to her than to the United States. Riots, and the destruction of machinery, were particularly rife throughout this year.

As a means of alleviating the present and prospective distress of the laboring classes, arising out of the instability of manufactures, the first savings institutions in this country were organized toward the close of this year. The "Saving Fund Society," of Philadelphia, Andrew Bayard, President, was opened for business December 2d, and the "Provident Institution for Savings," at Boston, was incorporated on the 13th. The latter, "intended to encourage industry and prudence in the poorer classes, and to induce them to save and lay by something of their earnings for a period of life when they will be less able to earn a support," received deposits as low as one dollar, and paid interest when they amounted to five dollars. The "Bank of Savings," in the city of New York, was formed under the auspices of the Society for the Prevention of Pauperism, in public meeting on 25th November. It was incorporated in March 1819, and received its first deposits, to the amount of $2,807, from eighty depositors, in sums of two dollars to three hundred dollars, on 3d July following.[1]

The dangers which appeared to threaten the national industry induced the American Society for the Encouragement of Domestic Manufactures, to issue at New York, on 31st December, an address to the people of the United States, inviting them promptly to establish throughout the Union, Societies for correspondence with them and with each other,

(1) On the 1st January, 1859, there were fifty-seven Savings Banks in the state, and sixteen in the city of New York; the latter having on deposit $36,804,419, and resources to the value of $38,757,860. The first Savings Bank in Baltimore, was formed early in 1818, and incorporated at the next session of the Assembly. It received, during the next three years, deposits to the amount of nearly $80,000.

and upon manufacturers, agriculturists, merchants, men of science, soldiers, and women every where to unite in upbuilding American Manufactures.

The Columbian Institute, for the promotion of Arts and Sciences, was instituted this year at Washington. It was merged in the National Institute on the expiration of its charter in 1830.

An interesting event of this year, was the introduction, in several different places, of the system of illumination by Gas Light. Lewis Enters and William Zeigler, of Georgetown, D. C., in February, memoralized Congress for its aid and patronage in carrying into execution a discovery which they had lately made of producing light from the gas of stone coal, for which they had already received a patent. In Baltimore a company was formed, composed of Rembrandt Peale, Wm. Lorman, James Mosher, Robert C. Levy, and Wm. Gwynn, who obtained a charter to furnish the city and individuals with gas light. They erected works on the south-west corner of North and Saratoga streets, and were the first in the United States to carry into operation the improved mode of illuminating towns. The corporation of New York, also, during the year, took measures for introducing gas light. Gas was introduced into a mill near Cincinnati, by Mr. William Green, and it was also proposed to light the streets of the city with it. On the 25th November, the New Theatre at Philadelphia was illuminated with gas lights under the direction of Dr. Kugler, being the first theatre on the continent illuminated in that manner.

A proposition was also made this year by Dr. John Rodman Coxe, professor of chemistry in the University of Pennsylvania, to establish an Electric Telegraph and to make signals at a distance by the decomposition of water and metallic salts, whereby a change of color would be produced.[1]

The manufacture of chemicals, paints, medicines, etc., was commenced at Baltimore, by Messrs. Howard Sims and Isaac Tyson, who erected a laboratory on Pratt street. They afterward removed it to Washington Avenue, and were incorporated in 1822. They became extensive manufacturers of copperas, and of chromate of potash, chrome yellow, and other chromic pigments from the chromate of iron at Bare Hills, Maryland, and in Chester County, Pennsylvania.

The first Steam Paper mill in the United States, went into operation at Pittsburg, with an engine of sixteen horse power, on the principle of Evans's. It employed forty persons, and consumed ten thousand bushels

(1) Thompson's Annals of Philosophy, vol. 7, p. 162.

of coal, and one hundred and twenty thousand pounds of rags, and made $30,000 worth of paper annually.

Five steamboats were built this year on the western rivers, of which the Vesta, one hundred tons, was the first ever built at Cincinnati. A small boat was built at Hendersonville, Ky. The Washington, of four hundred tons, constructed at Wheeling, with an engine made at Brownsville, was the first boat with her boilers above deck instead of in the hold, and was also the first to prove, by making a round trip from Louisville to New Orleans and back in forty-five days, the fitness of steamboats for the ascending trade. The increase of steamboats from this time was rapid. Shipbuilding was revived at Marietta, by the formation, in March, of a large commercial and exporting company at that place.

The first steamboat on Lake Ontario, was built this year at Sackett's Harbor. She was named the "Ontario," and made her first trip in April of the ensuing year.

Commercial intercourse with Europe was greatly facilitated by the commencement this year of the first line of Packet ships. Three ships of three hundred to four hundred tons, to sail on stated days about once a month, were put on the route by Jeremiah Thompson and Isaac Wright, and others.

By an act of Congress of 25th April, Congress appropriated one million dollars annually for eight years, for the general increase of the navy. Nine ships of not less than seventy-four guns each, and twelve of forty-four guns, including one seventy-four and three forty-four gun ships previously ordered, were to be built, and the engines and imperishable materials for three steam batteries were to be purchased. Under this act large contracts were made for timber and other materials, including 2,300 bolts of *American* canvas for about $49,700; eighty tons of lead for $10,398; 500 tons of iron for $52,558, and a steam engine of one hundred horse-power for $30,000. The Washington, of two thousand tons, one of the seventy-four gun ships referred to, was built at Portsmouth, N. H., and was the first United States ship of the line ever launched. She sailed May 8th, from Boston, under Commodore Chauncey, for Annapolis, to take out Mr. Pinckney as ambassador to Naples.

The manufacture of Cotton Sail Duck, commenced in 1809 by Mr. Bemis, near Boston, had been greatly increased on account of the scarcity of foreign sail cloth, and the amount required for privateers and merchant vessels, which raised the price of No. 1 duck to nearly one dollar a yard. It was made of Sea Island Cotton, costing then twenty to twenty-five cents a pound. During the first year of the war the manufacturers' sales were increased in Boston, and the article introduced to the southern markets; the article after 1812 being transported to

Baltimore, Alexandria, and Richmond, on his own teams, which, after an expedition of several months, returned with flour, tobacco, and other southern products; in 1812–13 his sales in Baltimore, by one house, were about $20,000; and by another, in the last and present year, over $21,000. He adopted this year the use of the Power Loom, which, with other improvements, reduced the price in the next fifteen years to thirty-five cents a yard, the manufacture having been commenced by others in the mean time.[1]

The encouragement given to woolen manufacturers by the tariff of this year, in which they were mentioned for the first time, prompted new enterprises in that branch. In addition to the Maryland Soap and Candle Factory, on a large scale, and the Warren Cotton Factory at Great Gunpowder Falls, incorporated this year in Maryland, an extensive woolen factory went into operation near Baltimore, and another at the Little Falls of the Potomac. In Ohio and neighboring parts of the west, where an improved quality of wool was now produced, woolen factories were increasing. At Steubenville, Ohio, a steam woolen factory, in addition to cotton, paper, and other factories, was in operation, owned by B. Wells & Co., and another large woolen mill, established by Thomas Roach, near Kendall, in Stark County.[2]

A new American Power Loom, to be worked by steam or water-power was invented and put in operation in Boston, this year, by Mr. E. Savage. It was of simple construction, and was adapted for weaving woolen cloths three yards wide, and the largest cotton sheets without a seam, fine shirtings, etc.

A patent was granted July 25th, to Cyrus Shepherd and J. Thorpe, of Taunton, Mass., for an upright power loom which was already in operation in the woolen mill of Mr. Shepherd, at that place. The same parties were also granted, October 14, a patent for a socket bobbin-winder, which was considered the best winding machine in use. It is related by the late Mr. Appleton, that while bargaining with Mr. Shepherd for the right of using the winders on a large scale, it occurred to Mr. Lowell or Mr. Moody, of the Waltham Factory, that he could spin the cops direct upon the bobbin, which cut short the negotiation and resulted in the last great improvement in connection with the power loom, that of spinning the filling directly on the cops without the process of winding. Mr. Moody took a patent (March 9) for winding spool yarn.

(1) Third Annual Report of Boston Board of Trade for 1857.

(2) At Richard Brown's woolen factory, Hollidays Cove, Va., four miles from Steubenville, the wool was shorn from a sheep in the morning, washed, carded, and spun into yarn of eighteen cuts to the pound, wove, dyed, filled, dried, shorn and made into a coat and worn in the space of twenty-four hours.

Jeptha A. Wilkinson, of Otsego, N. Y., patented (July 3) a machine for making loom reeds. This valuable machine, invented in 1813, was first successfully put in operation in the manufactory of Sharp, Roberts & Co., Dean's Gate, Manchester, England. In 1823, the inventor returned and established a manufactory of reeds in Providence, R. I., which, with the machine, he sold the same year to Arnold Wilkinson, by whom the machine was much improved. The factory has been since owned and much extended by Gorham & Angell, W. S. Humphreys & Co., and Frederick Miller, the present or recent owner.

Patents were taken out by Jos. and Stinson Demund, N. J. (Jan. 17), for making ardent spirits from corn and corn cobs; Daniel French, Bridgeport, Pa. (April 23), turning buttons; John Morton, Southington, Ct. (June 13), wooden mould buttons; Joseph Derby, Worcester, Mass. (April 30), stamping engravings on horn, etc.; Hez. Kelby, Brooklyn, N. Y. (May 17), extracting turpentine by steam; Nathan Weston, Reading, Mass. (May 24), cemented hats; David Beard, Guilford, N. C. (May 28), blocking hats; Eli Terry, Litchfield, Conn. (June 12), thirty-hour wooden clocks; Jesse Reed, Hanover, Mass. (August 1), making tacks. The inventor, a son of Ezekiel Reed, for whom the invention of cut nails and tacks has been claimed, had, at this time, six machines in operation at Pembroke, with one of which a single hand had made 60,000 in a day. Six others then building, were sold, with the right, to Elisha Hobart, of Abington, for $11,000. They completed the tack at one operation. George Ellicott, Baltimore (Sept. 20), rolling bar iron edgeways; David Thacher, Tuckerton, N. J. (Oct. 24), plan for erecting salt works; Benjamin Hanks, Albany, N. Y. (Nov. 4), moulding and casting bells; Peter L. Lannay, Baltimore (Dec. 4), elastic water-proof leather; John Adamson, Boston (Dec. 13), floating dry docks. This patent was renewed by act of Congress, March 3, 1831; Jacob Perkins and Thomas Gilpin, Philadelphia (Dec. 18), water marks in paper, and Thomas Gilpin (Dec. 24), making paper. This patent was for the first cylinder machine made or operated in this country. The patentee, who, in addition to extensive paper manufactures, had, during the war, erected large cotton and woolen factories on the Brandywine, after the peace, resolved to suspend the cotton works and to increase his paper manufacture. By the aid of all published drawings and works on the subject, and much skill in drawing as well as mathematical, mechanical and other scientific knowledge, he constructed a machine differing somewhat from those in use in Europe, and in February of the ensuing year, Poulson's "Daily Advertiser," in Philadelphia, was printed on paper cut from a continuous sheet made on his machine. A new edition of Lavoisne's Historical and Genealogical Atlas, was about two years after put to press by M. Carey & Sons, on paper made on his machines; and samples (one of them writing paper of superior quality) taken from a sheet 1,000 feet long and twenty-seven inches wide, were deposited by the Messrs. Gilpins with the American Philosophical Society in Philadelphia. The machine did the work of ten paper vats.

The dangers which had for some time been seen by prudent men to overhang the business of the country from an inflated and depreciated paper currency and other monetary causes, but especially from
1817 the enormous importations of foreign manufactures, began already to weigh heavily upon the manufacturing and laboring classes. By a resolution of Congress, paper money was not receivable for government dues after 20th February of this year, on which day the New York branch of the United States Bank went into full operation. On the same day the other banks of New York, Philadelphia, Trenton, Baltimore, and Richmond recommenced paying specie, and were followed, on 20th March, by the Bank of Pittsburg and by other private banks in the Middle, Western, and Southern States. The amount of paper in circulation was little reduced, however, nor had the banking mania been abated. When it reached its height in the following spring, about two hundred local banks had been projected in different parts of the Union. The drain of specie, to pay the heavy balance against the country for imports, continued to embarrass trade and soon forced the banks to contract, and many of them to break, involving an immense depreciation of property and entailing bankruptcy upon many individuals and companies.

The distress of the manufacturers—many of whom, particularly the cotton manufacturers of Rhode Island and other parts of New England, had, during the last year, entirely suspended operations—was made known, during the second session of the fourteenth Congress, by upward of forty memorials from ten different states, presented to that body between the 16th December and the 28th February. Of these petitions, twenty-two were upon the subject of bar iron and iron manufactures, principally in New York, New Jersey, and Pennsylvania, with several from Connecticut, Boston, Kentucky, and Vermont.

The cotton and woolen manufacturers of Rhode Island and Connecticut, and the umbrella manufacturers of Massachusetts and New York, and the lead manufacturers of Illinois, each sent a memorial. Others were presented on the subject of manufactures generally, viz.: two from Berkshire, Mass., five from New York, two from Oneida county, and one each from New Jersey, Pittsburg, Baltimore, and Philadelphia.

These memorials, to which were attached names of the highest respectability, though forcible in argument and pathetic in their appeals, and in many instances supported by agents at Washington, were all referred, without reading, to the Committee on Commerce and Manufactures, and few of them were ever reported upon. The Pittsburg memorial placed the prostrate condition of manufactures, resulting from unlimited importations and the inadequacy of the tariff, in a strong light, and was printed for the use of members.

The Oneida (N. Y.) memorialists stated, that that county contained a greater number of cotton and woolen manufactories than any in the state, and that $600,000 was invested in them. In spite of the utmost efforts of their proprietors, more than three-fourths of them remained closed, some of their owners having been wholly ruined and others struggling under the greatest embarrassments. They could not believe that the Legislature of the Union "would remain an indifferent spectator of the wide-spread ruin of their fellow citizens, and look on and see a great branch of industry, of the utmost importance in every community, prostrated under circumstances fatal to all future attempts at revival, without a farther effort for relief."

The distress exhibited in these memorials was common to the manufacturing portions of the Union. The representations of the memorialists, numbering many thousands, met with little more attention from the Senate than the House. Permission was successively granted them, on motion of a member of the committee to whom they were referred, to "withdraw their papers." A bill for the relief of the iron masters was, however, reported in February, but was never called up for a third reading.

The farming, planting, and shipping interests were as yet exempt from these embarrassments, in consequence of the failure of two successive corn crops in Europe, and the increased demand for cotton upon the resumption of manufactures after the general peace. Cotton, which had been down to twelve cents a pound, sold, during the last and present years, for about twenty-seven cents a pound. Flour rose from $9.50 a barrel in 1814, to $12.50 in 1816, and to fourteen dollars in February of the present year, in Philadelphia, and was exported to the value of $17,750,000. The price of tobacco also increased from seventy-four dollars per hogshead in 1814 to $185 in 1816, and an exportation of 62,365 hogsheads during the present year averaged $148. The agriculturists, particularly of the South, were greatly enriched by their crops. Although they enjoyed, under the recent tariff, that ample protection which they were reluctant to grant the manufacturers, their own prosperity was not of long continuance, and they soon experienced the value of a home market for their produce.

The measures which principally affected the agricultural classes, were the exclusion of American flour from British ports after November of this year, and the increased importations into that country of raw cotton from India, under the stimulus of high prices, induced by the rapid increase of the manufacture, which impaired the profits of the American planter. The importation of India cotton into England, had increased from 8,535 bags in 1802 to 117,454 bags in this year, and reached 247,604 in the next. The imports of cotton from America in 1802, were 107,494 bags, and this year 198,917, and in the next year was 205,881. The cotton from Brazil had more than trebled in the same time, and in the next five years American Uplands declined in price to nine and ten pence a pound.

The importance of fostering domestic manufactures as a support to the agriculture of the country, and as a national object, was referred to in the first inaugural address of President Monroe, as well as on subsequent occasions during his administration. They required the "systematic and fostering care of the government," and we ought not to be dependent upon other countries for supplies or capital, having abundant raw materials that would be enhanced in value by creating a domestic market.

Following the example of his predecessor, the President wore on this occasion, a suit of American cloth from a Pawtucket manufactory. Four fifths of the Legislature of Connecticut, were also, at this time, clothed in domestic fabrics; and at the close of its session, that body, by resolution, recommended the use of American fabrics by the people of the state, and declared the extension of cotton and woolen establishments to be connected with the best interests of the state. A joint committee of the New York Legislature, reported that the manufacturing policy of Great Britain was exclusive and calculated to crush American manufactures, involving immense suffering to the poor. It was resolved to move Congress to grant support and protection, and all officials of the government were recommended to wear home manufactures.

Among the acts of the National Legislature at this session, was one approved March 1st, which was the first bearing properly the character of a Navigation act, limiting importations to the vessels of the country in which the goods were produced, restricting the bounty to fishing vessels to crews of the United States, and excluding all but American vessels from the coasting trade.

A discriminating tonnage duty, of two dollars per ton, was also laid on 3d March, and, as a countervailing measure, the importation of plaster of Paris from Nova Scotia, was prohibited.

Four townships, each six miles square (92,160 acres), of vacant public land in Alabama—now Green and Marengo counties—were granted to Charles Villar and his associates, to encourage the cultivation of the vine and olive by French emigrants, who, ten years later, had 271 acres under cultivation with vines, and about 388 olive trees. The experiment did not, however, succeed.

In aid of efforts made to sustain manufactures, the "Delaware Society for promoting American Manufactures," was established at Wilmington, February 15, and the "Pennsylvania Society for the Promotion of Public Economy," at Philadelphia, May 13. The Delaware Society soon after issued a circular, calling for such statistics and observations upon practical economy as, aided by the voice of the people, might influence Congress in favor of American industry.

About the same time, the Philadelphia Society for the Promotion of National Industry, composed of ten influential members, was formed in that city. Its object was to advocate the protection of national industry in general, but more particularly for manufactures perishing for want of protection. It exerted considerable influence upon the public mind during the next few years, chiefly through a series of published addresses, most of them from the pen of Matthew Carey, who, in this connection, first appeared as the ardent and uncompromising advocate of protection, and for several years labored in behalf of the manufacturer with a zeal and a disinterestedness seldom equalled. These societies, the "Metropolitan Society" of Washington, Georgetown, and Alexandria, and others with similar objects in Baltimore, Lancaster, Rome and other places in New York, Middletown, Hartford, Litchfield, and elsewhere in New England, New Jersey, and the Western States, were organized early in this year, mainly through the efforts of the American Society for the Encouragement of American Manufactures, in New York, of which D. D. Tomkins, Vice President of United States, was president. It had published and circulated five thousand copies of an address to the people, and sent delegates to Washington, who held meetings in different places to excite a general interest in the subject. On 11th July, the American Society held a meeting and elected President Monroe, and Messrs. Adams and Jefferson, members of the Society, and were honored with the attendance of the President, then returning from a tour to the East, who commended highly the objects of the Society.

In April, the General Manufacturing Law of the State of New York, was so amended, chiefly through the agency of Gideon Lee, as to enable the manufacturers of Morocco and other Leather to become incorporated under the act, with capitals not exceeding $60,000, to be located only in Greene and Delaware counties.

Under this law, the "New York Tannery" was organized in May, by an enterprising company, and under the superintendence of William Edwards and Son, a tannery calculated for five thousand hides—the first wholly under cover in the United States—was erected at Hunter, in Greene County, on the Schoharie kill, twenty miles west of the Hudson, and in the midst of the hemlock forests of the Catskill Mountains, having twelve hundred acres of land attached. The first leather was sent to market from this region in the autumn of the next year. In 1822, the Messrs. Edwards, aided by Jacob Lorillard, whose name is associated with those of Edwards, Lee and Pratt, as one of the founders of the leather trade in the United States, purchased the real estate of the Company, which had been unsuccessful, and greatly enlarged the business and added new improvements in machinery. Other large tanneries had been erected in the mean time, and thenceforward the Catskill region became the principal source of leather for the New York market, previously supplied with hemlock leather from Connecticut, Massachusetts, and Vermont, and with oak-tanned leather from the Middle States of the Union.

On the 15th April, the Legislature of New York passed an act of the highest importance, creating a fund for the construction of the Erie, Champlain and Hudson Canal, the commencement of its stupendous system of internal improvements. A report of the commissioners, under an act of the previous year, estimated the cost at $5,752,738, but the actual cost amounted to $8,401,394. The judicious system of finance embodied in the act, and in the main embraced in the celebrated memorial drawn up by De Witt Clinton, and presented with more than one hundred thousand signatures to the Legislature, in 1816, included a duty on goods sold at auction, and raised the duty on salt made in the state from three to twelve and a half cents a bushel, pledging the revenues from these sources for the payment of the canal debt, which was effected in about nineteen years. Ground was first broken for this great work, at Rome, on the 4th July, and it was completed on 26th October, 1825.

The United States Salines, twenty-six miles below the mouth of the Wabash, recently leased by government to Messrs. Wilkins & Morrison, of Lexington, yielded at this time, about three hundred thousand bushels annually, and supplied the settlements of Illinois and Indiana at from fifty to seventy-five cents a bushel. Some beds of rock salt had been lately discovered on a fork of the Canadian, one of the head waters of the Arkansas river, between the latter and the Red river. Postlethwaites, and some other salt works on the Sabine and Red rivers, furnished that part of the country with salt at one to two dollars a barrel, from salt springs. Considerable salt was made at various salines throughout the west, but those of Kentucky and upon the Conemaugh and Kenhawa were by far the most productive.

Eight steamboats were built, this year, on the western rivers. On the 2d August, the General Pike, Captain Jacob Reed, a low pressure boat, built at Louisville, arrived at St. Louis, being the first that ever ascended the Mississippi to that placce. The first steamboat or vessel of any kind ever built in Alabama, was this year constructed at St. Stephens, by Messrs. Brown & Bell, natives of Darien, Conn., who had learned the business in New York, to which city they returned, in 1819, to conductfor many years an extensive business, in the ship-yard of their former employers, at the foot of Stanton street.

A manufactory of steam and fire engines, mill machinery, brass and copper castings, etc., but chiefly of engines for steamboats, was established in Cincinnati. It employed two air and one cupola furnace, fifteen smith's forges, with the requisite machinery, one hundred men, and a capital of $80,000, and manufactured products to the market value of $130,000, but was compelled entirely to suspend operations during the pressure of 1820–21. Another machine factory, established the next year, suffered great depression from the same cause ; as did also manufacturers of brass-work, wooden clocks, glass, printing presses, etc., etc.

Within the last and present years, an unusual number of manufacturing establishments, in different parts of the country, were destroyed by fire. On the 9th of August, a storm of wind and rain, of uncommon violence, caused an immense destruction of mill-dams, mills, factories, forges, bridges, etc., upon the Atlantic seaboard, particularly in Philadelphia, Baltimore and their vicinities.

The Fly-frame was this year introduced into England, from the United States, and was afterward patented there by J. C. Dyer, an American.

Thomas Amies, of the Dove Paper Mills, Lower Merion, Montgomery county, Pa., eight miles from Philadelphia, produced a sample of paper, thirty-six by twenty-six inches, weighing one hundred and forty pounds, and valued at $125 per ream, believed to be superior to any ever made in the United States. It was made from the finest linen rags, and the moulds and felts were of the best kind.

The patents issued this year numbered one hundred and seventy-three, or seventy more than the average of the twenty-seven years since the organization of the office. The list included the following: Benjamin and John Tyler, Claremont, N. H. (Feb. 1), manufacturing scythes; Genet Troost, Philadelphia (March 3), alum from lignite; John L. Sullivan, Boston (March 24), propelling boats by the application of condensed air; Joseph Webb, New York (May 3), rotary dry dock;

Phineas Dow and Daniel Treadwell, Boston (Aug. 8), manufacturing screws. This was for a machine to be operated by steam, water, or horse power, which, from a coil of wire, cut, headed, grooved, polished, and finished wood screws, at the rate of ten in a minute, and requiring no manual power except to coil on a reel, and apply one end of the wire. Jean B. Aveilhe, New York (Aug. 28), a sugar mill; Samuel Rogers and Thomas Blanchard, Boston (Oct. 3), a brad and tack machine. This machine was invented by Blanchard in 1806, at the age of eighteen, and several times improved by him while acquiring the means to introduce it. The material was put into a tube or hopper, and was delivered in the form of tacks, with heads and points more perfect than could be made by hand, at the rate of five hundred in a minute. A half ounce weight would balance a thousand. He sold the patent, for $5,000, to a company, who went extensively into the manufacture. W. R. Eagleston, Balimore (Oct. 4), setting natural and artificial teeth; George F. Hagner, Philadelphia (Oct. 13), manufacturing verdigris, and another of same date, for making white lead; Francis Hall, Charlestown, Mass. (Nov. 28), a lint loom; Moses Hall, Charlestown, Mass. (Dec. 31), dyeing and polishing morocco.

The number and species of arms made and repaired at the national armories, and the expenditures upon the works, from their establishment
1818 to the end of the last year, were as follows, viz: Muskets made at Springfield Armory, from 1795 to 1817, 128,559; repaired, 45,800; carbines made, 1,202; total expenditure, $1,820,122. At Harper's Ferry Armory, from 1798 to 1817, muskets made, 82,727; repaired, 5,379; rifles made, 11,870; pistols made, 4,100; expenditures, $1,858,398. The average cost, including transportation, etc., of each musket at Springfield, was $13.56; at Harper's Ferry, $14.25.[1]

An act of Congress, concerning navigation, approved April 18th, closed the United States ports against British vessels, coming from or touching at British colonial ports, from which United States vessels were excluded. The owners, or consignees of British vessels, taking on board produce or manufactures of the United States, were to give bond in double the value of such merchandise, not to land it in British colonial ports, from which American vessels were excluded.

By an act of Parliament, and order in Council, of 8th and 27th May, the ports of Halifax, Nova Scotia, and St. John, New Brunswick, were, in consequence, opened to American vessels.

On the 20th April, Congress repealed the discriminating tonnage, and other duties, so far as related to the Netherlands, and on 24th July, the

(1) Seybert, 627.

President, by proclamation, extended the principle of equality of trade to the free Hanseatic city of Bremen, which had abolished its countervailing and discriminating duties.

By an act of the same date, the following increased duties were to be levied, after the 30th June, in lieu of the existing rates: On articles manufactured wholly or principally from copper, and on silver plated saddlery, coach and harness furniture, twenty-five per cent. ad valorem; on cut glass, thirty per cent.; on tacks, brads, and sprigs, not exceeding sixteen ounces to the thousand, five cents per thousand; other tacks, etc., the same as nails; on brown Russia sheetings, one dollar and sixty cents; white ditto, two dollars and fifty cents per piece.

At the solicitation of the iron masters of New Jersey and Pennsylvania, who, through Mr. William Milnor, represented the prostrate condition of their manufacture, Congress also enacted, April 20th, the following increased duties, in place of those previously levied on iron and its manufactures, and upon alum. On pig iron, fifty cents, on iron castings, seventy-five cents per cwt.; on nails, four cents, spikes, three cents, and anchors, three cents a pound; on alum, two dollars per cwt.; on iron in bars and bolts, not manufactured by rolling, seventy-five cents per cwt., leaving it still charged with only one half the duty payable on rolled (English) iron. The collection laws were also amended to prevent numerous frauds.

Hammered bar iron, which, in 1814, was $125 to $145 a ton in the seaports of the United States, was at this time sold for $90 to $100, but in Pittsburg, was worth $190 to $200, and in Cincinnati, $200 to $220. Castings and hollow-ware in the latter place, were worth $120 to $130.[1] The duty was raised, by the above act, from nine to fifteen dollars per ton, and enabled many of the iron works which had been nearly ruined by the large importations the last two or three years, to resume the manufacture. In about twelve years the price of bar iron in the

(1) At Zanesville, Ohio, where Mr. Dillon had a large iron forge, foundry, and saw and flour mills, ordinary castings were made for $120 per ton, and for machinery eight cents a pound. The best Swedish bar iron (hammered) sold for $11.50, Juniata bars at $14, and Dillon's at $12.50 per cwt. The cost of transportation from Baltimore to Zanesville, was $10 per cwt., and from New Orleans to Shippingsport by steamboat, and thence by boats to Zanesville, $6.50 per cwt. The wages of laborers was $100 to $120 per annum and found. Coals delivered, eight cents per bushel.—*Cobbett's Year's Residence in the United States.* There were other furnaces and forges in Licking and Adams counties, and other parts of Ohio, Western Virginia, and Kentucky, and air-foundries at Steubenville and other places. On King's creek, eight miles from the latter, in Brooke county, Va., a forge and furnace were in operation in 1799. But bar and pig iron were still imported from the Juniata and Laurel Hill regions, in Pennsylvania, which had extensive iron works in the vicinities of Bedford, and Connelsville. A steel manufactory had been in successful operation at Brownsville, for several years.

Atlantic cities, fell to seventy-five or eighty-five dollars, and in the western cities above named, to about fifty dollars below the price at this time, or to $100 and $110.

The quantity of bar and bolt iron imported for the year ending 30th June, was, of rolled iron, 42,312 cwt., and of hammered, 462,193 cwt.; and the exports in the year ending September 30th, were, of cut and rolled 24,430 cwt., hammered 9,902 cwt.

An iron foundry at Cincinnati employed, at this time, eighty hands, and was engaged in making engines and iron works for seven steamboats.

The whole number of steamboats constructed this year on the western waters, principally on the Ohio, was about thirty, and their success having been fully established, the business thenceforward rapidly increased; Cincinnati and Pittsburg taking a lead in it. About twenty-seven steamboats, with an aggregate tonnage of near four thousand tons, traded with New Orleans from the upper and adjacent country. The Post-office Department was about to employ steamboats to carry the mails on the Ohio and Mississippi. John Allen, Esq., of Philadelphia, was granted, by the Emperor of Austria, the exclusive privilege for fifteen years, of carrying passengers and merchandise from Trieste to Venice by steam. In the harbor of New York, steamboats were successfully employed in towing large and heavily laden ships into port, at the rate of four miles an hour, against wind and tide. On the 28th May, the first Lake Erie steamboat, called after an Indian chief "Walk in the Water," was launched at Black Rock, on the Niagara river, near Buffalo, and on 23d August sailed, under Captain Fish, for Detroit. In the next two years she made three trips to Mackinaw with troops and stores, and in July following, with two hundred passengers and a large cargo went to Mackinaw and Green Bay, in Wisconsin, being the first steamer that floated on Lake Michigan. She was wrecked near Buffalo, in Nov. 1822.

The number of Manufacturing Companies established in the State of New York, up to June of this year, under the general act of that state, was one hundred and twenty-nine, with a capital of $7,742,500, in addition to many large individual establishments.

In July of this year the "American Journal of Science and Arts" was established, to be issued in four quarterly numbers, of not less than two hundred pages each with illustrations. It was the first journal in the United States which embraced in its plan the entire circle of the Physical Sciences and their applications to the arts. Under the editorship of Professors B. Silliman, B. Silliman, Jr., Dana, and other able collators, it has continued to the present time, a valuable vehicle of sound knowledge on these subjects.

On the 4th July, the "Association of Mechanics of the Commonwealth of Massachusetts," held their first public exhibition of premium articles. In making the awards, preference was given—other things being equal—first to apprentices and next to journeymen before master mechanics. The Society had existed twenty-three years, and been incorporated twelve years. Two years after, the Apprentices' Library, in Boston, was established under its supervision.

The imports, this year, were still very heavy, amounting to $121,750,000, of which over $102,250,000 in value was retained for consumption. The value of domestic exports, though greater than in any other year previous to 1833, only discharged $73,854,437 of the indebtedness. The drain of specie was therefore very great, and the ports of Boston and Salem are said to have exported five millions of specie within twelve months. The increase in the value of the exports, consisted largely of cotton, of which a greater quantity and value was exported than in any previous year, amounting to nearly 192,500,000 lbs., worth, as cotton then sold, $31,334,258, or more than forty-two per cent. of the whole domestic exports. The average price of all kinds of cotton at the place of shipment, was thirty-four cents, and in Liverpool, about twenty pence sterling, from which it soon after declined, notwithstanding the rapid increase of the manufacture in Europe and America.[1]

The returns of exports for the year, included the first from Alabama, to the value of $95,857; and those of South Carolina, Georgia and Louisiana, were largely increased, being in the last two greatly in excess of any previous year, and probably due, in a great measure, to the increased production of cotton and sugar. The States of Mississippi and Louisiana sold cotton to the value of two millions of dollars in New Orleans, which this year increased its trade more than one-fifth. The parish of Rapides alone produced crops which, at the current price of cotton, sold for $400,000. The price of lands and the incomes of planters were in consequence greatly augmented, many of the latter realizing $30,000, and in some instances $80,000, and even $120,000 per annum from the produce of their estates. Even laborers had been known, during the last winter, to make each $100 per diem with eight

(1) The quantity of cotton manufactured in England this year, was about 172,000,000 pounds, an increase of forty-seven per cent. in one year, and of nearly a hundred per cent. in two years. The city of Glasgow manufactured 105,000,000 yards of cotton cloth, valued at five million pounds sterling. The declared value of cotton manufactures exported from England, was $89,500,000.—*U. S. Treasury Report* 1835–36.

or ten mules, in dragging cotton a few hundred yards from the river to the warehouses, at the rate of one dollar per bale.

Many cotton mills, in Great Britain, were at this time adapted or built expressly to consume the cheaper cotton of Bengal and Surat, which consequently interfered greatly with the inferior qualities of Upland, from the United States. The exportation of cotton from India during the first six months of this year, was one hundred thousand bales in excess of the whole amount exported in the previous twelve months, and its consumption in England was increased twenty-six thousand bales, while that of American cotton was decreased twelve thousand bales. The price of cotton began therefore to decline rapidly toward the end of the year, and many shippers during the next ten or twelve months sustained heavy losses, computed in the aggregate at four millions of dollars to the mercantile classes, and at six millions in the incomes of the planters, a necessary consequence of the heavy importations of cotton from all parts of the world.

The first Cotton Factory in North Carolina, was established this year, at the Falls of Tar, or Pamlico river, in Edgecombe county, which was followed in 1822, by another near Lincolnton, on the Catawba. The former employed, in 1820, about twenty hands, and two hundred and eighty-eight spindles, and consumed eighteen thousand pounds of cotton.

The first annual message of President Monroe, in December of last year, spoke of the preservation of manufactures—which depended on due encouragement—as connected with the high interests of the nation. His second message, on 17th November of this year, referred to the provisions of the act of 20th April, amending the collection laws, as having secured to them all the relief to be derived from the protecting duties laid on imports, under which several branches had assumed greater activity, and others would probably revive and ultimately triumph over all obstacles. It suggested, however, the expediency of granting further protection.

The first Merino Sheep in Illinois—which was this year admitted as a state—were introduced into Edwards county, by Mr. George Flowers, an English gentleman, who, with Mr. Morris Birkbeck and a large number of their countrymen, formed a settlement at Albion. Mr. Flowers for many years bred improved stocks of sheep with much success, from twelve of the finest wooled merinos, selected by himself, from the royal flocks of Spain, and from those belonging to the monks of Paula and other Spanish convents.[1] Several hundred merinos were

(1) Hall's Notes on the Western States.

taken, during the last year, to Meadville, Pennsylvania, by Judge Griffith, of New Jersey, and H. J. Huidekoper, agent of the Holland Land Company, and became the source of many fine flocks in Crawford county.

Flannels were at this time made at Chelmsford (Lowell), Mass., by Winthrop Howe, and satinets by Thomas Hurd. Gunpowder was also made there by Moses Hale. Four years later, the gunpowder mills of Tileston, Whipple, and Hale, were on a large scale with a stamping mill of forty pestles, capable of making from three to four thousand casks, of twenty-five pounds each, per annum. The proprietors had nearly completed a much larger factory near the former, on the Concord river. Their manufacture was known as "Boston Gunpowder."

A Springfield, Mass., paper advertised for sale, one thousand yards of "Straw Carpeting," from four to six quarters wide, and at twenty-eight, thirty-seven, and forty-two cents a yard.

The manufacture of Jewelry in Providence, R. I., which had been nearly abandoned in the last two years, was revived this year, and in two more years reached double its former product, or $600,000 per annum.

Dr. Dyer, of Providence, planted about forty acres of land, near the city, with currant bushes, for the manufacture of currant Wine. It became profitable, and in a few years was expected to yield two hundred pipes of wholesome and pleasant wine.

At Vevay, Indiana, nearly five thousand gallons of wine, which sold at one dollar a gallon, was made this year. Each family had a small vineyard attached to its farm.[1]

The New England Glass Company, was incorporated and established at East Cambridge (Lechmere's Point), one of the most extensive Flint Glass manufactories in the country. Two flint furnaces and twenty-four glass-cutting mills, operated by steam, and a red-lead furnace, capable of making two tons of red lead per week, enabled them to produce every variety of fine, plain, mould, and the richest cut glass, as Grecian lamps, chandeliers for churches, vases, antique and transparent lamps, etc., for domestic supply, and exportation to the West Indies and South America. Virginia coal, New Orleans lead, Delaware sand, and other native materials, were used. The capital was about $80,000, and the annual product $65,000.

Salt works on a large scale, were erected at Lewistown, Delaware, to manufacture salt by solar evaporation.

The manufacture of copperas, alum, oil of vitriol, aquafortis, salts, soap, etc., was carried on at Steubenville, Ohio, by a Mr. Gibbs, from Scotland.

(1) Cobbett's Year's Residence, etc.

A large Sugar Refinery was put in operation in May, at Louisville, Ky., by Maltz & Jacobson, which made about three hundred loaves of five pounds each, or fifteen hundred pounds of refined sugar every twenty-four hours. The largest Soap and Candle factory in the western country, was at Louisville. It was owned by Peterson & Co., and produced twelve thousand pounds of soap per week, and one thousand pounds of candles daily, and had a capital of $20,000. Chewing tobacco, snuff, and segars, were made to the value of $8,000 per annum.[1]

A manufactory of Cloths, superfine and coarse Flannels, Blankets and Paper, at Lexington, Ky., said to be the largest and best supplied with machinery of any in the United States, was this year compelled to suspend operations on account of foreign importations. Its capital was $150,000, and it employed two hundred men, consuming one hundred thousand pounds of wool and one hundred tons of rags, the yearly product of which was $400,000. Of eight manufactories of cotton bagging, at the same place, only one was in operation in 1820, in which year there were in the county, five manufactories of cotton yarn, two of cassimeres, cassinets, cloths, etc., twelve of cordage, twine, and bagging, and one of cordage and sail duck; nearly all of which had either ceased operations or greatly reduced their business. There were other manufactories of cotton and wool, paper, gunpowder, soap and candles, red and white lead, etc.; bells and other brass and iron castings; beer, etc., in Lexington and vicinity.

The value of the rags collected in the United States for the use of paper makers, was estimated at $900,000 per annum.

PATENTS.—To Jeremiah Black, Northumberland, Pa. (Jan. 17), an Archimedean screw; Eb. Jenks, Colebrook, Conn. (Jan. 28), converting iron partially into steel; Cyrus Jackson, Otsego, N. Y. (Feb. 11), auger for boring square holes; W. S. Langworthy, Ballston, N. Y. (Feb. 28), and Lynus North, Otsego, N. Y. (May 28), metallic combs;[2] D. Pettibone, Philadelphia (April 10), machine for cutting combs; another to same (Aug. 11), for manufacturing combs; Sylvester Nash, Harper's Ferry, Va. (April 11), Seth Youngs, Hartford, Conn., (May 1), and Asa Waters, Middleburg, Mass. (Dec .19), each for turning gun barrels; also to D. Dana and A. Holmead, Canton, Mass. (Aug. 24), for lathes for turning gun barrels; Cyrus Eastman, Hillsborough, N. H. (April 16), rolling metallic tubes; Adam Ramage, Philadelphia (May 23), printing presses;[3] A. Wheeler, Concord, Mass. (June 10), dis-

(1) McMurtrie's Sketches of Louisville.

(2) A manufactory of brass combs made from brass wire was in operation in Saratoga county two years later, and the article was in much demand.

(3) A patent hand press, called the Co-

charging a gun seven or more times; John B. Breithler, New Orleans, La. (June 13), machine for grinding sugar cane; Samuel Rogers, Bridgewater, Mass. (June 24), rolling mill for sheet iron; Abraham L. Pennock and J. Sellers, Philadelphia (July 6), two patents, one for hose or leather tubes and one for mail bags. The first of these patents was an important improvement in fire apparatus, which had been eight or ten years in use, and consisted in making the hose of sole-leather by overlapping and riveting with copper or iron rivets, instead of sewing, and since exclusively practiced. Riveted hose was first introduced by the Philadelphia Hose Company, for whom it was executed by Messrs. Sellers, Pennock & Morris, No. 231 Market street, whose successors still carry on the business. The male and female connecting screw and swivel joint for connecting different sections of hose, was the invention of Jacob Perkins, who introduced it with the rivetted hose into England in 1819. George F. Valentine, Albany, N. Y. (Aug. 26), crystallizing tin; Edmund Warren, New York (Aug. 27), a loom. This improved loom, which was quite simple in construction, and cost only ten dollars, wound the cloth on the beam as it was woven, and the yarn was taken by the same process. It could be extended to weave any breadth, and a person accustomed to it could weave sixty yards a day. The patentee subsequently took out seven patents for threshing machines. Lewis Viales, New Orleans, La. (Oct. 29), a cotton inspecting machine; Aaron M. Peaseley, Boston, Mass. (Nov. 11), organs; David Mellville, Newport, R. I. (Nov. 13), argand lamps.

1819

The embarrassments which had been pressing heavily upon the manufacturing classes since the peace—chiefly in consequence of the unchecked importation of foreign goods, and the vitiated state of the national currency—culminated this year in the severest sufferings of a large portion of the community, which became involved in financial distress. Importations having been for several years, and still continuing greatly in excess of the exportations, according to the immutable laws of trade, the balance had to be paid principally in solid money, of which,

lumbian Press, was this year introduced in England in an improved form, by Mr. George Clymer of Pennsylvania, the inventor. In the style of finish and embellishment, with various devices emblematic of the art, it exceeded any thing known to the trade there, and the printed certificates and testimonials of masters and workmen, were much in its favor. The press of Mr. Ramage was probably an improvement upon the Scotchpress, invented by his countryman, Mr. Ruthven of Edinburgh, and introduced here about this time by the patentee. It was much esteemed for fine work, but was soon after superseded by the introduction of rollers for which it was not adapted.

the augmented trade with India and China,[1] had absorbed a large proportion. The Bank of the United States had been compelled to import specie, in the first sixteen months of its operations, to the amount of over seven and a quarter millions, at a cost of more than a half a million of dollars. The exportation of specie during the same period, was supposed to have exceeded the importation by the banks and individuals. The metallic currency remaining in the country, instead of entering into circulation, had, since the resumption of specie payments in 1817, remained in the vaults of the banks until drawn out at a premium for exportation. The paper currency had, at the same time, been violently contracted from an aggregate, in 1815 and 1816, of one hundred and ten millions to about forty-five millions at this time,—a reduction of fifty-nine per cent.,—thereby reducing prices, and checking enterprises created by its previous undue expansion. While the banks were thus contracting their discounts, the principal American staples began, toward the close of the last year, to decline rapidly from the high price they had commanded for a number of years in foreign markets. The reduction in the price of cotton and breadstuffs soon reached fifty per cent., and the losses thereby sustained, rendered additional loans necessary to the merchant at a time when it was most difficult to obtain them. The result was most disastrous both to the merchant and the agriculturist. But upon the manufacturer—overborne by unequal competition with his foreign rival, and suffering equally with the merchant and farmer, from the inability of all classes to purchase—the change fell with crushing weight. The price of raw cotton continued to decline with considerable uniformity, from this time forward, for at least a quarter of a century.

Flour had also gradually fallen off from its high price of ten to fifteen dollars a barrel in 1817, to five or six in the present year, in domestic ports; and tobacco, from $148 in 1817, to $110 in this year, and $75 in 1822. A like depreciation in other crops, greatly diminished the power of a large portion of the population to purchase manufactures, or even to discharge obligations already contracted in anticipation of their revenues. A general paralysis now fell upon all branches of industry. The distress became more general and severe than had ever been known, and but little alleviation was experienced for several years to come. The banks suffered from lack of specie. Bankruptcies over-

(1) The importation of specie into the single port of Canton alone, in one year, embracing portions of this and the preceding year, was $7,414,000, which was probably not more than one-half the total exports of solid currency to Europe and Asia.

took the mercantile and shipping interests, whose merchandise lay on their hands, and whose ships could neither be employed nor sold, save at ruinous losses. Rents and the value of all real estate were enormously depreciated. Farms were mortgaged or sold at one half and one third their value. Factories and workshops were everywhere closed. Manufacturers were forced to abandon extensive and flourishing establishments, reared as if by magic in the last few years, and with their operatives and multitudes of handicraft workmen entered into competition with the cultivators of the soil, and swelled the products of agricultural labor, for which there was no longer a market.

The suffering among manufacturers was more severe in Rhode Island, New York, and Pennsylvania, than elsewhere. The number of persons thrown out of employment since the peace was variously estimated at from forty to sixty thousand, and with their families, the number deprived of support was computed at one hundred and sixty to two hundred and forty thousand. The cities of Philadelphia and Pittsburg suffered extremely, and the Western country generally, participated in the common distress.[1] The extent of the suffering throughout Pennsylvania was forcibly portrayed in the report of a committee of the Legislature appointed to investigate its causes, and to prepare remedies.[2] A memorial was also presented to Congress from the western part

(1) A committee of the citizens of Philadelphia, appointed in August, reported in October, that in thirty out of sixty branches of manufacture there had been a reduction from the average of 1814 and 1816, in the number of persons employed, from 9,425 to 2,137; in their weekly wages, from $58,340 to $12,822; and in their annual earnings from $3,033,799 to $666,744. The actual loss of wages was therefore $2,366,935 per annum; and supposing the materials equal to their wages, the loss of productive industry in a single district, not forty miles in diameter, was $7,333,870. In the cotton manufacture the hands were reduced from 2,325, in 1816, to 149; in book printing, from 241 to 170; in the potteries, from 132 to 27; in the woolen branch, from 1226 to 260; in iron castings, from 1152 to 52; in paper hanging and cards, from 189 to 82. In the paper manufacture in their vicinity the hands were reduced from 950, in 1816, to 175, and their annual wages from $247,000 to $45,900; the annual production from $760,000 to $136,000. A committee of citizens of Pittsburg, in December, reported the whole number of hands employed in that town and vicinity, in 1815, to have been 1,960, and the value of their manufactures $2,617,833. In 1819 the hands numbered only 672, and the value of their manufactures was $832,000. In the steam engine factories the workmen were reduced from 290 to 24, and the value of their work from $300,000 to $40,000. In glass works and glass cutting the hands were reduced from 169 to 40, and the product from $235,000 to $35,000; the reduction in flint glass alone having been $75,000. In the manufacture of cotton, wire, umbrellas, yellow queensware, pipes, and linen, there was no longer a single hand employed.

(2) The actions for debt in the Pennsylvania courts this year were 14,537, and the number of judgments confessed was 10,326, exclusive of half as many more before justices. The imprisonments for debt in the city and county of Philadelphia were 1,808.

of the state, complaining that manufactures were in the last struggles of dissolution, estates were sacrificed, families ruined, agriculture was declining, internal trade was extinguished, capital was dormant, and thousands were idle.

"The wants and calamities of the people demanded an interposition radical in its character, and vigorous in the means of its accomplishment. Every man sees and feels that the excessive use of foreign goods has brought our country to the verge of destruction, and that nothing short of permanent and ample patronage to our own manufactures can afford any relief. The fallacy of buying at the cheapest market no longer stands in our way, nor will Congress be again alarmed with the danger of imposing regulations upon trade."

In Rhode Island, New York, and other manufacturing districts, similar reductions of labor, and sacrifices of mills and property for a fraction of their original cost, were quite common, many establishments being entirely broken up.

The question of protection to the manufacturing interests began once more to be agitated as indispensable, and numerous appeals were made from various quarters to Congress for its interposition. Many able advocates appeared in behalf of legislative measures, considered of vital importance to a class threatened with total ruin, and among the most able was Matthew Carey, of Philadelphia.

The duties on imports were already as high as Congress deemed it prudent to go. But the Secretary of the Treasury, on 8th February, in conformity with a resolution of the House of 20th April last, reported on the propriety of laying specific duties upon articles then charged ad valorem, and proposed a schedule of such articles, with specific rates attached, greatly higher than the existing ad valorem duties.

Acts were passed on 3d March, altering the duties on certain wines and the bounties to fishing vessels; also for the more effectual suppression of the slave trade and of piracy.

In consequence of a resolution of inquiry of December last, it was announced to the Senate by the Committee on Military Affairs, that by a regulation of the proper department, preference was now given to domestic manufactures in clothing the army, when they were to be had on reasonable terms, rendering a law on the subject unnecessary.

About the 24th May, the steamship Savannah, of 380 tons, the first that ever crossed the Atlantic, left Savannah, Georgia, for Liverpool, where she arrived on 20th June. Having consumed all her coal in ten or twelve days, the remainder of the voyage was made under canvas. She was built by Croker & Fickett, Corlears Hook, N. Y., and commanded by Captain Moses Rogers, who had been in command of Fulton's boat, the "Clermont," and of the Phœnix, on the Delaware. She proceeded to St. Petersburg, taking in Lord Lyndock at Stockholm, who presented the captain a silver teakettle, with an inscription expressive of his pioneer character, and in October returned to Savannah in twenty-two days under sail. She subsequently ran as a sailing packet between New York and Savannah, until lost in 1822.

On the 19th May, the steamboat Independence, Captain Nelson, built at Pittsburg in the last year, arrived at Franklin (Boonslick), on the Missouri, in seven sailing days from St. Louis, with flour, sugar, whisky, iron castings, etc., having been the first to stem the current of that river. Thirty-four steamers were built on the western rivers during the year, one of which, the Western Engineer, built near Pittsburg, under the direction of Major Long of the United States Topographical Engineers, for the expedition to the Rocky Mountains, was the first that ever reached Council Bluffs, 650 miles above St. Louis.

The Analectic Magazine for July (vol. 24, p. 67), contained the first published specimen of American lithographic printing, an art of recent introduction from Germany into England, where two silver medals were this year awarded by the Society of Arts for specimens on German and English stone. The design and execution of the print, from the drawing to the impression, were the work of Mr. B. Otis of Philadelphia, at the suggestion of Dr. Samuel Brown of Alabama and Judge Cooper. It was executed upon a stone from Munich—the birthplace of the art—presented to the American Philosophical Society by Mr. Thomas Dobson. Mr. Otis had also executed specimens of lithography, upon lithographic stone procured by Doctors Brown and Cooper, and Mr. Clifford, through Dr. Blight, from a limestone quarry, near Dicks river, Ky. Specimens of white lithographic stone were about this time deposited in the Troy Lyceum by Isaac McConike, Esq., who found it alternating with compact limestone in Indiana.[1] The lithographic art was introduced, in an improved form, in New York, in 1822, by Barnett & Doolittle, who had received regular instruction in Paris.[2]

A Society for the Encouragement of American Manufactures and Domestic Economy, established conformably to a resolution of the citizens of Baltimore in February, was incorporated during the year as the Maryland Economical Association.

The Society of Tammany, or Columbian Order, in New York, of which Clarkson Crolius was grand sachem, appointed a committee on the subject of National Economy and Domestic Manufactures, and to report an address to all members of the order throughout the Union. This

(1) Eaton's Geology of Northern States, 2d ed., pp. 232, 238–9.

(2) Silliman's Journal, ch. 4, p. 170.

was adopted on 4th October, and circulated through the public prints, explaining the causes and suggesting remedies for the national calamities. Resolutions were passed pledging the members to practice frugality, and to discontinue the importation and use, in their families, of every article of foreign manufacture which could be reasonably substituted by American manufactures, and recommending the same course to all their friends.

The universal interest awakened on the subject by these and similar organizations throughout the country, and the numerous memorials in preparation, asking of the Legislature an amendment of the tariff, induced the sixteenth Congress, on the 8th December, immediately after assembling, for the first time, to institute a standing Committee of Manufactures, to take charge of the accumulated business of what had now become one of the cardinal interests of the nation.

Messrs. Miller and Hutchins, of Providence, proposed to publish a periodical devoted to Domestic Manufactures, to be called The Manufacturers' Journal.

The price of Domestic Cottons, of the kind first made at Waltham, Mass., was at this time twenty-one cents a yard, or nine cents below the price in 1816. The Waltham Company, on account of its large capital and machinery, was enabled to withstand the financial pressure which carried away many of the cotton and woolen manufactures of New England, and was supposed to be unfavorable to an increase of duties. Several of its proprietors, in the midst of general depression, were looking for a suitable locality for a more extended business, which was soon after found in the water power of Lowell.

The first mill on the canal in the manufacturing borough of Manayunk, now in the city of Philadelphia, was built this year, by Capt. John Towers, and commenced running on 10th November. The first manufacturing in the place, was done by Isaac Baird. The first mill, since known as the "Yellow Mill," was afterward owned by a Mr. Rising, and still later by Mr. Joseph Ripka, to whose enterprise the growth of the place is principally due.[1] The second factory was erected by Charles V. Hagner, and the third by Mark Richards.

(1) Mr. Ripka, a native of Austrian Silesia, was, in 1814, the proprietor of a small cotton and silk factory at Lyons, and was at this time running a few hand-looms in Kensington, in the manufacture of cottonades. The superior quality and style of his goods made them popular, and soon after, in order to meet the increasing demand, he removed to larger premises on Poplar street, when the manufacture of his "Rouen Cassimeres," an article of pantaloon stuffs, was greatly extended, though he was still confined to hand-loom weaving. Having opened a warehouse in Front street, the profits of his manufacture enabled him, soon after, to fit up power looms on the Pennypack, near Holmesburg, and in 1828, he built his first mill at Manayunk, which then contained ten factories of

The Legislature of New York appropriated $20,000 for the promotion of Agriculture and Family Domestic Manufactures, to be equally divided among the County Agricultural Societies, and expended in two years. It also enacted a general law for the incorporation of Agricultural Societies, for which a new one was substituted in 1841. Similar appropriations to the above were made by the New Hampshire Assembly, in 1818.

The manufacture of Porcelain, of fine quality, from domestic materials, was commenced in New York, by Dr. H. Mead.

General Cass, accompanied by Mr. H. R. Schoolcraft, visited, this year, the copper mines of the Ontonagon and the southern shore of Lake Superior west to the Mississippi, including the Lead region of Missouri. Mr. Schoolcraft found forty-five lead mines at work in Missouri, thirty-nine of which were in Washington county. They were estimated to produce three million pounds of lead, and to employ eleven hundred hands. Mine à Burton and Potosi Diggings together, produced, between 1798 and 1816, 9,630,000 lbs. or half a million annually. The marshals, in 1820, reported four stone furnaces in Crawford county, Michigan, with a capital of $4,600, making bar lead at $4.50 per cwt., which found ready sales at south.

On the 10th November, Mr. Constant A. Andrews, of Pennsylvania, in connection with Messrs. Owens and Dixon, put in operation a saw mill, "not much inferior to any in the United States," upon Black river, a branch of the Mississippi, between Prairie du Chien and Lake Pekin, and about thirty miles east of the lake. It was probably the first in Wisconsin, and was erected by consent of the Sioux Indians, but was soon after burned, it is supposed, by the Winnebagoes.

Jacob Perkins, late of Philadelphia, took out a patent in England (Oct. 11), for "Machinery applicable to Engraving; transferring engraved or other work from the surface of one piece of metal to that of another;" (transferring difficult engravings for the production of bank notes.)[1]

Among the United States patents granted this year were the following: To James Barron, U. S. N., Norfolk, Va. (Jan. 12), for corks for

different kinds. employing six hundred and thirty-six hands. During the next fifteen or twenty years, he became the proprietor of five factories at Manayunk beside tenements, one in Northern Liberties, one at Chandlersville, Delaware, and of a large factory and print works on the Pennypack, employing, together, twelve hundred hands, and giving support to probably three thousand persons. The value of his manufactures exceeded one million dollars annually, and included Canton Flannel, which was extensively made and improved by him on its first introduction. His agencies extended to all the principal cities.

(1) Newton's London Journal, vol. 1, p. 159.

bottles; to the same (Feb. 20), for an air pump for extracting foul air from ships. For a cut and description of this ship ventilator of Commodore Barron, to whom both the above patents were renewed by special acts of Congress in 1833, and also for a plan, submitted by him to the Secretary of the Navy, for constructing vessels so as to prevent decay, see Portfolio for November, 1826. He took out seven or eight different patents, including one for constructing ships. To Samuel Morey, Oxford, N. H. (Jan. 19), for shooting with steam; John L. Wells, Hartford (Feb. 8), a printing press. This was the first in which long levers were introduced *end-wise* with success. Burgis Allison and William Elliott, Washington, D. C. (Feb. 20), printing by means of rollers; Silas Mason, Norfolk, Mass. (Feb. 20), manufacturing hats. This was for a carding machine, which produced the hat in its conical form at one operation. Francis Guy, Baltimore, Md. (Feb. 23), paper carpet; William Sheldon, Springfield, Mass. (Feb. 26), tanning with bark of chestnut trees, and John Lansing, Jr., Albany, N. Y. (April 30), tanning in hemlock; William Garret, New Lisbon, N. Y. (Feb. 27), manufacturing emory; A. W. Foster and J. Hugus, Greensburg and Hempford, Pa. (April 26), converting rectilinear into rotary motion; Robert Graves, Boston, Mass. (April 10), for cordage. This patent cordage, for which two other patents were granted in the following years, was extensively manufactured in Boston by Winslow, Lewis & Co., who used Graves's machinery, worked by horses, and in 1821, employed one hundred men and boys, and sold 746 tons of patent cordage, for $180,000. James Wiseheart, Wayne county, Ind. (May 25), making sugar from wheat, rye, &c.; William K. Clarkson, Jr., New York (June 26), velocipedes; Richard Bury, Albany, N. Y. (Aug. 21), glass strings for pianofortes; Daniel Pettibone, Boston, Mass. (Aug. 21), welding cast steel to iron; Jethro Wood, Poplar Ridge, N. Y. (Sept. 1), a plough. This was for the cast iron plough, which was the foundation of many subsequent improvements, and the patent was renewed by act of Congress, in 1834. Thomas Blanchard, Middlebury, Mass. (Sept. 6), turning gun stocks; Daniel Gillett, Springfield, Mass. (Sept. 15), preparing cotton seed for food; Cyrus Hawes, Bennington, Vt. (Dec. 15), carpenters' squares;[1] B. Croasdale, Byberry, Pa. (Dec. 21), machine for making brushes of broom corn; also, to Shadrach H. Weed, Poughkeepsie, N. Y. (Feb. 3), for broom making.

(1) The first manufacture of carpenters' steel squares, in the United States, was commenced at North Bennington during the ensuing year, and in 1842 two establishments in the village made from twelve to fifteen thousand annually, having nearly superseded the foreign article.—*Thompson's Gaz. of Vt.*

CHAPTER IV.

ANNALS OF MANUFACTURES.

1820—1830.

Evidence of the general and increasing embarrassments of every branch of industry continued to press itself upon the attention of the National
1820 and State Legislatures. Immediately upon the assembling of the sixteenth Congress, at its first session in December, memorials and petitions began to pour in from various bodies of manufacturers and others in different sections of the country, ascribing the pecuniary distress of the times to the immoderate use of foreign commodities, and complaining of the inadequacy of the general Tariff and existing revenue laws to afford suitable protection to the native industry against the combined efforts of cheap production, fraudulent invoices, protracted credits and unlimited sales at auction, whereby the country had been deluged with foreign merchandise, to the ruin alike of the farmer, the importer, and the manufacturer.

A Convention of the Friends of National Industry, composed of delegates from nine states, viz.: Massachusetts, Rhode Island, Connecticut, New York, New Jersey, Pennsylvania, Delaware, Maryland, and Ohio, who assembled in New York on the 27th August of the last year, to take into consideration the prostrate condition of manufactures, and to petition Congress—presented a memorial on the 20th December, in which the following measures were recommended as likely to remove the existing embarrassments of the country, and to restore life and vigor to the almost expiring manufactures. These were—to abolish credits on impost duties—to impose a restrictive duty on sales at auction, and to alter and increase the duties on imported goods.

The practice allowed by law of giving one to two years' credits on imposts upon East India and China goods, and the perversion of the system of auction sales from its original intention, it was conceived, exerted a most injurious effect upon the fair American trader, upon the manufacturer and the community in general, by encouraging speculation, and flooding the markets with cheap but worthless fabrics of silk, woolen, cotton, and other materials, manufactured in the East Indies and in Europe expressly for such sales, and which, by their high finish, concealed their flimsy texture until they reached the consumer.

It appeared, from the returns of the auctioneers themselves, that the sales of foreign goods at auction, in the city of New York alone, amounted, in the year 1818, to fourteen millions of dollars, and the quantity annually sold in the same way in the United States could not, it was believed, be less than thirty millions in value, a large part of which was on foreign account. Increased duties were asked for upon a number of leading articles, and the great disparity between the American and British tariffs upon several important articles of manufacture was shown, the United States ranging from seven and a half to thirty, and the British from forty-one and a half to seven hundred and fifty-five per cent. ad valorem. A memorial to the same effect, from the American Society of the city of New York, for the encouragement of domestic manufactures, presented April 24, prayed that the importation of cotton goods be restricted by law, to such only as were wholly manufactured from cotton grown in the United States. Memorials were also sent in from the manufacturers of paper, books, leather, etc., and from the inhabitants of different states and cities, urging suitable protection to manufactures, a change from ad valorem to specific duties, and other modifications of the revenue laws. Opposition to any proposed change was made by the agricultural and mercantile interests in various places, among which the Agricultural Society of Fredericksburg, Va., and the United Agricultural Societies of Prince George, Sussex, Surry, Petersburg, Brunswick, Dinwiddie, and Isle of Wight, in the same state, whose secretary was Mr. Edward Ruffin, were the first to denounce, in memorials presented on the 3d and 17th January, any increase of duties as a tax upon the agriculturists, who were the principal consumers.

A lengthy and able memorial, believed to be written by Judge Story, was also presented, January 31, from the merchants of Salem, Mass., whose India trade had been destroyed by the minimum duty on coarse cottons, against an increase of duties on imports, or any change of the revenue system in relation to credits and drawbacks. These remonstrances produced an elaborate memorial from the Pennsylvania Society for the Encouragement of American Manufactures, drawn up by Mr. Carey, and a second appeal from the New York Society, the latter of which stated that twelve thousand packages of goods, on which the duties were estimated at one million dollars, had been sold at auction in that city between the 1st of January and 15th of April,—the duties thereon had become so much active capital, loaned by the Government to foreign manufacturers, or their agents in this country, to aid them by

17

such operations in crushing the enterprise and industry of the nation. The Chamber of Commerce of New York and Philadelphia also opposed a change in the system of credits for duties, and the former likewise a tax on auction sales. The merchants of Baltimore were part in favor of a cash system, and another part opposed any change in the revenue laws.

The Legislature of New York, on 1st February, adopted resolutions to request its senators and representatives in Congress, to use their influence in obtaining such a revision and regulation of the tariff, as should reduce the importations and effectually protect manufactures, and also recommending all members of the Legislature, officers of government, their representatives in Congress, and citizens generally, to clothe themselves in fabrics of home manufacture, and to promote their introduction into general use in preference to foreign manufactures.

Notwithstanding the numerous petitions for a revision of the tariff, signed by at least thirty thousand persons, the views of the merchants and planters prevailed. A bill introduced by Mr. Baldwin, from the Committee on Manufactures, proposing a moderate increase in the duties, although it passed the House by a vote of ninety to sixty-nine on 28th April, was afterward lost in the Senate, where the vote stood twenty to twenty-one. The period of general relief was thereby postponed for another four years.

On the 17th March, Congress passed an act making provision for taking the fourth census of the population, the numeration to commence on the first Monday in August. The tenth section provided for taking, at the same time, under the directions of the Secretary of the Treasury, an account of the manufacturing establishments and manufactures, for which extra service the marshals were to receive twenty per cent. additional compensation.

A supplement to the Navigation Act of 18th April, 1818, was approved May 15th, by which United States ports were closed, after 30th September, to all British vessels arriving from colonial ports on the continent or in the West Indies, not included in the former act, and requiring the owner, consignee, or agent of British vessels, on taking in cargoes of the growth, produce, or manufacture of the United States, to give bond not to land the same in any of the British possessions described in either act, provided that the convention of 1815 was not infringed by the prohibition. No importations from any such British possessions were to be permitted after the above date.

The suffering produced in the West India Colonies by these retaliatory acts, gave rise to an appeal to Parliament, which resulted in the opening of the West India ports to American vessels, and consequent relief to the mercantile and agricultural interests of the United States.

On the third of May, the first permanent Committee of Agriculture was appointed by Congress to have charge of that branch of industry.

Among the petitions presented early in the session, was one from Mr. John Adlum, of the District of Columbia, calling the attention of Congress to the fact that he had succeeded in making wine of superior quality from native grapes. Mr. Adlum was one of the most zealous of the early promoters of the wine manufacture in this country, and especially in recommending the Catawba grape, but did not succeed in making good wine on a large scale, partly in consequence of the want of the means which he at this time solicited.

The General Assembly of Pennsylvania passed, March 6th, "An Act for the promotion of Agriculture and Domestic Manufactures," authorizing the incorporation of companies for these objects, by the Governor of the Commonwealth.

The Apprentices' Library, founded by voluntary contributions in Philadelphia, during the last year, and the Boston Apprentices' Library, commenced on 22d February, of the present year, under the supervision of the Massachusetts Charitable Mechanics' Association, were the first of that useful class of institutions established in this country, if not in the world. The Mercantile Library of Boston, was also founded on 11th March of this year, and the Apprentices' Library of Cincinnati, during the ensuing year.

The manufacture of Chain Cables was about this date commenced at Boston, by Cotton & Hill, who, for thirty years, were the only successful manufacturers of cables, in which they established a reputation at home and abroad. They were, however, ultimately compelled to abandon the business on account of the low price of English chains of inferior quality, but resumed it again in 1856.

Heavy Anchors were forged at South Canaan, Litchfield county, Connecticut, from the superior iron of that neighborhood, by the Hunt Brothers; who, during the year, made two, of eight and nine thousand pounds' weight respectively, for the seventy-four gun ship *Franklin*. Screws of the largest kinds for powerful machinery, were also made and cut by water power in their establishment. Anchors were made at twelve and a half cents a pound, in or near Baltimore, but were undersold by imported anchors of inferior English iron, which had already caused a suspension of the business.

Thirty Iron Works had been built in Pennsylvania during the last ten years, of which fourteen were charcoal blast furnaces, and sixteen bloomeries. The business labored under great depression on account of the limited demand, and a decline in the price of bar iron from $140 to $80 and $100 per ton, since 1818, chiefly occasioned by importations of iron and iron-wares, and the general prostration of all kinds of business. In Washington county, Maryland, an iron works consisting of two forges, and slitting mill, with a capital of $100,000, which had been in profitable operation for sixty years, was about to cease operations for want of demand. Pig iron sold for thirty dollars, and castings for seventy-five dollars per ton. In East Tennessee, which had between thirty and forty forges and furnaces, twelve of them in Carter county, and in other places remote from foreign competition, bar iron continued in good demand at ten to twelve and a half cents a pound.

The first regular commencement of the Anthracite Coal Trade of Pennsylvania, was made this year, by the shipment from the southern Anthracite region at Mauch Chunk, on the Lehigh, of three hundred and twenty-five tons or sixteen thousand bushels, to Philadelphia. It was sent by artificial navigation, opened by the Lehigh Navigation Company, and was mined by the Lehigh Coal Company, both of which were organized in July, 1818, and this year merged in one association, called the Lehigh Coal and Navigation Company, which was incorporated in 1832, and has since greatly developed the mineral riches of that region and improved the transportation. The coal was delivered at the doors of purchasers at $8.50 per ton. About seventy thousand bushels of stone coal were mined in Alleghany county, Maryland, this year, at a cost of six and a quarter cents a bushel; a part of which was sent down the Potomac in boats.

A steam ship, called the "Robert Fulton," of one thousand tons, was built this year at New York, for Messrs. Dunham & Lynch, by the eminent naval architect, Henry Eckford, who, during the late war, had constructed, with incredible dispatch, and to the entire satisfaction of the Government, a fleet upon the lakes, and had established the reputation of New York merchant ships, as equal to any in the country. The Fulton was intended for the New York and New Orleans trade, and attained a speed of nine miles an hour, which was regarded by the distinguished inventor, whose name she bore, as the maximum speed of steamboats, and was not surpassed for many years. The speculation was ruinous, however, to her owners, and the vessel having been sold, afterward became the fastest sloop of war (under sail) in the Brazilian navy.

The total value of the Book Publishing business of the United States, this year, was estimated, by the late S. G. Goodrich (Peter Parley), at $2,500,000, viz.: of school books, $750,000, classical, $250,000, theological, $150,000, law, $200,000, medical, $150,000, all others, $1,000,000. The relative proportions of British and American books consumed, was stated to be, of American thirty, and of British seventy per cent. of the whole. During the next thirty years, the proportions were reversed, the American forming seventy and the British thirty per cent. of the whole.

Of seventy paper mills in full operation in Pennsylvania and Delaware, at the close of the war, containing ninety-five vats, which cost about half a million dollars, and employed nine hundred and fifty persons, producing paper to the value of $800,000 per annum, but seventeen vats were at work at this time, producing $136,000 worth per annum. The number of hands had been reduced seven hundred and fifty-five, and the product $624,000, by the importation of paper, chiefly of low price, from the south of Europe. The manufacturers of these states, and of Baltimore, asked for a duty of twenty-five per cent. on foreign papers.[1] The whole annual value of the manufacture in the United States, was estimated at an average of three millions of dollars, the materials and labor at two millions, and the number of persons employed at five thousand. Congress, at this time, used English paper, although the Messrs. Gilpin, who employed near half a million capital in the manufacture, on the Brandywine, offered paper, allowed to be equally good, at twenty-five per cent. less price.[2]

The manufacture of starch from potatoes, for which a patent was granted, in 1802, to John Biddis, of Pennsylvania, had been recently established in Hillsborough county, N. H. The demand was principally for the cotton manufactories, which contained, in that county, exclusive of cotton and woolen factories, over four thousand spindles, and upward of fifty power-looms, employed on shirtings, tickings, checks, ginghams, yarn, etc. Many of these were idle at this time, or greatly depressed in consequence of a decline in the price of yarn of about fifty per cent., since 1812–13.

A manufactory of Vestings, Worsted, and Silk cloths, recently esta- in Providence, R. I., was said to be the only one of the kind in the United States. An infant manufactory of worsted stuffs, in Bristol county, calculated to run six hundred to eight hundred spindles, but having only seventy-two in operation, had, however, produced vestings of fine texture, and many other kinds of worsted and fine cloths, which had exceeded expectation.

Six establishments in Litchfield county, Conn., made 11,450 brass and wooden clocks, valued at $75,400, nearly the whole of which resulted from the industry and ingenuity employed on them.

The returns of the marshals represented a manufactory of Prussian blue, from leather shavings, to the value of $4,500 annually, in Rensselaer

(1) Memorials to Congress. (2) Munsell's Chronology of paper, etc.

county, N. Y., and one of hulled and pearled Barley to the value of $5,000 in Newcastle county, Del., as probably the only establishments of the kind in the United States.[1] The manufactures of Albany and vicinity were quite numerous, that of ale and strong beer being, next to flour, the most valuable, employing four breweries, which made to the value of $54,000 per annum, and were prosperous. The manufactories of the city and county of New York, embraced, among many others, two of oil of vitriol and chemical drugs in great variety; one of chrome and other colors, of red and white lead, of black lead-pencils and crayons, fancy transparent and perfumed soaps, patent floor cloths, types, etc., which had been several years in operation.

The manufacture of Iron Railing and House work, and of Needles and Fish hooks, imported in an unfinished state, and prepared for market at from one to twenty dollars a thousand, were among those of recent introduction.

The Salt manufacture of the United States employed, in Massachusetts, a capital of about $777,000, which yielded a product of $95,000; and seventy-nine establishments in the town of Salina, New York, upon land leased by individuals from the state, of which the product, inspected by the Government superintendent, for the year ending Nov. 7, was 554,776 bushels. On this a tax of one shilling a bushel was paid toward the canal fund. In Genesee county, about 83,000 bushels were made. In Kanawha, Va., twenty-three salt making establishments, with a capital of $696,000, and eighteen hundred and twenty kettles, etc., made salt at seventy-five cents to one dollar a bushel, but suffered by competition with foreign salt, brought from New Orleans in steamboats. Kentucky had upward of sixteen hundred kettles employed, and made salt worth about $190,000 per annum, and in New Hanover county, N. C., salt was made by solar heat to the value of $13,350. About $33,000 was invested in the same business in western Pennsylvania, and smaller amounts in other places.

The population of the United States in August, as returned by the fourth census, was 9,638,131, having increased 83.13 per cent. in ten years. The active population was distributed as follows: number engaged in Agriculture, 2,075,363, in Manufactures, 349,663, in Commerce, including country shop-keepers, 72,558.

The returns on the subject of manufactures, although the schedules furnished were more comprehensive than on former occasions, and

(1) The manufacture of Prussian blue was recommended, and the process described, with many original observations and experiments, in a volume of "*Chemical* and *Economical Essays*," published in 1790, by Dr. John Pennington, while a medical student.—See Mease's Archives, vol. iii., 129.

embraced nearly the same objects of inquiry as at present, were exceedingly defective, partly on account of the inadequate compensation allowed the enumerators, and partly from the inability or reluctance of manufacturers to give the details of their business. A digest of the accounts on this subject, which a resolution of Congress, approved March 30, 1822, authorized the Secretary of State to have made and published, was found, upon its completion, to be so imperfect an exhibit of this branch of the national industry, that the Secretary was only constrained, by the imperative nature of the requisition, to permit its publication, and the House of Representatives had nearly resolved to suppress the whole document, and tabled a resolution providing for the distribution of the books. The digest, however, when studied in detail, furnishes much useful information respecting the existing state of individual establishments and branches of industry, and shows the nature and extent of the embarrassments under which the manufacturers labored at this time. Although some branches of industry, particularly that of cotton, and others favorably situated, were tolerably prosperous, and there were indications of general improvement, large losses were reported as having been experienced within a few years. In all parts of the Union, machinery and fixed capital, to a large amount, were either lying idle, or were employed at a very meagre profit, in the hope of a favorable change. The products and the profits of manufactures had, in general, been greatly reduced, and much property had changed hands at ruinous sacrifices. The decrease in the aggregate value of manufactures returned, as compared with the census of 1810, was in part caused by the omission of all manufactures strictly domestic or household, in the fourth census, and which were included in the third.

From a report based on these returns made by the Secretary of State, in September, 1824, in obedience to a resolution of the Senate, we take the following:

STATEMENT OF THE AMOUNT AND VALUE OF DUTIABLE ARTICLES MANUFACTURED ANNUALLY IN THE UNITED STATES AND TERRITORIES; THE AMOUNT OF CAPITAL INVESTED, AND THE AMOUNT AUTHORIZED AND INCORPORATED BY STATE LAWS.

State and Territory.	Amount and Value of Dutiable Articles Manufactured.	Capital Invested.	Amount of Capital Authorized and Incorporated by State Laws.
Maine,	$424,648	$439,808	
New Hampshire,	740,894	893,065	$ 2,455,000
Massachusetts,	2,144,816	4,542,325	21,049,000
Rhode Island,	878,558	2,107,222	
Connecticut,	2,429,204	3,144,525	5,540,000
Vermont,	784,349	691,157	
New York,	4,844,387	7,774,049	18,304,000
New Jersey,	919,419	1,725,495	2,360,000

Pennsylvania, ...	5,049,276................	6,323,077................	1,115,000
Delaware, ...	561,500................	1,557,296................	
Maryland, ...	1,769,234................	5,671,837................	4,466,500
Columbia District,......	163,046................	45,200................	
Virginia,....................	2,708,077................	3,138,557................	
North Carolina,..........	473,656................	376,508................	
South Carolina,..........	70,922................	280,775................	
Georgia,.....................	494,752................	219,635................	
Alabama, ...	102,311................	36,501................	
Louisiana,..................	48,750................	33,025................	
Tennessee,.................	1,924,221................	976,229................	
Kentucky, ...	2,141,989................	2,575,522................	
Ohio,..........................	3,134,772................	3,955,839................	
Indiana, ...	142,692................	150,754................	
Illinois,......................	126,498................	74,465................	
Missouri, ...	160,419................	41,845................	
Michigan Territory,....	34,500................	60,835................	
Arkansas Territory,...	....	1,700................	
Total,	$32,271,984	$46,837,266	$55,289,500

The following table shows, probably, a nearer approximation to the actual condition of the cotton manufacture than is furnished by the general aggregates. It exhibits an increase of one hundred and seventy-six per cent., in the whole amount of cotton consumed, and of two hundred and thirteen per cent. in the number of spindles, given in Mr. Gallatin's Report, in 1810, but a decrease of about one hundred and seventy per cent. in the amount of cotton consumed in 1815, according to the report of a Committee of Congress.

STATEMENT OF THE RAW COTTON CONSUMED, AND OF THE NUMBER OF SPINDLES EMPLOYED IN EACH STATE, ACCORDING TO THE FOURTH CENSUS.

States.	Pounds of Cotton Annually Spun.	Number of Spindles.	States.	Pounds of Cotton Annually Spun.	Number of Spindles.
Maine, ...	56,500......	3,070	Pennsylvania, ...	1,062,753......	13,776
New Hampshire, ..	412,100......	13,012	Delaware, ...	423,800......	11,784
Massachusetts,.....	1,611,796......	30,304	Maryland, ...	849,000......	20,245
Rhode Island,......	1,914,220......	63,372	Virginia, ...	3,000......	
Connecticut,........	897,335......	29,826	North Carolina,...	18,000......	288
Vermont,............	117,250......	3,278	South Carolina,....	46,449......	588
New York, ...	1,412,495......	33,160	Kentucky, ...	360,951......	8,097
New Jersey,.........	648,600......	18,124	Ohio,.....................	81,360......	1,680
			Total,	9,945,609	250,572

Letters patent were granted for the following objects, among others: to Thomas Blanchard, Middlebury, Mass. (Jan. 20), for a machine for turning gun stocks. This was for the celebrated lathe, afterward adapted to turning irregular forms in general, as shoe-lasts, spokes, hat, tackle and wig blocks, etc., for which uses he was granted, by special act of Congress, in June, 1834, and again in 1848, a renewal of his patent, which has just expired (Jan. 1862), the author still living.[1] A. Woolworth, Waterbury county, also took a patent (June 15), for turning gun stocks; I. Kendall, Lincoln, Mass. (Jan. 28), preparing oxymuriate of lime (bleaching powder); A. Buffum and J. Kelly, Westfield, R. I. (Feb. 17), water-proof elastic hats; Robert Eastman and J. Jaquith, Brunswick, Me. (March 16), circular saw for clapboards, etc. This "improved rotary sawing machine" was the first application of the circular saw to the dressing of timber of large size, and the manufacture therefrom of staves, heading, clapboards, etc. One machine was capable of cutting two thousand feet of pine timber per diem. It was in general use throughout New England in 1822.[2] The patent was renewed by act of Congress, for seven years, in March, 1835. Henry and Jacob Day, New York (April 4), improvement in locks; Harvey Hackley, New York (April 21), brewing by steam; Shalor Ives, Chilicothe, Ohio (May 17), machine for spinning candle-wick; Duncan Wright, Medway, Mass. (Aug. 31), drying cloth by steam rollers; William Gilmour, Smithfield, R. I. (Oct. 28), improvement in the Power Loom. The Scotch power loom was first introduced into Rhode Island three or four years before by the patentee. Thomas Rowell, Hartford, Vt. (Nov. 24), making wooden pegs; Jonathan Fish, Medway, Mass. (Dec. 7), for five different improvements on the double speeder for spinning cotton, and one for a combination of these improvements in the double speeder; also to Paul Moody, of Waltham (Dec. 20), for double speeder for roping cotton; George P. Digges, Albermarle, Va. (Dec. 16), making oil from cotton seed; Thomas J. Bond, Baltimore (Dec. 21), iron boats. Improvements in propelling boats and vessels were patented by several persons.

Mr. Jacob Perkins, of Austin Friars, London, late of Philadelphia, and formerly of Newburyport, Mass., was this year awarded, by the London Society of Arts, two large silver medals, for his methods of

(1) This machine, the idea of which was suggested while operating a lathe, previously constructed for the Government Armory at Springfield, to turn gun barrels complete from end to end, was immediately introduced into the national gun factories at Harper's Ferry and Springfield, where the inventor was employed for five years. He there originated other improvements, and thirteen different machines, afterward generally adopted in the manufacture and stocking of fire arms. The Government allowance of nine cents upon each musket made in the two armories, was the only compensation he received, during the first term of his patent for the lathe, more than fifty of which had, in the mean time, been erected in different parts of the Union, in violation of his right, for turning lasts, spokes, handles, etc. He consequently applied for and obtained a renewal of the patent, as above stated, covering its application to irregular forms in general. For an interesting account of the origin of this and other inventions of the ingenious author, see *Howe's Memoirs of the Most Eminent Mechanics.*

(2) Silliman's Journal, vol. v., p. 154.

warming and ventilating rooms and the holds of ships, and for improvements in engine hose; also its large gold medal for an improved ship's pump, and its smaller or Vulcan gold medal for a method of freeing water wheels from back water. The thanks of the Society were also voted to Perkins, Fairman and Heath, for communicating to the society for publication, certain parts of their *Siderographic* process for multiplying copies of engravings, particularly with a view to the prevention of forgery.[1] The communication, pointing out the greater security and cheapness to be attained in the production of bank notes, and copies of engravings or illustrated works, requiring numerous impressions, and in the manufacture of printed calicoes, ribbons, earthenware, etc., by Perkins's method of decarbonating and hardening steel plates, etc., and the process of transferring, retransferring, and multiplying impressions and patterns, by aid of the geometrical lathe, invented by Mr. Asa Spencer, of Connecticut, accompanied by specimens of the art, together with accounts of the other inventions of Mr. Perkins, above named, will be found in the thirty-eighth volume of the Society's Transactions. In the thirty-ninth volume, for 1821, are also engravings and descriptions of an improvement in the warming and ventilating stove, for which Mr. Perkins received the thanks of the Society, and also of two instruments for ascertaining the trim of a ship more accurately than by the methods usually practiced, for which he was rewarded with the Vulcan gold medal. One of the instruments was designed to be placed in a line with the keel of the ship, and therefore denominated by him the *orthometer;* the other, placed at right angles to the keel, was called the *pleometer*, and the change in the relative positions of their indexes, showed when the vessel was in a proper trim for sailing.

The failure of the tariff bill, in the early part of the last year, was followed, in the next session, by several remonstrances against a renewal
1821 of the measure or any farther extension of the restrictive system, as destructive to revenue and to the interests of agriculture and commerce. The merchants and citizens of Petersburg, Va.; the commercial and agricultural citizens of Maine—recently admitted as a state; a convention of delegates representing the merchants and others interested in commerce, assembled at Philadelphia; the citizens of Charleston, S. C.; the delegates of the United Agricultural Societies of Virginia, in a

(1) Messrs. Murray, Fairman & Co., of Philadelphia, associates of the London firm, produced in this, or early in the following year, beautiful specimens of bank notes, showing all the improvements in the art of engraving, in part executed by very costly machinery, and of unrivalled excellence. They were in all respects equal to the specimens executed in London.

second petition, and the Roanoke Agricultural Society of Virginia, severally preferred their memorials. The proposed increase of duties and the whole system of bounties, premiums, prohibitory duties, or other enactments tending to limit the freedom of trade for the encouragement of manufactures, were deprecated with earnestness and ability, as calculated to embarrass the public finances, and promote smuggling; as partial and exclusive in their effects; as taxing the many for the benefit of a few; fostering single or local interests at the expense of every other, and as calculated to assimilate the national economy to the worst features of the European systems. The encouragement of manufactures by legislative interference, was denounced as alike impolitic and unjust. The auctioneers also petitioned against a duty on sales at auction, insisting upon the advantages of the system to the community in general, and particularly to the mannfacturers, to the smaller of whom, the auction was almost exclusively the medium of sale for his goods, which, in their own state, were exempted from duty by the Legislature.

Petitions were also laid before the House by the inhabitants of Belfast, Maine, and by the merchants and others of Richmond, Virginia, the former attributing to the tariff and cash payment bills repealed at the last session, a purpose to abolish the system of debentures and drawbacks, and depicting their ruinous effects upon commerce; and the latter imputing to the advocates of manufactures, less of a desire to promote internal manufactures than of enmity to foreign commerce and navigation, which it was their design in these bills to assail and eventually to destroy. These petitions were the subject of a report presented early in the session, by Mr. Baldwin, from the Committee of Manufactures, disclaiming any such objects in the bills or in their framers, and strongly rebuking misrepresentations and imputations so improper and unusual in reference to acts of the National Legislatnre.

The same Committee, on the 15th January, reported a new bill and accompanied it by a report of more than ordinary length and ability, in which the subjects of the various memorials, just referred to, were elaborately discussed, and the views of the Committee fully and freely stated.

An opposite view of this important question was also presented, at considerable length, on the 2d February, by the newly created Committee of Agriculture, to whom the second memorial of the United Agricultural Societies of Virginia had been referred.

The bill received some amendments, but was not called up for a third reading, either in consequence of its late introduction, or the strength of the opposition, a motion made four days before the close of the session, to go into consideration of the tariff and auction bills, having been negatived by a vote of sixty-two to fifty-three.

It does not appear that any great effort was made by the manufacturers generally to secure the passage of an act supposed to be exclusively for their benefit, although Mr. Carey, with his usual activity, issued, during the year, an address to the farmers of the United States, showing their interests to be involved in a change of policy, and also a review of a pamphlet on the tariff by Mr. Cambreleng, a prominent merchant and member of Congress, from New York, whose representations of the general prosperity of the country, and of the effects of a protecting system, were singularly at variance with the report of the Committee. For these and other services, the citizens of Wilmington, Del., in public meeting, voted Mr. Carey a piece of plate of the value of one hundred and eighty or two hundred dollars, subscribed by employers and operatives, which was presented in April, with an inscription expressive of their gratitude.[1]

The cotton crop of the United States, according to official tables, was this year about thirteen millions of pounds in excess of any previous year, and amounted to one hundred and eighty millions of pounds, being 28.5 per cent. of the whole quantity grown throughout the world, which was estimated to be six hundred and thirty millions of pounds. The quantity exported was one hundred and twenty-four millions of pounds, worth twenty millions of dollars, at the average price of sixteen cents per pound. The quantity manufactured in the United States was estimated at twenty millions of pounds.[2]

The cotton manufacture, offered at this time the most eligible investments of capital, and the success of the Waltham Manufacturing Company, which was the most extensive in the Union, and was said to have divided twelve per cent. upon its capital, during a period of general depression, induced others to engage in it. Messrs. P. T. Jackson and Nathan Appleton, principal owners in the Waltham factory, having instituted inquiries for a suitable water power, with the design of introducing the manufacture and printing of Calicoes on large scale, were directed to the Pawtucket Falls, in East Chelmsford, now Lowell, which they visited in September. In connection with Mr. Kirk Boot, they made, during the next month, the first purchase of lands, on the present site of Lowell, from the Pawtucket Canal Company, and other proprietors of the territory, which then contained less than two hundred inhabitants. Articles of association were signed on 1st December, and an act of incorporation was obtained on 5th February, 1822, under the name of The Merrimac Manufacturing Company, with a capital stock of six hundred shares, owned as follows: N. Appleton and P. T. Jackson, each one

(1) "A tribute of gratitude to Matthew Carey, Esq., in approbation of his writings on Political Economy, presented by some of the friends of National Industry, in Wilmington, Del., and its vicinity, April, 1821."

(2) Secretary Woodbury's Report.

hundred and eighty shares; Kirk Boot and John W. Boot, each ninety shares; Paul Moody, sixty shares. The following persons were permitted, at the next meeting, to subscribe to the amount of ninety-five shares, viz: Dudley A. Tyng, Warren Dutton, Timothy Wiggin, William Appleton, Eben. Appleton, Thomas W. Clark, D. Webster, Benjamin Gorham, Nathaniel Bowditch. The original shareholders also sold one hundred and fifty shares to the Boston Manufacturing Company, at an advance of ten per cent. Mr. Boot was elected treasurer and agent, and acted in the latter capacity until his death, in 1837. The corporation, early in the ensuing spring, proceeded to make additional purchases, toward acquiring control of the entire power of the Merrimac at that place, and to enlarge and extend the canal and locks sufficiently for fifty mill powers, at a cost of $120,000. They arranged, with the Waltham Company, for the transfer, for the sum of $75,000, of the patterns and patent rights of machinery, and of the services of Mr. Moody, and erected the first mill, a church, etc. The first wheel was started in September, 1823, and the capital was, the same year, increased to $1,200,000. In 1825, the first dividend of one hundred and sixty per share was made, at which time three additional mills were built, and five hundred dollars were appropriated for a library, and operations were commenced by the Hamilton Manufacturing Company. The original Company has continued, with few intermissions, to divide about twelve per cent. annually, to the present time. The Company commenced print works on a large scale, in 1823, but were anticipated by establishments at Taunton, Mass., and Dover, N. H.

The Great Falls Manufacturing Company was incorporated this year, by the States of Maine and New Hampshire, with a capital of $400,000, to erect works on the Salmon Falls, or Piscataqua river, which divides the states. The mills were built at Great Falls, now the beautiful manufacturing town of Somersworth, on the New Hampshire side, then containing only one house and a saw mill. Within ten years from this date, the place contained about two thousand inhabitants, and four large cotton mills, with 31,000 spindles, and a woolen mill, said to be the largest in America, two hundred and twenty feet long, six stories high, and having machinery for making 120,000 to 130,000 yards of fine broadcloth yearly, and a large carpet factory attached, capable of making 150,000 yards of best ingrain carpeting.

About four thousand looms were put in operation, in Philadelphia, in the first six months of this year, chiefly for weaving cotton goods. Calicoes of firm and fine texture were made and printed in Philadelphia, and sold as low as the poorer qualities of British calicoes. Preparations were made to carry on the business extensively, both by water and steam power. Domestic cottons had, at this time, in a great measure superseded the coarse plain cottons from abroad.

Money continued to be invested in woolen manufactures, and considerable quantities of Spanish wool were imported from Bilboa, and met with ready sale, the domestic supply of wool being then, as now, inadequate to the demand.

Mr. Macauley, the proprietor of a manufactory of woolen carpet, patent floor cloth, and oil cloth, which last were now made in different parts of the Union, contracted to supply a large quantity of ingrain carpeting, of his own make, to the new State House at Harrisburg.

The Wolcott Woolen Manufactory, at South Bridge, Massachusetts, was incorporated, with a capital of $144,000, for the manufacture of broadcloths and cassimeres, with thirty-two looms and other machinery valued at $40,000, but sunk, during the next five years, upward of $23,000. Boston was, at this time, the market for large supplies of domestic cloths, which were sought after, and the demand. for wool was increasing.

A manufacturer of power looms, who made about seventy per week, was unable to supply the demand.

An extensive steam mill was erected at Bath, in the State of Maine. The Copperas works, at Strafford, Vermont, produced about one hundred tons per annum, by the labor of four men. A manufactory of Alum was in successful operation at Salem, Massachusetts, and sulphate of copper (blue vitriol) was also made there, of superior quality, presenting crystals of extreme beauty.

The fifth annual message of President Monroe, read December 3d, held out the encouraging prospect, that, under the protection given to domestic manufactures by existing laws, the United States would become, at no distant period, a manufacturing country on a large scale. The resources of the country, in raw materials, food, mechanical skill, and improvements calculated to lessen the demand and cost for labor, would, under present duties, make our industry equal to any demand which, under a fair competition, could be made upon it. In proportion to our resources, and independence of foreign powers, would be the stability of the public happiness, and, with the increase of domestic manufactures and the demand for raw materials, the mutual dependence of the several parts of the Union, and the strength of the Union itself, would be proportionately augmented.

Miss Sophia Woodhouse (afterward Mrs. Wells), the daughter of a farmer residing at Weathersfield, Conn., in the early part of this year, sent, to the London Society of Arts, samples, in their raw, bleached, and manufactured states, of a new material for Straw Plait, consisting of a

Bonnet made in imitation of Leghorn, and dried specimens of the grass from which it was made, popularly known there as *ticklemoth*, a species of (*poa pretensis*), spear grass, or smooth stalked meadow grass, growing spontaneously in that port of the country. The Weathersfield bonnet was pronounced, by the principal dealers in London, superior in fineness and beauty of color to the best Leghorn, and the cultivation or importation of the straw was recommended as a means of supplying raw material of superior quality. The Society, at its next session, voted the large silver medal, and twenty guineas, to Miss Woodhouse, on conditions which would put the Society in possession of some of the seed, and the process of bleaching, which were sent by her with a description of the whole treatment of the culm, and a certificate that she was the original inventor of the art.[1] A patent was granted, in the United States, Dec. 25, to Garden Wells and Sophia Wells, of Weathersford, for making hats and bonnets of grass, in the manner above mentioned.

The Misses Burnap, of Merrimac, N. H., also claimed, not far from this time, the first discovery, in that region, of the manufacture of Leghorn bonnets. A grass bonnet of their manufacture sold this year, in Boston, at auction, for fifty dollars. In consequence of the high price of Leghorn hats and bonnets at this time, the manufacture had been commenced in a number of places, and many specimens rivalled, if they did not surpass the Italian. The importation of common straw hats had been long stopped by the domestic manufacture in Massachusetts, Connecticut, and elsewhere. Premiums as high as twenty dollars each were offered in New York for the finest specimens of bonnets, and the complete establishment of the business, it was thought, would soon be a saving of two millions of dollars annually to the country, and furnish an article for exportation.

Patents.—Paul Moody, Boston (Jan. 17), for frames for spinning cotton; to the same (Feb. 19), two patents for roping or spinning cotton, one being the double speeder. These and other improvements of Mr. Moody were introduced into the new factories at Waltham and Lowell, and aided in establishing the cotton manufacture in the United States, upon an improved and permanent basis. John Brown, Providence, R. I. (Jan. 23), for spinning and roping cotton and wool by hand; the same (Aug. 11), for a vertical spinner; George J. Newbury, New York (Feb. 1), printing with metallic and colored powder (bronzing); A. O. Stansbury, New York (April 7), and Samuel Rust, New York (May 13), improvements in the printing press. Mr. Rust's invention was known as the Washington press, which for some time was made by Rust &

(1) Trans. Soc. Arts, vol. 40., pp. 217-222.

Turney, afterward by Messrs. R. Hoe & Co., of New York, by whom they were greatly improved. Five different improvements in the cast iron plough were patented by inhabitants of New York State. Minus Ward, Columbia, S. C. (March 22), improvement in steam engines. This was for an alternating or rotary engine, which enabled the piston rod to describe a rotary motion upon its extreme end, when turning a wheel. Ross Winans, New York (June 26), fulling cloth by steam; Josiah Chapman, Frankford, Pa. (July 9), sail duck loom. Sail cloth, made by the improved method of the patentee, at Frankford, was tried on the boxer, in 1815, by Captain Porter, and was found superior to English or Russian, having twice the durability in hard service. James Richards, Paterson, N. J. (Aug. 10), sail cloth loom; Isaiah Jennings, New York (Sept. 22), repeating rifles; John Cook, Fayetteville, N. C. (Oct. 12), machine for packing cotton; Charles Williams, Boston, improvement in railways. The patentee, in a communication to the Richmond Whig, dated Fluvanna county, Virginia, December 13, 1845, claimed to have invented, in 1817, a wooden railway, to remove dirt, and during this and the following year to have planned a small engine, in Boston, to use steam, and therefore to have been the first to apply steam to railroads, the first locomotive of Stephens having been copied from his invention.[1]

The seventeenth Congress was memorialized during its first session, by Mr. Jefferson, the rector, and the visitors of the University of Virginia,
1822 and by the trustees of the Transylvania University, for a repeal of the duty on books imported into the United States, as being an obstruction to the progress of science, literature, and general improvement. The Senate Committee on Finance, on 8th Jannary, made a report adverse to the prayer of the trustees, because, by the tariff of April, 1816, philosophical apparatus, instruments, *books*, maps, statues, and other articles imported for the use of any society incorporated for philosophical or literary purposes, or for the encouragement of the fine arts, or by order and for the use of any seminary of learning, were exempt from duty. The interests of authors, publishers, paper and type makers, and of the revenue, forbade an exception, principally for the benefit of professional gentlemen or scholars of wealth and leisure, who might wish to obtain rare or elegant and expensive editions of foreign authors. On ordinary or cheap editions of English works for general circulation, the export bounty of three pence per pound weight, allowed in Great Britain, nearly balanced the American import duty of fifteen per cent.

(1) See Merchant's Magazine, vol. 14. p. 249.

ad valorem. It was, moreover, desirable that we should have American editions, adapted to our exigencies and tastes and less productive of foreign influence.

The subject of Protection to manufactures, which had strongly agitated the country for four or five years, was, on the following day, once more brought up in the House by a bill reported so late in the Session, that, after having been twice read and amended, the House, by a vote of sixty-two to fifty-three, refused to go into committee for the final consideration of that and the Auction Bill, and a new one was reported to the next Congress. Mr. Baldwin's bill proposed a very considerable increase in the rates of duty, and the substitution of specific rates on a large number of articles.

The Senate Committee on Commerce and Manufactures, instructed to inquire into the expediency of prohibiting the importation of foreign distilled spirits, reported toward the close of the session, that although agriculture and manufactures, and in a short time the revenue, would be benefited by the prohibition, its immediate effects would be injurious to the commercial interests of the United States, and would diminish the revenue, before an excise system could be brought into operation. They recommended, in preference, a gradual increase of duties to the extent of prohibition, for which purpose a bill must originate in the House as a revenue measure. Mr. Baldwin's tariff bill proposed to raise the duties on cottons and woolens, only eight and one third, and on iron, steel, copper, brass, and lead, five per cent., making them thirty-three and one third per cent. on the former and twenty-five on the latter.

The cotton crop of the United States amounted, this year, to 210,000,000 pounds or thirty millions of pounds more than that of 1821. The quantity exported was about 144,700,000 pounds, or nearly twenty millions of pounds more than in the last year. The heavy importations of the two years caused a reduction of the price in England, to an average, on the whole year, of eight and a quarter cents per pound. Some prime lots, which early in the season cost, in Charleston, eighteen and a half cents, sold in November for eight and a half pence, equivalent, with exchange at eleven per cent., to twelve and a half cents a pound. The average price of Upland cotton, toward the end of August, was as low as six and a half pence in Liverpool, or about nine and a quarter cents with exchange as above. The loss to shippers of cotton, was from twenty-five to thirty-three per cent., and was estimated to amount, on the exports of the whole year, to between four and five millions of dollars. The first cotton from Egypt was received at Liverpool the ensuing year.

The cotton culture was first commenced, this year, in Texas, by

Colonel Jared E. Groce, in the bottoms of the Brazos de Dios, where the first colony from the United States was planted in the last year, by General Stephen F. Austin, the father-in-law of Col. Groce. On the plantation of the latter the first cotton gin in Austin's Colony, and the second in the state, was erected in 1825, the first having been built by Mr. John Cartwright, of the Redlands.[1]

The most extensive Cotton pressing and Tobacco warehouse, at this time, in New Orleans, was that of Mr. V. Rillieux, and was furnished with three presses, with steam, water, and horse powers, and a fire engine. It was capable of containing eleven hundred and fifty bales of cotton, and cost $150,000.

The manufacture of Cotton Sail Duck was commenced in February of this year, at Patterson, N. J., by Mr. John Colt, who employed hand looms, and made it wholly of double and twisted yarn, without starch or dressing. In March, 1824, up to which time he had made only about five hundred pieces, Mr. Colt introduced the power loom, which had been used for several years by Mr. Bemis, the original manufacturer of the article. The business was from that time rapidly improved and extended by Mr. Colt, who, in 1831, made 460,000 yards, which quantity he has since more than doubled. His sail duck has always been in high repute. Two duck factories at Paterson, in 1823, owned by Mr. Colt and Mr. Travers, with fourteen hundred and thirty-three spindles and one hundred hand looms, consumed upward of a ton of flax daily, and in a great measure supplied the United States Navy with canvas. There were, at the same time, twelve cotton mills, with 17,724 spindles and one hundred and sixty-five power looms; three extensive woolen factories; three machine factories, one of which, Goodwin, Rogers & Co., was said to be the most extensive and complete in the United States, employing sixty-six hands; three extensive bleach greens; two brass and iron foundries, saw and grist mills, paper mill, rolling and slitting mill, nail factory, and reed factory. During the same year, cotton duck began to be made in Baltimore, by Charles Crook Jr. and Brother, who made from forty to sixty bolts per week, thirty-six yards in length by twenty inches wide, weighing forty pounds to the bolt. It was fifty per cent. stronger than required by the standard of the navy board, but the manufacturers were ruined by the enterprise, although it has since become a prosperous manufacture in Baltimore.

The cotton manufactory at Waltham, Mass., made, at this time, thirty-five thousand yards of cloth weekly, or about 1,820,000 yards in a year. It employed about five hundred operatives, nearly all of them Ameri-

(1) De Bow's Review, vol. 14., p. 74.

cans. The sheetings and shirtings, or domestics, as they began to be called, a quality of goods which originated with this factory, were becoming quite popular in all parts of the Union, and in foreign markets. Considerable quantities were already exported yearly to South America, where they were in much demand. Negro cloths of cotton and wool, also an American fabric, were fast superseding British cloth, as an article of clothing for slaves.

The first cotton mill at Lowell commenced the manufacture of calicoes this year, and propositions were made for the erection of a second factory. The second cotton mill in North Carolina, was erected at Lincolnton.

Messrs. David H. Mason and Matthew W. Baldwin, manufacturers of improved bookbinders' tools, in Philadelphia, commenced, about this date, the first engraving of Cylinders for calico printing in the United States. The establishment of print works on a large scale, at Taunton and Fall River and Lowell, Mass., Dover, N. H., at Baltimore, Columbiaville, N. Y., and elsewhere, within a few years, gave them a prosperous business, in which their numerous improvements enabled them to compete successfully with foreign artists. The invention and manufacture of tools and machinery adapted to their use, some of which were patented this year, led to the construction of calico printing machines, drying and calendering machines, for cotton, silk, or paper, drop and seal presses, engravers' machines, stationary engines and machinery in general, which was carried on at 14 Minor street. This business was soon followed by the construction of locomotives for railroads, of which Mr. Baldwin was one of the first, as he is now one of the most extensive builders in the United States.

Steam power was this year first introduced in the Sugar manufacture of Louisiana, which produced, at this time, about thirty thousand hogsheads, and in the next ten years, increased it to seventy thousand hogsheads. The first Steam Sugar mills and engines, were chiefly imported by Gordon & Forstall, and cost about $12,000. The use of steam did not become general until our own foundries had reduced the price to five or six thousand dollars.

The Bituminous Coal Basin of Richmond, or Chesterfield, Virginia, containing the oldest wrought collieries in America, and for many years the only domestic source for that species of fuel, produced this year, for exportation, forty-eight thousand tons, which was increased, in 1833, to 142,000 tons; from which the supply annually declined to sixty-five thousand tons in 1842.

The Iron Manufacture of the United States was much prostrated at this time. The importation of all kinds of iron this year, from Great Britain, was 15,000 tons, against 6,000 tons in the last year. The highest price of bar iron in the United States, from June, 1820, to July, 1824, was forty-six dollars, and the average about forty-two dollars per ton.

Among the iron works in operation, were two in Brandon, Vermont. One of these, owned by Mr. Roger Fuller, made thirty-six tons of bar iron annually, and also a very superior quality of shovels, said to be better and tougher than those imported from England. Mr. Conant's works, recently put in operation, made cast iron from the same ore. Castings, said to be the best in the country, were made by him to the amount of one hundred tons annually, and included Conant & Broughton's improved Cooking Stoves, patented the next year, which were so popular that the demand much exceeded the supply.

The first extensive or successful use of iron Conduit Pipes, in the United States, was made about this time in the service of the Fairmount Water Works, erecting in Philadelphia. They were cast in that city in sections of nine feet in length, and two to twenty-two inches diameter, upon the plan furnished by Mr. Walker, engineer of the New River water works, near London, where cast iron water pipes were in successful use. About 30,000 feet of pipe, and three to four thousand joints of peculiar construction had been laid, and the Schuylkill water was introduced into 3,945 private dwellings, 185 manufactories, and 401 private baths, in the city.

Elastic tubes or pipes of caoutchouc or India Rubber, for gaseous fluids, were made and used during this year by Thomas Skidmore, of New York, by a process devised by himself.[1]

Samples of white Flannel, made in the state of New York, sold in Charleston for one dollar a yard, and was considered equal to the best Welsh flannel.

Water-proof cloth, made by dissolving caoutchouc in petroleum (coal oil), and cementing the surfaces of two pieces of cloth by means of the solution, and then passing it between rollers, began about this time to be made in Glasgow, by Mr. McIntosh, the inventor of the process.[2] India rubber overshoes first began about this time to be imported into the United States.

The boldest enterprise yet attempted in the way of publishing in the

(1) Silliman's Journal, vol. 5, p. 153.

(2) In the second volume of the *Bee or Literary Weekly Intelligencer*, published in Edinburg, in 1791, is an account of the manner of obtaining and manufacture of elastic gum, or caoutchouc—then only used for erasing pencil marks, whence it derived the name of India Rubber—and suggested the numerous uses to which it might be put in the arts and manufactures, in which many of the present applications of that important material were recommended and foretold. The first patent for its application in the arts in England, was given, we believe, to Charles Baganelle Fleetwood, in 1824, "For a liquid and composition for rendering leather water-proof," (by dissolving caoutchouc in spirits with beeswax, etc.)

United States, was the completion at Philadelphia, during this year, of an American edition of Rees's Cyclopedia, revised, corrected, enlarged, and adapted to this country. It was in forty-one volumes, quarto, with six additional volumes of plates, containing 147 highly finished engravings. It consumed in the printing 30,000 reams of paper, and was the largest work in the English language.

The paper-makers, printers, and booksellers, who united to memorialize Congress against a reduction of the duty on imported books, stated that the cash value of books manufactured annually in Philadelphia was considerably more than one million of dollars, and every article used in the business was made at home.

An extensive paper mill on Bronx river, New York, was destroyed by fire, with its machinery and stock, and one of the large paper mills of the Gilpins, on the Brandywine, was carried away by a flood of great violence, reducing to a mass of ruins the first cylinder paper machine constructed in this country, the invention and improvement of which had cost Mr. Gilpin years of labor and expense.

A company was incorporated for the erection of a Shot Tower, in Baltimore, on the west side of North Gay street. It was 160 feet high, and built by Jacob Wolfe, under the direction of Col. Joseph Jamieson, president of the company.

Mr. Creswick, of New York, contracted to supply the United States Navy with Brass Buttons, which he struck off at the rate of nearly two dozen in a minute by a newly invented stamping machine, said to be the only one in America.

In nine years, since the enrolment and license of the first steamboat employed in trade on the Mississippi, there were eighty-nine boats enrolled at the port of New Orleans, with an aggregate admeasurement exceeding 18,000 tons. The whole number built on the Western waters, up to the end of this year, was 108, of which number ten were built this year, and seven in the last.

Patents.—A. C. Baker and M. F. Biddle, Albany, N. Y. (Feb. 7), transferring impressions from paper to wood; C. M. Graham, New York (March 9), artificial teeth, the first for that object; Wm. Hall, Boston (March 23), and Joseph Hastings, Cambridge, Mass. (Aug. 14), making isinglass or icthyocolla. This manufacture was thought to have been brought to great perfection by Mr. Hall, his isinglass being considered far superior to any imported. Robert Moore, Rowan county, N. C. (March 19), a mode of delaying buds from blossoming; George Murray, (March 23), and James Puglia, (Aug. 13), both of Philadelphia, making bank notes; Reuben Hyde, Winchester, Mass. (April 19), machine for making pales for fencing; B. and J.

Tyler, and J. B. Andrews, Windsor, Vt. (April 23), a threshing machine. This mill, invented two or three years before, was moved by two horses, and with a driver and four men would thresh and clean about twenty-five bushels of wheat in an hour; water and steam power could be used, and it would thresh cloverseed, rice or coffee, with equal success. John Ames, Springfield, Mass. (May 14), machine for making paper; Joshua Shaw, Philadelphia, (June 19), improvement in percussion guns;[1] John Rogers, Washington, D. C. (June 24), marine railway. This invention of Capt. Rodgers, President of the Navy Board, was the subject of a special message to Congress from the President, accompanied by a letter and description of the "inclined plane" dock and fixtures for hauling up ships, with estimates of cost, etc., and the committee to whom the documents were referred, reported a resolution to appropriate $50,000 for a dock, wharves, etc., at the Navy Yard, Washington. Eli Terry, Plymouth, Conn. (May 26), wooden wheel clocks; Moses Pennock, East Marlborough, Pa. (June 26), horse hay-rake; James McDonald, New York (Aug. 31), flax and hemp machine. This machine, for breaking and cleaning unrotted hemp or flax by one horse power, with a man and three boys to attend it, would clean from 1,600 to 2,000 lbs. in a day, yielding 400 to 500 lbs. when bleached. By attaching another machine, and adding another man and boy, it could clean with the same power 800 to 1000 lbs. of bleached fibre, at a cost of $5 per diem. Peter Force, Washington, D. C. (Aug. 22), printing paper hangings; N. Wright, Onondaga, N. Y. (Oct. 3), machinery for cooper's work. A cooper's ware factory employing this patent machinery, and a capital of $3,000 and six hands, was in opera-

(1) The invention of the percussion lock and cap has been ascribed to Mr. Shaw, some of whose patented improvements in percussion guns, pistols, and cannon, including the wafer primer for percussion cannon, were tested and approved by the United States government, from which he received $18,000 out of $25,000 granted him by Congress, in 1848, for the use of his patents, although he is said to have been entitled to, or claimed $170,000. He was a man of great ingenuity, and a native of Lincolnshire, England, whence he came to Philadelphia, in 1817, bringing with him, as a present to the Pennsylvania Hospital, from his friend Benjamin West, the American painter, the artist's great picture of "Christ Healing the Sick." He died at Burlington, N. J., in September, 1860, aged 83.

The invention of percussion fire arms has been claimed by different persons. The London Society of Arts, in 1818, voted Mr. Collinson Hall, of Mary-le-bone, a silver medal for a percussion gun lock, described in the 36th volume of the Transactions for that year, and in 1825, presented the gold Vulcan medal to Capt. T. Dickinson, of the Royal Navy, for the application of percussion powder by means of caps, to naval ordnance.—See Trans., vol. 43, p. 109, etc. Napoleon III. has also conferred a pension of six thousand francs upon Capt. Delvigne, as the inventor of the percussion lock. The first use of fulminating powder in guns adapted to its use, has also been ascribed to M. Beringer, in France.

tion at Onondaga, and was said to give a net profit of forty per cent., at wholesale prices, on the capital every time it was turned over, which could be done several times in the year. E. Heald, Norridgework, Me. (Dec. 4), machine for shearing cloth. Heald & Howard's patent cloth shearing machines were calculated to shear *two* pieces at one operation, and were made in Philadelphia, in 1828, by Benj. F. Pomroy. Christopher Cornelius, Philadelphia (Dec. 28), light-house lamps. Cornelius's Lamps for burning lard were on the solar principle of the Argand lamp, and were of great illuminating power, as shown by tests made under direction of the Treasury Department.

The subject of a revision of the tariff, with a view to the protection of domestic industry, continued to be one of paramount interest to the
1823 whole country. The sixth annual message of President Monroe to Congress, on 3d December last, adverted to the subject in these terms: "Satisfied I am, whatever may be the abstract doctrine in favor of unrestricted commerce (provided all nations would concur in it, and it was not likely to be interrupted by war, which has never occurred and cannot be expected), that there are other strong reasons applicable to our situation, and relations with other countries, which impose on us obligations to cherish our manufactures."

On the 9th January, Mr. Tod, of Pennsylvania, from the Committee on Manufactures, to whom this passage of the executive speech had been referred, along with sundry memorials, reported a bill for the more effectual encouragement and protection of certain domestic manufactures, which was read twice and committed to the Committee of the Whole on the State of the Union. It proposed to add five per cent. to the existing duties on woolen goods, making them thirty per cent. ad valorem, and estimating them at the minimum price of eighty cents per square yard, except blankets, flannels, and worsted or stuff goods, making the duty virtually prohibitory on all coarse woolens, but the most necessary ones. The duty on cottons was left as before, but a minimum price of thirty-five cents per square yard on checked and striped cloths, was proposed in part with the view of preventing foreign manufacturers from defrauding and discrediting American factories, by palming off worthless counterfeits of American cottons. On silk, linen, and hempen goods, the duty was increased to twenty-five per cent., and the minimum valuation of twenty-five cents a yard on the last two was established as on cottons. On Leghorn and silk hats an increase of one third was proposed, making the duty forty per cent., with a minimum price of one dollar. On hammered bar iron an addition of five dollars per ton was proposed, leaving rolled iron as before. On lead, hemp, nails, glass, and many other articles, an increase of duties, and change from ad valorem to specific rates were contemplated by the bill.

It was called up on 29th January, and Mr. Tod, in explaining its principles, stated the amount paid or due to foreign nations for manufactures of wool, cotton, linen, hemp, iron, lead, glass and earthenware imported in the last two years, was $55,453,951 (of which woolens formed over $19,000,000, and and cottons nearly $17,750,000). The annual average was $27,726,975, exclusive of all re-exportations, and exceeded, by above $8,000,000, the yearly expenses of the government and the interest of the national debt.

While such was the state of the import trade, foreign nations refused to reciprocate by taking American flour and provisions on like terms, in part payment. The grain-producing capacities of the country had been increased by new accessions of territory and internal improvements, from four to sixfold, since 1790; but the annual exports of flour, beef, and pork, etc., were only about equal to the average of the five years from 1790–94. As to the oft-repeated objection that duties on foreign manufactures enhanced the price to the consumer, a sufficient answer was furnished in the case of coarse cottons. These were supplied better and cheaper, by our own workmen, than the imported goods; yet these were the only articles legally protected by a prohibitory duty, like those of other nations. These were, moreover, the very articles, the duty on which had constantly been made, by the adversaries of protection, the theme of complaint as an instance of pernicious and oppressive legislation, as in the Salem memorial, and that of the United Agricultural Societies of Virginia.

The bill had not, therefore, been framed solely nor chiefly for the benefit of the manufacturer. If protection now enabled the poor man and the farmer to obtain coarse cottons at a price, considering the quality, one half (he would say one third) that formerly paid for the imported article—as it was notorious he could do—the same effect might be expected to follow the exclusion of other articles, with the further advantage of having constant employment for his family, or a market for his produce if living near a factory. Mr. Holcombe, from New Jersey, who ably supported the bill, remarked that the manufacturing question was very different from what it was ten years before. It was no longer whether we could manufacture any article as profitably as we could purchase it, but whether, by additional protection, we could not sell profitably abroad as well as supply the domestic market.

The bill was strongly opposed by most of the members from the planting districts, and by several from the commercial and manufacturing towns of the north; among whom, were prominent Messrs. Cambreleng, of New York, Tatnall, of Georgia, Gorham, of Massachusetts, Durfee, of Rhode Island, and others, some of whom used very strong language and even threatened or counselled resistance. It was supported with energy by Messrs. Tod, Holcombe, of New Jersey, Mallary, of Vermont, Eustis, of Massachusetts, and many others. Having been warmly debated for several days, Mr. Tod, on 14th February, made a motion, with a view of having the bill brought directly before the House for final action, which produced much excitement; after which it was laid aside for other business and was not again considered during the session.

The revenue laws were amended by an act, approved March 1, decreeing that no goods imported, subject to ad valorem duties, should be admitted to entry, unless the true invoice was produced, excepting goods from a wreck.

By an act of the same date, United States ports were opened to British vessels from colonial ports in America.

On the third March, the act of 15th May, 1820, imposing a tonnage duty on French ships, was repealed, and a discriminating duty of two dollars and seventy-five cents per ton on French goods imported on French bottoms was laid, and after two years was to be diminished one fourth annually.

An act of the same date, to establish a National Foundry on the Western waters, appropriated $5,000 for the employment of engineers and others, under the direction of the President, to examine and report, on the most suitable site, the cost of erection, etc.

The report of the commissioners, made at the next session, in conformity with the last mentioned act, described three localities on the waters of western Pennsylvania, and made the following estimate of the cost of steam power, etc., at Pittsburg, for such an establishment, one of the proposed sites being near that town. The total annual cost for four steam-engines, working three hundred and thirteen days, would amount, for one hundred and sixty bushels coal per diem, at three cents a bushel, for oil, and four packings each, and for the wages of four engineers, at $400 each, to $3,225.60. It also stated that there were employed in Pittsburg at this time fourteen engines, from twenty to eighty horse power each, whose united power exceeded that of the whole extent of the Muskingum river, with a head of eight feet.

With the general revival of business, about this time, the building of Steamboats was resumed at Marietta, by James Whitney and others, who, in the next fifteen years, built about forty boats. The business also received a new impulse in other river towns, among which Pittsburg and Cincinnati took the lead. At Pittsburg, seven boats, measuring together about nine hundred and sixty tons; and at Cincinnati four boats, whose tonnage was seven hundred and ninety, were built in this year; and four others at Steubenville, Marietta, and Louisville.

A stern wheel boat, the Virginia, first ascended the Mississippi by steam, as far as Fort Snelling, in May of this year.

The progress of steam navigation on the Western rivers had already effected a great saving in the time and cost of travel and transportation.

The average time and rates of passage between certain ports were as follows: New Orleans to Cincinnati, a distance of fourteen hundred and eighty miles, sixteen days, fare fifty dollars, down passage eight days, twenty-five dollars; Louisville to Cincinnati, one hundred and thirty miles, thirty hours, six dollars; downward, fifteen hours, four dollars; Cincinnati to Pittsburg, four hundred and forty-nine miles, five days, fifteen dollars; downward, sixty hours, twelve dollars.

During the year, 68,932 tons of merchandise, valued at $3,590,000, exclusive of iron castings, salt, gunpowder, white lead, and other manufactures not estimated, descended the falls of the Ohio at Louisville. It was the growth and manufacture of 1822, and came from all parts of Ohio, except the lake border, from two thirds of Kentucky, one half of Indiana, and small portions of western Pennsylvania and Virginia. The value of produce and manufactures shipped from Cincinnati and its immediate vicinity, in the year ending in April, was estimated at over $1,000,000, and included types and printing material worth $10,000, paper $15,000, cabinet furniture $20,000, chairs $6,000, hats $6,500.[1]

The first Railway Act in America was passed 31st March, by the General Assembly of Pennsylvania, to incorporate a company to erect a railroad from Philadelphia to Columbia, in Lancaster county, under the name of "the President and Directors of the Pennsylvania Railroad Company," the stock of which was limited to six thousand shares, of one hundred dollars each. The act was passed, as the preamble declares, in consequence of the memorial of John Stevens and his associates, which stated that it would facilitate transportation, and that Mr. Stevens had made important improvements in the construction of railways. The road was to be built under his superintendence, but this first link in the great chain of communication with the west was finally completed by the state.[2] During this year also, the Champlain Canal, connecting the

(1) Niles's Register, vol. 25, p. 95.

(2) Mr. Stevens and his partners in the enterprise, having failed to carry out their design, the act was repealed April 7, 1826, by an "act to incorporate the Columbia, Lancaster, and Philadelphia Railroad Company," and on 28th March, 1828, the Legislature authorized its construction, at the expense of the commonwealth. It was soon after located, and begun the next year, and completed from Philadelphia to Columbia, eighty-one and a half miles, in October, 1834. The Danville and Pottsville Railroad Company was also chartered 8th April, 1826.

Hudson river at Albany with Lake Champlain, and the first portion of the great system of internal navigation, between New York and the basins of the St. Lawrence and the great lakes, was completed. The grand Erie Canal was so far completed that ten thousand barrels of flour were embarked at Rochester, for New York and Albany, and with the first boats passed on 8th October.

About thirty-five Manufacturing Companies, with a total capital of over two and a quarter millions of dollars, were incorporated in New York State, under the general act of 1811, since June 1818. The whole number of incorporated manufacturing companies in the state on 1st October, was two hundred and six, whose capital stock amounted to $20,350,500. Among these there were, for manufacturing cotton and woolen goods, sixty-two; for cotton goods only, thirty-six; for woolen only, sixteen; for cotton, woolen, and linen cloths, twelve; for glass, ten; ironmongery, five; coarse salt, three; and some others. Some of these had probably ceased to exist, but there were, in addition, hundreds of private and unincorporated companies.[1] The general law of 1811 was amended, in April of last year, to enable the trustees of such companies to mortgage the property of the corporation for the payment of debts, etc.

Oneida county contained, beside other manufactories equally extensive, a woolen mill, working up 80,000 lbs. of wool, six cotton factories, with 6,356 spindles, and 128 power looms, and a cotton and woolen factory, with seven hundred spindles and twelve power looms.

New Hampshire contained twenty-eight cotton and eighteen woolen factories, twenty-two distilleries, twenty oil mills, one hundred and ninety-three bark mills, three hundred and four tanneries, twelve paper mills, and fifty-four trip hammers. Dover, Exeter, Peterborough, and Pembroke, were the principal manufacturing towns, of which Dover was the most important, on account of the extensive cotton, woolen, and iron works erecting there. The Dover manufactories on the Cocheco, with a capital of half a million dollars, had in full operation twenty-five hundred spindles, and eighty-six looms, making forty-inch sheetings and thirty-inch shirtings to the amount of ten thousand yards per week, and had also a bleachery attached. A rolling and slitting mill, and nail works machine shop, were also in course of erection.

A cotton mill was building in the state, calculated for twenty thousand spindles, probably that of the Nashua Manufacturing Company, incorporated this year, which became the centre of extensive manufactures of cotton, iron, etc., on the Nashua river, the valuable water power of which was overlooked by the founders of Lowell.

A new manufacturing village arose, about this time, upon the south side

(1) Niles's Register, vol. 25., p. 71.

of the Chicopee river, near Springfield, Massachusetts, upon land purchased in the last year by J. and E. Dwight, of Springfield, who, associated with other gentlemen of Springfield and Boston, were incorporated, in January of this year, as the Boston and Springfield Manufacturing Company, with a capital of $500,000. A dam and canal were made, and a cotton mill completed in 1825, to which two other mills and a bleachery were added, in the next two years, by the corporation, which, in 1828, assumed the name of the Chicopee Manufacturing Company, and now has four large mills, one of them containing over twenty thousand spindles and nearly seven hundred looms. It has other extensive manufactures of cotton, paper, arms, swords, hardware, castings, etc., the last mentioned business having been carried on there since 1786.

The rapidly increasing cultivation and consequent low price of Cotton in the United States, the success of the Waltham cotton establishment, which was regarded as the pride of America, and more recently of the new works at Lowell, and the increasing popularity of the domestic cottons, at home and abroad, which had already caused them to be counterfeited by foreign manufacturers, led to extensive preparations in different parts of the country, to prosecute the cotton manufacture, with all the advantages of associated capital and the most improved machinery. Calico printing, on a large scale, was also contemplated in several places, and had already been commenced in two or three. American Calicoes, or chintzes, of seven or eight colors, fast and brilliant as any imported, accompanied by specimens of jaconet muslin, suitable for gentlemen's neck cloths, spun and woven on the Brandywine, were sent early in the year to the editor of the Register at Baltimore. The printed cottons, being made of American cotton, were better than English prints of similar kind, which were usually made of the inferior Bengal or Surat cotton. They could be sold for twenty-five cents a yard. About forty thousand dollars were said to be invested in their manufacture. The Warren factory, at Baltimore, was making large preparations to manufacture calicoes, and finished its first bale in July of the ensuing year. Print works were erecting at Taunton and Lowell, Massachusetts, at Dover, New Hampshire, and were in operation on a smaller scale in Philadelphia.

Rhode Island, in proportion to its population, was more largely engaged in manufactures than any other state. The number of cotton manufactories in that and the adjacent parts of Massachusetts and Connecticut, chiefly owned in Providence, was estimated at one hundred. Among the largest were the establishments of Almy, Brown, and Slaters, at Smithfield, and that of the Blackstone Manufacturing Company, at Mendon, Massachusetts, the former having one hundred and sixteen, and the latter one hundred and fifty power looms, with six thousand spindles each, with bleach and dye houses, and other collateral works, and the Coventry Manufacturing Company, with four thousand spindles and seventy-two power looms, machine shop, saw and grist mill, etc.

Among other associations in the state, were the R. I. Society, for the Encouragement of Domestic Industry, with a fund of $12,000, the interest of which was awarded in premiums at their annual cattle show and exhibition of domestic manufactures, and the "Hamilton Society," in Providence, for the encouragement of manufactures.

The manufacture of Lace was carried on quite largely, at Medway, Massachussetts, by Dean Walker & Co. They employed machines, one of which would make daily fifty yards, five inches wide, which sold for two dollars a yard, or below imported lace of similar quality.[1] Several manufactories of silk, in New York, Boston, and elsewhere, were said to be doing well. Printed Silk handkerchiefs produced by them were highly spoken of. At the fair, in Providence, Rhode Island, Dr. Benjamin Dyer, of that town, wore a complete suit of silk from materials produced and manufactured in his own family.

The manufacture of plain Straw Hats and Bonnets, which had been gradually increasing for twenty years, was nearly suspended at this time by the demand for Leghorn goods and their extensive importation. In Massachusetts, where about three hundred thousand bonnets had been made and sold in a year, at an average price of $2.75 each, giving employment to twenty-five thousand persons, chiefly young females—the price was reduced to $1.25. The hats and bonnets imported during the last year, as stated in Congress, amounted to the value of over $700,000, of which $600,000 worth were from Leghorn and Malta. Many females in New England, New York, and elsewhere, were turning their attention to the manufacture of fine straw or grass bonnets, in imitation of Leghorn, for their own use or for sale, and specimens of these fashionable articles often sold for thirty to forty dollars apiece.

There was a Glass Globe Manufactory in Albany, New York, on a scale which promised to supply the United States with the article.

Lechmere Point, in Cambridge, near Boston, now contained a popu-

(1) This loom was of singular construction, and was made in the United States, from the recollection of a machine seen in England by the constructor. The warp was wound on twenty-six spools, each having a compound motion, and the spools, with twelve hundred and thirty shuttles, traversing side by side within a space of fifty-six inches, were kept in motion by one man, by means of two handles, three treadles, and two thumb pieces, producing a web of plain lace fifty-six inches wide. By drawing single threads, the web was divided into twenty-six pieces, from one and a half to five inches wide, which were afterward finished with ornamental needle work, by female hands.

lation of more than one thousand. Its recent and rapid growth was principally ascribed to its manufacturing and provision establishments. In the glass house, cutting house, and other appendages to the manufactory, one hundred and forty workmen were constantly employed. There were manufactured there 22,400 lbs. of glass vessels per week, many of which were beautifully cut and sent into Boston, and to various other places for sale. The annual amount of sales was $150,000. Besides an immense amount of provisions packed in the place, and large manufactories of candles and soap, there were at the Point an extensive pottery, a brewery, and two large carriage manufactories, and one hundred and fifty men were employed in the vicinity in making Bricks from an inexhaustible bed of clay.[1]

Mr. Jonas Booth, of New York, was said to have in operation the first Steam Printing Press in the United States, from which the first book printed was an abridgement of Murray's English Grammar.[2] The first power press in the country, is also said to have been used during the ensuing year, in the establishment of Shadrach Van Benthuysen, at Albany.[3]

Savings Banks were incorporated this year, at Troy, New York, and Portsmouth, New Hampshire. The savings banks and friendly societies of England and Ireland, had, at this time, $8,500,000 deposited in the government funds on behalf of the industrious classes.

Nicholas Longworth, Esq., of Cincinnati, about this time made his first essay in Wine Making. It was made from the Schuylkill, Muscadel or Vevay grape, which had been previously employed for many years by the Swiss settlers at Vevay, Indiana, in making wine of an inferior quality, which had, at this time, been altogether superseded by imported wines. By an improved method, Mr. Longworth made a wine resembling Madeira of the second quality, but having, soon after, received from Major Adlum, of Washington, some of the Catawba and other native grapes, he has since, by the aid of ample capital and an improvement on the process of Mr. Adlum, succeeded in establishing a permanent and yearly increasing manufacture of wine, chiefly from the Catawba, in the valley of the Ohio. He long since expressed his concurrence in the prediction made to him by Major Adlum, who said: "In introducing this grape to the public notice, I have done my country a greater service than I should have done had I paid the national debt" Mr. Adlum published this year, "A Memoir of the Cultivation of the Vine in America, and the best Mode of making Wines." The cultivation

(1) Holmes's Annals.
(2) Niles's Register, vol. 24, p. 256.
(3) Merchants' Mag., vol. 21, p. 56.

of the vine was still continued in Indiana, and six vine dressers made, during this season, about five thousand five hundred gallons of wine. Mr. Eichelberger, of York, Pa., made also about forty barrels of wine, having ten acres of land covered with Lisbon, white, and other grapes He proposed to extend his vineyard to twenty acres.

The Farmers' Brewery, an extensive establishment built in the last year, at the corner of Tenth and Filbert streets, Philadelphia, by a company of farmers and farm-holders, for the purpose of manufacturing their own barley, and to increase the consumption of malt liquors, commenced operations early this year. There were fourteen or more breweries in the city, including the Farmers', Gauls', and some others still in operation.

The first lease of lands in the Lead region of the upper Mississippi, authorized by the act of March 3, 1807, which reserved such lands to the Government, was issued this year to Colonel James Johnson, of Kentucky, who commenced smelting the ore with a large force the following year, causing an active emigration during the next five or six years. The Government received ten per cent. in lead as rent, which was afterward reduced to six per cent. The amount of lead manufactured in the Galena Lead region, from 1821 to September of this year, was 335,130 pounds, chiefly by Indians; but rapidly increased from this time until 1829, when upward of 31,750,000 pounds had been taken out, and having been overdone, the business again declined.

On the 2d December of this year, the London Mechanics' Institute was established, and formed an epoch in the history of industrial education, as having first awakened public attention to the importance of instruction in elementary and practical science for the mechanic and artizan, and led to the general establishment of Mechanics' Institutes and other schools of art throughout the world. The suggestion of such an institution in London, was first made by the editors of the Mechanics' Magazine, October 11, of this year, and was carried out, primarily through the agency and at the expense of Dr. George Birkbeck, aided by Mr. Brougham and others, to the former of whom belongs the honor of having, twenty-three years before, in connection with the Andersonian Institute, at Glasgow, first made instruction in mechanical philosophy and chemistry accessible to the working classes.[1]

(1) Hole's Prize Essay on Literary, Scientific and Mechanics' Institutions, London, 1853. London Mechanics' Journal, vol. 4, pp. 232–240. The London Institute, though not strictly the first institution of its class, has the merit of having first caused them to be appreciated. The "Mechanics" class of the Andersonian University, established in the year 1800, by Dr. Birkbeck, and, since 1804, conducted by Dr. Andrew Ure, was, about July of this year (1823), organized into the Glasgow Mechanics' Institute, and

In November, 1822, a similar measure for the promotion of the Mechanic Arts was discussed, but finally abandoned, by a number of gentlemen in Philadelphia, but was revived by others during this year. On the 9th December, a meeting was held in the hall of the American Philosophical Society, when both of the previous propositions were considered and so combined as to result in the establishment of an institution, which was incorporated on the 20th March, 1824, as the "Franklin Institute, of the State of Pennsylvania." Its constitution, framed by a committee appointed at the meeting above named, states the objects of the association to be "For the Promotion and Encouragement of Manufactures and the Mechanic and Useful Arts, by the establishment of popular lectures on the sciences connected with them; by the foundation of a library, reading room, and a cabinet of models and minerals; by offering premiums on all subjects deemed worthy of encouragement; by examining all new inventions submitted to them, and by such other means as they may deem expedient."

Much sensation was created in the scientific and manufacturing world, both in England and the United States, by an improved steam engine, in use in the establishment of Mr. Jacob Perkins, in London, for which letters patent were sealed to him in that country, 10th December, 1822, and for other applications of the principle, in November and December of this year. It combined, with great simplicity of construction and economy in the cost, weight of metal, space and quantity of water and fuel required, which adapted it for navigation purposes—a great increase of power. A cylinder two inches in diameter, eighteen inches long, with a stroke of only twelve inches, gave the power of ten horses, at an expense of only eighteen hundred and forty-eight cubic inches of water, and two bushels of coal daily. No new principle was claimed, but a new application of known principles, and these were also made applicable, during this year, to boilers of the old construction, and the heat was at

the "Liverpool Mechanics' Institute and Apprentices' Library" was established the same month, both of which had, however, been preceded by the Edinburg School of Arts (now the Watt Institution), founded in April, 1821, by Mr. Leonard Horner. A mechanical institution had been formed as early as 1817, in London, and others the same year in Glasgow, Liverpool, and Haddington, but none of them attracted general attention until the London Institute was established, from which the history of Mechanics' Institutes is usually dated. It is proper to remark, that previous to the formation of any association of mechanics for mental instruction in Europe, a public-spirited gentleman of New York, favorably known for his scientific and literary publications and as a public lecturer, is said to have resolved to attempt to unite the mechanics of that city into an institution for the promotion of the mechanic arts, by lectures and other judicious means. Between July of this year and May, 1824, no less than thirty-three Mechanics' Institutes were established in Great Britain and elsewhere.

the same time made to return to the boiler, and perform its service the second time. The improvements related chiefly to the boiler or generator, and were also claimed by Mr. James Scott, of Providence, R. I., and by others in New York and Baltimore. It was regarded in England as one of the greatest improvements of the age.

PATENTS.—Lucy Burnap, Merrimac, N. H., Feb. 16, for weaving straw and grass for hats and bonnets; Wm. Knapp, Milford, N. Y., April 5, mode of extracting tannin; D. Roe, C. F. Kellogg, and J. W. Gazley, Cincinnati, Ohio, Oct. 3, mode of procuring tannin by the pyroligneous acid; and Horace H. Hayden, Baltimore, Nov. 26, pyroligneous oil and acid for tanning; Thomas Ewbank, N. Y., May 9, manufacturing and plating lead pipes with tin, for stills, and May 30th, manufacturing tinned sheet lead. This, we believe, was the first application in this country of tin as a lining or coating to metallic tubes and plates. Adam Ramage, Philadelphia, May 19, printing press for proofs; Amos Miner, Elbridge, N. Y., July 9, machinery for making window sash. This machinery had been several years in operation in Onondaga county, and the product was rising in demand. Henry Western, Philadelphia, July 23, improvement in the machine for making pins;[1] Archibald Smith, Rhinebeck, N. Y., Aug. 30, converting measured rectilinear motion into rotary; James Delliba, Watervliet, N. Y., Sept. 26, improvement in crucibles; E. L. Losey, New Brunswick, N. J., Nov. 20, converting iron partially into steel (antedated Dec. 30, 1837). A cutler and surgical instrument maker, of New York, early the next year, testified to having used two samples of New Brunswick patent steel, made by S. Seymour & Co., one of bloomery iron, of Morris & Co., of which he made penknife blades, the other from Swedish iron, of which he made a razor, and found both superior to any English blistered steel. For coarser kinds of edged tools, either was little inferior to cast steel. John Conant, Brandon, Vt., Dec. 13, improvement in stoves for cooking.

President Monroe, in his seventh annual message, delivered to the eighteenth Congress, at its first session on 2d December, 1823, once
1824 more referred to the subject of manufactures, and declared that his views, as stated in his previous message, remained unchanged, and were confirmed by the state of those foreign nations, with which the

(1) Mr. H. Whittemore had in operation, in New York, a small pin machine, of American invention, which he had so improved that it would make, head and point, thirty solid headed pins in a minute, from the simple wire, and required only one man to keep it in motion. In London they were only able, at that time, to make fourteen pins in a minute, and they were less perfectly made.

19

United States held the most intimate political and commercial relations. He recommended "a review of the tariff for the purpose of affording such additional protection to those articles which we are prepared to manufacture, or which are more immediately connected with the defence and independence of the country." In relation to the general progress of the country, he adds, "If we compare the general condition of our Union with its actual state at the close of our revolution, the history of the world furnishes no example of a progress in improvement, in all the important circumstances which constitute the happiness of a nation, which bears any resemblance to it."

Notwithstanding the unexampled progress of the United States in all the essential elements of the public welfare, as adverted to in the executive message, many professed at this time to discover evidences of a general impairment of the great sources of national prosperity, since the peace of 1815, and of the threatened overthrow of some important branches of American industry. The manufactures of the country were believed to have been long undergoing a slow disintegration from the effects of foreign rivalry. The public finances had been so far impaired as twice to compel a resort to loans, during a period of profound peace, in order to meet the ordinary demands upon the Treasury. The agriculture and commerce of the Union were already suffering from causes which had dried up the sources of public and private revenue.

The conviction, which had long been gaining strength, that the industry of the country was inadequately protected against the superior advantages, encouragements, and arts of the foreign manufacturer, by the commercial regulations of the United States, and which had produced several ineffectual attempts to procure a revision of the tariff act of 1816, resulted, during this session, in the passage of a new law, which extended, to several branches of manufacture, a more decided measure of protection than any before enacted.

The measure was pressed upon the attention of Congress by an unusual number of memorials and petitions, from various sections and interests in the country. It was also the subject of numerous remonstrances and memorials, from the commercial classes, and from the cotton and sugar growing interests, which were opposed to any change in the tariff, or to any further legislative encouragement to manufactures. Resolutions of the General Assemblies of Pennsylvania and Ohio were also read in favor of further aid by Congress to domestic manufactures.

The total value of dutiable imports, during the last four years, was $264,962,457, and the duties which accrued thereon amounted to $90,430,612, being an average of thirty-five per cent. The new tariff, enacted this year, raised the average rate of duty to forty and a half per cent., on a total importation, during the next four years, of $301,558,885, on which duties were paid to the amount of $121,637,942.

The new bill, to amend the several acts imposing duties on imports, which was introduced by Mr. Tod, chairman of the Committee on Manufactures, on the 9th January, was taken up in Committee of the Whole on the State of the Union, on the 10th February, and its objects and principles explained by Mr. Tod. The duties proposed were to be laid upon two distinct classes of articles, one embracing silks, linens, cutlery, spices, and others of less importance, which were by no means necessaries, and did not interfere with any home production or manufacture for which the country was prepared. Most of these were charged with the rates recommended by the Secretary of the Treasury, and chiefly for revenue, and to supply the deficiency occasioned by checking the excessive importation of other articles. But the important duties in the bill were for the purpose of protection, and included those upon iron, hemp, lead, glass, wool, and woolen goods.

As to the details of the bill, it was not proposed to change the duty on cottons, except that the minimum valuation was raised from twenty-five to thirty-five cents the square yard, in order to protect fabrics two or three grades finer than was now done. The protection was already effectual on the three lowest grades of cotton, which would never be imported. On cotton bagging, a specific duty of six cents a square yard was proposed, intended to be protective and prohibitory, for the benefit of Kentucky and the Western States, which consumed large amounts of cotton already protected by three cents a pound. This duty was strongly resisted by the members from the cotton states, who regarded it as a tax of over $200,000 per annum upon the cotton growers, who used some four million yards annually, for the benefit of a few hundred workmen in Kentucky. The duty was consequently reduced to three and three-quarter cents a yard. Upon all manufactures of wool, a duty of thirty per centum ad valorem, and, after 30th June, 1825, thirty-three and one third per cent., with minimum valuations of forty and eighty cents respectively, upon milled and unmilled goods, excepting blankets and stuff goods. The rate was, however, reduced to twenty-five cents per square yard, on goods costing less than thirty-three and one third cents per square yard, and after June 30th, 1825, thirty-three and one third per cent. on those costing more than that.

The encouragement of wool growing being an object of the bill, that article was charged with twenty-five per cent. ad valorem when costing over ten cents a pound, to be raised to thirty, forty, and fifty per cent., which was to be the permanent rate after June, 1827. These rates were reduced to twenty, twenty-five, and thirty per cent., which last was to be the duty, after June, 1826, upon all wool costing over ten cents a pound at the place whence imported, and fifteen per cent. on wool costing less than ten cents. On Leghorn, straw, and chip or grass hats and bonnets, and braid or plat, fifty per cent. On hammered iron, $1.12 per one hundred and twelve pounds, reduced to ninety cents or eighteen dollars per ton, rolled iron being left as before. On window glass, from three to four dollars per hundred feet, according to size, and on black glass bottles, from two to three dollars per gross; on hemp two cents a pound, reduced to thirty-five dollars per ton, ad valorem; on pig lead the duty was raised from one to two cents a pound, and on red and white lead from three to four cents; on alum, the duty was increased from one to two dollars and fifty cents a hundredweight; on copperas, from one to two dollars; on oil vitriol and refined sulphate, the duty was changed from seven and a half per cent. to three cents a pound; Epsom salts three cents, Glaubers salts two cents a pound. The increase of duties on these and other chemicals, was followed by a remarkable reduction of the price, within a few years, and by the firm establishment of the manufacture of most of them.

The bill was the subject of a protracted debate, and received the able support of Mr. Clay, Speaker of the House, who, on the 31st March, in reply to Mr. Barbour, of Virginia, and other opponents, spoke between four and five hours, and on the following day concluded a brilliant and elaborate argument in favor of protection. He described the prostrate condition of every branch of domestic industry, and the suffering of every class of the community, tracing the causes in the foreign policy of the Government. He enunciated his belief that the true remedy was to be found in the abandonment of that policy and the adoption of "a genuine American System" of encouragement to domestic industry, in imitation of the prevailing policy of other nations, which had always promoted their prosperity and depressed our own. Mr. Buchanan, of Pennsylvania, spoke on the same side, chiefly in reference to the shipping, tonnage, and iron interests. Their views were ably combated by Mr. Webster, who represented the commercial and shipping interests, and opposed high duties on hemp and iron, and some other provisions of the bill. He quite dissented from the Speaker's opinion, as to the general condition of the country, which he considered one of extraordinary prosperity, with the exception of diminished prices and profits, and some pecuniary embarrassments, in the payment of debts contracted when prices were high, attributable to other causes than a diminution of exports. Messrs. Randolph, of Virginia, McDuffie, Tucker, and Hamilton, of South Carolina, and others from the cotton states, denounced the whole system of protection, and argued that foreign nations would no longer take their supplies of cotton if we did not take their manufactures. It was also opposed by Mr. Foote, of Connecticut, and others, and well defended by Mr. Holcombe, of New Jersey, Mallory, of Connecticut, and others who spoke on the same side. The Committee of Agriculture reported in favor of the bill, which, with some amendments, passed the House on the 16th April, by a vote of one hundred and seven to one hundred and two. Having been considerably modified in the Senate, the House, after a Committee of Conference, rather than lose the bill altogether, concurred in most of the amendments and reductions, and it finally passed on 19th May, by a vote of one hundred and twenty-five to sixty-six, and was approved on the 22d.

An act was also approved, January 7th, suspending the discriminating duties of tonnage and import, so far as they related to the vessels, produce, or manufactures of the Netherlands, Prussia, Hanseatic cities, Norway, Sardinia, and Russia, so long as United States vessels were exempt from like discriminations in their ports; and authorizing the President to proclaim reciprocal exemption from such duties, on evidence that any foreign nation had abolished its discriminating duties on goods and vessels of the United States.

An act of May 26, allowed to vessels in the cod fishery, lost or wrecked on their return to the United States, the same bounty as if they had returned to port.

The Franklin Institute, of Pennsylvania, incorporated March 30th, commenced, on 28th April, the first course of instruction in mechanical science in the United States, by a lecture delivered at the Philadelphia Academy, on north Fourth street. The first course was attended by twenty-seven junior students, the second by one hundred and twenty-six, and the third by one hundred and eighty. On the 2d June, a letter from the Secretary was read to the members of the London Mechanics' Institute, announcing its formation, with objects kindred to those of the London Institution. Soon after its formation, "a regular system of lectures was adopted, four professorships created, namely, of Natural Philosophy, Chemistry and Mineralogy, Architecture and Mechanics. One evening in each week was set apart for lectures on miscellaneous subjects. A library, a mineralogical collection, a museum, and a cabinet of models were commenced. An exhibition of manufactures was held, at which premiums were awarded." The first annual exhibition of the products of domestic industry, took place on the 18th and two following days in October, when gold, silver, and bronze medals were adjudged for the best articles, and proved serviceable by exciting competition.

The Rensselaer Institute was this year established and endowed at Troy, New York, by Hon. Stephen Van Rensselaer, for the instruction of young men in the application of mathematical science to civil engineering, and in natural science.

In July, a school was established, at Baltimore, for the instruction of poor girls in the various branches of straw plaiting, from the simple plait to the finished bonnet. It was supported by contributions from a few individuals, and was known as the Baltimore Plaiting School, but was not self-sustaining at the end of the first year.

The amount of manufacturing capital authorized and incorporated by state laws, since 1820, was, in New Hampshire, $5,830,000; in Massachusetts, $6,840,000; in Connecticut, $1,300,000; and in New York, $797,000, which, added to the amount authorized and employed in seven states, in 1820, made a total of $70,656,500.[1]

The New Jersey Bleaching, Printing, and Dyeing Company, at Belleville, nine miles from New York, was incorporated in December, with a capital of $150,000, and erected one of the largest and most complete manufacturing edifices in the United States. The printed calicoes ranked with those of the Taunton and Chelmsford factories. Within ten years the calico print works of Andrew Gray, the silk printing establishment of Duncan & Cunningham, a brass rolling mill and button factory, two copper foundries and rolling mills, a britannia metal factory, lamp factory, and large grist mill, in the place, produced articles valued at two millions of dollars per annum.

The Merrimac Manufacturing Company was at this time making about twenty-five hundred yards of printed cottons daily. Calicoes were this year first made in the Warren factory, at Baltimore.

Flannel was woven by water power, in Massachusetts, and specimens exhibited at the fair, in Brighton, in November, gave general satisfaction. Within forty miles of Boston, about fifteen thousand pieces of flannel, of forty-six yards each, were made in the last year, and new mills were erecting, which, with the enlargement of old ones, would make thirty thousand pieces this year. There were factories of the same article in New York and Connecticut.

Philadelphia had, at this date, upward of thirty cotton mills, some of them quite extensive. They averaged fourteen hundred spindles each, and together employed nearly five thousand looms and three thousand persons. There were in the city fifteen breweries, and umbrellas were manufactured there to the value of $400,000 annually.

In the borough of Reading, Pennsylvania, about six thousand pounds of wool were wrought up into fifteen thousand pair of fine wool hats, giving employment to five hundred persons.

(1) Report of Secretary of State in obedience to Resolution of Senate of March 1, 1823.

On the 27th of January, a charter was granted by the State of Virginia to the Chesapeake and Ohio Canal Company—subject to the approval of Congress, and of the States of Maryland and Pennsylvania, which was obtained the next year—for the construction of a canal from tide water above Georgetown, D. C., on the Potomac, to Pittsburg, a distance of three hundred and forty-one miles. The capital stock was six millions of dollars, with power to augment it, which it beeame necessary to do.

The Legislature of New Jersey also, on the 31st December, granted acts of incorporation to companies authorized to construct the Delaware and Raritan canal, and the Morris canal, the former suggested in Mr. Gallatin's Report, in 1808, and the latter surveyed and leveled, in conformity with an act of the state, passed in November, 1822. The last of these important works of internal improvement opened up communication between the Delaware river at Phillipsburg, opposite Easton, and the Passaic at Newark, over mountains, in the district of Warren, Morris, and Essex counties, nine hundred feet above sea-level, which were overcome by locks and inclined planes. It gave access to the anthracite mines of Pennsylvania, and a cheap outlet for the iron of that region, which at one time contained eighty-one forges and twelve furnaces, of which thirty of the former and nine of the latter had, at this time, gone to decay, in part from the scarcity of fuel and the increasing cost of transportation.

The steamboat "Erie Canal" arrived in December, at Genesee Landing, having passed through the feeder at Rochester. She was the first boat upon that river, and was supposed to have shown the practicability of navigating canals by steam, without injuring them.

Nine daily newspaper offices in New York city were estimated to issue 85,600 newspapers every week, exclusive of eight or ten weekly papers, of which the circulation was unknown. An official return to the Postmaster General, stated the whole number of newspapers published in the United States at one hundred and ten, of which eighteen were issued in Philadelphia, eleven of them being dailies.

The first Book Trade Sale in Philadelphia was held this year, according to the suggestion and plan of Mr. Henry C. Carey. The auctioneer was Moses Thomas, by whom these sales are still conducted semi-annually, under the name of Moses Thomas & Sons, having, during a part of the intermediate time, been under the management of Cowperthwait & Lord, Lord & Carlisle, and George W. Lord & Son. The city contained, at this date, fifty-five printing offices, with one hundred and twelve presses, supporting about one hundred and fifty workmen.

Land and water power were this year purchased, in Greene county,

New York, by Zadoc Pratt, who established at the village, since called Prattsville, on Schoharie creek, a mammoth tannery, for the manufacture of hemlock-tanned leather—the forest, on either hand, to the very tops of the mountains, being covered with a dense growth of hemlock, adapted to his purpose. His tannery was five hundred feet long, containing over three hundred vats, requiring a consumption annually of fifteen hundred cords of wood, and six thousand cords of hemlock bark in the manufacture of six thousand sides of sole leather, which he annually sent to market, or more than a million sides in twenty years. He employed a capital of over $250,000, it is said, without a single litigated lawsuit, or the loss of one dollar in bad debts, or having a single hide stolen. To his enterprise and public spirit the village of Prattsville owes its growth, and the Catskill region much of its prominence as the principal leather producing district of the United States. The first hemlock-tanned leather in England was sent, in 1842, from the Prattsville tannery.[1]

An improvement in tanning was introduced this year, and patented the next, by Mr. Joseph Giles, of Guilford, or Brattleborough, Vermont, by the use of a liquid extract, or essence of oak and hemlock bark, so concentrated as to tan calf skins in forty-eight hours, one hogshead containing the tannin of four cords of bark. He began the erection of extensive works for the manufacture of the article. Tanneries about this time began to be provided with roofs, instead of being open as formerly.

The sugar crop of Louisiana was estimated at forty thousand hogsheads.

The manufacture of Isinglass, from the swords of hake fish, for the use of cotton manufacturers, was commenced at Gloucester (now Rockport), on Cape Cod, in Essex county, Massachusetts, which a few years later was the only place in the United States where it was made.

In Albany, New York, were five extensive breweries; that of Fiddler & Taylor, supposed to be the largest in the United States, was capable of manufacturing two hundred and fifty barrels of beer in a day.

The Company owning the large manufacturing establishment called

(1) This eminent manufacturer, who probably tanned more sole leather than any man in the world, was himself the son of a tanner, and rose from the humble position of a journeyman, by the force of his own energy and character, to places of honor, influence, and public trust. He was not less distinguished for uprightness, benevolence, and public usefulness than for perseverance, intelligence, and success in business. In Congress, to which he was elected in 1836, he proposed many important measures, among which were the introductión, through the United States consuls and national vessels, of foreign seeds and plants for general distribution by the Patent Office, and the publication and engraving of all the important patented inventions for circulation throughout the country, and the establishment of a Bureau of Statistics.

Ramapo mills, in Rockland county, New York, was incorporated this year, with a capital of $400,000. The Company owned four thousand acres of land, and the village contained, in 1833, rolling and slitting mills, cut nail factory, large cotton mill, grist and saw mills, etc., the first of which had been many years in operation.

The Glenham Woolen Manufacturing Company, composed of Messrs. P. H. Schenck, G. E. and S. S. Howland, John Jacob Astor, Philip Howe, and others, was incorporated in the State of New York. The factory was erected, during the last year, by Mr. Schenck, upon the Matteawan, or Fishkill creek, in Dutchess county, two miles above the extensive Matteawan Cotton Factory of the Messrs. Schenck and others, built in 1814. It manufactured superfine blue and black broadcloths, but sunk considerable money during the next three years. The average value of its manufactures, during twenty years, was $100,000. The Messrs. Schenck were also interested in an extensive flour mill, foundry, and machine shop at this place.

The Tufts Manufacturing Company, at Dudley, and the Ware Manufacturing Company, at Ware, Massachusetts, were incorporated, and commenced operations about this time. The Boston and Ipswich Lace Factory was this year incorporated, with a capital of about $150,000, for the manufacture of lace by machinery, the business having been carried on there by hand for nearly half a century.

Patents.—Gilbert Brewster, Norwich, Conn., Feb. 27, patented an improvement in the wool spinning wheel, and March 13, received three patents, viz.: for a spinning machine and method of receiving rolls from the machine; for an improvement on spinning wool, and for a spindle for throstle spinning. These, and later improvements in cotton and wool spinning machines, by Mr. Brewster, came into quite extensive use, and a few years later were manufactured by him to a large extent at Poughkeepsie, N. Y. George Danforth, Morton, Mass., Sept. 2, counter twisting spinning speeder. The Danforth throstle frame was an important improvement upon the ordinary throstle, which had superseded the water frame. It dispensed with a flyer, and produced yarn less wiry and more economically from certain kinds of goods, than the common throstle. It was patented in England, about 1830, by John Hutchin, Esq., of Liverpool, and gave rise to numerous later inventions for the improvement of the original throstle.[1] Some fourteen or more patents were this year granted for improvements in spinning wheels, and other cotton and wool spinning machinery. Joseph P. Rossiter, Selina, N. Y., March 2, improvement in making fine and coarse salt; and Peter

(1) Ures' Cotton Manufacture.

Cooper, New York, Dec. 23, mode of manufacturing salt; Samuel Brown, London, England, March 2, gas engines, and Maximin Isnard, New York, Dec. 11, improvement in gas engines; Jeremiah Dewey, Chelsea, Vt., April 2, improvement in the spring lancet, and Thomas R. Williams, Newport, R. I., July 16, retreating spring lancet; John R. Averill, Manchester, N. Y., May 27, cast iron steam boilers. Numerous improvements in the steam engine and boiler were patented this year. John Stevens, Hoboken, N. J., June 8 and Oct. 23, improvements in railways; the same, June 8, rendering rapids and shallow rivers navigable; John Brown, Providence, R. I., June 28, improvement in making razors; Henry and Ezra Hoopes, Wilmington, Del., July 26, improvement in revolving hay rakes; Moses Pennock, Kennett Square, Pa., Nov. 23, improvement in revolving horse hay rakes; John A. Wadsworth, Newport, R. I., July 3, horse scythe; David Henderson, Jersey City, N. J., Sept. 17, improvement in lithography.

On the 3d of January of this year, Eli Whitney, the inventor of the saw gin, and one of the most eminent mechanics of his age, died,
1825 at the age of fifty-nine. He had lived to see the cotton crop of the United States increased, from about five millions of pounds to two hundred and fifteen millions, and the exports of the article augmented from less than half a million pounds to one hundred and forty-two and a quarter millions of pounds, the result in no small degree of the benefits conferred upon the planter by his invention.

In the early part of this year considerable speculation was indulged in the exportation of cotton, which, during the year, reached the large amount of 563,129 bales, 176,500,000 pounds, valued at $36,846,649, being more than thirty-two millions of pounds in excess of the total importations from all countries into Great Britain. The average price was in consequence advanced in the United States from fifteen in the last year to twenty-one cents in the present, the extreme prices of Uplands in Charleston being thirteen and a half to thirty-two cents per pound. Nothwithstanding an advance in the price in England, from about eight and a half to eleven and a half pence, the excessive speculation involved many shippers in ultimate loss, the average price having declined to eleven cents in the United States, and to nine and a half pence in England during the next year. The amount grown this year in the United States was two hundred and fifty-five millions of pounds. Some apprehension was felt at the increased importation of Egyptian cotton in England, which, commencing in 1823 with 5,623 bales, reached this year to 111,023 bales, but immediately fell off again as rapidly.

The caterpillar or cotton moth, which had only occasionally appeared since 1804, renewed its visits in South Carolina with devastating effects, and during several subsequent years continued with some intermission to lay waste the cotton fields.

The number of spindles employed in cotton factories in the United States, at this time, was 800,000, and the domestic consumption of raw cotton was about 100,000 bales.

Several important improvements were made in cotton machinery in England this year, among which the most important were the mule spinner, patented by Mr. Roberts, of Manchester, M. De Jong's self-acting mule, and the tube frame, introduced from America by J. C. Dyer, who also took another patent for wire cards, and for other objects. In and around Glasgow, within a circuit of two miles, steam engines of eight hundred and ninety-three horse power were employed in spinning cotton, and the number of factories in the neighborhood of Manchester was one hundred and four; at Preston, forty; Stockport, forty-seven, and Staley Bridge, twenty-five.

At Columbiaville, near Hudson City, N. Y., were three cotton factories, employing two hundred and fifty persons. Two of them made about 340,000 yards of cotton shirtings yearly, worth thirteen cents a yard, and a new mill on the south side of the creek was calculated to produce 360,000 yards of a finer fabric, worth twenty-four cents a yard. The city of Hudson was the third town in the state in regard to manufactures, and in 1822 had eight factories, employing five hundred hands, and working 364,300 pounds of wool into 711,200 yards of cloth.

Cutts, or Factory island, at the Falls of the Saco river, in Maine, was this year purchased by a company, principally from Boston, for the purpose of erecting an extensive cotton factory. The whole cost to the company was $110,000, to which was added $10,000, for a considerable part of the privileges on the opposite side of the river, purchased at the same time. During the next year a canal was cut from the head of the falls to the mill site, and a factory erected two hundred and ten feet long by forty-seven wide, seven stories high. It was the largest factory ever attempted in America, and was calculated to operate twelve thousand spindles and three hundred looms. The machinery was completed in 1830, at a cost of $200,000, but the whole establishment was the same year burned to the ground, with a loss to the company of all the stock. Another company was formed, and the mill was rebuilt.

The Merrimac Manufacturing Company, at Lowell, whose mills, since the death of Mr. Ezra Worthen, in the last year, were superintended by Warren Colburn, and their print works by Allan Pollock, who was succeeded next year by John D. Prince, of Manchester, England, increased their capital to $1,200,000, built three additional mills, and made their first dividend of one hundred dollars per share. A canal company was organized by the stockholders, to which was transferred all the surplus water power, and the price for a mill power, with a suitable quantity of land, and the privilege of drawing twenty-five cubic feet of water per second, on a fall of thirty feet, equal to about sixty horse power, was fixed at $14,336, of which $5,000 was to remain, subject to an annual rent of $300. The average price of its Prints, at this time, was 25.07 cents a yard. The first sale was made this year to the Hamilton Manufacturing Company, the second of the large corporators of Lowell, which was chartered this year with a capital of $600,000, afterward increased to $1,200,000. Mr. Samuel Batchelder, of New Ipswich, now Treasurer of the York Manufacturing Company, at Saco, was appointed superintendent, and under his skillful management the power loom was first applied to the weaving of twilled and fancy goods, with great success. Cotton Drills, an American fabric, which soon became one of much value in the export trade, were first made in this establishment. The company established print works in 1828, under Mr. William Spencer, who is still the superintendent.

The Middlesex Mechanics' Association of Lowell was incorporated this year, and now owns a hall, with a library of five thousand volumes, a cabinet of natural history, and paintings of Washington, Webster, Kirk Boot, P. T. Jackson, Abbott Lawrence, N. Appleton, and John A. Lowell.

The Pontoosuc Manufacturing Company, of Pittsfield, Massachusetts, was chartered, and built a mill this year for the manufacture of all wool and cotton warp broadcloths, and was long celebrated for the manufacture of a superior quality of drab cloth for carriage linings, which was distinguished for its purity of color and beauty of finish. The first broadcloth power loom in Berkshire county was set up this year.

Agreeably to a proposition made at a meeting of manufacturers in Philadelphia, during the last year, an exhibition of domestic manufactures was held in Washington in February of this year, for which purpose Mr. Little, superintendent of the Capitol, tendered the use of the Rotunda. Among the articles exhibited were cloths from the factory of Mr. Wells, Steubenville, Ohio, at from three to twelve dollars a yard; blankets, much admired for substance and fleecy whiteness, at twelve to fifteen dollars per pair, by Mr. E. Patterson, of the District of Columbia; fine flannels by Mr. Van Croft, on the Brandywine; specimens of flannel and grass cloth from New Harmony, Ind.; excellent lace bobbinet and thread from Dean, Walker & Co., Medway, Mass.; coach bindings by Catharine Gattie, of Baltimore; improved hats by Mr. Hamelin, of Baltimore, made of Russia cotton duck, and varnished, which were much approved of by the Department for Seamen; machine cards by Mr. McCoy, of Baltimore; improved saddles by Mr. Prettyman, of Alexandria; oil cloth by Mr. Macauley, of Philadelphia, in great variety of patterns, and some of the finest quality for taste and design, and beauty of execution; stair carpets by Mr. Wilson, of Baltimore; shovels and spades by Mr. Harvie, of Richmond, Va., of the finest workmanship and material, as were also the axe heads from Baltimore, by Mr. Kinsey.

Pittsburg contained at this time seven steam rolling mills in active operation, making bar and sheet iron, nails, etc., and one of them in addition axes, scythes, sickles, shovels, etc. There were also eight air foundries and a cupola furnace, making stoves, grates, hollow ware, sad irons, shafts and wheels for steam machinery, common wagon boxes, plough castings, and other articles, from a quarter pound weight to four tons. McClung's "Pittsburg foundry" had a mill for boring cylinders, turning rolls and shafts, grinding sad irons, etc. Metal castings averaged from sixty-five to seventy dollars per ton. There were also six steam engine factories, some of which built six engines during the season, and Mark Stackhouse constructed one of one hundred horse power for the Phœnix Iron Works, near Philadelphia. Eichbaum's wire factory had been recently put in operation again, with an engine of ten horse power. There were five blast furnaces north of the Allegheny river, supplying metal to Pittsburg, viz.: two in Butler county, one in Armstrong, one in Venango, and one in Crawford, besides several in Fayette, Westmoreland and Beaver counties, and a new one just erected by J. W. Biddle, on a large scale, on the Kiskimenitas, in Armstrong county. There were nine paper mills in Western Pennsylvania, four of them owned in Pittsburg, besides two in Jefferson county, Ohio; six of them contained two vats each, and one three vats, with water power. Three others were worked by steam, one having three vats and a twenty horse power engine, the others four and six vats, respectively, with engines of thirty horse power. The product of all the mills was estimated at $150,000, and the rags consumed, at $58,000 per annum. Seven glass works, including that established by Mr. Gallatin, at Geneva, made 27,000 boxes of glass annually, valued at $135,000, in addition to $30,000 worth of white and flint glass, and about $100,000 worth of the product was probably exported. Pittsburg glass undersold the imported in Eastern cities, and received the premium of the Franklin Institute in the last year, over numerous specimens. Within the last three years twenty-one steamboats, whose tonnage was 3,720 tons, were built at or near Pittsburg, and one was building at Brownsville to draw only two and a half or three feet of water, with her engine in. At Walker's boat yard, at Elizabethtown, a keel boat was launched every month during the past year, worth, on an average, $275 each.[1] The manufactures of Pittsburg, during this year, were estimated at $2,500,000. In consequence of its profitable manufactures, Pittsburg experienced little of the pecuniary distress which this year visited many portions of the country.

The Harmony Society, under Mr. George Rapp, having returned to Pennsylvania from Indiana, commenced operations at Economy, eighteen miles below Pittsburg, in Beaver county, where they built a large town—an elegant church, a large cotton and woolen factory, store, tavern, large steam mill, a brewery, distillery, tanyard, and other workshops. Their factories and workshops were warmed by means of pipes connected with the steam engine, and in other respects the Society were ready to adopt the latest improvements. They purchased annually from sixty to seventy thousand dollars' worth of wool, and twenty to thirty thousand dollars' worth of other articles for manufacture and consumption, and three years after commenced the culture and manufacture of silk.

The completion of the Erie canal opening internal communication between the waters of Lake Erie, at Buffalo, and the Atlantic Ocean, was celebrated on the 26th October, at Albany. Cannon were fired along the whole line, and a flotilla of boats conveyed Governor Clinton and the Commissioners over the route to New York, where the first boat arrived, November 4th. Its cost was about eight millions of dollars.

The licensed tonnage of all the lakes above the Falls of Niagara, consisted of three steamers of 772 tons, and fifty-four sailing craft of 1677 tons, making an aggregate of steam and sailing tonnage entering the ports of Buffalo of only 2,449. It was increased in the next five years to 16,300 tons, or 113 per cent. In the United States nine hundred and ninety-four vessels, including thirty-five steamers, were built in the year, whose tonnage was 114,997.

The Buffalo Steam Engine Works, or furnace, was incorporated for the manufacture of steam engines, mill gear, and other castings.

A small cupola furnace, the first in the city, and said also to have been the first in the state, was erected by Mr. William A. Wheeler, at Worcester, Massachusetts, where the manufacture of tools and machinery has since become extensive. His principal business was machine castings, and ten years after he is said to have made the first hot air furnaces, for warming houses, in New England.[2]

(1) Portfolio for September, 1825.

(2) The first heating of houses by flues, from anthracite furnaces, is stated by Professor Walter R. Johnson, in his American edition of Knapp's Chemical Technology, (vol. 2, p. 58), to have been made, as far as he knows, in his own family, during the last or present year. A large house was heated by means of a furnace in the cellar, surrounded by an air chamber of brick-

The manufacture of paper, by the Fourdrinier machinery, commenced about this time at Springfield, Massachusetts. One of the mills of J. & J. Gilpin, in Delaware, where machinery was first employed in this country, was this year destroyed by fire. The paper manufactory of Messrs. D. & J. Ames, at Springfield, was said to be the most extensive at this time in the United States, employing twelve engines, and more than one hundred females, besides the usual number of male hands.

A Geological reconnoisance of the State of North Carolina, made during the last year by Professor Olmsted, directed public attention to the gold-bearing region of the state, which he estimated to embrace an area of over one thousand acres. All the gold obtained in the state up to this time was from washings, at three principal localities. But gold having about this time been found in place by M. Barringer, of Montgomery county, attention was thenceforward directed from the "deposit mines" to the "vein mines." The first native gold from Anson county was this year coined at the mint, and valuable quartz veins were soon after found in Mechlenberg county.[1]

Anthracite coal was this year sent to market from the Lehigh mines in Pennsylvania, to the amount of 28,396 tons, and 6,500 tons were sent also from the Schuylkill region, being the result of the first mining operations in the latter place. The whole quantity from both sections was 25,355 tons in excess of the last year's product.

The first successful attempt to generate steam, with anthracite fuel, was made this year at the Phœnixville Iron works, by Messrs. Jonah and G. Thompson, of Philadelphia, who completed in January a steam engine for their Nail works on French creek, in which anthracite was employed.

Sewing silk and raw silk were produced this year in Windham county, Connecticut, to the value of $54,000, being double the quantity produced by the county in 1810. Sewing silk formed a part of the circulating medium, and was readily exchanged at the stores for other articles, the buyer giving the balance in silver when the account was in favor of the seller. The only machines used were the common domestic small and large wheels. Three fourths of the families in Mansfield were engaged in raising silk, making annually from five to ten, twenty, and fifty pounds in a family, and some as much as one hundred pounds in a season. It was thought that three or four tons were made annually

work, whence the gaseous products of the combustion were carried through the building, passing through cylindrical drums on the first and third floors, and out at the top. This mode of warming buildings doubtless contributed to the general use of anthracite fuel in the Atlantic states.

(1) Whitney's Metallic Wealth of the United States.

in the town and vicinity. The increased attention given to the business in that place directed interest in other parts of the country to the subject, and Congress, on the 29th December, adopted the following resolutions, introduced by Mr. Miner, of Pennsylvania.

"*Resolved,* That the Committee on Agriculture be instructed to in quire whether the cultivation of the mulberry tree, and the breeding of silk worms for the purpose of producing silk, be a subject worthy of legislative attention; and should they think it to be so, that they obtain such information as may be in their power respecting the kind of mulberry tree most preferred, the best soil, climate and mode of cultivation, the probable value of the culture, taking into view the capital employed, the labor and the product, together with such facts and opinions as they may think useful and proper.

"*Resolved,* That the same Committee inquire whether any legislative provisions are necessary to promote the production of silk."

The report was made in May following.

PATENTS.—E. Daggett, and T. Kensett, New York, Jan. 19, for preserving animal substances; T. Rowell, Hartford, Vt., Feb. 10, pointing, splitting, and waxing wooden pegs; S. H. Weed, Poughkeepsie, N. Y., Feb. 28, making brushes and brooms of grasses; Lemuel W. Wright, Manchester, England, March 12, improvement in machine for making pins. This machine for making solid-headed pins was patented in England, in May, 1824, by Mr. Wright, a native of New Hampshire, who, in 1826, had a manufactory in operation at Lambeth, which proved ruinous to himself and partner. The same machinery was set up in 1832 or '33, at Stroud, in Gloucestershire, by his former partner, and the first solid-headed pins in the English market were made with it. It was however defective in forming the point.[1] Isaac Macauley, Philadelphia, April 4, improvement in making oil cloth—Mr. Macauley had carried on the manufacture for many years in Philadelphia, and was probably the first in this country—Joseph B. Nones, Philadelphia, April 28, making yellow and buff nankeen; Joseph Grant, Providence, April 28, setting up hat bodies (first patented, 1821). A large steam factory for making hat bodies, under this patent, was carried on in Pittsburg in 1837, by D. P. Ingersoll. John Giles, Guilford, Vt., April 11, improvement in Desmond's mode of obtaining tannin; Daniel Stansbury, Belleville, N. J., April 15, furnaces for fossil coal; Oliver Woodruff, New York, Nov. 7, and John L. Sullivan, New York, Nov. 26, furnaces for anthracite; Eli Terry, Plymouth, Conn., May 18 and Sept. 9, wooden-wheeled thirty-hour clocks; Josiah Durden, Washington, Ala., June 25, water power cotton press; Lewis Lyssard, Halifax, N. C.,

(1) Newton's London Journal, vol. 9. Ure's Dictionary.

Sept. 28, machine for packing cotton; J. N. Gordon, Plymouth, N. C., Oct. 8, improvement in machine for pressing cotton; J. P. Bakewell, Pittsburg, Pa., Sept. 9, improvement in making glass furniture knobs.

Considerable interest was about this time excited in Europe by the experiments of Jacob Perkins, with steam artillery, exhibited for several years at the Adelaide Gallery, in London. In his exhibitions before the Duke of Wellington and eminent engineers, iron targets were shattered to atoms at thirty-five yards, and afterward the balls were shot through eleven one-inch planks of the hardest deal, placed in a line at a distance from each other, and balls were discharged at the rate of one thousand per minute.[1] Experiments were also made at Greenwich, before Prince Polignac and French engineers, but the engineers of both nations regarded the steam gun as practically useless, although displaying extraordinary ingenuity in the inventor.

With the commencement of this year, the Franklin Institute, in Philadelphia, which already numbered about one thousand members, issued
1826 the first number of the Franklin Journal, now the oldest periodical in the United States devoted to the mechanical and manufacturing arts, and containing for many years the only record of American Patents as they were issued. It was published in monthly numbers at five dollars a year, and has continued to the present time, a valuable and leading repository of original and selected papers, theoretical and practical, in mechanics and the useful arts, being held in deserved esteem as well in foreign countries as in the United States. The several series of the work up to the close of 1860, comprise about seventy volumes of well digested matter relating to the progress of mechanical science in Europe and America.

The Maryland Institute, formed during the last year at Baltimore, through the exertions of J. H. B. Latrobe and others, for the benefit of the mechanical and laboring classes, was incorporated in the course of the present year, by the Legislature of Maryland. It continued in successful operation until 1835, when the library, apparatus, and other property, were destroyed by the burning of the Athenæum building, and the Society disbanded. In 1848 the new society was organized, and the present Institute was incorporated in 1850.

On the 3d March, the New England Society, for the Promotion of

(1) "Five hundred balls per minute, shot,
Our foes in fight must kick the beam;
Let Perkins only boil his pot,
And he'll destroy them all by steam."
"Steam, a Poem," *in the London Mirror, February*, 1825.

Manufactures and the Mechanic Arts, organized in the last year, by citizens of Boston, who were desirous to promote American Industry and talent wherever found, received a charter from the General Assembly of Massachusetts. It was empowered to hold public exhibitions of the products of American industry, and to award premiums for new and useful inventions, and for the best specimens of the skill and ingenuity of manufacturers and mechanics. All goods sold under its direction at the regular semi-annual sales, which were held in the Spring and Fall, were, by the act of incorporation, exempted from the auction duty, and an ordinance of the City Council granted the use of the halls over the Faneuil Hall Market, for the Society's fairs, free of expense. The first public sale was commenced on 12th September, and the amount received from the first five sales was nearly two millions of dollars. An exhibition was also held in October of this year, when fifteen medals were awarded, and twenty the next. A standing committee awarded premiums for new inventions, machinery, and experiments in chemistry and natural philosophy, tending to advance improvements in the arts. The common premium was an elegant silver medal, struck from highly finished dies, made by Mr. Gobrecht, an eminent artist of Philadelphia. The payment of two dollars admitted to annual, and twenty-five dollars to life membership. The Society exerted a favorable influence upon the progress of useful arts in their vicinity.[1]

In December, an association called the "Pennsylvania Society, for the Promotion of Manufactures and the Mechanic Arts, was formed at Philadelphia," a principal object being the spread of information on the subject of legislative protection.

A paper read before the Pennsylvania Society for the Promotion of Internal Improvement, January 10th, stated that there were thirty-five salt works upon the Connemaugh and Kiskiminetas, three upon the Alleghany, and many others in course of preparation upon these waters, one of them expected to yield fifteen hundred bushels daily. The wells were sunk from four to five hundred feet deep. The increase of the manufacture had been rapid beyond example, and improved transportation would enable the manufacturers to supply the middle and eastern parts of the state, with salt cheaper than the foreign. A steady market, it was believed, would insure 750,000 bushels per annum, or with the new well 1,200,000 bushels. The quality of the Pennsylvania salt was excellent, and daily improving. Its price was twenty to twenty-five cents per bushel at the works, and on the river had been sold as low as twelve and-a-half cents. Its price in the middle counties was one dollar

(1) Bowen's Picture of Boston, p. 60.

to one dollar twenty-five, and the average quantity used there was estimated at half a bushel for each person. If a canal were cut, the salt makers would contract to deliver the best salt at forty cents a bushel in Harrisburg.

The New York Salines produced, in the last year, only 736,632 bushels, against 820,926 in 1825, but in the following year yielded 1,104,542.

The quantity of Salt made in the United States during the year, as stated in documents laid before the United States Senate, relative to the repeal of the duties, amounted to 4,113,000. The quantity imported for the year, ending 30th September, was 4,564,720, whereof 30,680 bushels were reshipped. The duties collected on the importation were $912,944. The price of Turks Island salt, in New York, was forty-nine to fifty cents. It cost in the British West Indies about eleven cents a bushel.

Huntingdon county, in Pennsylvania, contained at this time eight furnaces and ten forges, one paper mill, three powder mills, one hemp mill, one slitting and rolling mill, and one nail factory, in addition to grist and saw mills, distilleries, etc., etc. The rolling mill and nail works belonged to the extensive Tyrone works of Gloninger, Anshultz & Co.

Mr. Marcus Bull, on the 7th April, read before the American Philosophical Society, a memoir on Fuel, containing the result of his careful analysis and experiments upon the relative heating power, and other properties of different species of American woods. The practical value of his researches, extending altogether to forty-six different species, has been highly appreciated both in Europe and America.

In obedience to the resolution of the House of December 29th, Mr. Van Rensselaer, from the Committee on Agriculture, on the 2d May, presented a report on the expediency of encouraging, by legislative measures, the planting of mulberry trees, and the breeding of silk worms for the production of Silk. The committee stated that mulberry trees were indigenous in the United States, and that silk could be raised with facility. Measures had been recently adopted at Savannah to renew the culture, which had been suspended by the Revolution. Considerable sewing silk was at this time made in Kentucky, and the business was prosperous in Connecticut. The total value of silks imported in the five years, from 1821 to 1825, inclusive, was $35,156,494, of which $7,968,011, was exported. The exportation of breadstuffs, on the other hand, had fallen off from $20,374,000, in 1817, to $5,417,997, in 1825, in which year the silk imported reached the value of ten and a quarter millions of dollars! The committee submitted a resolution, which was adopted on the 11th, directing the Secretary of the Treasury to cause to be prepared, and laid before the House, early in the next session, "a well digested manual on the growth and manufacture of silk." The report of the Secretary, the late Richard Rush, was made in February, 1828, and six thousand copies of the report and manual were printed. This, with other measures soon after adopted by Congress for circulating information on the subject, first directed public attention strongly to the silk culture in the United States, which, for several years, was prosecuted with an enthusiasm probably unequalled in our industrial history, and which proved ultimately injurious to the object it was designed to promote. In the course of this year, Dr. James Mease of Philadelphia, to whom the preparation of the manual was intrusted by the Secretary, imported from Genoa the first Piedmontese silk reel for winding silk from the cocoons. It answered well, and the manufacture was commenced in Philadelphia by Mr. Tees and Mr. B. F. Pomeroy. During this year or the following spring, the first specimen of the Morus Multicaulis, or Mulberry of the Philippine Islands, was imported into the United States from Tarascon, near Marseilles, where it cost five francs, indicating the high value placed upon it even there. The plant—which had been first introduced into France in 1821 from Manilla, by Mr. Perottet, who gave it its botanical name—was planted in the Linnean Botanic Garden of William Smith & Sons, commenced in 1750, at Flushing, on Long Island, by a descendant of Governor Thomas Prince of Plymouth. Its qualities, however, first became known in 1829, through Mr. Gideon B. Smith, of Baltimore, and Dr. Pascalis, of New York, who wrote on the subject. Silk worms were this year reared in Massachusetts by Mr. Cobb, who soon after called the attention of the Legislature to the subject, and prepared, under its authority, a manual on the mulberry tree and silk culture.

The number of distinct factory buildings devoted to the cotton manufacture in New England, was estimated at four hundred, averaging seven hundred spindles each, or 280,000 in all. The new ones were very large, the old ones quite small. Each spindle was estimated to consume about one half pound of cotton daily, or 140 pounds per annum, which for 280 work-days, gave about 39,200,000 pounds, or 98,000 bales, as the annual consumption. About one third of the buildings employed power looms, one third hand looms, and the others spun yarn and twist for the Middle and Western States, where, as in Philadelphia, it was woven by hand under contract or in families. The factories were distributed about as follows: in Massachusetts, 135; Rhode Island, 110; Connecticut, eighty; New Hampshire, fifty; Maine, fifteen; Vermont, ten. The larger manufacturing villages, where much capital was employed, were the following, in the order of their size, viz.: Chelmsford (Lowell), Mass.; Somersworth, Dover, and Dunstable, N. H.; Pawtucket, R. I.; Fall River, Mass.; Blackstone, Mass.; Slatersville, R. I.; Taunton, Mass.; Pawtuxet, Kent county, R. I.; Ware and Waltham, Mass.; New Ipswich, and New Market, N. H.; Springfield and Lancaster, Mass.; Norwich, Conn. Large companies were forming at Saco, Maine; and Haverhill, Mass. Calico printing was carried on at Chelmsford, Taunton, and Pawtucket, and they were preparing to print at Ware, Dunstable, Somersworth, Dover, and elsewhere. They already printed in New England sixty thousand yards a week. One third of all the mills in New England, including all the new ones, had their machinery from the best models used in England. The new establishments had several inventions of their own, which saved one third the work in some processes, and which were not yet used in England. The number of cotton factories in all the other States, was estimated at 275, of the same average size, which would make the total consumption of cotton, 150,000 bales per annum.

The price of Cotton Machinery in the United States, which in 1810 was three to four hundred times as much as in England, and in 1820 was about double, amounted on an average at this time to about fourteen dollars per spindle, with the appurtenances, or fifty to sixty per cent. more than in England. Spindles of the throstle kind were made for about eight dollars each, those of the mule kind for less.[1]

The Hudson Calico Print Works, at Columbiaville or Stockport, five miles above Hudson city, N. Y., were established this year on a small scale, by Joseph and Benjamin Marshall. One printing machine, a small dye-house and bleachery, sufficient to print about three hundred yards daily, were increased in 1828, by the importation from England of three more printing machines, with steam dyeing appurtenances, etc.; and in 1836 the print works of Marshall, Corville & Taylor, employed 250 hands, and printed on an average eighteen thousand yards daily, or 5,400,000 yards annually, worth eighteen cents a yard, of good permanent madder colors. Their madder dye-house, two hundred and eighty-six by fifty feet, was probably the largest ever built for that purpose.

The Cohoes Company, of New York, was incorporated in March, with a capital of $250,000, afterwards increased to $500,000, to improve the immense water-power at the Falls of the Mohawk, on the Erie canal, eight miles north of Albany. They built a dam and canals, which made the whole fall of 103 feet available for mill sites five times at five different levels, which have since been occupied by extensive cotton, iron,

(1) Report of Secretary Woodbury.

and other manufactures, to the value now of nearly two millions annually.

In the returns for this year, the values of domestic cotton goods exported are given for the first time, and were as follows, viz. : white piece goods, $821,629; printed goods, $68,884; Nankeen, $8,903; twist, yarn, etc., $11,135; all others, $227,574; total, $1,138,125. Of the white goods, the value of $671,266 was sent to South America, Central America and Mexico.

The manufacture of Cotton Bagging was at this time attempted at Nashville, Tenn., by a Mr. Allen, who received a contract from some gentleman of Huntsville, for twenty-five thousand yards. Mr. Rapp, of Economy, Pennsylvania, also received a commission from Adams county, Mississippi, for twenty thousand yards, at twenty-three cents a yard. Premiums were offered in the same county, for cotton cordage, cotton bagging, blankets, and negro clothing. The large factories of hempen bagging at Lexington, Paris, Danville, Shelbyville, and other towns in Kentucky, almost exclusively employed negro operatives, few others being seen, except managers and machinists.

The manufacturing establishments of Cincinnati, which had greatly increased within two years, embraced five steam engine and finishing shops, with 126 hands; four iron foundries, fifty-four hands; eleven soap and candle factories, forty-eight hands (making 451,000 pounds of soap and 332,000 pounds of candles); ten tanner and currier shops, sixty-six hands; thirteen cabinet furniture shops, 104 hands; four ropewalks, thirty-one hands; two breweries, eighteen hands; seven hatters' shops, ninety-five hands; twenty-nine boot and shoe shops, 257 hands; two wall paper factories, nine hands; six chair factories, thirty-eight hands; one type foundry, twenty-three hands; one clock factory, eighteen hands; three plough factories, eleven hands, two woolen and cotton factories, six hands; two cab factories, six hands; one chemical laboratory; one paper mill, forty hands; fourteen brickyards, 210 hands (10,000,000 of bricks); one white lead factory, eight hands; three steamboat yards, two hundred hands; nine printing establishments, and numerous other factories and machine shops, whose aggregate manufactures amounted to the value of $1,850,000.

The Printing-offices issued during the year, in addition to about one hundred and seventy-five thousand newspapers, nearly two hundred thousand copies of pamphlets, almanacs, school and other books, etc. The whole number of steamboats that had been built there since 1816, was fifty-seven, whose total tonnage was 10,647 tons, of which seventeen boats, with a tonnage of 3,139, were constructed the present year. There were, at this time, 143 steamboats, carrying about twenty-four thousand tons, running upon the western waters. Of these, forty-eight were built at Cincinnati, thirty-five at Pittsburg, ten at New Albany, seven at Marietta, five at Louisville, four at New York, and the others at different places on the Ohio, the engines for which were nearly all furnished by Cincinnati and Pittsburg. The imports of Cincinnati for the year, amounted to $2,528,590, and the exports to $1,063,560.[1]

The first Railroad constructed in America, was built this year from the granite quarries of Quincy, Mass., to tide water on the Neponset river, a distance of three miles, having a single track and one inclined plane 275 feet in length. Pine rails were laid and covered with oaken rails, and these with iron plates three eighths of an inch thick. It was used only for transportation of granite. On the 8th January following, the Mauch Chunk railroad, nine miles in length, for the transportation of coal from the Summit mines to the landing on the Lehigh, was commenced and finished in about three months at a cost of $3,500 per mile. Both roads went into operation in 1827, and were the commencement of railroad enterprises in the United States. The Hudson and Mohawk railroad, between Albany and Schenectady, was also chartered this year, and the Baltimore and Ohio Railroad in February of the next year.[2]

An Electric Telegraph was erected on Long Island, in New York, by Mr. Harrison Gray Dyer, who used frictional electricity and dyed marks on chemically prepared paper, by means of electric sparks.

Patent or Japanned Leather, was about this time made in Newark, N. J., by Mr. Seth Boyden, an ingenious citizen, who obtained letters patent for several improvements in manufactures. He erected a factory for making Patent leather, which he was probably the first in the United States to make. Mr. David Crockett commenced the business a few years after.

The first manufacture of Palm Leaf Hats in this country, was commenced this year in Massachusetts. The material was imported from Cuba and was made up chiefly by young girls. The manufacture in 1831, reached the number of two millions, nearly one half of which were made in Worcester county. They are still somewhat extensively made in Shutesbury and many other towns, and form a large item in the export trade of Boston.

The manufacture of Axes and other edge tools, was commenced at Hartford, Conn., by the brothers Collins, under the style of "Collins

(1) Drake and Mansfield's "Cincinnati in 1826," 64–66, 74–76.

(2) The Stockton and Darlington Railroad in England, opened on 26th September, 1825, was the first passenger railroad ever built to the extent of twenty-five miles. It used edge rails, and employed locomotives, stationary engines and horses.

& Co.," still retained on their celebrated wares. They were the first to supply the markets of this country with cast steel axes, ready ground for use. The manufactory was soon after removed to its present locality, on the Farmington river, where it has since been carried on extensively, under a charter, by the "Collins Company," with labor-saving machinery, much of which was invented, patented and constructed, by themselves. Their axes soon altogether superseded the foreign article.

At the Exhibition of the Franklin Institute this year, there was a pair of scissors, of Philadelphia manufacture, which weighed only one fifth of a grain, showing the improved dexterity of her mechanics. A Lace dress was made in Pawtucket, R. I., which took there a premium of ten dollars, and was afterwards purchased by the President of the United States, showing the progress of the finer manufactures.

The total capital employed in manufactures was estimated at $156,500,000, of which, $30,000,000 was given to Pennsylvania, $28,000,000 to New York, and $26,000,000 to Massachusetts. It included every species of manufacture, except food, in which the capital was estimated at $200,000,000.

At Middletown, Conn., where Swords of fine quality had been made for many years, Mr. Nathan Star made several, considered almost equal in temper to the famous "Damascus Blades." They were presented to Generals Jackson, Gaines, Johnson, and Commodore Hill.

Patents.—David H. Mason, Philadelphia, January 26, ornamental rolls and stamps for bookbinders; John S. Gustin, New York, February 23, power loom for weaving wire; Daniel Treadwell, Boston, March 2, power printing press—this press was about this time in operation in the office of the "National Intelligencer," and was considered by the proprietors, Messrs. Gales & Seaton, one of the most valuable discoveries ever conferred upon the art. It was said to be the only press on the cylindrical principle, adapted to book printing, which it executed in the most beautiful manner. Wm. Hoyt, Brookville, Indiana, March 3, cast-steel triangular bells; Jessie Delavo, New York, March 7, wrought iron fireproof chests; E. Nott, Schenectedy, N. Y., three patents, March 23, June 21, and December 29, for the evolution and management of heat, which was the subject of five subsequent patents by the same person, and covered the construction of Nott's highly popular and beautiful stoves. Benjamin Bull, New York, June 20, machine for weighing canal boats; W. Hunt & W. Hoskins, Martinsburg, N. Y., June 22, machine for spinning flax and hemp. This machine, invented by the late Walter Hunt, whose patented and other inventions and improvements were very numerous, was the result of numerous experiments made to revolutionize the flax manufacture, as that of cotton had been by labor-saving machinery, and came nearest to the object of any introduced up to that time. John M. Brookings, Wiscasset, Maine, June 23, and several others, machines for moulding and pressing bricks; Henry Bostwick, New York, August 2, representing genealogy and chronology by lines; Joseph Eve, London, England, August 16, improvement in steam engines. Eve's steam engine, for which he obtained a patent in 1818, while a resident of Georgia, excited considerable interest in England for its novelty, having no parts in common with ordinary engines, "no cylinder, piston, valve cock, fly wheel, crank, condenser, or reciprocating parts whatever." It was rotary and high pressure, and was impelled by the direct impulse of the steam acting on surfaces at right angles with the motion, securing its whole power under favorable circumstances. D. Collings & J. D. Galup, Wilkesbarre, Pa., October 12, generating steam by Anthracite; Wm. G. Berry, and J. T. Osborn, Cincinnati, Ohio, November 26, a locomotive steam saw mill; Isaiah Lukens, Philadelphia, December 30, improvement in the lithontripter. A patent was granted in England on 15th September, 1825, to Mr. Lukens, machinist, of Adams street, Adelphia, County of Middlesex, "for his new invented surgical instrument, for destroying the stone in the bladder without cutting, which he denominates lithontripter." This valuable surgical instrument appears to have been the invention of an American.

1827

In the expectation that a permanent system of adequate protection to domestic industry, would be engrafted upon the national policy, and in consequence of the tariff of 1824, which raised the duties upon woolen goods from twenty-five up to thirty-three and one third per cent., a large amount of capital had, during a number of years past, been attracted to the Woolen Manufacture. Enterprise had been still farther invited into that and other branches of manufacture on account of the depressed state of the foreign commerce, and of agriculture resulting from the low price of American staples in the markets of Europe, to which may also be added a general improvement in the financial condition of the world. The augmentation of the duty on imported woolens, was, however, immediately followed in Great Britain by a reduction of the duty upon foreign wool from six pence to one penny per pound (and soon after to one halfpenny), for the acknowledged purpose of enabling the British woolen manufacturer to send his goods into the United States at a reduced cost. As a consequence of the combined foreign and domestic competition, increased in the former case by the great improvements in machinery, the low price of wool in

Europe, and the revulsion of 1825, which stimulated the exportation of woolens, under the various devices employed for evading the duties and breaking down the American manufacturer, the woolen interests at this time, as well as the agricultural branches connected with them, found themselves suffering under the severest depression and unable to struggle with the various adverse influences by which they were surrounded. The amount of capital employed in woolen manufactures, had increased since the peace, from ten millions to fifty millions of dollars in the present year. A corresponding increase had taken place in the number of sheep raised, and in the production of wool, which found a ready sale so long as the manufacturer was prosperous. But by the ruin of the woolen manufacturer, or the suspension of the mills, which at this time threatened to become general, the farmer found himself without a domestic market for his wool or his breadstuffs, at the same time that he was deprived of a foreign market for his products. Numerous memorials were in consequence sent up to the nineteenth Congress, at its second session, from the manufacturers and farmers of different sections of the Union, asking its interposition to save those valuable interests from total overthrow, and to raise up a domestic market for the perishing and unsalable production of the soil, by a revision of the tariff. With a view of securing to the manufacturer of Woolens, and to the country, the benefits intended by the act of 1824, and which had accrued both to the manufacturer and consumer of coarse cottons, under the minimum duties of 1816, whereby foreign low-priced cottons were wholly excluded, and a greatly superior article was supplied by our manufacturers at about one half the former price, Mr. Mallory of Vermont, from the Committee on Manufactures, reported on the 10th January, a bill having especial reference to the protection of that branch. The bill left the rate of duties unchanged on woolen manufactures, but all manufactures of wool, except worsted stuff goods and blankets, whose actual value at the place whence imported was less than forty cents, between forty cents and $2.50, or between $2.50 and $4 per square yard respectively, were to be deemed and taken to have cost those prices. All unmanufactured wool then chargeable with a duty of thirty per cent. ad valorem, was to pay thirty-five per cent. during the first year, and after 1st June, 1827, forty per cent. ad valorem, with a minimum valuation of forty cents per pound on wool costing between ten and forty cents. Having been taken up in Committee of the Whole, on 17th January, Mr. Mallory advocated its passage as alike demanded by the prostrate condition of the manufacture and as a benefit to the agricultural interests. He estimated the capital employed in the woolen branch to be at least forty millions, giving employment to sixty thousand persons, and the capital devoted to wool growing at as much more. The number of sheep was estimated at fifteen to sixteen millions. The principal causes of the present depression which the bill sought to remove, were the evasion of duties under the ad valorem system, by means of foreign agents residing in the country, to whom unfinished goods were consigned at a low valuation, and finished by foreign workmen in their employ in this country; the irregularity of the market in consequence of sudden influxes of foreign goods; the credits on duties; sales at auction; and the practice of the manufacturer, always to sell his surplus stock in this country, rather than depress his own market when compelled to sell at reduced prices. The bill was opposed by Mr. Cambreleng, of New York, who declared that it was an attempt to levy a duty of two hundred per cent., disguised under the minimum rule as one of thirty-three and one third per cent. only, and that it would be in effect entirely prohibitory of coarse woolen goods, much needed by the poorer classes, for the benefit of manufacturers, who were suffering only from a reaction of trade, the result of their own over-speculation and production. After further opposition from Mr. Buchanan of Pennsylvania, who favored protection as in 1824, but was opposed to this bill, and from Messrs. Mitchell, Hamilton, Drayton, and McDuffie of South Carolina, Archer of Virginia, and others, and having received the advocacy of Messrs. Tristram Burges of Rhode Island, Dwight and Davis of Massachusetts, Stewart and Ingham of Pennsylvania, and many others, the bill in an amended form passed the House on the 10th February, by a vote of one hundred and six to ninety-five. It failed, however, to become a law, having on the 28th, on motion of Mr. Hayne, been laid on the table in the Senate, by the casting vote of the Vice President, chiefly in consequence of its late introduction and want of time to discuss it.

The failure of the Woolens bill was immediately followed by efforts on the part of manufacturers, to secure, by combined and systematic action, an early attention at the next session of Congress to the important interests which appeared to be consigned to inevitable ruin. A convention of delegates from the friends of domestic industry in thirteen New England and Middle States, assembled at Harrisburg, Pa., on the 30th July, when the subject was fully discussed. A memorial drawn up by C. J. Ingersoll, was presented and adopted, and having been laid before the next Congress, with the draft of a bill containing a higher schedule of duties, resulted in the passage of a new Tariff act, giving a greater measure of protection to the manufacturing interests, although an increase of duties was opposed by an elaborate and able report of a committee of citizens of Boston, published November 30, of this year.

On the 6th of August, a Convention of Commerce between Great

Britain and the United States was signed at London, whereby the provisions of the commercial treaty of July 3, 1815, which had been continued for ten years by the convention of 20th October, 1818, were again continued and extended indefinitely.

A remonstrance from Massachusetts against a bill for the repeal of the duty on foreign Salt, which passed the Senate on 5th February, stated that the manufactories were numerous along the sea coast of that State, and employed upward of one thousand persons, producing annually six hundred thousand bushels of the best salt. In Barnstable County alone, there were fifteen million feet of vats, worth $1,300,000. The duty of twenty cents a bushel, imposed in 1813, had revived and extended the manufacture, and within three years past the domestic and foreign competition had reduced the price about thirty per cent. It had been as high as sixty cents a bushel, but was now sold for thirty-three or thirty-five cents, which was less than it could be afforded. The total salt manufacture of the Union was estimated at 4,151,182 bushels, of which about one fourth, or 1,104,452 bushels, was made in New York, and 929,848 in Virginia.

The general introduction, about this date, of grates and furnaces for burning Anthracite coal, considerably increased the coal trade of Pennsylvania, which was still more promoted by the completion in the spring of this year, of the Mauch Chunk railroad and the use of rail cars drawn by mules in the "drifts" of the coal mines.

The General Mining Association, sole lessees from the creditors of the Duke of York, of the immense bituminous coal fields of Nova Scotia, at the same time commenced operations at Sydney, in Cape Breton—where coal had been mined on a small scale for sixty years—and at the Albion mines in Pictou.

The Boston Mechanics' Institute was incorporated June 15, for the promotion of science and the useful arts by lectures and other means. A course of lectures was commenced three weeks after its organization, and a second course in November, and it numbered among its early lecturers such men as Messrs. George B. Emerson, Professors Farrar and Webster, Daniel Treadwell, Edward Everett, Dr. John Ware, Dr. Bigelow, and others.

On June 25, there were in Philadelphia and its vicinity, one hundred and four warping mills at work, sufficient to employ forty to fifty weavers each, or forty-five hundred in all, over two hundred dyers, three thousand spoolers, two thousand bobbin winders. Weavers, dyers, and warpers, could average five dollars per week in wages, and spoolers fifty cents to one dollar and a half, and bobbin winders one dollar and found. The manufacturing establishments were over fifty, at an average rental of one hundred and eighty dollars; the houses occupied by weavers about fifteen hundred, at sixty to eighty dollars; indigo used weekly, twenty-two hundred pounds; flour used as sizing, thirty to forty pounds; the goods produced daily were eighty-one thousand yards, at an average value of sixteen cents a yard. The whole wages of operatives amounted to $1,470,000 per annum; rents to $114,000; indigo at two dollars per pound, $228,800; flour for sizing to $9,100; and the goods manufactured to 24,300,000 yards, worth at sixteen cents, $3,888,000, and requiring, at four yards to the pound, 6,075,000 pounds, or 20,250 bales of cotton, equal to sixty-nine bales per diem, and worth at ten cents, $607,500 per annum. The goods were ginghams, checks, bedtickings, and stripes, which were exported in large quantities, to supply as well the Eastern and Western as the Southern States, many being sent to Boston by every packet.[1]

The City of Paterson, N. J., had become, in consequence of its manufactures, a place of 6,236 inhabitants, with seven houses of public worship, seventeen schools, a philosophical society, fifteen cotton factories, employing 25,998 spindles, and two duck factories, with 1,644 spindles, besides extensive machine shops and iron works. Its manufactories employed 1,453 hands, whose annual wages were $221,123. They consumed six thousand bales, or 1,843,100 pounds of cotton, 620,000 pounds of flax, 1,630,000 pounds of cotton yarn, and 430,000 pounds of linen yarn were spun, besides 630,000 yards of linen and duck, and 3,354,500 yards of cotton cloth. New factories were in progress of erection.[2]

The first importation of United States Cotton into Genoa was made this year by the house of Antonio & Andrea Ponti, proprietors of the oldest and largest cotton mill in Lombardy, established in 1810. It was purchased in New Orleans by a member of that house, one of whom afterward resided eleven years in the United States, and greatly increased the exportation of American cotton to the Mediterranean.

The total consumption of Cotton in the United States was estimated at 103,482 bales. The demand for American domestic cottons in Brazil, was considerably affected by imitations of them made in Manchester, and offered there at lower prices, although they could be made as cheaply in the United States as the same quality could be produced in that city. The progress of the cotton and woolen manufacture in the United States was a subject of some anxiety in England, and the Leeds Mercury about this date, stated that the Americans had even succeeded in applying the power loom to the woolen manufacture, "in which the English have hitherto failed."

During this, or the following year, subscriptions to the requisite amount

1) Hazard's Register of Pennsylvania, vol. 1, p. 16.

(2) Gordon's Gazetteer. Montgomery on the Cotton Manufacture.

were made, for the establishment of the first Virginia cotton factory, at Petersburg, where ample power was afforded by the falls of the Appomattox. Two large cotton mills were afterward erected at Matoaca, on the north bank of the river, four miles above Petersburg. A company for the manufacture of cotton and woolen cloths, and linens, was also about this time projected by the people of Fredericksburg and Falmouth.

The value of Flannels, made by three mills in the vicinity of Newburyport, Massachusetts, for one year, was estimated at $684,000.

The number of incorporated manufacturing companies in Massachusetts, at this time, was one hundred and sixty-one, with capitals varying from $20,000 to $650,000. The whole amount of capital was $21,465,000.

The Bobinet factory at Ipswich, which had employed eight hundred young women in lace work, was compelled to discontinue operations, on account of the British manufacturers having so much improved their machinery as to undersell them. A new Net factory was, however, about to be started at that place. A Lace school at Newport, R. I., also employed about five hundred young women.

In Windham and Tolland counties, in Connecticut, the following quantities of Silk were made this year: Mansfield, 2430 pounds; Chaplin, 550 pounds; Ashfield, 500 pounds; Hampton, 467 pounds; Coventry, 350 pounds; total, 4,297 pounds, worth four dollars per pound. It was made in several other towns, from which there were no returns. Two attempts made, during the last and present years, by the Messrs. Terhoeven, near Philadelphia, to rear two crops of worms in a season, proved failures, although two crops had been produced at Bethlehem in 1825, by Messrs. Weiss & Youngman. The Messrs. Terhoeven, brothers, about this time invented a simple and ingenious machine for winding silk from the cocoons, and for doubling and twisting at the same time—operations believed to have never before been united in the same machine. It gave perfect satisfaction, and the inventors were awarded a medal and twenty dollars, from the fund left by John Scott, of Edinburgh, to the corporation of Philadelphia, for the distribution of premiums "to ingenious men and women, who make useful inventions and improvements."[1]

A manufactory of Ingrain or Kidderminister carpets and shawls, was carried on at Tariffville, Connecticut, by an incorporated company, under the direction of H. K. Knight; some of its productions were considered elegant, and four years after, it employed a capital of $123,000 and ninety-five male weavers.

The first Lithographic establishment in the United States was this

(1) Rush's Manual, pp. 26, 39, 178.

year established at Boston, by Wm. S. Pendleton, who imported artists and materials from England, and produced portraits, music titles, and other beautiful specimens of the art, with great facility and correctness.[1]

A large manufactory of American China or Porcelain was in successful operation at Philadelphia. It was owned by William Ellis Tucker, whose warehouse was at 40 North Fifth street, and who was believed to be the only person who had brought the domestic manufacture of China to any considerable degree of perfection. A company of English artificers, this year, established the same business near Pittsburg, where suitable clay was found. A porcelain factory at Jersey City, near New York, was also said to be doing well. It employed one hundred persons and $200,000 capital. A glass factory, of the same size, was in operation there, and a carpet factory, making twenty-five hundred yards weekly.

Stained glass of fine finish and design, was also made in considerable quantity in the vicinity of New York. Glass decanters of great beauty and solidity were made at Wellsburg, Va., where white, flint, and green glass wares, within a few years, rivalled the foreign.

The first Bell made from blistered bar steel, or cast steel, melted, was manufactured this year at the works of the New York Steel Manufacturing Company, in New York city, under the superintendence of a gentleman from Baltimore, who was said to have a patent. It was equal in sound to composition bells, and could be made as light as they at a cost of twenty to twenty-five cents per pound. The West Troy bell foundry, of A. Meneeley's Sons, was established about this time.

Orders were this year received from France and England, for some of the card making machines, invented by Mr. Whittemore of Cambridge. The English machinists are said to have been unable to put them

(1) This enterprise appears to have been immediately successful, and having passed through different hands, was recently owned and conducted by S. W. Chandler & Brother, at 204 Washington street. The second lithographic establishment was the next year attempted at Philadelphia by Kennedy & Lucas, but for want of practical printers, soon ceased, and was followed, near the same time, by the third establishment, started in the same city by Messrs. John Pendleton, Kearney & Childs, who employed as draughtsmen the late Rembrandt Peale, the eminent portrait painter, and Mr. Swett. Mr. Pendleton soon after left, and set up the first lithographic house in New York, and the fourth in the Union; while in Philadelphia, the business was continued by C. J. Childs and H. Inman, the latter also a painter of great merit. In about two years, Mr. Lehman took the place of Mr. Inman, and Childs & Lehman conducted it until 1834, when P. S. Duval, their printer, succeeded Mr. Childs, under the firm of Lehman & Duval, and in 1836 the former retired, leaving Mr. Duval sole proprietor of the business, which he has since conducted.

together when they arrived, and the persons ordering them were obliged to send to Boston for an American machinist.

Mr. Richardson, of Baltimore, this year constructed a steam flouring mill, on the American plan, for the Netherlands.

PATENTS.—Isaac Tyson, Baltimore, February 15, making copperas; John Sitton, Pendleton, S. C., February 15, and Cyrus W. Beach, Schoharie, N. Y., March 16, wheelwrights' assistant; William A. Hart, Fredonia, N. Y., Feb. 20, Marvel Davis, Mayville, N. Y., July 10, and Joseph Shattuck, Jefferson county, Ohio, Nov. 10, all for percussion gun locks, and John Ambler, jr., New Berlin, N. Y., Oct. 16, lever percussion lock; David Myerle, Philadelphia, March 3, machinery for laying ropes; Robert Groves, Brooklyn, N. Y., July 25, making cordage. [Messrs. Tiers & Myerle, of Philadelphia, purchased afterward the patent of Mr. Groves, originally taken out seven years before, and established a large factory for the manufacture of cordage on a new principle; the threads being placed on different revolving spools, passed through perforated cast-iron plates, and then through a cast-iron tube of suitable diameter for any sized rope. D. Myerle & Co., also established a large steam rope factory at Wheeling, Va., and another, fourteen hundred feet long by twenty-five wide, at Louisville, and others, we believe, at Cincinnati and St. Louis. His machinery was also used at Pittsburg and elsewhere, and was a valuable mprovement.] Oliver Ames, Easton, Mass., March 5, making shovels; Lemuel Hedge, Windsor, Vt., June 20, engine for dividing scales, which was adapted for stamping Gunter's scales; Denison Olmsted, New Haven, Ct., July 21, making gas light from cotton seed; Simeon Brown, N. Y., July 31, removing buildings with chimnies, furniture, etc.; Horace Baker, North Salem, N. Y., August 30, loom for weaving figured goods; John Robinson, Pittsburg, Pa., Nov. 14, glass knobs pressed at one operation; John McClintic, Chambersburg, Pa., Oct. 8, mortising and tenoning machine: this, though not the earliest patent, is regarded as the first practical contrivance of the kind, and the parent of the foot mortising machine for wood, since universally adopted in workshops, and the subject of numerous patented improvements. Charles Miner, Lynn, Ct., Oct. 12, and Nov. 16, raising ships, etc., by cradle screw; David H. Mason and M. W. Baldwin, Philadelphia, October 30, biting figures on steel cylinders for printing calicoes; Nathaniel Bishop, Danbury, Ct., Nov. 17, rolling the backs of tortoise shell combs.

Jacob Perkins patented in England, March 22, a steam engine and tubular boilers.

The excitement which had for several years agitated the whole country on the subject of legislative protection to domestic manufactures, received intensity in consequence of the organized effort of the manufacturers to influence Congress, through the Harrisburg Convention held in July of the last year, following the defeat of

1828

the Woolens Bill in the Senate. The hostility of the planting interests of the South, to an increase of duties on imports, with a view to encouraging manufactures, as being sectional, oppressive to themselves, and likely to produce retaliating discriminations against their great staples, in addition to its being a tax upon the consumer, had gathered strength at each attempt to remodel the tariff since 1816. An increasing degree of asperity was manifested in the South, on the subject of protection, and amid the severe denunciations, and counteracting efforts, which were fast making the question of prohibitory and protective duties a principal issue between the great political parties of the country, the twentieth Congress assembled in its first session on 3d December of the last year. The continued distress of the woolen manufacturers, who had been fast sinking under foreign competition, or with very few exceptions had barely sustained themselves in the hope of some permanent measures for their relief, and the equally depressed condition of the iron interests, produced, on the 31st December, a resolution of the House, empowering the Committee on Manufactures "to send for and examine persons on oath, concerning the present condition of manufactures, and to report the minutes of such examination to the House," preparatory to a revision of the tariff. Subpœnas were issued and numerous witnesses were examined relative to iron, wool, woolens, steel, paper, glass, hemp, flax, sail duck, shirts, and cotton cloth.[1]

(1) On the subject of wool and woolens, the following proprietors and representatives of leading establishments, were examined by the committee, viz.: Simon A. Dexter, of the Oriskany Manufacturing Company, Whitesboro', N. Y., commenced 1810, making kerseymeres and broadcloths; Hon. A. Tufts, of Tufts' Manufacturing Company, Dudley, Mass., commenced 1824, capital $40,000: loss, exclusive of interest, in eighteen months, $5,000; Col. James Shepherd, of Shepherd Woolen Manufacturing Company, Northampton, Mass. (the largest in the United States), capital $130,000, made broadcloths and cassimeres: lost in two years about $30,000; Wm. Phillips, of Phillipsburg Factory, Walkill, N. Y., capital $20,000, broadcloth; Abraham Maitland, Andover, Mass., capital $42,000, flannels altogether, to amount of 3,200 pieces in 1827, with improving sales; Wm. W. Young, Brandywine, Del., commenced 1813, capital $100,000, blue cassimeres and coarse wool satinetts, losing business since 1825; William R. Dickerson, Steubenville, Ohio, commenced 1815, capital $100,000, six to seven-quarter broadcloths and some flannels: losses in three years about $8,000; A. Schenck, Glenham Company, Matteawan, N. Y., incorporated 1824, capital $91,531, broadcloths: lost in 1826-7, $5,500, and in 1825-6, $1,795: made also, machinery in last year to amount of thirty or forty thousand dollars, which was a profitable business; James Wolcott, Jr., of Wolcott Woolen Manufactory, South Bridgewater, Mass., incorporated seven years before, capital $126,000, broadcloths, principally indigo-blues, stock depreciated fifty per cent.: lost in 1826 $23,095, exclusive of interest on

The Committee, acting upon the evidence thus obtained, made a report, of which six thousand copies were printed, and accompanied it by a bill drawn up by Mr. Silas Wright of New York, and framed with especial regard to the protection of the woolen manufacturer, wool grower, and farmer, and the producer and manufacturer of iron, by encouraging the consumption of domestic materials in preference to foreign, and giving to both the command of the home market. Mr. Mallory, chairman of the committee, through whom the bill was reported and called up in Committee of the Whole on the 4th March, explained its provisions, and forcibly argued in favor of protection, while he disapproved of some of

capital, not paying expenses; Jonas B. Brown, of Goodall Manufacturing Company, Millbury, Mass., capital $80,460, broadcloths and satinetts: latter a losing business; Joshua Clapp, Litchfield, Conn., also a factory at Northampton, Mass., uses his factory rent free, made broadcloths: lost in 1825–6, $8,995, including commissions, and in 1826–7, $3,895; Benjamin Poor, of Saxon and Leicester Factories, Worcester and Middlesex counties, Mass., capital $150,000: loss to July, 1827, $26,394; Elenterre Irene Dupont, near Wilmington, Del., capital over $70,000, coarse cloths and kerseys for the army of common country wool, and of coarsest country wool linseys for negro clothing—business always being a losing one; Joshua W. Pierce, Salem Falls Manufactory, Souerswitt, N. H., capital, in November, $362,000, broadcloths only: profits in 1825, $6,772, losses in 1826, $17,059.

In these factories the aggregate amount of wool consumed was 716,559 lbs. It was stated that purchasers generally preferred English goods—they complained especially of the dyes of blue cloths, the others being as good as English. The prejudice excited against American cloths by foreigners was equal to twenty-five per cent. against the manufacture. The manufacturers considered that they could make cloths as cheaply as the English, wool being of the same quality and price. More female labor and machinery were used here than in England. Four fifths of the consumption of woolens was of American manufacture, and the whole amount was estimated at $50,000,000 annually. Small establishments and medium capital answered better, under their sole proprietors, than incorporated companies. Manufacturing was considered favorable to morals, as the education of children was attended to in most of the large factories, particularly by Sunday-schools. The best wool, say half to full-blood merino, was preferred, but for negro cloths the coarse Smyrna and South American wools were employed. Fine and coarse wools were imported from Germany, Spain, Portugal and England, and coarse from Smyrna, Adrianople and Buenos Ayres. They varied much in price—Saxony cost sixty-one to one hundred and sixty cents; Spanish, thirty-five to eighty-five; Merino, thirty to one hundred and twenty-five; Italian, thirty-two and a quarter; German coarse wool, sixteen to twenty; Russian, thirteen; Smyrna, sixteen to twenty-two; spring wool, thirty to forty-one; pulled wool, thirty to thirty-five; common domestic (native), twenty to twenty-five cents. [Its price has depreciated since 1852, twenty-five to thirty-three and one third per cent., owing to the depressed state of the manufacture, that which cost seventy-five now selling for fifty to fifty-five. It was still fifty to seventy-five per cent. higher than in England. A lot sold in New York in October last for seventy-six cents, which cost in London two shillings and one pence, or forty-six cents, and a lot purchased in Boston at fifty cents was valued in London at twenty-three and one half cents. Wool, costing twenty to seventy-five cents, was about half the price of the plain cloth. There was no wool more suitable for blankets than native wool, but its price had always been too high.]

the details of the bill, especially the duty on certain kinds of wool, as positively injurious to the manufacturer and of no advantage to the farmer. The bill proposed to increase the duty on hammered iron, from $18 to $22.44, and on rolled iron from $30 to $37 per ton, making the first equal to about sixty-seven per cent. and the latter one hundred and twenty-one per cent.; on pig iron, from fifty to sixty-two and a half cents per cwt., and increased the duty on wire one cent per pound, on hardware ten per cent., and on steel from one to one dollar and a half per cwt. Upon wool and woolens, which were the great interests regarded by the bill, as suffering most from the low price of foreign wool, auction sales, credits for duties, and various defects of the revenue system, the following duties were proposed: on unmanufactured wool, seven cents per pound (reduced to four cents), with an addition of forty per cent. and an annual increase of five per cent., until it reached fifty per cent. ad valorem. Manufactures of wool (except carpets, blankets, worsted stuff goods, bombazines, hosiery, mits, gloves, caps, and bindings), the actual value of which, at the place whence imported, was not over fifty cents, were to pay sixteen cents the square yard—changed to an ad valorem duty of forty per cent. until 30th June, 1829, and forty-five per cent. thereafter on a minimum valuation of fifty cents. On woolens valued between fifty cents and one dollar per square yard, a duty of forty cents; on those between one dollar and two dollars and a half per yard, one dollar. Those costing between two and a half and four dollars, were to be taken to have cost four dollars and pay forty per cent. ad valorem. Woolen blankets having nuts, etc., thirty-five per cent. These rates were finally changed to a uniform duty of forty per cent., until 30th June, 1829, and forty-five per cent. thereafter, on the first three classes, with minimum valuations respectively, of one, two, two and a half, and four dollars the square yard; and woolens costing over four dollars per yard, were to pay forty-five per cent. before and fifty per cent. after the above date; ready-made clothing fifty per cent.; Brussels, Turkey, and Wilton carpets and carpetings, seventy cents; Venetian and ingrain carpetings, forty cents; other carpeting, thirty-two cents; patent floor cloth, fifty cents a yard, etc. On unmanufactured hemp and flax, forty-five dollars per ton, and five dollars per ton additional per annum, until it reached sixty cents; and sail duck nine cents the square yard, to which was added four and a half cents the square yard on cotton bagging, and after June 1829, five cents. On molasses, ten cents per gallon, and on distilled spirits, ten cents in addition to the existing duty, altered to fifteen cents. The bill having been thus amended and discussed, passed the House on the 21st April, by a vote of one hundred and five to ninety-four, and was sent to the Senate, where it received farther amendments, which were agreed to by the House. Mr. Benton proposed an annually increasing duty on indigo until it reached one dollar per pound. It was advocated by others but opposed by Mr. Hayne of South Carolina, who was unwilling that the South should participate in the American system, and the duty was fixed at an increase of five cents the first year, and ten cents annually afterward up to a maximum duty of fifty cents a pound. A duty of thirty per cent., and after June 1829, an additional duty of five per cent. on all silks beyond the Cape of Good Hope, and of twenty per cent. on other manufactures of silk, was added to the bill.

Duties of four to nine dollars per ton on roofing slates, and of thirty-three and one third per cent. on school slates, were also added by this bill, and the minimum value of cottons was raised to thirty-five cents the square yard.

Under the minimum principle, which was now applied generally to woolen manufactures, the five several grades of woolens paid respectively, at the rate per yard of fourteen, twenty-two and a half, forty-five, one hundred and twelve and a half, and one hundred and eighty cents per yard. But the increased duties upon woolens which gave to this measure the name of the High Tariff, were materially modified in their effect by the high duty on wool, which, as originally reported, would have effectually counteracted its benefits to the manufacturers of coarse wool—an article extensively imported but not produced in the country.

The act, which was to go into immediate effect after the 30th day of June, notwithstanding strong remonstrances from the Legislature of South Carolina and from unofficial sources, and various efforts to defeat it, finally passed the House on the 15th May, when the last of the Senate's amendments was agreed to by a vote of one hundred and twenty-two to sixty, and it became a law on the 19th.[1] It was the first act regarded by the manufacturers as really protective of their interests, and greatly promoted the growth of certain branches.[2] No protection was asked for manufactures of glass, paper, or iron, except hammered bar iron. On the 5th January Mr. Rush, Secretary of the Treasury, in obedience to a resolution of the House of 29th December, 1825, made a report accompanied by a manual prepared under his direction in conformity with the resolution of 11th May, 1826, on the growth and

(1) Under the tariff of 1824, in part repealed by this act, the total importations in four years amounted to $301,558,885, and the duties to $121,637,942, an average of forty and a quarter per centum.

(2) The passage of this act produced much dissatisfaction and threats of retaliation both in England and the Southern States. At public meetings, resolutions to abstain from the use of every thing produced in the tariff states, and even from communication with them, with various propositions of a retaliatory kind were passed in Baldwin county, Georgia, and Barnwell district, South Carolina, and much excitement was manifested elsewhere.

manufacture of silk, of which reports the Senate ordered six thousand copies to be printed.[1] The manual was a valuable digest of information upon the history and management of silk worms, and the manufacture of silk with plates of the most approved machinery. It contributed to the general interest at this time awakened on the subject of silk culture, and to the diffusion of correct knowledge in relation to it.

The Pennsylvania Society for the Promotion of the Culture of the Mulberry and the raising of silk worms, offered on 2d April the following premiums to promote the objects for which it was organized, viz. : sixty dollars for the greatest quantity of sewing silk of the best quality, produced within the state, from cocoons raised therein by one family, not less than twenty pounds, and smaller sums of forty and twenty-five dollars for the next greatest quantity not less than fifteen and ten pounds; premiums of fifty and thirty dollars for the greatest quantities of cocoons not less than one hundred and fifty pounds; fifty dollars for the largest lot of white mulberry trees, not less than four hundred, within twelve miles of the city, and sums of thirty and twenty dollars for smaller lots. The culture of the mulberry was this year commenced at Economy, in Pennsylvania, by Mr. George Rapp and his associates, whose experiments with the white Italian mulberry and the morus multicaulis, and in the manufacture of silk, were among the most successful in the country.

On the 11th June of this year, the Congress of Peru "considering that new states ought to encourage, above all, their own manufactures and industry," decreed that within ten months from Europe, and eight months from the states of America (Feb. 11, 1829), all articles then paying ninety per cent. duties should be totally prohibited. These articles embraced American bleached and unbleached cottons, hats, shoes, soap, tobacco, etc.; and the prohibition was also extended to flour, butter, rice, and some other articles. In consequence of a revolution in the following year, the decree was annulled by the new administration on June 15, 1829.

The largest wool sale in the United States up to this date, took place in Boston on 10th June, at the hall over the new market house, when Messrs. Coolidge, Poor, and Head, offered 1536 bales of Saxony, Spanish, and other foreign and American wool, amounting to four hundred thousand pounds, valued at from two to three hundred thousand dollars.

The manufacturing borough of Manayunk, Pennsylvania, contained at this time, ten mills in operation and in course of erection, including Richards' rolling and nail mills. The former employed 636 persons, and

(1) Senate Document, No. 175, 20th Congress, 1st Session. Wm. A. Vernon, Esq. of Rhode Island, published this year a translation of the work of M. De Labrousse on the cultivation of Mulberry trees, with valuable notes by the translator.

embraced manufactures of flour, drugs, saw grinding and polishing, carding and filling of cloth, cotton and woolen goods, paper, etc., nearly all of which had grown up within six years.

Lexington, Kentucky, contained ten manufactories of cotton bagging and bale rope, in which five hundred persons were employed, of whom not over two per cent. were white. There were in other parts of the state as many more. The annual produce was nearly one million yards of cotton bagging and two million pounds of bale rope, beside large quantities of twine and yarns. There were also ten cotton manufactories. The Fayette factory, near the town, spun weekly, between four and five thousand dozens of cotton, and had recently put up looms to make about fifty pieces of muslin, thirty yards each, per week. Mr. James Weir's cotton factory worked up about two hundred and fifty bales of cotton annually. There were three woolen factories. The Lexington white lead factory made annually from eighty to one hundred thousand pounds of white and ten thousand pounds of red lead. The stock was about six thousand dollars, and the dividends about eight per cent. per annum. This city had numerous other establishments, as grist mills, breweries of beer and porter, paper mills, ropewalks, distilleries, foundries, nail works, etc. About two thousand tons of hemp were annually raised in the vicinity, and the culture had greatly increased of late.

The Covington Cotton Factory, at Covington, in the same state, opposite Cincinnati, was built this year, at a cost of sixty-six thousand dollars.

One or more cotton spinning mills were in operation at Vincennes, Indiana, owned by Messrs. Reynolds & Bonner, and H. D. Wheeler.

Notwithstanding the hostility of the South to the tariff act, several cotton manufactories were projected within a few months, and others were about to go into operation—one at Augusta, two at Milledgeville, and another at Indian Springs in Georgia. The Petersburg Virginian contained an essay in favor of their establishment at that place, and efforts were made to establish cotton and woolen factories at Fredericksburg in that state.

Two more of the large manufacturing companies of Lowell, Massachusetts, were this year incorporated, and commenced operations, viz.: the Appleton Company, and the Lowell Manufacturing Company. The Lowell Bank was also chartered.

A charter was granted in Connecticut to the "Norwich Water Power Company," with a capital of forty thousand dollars, for the construction of works to bring into use the immense and previously unoccupied water power of the Shetucket, below its junction with the Quinelaug, at

Norwich. A substantial stone dam, 280 feet in length, and a canal, were built, which furnished power for sixty thousand spindles. Within four or five years five large factories were erected, the largest, that of the Thames Company for the manufacture of cotton cloths, being one of the finest in New England.

Colonel Breethaupt, agent of a manufacturing company in South Carolina, visited the New England factories in October, and in proof of the superior character of the machinery made there, stated that the agent of an extensive cotton factory, about to be established in Prussia, after visiting England, gave the preference to American machinery, and ordered at one factory $100,000 worth. The shops, he said, were filled with orders.[1]

Considerable excitement existed at this time in South Carolina, growing out of the improvement in the texture of Sea Island cotton. Kinsay Burden, sen., of St. John's Colleton, in 1804 or 1805, had produced a "packet" of cotton, worth in the English market twenty-five cents a pound more than any other kind. He had since assiduously employed his botanical knowledge, in effecting further improvements in the staple, the method remaining undiscovered by others. In 1826 he sold his first full crop of sixty bags for one hundred and ten cents per pound. In the following March, Mr. Whitemarsh B. Seabrook read, before the Agricultural Society of St. John's Colleton, of which he was secretary, a "report, accompanied by sundry letters, on the causes which contribute to the production of fine Sea Island cotton," which directed attention still more to the subject and especially to the selection of proper seed. The experiments were successful and resulted in the rejection of the clean seed, and the use of the downy retained for planting. During this year, Hugh Wilson, sen., of the same parish, obtained ninety cents for ten bags, and from his two succeeding crops one dollar and one dollar and twenty-five cents per pound. Two bags of extra fine, raised by him this year, sold for two dollars per pound, the highest price ever obtained in any country for cotton. So valuable was Mr. Burden's secret deemed, that he offered to sell to the Legislature for $200,000 all his seed, and to communicate the method of perpetuating the silky properties of the new cotton fibre, for which knowledge, it is said, Mr. William Seabrook of Edisto, proposed at one time to give $50,000, although both offers were subsequently withdrawn. This revolution in the cotton culture is believed, however, to have been injurious to the planters generally. The staple has been continually improving in quality, at the expense of its quantity, and in consequence of the fall in prices, has resulted in loss, except to a few individuals.[2]

(1) Niles's Register. (2) The Cotton Plant.

At the exhibition of the Franklin Institute, held in Philadelphia, October 8th to 16th, a premium was awarded to Seth Boyden of Newark, New Jersey, for an assortment of buckles, bits, and other castings, of annealed cast iron, remarkable for smoothness and malleability. It was the first attempt in this country, known to the committee, to anneal cast iron for general purposes. Premiums were also awarded for japanned waiters and trays, to J. V. Blackmar of Philadelphia, and to the Merrimac Manufacturing Company of Massachusetts, for the best specimens of calicoes or prints for ladies' dresses. Prints were exhibited also by the Taunton Company, deemed nearly equal to them, and others by the Warren Factory of Baltimore.

Among the premiums were also the following: to S. P. Wetherill & Co., Philadelphia, for samples of one thousand pigs of lead, the product of the Perkiomen mines, smelted by them; to Wm. and T. H. Day, for safety door locks of their invention; for flannel, from the Yantic factory, Connecticut, for hearth rugs, the first product of machinery invented by Lloyd Mifflin; to Messrs. Terhoeven, for pins made by them. Pianos were exhibited from eight different manufacturers, and honorary mention was awarded to Mr. Rowland of Philadelphia, for superior mill, pit, and cross-cut saws; to George W. Carpenter, for pharmaceutical preparations; to the Maryland Chemical Company, for bleaching salts, preferred by many to the celebrated Tennants of Glasgow, for magnesia, etc.;[1] to Jones, Keim & Co., of Windsor Furnace, near Harrisburg, Pennsylvania, for the most perfect specimens of castings known of this country's production, rivaling the most splendid Berlin medals; and to George C. Osborne of Philadelphia, for water colors, and to other exhibitors.

The first manufacture of Varnish, except for individual use, is said to have been this year commenced in New York, by P. B. Smith, 202 Bowery, who the next year was joined by a Mr. Hulburt, and in the following year, Tilden & Hulburt started the second factory. Mr. Smith, subsequently (1836), commenced the business with D. Price, at Newark, New Jersey, where seven or eight establishments now manufacture the well known *Newark varnishes*—Mr. Smith's being one of the oldest and largest in the United States.[2] Copal varnish had been made

(1) The London Mechanics' Magazine for this year, stated that the United States was now wholly supplied with Epsom Salts, which it formerly received from England, by the "factory established in Baltimore, making a *purer* salt than in Europe and at *much less price*." It was made by Messrs. McKim, Sims & Co., who produced the next year over 1,500,000 pounds. Sulphate of Quinine was worth this year seven or eight dollars an ounce, but its manufacture was soon after commenced, and in 1831 it sold in Baltimore for $1.40 per ounce.

(2) Coach-makers' Magazine, vol. 1, p. 212.

on a small scale in Philadelphia, before this time, by Mr. Christian Schrack, who, in 1830, devoted his whole attention to its manufacture.

Castor oil was manufactured in considerable quantities from the palma christi or castor bean, in Illinois and some other parts of the West. Mr. Adams of Edwardsville, Illinois, in 1825, made five hundred gallons, which sold at $2.50 per gallon; in 1826, eight hundred gallons; in 1827, one thousand gallons, which brought $1.75; and this year, eighteen hundred gallons, at one dollar per gallon. Two years after, he started two presses and made over ten thousand gallons, which sold for seventy-five to eighty-seven cents per gallon.

The Lead regions of that state were at this time filled with miners, speculators, and others, attracted thither during the last few years for mining purposes. The lead manufactured this year amounted to 11,105,810 pounds.

The sugar plantations of Louisiana, as ascertained by personal visitation to each estate, yielded this year 87,965 hogsheads of sugar, and 39,874 of molasses. There were besides, two hundred and six planters, who produced nothing this year, but would the next. The largest plantation was that of General Wade Hampton, seventy miles above New Orleans, which yielded 1640 hogsheads of sugar and 750 of molasses. The sugar estates in operation numbered 308; their manual power was twenty-one thousand slaves; the steam power, eighty-two engines; horse power, 226; capital invested, about $34,000,000. Since 1816, when the state produced fifteen thousand hogsheads of sugar, the business has greatly increased under the protecting duty then laid, and now supplies nearly two thirds of the domestic consumption. Upward of thirty-nine thousand hogsheads of sugar, and about eighteen thousand five hundred hogsheads of molasses, were sent from Louisiana to northern parts of the Union, and nearly as much up the river in the year ending September 30. Its price at Louisville, Kentucky, was seven and a quarter cents by the barrel.

The iron manufacture of Pennsylvania amounted to 22,600 tons of bar and rolled iron, and 14,000 tons of castings, equal to 48,000 tons of pig metal. The Champlain region of New York produced about 3,000 tons of bar iron, and the state an amount equal to 13,500 tons of pig iron; Virginia, 10,500; Ohio, 5,000; Kentucky, 4,500; Tennessee, 5,000; New Jersey, 4,000; Maryland, 3,000; North Carolina, 1,800; the six New England states, 1,200; and the rest of the states about 4,500 tons; total, 101,000 tons. The whole number of furnaces in operation has been elsewhere estimated on reliable data at 192, and the product in pig iron and castings at 123,404 tons. The price of American hammered bar iron, which had advanced within three or four years, was in the seaports $105 per ton, and on the Ohio, $115 to $125.[1]

The first locomotive trip upon a railroad in America, is said to have been made during this year upon the Carbondale and Honesdale railroad, extending from the western terminus of the Lackawaxen canal to the Lackawanna river, and connecting the canals of the Delaware and Hudson Canal Company with their coal mines in Luzerne county, Pennsylvania, whence the first coal was sent the next year. The engine was imported from England, where the use of locomotives was by no means established, and even appears to have been in some instances abandoned in favor of stationary engines for railways.[1] The engineer was Mr. Horatio Allen, of New York, since engineer of the New York and Erie railroad, who made the experimental trip alone, crossing the Lackawaxen, on trestle work thirty feet high, with a curve of 355 to 400 feet radius, and returning in safety, contrary to the expectations of many spectators. The engine proved afterward to be too heavy for the road. The first American patent for a locomotive engine, was taken out this year, by W. Howard, of Baltimore.

The Daily Advertiser, and several other newspapers in Boston, were at this time printed on Treadwell's Power Presses, which were moved by steam, and threw off about six hundred impressions per hour. The newspapers of that city numbered thirty-four, including seven dailies, and a weekly paper called the "American Manufacturer." The number of printing offices in the United States at this time, was not less than nine hundred, an increase of 525 since 1810. The newspapers of the whole Union were estimated to consume 104,400 reams of paper yearly, worth $500,000, and those of New York, 15,000 reams, worth four to five dollars per ream.

(1) Evidence before a committee of Congress.

(2) Early in this year, a deputation of the Liverpool and Manchester Railway Company, whose double track road, the first great experimental work of the kind in England, was approaching completion, reported in favor of *stationary engines*, as a tractive power. But the directors, encouraged by their engineer, Mr. George Stephenson, whose opinion that a locomotive could be constructed to travel fifteen or twenty miles an hour was ridiculed before a committee of Parliament, and by others, decided to make a trial of locomotives, and offered a premium of £500, for the best locomotive engine, to draw on a level three times its own weight (which was not to exceed six tons), at the rate of ten miles an hour, and to cost not over £550. At the trial on the 8th October, four engines competed for the prize, which was given to Stephenson's "Rocket," which traversed the prescribed route, at a speed varying from twelve to twenty-nine miles an hour, establishing the epoch of land locomotion by steam, and procuring for Mr. Stephenson the title of the "father of the locomotive system." The first Stephenson engine imported into the United States, was the "Robert Fulton," for the Mohawk and Hudson Railroad in 1831, about which time their construction commenced in this country.

Several additions were about this time made in the manufacture of Paper. William Morgan, of Meadville, Pennsylvania, commenced at that place on a small scale, the first manufacture of paper from straw and hay, for which he obtained a patent. The paper was of a yellow color, but strong and smooth, and an edition of the New Testament is said to have been printed upon it, which cost only five cents a copy. On the 28th November, a canal boat was launched at Meadville, built of materials growing upon the banks of French creek the day before, which left for Pittsburg on the 30th, with twenty passengers and three hundred reams of straw paper.[1] Machinery was also erected this year, or the next, at Chambersburg, Pennsylvania, for the manufacture of paper, from straw and blue grass, to the amount of three hundred reams daily. In September of the next year, it was made at Baltimore by hand process. A patent was taken out by E. H. Collier of Plymouth, Massachusetts, for making paper from sea grass (*ulva marina*), and by several others for mechanical processes and machines connected with paper making.[2]

An improvement in the vibrating apparatus of the Fourdrinier or endless wire-web paper machine, was this year patented in England by Mr. George Dickinson, and came into extensive use.

The amount of fees received for patents, etc., by the Patent Office, from its organization to December 31, was $160,659.37. Among the patents issued this year were the following:

William H. Folger, Spartansburg, S. C., Feb. 13, for separating gold and silver from earth, for which he received two other patents the next year; William Magaw, Meadville, Pa., March 8, making paper, and to the same, May 22, for making paper from hay and straw; Elisha H. Collier, Plymouth, Mass., April 15, paper from sea grass; Wm. Hoyt, Vernon, Ind., April 29, corn sheller, reissued June 13, 1831; Richard Waterman & George W. Annis, Providence, R. I., Aug. 30, making double paper on machines, by which any number of thicknesses might be made by pressure between rollers, etc.; Mason Hunting, Watertown, Mass., Oct. 20, improved top press roller, for making paper (of any thickness at one operation);[3] Marsdan Haddock, New York, July 17, making paper by the flat press in sheets (by the dipping process); Richard Mitchell and N. Butterworth, Troy, Mass., March 22, satinett power loom; Cyrus Durand, New York, May 22, copper plate printing press; Charles G. Williams, New York, March 29, cylindrical printing press; E. Burt, O.

(1) Day's Historical Collection of Pennsylvania, pp. 256, 258.

(2) See Patents.

(3) John Dickinson of Nash Mills took out a patent in 1830, in England, for making paper of any thickness by uniting the surfaces of two or more sheets.

D. Boyd, & A. H. Boyd, Manchester, Ct., Aug. 19, power loom for weaving check and plaid; this loom, invented by Rev. E. Burt, was the first American check loom; William M. Johnson, New York, Aug. 21, and George F. Peterson, New York, Oct. 13, casting printers' types. The machine of Mr. Johnson, secured a much sharper outline and better face to the letter by the use of a pump to force the liquid into the matrix, and has been much improved since. Samuel S. Williams, Roxbury, Mass., Aug. 22, making mats from manilla and other grasses; Charles Danforth, Ramapo, N. Y., Sept. 2, bobbin and flyer; Thomas W. Dyott, Philadelphia, Oct. 10, melting and fusing glass by the use of rosin; Allen Ward, Philadelphia, Oct. 11, triangular measure case ruler for garments—these instruments are still in use we believe; Isaac Sanford, Blockley, Philadelphia, Oct. 11, carding, winding, and making of hats—the model of this machine was deposited in the office, and the money paid in February, 1799, since which, the invention had lain dormant; Joshua Shaw, Philadelphia, Oct. 24, percussion lock for cannon; H. F. West and A. F. Stevens, Richland, N. Y., Oct. 29, mode of forming hat bodies; William Coburn, Gardner, Maine, Nov. 1, extracting tannin by steam; B. B. Howell, Philadelphia, Nov. 6, making malleable iron; Lemuel W. Wright, London, England, Dec. 6, arranging machinery for manufacturing wood screws. [This apparatus, by the patentee of the pin machine, was also patented in England in March, 1827, and an amended patent was given in September of this year. It was somewhat complex.] William Howard, Baltimore, Dec. 10, locomotive steam engine (the first recorded in this country); William Woodworth, Hudson, N. Y., Dec. 27, planing, tongueing, grooving, and cutting boards, etc., and dressing brick, or other mineral or metallic substances. This patent is remarkable for the amount of litigation arising out of it for many years after, and for having been longer extended than any other patent, as well as for the great profits it has yielded to its owners.

The relations of the General Government to the subject of protecting duties, upon which the public mind continued to be exercised to a degree
1829 that threatened the harmony of the Union, was brought to the notice of Congress by the last annual message of President Adams. Having observed that the imports and exports, under whatever tariff, had always nearly corresponded in amount, and were both likely to be much increased by the recent removal of the interdict against American breadstuffs abroad: that the great interests of agriculture, manufactures, and commerce, were inseparably united, and were alike under the protecting power of the Legislature, and that taxes for revenue

should be adjusted as equally as possible, but that countervailing regulations, such as the legislation of England, in excluding nearly all our great staples, except cotton, which she needed in times of scarcity, must often bear heavily on some, the message proceeds:

"Is the self-protecting energy of this nation so helpless that there exists no power to counteract the bias of this foreign legislation? That the growers of grain must submit to this exclusion from the foreign markets of their produce; and the shippers must dismantle their ships; the trade of the north stagnate at the wharves, and the manufacturers starve at their looms, while the whole people shall pay tribute to foreign industry to be clad in a foreign garb? That Congress is impotent to restore the balance in favor of native industry, destroyed by the statutes of another realm? More just and more generous sentiments will, I trust, prevail.

"If the tariff adopted at the last session of Congress shall be found by experience to bear oppressively upon the interests of any one section of the Union, it ought to be, and I cannot doubt will be, so modified as to alleviate its burdens. To the voice of just complaint from any portion of their constituents, the representatives of the states and the people, will never turn away their ears. But so long as the duty of the foreign shall operate only as a bounty upon the domestic article—while the planter, and the merchant, and the shepherd, and the husbandman, shall be found thriving in their occupations under the duties imposed for the protection of domestic manufactures, they will not repine at the prosperity shared with themselves by their fellow citizens of other professions, nor denounce as violations of the Constitution the deliberate acts of Congress, to shield from the wrongs of foreign laws the native industry of the Union."

The strong dissatisfaction of the people of the Southern States, and of some other portions of the Union with the tariff act of the last session, was manifested by various measures of a public character, and soon after the reassembling of Congress, several earnest remonstrances were presented to the Senate on the subject from legislative and other bodies. At the suggestion of Governor Forsyth, who, in his message of Nov. 4, advised the people of the state to substitute as far as possible, their own household manufactures for those of Europe and the Northern and Eastern States, the Legislature of Georgia, on the 10th December, adopted a solemn protest against the recent act, and demanded its repeal, as fraudulent, oppressive, partial, unjust, and a perversion of the powers of Congress, which was presented to the Senate on the 12th January, for the purpose of being preserved among the archives of that body. On the 12th February, the Legislature of South Carolina presented, through Messrs. Smith and Hayne, the protest against the act as unconstitutional, oppressive, and unjust, but declaring their anxious "desire to live in peace with their brethren, to do all that in them lies to preserve and perpetuate the Union of the States and the liberties of which it is the surest pledge."

A committee of the Assembly of Virginia, acting upon the resolutions of Georgia and South Carolina, also reported, on 21st February, a series of resolutions, which were adopted, condemnatory of the tariff as a violation of constitutional authority; and, on the 28th, a protest of the Alabama Legislature, to the same effect, was read in the Senate of the United States. North Carolina also entered her protest. The remonstrances from Georgia and Alabama, claimed the right of resistance to acts which transcended the legislative powers of Congress, and trespassed upon the reserved rights of the States.[1] A meeting of merchants and others of Boston, opposed to the tariff, also adopted, on 13th Jan-

(1) Much language of an inflammatory nature was about this time used in public meetings and by the press. The Milledgeville Journal said, "The memorable scenes of our Revolution have again to be acted over." A meeting in St. John's Parish, S. C., declared, "We have sworn that Congress shall at our demand repeal the tariff. If she does not, our State Legislature will dissolve our connection with the Union, and we will take our stand among the nations, and it behooves every true Carolinian to stand by his arms, and to keep the halls of our Legislature pure from foreign intruders." That the tariff acts "ought not to be submitted to," and that "the adhesion of the State of South Carolina to the Union, shall depend upon the unconditional repeal of the tariff laws of 1816, 1824, and 1828, so far as they are inconsistent with the constitutional rights of our citizens." "This is not the language of vain-glorious boasting, of hot-headed enthusiasm," it was said on an another occasion. "It is the resolute voice of despair. It is useless to disguise matters, or to shut our eyes upon the possible (must we say probable?) consequences. If this spirit spreads over the South—and what can prevent it?—civil war must follow, and the bonds of the Union are broken."

Mr. George Canning, while prime minister, is said also to have declared that "he would make the people of America reduce their tariff or dissolve their Union." This led to a correspondence with the leading opponents of the act in this country, and laid the foundation of nullification in South Carolina, which resulted in the compromise tariff of 1833.

In consequence of the excitement on the subject, M. Carey, toward the close of the last year, published a series of "common sense doctrines" to the Southern people, and endeavored by means of a lengthy circular, to organize a "society of Political Economists" for the diffusion of what he considered sounder views of the principles of protection, in the hope of allaying the ferment. Failing to meet with support, he finally abandoned the active advocacy of the cause about this time, and devoted his energies to various benevolent and charitable objects, in which he was always prominent.

With the commencement of this year, Mr. Condy Raguet issued the "Free Trade Advocate," a monthly journal devoted to the support of Free Trade principles, adopting as his motto the answer of the French minister Colbert "*Laissez nous faire*," "let us alone," which was the favorite maxim of the anti-tariff party. The Advocate, after the appearance of two volumes, was merged in the "Banner of the Constitution," a semi-weekly paper under the same editorial management.

uary, resolutions declaring the acts partial, oppressive, and contrary to the spirit of the Constitution, and a memorial to Congress on the subject.

An act was passed, January 21st, allowing an additional drawback of five cents a pound on sugar refined in the United States when exported therefrom.

Acts of the 3d March authorized the President of the United States to cause the reserved salt springs in the State of Missouri, and the reserved lead mines in the same state to be exposed to public sale, as other lands. The lead mines had been worked for many years imperfectly, with but little public benefit, but the act did not apply to the mines of the upper Mississippi, which had been worked since 1720.

A report made to the New York Legislature, February 19, recommending a bounty on domestic salt, stated that the supply of brine at the Salina springs was inexhaustible, and the strongest in the United States, making fifty-six pounds of salt to every forty-five gallons. Salt was made at Salina at a fair profit of twelve and a half cents per bushel of fifty-six pounds. The state duty was twelve and a half cents, freight and toll to Albany nine cents, and transportation thence to New York four cents, which, with two cents allowed for waste, made it cost in New York forty cents a bushel. St. Ubes salt was about thirty-five cents per bushel.

The capital employed in the manufacture of salt in the United States was estimated to be $6,964,988, and the product 4,444,929 bushels. The quantity imported during the fiscal year was 5,945,547. England, the British West Indies, and Portugal, were the principal sources of supply. Key West, in Florida, the most southern settlement in the Union, became about this time a new source of domestic supply, the ponds yielding this year about four thousand bushels.

A decree of the Liberator President of the Republic of Columbia, at Quito, dated May 8, imposed for purposes of revenue a tariff of duties on imports, which was almost prohibitory of many articles of export from the United States.

A decree of the Mexican government, dated May 22, prohibited, under the penalty of confiscation, the importation into that republic of a large list of raw and manufactured articles, including many of the leading products of American manufacture.

At a meeting of the cotton manufacturers of Philadelphia, on 3d February, resolutions were adopted to establish one or more private houses for the sale of their goods, and to discontinue sales at public auction, as having a tendency to reduce the prices below value, and injurious to the interests of manufacturer, workman, dealer, and consumer.

The Boston Daily Advertiser, of the 2d March, gave the names of twelve cotton factories destroyed by fire within one hundred and fifty miles of that city, since the first of January, involving a total loss in six of them of $215,500, and the insurance amounting to $42,500. The burning of the Byram and Phillipsburg factories, in Pennsylvania, about this time, increased the loss to $321,600.

An unusual degree of distress prevailed at this time among the manufacturers of New England, particularly in the cotton branch, producing numerous failures and great depreciation of the value of stocks. The cause was by some ascribed to the disappearance of specie, and by others to over-speculation, which had tempted great numbers into manufacturing, with insufficient capitals, and a consequent over-production.

The number of incorporated manufactories in Massachusetts at this date was stated at two hundred and thirty-five. A large proportion of them manufactured cotton, wool, and iron; but there were also incorporated companies for the manufacture of glass, hair, leather, wire, files, lead, duck, pins, soapstone, cordage, salt, calico, brass, copper, lace, umbrellas, linen, hose, ale, beer, type, cotton, cards, gins, glass bottles, lead pipe, etc.

The State of Rhode Island contained one hundred and thirty-nine cotton factories. The towns of Warwick and Smithfield had each twenty woolen and twenty cotton factories. The use of Turkey red in calico printing, which had long given the French an advantage over English and American prints, was this year successfully introduced by the manufacturers of Lowell. A fire department was also established in that town, and the Lowell Institution for savings was incorporated.

About twelve thousand pieces of calico were this year made at the new print works of Mr. Marshall, near Hudson, New York. A new establishment also went into operation at Baltimore, for weaving stuffs for calicoes, having one hundred power looms driven by steam, making fifteen thousand yards weekly.

On the 26th March, the corner stone of a factory was laid at Athens, Georgia, which was about the commencement of manufactures in that state since the war. The building was burned soon after, but was rebuilt.

About five hundred bales of cotton were this year grown in Texas.

The town of Lynn, in Massachusetts, had a population of over five thousand, chiefly supported by its shoe manufactures, the product of which was estimated at 1,200,000 to 1,400,000 pairs of shoes annually, at an average value of seventy-five cents each, or $1,000,000. The females of the town earned more than $60,000 annually by binding and ornamenting. Large quantities of low-priced fancy shoes were exported to South America, and sold at a profit. About sixty tons of chocolate were annually made by a factory at Lynn.

The paper mills in Massachusetts, in November, numbered sixty, in six of which machinery was used. They consumed seventeen hundred tons of rags, junk, etc., and made paper to the value of $700,000 per annum. The entire paper manufacture of the United States was estimated to amount to the yearly value of over $6,000,000, and to employ upward of ten thousand persons. Large quantities of rags were imported from Germany and Italy. Several improvements were patented in the manufacture of straw and other paper, including an improvement in the cylinder machine, by Isaac Sanderson, of Milton, Massachusetts, by which greater equality of strength in machine-made paper was secured. Straw paper began to be somewhat extensively used for wrapping in Philadelphia. It was also used in printing Niles's Weekly Register, which had an extensive circulation; being regarded as the best and cheapest paper then made for that purpose. It was principally made at Chambersburg, by machinery, and cost less than two dollars per ream, imperial size.

The town of Paterson, New Jersey, contained 7,033 inhabitants, and had four machine shops, one of which, Goodwin, Rogers & Company, made, in the last year, 15,048 spindles with all the necessary accompaniments, worth, at twelve dollars each, $180,576, in addition to 1,020,000 pounds of iron, and 35,000 pounds of brass castings, made in a foundry connected with it. A rolling and slitting mill and nail factory made 672,000 pounds of nails. There were seventeen cotton factories, with 32,000 spindles, of which fourteen factories and 27,679 spindles were in operation, and worked up 2,179,600 pounds of cotton into 1,214,450 pounds of yarn, 150,000 yards of cotton duck, and 1,861,450 yards of other cotton cloth annually. In the town were four hundred and eighty-seven hand and power looms, and 33,965 cotton and flax spindles.

Pittsburg, Pennsylvania, contained eight rolling mills, employing three hundred hands, and using six thousand tons of blooms, chiefly Juniata, and fifteen hundred tons of pig iron. A nail factory employed one hundred and fifty hands, and made eighteen tons of nails. There were seven steam engine factories, with two hundred and ten hands, which had made several engines for the northern lakes, a few to go east of the mountains, and one to Mexico. Within two or three years the casting of sugar kettles, sugar mills, and small steam engines for the planters of Louisiana, had become an important branch of industry. The plow factory was established this year by Samuel Hall. In October, the mechanics and artizans of the town bore public testimony to the excellence of the files made by Broadmeadow & Co., who had recently established a large manufacture of files and rasps, from steel of their own make, and of finished workmanship. Some penknives were also made there.

The manufacture of penknives and pocket knives, articles almost exclusively imported up to this time, was commenced somewhat extensively at Worcester, Massachusetts, by Moses L. Morse & Co., the former of whom had invented a pin machine several years before, and superintended the business. The several parts of the knife were made by machinery, and each by appropriate sets of workmen, with such success as to be with difficulty distinguished from English cutlery. Two other cutlery establishments were commenced in the vicinity within two years after. Superior table knives and forks were made at Philadelphia.

The Lemnos factory for the manufacture of edge tools in almost every variety was about this time established in the borough of Chambersburg, Pennsylvania, by Messrs. James Dunlop and George A. Madeira, by whom an axe and hatchet, of superior quality, were presented to President Jackson, in April of the next year. The hardware and cutlery manufacture received a considerable extension about this time.

The aggregate value of goods sold at the sixth semi-annual sale of the New England Society at Boston, in March of this year, was estimated at $1,300,000.

On the 2d May, the "American Institute, of the city of New York, for the purpose of encouraging and promoting domestic industry in this state and the United States, in agriculture, commerce, manufactures, and the arts," was incorporated by the Legislature. With purposes similar to those of the "Conservatory of Arts and Trades" in Paris, and the "National Repository" in London, it aimed to promote its objects by an annual exhibition of machinery, manufactures, etc., by awarding premiums, by the formation of a repository of models, and a library of books relating to agriculture and the arts, and was empowered to hold property yielding an income of thirty thousand dollars per annum. The first annual fair of the Institute was held at Castle Garden, in November, when premiums were awarded for the following articles of domestic manufacture. For broadcloths, cassimeres, etc., twelve premiums; manufactures of cotton nine, of iron six, of glass four, hats three, pianos four, paper seven, books and printing four, stoneware six, hemp and flax three, leather four, ladies' apparel six, machinery three, miscellaneous articles thirty-seven. The Phœnix mill of Mr. Colt, of Paterson, New Jersey, received the premium for the best article of cotton bagging, which was made of Sea Island cotton, and excited much curiosity. The exhibition of manufactures at the Franklin Institute this year exceeded any previous one. Samples of osnaburgs bagging and negro cloth were exhibited by the South Carolina Manufacturing Company of Darlington, the last of which could be retailed at twelve and a half cents per yard.

A large cloth manufactory, and a carpet factory, was at this time in operation at Martinsburg, Virginia, both of which produced fabrics of beautiful pattern and excellent quality. Felt carpeting was made this year at Catskill, New York, and was considered durable and cheap. A flannel factory was established at Barnet, Vermont, by water power, capable of finishing three thousand yards weekly, from which the first bales were on a team to Boston on 13th October. It belonged to Mr. Henry Stevens.

The manufacture of damask table linen was commenced at Philadelphia in December, by Hamilton Stewart, who made some very elegant patterns.

It was estimated that twenty-five hundred Piano Fortes, of the aggregate value of $750,000, were made this year in the United States, of which nine hundred were made in Philadelphia, eight hundred in New York, seven hundred and seventeen in Boston, and a considerable number in Baltimore.

Handsome silk ribbons, in great variety, were manufactured in Baltimore, from American silk. Silk to the value of twenty-five thousand dollars was made at Mansfield, Connecticut, chiefly by women and children. The first attempt in the United States to manufacture sewing silk by machinery was made at Mansfield this year, by Captain Joseph Conant, afterward of the firm of Conant & Smith, Northampton, Massachusetts, and Mr. Atwood, subsequently of the firm of Atwood & Crane, Mansfield, by whom the business was continued. After many losses and discouragements, they succeeded in making a good article. Silk pocket handkerchiefs by Mr. Bryant, and other silk goods by James Reed, were exhibited at the American Institute fair. A powerful interest in the silk culture was excited by some essays and experiments on American silk, published in July of this year, at the suggestion of John Vaughan, Esq., by Mr. D'Homergue, a practical silk manufacturer, of Marseilles, who had been invited to the United States by the American Silk Society in Philadelphia. He advocated, in conjunction with P. S. Duponceau, Esq., a filature system as the only effective means of promoting the silk culture, and their efforts were followed by the introduction, soon after, in Congress, of the famous silk bill, which was ultimately defeated, an experimental filature having, in the mean time, been started in Philadelphia by them, in 1830.

There were at this date two watch crystal manufactories in the United States, one at Boston and one at Pittsburg, Pennsylvania. Watch glasses were also made to some extent in the glass factories at Jersey City, New Jersey.

Tin was this year discovered by Professor Hitchcock, of Amherst, Massachusetts, at Goshen, in Connecticut, being the first discovery of tin in the United States. It consisted of a single crystal of oxide of tin (cassiterite, or tin stone), weighing fifty grains, contained in granite. It has been since found in small quantities in different places by Professors Sheppard, Rogers, and others.

Specimens of gold, weighing ten pounds, four pounds, and others of less weight, were discovered in Anson county, North Carolina. The first gold received at the mint from Virginia, was deposited this year to the value of $2,500; and the first from South Carolina, to the value of $3,500. The first from Georgia was sent the next year to the amount of $212,000. A map of the gold region of North Carolina, published by Professor Mitchell, indicated nine different mining localities in that state, three in the "primary," and six in the "transitive, or slate" rocks.

A furnace was erected at Strafford, Vermont, for smelting copper pyrites, which occur there with sulphuret of iron, being employed there in the manufacture of copperas, which was made at this time to the amount of ten thousand tons annually, the works having been extended in the last year.

The manufacture of bricks by machinery was successfully commenced in New York. The machines made twenty-five thousand bricks per diem of twelve hours, ready for the fire as soon as they left the machine. They sold readily at five dollars to eight dollars per thousand. The Salamander Fire-brick Works, at Albany, was established at this date by Jacob Henry; and Mr. Berry and others of Baltimore, were so successful about this time in the manufacture of fire bricks as to stop the importation.

At the Springfield Armory, in Massachusetts, the arms, etc., manufactured since 1795 to December 31st, amounted to 296,982 muskets, 250 rifles, 1,000 pistols, 1,202 carbines, 12,840 ball screws, 93,631 wipers, 139,700 screw-drivers, 12,720 sprig vices, 1,936 sets of verifying instruments for muskets, 2,890 arm chests, and 46,545 muskets repaired. The expenditure, including pay of officers and workmen, had been $3,700,559.76. The cost of each musket, exclusive of repairs, improvements, machinery, etc., for 1829, would be about $10.66, a reduction of $1.68 since 1815.

The number of steamboats built on the western rivers since 1811 was three hundred and twenty-one, of which one hundred and eighty-eight were still running.

PATENTS.—William Delit, East Hartford, Conn., Jan. 13, machine for cleaning rags for paper; John C. Ely, New York, Jan. 28, screw dock; John Goulding, Dedham, Mass., two patents, dated Feb. 16, and two others June 11 and July 21, for manufacturing wool; G. H. Burgin, Philadelphia, April 3, use of ley from soap as a flux for glass; S. Beckwith, S. Beckwith jr., and E. Beckwith, Jan. 27, machine for making shoe pegs; Joseph Soxten, Philadelphia, April 11, improvement in ever-pointed pencil cases, and William Jackson, Philadelphia, July 27, a slide instead of a screw in ever-pointed pencil cases; S. G. Reynolds, Bristol, R. I., April 13, machine for making nails and rivets. This was for making wrought iron nails, etc., by machieery, almost as cheaply as cast iron nails. Isaac Sanderson, Milton, Mass., April 18, cylindrical machine for paper making; Amasa Stone, Providence, R. I., April 30, improved power loom; John W. Cooper, Washington, Pa., Feb. 7, whitening straw and rags for paper making; R. Fairchild, Trumbull, Conn., May 4, agitator in paper making; Nathan Leonard, Merrimac, N. H., June 11, machine for pegging boots and shoes; Frederick B. Merrill, Buffalo, N. Y., June 13, chandelier of crystallized salt; John Arnold, Norwalk, Conn., July 15, forming the web of cloth without spinning or weaving; Reuben Wood, Erin, N. Y., Aug. 25, dyeing by steam; R. S. Tilden, Lynchburg, Va., Sept. 10, covering roofs with tin; Henry Korn, Philadelphia, Sept. 12, fly nets for horses, two patents reissued in 1834 and 1836; J. Rynex, J. Haskins, and S. Knower, Boston, Sept. 23, perpetual polished water proof boots and shoes; Daniel Baldwin, Ithaca, N. Y., scalding and napping hats; Anthony Doolittle, Ann Arbor, Michigan Territory, Nov. 10, distilling maize; David H. Mason and M. W. Baldwin, Philadelphia, Dec. 2, Bramah's hydrostatic press; William H. Bell, Fortress Monroe, Va., Dec. 8, elevating cannon. This patent was purchased by the United States government in 1836. John Thorp, Providence, R. I., Dec. 22, weaving narrow stuffs, such as ribbons, webbing, tapes, ferrets, girthings, chaise lace, fringes, etc., without the use of shuttles.

The number of patents in force in England at this date was 1,855, of which 152 were granted in 1828. Patents had to be taken out separately for England, Scotland, and Ireland, and the aggregate cost was $1,656, while in the United States it was only thirty dollars.

CHAPTER V.

ANNALS OF MANUFACTURES.

1830–1840.

THE attention of Congress was once more called to the subject of the Tariff, which continued to be violently discussed by the opponents of the late act. President Jackson, in his first annual message to the
1830 twenty-first Congress, at its first session, December 8th, 1829, made the following remarks:

"To regulate its conduct so as to promote equally the prosperity of these three cardinal interests (agriculture, commerce, and manufactures), is one of the most difficult tasks of government; and it may be regretted that the contemplated restrictions which now embarrass the intercourse of nations, could not by common consent be abolished and commerce allowed to flow in those channels to which individual enterprise, always its surest guide, might direct it. But we must ever expect selfish legislation in other nations, and are therefore compelled to adapt our own to their regulations, in the manner best calculated to avoid serious injury, and to harmonize the conflicting interests of our agriculture, our commerce, and our manufactures. Under these impressions I invite your attention to the existing tariff, believing that some of its provisions require modification. The general rule to be applied in graduating the duties upon the articles of foreign growth or manufacture, is that which will place our own in fair competition with those of other countries; and the inducements to advance even a step beyond this point, are controlling in regard to those articles which are of primary necessity in time of war."

The committee to which this part of the message was referred, reported against the expediency of any alteration of the tariff, but Mr. Cambreleng, from the Committee of Commerce and Navigation, on the 8th February, made a lengthy report, which was printed, recommending a modification of the existing tariff and revenue laws as incongruous and absurd in their provisions. On the 30th April, he introduced a bill to amend the navigation laws so as to secure a reciprocity of trade, at a uniform duty of thirty per cent. upon imports from such nations as would admit American products on like terms. The bill did not prevail, and another introduced in the Senate, by Mr. Benton, on the 23d of the same month, was also laid on the table on motion of Mr. Webster, and never taken up. The latter was entitled "A bill for the abolition of unnecessary duties, to relieve the people from sixteen millions of taxes, and to improve the condition of the Agriculture, Manufactures, and Commerce, of the United States," and provided for the repeal or the reduction of the existing duties on the principal imports, in favor of such nations as would reciprocate by treaty, and laid a duty of thirty-three and one third per cent. on furs and raw hides imported.

A bill introduced early in the session, by Mr. Mallory, from the Committee on Manufactures, in alteration of the several acts laying duties on imports, providing for the more effectual collection of the duties, and to prevent evasions of the revenue, became the subject of earnest discussion, upon the presentation of a new bill by way of amendment, by Mr. McDuffie of South Carolina. The substitute, which was rejected, proposed to repeal the acts of 1824 and 1828, so far as they imposed increased duties on woolens, iron, hemp, flax, cotton bagging, molasses, indigo, and manufactures of cotton—and to reduce the duty on salt to ten cents a bushel. Mr. McDuffie entered into a protracted discussion of the whole policy of protecting duties, designed to show their pernicious effects upon the various interests of the country, and particularly upon the South, which he represented to be suffering extremely from that cause. He repudiated with much severity of language, a constitutional right in the majority to govern, and was supported by Mr. Blair of the same state, who, also spoke in strong language, and declared that the time was at hand, when the rights and interests of his state, in common with those of the South, must be respected, or she would seek a remedy herself. The bill, after receiving several amendments, and the support of Messrs. Crawford of Pennsylvania, Everett of Massachusetts, Burgess of Rhode Island, and others, who spoke of the prostrate condition of New England manufactures, passed on 13th May, by a vote of one hundred and twenty-seven to forty.

On the 20th May an act was approved, reducing the duty on coffee, tea, and cocoa; and on the 29th, the duty on molasses was reduced to six cents a gallon, and a drawback allowed of four cents a gallon on spirits distilled from foreign molasses. An act, of the same date, reduced the duty on salt to fifteen cents a bushel until 31st December, and to ten cents thereafter.

In the discussion of these measures, and the question of internal improvements, in Congress and by the leading journals of the South, to which Dr. Cooper of Columbia College, South Carolina, was a prominent contributor, the doctrine of state sovereignity, and of the right of the local governments to annul any act of Congress, which a state might deem an encroachment upon its reserved rights, began to be distinctly asserted, particularly by the people of South Carolina. The right of Nullification, therefore, became the issue, in the great debate in the Senate, in January, between Mr. Hayne of South Carolina, and Mr. Webster of Massachusetts, upon the resolution of Mr. Foot, to limit the sale of public lands. Resolutions affirming the constitutionality of the tariff act of 1828, were adopted by the Legislatures of Vermont, Delaware, Louisiana, and perhaps others.

By an act approved May 31, the tonnage duties on ships and vessels of the United States, and of such nations as had abolished their discriminating and countervailing duties were repealed.

A bill before the Senate to recompense the heirs of Robert Fulton by the grant of a township of land, in consideration of the benefits rendered by him to the country, was rejected upon constitutional grounds.

Mr. Spencer, from the Committee on Agriculture, on 12th March, made a report, accompanied by a bill to promote the growth and manufacture of silk in the United States. The report, based upon the essays, and other information furnished by Mr. John D'Homergue, the son of an eminent silk manufacturer of Nismes, assisted by Mr. P. S. Duponceau, tended to establish the fact that American silk worms were more productive of silk than those of any other country,[1] but that the manufactured silk of the country was inferior, for want of practical knowledge and suitable machines for reeling, whereby it was rendered unfit for the finer fabrics; that every state was adapted to the cultivation of mulberries and the production of silk, and that if the culture were zealously prosecuted, the large importations of foreign silk, amounting in the last year to eight and one half millions, would be compensated by the export of raw silk, and the manufacture of silk stuffs be necessarily introduced. The bill drawn up, at the request of the committee, by Mr. Duponceau, after consultation with Mr. D'Homergue, proposed to devote forty thousand dollars to the establishment of a normal filature at or near Philadelphia, under the charge of the latter, whose departure from the

(1) The proceedings of the Chamber of Commerce at Lyons, published early in the year, in relation to American silk, state that a sample of silk, reeled in Philadelphia by Mr. D'Homergue, was assayed by a sworn and licensed assayer, and was declared to be of an extraordinary quality and admirably adapted to the uses of fabrication. Its degree of fineness was sixteen deniers, and it would produce singles of fifty, organzine of thirty-two, and tram of wool and silk of thirty duts, a quality extremely rare in our country. American silk is fine, nervous, good, regular, clean, of a fine color; in short, it unites all the qualities that can be wished for. Its value was estimated at twenty-six francs (five dollars) a pound.

country the committee thought would be a national misfortune, and he was to be required to instruct gratuitously sixty young men in the art of reeling silk and preparing it for exportation, so as to become afterward directors of filatures, and at least twenty women, who were to be paid for their labor. The balance of the appropriation, after deducting expenses, and the materials, were at the end of two years to be the property of Mr. D'Homergue. No opportunity was found to discuss the bill during this and the following session, and it was lost in the next.

An experimental filature, with ten reels and twenty women, was, however, put in operation in Philadelphia during this year, by Mr. Duponceau, under the charge of Mr. D'Homergue, who was a skillful reeler. Two banners of Pennsylvania silk, of light but beautiful texture, each twelve feet long and six feet wide, were woven by the latter for Mr. Duponceau, and having been dyed by some Germans in the city, were exhibited with some smaller articles, as cravats, handkerchiefs, etc., at the Fair of the Franklin Institute, and at the ensuing sessions were presented, one to Congress and the other to the Legislature of Pennsylvania, and received with appropriate acknowledgments.

Mr. Rapp of Economy, Pennsylvania, who commenced the silk culture in 1828, and made from his first crop fifteen or eighteen yards of striped silk for female apparel and vestings; also made during the last year some black figured silk vestings, and one hundred black silk handkerchiefs, the first ever made west of the mountains, and wholly the product of his Society from the worm to the looms. Spirited efforts began to be made in nearly every part of the country, to produce raw silk for exportation. The "silk mania" may be said to have commenced at this date.

In accordance with an act of 29th May, the President issued a proclamation on 5th October, opening to British vessels the trade between the British colonial possessions and the American ports, having received satisfactory assurance that the colonial ports of Great Britain in the West Indies, South America, the Bahama and Bermuda Islands, would be opened to American vessels, which was accordingly done by an order in council, dated Nov. 5th.

It was estimated that there were at this time completed within the United States, 1343 miles of canals and other artificial navigation; 1828 miles in progress, and 408 projected. Of railroads, forty-four miles were completed, 422 in progress, and 697 projected. A valuable improvement in Western navigation, was the opening of the Louisville and Portland canal, around the Falls of the Ohio, on the 5th December, at a cost of $750,000.

The first locomotive constructed in the United States, is said to have been built this year at the West Point Foundry in New York. It was named the "Phœnix," and was built for the South Carolina Railroad, for which a second engine, called the "West Point," was built at the same place during the year. A third one, "the Dewitt Clinton, was constructed there in the following Spring, for the Mohawk and Hudson railroad, which, about the same time, imported the first Stephenson locomotive, afterward rebuilt, and called the "John Bull."[1] A model locomotive engine was built this year for the proprietor of Peale's Museum, in Philadelphia, by Mr. M. W. Baldwin, and attracted much attention during the next year, by its performance with a train of loaded passenger cars. A rotary steam engine, for propelling carriages on railroads, was patented this year, and exhibited by Mr. Ezra Child of Philadelphia, and recommended by Mr. Jones, editor of the Franklin Journal.

A new branch of the Carriage Manufacture, was about this date introduced by the construction of the first "Omnibus" in New York. During the next year, Mr. John Stephenson commenced the business on Broadway, where he built his first omnibus, and the second in that city. He has since been extensively known in connection with this branch of the trade, recently superseded in our principal cities by the introduction of horse railroads.

The manufacture of sugar mills for Louisiana and the West Indies, had become an important business at Cincinnati and Pittsburg. In addition to cotton, woolen, and other machinery, one hundred and fifty steam engines, and fifty sugar mills, were built this year at the former place, and one hundred steam engines at Pittsburg. Five rolling and three slitting mills, had been erected in Pittsburg in the last two years, and of the iron made there in the same time, six hundred tons were converted into other articles before leaving the city. The iron rolled this year was 9,282 tons.

The number of iron works built in the state, in the ten years ending January 1, was forty-nine, of which thirty were blooming forges and rolling mills, one a mineral,[2] and sixteen charcoal blast furnaces. The whole number of iron furnaces in the United States was estimated at 202, and their product 137,075 tons of pig iron, and 18,273 tons of castings: total, 155,348. In east Jersey, in a part of Connecticut, in a large district of New York, and in Vermont, bar iron was extensively made, by the process technically denominated "blooming," only a single operation from the ore, without the intervention of the blast furnace.

(1) Historical Magazine, vol. 3, p. 150.

(2) The Mauch Chunk anthracite furnace, owned by the Lehigh Coal and Navigation Company, erected in 1826.

The total amount of iron made in the United States, was estimated as follows: bar iron made, 112,866 tons; bar iron castings, etc., estimated as pig iron, 191,536 tons, value $13,329,760; men employed, 29,254; persons subsisted, 146,273; annual wages, $8,776,420; paid for food furnished by farmers, $4,000,490. The average price of hammered iron was $96.66⅔ per ton; and of castings, sixty dollars, though much sold higher; and from the air furnace and cupola at four and one half cents a pound. The annual consumption of bar iron was about 130,007. The quantity of iron annually imported was about 33,986 tons.[1]

The value of domestic manufacturers exported this year was $5,320,980, which was a little below the average of the last five years. It included cotton manufactures to the value of $1,318,183, viz.: white piece goods, $964,196; printed goods, $61,800; Nankeen, a new manufacture, $1,093; twist and yarn, $24,744; all others, $266,350.

The cotton goods manufactured this year were estimated at 250,000,000 yards, including every kind, and worth, at ten cents a yard, $25,000,000. Four additional manufacturing companies were chartered in Massachusetts, to carry on the cotton manufacture at Lowell, viz.: the Middlesex Company, Suffolk Manufacturing Company, Tremont Mills, and Lawrence Manufacturing Company. The reduction in the price of water privileges, caused by the financial revulsion of the last year, which prostrated many cotton manufacturers in England, and those of slender capital in the United States, induced Messrs. Amos and Abbott Lawrence to enter largely into the business, in connection with the corporations above mentioned. The Boston and Lowell railroad was also incorporated and opened in 1835, and the town (now city) hall was built. The population of Lowell was 6,477, and six daily and one tri-weekly stage ran between it and Boston. The merchandise passing to and from Boston, for the corporations alone, amounted to ten thousand tons annually. The average price of Merrimac prints was 16.36 cents per yard, a reduction of 6.71 cents since 1825.

The manufacturing town of Fall River had increased in population, from 1,594 in 1820, to 4,259, and contained 20,357 cotton spindles, and 575 looms, making 100,105 yards of cloth weekly, a large calico printing establishment, rolling mill, and nail factory, a large woolen establishment, etc. The Exeter (N. H.) Cotton Factory went into operation in March, with a capital of $200,000, and 5000 spindles and 175 looms, employing 256 operators.

Cotton bagging of good quality was made in Providence, Rhode Island, from the waste of the factory. It was strong and heavy, weighing one and three quarter pounds to the yard, or one quarter

(1) Report of the New York Convention of the Friends of Domestic Industry, 1831.

pound more than the best hemp bagging, and was sold at eighteen cents a yard.

The manufacture of cotton bagging, etc., by steam power, was commenced this year at Newburyport, Massachusetts, which contained the only stocking factory of any size then in the country. The latter, recently established by the Newburyport Hosiery Manufacturing Company, contained a number of looms worked by females, at each of which, about twenty stockings were made daily by one person. The hosiery was of every variety—wool, lamb's wool, worsted, and cotton, and successful attempts had been made with silk. The articles being deemed superior to English hose, were in great demand.

The manufacture of Hats and Bonnets of straw was a prosperous business in New England, where it had greatly extended within a few years. The annual manufacture of these articles in the United States, was estimated at more than one and a half millions. They were made in large quantities from rye straw by the females of Boxford, in Massachusetts, whose bonnets were sold in the cities as English bonnets, at ten to fourteen dollars each, the cost being only two or three. The machine in general use at this time, for pressing straw hats, consisted of three blocks, with a lever and pressing flat attached to each, and the rim, crown, and top were pressed by hand at three separate operations, by being removed successively from one to the other. Several improved machines were introduced within a few years after.

The domestic manufacture of Lace was estimated to be worth at least half a million dollars, and Artificial Flowers were made in many towns and villages of the country, a large proportion of those on sale being of American manufacture.

Nearly every description of Carpeting made in Europe, was at this time produced in the United States, of a quality nearly equal to the imported, and supplied much of the demand.

Gloves and Mittens of buckskin, to the value of $130,000, were annually made in Johnstown, New York, where the business was commenced many years before and is now extensive.

Many articles of hardware, and the finer manufactures of metals, began to be produced at this time in considerable quantity. Upwards of forty trading houses in Philadelphia, were supplied with gilt Buttons from the factory of Mr. Robinson, at Attleborough, Massachusetts, in which the labor was principally performed by females, assisted by machinery invented and patented by the proprietors within the last twenty-five or thirty years. There were several other button factories in the country whose manufactures were said to be cheaper than the imported. The manufacture of American wire-eyed buttons was about this time commenced, under a patent, at Haydenville, Massachusetts, by two brothers, named Hayden, of Waterbury, Connecticut, who, in 1838, employed two hundred hands, and a capital of $100,000, and in the following year added to it the manufacture of steel pens.

The large button factory of Messrs. Scoville & Co., at Waterbury, Connecticut, was destroyed by fire in March. That town contained three factories of gilt and other metal buttons, and one of ivory.

A manufactory of steel buttons, clasps, ornaments, and other fancy articles of iron and steel, with twenty hands, and a gilt button factory with twenty hands, making nine thousand gross per annum, worth $4.50 per gross, and not surpassed in quality, it was thought, by any imported, was in operation about this time at Paterson, New Jersey. About three thousand gross of Pearl and Bone buttons and moulds were annually made, by Daniel Buzzel, in Philadelphia, and metal, cloth, and other buttons, were made in many other places at this time, in great profusion.

An extensive manufactory of Brass Hinges, was established about this date at Troy, New York, the products of which, in quality and cheapness, rivalled those of Birmingham. The Globe Sickle Factory, at Pittsburg, was also established, and the manufacture of large circular, mill, pit, and cross-cut cast-steel saws, was commenced in Boston by Mr. Charles Griffiths, an English manufacturer, and under the firm of Welch & Griffiths has been continued to the present time. Carpenters' small cast steel saws were also made in New York, by Mr. Nichols, and by Mr. Rowland and perhaps one or two others in Philadelphia. Swords for the army and navy were furnished by N. P. Ames, of Chicopee, Massachusetts, by contract with the government.

About one and a half million pounds of American cut nails were this year exported to foreign countries.

Roofing slates were extensively manufactured at Easton, Pennsylvania, by James M. Porter, and in May a manufactory of roofing slates and slate pencils of superior quality was established at Baltimore by Thomas Symington, who employed machinery patented by him in November 1828. The price of roofing slates was said to have been reduced one third, under the existing duty.

Six shot factories had been erected in the Atlantic States since the duty on foreign shot was laid, and there were several others on the Mississippi. The shot tower of Paul Beck, on the Schuylkill, near Philadelphia, was said to be capable of supplying the whole United States with that article.

An improvement in the manufacture of Caoutchouc was made this year by Dr. J. K. Mitchell, of Philadelphia, who showed that India rubber bags, after maceration in sulphuric ether, could, by successive inflations and collapses, or by being rolled in its soft state, be made into thin bottles, or sheets of great size, and that after being cut with a wet knife, the edges would adhere so that the place of union would be scarcely visible. A similar discovery had been announced in England by Mr. Hancock, but his process was kept a secret.

A Fourdrinier paper machine is said to have been first successfully made in the United States this year, at Windham, Connecticut, since which time few, if any, have been imported. Cylinder machines, somewhat resembling the endless web machine, had been constructed and used many years before by Mr. Gilpin, of the Brandywine Paper Mills, who this year also patented an improved mode of finishing paper by passing it between calenders or cylinders to give it a polished surface. The Messrs. Ames & Co., of Springfield, Massachusetts, employed sixteen engines, and used on an average three tons of rags every twenty-four hours, making at the rate of eighty reams of the largest sized printing paper, and one hundred and eighty of foolscap or letter, equal to three hundred and ninety of the latter. They used machinery which produced the paper in an endless sheet, and was patented by them. It enabled one man to do the work of over thirty, and was considered superior to the foreign machine. The paper manufacture of the United States was further improved and cheapened about this date by the use of chlorine for bleaching colored rags, not previously used in making writing paper Patents were also obtained this year for making paper from wood, at the rate of five to seven reams to the one hundred pounds. Paper was also made in western Pennsylvania from fibres of the lime and aspen. Leathern paper, made from the refuse shavings and parings of leather, was also the subject of a patent. It was adapted to sheathing vessels. A manufactory of parchment was established at Pottsville, Pennsylvania.

The value of the books published in the United States this year was estimated at $3,500,000, of which $1,100,000 were school books alone. The increase, since 1820, was over forty per cent.

According to a report to Congress, the number of steamboats of all kinds on the waters of New York state, in November, was eighty-six, those on the North river and the Sound being the largest. They varied from three hundred and six to five hundred and twenty-seven tons. On the Mississippi there were one hundred and thirty steamboats, one hundred of which were of large size, averaging three hundred tons each.

The patents granted this year by the United States Patent Office, numbered five hundred and forty-four, of which one hundred and ninety were to New York, one hundred and forty-six to New England (fifty-two to Connecticut), eighty-eight to Pennsylvania, twenty-six to Virginia, twenty-four to Maryland, eight to New Jersey, nineteen to Ohio, one to Mississippi, one to Alabama. Twenty-seven were for threshing machines, chiefly to New York, eight for spinning jennies, six for machines for making hats, seven for steam engines, seven for grist mills, twelve relating to railroads, nineteen for churns, and twenty-one for washing machines. The following were among the number:

Eleazer Cady, Canaan, N. Y., Jan. 6, weighing boats and cargoes (called the tongue metre); E. F. Blank and Thomas Blank, New York, Feb. 16, making paper of leather cuttings and parings, etc.; Zechariah Allen, Providence, R. I., Feb. 23, dressing and finishing cloth; Charles Danforth, Paterson, N. J., April 1, spinning threstle. This valuable machine was introduced into England during the last year, where it was patented by J. Hutchin, Esq., and came into extensive use. Samuel Lane, Hallowell, Me., May 17, endless chain and railway horse power; Thomas Ewbank, New York, June 8, preventing explosion of boilers; Aaron B. Quimby, Hagerstown, Md., Oct. 1, preventing explosion of boilers; I. Loughead and J. B. Chapman, Philadelphia, June 11, guard for explosion of boilers; S. P. Mason, Leesville, Conn., June 24, reissued Dec. 29, cotton roping spinning speeder; Thomas Gilpin, Philadelphia, June 25, paper finishing machine; B. Toll and J. Doyle, Baltimore, Md., July 19, and John Kennedy, Baltimore, Oct. 1, making soap by steam; Lewis Wooster and J. B. Holmes, Meadville, Pa., Aug. 3, manufacturing paper from wood; E. H. Thomas and Nathan Woodcock, Brettleborough, Vt., Aug. 11, pulp dressers for making paper; Benjamin Greet, New York, Oct. 1, water proof hats of paper; Jacob Senneff, Philadelphia, Oct. 1, loom reeds; Joseph C. Dyer, Manchester, England, Oct. 1, twisting spinning speeder; John P. Bakewell, Pittsburg, Oct. 1, glass wheels for clocks; Festus Hayden, Waterbury, Conn., Oct. 1, American wire-eyed buttons; Isaac Adams, Boston, Mass., Oct. 4, power printing press; Richard Wood, New York, Nov. 4, apparatus of Neal's printing press; Isaiah Jennings, New York, Oct. 16, producing light by a combination of liquids to lamps without wicks. This was for the combination of alcohol and turpentine, since so extensively used under the name of patent "burning fluid."

The second annual Message of President Jackson to the twenty-first Congress, adverted to the subject of the impost revenue as a cause of
1831 congratulation, inasmuch as it promised the means of extinguishing the public debt sooner than was anticipated, and furnished a strong illustration of the practical effects of the present tariff upon the

commercial interests. 'Upon the constitutionality and effects of the tariff, we find the following arguments:

"The power to impose duties on imports originally belonged to the several states. The right to adjust those duties, with a view to the encouragement of domestic branches of industry, is so completely incidental to that power, that it is difficult to suppose the existence of the one without the other. The states have delegated their whole authority over imports to the General Government, without limitation or restriction, saving the very inconsiderable reservation relating to their inspection laws. This authority having thus entirely passed from the states, the right to exercise it for the purpose of protection does not exist in them; and consequently if it be not possessed by the General Government, it must be extinct. Our political system would thus present the anomaly of a people, stripped of the right to foster their own industry, and to counteract the most selfish and destructive policy which might be adopted by foreign nations. This surely cannot be the case; this indispensable power thus surrendered by the states must be within the scope of the authority on the subject expressly delegated to Congress. In this conclusion I am confirmed as well by the opinions of Presidents Washington, Jefferson, Madison, and Monroe, who have each repeatedly recommended the exercise of this right under the constitution, as by the uniform practice of Congress, the combined acquiescence of the states, and the general understanding of the people. * * * * *

"The effects of the present tariff are doubtless overrated, both in its evils and its advantages. By one class of reasoners, the reduced price of cotton and other agricultural products is ascribed wholly to its influence, and by another the reduced price of manufactured articles. The probability is that neither opinion approaches the truth, and that both are induced by that influence of interests and prejudices to which I have referred. The decrease of prices extends throughout the commercial world, embracing not only the raw material and the manufactured article, but provisions and lands. The cause must therefore be deeper and more pervading than the tariff of the United States. * * * * *

"The present tariff taxes some of the comforts of life unnecessarily high; it undertakes to protect interests too local and minute to justify a general exaction, and it also attempts to force some kinds of manufactures for which the country is not ripe. Much relief will be derived in some of these respects from the measures of your last session."

Mr. Mallary, chairman of the Committee on Manufactures, to which this portion of the message was referred, made a report on the 13th January, which concurred in the President's glowing view of the prosperity of the country, and in the benefits as well as the constitu tionality of the tariff, but dissented from his opinion that its chief object should be revenue and protection a secondary one, when, as was then feared, the revenue was about to become too abundant. Protection "should be the *primary* object. The protecting power having once belonged to the states, and now transferred to the General Government, it may be used as the good of the nation demands, for a primary, not a secondary object. It ought not to be loosely attached to the skirts of revenue. Domestic industry is a single, great, ever pre-eminent interest of the nation." Other views of the principles and details of the tariff contained in the message were reviewed, and the soundness and natural character of its provisions were affirmed by the Committee, who believed that any attempt to change them after so recent a revision would be impolitic. A minority report on the subject from the same committee was also presented by Mr. Morrell, which also concurred in the President's favorable view of the practical operation of the tariff, which had not produced the injuries predicted to Congress, and in the soundness of his argument upon the constitutionality of protective import duties; but also agreed with him that a portion of the duties on necessaries and comforts of life should be repealed or reduced, and to adjust the whole revenue of the country, with a view to the protection of domestic industry.

A resolution submitted by Mr. Trevzant on 10th January, for instructing the Committee of Ways and Means to report a bill to reduce the duties on imported goods, to take effect after the payment of the public debt, was repealed by the House.

The Committee of the Senate on Manufactures, on 16th February, reported on a bill to reduce and fix the duties on imported sugars, stating the produce of the crops in Louisiana in the last year at one hundred thousand hogsheads, and that the land adapted to its cultivation would yield a sufficient supply for the whole United States, for fifty years to come. Under the duty of three cents, imposed in 1816, the sugar establishments had rapidly increased, and the price had as constantly decreased, and would continue, since the profit of capital employed in producing sugar was greater than that employed in product of rice, cotton, and tobacco, and would attract capital from those articles, until there was an equality of prices among them. Increased competition would reduce the prices. The sugar culture was an object of national importance, and should not be destroyed or checked, while in a train of successful experiments, by a reduction of the duty. An indefinite postponement of the bill was therefore recommended.

Judge Spencer, from the Committee on Agriculture, reported a resolution that the flag bearing the colors of the United States, presented to the House by Peter S. Duponceau, of Philadelphia, made of American silk, and prepared and woven by John D'Homergue, silk manufacturer, in the city of Philadelphia, be accepted by the House, and it be displayed in some conspicuous part of the hall of sittings of the House. The report was accompanied by the bill for promoting the growth and manufacture of silk, reported at the last session, and by further communications from Mr. Duponceau on the subject of the bill.

The same committee, on 3d February, reported on the memorial of the manufacturers of salt, in Kenhawa county, Virginia, praying for the restoration of the duty on imported salt, that the laws of the last session, reducing the duty, ought to be suspended. The article was one of the first necessity, the domestic sources adequate to a full supply, and the manufacture already existed in nineteen out of the twenty-four states. But it was in few hands and easily prostrated by a fall in price, while the importation was as easily monopolized, and the prices raised by a few merchants. About 2,400,000 bushels were made on the western waters in the last year, and the consumption was 2,800,000 bushels. The total manufacture on an average of the last five years, was 4,250,000 bushels, the importation 5,500,000, and the annual consumption 9,750,000. The price had steadily and rapidly declined in the western country, from two and three dollars a bushel, in 1820, to seventy-five cents, the average of the last year, and sixty-two and a half cents, the present price, and in some places as low as fifty cents. The manufacture, on any considerable scale, was but little over fifteen years old, and had been much extended and improved by the act of last session. They reported a bill to repeal so much of the act of May 29th, 1830, as had not gone into operation, which was finally laid on the table, as was also a bill supplementary to the same act, from the Senate.

A select committee, to whom was referred the petition of upward of three hundred mechanics, citizens of the city and county of Philadelphia, employed in the various branches of the iron manufacture, and that of the journeymen blacksmiths, of the same place, employed in manufacturing anchors and chain cables, reported on 28th February. The high duty imposed on bar iron by the act of 1828, was represented to be extremely unfavorable to the manufacturers of hardware, blacksmith's work, and chain cables, etc., which last could now be imported cheaper than the rods out of which they were made. Relief could only be afforded by a reduction of the duty on raw iron.

A bill, reported by Mr. Ellsworth, from the Committee on the Judiciary, to amend the several acts respecting copyrights, was passed and approved on 3d February, securing to authors a copyright for twenty-eight years, with a right of renewal for fourteen years more, if at the end of the first period he should be living, or leave a family. The previous act was for fourteen years without the privilege of renewal by his family in case of his decease.

The English excise duty of three pence the square yard on printed cotton goods, which was imposed in 1774, and raised in 1806 to three and a half pence, was repealed on the first March, of this year, and by way of partial compensation for loss of revenue thereby, the duty on foreign cotton wool was raised from six per cent. ad valorem to five shillings and ten pence per cent., but was reduced two years after to two shillings and eleven pence, cotton from British possessions paying only four pence per cent.

A very considerable decline in the price of cotton took place in the Southern States. Heavy failures occurred in June at Macon, Georgia. Cotton which had sold at nine and a half to eleven and a half cents, in the last autumn, was then worth only five to seven and a half cents.

The tariff of the United States, to which it was customary to ascribe the low price of cotton and other staples, was still the subject of much excitement. On the 3d August, an anti-tariff convention assembled at Augusta, and others were held in different states, at which delegates were appointed to meet in general convention at Philadelphia. The Free Trade Convention, which met accordingly at Philadelphia, on 30th September, and adjourned on 7th October, was proposed by Mr. H. D. Sedgwick, of Massachusetts, through the New York Evening Post, and was composed of about two hundred delegates, from fifteen states, who were presided over by Judge P. P. Barbour, of Virginia, Mr. Condy Raguet, of Philadelphia, acting as secretary. The Convention adopted a series of resolutions expressing attachment to the Constitution, and declaring the existing tariff laws of Congress, so far as they went to protect manufactures, to be a manifest violation of the true intent and spirit of the Constitution, inexpedient, unequal, oppressive and unjust, especially the act of May, 1828, which was oppressive to agriculture, commerce, and manufactures; that a solemn appeal should be made to the people, to unite in obtaining such a modification of the tariff as might be essential to all the important interests of the people, and calculated to quiet the fears and satisfy the reasonable demands of every section of the Union. An address to the people of the United States, of like import, was adopted, and a committee for each state was appointed, and instructed to draft a memorial to Congress, which they were to present at its next session, and promote, by their personal attendance, or by a sub-committee, in order to impress the views of the convention upon that body. The memorial, prepared by Mr. Albert Gallatin, was presented to Congress in February, 1832.

On the 26th of October a Tariff Convention of the Friends of

Domestic Industry, composed of upward of five hundred delegates from the New England and Middle States, Maryland, Virginia, Ohio, and the District of Columbia, met in New York, "for the purpose of taking into consideration what proceedings might be necessary for the support and further extension of the American system, as involved in the protection of the various pursuits of domestic industry." The Convention was organized, with William Wilkins, of Pennsylvania, as president, four vice presidents, and four secretaries, of whom Hezekiah Niles, of Baltimore, was principal. Committees composed of one delegate from each state were appointed to prepare an address to the people of the United States, affirming the constitutionality of a tariff that would protect the interests of agriculture, commerce, and manufactures, which was written by C. J. Ingersoll, of Pennsylvania, chairman of the committee. 2. To prepare a memorial to Congress, enforcing the propriety of continuing the protection of domestic industry, whatever reduction of duties might be expedient on articles not conflicting with that industry. 3. To inquire and report upon the effect of the existing tariff upon the agriculture, manufactures, mechanic arts, internal trade, and foreign commerce of the country—A. H. Everett, of Masssachusetts, chairman; and, 4. A committee of seven to inquire and report upon evasions of the existing revenue laws. To the foregoing were added special committees to consider and report, severally, upon the production and manufacture of iron and steel, sugar and molasses, copper, lead, cotton, salt, wool, hats and cabinet furniture; paper, glass, porcelain and other manufactures of clay; culture of silk and hemp; on chemistry, on the currency, and on foreign tariffs.[1]

These conventions were each composed of men eminent for their respectability and practical knowledge of the important subjects discussed, and the addresses and memorials prepared under their direction are among the ablest expositions of the two great parties which now divided the country, on the subject of protecting duties, in our political annals. They had the effect of bringing the subject of the tariff once more before the National Legislature, at its next session, with such effect as to result in an entire review of its principles, and an attempt to reconcile the conflicting interests.

The reports of the several committees of the New York convention, after its adjournment, to the permanent committee, embodied a large amount of statistics and valuable information, derived from the members and from other sources, some of which has been given under

(1) The thanks of the convention were voted to Matthew Carey and Hezekiah Niles for their long and able advocacy of the cause of domestic industry, and twenty thousand copies of the address were ordered to be printed.

previous dates. We give the result of their inquiries as containing what have been deemed reliable data respecting several branches of industry, and, in the absence of the usual official census of manufactures, at this time more to be depended upon than the voluminous report of the Secretary of the Treasury, made in obedience to a resolution of Congress at its next session, based upon information very imperfectly and hastily obtained, in answer to circular letters, and of which no digest has ever been made, or seems possible to be made with advantage.

From the best information that could be obtained, the Committee on Cotton, of which P. T. Jackson, of Massachusetts, was chairman, estimated the crop of the United States, after the year ending October 1, to be, in the Atlantic states, 486,103 bales of 306 lbs. each, equal to 148,747,518 lbs., and in the Southern and Western States, 552,744 bales of 411 lbs., equivalent to 227,177,784 lbs., giving a total crop of 1,038,847 bales, or 375,925,302 lbs. The domestic consumption amounted to more than one fifth of the whole crop; and the value of the product, allowing it to be increased fourfold in the process of manufacture, probably four fifths that of the cotton crop, and equal to the value of the whole quantity exported.

The following is a summary of the detail of the cotton manufacture in the twelve Eastern and Middle States, including Maryland and Virginia. But owing to misapprehension of the question respecting capital, only that employed in fixtures was returned, and some manufacturers were reluctant to give the details of their business, for which reasons it was thought that one fourth to one third might be safely added to the account. The statement was exclusive of no less than thirty establishments returned from the Southern and Western States, from which no accurate details were received, and also of family manufactures. The cotton mills in the twelve numbered seven hundred and ninety-five.

	Total in Cotton Mills.	Machine Shops.	Bleacheries.	Printeries.	Total.
Capital (principally in fixtures) in dollars,	40,614,984	2,400,000	900,000	1,000,000	44,914,934
Spindles in operation, ...	1,246,503				
Yards of cloth made, ...	230,461,900				
Pounds of yarn sold, ...	10,642,000				
Pounds of cotton used (214,822 bales),	77,757,316				
Hands employed (females 38,927), . .	62,157	3,200	738	1,505	67,600
Pounds of starch used, ...	1,641,253		429,625		2,070,873
Barrels of flour for sizing, . . .	17,245			1,300	18,455
Cords of wood, ...	46,519			30,000	76,519
Tons of coal, ...	24,420		19,250	2,250	45,920
Bushels of charcoal, ...	39,205				
Gallons of oil, ...	300,338			2,800	303,138
Value of other articles in dollars, .	599,223	1,960,212	276,625	935,585	3,766,285
Spindles building, ...	172,024				
Hand weavers, ...	4,760				
Total dependents, ...	117,625	9,600	1,403	2,860	131,489
Annual value in dollars, ...	26,000,000	3,500,000	1,036,760	1,500,000	32,036,760
Aggregate wages, ...	10,294,944	1,248,000	209,814	402,965	12,155,723

Without opportunity for further inquiry, the Committee on Iron and Steel was able to enumerate fourteen steel furnaces, then in operation, capable of supplying sixteen hundred tons annually, an amount equal to the whole importation, but believed to be far short of the quantity really made. The furnaces were at the following places, viz: at Pittsburg two, Baltimore one, Philadelphia three, York county, Pennsylvania, one, New York three, Troy one, New Jersey two, Boston one. American steel was considered quite equal to English steel for agricultural purposes, and had excluded the latter altogether, the only steel imported being of a better quality, such as Swedish, blister, and sheer and cast steel. Iron of similar or equal quality to that which had given Great Britain the manufacture of the best articles of cutlery, had been recently made by improved processes, from Juniata ore, and that of Aucrim, New York, and Salisbury, Connecticut. Steel was made in Pittsburg, and could be made in New York and Connecticut, bearing a fair comparison with the best hoop L or Danamoura steel from England, all the iron made from Danamoura ore being monopolized by a firm in Hull. The second quality, or sheer steel, also an English monopoly, was now made by English artists in the United States, but attempts to make cast steel in the United States had not succeeded, owing first to a want of the best quality of blister steel, as a material, at reasonable price, and secondly to the want or expense of proper crucibles. These difficulties, it was thought, would be removed by the superior quality of Juniata iron for blister steel, and by the recent discovery of clay in Clinton, Clearfield, and Lycoming counties, Pennsylvania, and near to Baltimore, believed to be identical with the Stourbridge.

A statement of the iron and other manufactures in Litchfield county, Connecticut, gave the pig and bar iron made at $293,000; the manufactures of iron, including scythes, hoes, axes, tacks, shovels and spades, augers, steel, pitchforks, ploughs, etc., at $177,650,000; wool, woolen cloths, cotton cloths and hats, shoes, clocks, leather, buttons, etc., etc., $1,414,200; total, $1,884,850.

Mr. J. P. Crozer, from a committee of Delaware county, Pennsylvania, reported to the Convention the following establishments in that county, viz: rolling and slitting mills, four; nail factories, two; till mills (making edge tools, spades, and shovels), four; paper mills, thirteen; cotton spinning mills, thirteen, with 17,350 spindles; cotton weaving mills, three, with 420 looms; woolen mills employing 350 persons; total value of manufactures, $1,372,175; persons employed, 2,185.

The annual manufacture of hats in the United States was estimated at ten millions of dollars, and employed 15,000 men and 3,000 women, whose wages were $4,200,000. A foreign hat was seldom to be seen, American hats being regarded as cheaper, and about $500,000 worth were exported. The manufacture of caps was also extensive; one of three or four factories at Albany employing about 600 persons, and paying about $100,000 per annum in wages. The value of hats and caps for men's wear was put down at fifteen millions of dollars annually.

The Committee on Glass and Manufactures of Clay reported twenty-one furnaces in the United States (six of them in Boston and its vicinity), containing one hundred and forty pots for the manufacture of flint glass. Their total product of flint glass was $1,300,000, of which $400,000 was made in two of the largest at Boston, much of the latter consisting of cut glass. They were estimated to use 1,450 tons of lead, 900 tons of pearl ashes, 2,600 tons of sand, 1,000 tons of fire clay, and 100 tons of saltpetre. The manufacture had been greatly improved and extended under the protective duty of 1824, and the price was fully one third less than in 1816. Few if any orders were sent abroad for flint glass by American merchants. But one factory of black glass bottles, carboys, etc., was known to exist, and that was near Boston, with a capital of $50,000, and employing sixty-five men and boys. Its product was six thousand gross annually. The New England Crown Glass Company, near Boston, with a capital of $450,000, made crown window glass to the value of $100,000, and was the only factory of the kind except one recently erected at New York. The largest manufactory of green bottles, demijohns, druggists' wares, etc., was that of Dyott, near Philadelphia, employing two hundred and fifty to three hundred men, and melting about 1,200 tons per annum. There were twenty-three manufactories of cylinder window glass, four of which were at Pittsburg, four at Burnsville, Pennsylvania, and two at Wheeling, Virginia. The total value of the glass manufactured in the United States was about $3,000,000; the number of persons employed 2,140; persons subsisted 10,800; wages annually paid $720,000.

The value of Cabinet wares made was ascertained to be ten millions of dollars. The price was thirty per cent. less than it was a few years before, and a considerable value was annually exported to Canton, South America, and the West Indies.

The number of sugar plantations in Louisiana alone exceeded five hundred, one half of which were supposed to be worked by steam, the remainder by cattle and horses, and there were infant establishments in Georgia and Florida, all of which, it was thought would be ruined by a reduction of the duty of three cents on sugar.[1] The sugar refineries

(1) It was argued in favor of the reduction of the duty on sugar for the refineries, that Lousiana could not produce sugar of sufficient strength for their use. The objec-

numbered thirty-eight, of which three were in New Orleans, eight in Baltimore, eleven in Philadelphia, eleven in New York, three in Boston, and one each in Salem, Massachusetts, and Providence, Rhode Island. A continuance of the duty would secure a large proportion of the refinery business to the United States.

The number of sheep in the United States was estimated at twenty millions, worth, on an average, two dollars a head. The capital invested in sheep and lands to feed them was about $105,000,000. The fixed and floating capital invested in the woolen manufacture was about forty millions of dollars, total capital in the growth and manufacture and the support of the manufacturers, $167,500,000. The number of persons employed, 162,000, requiring, for materials and subsistence, $250,000,000 worth of agricultural products yearly. New York probably produced one fourth of all the wool in the United States, and Massachusetts manufactured one fourth. Vermont, in the last year, sold wool worth $1,200,000.[1]

There were at least thirty chemical establishments in the United States, with an aggregate capital estimated at $1,158,000. They produced articles worth fully one million of dollars annually. Alum, copperas, and some other articles were produced to the almost total exclusion of the foreign. The manufacture included calomel and various other mercurial preparations, Glaubers and Rochelle salts, tartar emetic, ammonia, sulphate of quinine, oil of vitriol, tartaric, nitric, muriatic, oxalic and acetic acids, aqua fortis, Prussian blue, chrome yellow, chrome green, barilla, chloride of lime and of soda, refined saltpetre, refined borax, refined camphor, acetate and nitrate of lead, prussiate of potash, bichromate of potash. Additions were daily made to the list. Nearly all the materials used were the products of the United States, the only important exceptions being brimstone, saltpetre, cream tartar, and Peruvian bark, which few of the rival manufacturers possessed in their own countries.

The following estimate was made of the value of manufactures in the United States this year, viz:

Leather, thirty-five millions of dollars; hats and caps, fifteen; household and kitchen furniture, fifteen; wagons, coaches, carriages, etc., and agricultural tools, ten; coats, vests, and other tailors' work, ten; paper,

tion was about this date removed by the introduction of Howard's process of boiling *in vacuo*, after previous concentration in open kettles. Thomas A. Morgan, and Godon & Forstell, were among the first to use the vacuum pan and process of Howard in Louisiana.—*De Bow's Resources*, vol. 3, p. 276. *Patent Office Report*, 1848, p. 218.

(1) The quantity of wool imported into Boston, in the first three quarters of this year, was 2,491,846 lbs., and the average of the two previous years was over half a million of pounds.

books, binding, newspapers, and stationery, ten; ladies' hats, caps, and bonnets, lace, artificial flowers, umbrellas, etc., eight; soap, candles, tobacco, buttons, penknives, wooden clocks, etc., seven; manufactures of iron, lead, and other metals, wool, cotton, etc., ninety millions; total, two hundred millions of dollars.[1]

Among the articles presented for the first time at the seventh exhibition of the Franklin Institute, in Philadelphia, in October, were samples of the natural yellow nankeen, made without dye, by Collett & Smith, of Paterson, New Jersey, black silk plush, made of American silk, with a very small admixture of foreign material, and remarkable for the quality of the silk, and the excellence of the manufacture, color, etc. The latter article was from the factory of Joseph Ripka, at Manayunk, who also received an extra premium for his green summer cloths, of cotton and worsted, the only imitation of the English article ever seen by the committee. Cutlery was also a new article. The Hon. John Forsyth, Senator from Augusta, Georgia, was awarded an extra premium for his enterprise in cultivating the variety of short staple cotton, from which the Aerumna nankeens, and those above mentioned, were made, as a substitute for the Indian fabric.[2] Col. John E. Calhoun, of Pendleton, South Carolina, was rewarded for cotton and woolen blankets for plantation use, made by him in the first manufactory of the kind in that state. Great improvements were noticed in the quality of the carpets exhibited, among which imitation Brussels carpets from the Lowell factory, and that of Mr. Givens, at Carlisle, Pennsylvania, were conspicuous—also, in flannels, printed cottons, stoves for anthracite, writing paper and Britannia ware, especially that of the Taunton Britannia Manufacturing Company of Massachusetts,[3] and in buttons, from Attleboro, Massachusetts, and Waterbury, Connecticut.

The Rockland flour mills, eight miles from Baltimore, were converted into a calico printing establishment, by Mr. Mellier, and printed 8,000 yards daily.

The number of pairs of ladies' boots and shoes made at Lynn, Massachusetts, in the year, was 1,675,781, valued at $942,171. The business employed 1,741 men, 1,675 women, and consumed $413,350 worth of materials.

The manufactures of Hampden county, Massachusetts, were ascer-

(1) Niles's Register, vol. 39, p. 148.

(2) Georgia nankeen cotton was manufactured at Lonsdale, Rhode Island, in 1834.

(3) The Taunton factory of Reed & Barton, a firm still in existence, was probably the first to make rolled Britannia ware, and their work took the lead. Britannia teapots were also made by T. D. & S. Boardman, of Hartford, and Eben Smith, of Beverly, Massachusetts, and perhaps others.—*Letter from J. W. Quincy, Esq., of New York.*

tained to amount to the value of $2,191,000. The principal articles were cotton and woolen cloth, firearms, paper (39,324 reams), saddlery, harness, and trunks, whips, and leather. The cotton factories were sixteen, spindles 30,766, looms 712, artizans 4,099. At Chicopee 20,000 spindles were at work, and 13,500 yards of cloth made daily. Berkshire county had invested in manufactures $2,087,930, and the value of the products $2,006,965.

The Trenton Falls Company was incorporated in New Jersey, February 16, for the improvement of the extensive water power of the falls of the Delaware, and of the Assunpink creek, at Trenton.

The fine Porcelain and Chinaware manufactures of Philadelphia were pronounced by competent judges to be second only in point of perfection to those of France. The business was first commenced by William Ellis Tucker, whose experiments, during several years, in the manufacture and coloring of various clays, induced him, in 1825, to enlarge his operations by starting the first American Queensware manufactory in the old city water works, in Philadelphia. By successive improvements and much expenditure he was enabled to produce wares, comparing favorably in color, surface and gilding with the French. He was this year joined in the business by Judge Hemphill, of Philadelphia, and they established on a larger scale the American Porcelain manufactory, at Nineteenth and Chestnut streets, which, after Mr. Tucker's death the next year, was carried on by Thomas Hemphill, under his brother's patronage. They owned a fine bed of kaolin in Chester county.

A large steam cotton factory, two hundred feet long, commenced in July at Olneyville, Rhode Island, and another two hundred and seventy-five feet long, nearly completed at Fall River, Massachusetts, were among the largest in the country. A cotton factory was also projected at Nashville, Tennessee. At the cotton factory in Richmond, Virginia, slave labor alone was employed, except in superintendence.

Many useful and ornamental articles, as inkstands, sand-boxes, toys, etc., were made in Pennsylvania out of anthracite coal and lignite, for which a Mr. Kirk, this year, obtained a patent, under which Kirk's Patent Anthracite Wares Manufacturing Company, with a capital of $100,000, afterward commenced the business with a charter granted by the state, in March, 1838.

About sixty out of one hundred steam engines, at this time employed in Philadelphia, used anthracite coal for fuel.

James D. Allaire, proprietor of the Allaire works, Cherry street, New York, employed two hundred hands in the manufacture of steam engines, and other heavy iron work, to the amount of $140,000, in six months. He had other factories for making hollowware, sadirons, etc., in which four hundred hands were employed. In Pittsburg cast iron began to be used for pillars, the caps and sills of windows, etc.

The manufacture of corn brooms had become a large business in the United States, and was valued at several hundred thousand dollars. A machine had been recently invented by a young American for cleaning the material with great rapidity.

American power looms had nearly superseded the English, and were about this time introduced into England, where they became very popular. An improved power loom for weaving checks was at this period invented by Mr. Alfred Jenks, of Bridesburg, Pennsylvania, and was introduced into the Kempton mill, at Manayunk.

The public interest in the silk culture continued to extend, and raw silk was produced in small quantity, by individuals, in many parts of the country. The silk bill before Congress attracted attention to the subject, and much was expected from the Chinese mulberry and Morus Multicaulis, which was this year introduced into New England. The Legislature of Massachusetts manifested its interest by appropriating six hundred dollars for the completion and printing of a manual on the silk culture, for distribution throughout the state. The work, entitled a "Manual of the Mulberry Tree and the Culture of Silk," was prepared by Jonathan H. Cobb, of Dedham, Massachusetts, an early cultivator of the Multicaulis, and inventor of an improved silk reel, and contributed much useful information on the subject, although it contained many extravagant estimates of the profits of silk raising.

The American Railroad Journal was established this year, devoted to the interests of railroad enterprises, which had grown to considerable magnitude. It was edited and published by D. K. Minor and Henry V. Poor.

The "American Steam Carriage Company," composed of Col. Stephen H. Long, United States Army, William Norris, and others, was formed at Philadelphia in March, to build "locomotives" according to the plans of Col. Long, afterward secured by letters patent, and intended to use anthracite fuel. The first engine was built under Col. Long's superintendence, at the Phœnix Foundry, Kensington, but at its trial, on the fourth of July of the next year, proved a failure. A second one, finished in June, 1833, was successful, and in the following year three others were built by Messrs. Long and Norris, the latter of whom became about the same time sole proprietor of the business, which has since become one of the most extensive in the city, the works being known as the Norris Locomotive Works.

The first of a series of eight reports on the Geology of the State of Tennessee, was this year communicated to the General Assembly of the

State, by Professor Gerard Frost. The final report was made in 1846. Sixty patents were granted during the last and present year for threshing machines.

PATENTS.—Elizabeth Oram, New York, Jan. 12, globe for teaching geography; Charles Goodyear, Philadelphia, Jan. 12, manufacturing buttons, called the "safe-eye button;" De Grasse Fowler, New Brantford, Conn., June 13, manufacturing dead-eyed wooden buttons; Joseph Boston, New York, Feb. 11, manufacturing gas for illumination, etc.; Solomon Andrews, Perth Amboy, N. J., April 15 and May 5, manufacturing gas from oil and by spirit lamp; Henry Robinson, Boston, March 10, gas meters; Seth Boyden, Newark, N. J., March 9 and April 6, malleable cast iron; Thomas Blanchard, Springfield, Mass., March 25, steamboats for passage of rapids;[1] Asa G. Bill and George Spalding, Middletown, Conn., March 28, loom for weaving webbing, tape, etc.; Richard Willcox, Paterson, N. J., April 5, three patents for metallurgical apparatus, with anthracite and bituminous coal and charcoal; Moses Isaacs, Philadelphia, April 7, making coke from anthracite, etc.; George H. Richards, Washington, D. C., April 11, fluid caoutchouc to render articles water-proof—the first patent for this class of articles recorded; Daniel Strobel, jr., Washington, D. C., May 9, concentrating syrup and cane juice by steam; Thomas Oxmard, Cumberland, Maine, Aug. 6, apparatus for filtering syrup and washing animal blood used in clarifying sugar; John F. Nunns, New York, May 5, and Jesse Thompson, New York, August 6, action piano fortes; E. Fairbanks and T. Fairbanks, St. Johnsbury, Vt., June 13, balance for weighing heavy bodies, (reissued March, 1834, and again Feb. 1837.) This was for the valuable "platform scale," which has effected a great change in the system of weighing. Daniel Loring, Newark, N. J., Aug. 23, and Jas. Coulter, Philadelphia, Oct. 13, balances for weighing canal boats and loaded wagons, etc.; James Stimpson, Baltimore, Md., Aug. 23, wheels for railroad carriages; Samuel Krauser, Reading, Pa., Nov. 2, wheels for railroad cars, to prevent friction; D. Ames, jr., and John Ames, assignees of Samuel Eckstein, Philadelphia, June 13, machine for washing rags for paper—consisting of a wire cloth cylinder, to carry off the dirt beaten from the rags, as a substitute for the screens and washers then in use; Josiah W. Kirk, Schuylkill county, Pa., June 13, ornaments from anthracite coal, etc.; Peter Mintzer, Philadelphia, July 20, and W. H. Horstmann, Philadelphia, July 28, fly harness nets for horses; Isaiah Jennings, New York, Aug. 1, lamps for burning evaporable ingredients; Charles Goodyear, Philadelphia, Sept. 7, steel

(1) This was a practical and ingenious improvement, for an account of which see Howe's Memoirs of Eminent Mechanics, p. 207.

spring fork; E. N. Sherr, Philadelphia, Oct. 6, guitar; James R. Stewart, New York, Nov. 11, dyeing cotton in the staple or cotton wool.

The first message of the President to the twenty-second Congress spoke of the prosperous condition of Agriculture, Manufactures, and internal improvements, and of the scarcely less prosperous state of the foreign trade and navigation, which, in consequence of the improved relations of the country, had resulted in an increase of the revenue beyond the most sanguine expectations of the Treasury Department. The revenue of the year would not fall short of $27,700,000; and the expenditures for all objects, other than the public debt, would not exceed $14,700,000. The payments on account of the principal and interest of the public debt would exceed sixteen and a half millions; and the sum so paid since his inauguration would exceed forty millions of dollars. The condition of the public finances, and the certainty of the extinguishment of the public debt by redemption or purchase within the four years of his term, furnished an opportunity for carrying more fully into effect the policy recommended in his previous messages in relation to import duties: "A modification of the Tariff which shall produce a reduction of the revenue to the wants of the government, and an adjustment of the duties on imports with a view to equal justice in relation to all our national interests, and to the counteraction of foreign policy so far as it may be injurious to these interests, is deemed to be one of the principal objects which demand the consideration of the present Congress. Justice to the interests of the merchant as well as the manufacturer, requires that material reductions in the import duties be prospective; and unless the present Congress shall dispose of the subject, the proposed reductions cannot properly be made to take effect at the period when the necessity for the revenue arising from present rates shall cease. It is therefore desirable that arrangements be adopted at your present session to relieve the people from unnecessary taxation, after the extinguishment of the public debt. In the exercise of that spirit of concession and conciliation which has distinguished the friends of our Union in all great emergencies, it is believed that this object may be effected without injury to any national interests."

1832

On the 9th January, Mr. Clay, recently elected to the United States Senate by the Legislature of Kentucky, submitted to that body the following resolutions:

"That the duties on articles imported from foreign countries, and not coming into competition with similar articles made or produced in the United States, ought to be forthwith abolished, except the duties on wines and silks, and that they ought to be reduced.

"That the Committee on Finance report a bill accordingly."

To the first resolution, Mr. Hayne, of South Carolina, moved an amendment to the effect that the duties be so reduced that the public revenue should be sufficient to defray the expenses of government according to their present scale, after the payment of the public debt; and that a gradual reduction of the high protecting duties take place until the rates should be equalized on all imports. This proposition, which was the utmost he could yield as a representative of South Carolina, was finally rejected; though ably supported by him and others opposed to the American system, which they declared unequal, unjust, and ruinous to the South, whose condition, Mr. Hayne assured the Senate, was "not merely one of unexampled depression, but of great and all pervading distress. Joint stock companies at the North had made large dividends, and flourishing villages had grown up under it, but the condition of the masses had not been improved, and the proposed reduction of duties on luxuries was only a measure to relieve the rich manufacturers of a portion of these burthens and to add to those of the South."

On the 19th January, the House of Representatives passed resolutions calling upon the Secretary of the Treasury to furnish information respecting the extent and condition generally of the manufactures of wool, cotton, hemp, iron, sugar, salt, and other articles manufactured to a considerable extent; and to accompany it by such a tariff of duties on imports as he might think best adapted to the advancement of the public interests;—also to obtain and lay before the House information as to the quantities and kinds of the several articles manufactured in the United States, particularly those of iron, cotton, wool, hemp, sugar, etc., and the cost thereof, as well as the quantities and cost of similar articles imported from abroad during the same year.

In conformity with these requisitions, the Secretary, Mr. McLane, issued circular inquiries calculated to elicit the information sought; and on the 27th April submitted a report, accompanied by a tariff bill repealing the act of 1828, and so altering and reducing the rates of duty on a large number of articles as to reduce the whole annual revenue from customs about ten millions, and that arising from protected articles about three millions; and the average rate of duty from about forty-five to twenty-seven per centum, leaving the total revenue from customs equal to about twelve millions annually. It was framed in accordance with these principles, and intended to harmonize both parties, but was satisfactory to neither.

Mr. McDuffie, of South Carolina, from the Committee of Ways and Means, also made a report to the House on the 8th February, along with a bill "to reduce and equalize the duties on imports." It proposed a uniform rate of twenty-five per cent. ad valorem on the more important articles, which rate was to be further reduced within one year to eighteen and three-fourths per centum, and within two years to twelve and one-half per centum and no more, on articles not already free or charged with a lower duty than twelve and one-half per centum.

Other measures were brought forward during the session by Messrs. Stewart, Dickerson, and Doubleday. The leading measure of the session, however, was a tariff bill reported by Mr. Adams, chairman of the Committee on Manufactures, on 23d May, "to alter and amend the several acts relative to duties on imports;" which was accompanied by a report on the subject. It was framed on the basis of the bill submitted by the Secretary of the Treasury, but was somewhat more favorable to protection. It passed the House, with some amendments, on 28th June; and, having received several additional amendments in the Senate, became a law on the 14th July, and was to take effect on 3d March following. This tariff made additions of some two hundred articles to the free list, enlarging it to about two hundred and seventy articles, including wool costing less than eight cents a pound, the teas of China and India, most tropical productions, and others not competing with domestic productions, many drugs, dye-stuffs, and chemicals. It reduced the duties on a large number of articles, and increased them upon a few, as china, stone and earthenware; but preserved the characteristics of a protective measure.

An official statement, emanating from the Treasury Department, estimated the amount of duties that would accrue under this tariff, calculated upon the importations of the year ending September 30, 1830, at $12,101,567, after deducting drawbacks and expenses—a reduction of $5,187,078 from the amount realized under the act of 1828.

The intense interest felt throughout the country on the subject of the tariff, as manifested by the memorials laid before Congress during the session from the Free Trade and Anti-Tariff Conventions of the last year, the numerous memorials and resolutions adopted by several of the local Legislatures, and by unofficial meetings held in various parts of the Union, approving or condemning any modification of the revenue system, was in no wise allayed by the passage of this act, which, though adopted with a view to conciliation, was unsatisfactory to the extremists of both parties. The agricultural interests of the South were generally arrayed against any measure retaining the features of a protective policy; and in South Carolina the spirit of Nullification had become exceedingly rife. At a State Rights and Free Trade Convention of delegates from every district but one in the state, held at Charleston on

23d February, at which Governor Hamilton presided, it was resolved to publish and circulate among the people tracts to explain and inculcate *Nullification* as the legitimate, peaceful, and rightful remedy for all oppressive and dangerous violations of the federal compact. An address to the people of the state was adopted, which characterized the bills before Congress as attempts to fasten the restrictive system upon the country, and to produce in effect "a steady discriminating *duty* of fifty per cent. on Southern, and a *bounty* of fifty per cent. on Northern industry." They did not propose to moot constitutional questions. That argument had been exhausted. They desired to give a more practical scope to their reflections. "The state looks to her sons to defend her in whatever form she may choose to proclaim her purpose to *resist.*"

The Senators and Representatives of that state in Congress having issued an address to the people announcing that, by the passage of the tariff bill, the protecting system must be regarded as the settled policy of the country, that all relief from Congress was irrecoverably gone, and that it remained with the sovereign power of the state to decide what course to pursue. Another convention was accordingly assembled at Columbia in November, which, on the 24th, passed the famous ordinance to nullify the acts of Congress. It declared that the tariff laws of 1828 and July 14, 1832, were "unauthorized by the constitution of the United States, and violate the true meaning and intent thereof, and are null and void, and no law, nor binding upon this state, its officers, or citizens," etc. It was declared unlawful for any constituted authorities of that state or the United States to enforce the payment of the duties within the limits of the state; and the Legislature was instructed to pass acts to give full force to the ordinance after the 1st February following. Addresses were issued to the people of the state, calling upon them to prepare for the crisis; and to the people of the United States, explaining the causes of their hostile attitude to the General Government. An act of replevin was promptly passed by the Legislature, and an act to empower the Governor to employ the naval and military force of the state, and to subject all officers of the state to a test oath, with a view of enforcing the ordinance. The plan of taxation in which the convention declared itself willing to acquiesce "in a liberal spirit of concession, provided they were met in due time, in a becoming spirit, by the states interested in manufactures," was, the "whole list of protected articles should be imported free of all duty, and that the revenue derived from import duties should be raised exclusively upon the unprotected articles; or that whenever a duty is imposed upon protected articles imported, an excise duty of the same rate shall be imposed upon all similar articles manufactured in the United States"! The impolitic measures proposed by South Carolina in case this spirit of "concession" was not met by a tariff substantially uniform on all foreign imports, and limited to a revenue standard, called forth from President Jackson, on the 10th December, a proclamation, warning the authorities of the consequences of following the dictates of the Convention, and of the course he would be compelled to pursue. Under instructions from the state Legislature, then in session, a counter proclamation of open defiance was issued ten days after by Governor Hayne, the late Senator, who was succeeded in the senatorship by Mr. Calhoun, the reputed parent of the doctrine of state sovereignty, and of its legitimate fruit, nullification and secession, the latter having resigned the vice-presidency of the United States to occupy the Senate.

The nullification measures of South Carolina were condemned by different legislative and other public assemblies of states, north and south, many of whom were as much opposed to the tariff as herself. The energy of the executive was effectual in maintaining the authority of the laws; and on the 18th March of the ensuing year another state convention rescinded the nullification ordinance; but passed another to nullify what was called the force bill, for the collection of duties on imports, approved March 3, 1833.

In consequence of the intense feeling excited in Congress on the subject of the tariff, which had rendered the very word *manufacture* distasteful to many, the Silk bill, which had been pending during two sessions, having been pressed to a decision by its friends, was finally rejected by a small majority, chiefly, it is believed, on party grounds, under the plea that it was unconstitutional.

That measure, which was the first important evidence of a national interest in a branch of industry that promised to be renewed, or established with permanent benefit to the country, had excited no little attention in England, as opening a new source of supply of raw silk for her manufacturers, and had drawn to the United States a number of silk throwsters, weavers, dyers, and others skilled in the silk business, in the vain hope of finding employment. Specimens of *Gros de Naples*, made in England from silk sent to that country by the venerable P. S. Duponceau, President of the American Philosophical Society, by whom the bill had been drawn up at the request of a committee of Congress, arrived during the session, and were distributed among the members, and other fabrics from France were received after the adjournment. The measure is believed to have met with the private opposition of the French minister, M. Serurier, as one likely to conflict with an established industry of his own country. Though supported by many ardent friends, by memorials in its favor, and by the personal influence of Mr. Duponceau, whose character and patriotism commanded the highest esteem, the bill, after an animated discussion, was thrown out. The filature, established by that gentleman in Philadelphia, was suffered to go down, and public attention was prematurely turned to the more difficult art of manufacturing the native silk into fabrics for use, rather than the production of a raw material for exportation, by which it is possible silk raising might have been added to the staple industries of the country. Under the expectations created by the discussion of this subject in Congress, and by the press, the attention of agriculturalists, associations, and families throughout the Union, was earnestly given to this branch; and specimens of raw silk, sewings, and various silk fabrics, produced by private enterprise, continued to be received from sections of the Union widely remote, and gave abundant evidence of the facility with which the material could be produced in the United States. Connecticut offered a bounty of one dollar per hundred for mulberry trees, and fifty cents a pound for reeled silk, suitable for manufacture. A bill to encourage the propagation of the white mulberry, which was becoming the favorite variety, and the culture of silk, was introduced into the New York Legislature, and various measures to promote the same objects were adopted in other states.

The General Assembly of Pennsylvania, on the 4th of May, passed a general "Act to promote the Culture of Silk," authorizing the Governor to incorporate in each county a Society for the cultivation of the White Mulberry, with the privilege of establishing and conducting a manufactory of the raw material; and also to cultivate a farm, and establish a school or academy for the education of youth, to be so conducted as to combine labor and instruction,—the whole art and mystery of raising and manufacturing silk, to be taught, if desired by the students.

On the 14th July an act was approved, to release from duty iron imported for, and actually laid on railways or inclined planes.

The low price of railroad iron in England, occasioned by the extensive use of the process of coking bituminous coal for fuel, an art not then introduced into the United States, caused a greater part of such iron to be imported. It appears from a report to the Senate of Pennsylvania, that among the proposals to furnish railroad iron for the Columbia and Philadelphia Railroad, received in May of the last year, there were none for American iron, and contracts were made in England for the whole quantity, at £6 17*s*. 6*d*. per ton.

The first attempt was about the same time made to introduce the use of coke in the iron manufacture, by a bill to incorporate the "Pennsylvania Coke and Iron Company." It passed the Senate, but was lost in the House, and having been again brought forward in this year passed the House, after strong opposition, on the 16th of February, by a vote of fifty-one to forty-six. In Berks county, of that state, there were eleven iron furnaces and twenty-two forges. At Reading, where manufacturing operations first commenced about this time, the beautiful anthracite stoves of Dr. Nott's invention were cast. One of them, either from this furnace, or from Albany, is said to have been presented about the same time to the monks of St. Bernard, on the summit of the Alps. The counties of Sussex, Warren, Morris, and Bergen, in New Jersey, contained fifteen furnaces, and eighty-seven forge fires in operation. Great importance had been given to the iron mines of that region by the completion of the Morris Canal.

Eight joint stock companies, with an aggregate capital of four millions of dollars, were incorporated this year in Indiana, to construct railroads from the Ohio river to Indianapolis, and different places on the Wabash.

The number of railroads completed and in progress, on the first of January of this year was nineteen, of an aggregate length of nearly fourteen hundred miles, upwards of one hundred of which were already completed.

A company was incorporated in Mississippi, in March, to establish a Cotton manufactory, to be carried on by slave labor.

The eminent American naval architect, Henry Eckford, of New York, died on the 12th November, in the service of Sultan Mahmoud, of Turkey. In June of the last year, he finished for the emperor a sloop-of-war, and having soon after visited Constantinople, was offered and accepted the situation of chief naval constructor for the empire, and proceeded to organize a navy yard, and to lay the keel of a ship-of-the-line, in which service he died suddenly at the age of fifty-seven, when about to be made a Bey of the Empire, in acknowledgment of his professional abilities. He had previously furnished President Jackson with a plan for the entire reorganization of the American Navy, and made preparations to publish a work on Naval Architecture, and had also laid aside $20,000 to establish a professorship of Naval Architecture in Columbia College, under Mr. Doughty, an eminent naval constructor.

Works were erected at Jaffrey, N. H., for the manufacture of sugar and molasses from potatoes, according to a process described in Silliman's Journal.

The Patent Laws underwent some modification during this year. Among the patents issued were the following: to E. and T. Fairbanks, St. Johnsbury, Vt., Feb. 21, for balance for weighing heavy bodies; and to the same, Sept. 22, two patents for balance steelyards, etc.; John and Charles Bruce, Kings county, N. Y., March 13, machine for cutting crackers and biscuit. [It performed the whole work of the "batch," and turned out complete about two hundred pounds of biscuit per hour.] Eliphalet Snow, Mansfield, Conn., March 16, and Charles C. Greene, Windsor, Vt., May 31, for silk reels; Frederick A. Taft, Dedham, Mass., May 11, manufacturing paper for covered buildings; John Ames, Springfield, Mass., March 12, reissue of patent of May 14, 1822; to the same, Sept. 1, for sizing paper; to A. H. Jervis and Thomas French, Ithica, N. Y., Nov. 6, hot and cold cylinder paper press; Thomas Ewbank, New York, May 16, coating pipes with tin; John J. Howe, North Salem, N. Y., June 22, manufacturing pins. [This valuable machine formed the head of a coil of fine wire by dies, completing a pin at each turn of a crank, at the rate of forty to fifty per minute. The machines were introduced the next year by the Messrs. Hoe & Co., of New York. In 1835, the Howe Manufacturing Company was organized in that city to carry on the manufacture under the patent. It was also patented in England and France afterward.] Eliphalet Nott, Schenectady, N. Y., Oct. 25, anthracite coal stoves; Felix Fossard, Pittsburg, Pa., April 23, dyeing with alkaline prussiates;[1] Edward Evans, Salem township, Pa., tanning without the use of lime, or sweating hides. This method of unhairing hides by sweating had been previously known in Pennsylvania, Maryland, and Jersey, and about this time was generally adopted in the large sole leather factories of New York and other places.

1833 In view of the great discontent manifested toward the tariff, by the Southern people, and which even threatened a disruption of the Union, as well as on account of the ample means in the public treasury for extinguishing the remainder of the public debt, amounting on the first of January to a fraction under seven millions of dollars, the President once more recommended to Congress a reduction of the duties on imports, to a scale adapted to a strictly revenue standard, as soon as practicable. "In effecting this adjustment," he says, "it is due in justice to the interests of the different states, and even to the preservation of the Union itself, that the protection afforded by existing laws to any branch of industry, should not exceed what may be necessary to counteract the regulations of foreign nations, and to secure a supply of those arti-

(1) Specimens of blue broadcloth, denominated Lafayette blue, made at Dedham, Mass., and dyed by F. Tassard, Philadelphia, with prussiade of potash, were exhibited at the Fair in the American Institute, New York, in the following year. The mordante used was sulphate of iron, and the dye was believed to have many advantages over indigo. No country possessed so many facilities for the manufacture, which has since become an important one. This appears to have been the first use of Prussian blue or dye in this country.

cles of manufacture essential to the national independence and safety in time of war. * * * *

"Those who take an enlarged view of the condition of our country, must be satisfied that the policy of protection must be ultimately limited to those articles of domestic manufacture which are indispensable to our safety in time of war. Within this scope, on a reasonable scale, it is recommended by every consideration of patriotism and duty, which will doubtless always secure to it a liberal and efficient support. But beyond this object we have already seen the operation of the system productive of discontent. In some sections of the republic its influence is deprecated as tending to concentrate wealth into a few hands, and as creating those germs of dependence and vice which in other countries have characterized the existence of monopolies, and proved so destructive of liberty and the general good. A large portion of the people in one section of the republic declare it not only inexpedient on these grounds, but as disturbing the equal relations of property by legislation, and therefore unconstitutional and unjust."

Calculated upon the average importations of the last six years, the revenue from customs, at the rates payable after the 3d March of this year, were estimated by the Secretary of the Treasury in his annual report at eighteen millions annually; and the aggregate revenue from all sources at about twenty-one millions a year. The probable expenses of government for all objects other than the public debt were placed at fifteen millions, leaving a surplus of six millions. In conformity with the views of the President, and the reasons urged in the last annual report of the department, Mr. McLane proposed to limit the revenue to a sum consistent with an economical administration of the government; and expressed his conviction that "by a tariff formed on proper principles, the reduction of six millions now recommended might, for the most part, be made upon those commonly denominated protected articles, without prejudice to the reasonable claims of existing establishments."

By a resolution of the Senate of December 13, the Secretary was therefore called upon, with as little delay as possible, to furnish the project of a bill for reducing the duties on imports, in conformity with suggestions contained in his annual report.

The Committee of Ways and Means,[1] through Mr. Verplanck, a few days after, reported to the House a bill "to reduce or otherwise alter

(1) The Committee on Manufactures in the House, to whom that part of the President's message relating to the tariff was referred, were unable to agree in a measure upon the subject, and asked to be discharged; but a very able report was made, on the 28th February, by Mr. Adams, on behalf of the minority, who dissented from the views expressed in the message.

the duties on imports." It went to repeal the act of 1832, passed after mature deliberation, and which had not yet gone into operation, and contemplated an annual revenue of fifteen millions of dollars, twelve and a half millions of which were to be derived from customs upon sixty to seventy millions of dutiable commodities annually imported. The rates proposed were from ten to twenty per cent., with variations in special cases, as upon lead, iron, spirits, wines, silks, etc.; and the bill was framed on the basis of the acts of 1816 and 1818, which were believed to have given ample protection to manufactures, as shown by their great increase from 1816 to 1824. The bill restored the duties on tea and coffee, and was favorable to the iron, coal, tobacco, and some other interests; but the duties on foreign cottons and woolens, by the abandonment of the minimum system, were lower than under the act of 1816, but the duty on wool and other materials was also reduced. This bill, which was intended as a concession to the South, the committee said, if adopted, might "serve as a basis for a financial system for many years." After a protracted debate, Mr. Verplanck's bill was recommitted to a committee of the whole, with instructions to report Mr. Clay's bill from the Senate instead, which passed the House on the following day by a vote of 119 to 85.

This measure, known as the *Compromise* Act, was introduced in the Senate on 12th February, by Mr. Clay, who, in explaining the principles by which he was guided in submitting a modification of the tariff, declared that he considered the protective system in imminent danger, and said: "When I look to the variety of interests which are involved, to the number of individuals interested, the amount of capital invested, the value of buildings erected, and the whole arrangement of the business for the prosecution of the various branches of the manufacturing arts which have sprung up under the fostering care of this government, I cannot contemplate any evil equal to the sudden overthrow of all these interests. History can produce no parallel to the extent of the mischief which would be produced by such a disaster. The repeal of the Edict of Nantes itself was nothing in comparison with it."

The act provided that where the duties upon imports exceeded twenty per cent. on the value thereof, there should be deducted, after the 31st December of this year, one tenth of the excess above twenty per cent., and that a like reduction of one tenth should be made every second year until the 31st December, 1841, when one half of the residue of such excess should be deducted, and the remaining half after the 30th June, 1842, from which time the duties upon imports were to be twenty per cent. The valuation was to be made at the port of entry, and the duties were to be paid in cash, the credit system being abolished.

Coarse woolens, costing not over thirty-five cents a yard, which, by the act of 1832, were admitted, as negro clothing, at five per cent. duty, by way of concession to the Southern States, were restored to the duty of fifty per cent. with other woolens, subject to the deductions provided for. Linens, stuff goods, and silks (except sewing, which paid forty per cent.) were admitted free of duty after June, 1842, as was also a considerable list of articles, including many chemicals, dye-stuffs, tropical products, and raw materials.

The bill having passed the House without much discussion, was carried in the Senate on the 1st March by a vote of twenty-nine to sixteen, and was approved on the 2d, and Congress adjourned on the following day. This act, by which discrimination in favor of domestic industry was practically abandoned for the time as an act of conciliation, was afterward regarded by the opponents of protection as in the nature of a compromise between the North and South, and therefore unalterable by subsequent legislation.

An amendatory act of 2d March restored the duty repealed by the act of July, 1832, on copper bottoms, still boilers, braziers, copper, and unmanufactured tobacco; and sheet and rolled brass were made subject to a duty of twenty-five per cent.

A bill (which passed and was approved on the same date) to provide for the collection of duties on imports, and known as the Enforcement Act, was introduced on the 21st January, and drew from Mr. Calhoun a series of resolutions defining the powers of government, and asserting the sovereignty of individual states; and, with the tariff discussion, elicited resolutions upon the subject of the tariff which Georgia and North Carolina pronounced unconstitutional. The new act, however, was regarded as acceding to their demands, and South Carolina, in convention, revoked her nullification ordinance two weeks after the passage of the act.

A report on the subject of Live Oak, made early in the session by the Secretary of the Navy, stated the number of live oak trees suitable for ship building growing on the public lands of the United States to be about 144,655. At an average of twenty cubic feet per tree they would furnish 2,893,100 cubic feet of timber. But the average was by some estimated at eighty cubic feet each, and a mean between the two of fifty feet would give 7,232,750 cubic feet. The first-named quantity would build one hundred and seventy-three vessels, one-fourth of them ships of the line, one-fourth frigates, and one-half sloops and schooners in equal proportion. The medium quantity would suffice for four hundred and thirty-three vessels, and the highest estimate six hundred and ninety-three vessels. The trees reported to be growing on private lands were 8,975, sufficient on the above estimate for ten to forty-three vessels. The actual use of live oak timber for small repairs of live oak vessels during the last thirty-five years was estimated at one thousand feet annually; and during the last ten years twelve hundred feet annually. The future demands were estimated at three thousand four hundred feet annually, for small or ordinary repairs. All the timber used in the frames of public vessels constructed since 1797 was about 974,363 cubic feet, or 27,838 per year on an average. The price for live oak timber suitable for ships of the line, delivered at the yards, was in 1799 $1.33 per cubic foot; in 1801, $2; in 1816, $1.55 for frames of seventy-fours; in 1827, $1.37 for the same; and in this year for frames for frigates $1.09 to $1.50. No further purchases of live oak lands or artificial cultivation of the tree was recommended.

A report was made, February 21, by the Committee on Military Affairs, in accordance with a resolution of the House, upon the expediency of employing a suitable person, in aid of the Topographical Bureau, to ascertain the mineralogy and geology of each of the several states of the Union, with a view to the construction of a mineralogical and geological map of the United States. The subject was recommended as one of great national importance, and an appropriation for the purpose suggested. The report said: "Whilst all the resources of industry in the United States have been deemed worthy the attention and protection of the government, the development of our immense mineral wealth has been left entirely to accident, and has not been fostered by that public encouragement which would have been followed by so many advantages to our own citizens, or would have raised the scientific character of our country abroad."[1]

A memorial from merchants of Baltimore asked for a reduction of the duty on common salt, or an increase of the duty on fossil salt; which last was imported at a duty of one cent a bushel, at a low freight, in British ships coming empty to Nova Scotia for timber, greatly to the benefit of the British and the injury of American shipping. A manufactory of rock salt in the State of Maine, using the imported article, was complained of as a monopoly, ruinous to the manufacturers of common salt. It was able to make and sell rock salt at twenty-five cents a bushel, while Liverpool common salt cost thirty-five cents, under a duty

(1) The first complete geological survey of a whole state, under authority of government, was that of Massachusetts, made by Dr. Edward Hitchcock, who was appointed in 1830, and in 1831 made his first report on the Economic Geology of Massachusetts, and this year published a "Report on the Geology, Zoology, and Botany of Massachusetts," with plates.

of ten cents a bushel; and it was estimated to have made in the last year a clear profit of $100,000.

The House ordered two thousand copies of the Manual on Silk, published by J. H. Cobb, under the patronage of the Massachusetts Legislature, to be published for distribution by the members. About one dozen mills for the manufacture of silk goods had been erected in the United States, chiefly in New England, since 1828, with a view of using imported raw silk until a domestic supply could be had. By increased attention, several persons this year succeeded, as a few had done before, in raising two crops of silk, some of which was exhibited at the Fair of the American Institute in New York. The morus multicaulis was used as food for worms. A silk factory at Mansfield, Conn., under an English manufacturer, with swifts for winding hard silk, employed thirty-two spindles for soft silk winding, and two broad and one fringe silk loom. It had machinery enough to employ thirty broad looms and fifty hands.

The New England Lace Factory, at Newburyport, Mass., with a capital of $150,000, was incorporated; but was compelled to suspend operations four or five years after.

The manufactures of Meriden, Conn., amounted to about one million dollars in value. One company employed two hundred and fifty hands in the manufacture of Britannia wares, such as coffee pots and mills, spoons, waffle irons, signal lanterns, etc., to the value of $200,000 per annum, and another made to the amount of $25,000. The other manufactures were, wooden clocks to the value of $50,000; ivory, wood, boxwood, and horn combs, worth about $40,000; auger bits and rakes, $20,000; tinware, (its earliest extensive manufacture,) about $90,000; also Japanned ware, boots, shoes, etc. *Middletown*, in the same state, had manufactories of arms for the United States service, one factory making annually fifteen hundred rifles, milled in all the parts; another two thousand milled muskets; another twelve hundred guns, which were cast. There were also large factories of cotton yarn, broadcloth, webbing, combs, Gunter's scales, machinery, pewter, axes, tinware, paper, gunpowder, and jewelry; and about two hundred thousand coffee mills were made annually. The yearly value of its manufactures was about $700,000.

The capital invested in Manufactures in Lowell, Mass., was $6,150,000. The number of large mills (five stories high) in actual operation was nineteen, the spindles 84,000, looms 3,000, operatives 5,000, of whom 3,800 were females. 27,000,000 yards of cotton were annually manufactured from 200,000 bales of cotton, 150,000 yards of cassimeres, and 120,000 yards of ingrained, Brussels, and other carpeting, for all which the workmen received $1,200,000 per annum. There were two hundred machinists, who worked up six hundred tons of iron annually into machinery. Upwards of five thousand tons of anthracite coal, besides other fuel, it was computed, were consumed annually. There were only five factories in operation in 1831, which made from twelve to fourteen millions of yards of cloth per annum, equal to one yard per second.

Fall River, Mass., where the first cotton mill was erected in 1812, now contained thirteen cotton factories, one satinet factory, employing one hundred and fifty hands, and the Anawan iron works and nail manufactory. The cotton factories made about 9,160,000 yards annually. The largest was the Massasoit, which ran 10,000 spindles, 350 looms, and employed 400 hands, using 810,000 pounds of cotton. The whole number of spindles was 31,500, looms 1,050, hands employed 1,276, and the cotton consumed was 2,290,000 pounds. The calico works alone employed 260 hands, and the iron works consumed one thousand tons of iron annually. Population about five thousand.

The York Manufacturing Company, of Saco, Me., completed a new four story cotton mill in the place of the first one, which was destroyed by fire in 1830. They commenced operations under the superintendence of Mr. Samuel Batchelder, with eight thousand spindles, and within the next four years added two other large mills. They had also at this time a rolling mill and nail factory, which made four hundred tons of nails annually.

The high duties levied in Peru upon the principal American exports had caused a great decline in the trade with that country. With the republic of Chili, however, a treaty of amity and commerce had been made, and a valuable trade existed with its ports, which were the resort of American fishing vessels. From the 20th to 30th August of this year, 2,603 bales of one thousand yards each of American manufactured cottons arrived at Valparaiso. These fabrics had driven the English cottons out of the market; and the proceeds being paid chiefly in gold, enabled the ships to make a profitable return voyage by way of China. The exports to Chili this year amounted to $1,463,940.

The whole value of domestic cotton manufactures exported this year was $2,532,567; of which about $36,000 went to the East Indies, $213,000 to China, upward of $900,000 to Mexico, and the rest principally to Central America, Columbia, Brazil, Buenos Ayres, and Chili.

A locomotive engine, called the Pennsylvania, invented by Col. S. H. Long, U. S. A., and built in the last year by Matthew W. Baldwin of Philadelphia, was put upon the Philadelphia and Germantown Railroad in January of this year. This engine, which was about the first successful American locomotive, is said to have run a mile in less than a minute, and drew thirty-two tons at the rate of fifteen miles an hour. Its performance was not exceeded for several years. During this and the following year, five engines were built at the same factory; and the present extensive works of the proprietor on Broad street were completed. In the next three years about one hundred locomotives were built there, and numerous improvements have been made in the construction of locomotives by Mr. Baldwin and his associates.[1] A very successful locomotive was also constructed at this time by Mr. R. L. Stevens, of Hoboken, and placed on the Camden and Amboy Railroad, which then had but two others.

Nine railroad companies, with a capital of $7,140,000, were incorporated in New Jersey previous to this year. Since March, 1801, fifty-four turnpike companies were authorized in that state.

The New York Mechanics' Institute was incorporated April 24. It has established classes in modeling, machinery, architectural and ornamental drawing, a winter course of lectures, reading room, and library of six thousand volumes; all of which are free to mechanics, working-men, and apprentices of the city.[2]

Mr. Mariner, of New York, this year introduced a process for coating leather, cotton, linen, silk, etc., and for making them into water proof India rubber garments. These fabrics were made by George Spring, 55 Pine street. India rubber shoes, hose, coats, life preservers, carriage traces, etc., were made at this time at the first American rubber manufactory, established in Roxbury, Mass. The foreman of the factory claimed the invention of a new and cheap solvent for caoutchouc, the receipt for which he kept secret, and deposited under seal in one of the banks, for the benefit of his heirs. Boots made in New York, and sent to South America, to be varnished with the fresh juice as it exuded from the tree, to be returned and sold as gum elastic boots, were exhibited at the American Institute Fair this year by J. M. Hood, of Wall street; along with garments from the Roxbury factory, a diving dress from Boston, etc. India rubber carpets were about this time made by Dr. Alexander Jones, of Mobile, of rich figures and beautiful colors, and impervious to water or grease, by covering successive layers of paper and wall paper glued to canvas with a varnish of India rubber. Neat durable carpets, made of good papering, cost about thirty-seven and a half cents per yard; and richer ones, adorned with gold or silver leaf, for one dollar to one dollar and fifty cents per yard.

A single publishing house in Philadelphia—that of Cary, Lea & Blanchard—were said to have paid annually during the last five years to American authors and writers the sum of thirty thousand dollars. The

(1) Leading Pursuits and Leading Men, by E. T. Freedley, p. 302.

(2) French's Gazetteer of New York, 1860.

brothers James and John Harper, of New York, who in 1816 were journeymen printers, working at hand-presses in that city, now owned an establishment of their own, which was one of the largest in the city. It employed seven hand-presses, one horse-power press, (doing the work of seven hand-presses,) and 140 workmen; and they paid $100 per diem in wages, $200 for paper, and $1,000 per annum for postage.

The town of Newark, N. J., contained sixteen extensive factories of saddlery and harness, employing 272 hands, a capital of $217,300, and yielding a product of $346,280 per annum; independently of the coach makers, who made their own saddlery and harness. Ten carriage factories, having 779 workmen, and a capital of $202,500, produced carriages to the value of $593,000, including plating and lampmaking, etc., which was generally done by themselves. The shoe factories were eighteen in number, with 1,075 hands, and a capital of $300,000; and their product was $607,450. They consumed $400,000 worth of leather. Nine hat manufactories employed 487 hands; capital, $106,000; product, $551,700. Thirteen tanneries, with 103 hands and $78,000 in capital, returned an annual product of $503,000. In addition to these principal manufactures, there were also considerable manufactures of soap and candles, iron and brass castings, malleable iron, coach springs, tin and sheet ironware and stoves, a hardware manufactory, and two patent leather manufactories.[1] About two hundred thousand dollars worth of manufactures, principally shoes, were sent to New York in two days during this year.

The Novelty Works, for the manufacture of platform scales and domestic hardware, was established at Pittsburg, Pa., by L. R. Livingston.

There were Gimlet factories at Whately, Buckland, Keene, and in Franklin county, N. H., and one in Connecticut. The new twist gimlet was considered as much superior to the old English as the American screw-auger was to the old auger.

Patents.—William Edwards, Masonville, N. Y., Feb. 13, softening, breaking, and fulling hides. This hide mill, for softening and preparing hides by a process similar to the fulling of cloth, instead of soaking and breaking over the beam as formerly, was a valuable improvement. Robert C. Manners, Boston, Feb. 13, lithography applied to the printing of books; Sereno Newton, New York, Feb. 26, double cylinder register printing press—also for a double Napier printing press; Robert L. Stuart and Alexander Stuart, New York, March 7, applying syrup by steam in the manufacture of confectionery; Charles J. Gayler, New York, April 12, fire-proof iron chest; Joseph Francis, New York, April

(1) Gordon's Gazetteer of New Jersey.

23, portable screw boats; Samuel D. Breed, Philadelphia, June 29, hose from cloth and gum elastic; Matthew W. Baldwin, Philadelphia, June 29, wheels for locomotive carriages and railroad cars; John Elgar, Philadelphia, Nov. 29, wheels for railroad carriages; James Bogardus, New York, Sept. 17, metallic slides and cases for ever-pointed pencils; Edward M. Converse, Southington, Conn., Nov. 19, a wiring machine for tin plate ware; Herrick Aiken, Dracut, Mass., Dec. 16, sockets or hafts for awls and other tools. [The pegging haft is deemed one of the most useful among the minor inventions connected with the shoe manufacture.] F. W. Geisenhainer, New York, Dec. 19, making iron and steel by anthracite coal; Obed Hussey, Cincinnati, Ohio, Dec. 31, machine for cutting grain. A public trial of this valuable reaper was first made in July of this year, before the Hamilton County Agricultural Society, near Carthage, Ohio; and the next year it was introduced in Illinois and New York, and soon after in other states. In 1838 the patentee established a manufactory in Baltimore. This machine, though not the first horse-power reaper, was superior to any in use, and cut grain as fast as eight persons could bind it.

The usual excitement arising from the question of protective duties gave place, during the first session of the twenty-third Congress, to discussions growing out of the conflict between the executive
1834 department and the United States Bank. The President, in view of the expiration of the charter of that institution, on the 3d March, 1836, and in doubt of its constitutionality and solvency, and purity of action, as intimated in his message to Congress, directed the Secretary of the Treasury, before the re-assembling of Congress, to withdraw the government deposits from its vaults, and to lodge them with certain state banks, notwithstanding a vote of the House that they might be safely continued in that bank. The reasons for the removal of the deposits were communicated to Congress by Mr. Secretary Taney at the present session, and the act was virtually allowed; although numerous petitions were presented for the restoration of the government monies to the national bank.

The number of banking institutions in the United States had increased from three in 1791, with a capital of two millions of dollars, to 246, with an aggregate capital of $89,822,422, in 1816, when the United States Bank was chartered, until on the first of January of the present year, the number was 502, their united capital $168,827,803, their issues $78,342,528, and the specie in their vaults $17,368,430; the deposits amounting to $66,216,087. Including the bank of the United States, the whole banking capital of the Union at this time amounted to

$203,827,883; the issues to $97,550,907; specie in vaults, $27,394,667; deposits, $77,181,462; and discounts, $325,599,843.

The banks were distributed as follows: in New England 241, the proportion of whose notes to their capital was thirty-three per cent.; in New York, New Jersey, Pennsylvania, Delaware, and Maryland, 173, proportion sixty per cent.; Virginia, North and South Carolina, Georgia, and Florida, thirty-nine, proportion of notes seventy per cent.; Alabama, Mississippi, and Louisiana, eighteen, proportion of notes twenty-six per cent.; Tennessee, Kentucky, Ohio, Indiana, Illinois, Missouri, and Michigan, thirty-one, proportion fifty-five per cent. The whole circulation of the state banks was about forty-six per cent. of their capital; and that of the United States, including the national bank, a little less than fifty per cent. of their capital.[1]

Among the acts of the session was one of February 26 to authorize G. B. Lamar, of Savannah, Ga., to import, free of duty, an iron steamboat, with its machinery and appurtenances, for the purpose of making an experiment of the aptitude of iron steamboats for the navigation of shallow waters; one of June 30, empowering the Secretary of the Navy to examine and test a steam engine devised by Benjamin Phillips of Philadelphia, and such other improvements in the same line as might thereafter be presented, for which five thousand dollars were appropriated; one of the same date, appropriating eight hundred dollars to procure a marble bust, executed by an American artist, of the late Judge Ellsworth; and one modifying the duty on manufactures of lead.

A report on the subject of the coal trade, made by a committee of the Senate of Pennsylvania, stated that among other points they had been led to consider "whether the bituminous coal of Pennsylvania can be brought into general use east of the mountains for manufacturing purposes; and be transported to the eastern markets upon such terms as to supersede the use of foreign coals." The price of coals, since the commencement of the trade, appeared to have been little influenced by the tariff, but almost entirely by the scarcity and demand. In 1815, when the duty on foreign coals was three dollars and sixty cents, the price in New York was twenty-three dollars per chaldron of thirty-six bushels; from 1816 to 1823, under a duty of one dollar and eighty cents, the average price was about eleven dollars. Its price in 1821, under that duty, was fourteen dollars; and in 1830, when the duty was two dollars and sixteen cents, the price was only eight dollars. The average price from 1824 to 1834 was ten dollars; and in the latter year it declined to five dollars and five dollars fifty cents. The average increase in the

(1) Pitkin's Statistics, 2d ed.

consumption of Pennsylvania coal since 1820 was a fraction more than one third yearly.

The existence of bituminous coal in Alabama was at this time first noticed by Dr. Alexander Jones, of Mobile.

In the manufacture of Carpets, which had rapidly increased in the United States within a few years, it was ascertained that there were in operation in December eighteen to twenty factories, containing at least 511 carpet looms. Of these, eighteen were for Brussels, twenty-one for treble-ingrained, 424 for other ingrained, forty-four for Venitian, and four for damask Venitian. They produced the following quantities of the several kinds, at an average value of one dollar per yard, viz.: Brussels, 21,600 yards; three-ply, 31,500; other ingrained, 954,000; Venitian, 132,000; damask Venitian, 8,400; total, 1,147,500 yards.

The American market was in a great measure supplied with domestic carpetings of all kinds. The average quantity imported from 1828 to 1832 was 536,296 yards, valued at the place of export at $416,944; and in 1833 the quantity was 344,113 yards, worth $319,592. In some states large quantities of carpeting of inferior quality were made in families, and in 1832 it was officially reported that four counties of New Hampshire exported to other states carpeting of household manufacture probably exceeding in value all the foreign articles consumed in them.

The total value of the domestic woolens and cottons consumed in the United States, with a population taken at fourteen millions—estimated according to the consumption in Great Britain, which was equal to $160,000,000, or ten dollars per head, and including Ireland, eight dollars per head—was $122,000,000; or at the lower estimate $94,000,000.

The aggregate value of all the manufactures of the United States was estimated at not less than three hundred and twenty-five to three hundred and fifty millions per annum.[1] The foreign articles consumed in the country, after deducting teas, wines, coffee, and spices, did not exceed fifty millions of dollars per annum.

The product of raw cotton throughout the world was this year officially estimated at nine hundred millions of pounds, of which the United States produced four hundred and sixty millions, in the following proportions: Alabama and Mississippi each eighty-five millions, Georgia seventy-five, South Carolina sixty-five and a half, Lousiana sixty-two, Tennessee forty-five, Florida twenty, Virginia ten, North Carolina nine and a half, and Arkansas half a million pounds. The total value of the crop was computed to be seventy-six millions of dollars, and the quantity exported was three hundred and eighty-four

(1) Pitkin's Statistics.

millions of pounds, worth forty-nine millions of dollars, which included eight millions and eighty-five thousand pounds of sea island cotton from South Carolina and Georgia.[1]

The quantity of cotton long cloths imported this year from the United States into China was 134,000 pieces, and of cotton domestics 32,743 pieces; while of cotton goods the whole importation into that country in British vessels was only 75,922 pieces. The importation of American piece goods was nearly double that of the previous year, amounting to 24,745 pieces. An extensive manufacturer of Glasgow, who had for several years supplied Chili with cotton domestics, spun and woven in his own works to the best advantage, had latterly been obliged to abandon the trade to American competition. At Manilla, 35,240 pieces of thirty inch and 7,000 pieces of twenty-eight inch American gray cottons were received, and only 1,832 pieces of Belfast manufacture. The ports of Rio de Janeiro, Aux Cayes, of Malta, Smyrna, and the Cape of Good Hope, were also overstocked with American unbleached cottons, to the exclusion of British goods, which they undersold.[2]

The rise in price of raw cotton during the last autumn caused many New England factories to stop work. The establishment this year of a cotton factory on a large scale, with the best machinery and many advantages, at Lynchburg, Va., was regarded as opening a new era to that section of the country.

The manufacture of cotton gins on an extensive scale was commenced at this time in Autauga county, Ala., by Daniel Pratt, a native of New Hampshire, who had been previously engaged in the business with Mr. S. Criswold at Clinton, Ga. The reputation of his gins extended rapidly throughout the Southwest, and in 1839 he laid the foundation of the flourishing village of Prattville, Ala., by building a saw mill, planing mill, flour and grist mill—the first of any note in the state—gin manufactory, etc.; and in 1846 added a large cotton factory, iron foundry, and other works. In the first seventeen years he manufactured about eight thousand cotton gins.[3]

A large manufactory of oil from cotton seed was established in the last year at Natchez, Miss., and others were building at Mobile, Ala., Florence, Ga., and Petersburg, Va. The oil was used for making paints, and when refined was said to burn well in lamps; and the oil cake was used as food for cattle.

A new machine for spinning flax and hemp for cordage was introduced about this time by Joseph Westerman of New York, which spun rope

(1) Secretary Woodbury's Report.

(2) Ure's Cotton Manufactures, Bohn's Ed., vol. i. pp. xliii–iv.

(3) De Bow's Review, volume 10, page 226.

yarn from hemp without previous hatcheling, and without the consequent loss of eight to ten per cent. from that cause. The saving was so great that the rope manufacturers of Brooklyn dare not, it was said, introduce it into their factories in consequence of combinations among the spinners. The machinery to spin a ton of hemp per diem, including four machines called breakers, six finishers, two spinning and three doubling frames, a four horse power engine, etc., cost nine thousand dollars; and the total cost of spinning a ton of hemp was $17.50.

The manufactures of Manayunk, Pa., consisted at this time of Ripka's Silesia factory, with 7,176 spindles, 224 looms, and 300 hands; seven cotton mills, with upward of twenty-two thousand spindles and about one thousand hands; Hays' woolen factory, with fifty-seven hands, and Darrock's woolen and hat factory, employing fifty-seven hands; Newman's dyeing establishment, with eleven large vats and twenty-one hands; the Flat Rock Iron Works, with thirty-six hands; Rowland's saw finishing mill, turning out sixty mill-saws per week; Eckstein's paper mill, making three hundred reams weekly; and two flour mills, making two hundred and fifteen barrels of flour daily.

An act of the New York Legislature reduced the duty on salt made in the state from twelve and a half to six cents per bushel; and an amendment to the constitution, proposed this year and adopted the next, authorised the transfer of the salt duties, after payment of the canal debt, from the canal to the general fund of the state.

A State Geological Survey of Maryland was commenced this year by Dr. J. T. Ducatel, and was completed in seven annual reports.

A report to the Senate of Pennsylvania gave the quantity of anthracite coal sent to market from the Schuylkill coal region in the last year as 429,933 tons; and the capital invested was $5,022,780. The whole capital invested in the mining and transportation of coal, in canals, railroads, coal lands, working capital, etc., was $19,176,217, exclusive of storehouses, wharves, landings, vessels, etc., in Philadelphia and other places.[1]

During the last four or five years, many thousands of persons had engaged in gold washing in the Southern States; and the amount collected at this time in Virginia, North and South Carolina, and Georgia, was about one million dollars per annum. The product thenceforward fell off to one half that amount, until mining in the solid rock was attempted.

The number of Steamboats on the western waters was two hundred and thirty, and their tonnage was estimated at thirty-nine thousand

(1) Taylor on Coal, 2d Am. Ed., p. 354, 362.

25

tons, and the expense of running them at $4,644,000. The number of American steamers on Lake Erie was thirty-one, which, with 234 schooners and three brigs, had a tonnage of 30,168. The first Association of steamboat owners was formed at Buffalo during the last year, where eleven steamboats, costing $360,000, were employed; and three trips were made to the upper lakes, two to Chicago, and one to Green Bay. One of the trips to Chicago occupied twenty-five days, and another twenty-two days; it has since been made in four days by a sailing vessel. The association employed eighteen boats this year, worth six hundred thousand dollars.

Refined Sugar, which had become an article of exportation, employed at this date thirty-eight refineries in the United States, the total product of which was estimated to equal at least two millions of dollars. Prime Louisiana sugars had proved on trial to be equally valuable for refining with those of the West Indies. A large refinery, lately established near New Orleans, used thirty hogsheads of raw sugar per diem. A knowledge of the art was promoted by the publication this year of a "Manual on the Cultivation of the Sugar Cane, and the fabrication and refinement of sugar," prepared by Professor Silliman, in compliance with a resolution of the House of Representatives of January 25, 1830.

Great perfection was at this time exhibited in the art of casting in iron. The product of different establishments in the United States showed fineness and beauty of workmanship, as well as elegance of design. The iron castings made at Albany, New York, were particularly noted for their excellence, and were considered equal to any in the world. The hollowware of Bartlett, Bent & Co. was preferred to the best Scotch castings, and the stoves of Dr. Nott received the preference wherever known. The machine castings of Maury & Ward were equal to those of any country. Five establishments in the town melted annually about 2,500 tons of iron, and gave support to about four hundred persons. Elegant fruit dishes, with open flower work, cast, and then rendered malleable so as not to break, as well as breastpins of Napoleon, and other iron ornaments, rendered fashionable in Europe by the example of the Queen of Prussia, were made at the foundry of Seth Boyden, in Newark, New Jersey, who held letters patent for the process of rendering castings malleable. Beautiful specimens of small statuary, and other fine castings, rivalling those of Germany, were made at the foundry of Mr. Francis Alger, in Boston.

The recent progress in the manufacture of American Hardware was indicated by the increasing number of articles of domestic production which began to compose the ordinary stock of the hardware merchants, as well as by the improved quality of the goods. Several dealers in the principal cities were at this time chiefly, or altogether devoted to the sale of the American hardware, generally consigned to them by the manufacturers, and sold almost exclusively to the trade.[1] The samples

(1) Upon the early history of the American Hardware trade, we have been favored with communications from gentlemen connected with it from its origin. Some interesting reminiscences upon the subject have been sent to us by John W. Quincy, Esq., of New York, who has been identified with this branch of the trade from its commencement to the present time—first in Boston, and for the last quarter of a century in New York. His large and intelligent acquaintance with the subject gives authority to his communication, which we should be glad to give entire if our space permitted. We learn from him, and Mr. Hand of Philadelphia, that about the year 1827, or 1828, Mr. Amasa Goodyear, a manufacturer for many years of hay forks, buttons, and other articles at Salem village, near Waterbury, Connecticut, (who had been accustomed to take orders by semi-annual visits to the city, storing his goods in the warehouse of Mr. David W. Prescott,) opened in Church alley, in connection with his son, the late Charles Goodyear, of India rubber celebrity, and under the management of the latter, a small store, which, it is believed, was the first in the United States for the sale of American hardware. A. Goodyear & Son having failed, through speculations of the junior partner in real estate, the business, in January, 1831, passed into the possession of Messrs. Curtis & Hand, by whom it is still conducted, and who exerted themselves to give currency to various articles of home manufacture. About the former date the business was also commenced in New York by Christopher Hubbard, afterward Casey and Hubbard, who were followed in 1829 by George H. Gray & Co., and Hasner and Green, of Boston. At that time there was but one hardware store in the country of one hundred feet in depth, those of forty to sixty feet deep being considered first class stores, and a rent of $1,000 per annum rather a high one. The number of articles of domestic hardware, kept or to be obtained by the largest dealers was quite limited, and embraced many small articles, as shell and other buttons, which have since passed to other branches of trade. Among the staple articles kept by the earliest dealers were Goodyear's patent molasses gates, Fenn's patent cockstop and leather faucets, cast bits and screws (not very saleable), nail, shoe, and side strap hammers (among which those of Charles Hammond, of Philadelphia, and Mr. Eastman, of Concord, New Hampshire, were well known), wooden awl handles, Rowland's mill saws, the circular and hand-saws, and wood-saw web, of Welch and Griffiths, of Boston (whose brand was already in repute), spinning-wheel heads of home invention, Britannia wares, carpenters' planes, manure and hay forks, shovels, scythes, &c. Even all of these had not come into use as early as 1828 or 1830, but the list of American articles purchased and sold by hardware dealers, at the close of this year (1834), embraced the following goods furnished by Mr. Quincey from a record before him. Some of these articles were still more or less largely imported as well as made here, and are marked thus [*]. Iron and brass wire seives, cotton, cattle and wool cards, board coffee mills, brass andirons, *brass head shovel and tongs, cast iron circular gridirons, bung borers and reamers, *iron wire, *Britannia tea and coffee pots, wood faucets, wheel-heads, hoes (not planters'), *scythes, cow bells, japaned lamps, black-ball, *bulls-eye and dark pan hand-bells, pewter faucet and molasses gates; lines, mackerel and small hemp, bed cords, clothes lines, window cord, coil rope of hemp and manilla; *brushes, viz., scrubbing, floor, paint, furniture, horse, shoe, hair, varnish, dust, sash, hearth, etc.; sand boxes, *scale beams, sad iron stands of zinc; sleigh bells, raw hides, *inkstands, *gunter scales, *board rules, gauging rods, *pocket rules, two and four-fold; britannia tumblers and ladles; whipthongs, mouse traps, *guns, bellows, *coopers' axes, *adzes and draw-

were generally limited to a few shelves, and the profits were extremely small, compared with those on hardware. The general prejudice was strongly in favor of foreign goods, and the introduction of a new article of domestic manufacture was extremely slow and difficult for many years, the prejudice only giving place by degrees to the manifest superiority in quality or cheapness of the latter. The limited and fluctuating character of the protection, as yet afforded by the tariff, also retarded the growth of this branch.

Hammered brass kettles or battery, began at this time to be first made in the United States, at Wolcottville, Connecticut, by Mr. Israel Coe. It has since been extensively manufactured by rolling at Birmingham, in the same state and elsewhere.

Wood screws were this year first made by machinery at Providence, Rhode Island, where the New England Screw Company, and another company in the same business, were organized within a few years, and employed a capital of $200,000, making daily two thousand gross of brass and iron screws. The quality of the screws made there was such that they soon superseded James' celebrated English screws, notwithstanding the mercantile prejudice in favor of foreign articles. The business in that city has recently exceeded the value of one million dollars per annum.

N. P. Ames, and his associates, who employed at Chicopee Falls twenty-five to thirty men in making cutlery, and finishing swords by contract with the United States government—having been incorporated as the "Ames' Manufacturing Company," commenced operations this year in a new establishment, erected at Cabotville. They employed a capital of $30,000, afterward increased to $200,000, in the manufacture of arms, tools, cutlery, etc., to which they added, two years after, a foundry for casting bronze cannon and church bells, and in 1845, an iron foundry for machinery, etc., nearly all of which branches are still carried on extensively, in addition to some others. Gold and silver-mounted swords were made also by W. F. Widmann, of Philadelphia,

ing knives, *steelyards; cut tacks and brads, sheet nails, patent awls, *iron candlesticks, mahogany knobs for drawers, steel squares, *brass spring door catches, *screw drivers, *plated squares and bevils, *brass nails, *awl hafts, *mincing knives, *spring shoe punches, *gimblets, coopers' braces, gut and bone whips, *japaned door latches, *circular saws, glass knobs, timber scribes, shingling, lath and axe hatchets, scratch awls, hooks and eyes, silver ever-point pencil cases, *razor strops, screw augers, auger bits, *pocket books, *lead pencils, bone mould and suspender buttons, *soap, axes, waffle irons, oil stones, blind fasts, *mill, cross-cut and tenon saws, manure and hay forks, *shovels, spades, *glue, planes, *sadirons, *Bristol brick, cast iron cart and wagon boxes, brass head dogs, scythe-rifles, wood-saw frames.

and a year or two later, the largest manufacturer of swords in the country was Robert Keyworth, of Washington city.

Tailors' cast steel shears, with German silver and malleable iron handles, and carving knives, made by R. Ward and R. Heinish, of New York; framing chisels, by Wolcott & Russell; mortice chisels, by Gay & Galloway; augers, by Dwight & Sons; bank and store locks, with 16,382 combinations (afterward picked and improved upon by Newell), made by Andrews & Co., of Perth Amboy; with brass and copper wares, from Ludlam's factory, were among the goods exhibited at the American Institute, during the last autumn.

American axes and locks were acknowledged to be the best in the world. There were two axe factories at New Haven, Connecticut, those of Alexander Harrison, and of Collins & Company—the latter was capable of finishing two hundred axes per diem, the former one hundred and fifty. The steam axe factory of Mr. Maule, twelve miles from Wheeling, Virginia, manufactured to the value of $10,000 per annum. Door locks began to be made there the next year by Pierpont & Hotchkiss.

Oliver Ames, of Easton, Massachusetts, had at this time three extensive shovel factories—one at Easton, one at Braintree, and one at West Bridgewater. He employed nine tilt hammers, and could turn out forty dozen shovels a day, each shovel passing through twenty different hands, and his profits were estimated at $15,000 per annum.

A factory, which employed one hundred and fifty saws, was erected at Black river, in Plymouth, Vermont, for the manufacture of marble, from the white and variegated primitive limestone. *Scagliola*, or composition marble, both plain and sculptured, of various colors and fine polish, was about this time first successfully made in New York, by Clark and Dougherty. Friezes, capitols, and other composition ornaments, are noticed as new articles in New York, at this date.

Experiments made by Dr. Jones, of Mobile, showed that paper of excellent quality could be made from the husks of Indian corn, and various kinds of wood and bark, particularly that of several kinds of poplar, birch, and other trees. Several reams of good printing paper were made this year by Dr. Daniel Stebbins, of Northampton, Massachusetts, from the foliage and bark of the mulberry tree, as in China. During the year Mr. Stebbins obtained from China probably the first seeds received in this country of the genuine Canton or Chinese mulberry tree, and in order to encourage the making of bark silk paper, etc., from its bark and leaves, he erected a large cocoonery, and kept up a nursery of the trees for many years, without eventual success.

The manufacture of "pressed glass," by means of metallic moulds, in imitation of cut glass—an American invention—was this year introduced into England by Messrs. Richardson, of Strowbridge.

PATENTS.—Samuel P. Mason, Killingly, Conn., Jan. 17, spinning cotton and silk; Charles Goodyear, Philadelphia, Feb. 5, faucets or molasses gates; Nathaniel Benedick, jr., Abel Benedick, and A. H. Hotchkiss, Sharon, Conn., Feb. 10, cast iron sleigh runners; Lot Brees and Ezra Brees, Luzerne county, Pa., Feb. 10, double grooved cast iron sleigh shoes; John H. Hagenmacker, Philadelphia, Pa., Feb. 11, new American silver; Daniel Neall, Philadelphia, Feb. 13, Wm. R. Collier, Washington, D. C., April 11, Otis Tufts, Boston, Aug. 22, and Adam Ramage, Philadelphia, Nov. 19, each for a printing press; James Sellers, Philadelphia, Feb. 18, covering window and other frames with wove wire; Margaret Gerrish, Salem, Mass., manufacturing the external fibres of the Asclepias Syriaca; James Bogardus, New York, April 7, gold cleaner; Levi Ward, assignee of Phœbe Atwell, Walworth, N. Y., April 30, extracting fur from skins and manufacturing it into yarn; Edwin M. Chaffee, Roxbury, Mass., May 17, making boots and shoes from India rubber leather; Isaac Fisher, jr., Springfield, Vt., June 14, four patents for making, softening, etc., sand paper; Cyrus H. McCormick, Rockbridge Co., Va., June 21, cutting grain of all kinds. [This was for the celebrated reaping machine, which took the great medal at the World's Fair, in London, in 1851. It will cut twenty acres a day. The patent was renewed in 1845, and has recently expired, having yielded the patentee between one and two millions of dollars.] James Rennie, Lodi, N. Y., Aug. 9, dyeing and printing with two or more colors at one impression; Samuel Guthrie, Sacketts Harbor, N. Y., Aug. 21, percussion powder for discharging arms; M. W. Baldwin, Philadelphia, Sept. 10, steam engine, locomotive, and cars; Henry Blair (colored man), Glenross, Md., Oct. 14, seeding corn planter; Henry Burden, Troy, N. Y., Oct. 14, furnace for heating bar iron; Patrick Mackie, New York, Oct. 16, and Dec. 3, covering ropes with caoutchouc; John W. Cochran, Lowell, Mass., Oct. 22, rotary cylinder cannon; reissued for many-chambered cannon, March 23, 1836, in which year a factory in Springfield, Mass., made eight of Cochran's many-chambered rifles weekly; Dennison Olmstead, New Haven, Conn., Nov. 5, furnace for anthracite; reissued Oct. 14, 1835; Charles Woodworth, Barre, Me., Nov. 17, and Dec. 23, machine for splitting palm leaf.

1835

The State of New York contained in January of this year, according to the State Census, among other manufacturing establishments, one hundred and twelve cotton factories, two hundred and thirty-four woolen, thirteen glass, sixty-three rope, seventy paper, and twenty-four oil cloth factories, and two hundred and ninety-three iron works.

The cotton mills employed a capital of $3,669,500, spindles 157,316, hands 12,954, and produced upward of twenty-one million yards of cloth. The woolen, cotton, and linen cloths made in families, amounted to more than eight and a half million yards. The number of sheep in the state was about four and a half millions.

An official but defective census of Illinois, gave in that state three hundred and thirty-nine manufactories, nine hundred and sixteen mills, eighty-seven manufacturing machines, and one hundred and forty-two distilleries.

Samuel Slater, the father of the American cotton manufacture, died at Webster, Massachusetts, on the 20th April, in the sixty-seventh year of his age.

Considerable excitement began about this time to be manifested, particularly in New England, on the subject of the silk culture, and the rearing of the mulberry tree. The interest shown by Congress, and by several of the state legislatures, within the last few years in the promotion of silk growing, by means of publications, bounties and other measures, had turned the attention of many agriculturalists and others to the cultivation of different kinds of mulberry. Among these the Morus Multicaulis, Chinese, or Perottel mulberry, recently introduced into Europe and America, though not superior if it was equal to some others, began to be regaraed as the best for feeding silkworms. Its supposed ability to stand the coldest winters, to afford two crops of foliage in a season, the size and profusion of the leaves, and the facility with which they could be collected from its numerous low stalks, and the ease with which the tree could be propagated by layers and cuttings, contributed to its popularity.

Large profits were made by the sale of the young plants of that and other species and varieties of mulberry, which severally had their advocates, and many were induced to engage in the "silk business," as it was called, and which a few years after degenerated into a mere speculation in trees, to the permanent discredit of silk raising in the United States. Among those whose successful enterprise at this time added to the prevalent excitement was Mr. Whitmarsh, of Northampton, Massachusetts, who, during the last year, visited Italy and France to obtain information from the best sources, and returned with a considerable quantity of seeds of a variety of the Chinese mulberry in repute there, which he denominated the Alpine, and added to his collection. He was said to have sold, before the close of this year, mulberry plants to the value of over twelve thousand dollars, the cost of which was less than one thousand. He had also a large Cocoonery erected about this time, with a small engine for moving the reals, designing to use exclusively the Multicaulis, on which he subsequently published a treatise. Mr. William Kenrick, an eminent horticulturist of Newton, Massachusetts, had also a nursery of the same kind of trees, which he was instrumental in bringing into popular favor. He also published this year a useful manual, called the "American Silk Growers' Guide," recommending an American system or successive crops of silk in the same season.[1] A plantation of 25,000 mulberry trees was also commenced in Ohio, one of 40,000 trees near Fredericksburg, Virginia, where others were to be commenced, and five large orchards were planted in Baltimore county, Maryland. These and similar efforts throughout New England, and in other states, indicated the general enthusiasm.

Several attempts were also made to improve the winding, and other mechanism connected with the preparation and manufacture of raw silk, and several companies were organized for the manufacture of silk fabrics, generally in connection with the production of the raw material, the excitement as yet having only a healthy tendency to practical results.

Mr. Gamaliel Gay, of Poughkeepsie, New York, invented and patented this year a new mode of winding silk for the cocoons, upon spools or bobbins, instead of reels, which it superseded. He also this year received a patent for a power loom for weaving silk, which it was said to accomplish more rapidly than cotton of the same relative fineness could be woven. Both inventions were deemed valuable, especially the latter, which was introduced into establishments of the Rhode Island Silk Company, late the Valentine Company, conducted by Messrs. Dyer, at Providence, which employed a capital of $100,000, and had a cocoonery one hundred and fifty feet long, and a nursery about to be increased to 40,000 trees. Ten or twelve different fabrics of silk, and cotton and silk, woven in this establishment upon Mr. Gay's looms, were exhibited in the following March at Albany, and it was followed by the organization of a company at Troy for the manufacture of silk, and another large establishment about this time commenced operations at Poughkeepsie. The Atlantic Silk Company at Nantucket was also formed this year, to establish a manufactory of foreign and domestic raw silk, with machinery erected under the superintendance of Mr. Gay, and propelled by an engine of sixteen-horse power. The Concord Silk Company, in New

(1) Among the publications, wholly or in part devoted to the Silk Culture at this time, were Fessenden's "New England Farmer," a weekly; Fessenden's "Silk Manual and Practical Farmer," a monthly; "The Silk Culturist and Farmer's Manual;" a monthly, edited by Judge Comstock, of Hartford, Connecticut; "The Silkworm," a monthly, by S. Blydenburgh, of Albany, commenced in May; "The Albany Cultivator," monthly, by Judge Buell; "The American Farmer," formerly edited by Gideon B. Smith, of Baltimore, a practical silk grower; "The Farmer's Register," by Edmund Ruffin, of Virginia, and several other Agricultural journals.

Hampshire, was formed in June of this year, and incorporated with a capital of $75,000, and purchased a farm of two hundred and fifty acres near Concord, for the raising of mulberry trees and silk worms. Many foreign workmen were employed in a new manufactory of silk, at Lisbon, Connecticut, under Mr. William Carpenter, a silk manufacturer from Spitalfields, and also at Mansfield, where Mr. W. Atwood, the next season, manufactured about 30,000 sticks of twist, worth $4.50 per hundred. A new incorporated company, called the Connecticut, had recently commenced at Hartford, and employed a capital of $30,000, and upward of one hundred looms, chiefly in weaving Tuscan braid, the straw being imported at a cost of about one dollar a pound. Nurseries of mulberries existed in a number of towns. Massachusetts passed this year an act to encourage the silk culture, but repealed it the next year, and gave a bounty of ten cents a pound for cocoons, and one dollar for raw silk, made in the state. The New England Silk Company, at Dedham, had commenced operations recently under the superintendence of J. H. Cobb, with a capital of $50,000. It employed sixteen sewing silk machines, and under the protective duty of forty per cent. on sewing silk, made arrangements to manufacture two hundred pounds per week. It made also, during the next year, about $10,000 worth of silk and mixed fabrics. The Massachusetts Silk Company, formed about this time at Boston, for producing and manufacturing silk, had a capital stock of $100,000, and purchased a tract of land at Farmingham, where they soon had two hundred thousand white and ten to twenty thousand Multicaulis mulberry trees growing. The Messrs. Montogul had an establishment on Washington street, Boston, which had been three or four years in operation. It constantly employed about three hundred females, and one hundred and fifty to two hundred looms in weaving Tuscan Braid in a great variety of elegant patterns. Silk formed the warp and the filling was of imported Tuscan straw with occasional admixtures of Manilla grass or fine strips of whalebone, both of which gave the braid an elegant appearance by their white and shining appearance. From eight hundred to twelve hundred bonnets were made weekly at the last mentioned factory, of a variety of beautiful forms and patterns, which sold readily in the North, South and West, at from $2.50 to $4.00 each. Much gimp was made and used in the manufacture of bonnets at the same place, by very simple but effective machinery, and a ribbon loom with a dozen spring shuttles wove a dozen ribbons at a time by a single hand. Twenty pieces of galloon were woven at the same time in another loom, by the aid of as many shuttles impelled by a single hand. From thirty to fifty pounds of silk imported from China direct or from France, at eleven dollars per pound, were used weekly in the establishment, which had also a throwing mill for making organzine and tram or warp and filling.

A variety of silk fabrics had been for several years made by Mr. Rapp, at Economy, Pa. The Beaver Silk Culture and Manufacturing Company was this year formed in Philadelphia, and purchased land to the value of thirty or forty thousand dollars near the Falls of Beaver. The Chester and Philadelphia and other silk companies were also organized in the state within a year or two, and associations were formed for similar objects in most of the states during the next five or ten years. Many of those already mentioned, and others which engaged in the silk business, were ruined by the speculation.

The value of foreign silks which were imported this year, amounted to $16,597,983, and in the following year reached the enormous sum of $25,033,200.

There were at this time only two manufactories of Hair Cloth in the United States. One of these, the first in New England, had recently been started at Deerfield, Mass., by Elias Willis. The Hair cloth used at this time was principally imported from England, and was only employed for covering furniture and making elastic stock bodies.

Six companies had at this date been incorporated by Massachusetts for the manufacture of India Rubber goods. The "Roxbury," incorporated in 1833, E. M. Chaffee and others, proprietors, had its capital increased in the last year to $300,000. The "Boston and Lynn," located at Lynn, capital $200,000; the "Boston" $100,000; the "New England" $70,000; the "South Boston" $50,000, and the "Suffolk" $150,000, were all incorporated in 1834.

The Boot Cotton Mills at Lowell, which now consist of five mills and 54,936 spindles, were incorporated. The Boston and Lowell Railroad was opened for travel in June, and the Nashua and Lowell Railroad was incorporated. A cotton factory was erected at St. Francisville, Louisiana, this year, and a paper mill in Boone County, Mississippi. A large paper mill at New Orleans made from one hundred to two hundred reams daily.

It was estimated that two million pairs of shoes were made at Lynn this year. Chocolate was made there in large quantities, amounting in the next year to one hundred tons.

The material and intellectual resources of Ohio had been greatly developed during the last five years. It now contained about one million inhabitants, and had one hundred and twenty newspapers in sixty-five different towns, thirty-two of which are still published under their original names. The first cylinder printing press in the West was purchased this year for the Methodist Book concern at Cincinnati.

The proprietors of the Cincinnati Gazette, who started this year under the editorship of J. H. Wood, the first commercial paper in the North-west, called the "Price Current," also employed the first newspaper express ever run in the West. They obtained the President's Message from Washington in sixty hours, at a cost of $200. Cincinnati was at this time seven days distant from Pittsburg, twenty-one from New Orleans and fourteen from New York. Messrs. Corey and Webster, publishers of that city, had issued during the last three years, 771,000 volumes of school and other books, including six hundred thousand copies of Webster's Spelling Book. There were many other publishers, some of whom had probably published nearly as many. There were in successful operation in the city over fifty steam engines, besides four or five in Newport and Covington. More than one hundred steam engines, about two hundred and forty cotton gins, upward of twenty sugar mills, and twenty-two steamboats, were built in the city during this year. Its population was thirty-one thousand. The State of Ohio this year first began to export breadstuffs, wool, ashes, etc., by way of the lakes. The shipments of breadstuffs were equivalent to 543,815 bushels of wheat, and was increased in the next five years to an amount equivalent to 3,800,000 bushels.

The Newport Manufacturing Company, opposite the city, employed, during the last year, two hundred hands, and made woolen goods, cotton bagging, cotton yarn and bale rope to the value of $281,160. The manufactures of Covington for the same year were estimated at $508,500, of which value $200,000 was the product of an iron rolling mill and nail works in the town.

An official table gives the number of steamboats built on the western rivers since 1811 as 684, measuring 106,135 tons, an average of 155 tons each, of which fifty-two were built the present year. The number running on the Mississippi and twenty-two of its tributaries at the beginning of the last year was two hundred and seventy, whose tonnage was 39,000 tons. More than eight thousand miles were traveled by them. Of the whole number, three hundred and four were built in Pittsburg District (one hundred and ninety-seven in the town), two hundred and twenty-one at Cincinnati, one hundred and three at Louisville, nineteen at Nashville, and thirty-seven at other places. The arrivals of steamboats at New Orleans this year were estimated at twenty-three hundred, an increase of seven hundred since 1832.

The "Howe Manufacturing Company" was established in December of this year, at New York, by John J. Howe and his associates, for the manufacture of "Spun Head" Pins under Mr. Howe's patent. They established a manufactory at Derby, Connecticut; and some five years after, having obtained a new patent for "solid-headed" pins, Mr. Howe commenced the manufacture of them. Mr. Samuel Slocum, of Rhode Island, obtained a patent in England this year, for his machine for making solid-headed pins, since extensively used at Poughkeepsie, New York, and Waterbury, Connecticut.

Several experiments were made during the past and present years, by the late Walter Hunt of New York, to produce a Sewing Machine. Notwithstanding many ingenious devices, it was never perfected so as to be patentable, and was laid aside until after the invention of a practical machine by Elias Howe, in 1845, when claims were made on Hunt's behalf to the original invention.[1]

The manufacture of Locomotives was commenced in New York by Thomas Rodgers, an eminent manufacturer of cotton machinery, railroad work, etc. Fourteen locomotives were built this year in Philadelphia, by M. W. Baldwin, and about forty the next year. The Norris Locomotive Works in the same city were also in operation on a smaller scale, and about this time turned out the engine "George Washington," which, on the 10th July, 1836, ascended the inclined plain, on the Columbia and Philadelphia railroad, thereby demonstrating the fact that heavy grades could be ascended without the aid of stationary engines and ropes. This resulted in a new principle of construction for railroads and great saving of expense in grading. It established the reputation of the builder, who added other improvements the same year, and became known in Europe and America as a skillful constructor.

Nearly one hundred thousand wood and brass clocks were made this year in the towns of Bristol, Plymouth, and Farmington, Connecticut. Many women were employed, chiefly in making and painting the dial-plates.

PATENTS.—Artemas L. Brooks, Lowell, Mass., Jan. 7, improvement on Woodworth's Planing Machine. It made use of two revolving cutters for planing both sides of a board at once, instead of one as in Woodworth's machine, in the patent of which he owned a right. Peregrine Williamson, New York, March 30, manufacture of metallic or steel pens—an improvement upon his pen patented in 1809—Charles Jackson, S. S. Potter and John Miller, Providence, R. I., April 2, combined rotary and stationary spindle for spinning. C. Whipple, J. Sprague, and M. D. Whipple, Douglas, Mass., April 3, lathe for turning lasts and other irregular forms.—This patent was assigned to Carter & Hender of Boston, principal owners of Blanchard's earlier

(1) Gifford's Argument on Howe's Application for Renewal of Patent.

patent for the same purpose, from which this differed somewhat. S. S. Allen, Saratoga Springs, N.Y., and John Brandon, Williamsport, Pa., April 8, each a portable horse-power. [In both these horse powers the animal walked around the machine.] Lemuel Hedge, Brattleborough, Vt., April 22, constructers of the joints of carpenters' rules; Henry Blynn, Newark, Essex Co., N. J., May 9, machine for stiffening hat bodies. [This mode of stiffening by immersing the crown and brim in stiffening liquors of different strength and passing between rollers, was an improvement which enabled one man to do the work of five by the old process, and is still in use.] Lucilius H. Mosely, Poughkeepsie, N. Y., May 9, throwing and twisting silk; Gamaliel Gay, Poughkeepsie, N. Y., Aug. 17, unwinding silk upon spools instead of reels; to the same, Sep. 26, a power loom for weaving silks; P. M. Gilroy, Warwick, and Abner S. Tompkins, North Providence, R. I., May 9, improvement in the damask loom by the application of water or other power to drive it; Elwood Mears, Philadelphia, June 26, ever pointed lead pencils; Guy C. Baldwin, Ticonderoga, N. Y., Dec., making pencil points and composition therefor; Dayton, Hoyt & White, Salina, N. Y., June 6, and John White, New York, July 18, making coffins from hydraulic cement, and to John White, July 18, for coffins of artificial stone or marble; Preswick and Fisher, New York, Aug. 17, preparation of oil of hazel; Amasa Stone, Johnston, R. I., Aug. 17, power loom and taking up motion. This improvement upon a former patent was introduced by the patentee into England, and was considered a valuable mechanism. Jesse Marden, Baltimore, Md., Sep. 9, balance platform scale for weighing—a useful invention still in demand; Charles Goodyear, New Haven, Ct., Sep. 9, gum elastic cement. Four other patents were granted for making and using hydraulic and other cements. J. S. Brown and J. J. Barker, also to W. Bradly and M. L. Worthley, all of Philips, Me., Oct. 14, for machines for cutting felloes for wheels; William Gates, Hanover, N. Y., Nov. 14, for Japan applied to leather; John Scott, Philadelphia, Nov. 26, use and application of asbestos to stoves, grates, crucibles, etc.; F. Goodwell and F. H. Harvey, Ramapo, N. Y., Dec. 2, power loom for weaving stock frames; Joseph Curtis, New York, Dec. 28, three patents for an amalgam mill for separating gold from ore.

An act of Congress of March 3 authorized letters patent to Francis B. Ogden, for "an engine for producing motive power whereby a greater quantity of power is obtained by a given quantity of fuel than heretofore," as the assignee of John Ericsson, "a subject of the King of Sweden," the true inventor, whose improvements in steam propulsion have since excited much attention.

A Report on the cultivation, manufacture, and foreign trade of cotton, accompanied by a series of tables, giving its statistics since the year
1836 1789, was communicated to Congress on the 4th of March, by the Hon. Levi Woodbury, Secretary of the Treasury. The capital invested in the production of cotton was estimated at eight hundred millions of dollars, and the average production of the last ten years was 2,137,000 bales. The foreign trade in raw cotton of the whole world, which was small compared with the whole growth and consumption, did not probably exceed five hundred and thirty-five millions of pounds, and of that the United States exported about three hundred and eighty-four millions of pounds, or almost three-fourths. The average price of Upland cotton, at the place of exportation in the United States, during the last year, was sixteen and a half cents, and in England twelve and a half pence sterling—sea Island cotton being usually worth two hundred and fifty per cent. more than other kinds. Of the exports in the last year 253,000,000 pounds went to England, 100,333,000 to France, and 16,750,000 to other places, of which Holland and Belgium, Trieste, and the Hanse Towns, were the principal.[1] The quantity of raw cotton manufactured in England, during the last year, was about 320,250,000, and in the United States about 100,000,000 of pounds. The capital employed in manufacturing, by machinery, amounted in England to $185,000,000, and in the United States to $80,000,000, the value of the product in the latter being forty-five to fifty millions of dollars. The spindles employed in cotton manufactures in the United States, were estimated at 1,750,000. The value of the exports of cotton goods from England, in 1835, was placed at $88,500,000, and in the United States, in 1834, at $2,200,000. The exports of cotton manufactures from England had been for some years, and were now, nearly equal to one half of her exports of every kind; and in 1834 about one third of the value was in yarn, which in some years constituted one half the weight.

The best cotton goods were supposed to be made in Switzerland, where the skill and machinery were good, and the climate congenial. But the raw material, being carried so far by land, was expensive, and

(1) The value of raw cotton exported this year (1836), from the United States, amounted to 423,631,367 pounds, valued at $71,284,925. The value of cotton manufactures imported was $17,876,087, of which $14,092,477 were from Great Britain, and $2,321,008 from France, whereof $2,765,676 were re-exported chiefly to Mexico, Cuba, and South America. The exports of domestic cotton goods this year were valued at $2,255,734, chiefly to Cuba, South America, and Africa. Cotton bagging, worth $1,701,451, was exported this year, nearly all of it from Great Britain, and the Hanse towns.

the manufacturer could not compete with England, though twenty per cent. cheaper than in France.

In France many fine goods were made by skill and experience, but the machinery was poorer and cost more. Hence the prices in those two countries of the cloth made from a pound of raw cotton exceeded on an average fifty cents, while in England they were about fifty cents, and in the United States were now somewhat less. We made more coarse and substantial cloths of cotton than England, and they could be afforded cheaper by two or three cents per yard. They were in greater demand abroad, as we put more staple into them, the raw material being cheaper here. But the English laces being made chiefly of Sea Island cotton, with a very little silk, enhanced the value of each pound to over five dollars; and the whole manufacture of it equalled $9,000,000 per annum, or 30,750,000 square yards.

In regard to improvements in machinery, it was remarked that a spindle now sometimes revolved eight thousand times in a minute instead of only fifty times as formerly, and would spin on an average from one sixth to one third more than it did twenty years previous. Indeed, in 1834, it was said that one person could spin more than double the weight of yarn in a given time than he could in 1829. The quantity of raw cotton spun by one spindle depended of course on the fineness of the thread, and the quality of the machinery. In England, where a considerable portion of the yarn was finer, the average was about eight and a half ounces weekly, or from twenty-seven to twenty-eight pounds yearly; while the average in the United States was about fifty pounds yearly, of yarn number twenty and twenty-five in fineness, and about twenty-six pounds of number thirty-five and forty. In 1808, the average was computed at forty-five pounds per spindle of cotton, yielding thirty-eight pounds of yarn. The loss from dirt and waste was estimated at from one twelfth to one eighth. At Lowell one hundred pounds of cotton yielded eighty-nine pounds of cloth, though the average here used to be estimated at only eighty-five pounds, when cotton was not so well cleaned, and machinery less perfect. One spindle at Lowell produced, through looms, etc., on an average one and one tenth yards of cloth daily, but this result differed greatly with the fineness of the thread, excellence of the looms, width of the cloth, etc.

In 1830, it was computed that thirty-seven spindles were necessary to supply one loom; though in 1827, at Lowell, the actual proportion was only twenty-six; at Exeter, in 1831, it was twenty-nine, and now at Lowell it is eighteen hundred and thirty-one. The number of looms in England, in 1832, was only one to about forty spindles, (so much more yarn is made and not woven there,) and these were mostly hand looms.

But in 1834, the number of them was about one hundred thousand power looms, and two hundred and fifty thousand hand looms, or in all, about one to thirty. One loom formerly wove about twenty yards of cloth of the ordinary seven eighths width, more of the twenty-six inches in width used for calicoes, and less of the five quarter wide. The average new was from thirty to forty yards of number twenty. At Lowell, in 1835, it was thirty-eight to forty yards of number fourteen and twenty to thirty yards of number thirty. It required from four to five yards of number twenty to twenty-five yarn to weigh one pound, and five to six yards of numbers thirty-five to forty.

In making cloth of plain ordinary width and fineness, one person was needed to conduct all the business from the raw cotton to the finishing of the cloth for every twenty spindles. If the cloth was colored, printed, or stamped, one person was required for every seven spindles. This would be about two hundred and fifty persons for all purposes in a factory of five thousand spindles, making plain thin cloth. One person could manage from two to three power looms.

The average number of spindles in new mills was now five to six thousand. In Lowell, in 1836, they had in twenty-seven mills one hundred and twenty-nine thousand eight hundred and twenty-eight spindles, or a little under five thousand to each, though they printed, etc., in some. A factory with five thousand must be about one hundred and fifty-five feet long and forty-five wide, four stories in height, and contain about one hundred and forty looms with other suitable machinery for picking, working, and sizing. Such an one would cost, with a few shops and outhouses appurtenant, and land and water privilege, $140,000 to $220,000, according to the materials for building, distance from navigation, etc. If bleaching or printing cloths be added, more expense would be necessary, and more than two hundred and fifty persons, making a permanent investment in buildings, water power, machinery and appurtenances, equal to twenty-eight or forty-four dollars per spindle, independent of temporary investments in raw material and wages.

Spindles, which were about half the expense of all the machinery, formerly cost in France ten dollars, and in 1832 eight dollars each, now cost here four dollars and a half if of the throstle kind, and two dollars and a half if of the mule kind; but in some places in the United States five per cent. higher. Throstles in 1826 cost here, it was said, eight dollars each. The spindle used in the filling frame quite extensively at this time, cost about six dollars.

About forty-two and a third pounds of flour were used to each spindle per annum, for sizing, or four pounds weekly to each loom; in England and here about one pound weekly to each loom, but at Lowell nearly four pounds each per week. In England three times as many spindles and factories were moved by steam as by water. In the United States not one in a hundred factories was moved by steam. The power to move all the cotton mills in England equalled that of forty-four thousand horses, of which only eleven thousand was by water wheel. In 1824 the whole power was estimated at only 10,572 horses. Each factory of common size and employment required from sixty to eighty horse power here or about eleven and a half horse power to one thousand spindles.

On the fourth of July an "act to promote the progress of the useful arts, and to repeal all acts and parts of acts heretofore made for that purpose" was approved, and became substantially the foundation of the present system of protection to inventors and discoverers in the United States. By this law, which has been amended by several subsequent acts[1] regulating the details of organization and business, the Patent Office was entirely reorganized and erected into a separate bureau or department of state with enlarged powers, under a chief to be called the Commissioner of Patents,[2] to be appointed by the President of the United States, with a chief clerk, examiner, and three subordinate clerks. Patents were to be issued under a special seal of the office, and to be signed by the Secretary of State and countersigned by the commissioner. Among other provisions of the act, the examiners, instead of merely making, as formerly, a comparison of the specifications, drawings and model, to ascertain their agreement, were required to entertain the question of novelty, utility and priority of invention, in aid of which increased labors a library of scientific works and periodicals was provided. Models and specimens of manufactures, works of art, etc., whether patented or unpatented, were to be arranged and classified in suitable rooms or galleries, and to be open at suitable hours for public inspection. The first commissioner was Hon. Henry L. Ellsworth, appointed July 4 of this year.

On the 15th December the Patent Office with all its contents, occupying a part of the General Post Office building, was destroyed by fire, obliterating the records and models which had accumulated during many years.

The Trustees of the American Institute in New York on the 30th March, issued a circular to the friends of the useful arts and national industry announcing the establishment of a Repository of Arts of the

(1) Subsequent acts were approved March 3, 1837, March 3, 1839, August 29, 1842, May 27, 1848, and March 4, 1861.

(2) The chief of the Patent Office in 1821, received by courtesy, the title of Superintendent, and the incumbents of that office were William Thornton, appointed July 1, 1821, Thomas B. Jones, April 12, 1828, John D. Craig, —— and J. C. Picket, Jan. 31, 1835.

American Institute, at No. 187 Broadway, to be opened in May. It was intended to collect into one great hall, machines, models, specimens and drawings of all the important improvements and inventions which the country afforded, and for that purpose manufacturers, mechanics, artizans, inventors and producers generally throughout the country were invited to contribute their varied products. A library was opened to the public, and a monthly journal of the proceedings of the institute was published at the Repository. They also commenced the publication of an annual volume of the transactions, continued to the present time.

A law was enacted in Massachusetts prohibiting, under penalty of fifty dollars, the employment of any child under fifteen years of age, in any manufacturing establishment, unless such child had received school instructions under a legally qualified teacher, in orthography, reading, writing, English grammar, geography, arithmetic, and good behavior, for at least one term of eleven weeks in the year preceding its employment, and for the same period during any and every twelve months in which the child was so employed.

Charters were this year granted in Massachusetts to seventy-three manufacturing corporations, with an aggregate capital of $10,729, in addition to thirteen railroad companies with $5,675,000 capital, and twenty-eight companies for other purposes representing $6,172,500 capital—total $22,576,500.

The Legislature of Pennsylvania passed on 16th June, an "Act to encourage the manufacture of Iron with coke or mineral coal, and for other purposes." It authorized the formation—with the usual corporate privileges—of associations with capitals of not less than $100,000 nor more than $500,000, in shares of fifty dollars each, exclusively for the manufacture, transportation and sale of iron made with coke or mineral coal, each corporation to hold two thousand acres of land and to make an annual statement of its transactions to the Legislature.

The first manufacture of Wrought Iron Tubes and fittings for gas, steam and water works in the United States, was commenced this year at the Pascal Iron Works, Philadelphia, by Morris, Tasker & Morris. The senior member of the firm had carried on, for fifteen years previously, the manufacture of coal grates, stoves, and general smith-work, and they afterward added to their business the making of cast-iron gas and water mains, lapwelded flues for boilers, gas and steam fitters' tools, etc., employing machinery of a very perfect description, in which they now consume over six thousand tons of anthracite fuel annually.

A Geological Survey of the State of Virginia, by Prof. W. B. Rogers, was commenced under an act of the last year, and was completed in six annual reports. State geological surveys of Pennsylvania and New

Jersey were ordered by their respective legislatures, to be conducted under the direction of Prof. Henry D. Rogers, now of the University of Glasgow. The first report of New Jersey was made this year, and the final one in 1840. Several annual reports of the Pennsylvania survey were made, and in 1859 Professor Rogers published in Edinburg, in two quarto volumes, accompanied by maps and illustrations in the highest style of accuracy and beauty, his final report on the Geology of Pennsylvania. Professors Emmons, Matthew L. Vanuxem, L. C. Beck, T. A. Conrad, and James Hall, were appointed by the State of New York to make a geological survey of that state. Five annual reports were made, and have been followed by several volumes of a final report, embracing the Natural History of the state in general and a geological map.

J. R. Cotting was this year commissioned to make a state survey of Georgia, which appeared in 1841. D. Trimble reported on the Geology of Kentucky during this year.

One of the most extensive Copper Mines in the country was opened about this time at Bristol, Connecticut, which yielded the proprietors, for many years, large quantities of ore containing thirty-two per cent. of copper. In Flemington, New Jersey, was a copper mine lately opened, which was the only one in that state that was wrought at this time.

The productive value of all branches of manufactures, including raw material, in the city of Pittsburg, was estimated this year at $15,575,440, the largest items being $4,160,000, the products of nine rolling mills in operation, and $2,130,000, produced by eighteen iron foundries, steam engine factories, and machine shops—six cotton factories produced about $500,000 worth of goods. Sixty-one steamboats, valued at $960,000, were built there this year. Messrs. Lippincott & Brothers, and Kings, Highby & Anderson, manufactured eight thousand dozen shovels and spades, one thousand six hundred dozen hoes, and six hundred dozen saws. Owen Waters, on Chartier's creek, and E. Estep, at Lawrenceville, made axes, shovels, and spades, etc., to the value of $90,000. The manufactures and mechanical products and sales of all kinds, foreign and domestic, were estimated at from twenty to twenty-five millions of dollars. Nine million feet of lumber from the Alleghany were measured in the last year, and over seven million feet this year. The whole quantity of lumber sent down the Ohio from the Alleghany, was computed to be thirty million feet.[1]

In the city of Wheeling, Virginia, were one hundred and thirty-six establishments for the manufacture of domestic goods, employing more

(1) Syford's Western Address Directory, pp. 92–112.

than seventeen hundred hands and twenty-eight steam engines, equal to nine hundred horse power. Their annual product was worth at least two million dollars. Within a circle of twenty-five miles were one hundred and thirty-four flour mills, making at least two hundred and eighty thousand barrels of flour, worth $6.75 per barrel. Eleven steamboats valued at $198,000, were built there during this year. Coal cost there in no case over three cents a bushel, and in the rolling mill and nail works of D. Agnew & Co.; cost only one and a half cents a bushel.

Dayton, Ohio, contained within its corporate limits water power sufficient for thirty-five pairs of mill-stones, or seventeen thousand five hundred cotton spindles; and improvements were contemplated which would increase it fourfold, by making nearly the whole power of Mad river available. The capital employed in trade and manufactures exceeded one million dollars. The principal factories were three or more cotton mills, two gun barrel factories, the Dayton Carpet Factory incorporated and recently put in operation, an extensive machine shop, flouring mill with three run of stones, carding and fulling mill, clock factory, last factory, iron foundry in operation six years, two soap and candle factories, etc. During this year eighty-one houses were built and nearly three millions of bricks were laid.

A Cotton Factory capable of running one thousand spindles was put in operation on the 4th July, at Fayetteville, North Carolina. Two cotton mills three stories high, with machine shop and sizing house, had been recently erected on the Appomatox, four miles from Petersburg, Virginia. They would contain about four thousand spindles and one hundred and seventy looms. The silk business was about to be commenced at Petersburg. Among the numerous companies chartered this year in Massachusetts, was the Perkins Mills, at Chicopee, with a capital of $400,000, afterward increased to half a million.

The Hudson Calico Print Works of Marshall, Carville & Taylor, was in a high state of efficiency, having forty-two block hand printers and five printing machines, two of which printed four colors at a time, and three of them three colors. The machines were all of the best models in England, whence they had been recently imported, and could print eighteen thousand yards or 5,400,000 yards per annum. Mr. Benjamin Marshall, of Troy, at this time proprietor of the New York Mills, made the finest shirtings in the country as well as the finest printing cloths.

The quantity of calicoes printed in the United States during the year ending April 1, was one hundred and twenty millions of yards. There were several establishments in the country for printing silks and ginghams, of which the Phillips Mills, at Lynn, Massachusetts, was probably the largest.

Silk Societies and Stock Companies continued to be formed and incorporated in different parts of the country. Additional interest in the subject was excited by a communication from General Tallmadge—then on a tour through the silk countries of Europe—which appeared in the Journal of the American Institute. In Massachusetts a legislative bounty of ten cents a pound for cocoons, and one dollar for raw silk made in the state, was offered April 11th, but only $85.20 was claimed during the year. Maine offered bounties of five cents for cocoons and fifty cents for raw silk, and New Jersey fifteen cents a pound for cocoons raised in the state for five years. The latter act excepted "bodies corporate and politic," and was repealed the next year.

The general prosperity of the country was indicated by the importation during this year, of silks—chiefly manufactured goods—to the value of twenty-two millions of dollars or more than double the average of former years. The total importations of the year amounted to one hundred and fifty-nine millions, and averaged for the last three years one hundred and twenty-two millions per annum, against an average of seventy millions annually for the five years under the tariff of 1828.

A large Ingrain Carpet Factory, afterward Petton's, was established this year at Poughkeepsie, New York, by Henry Winfield, which, four years after, turned out, of three-ply, superfine, fine and common ingrain carpeting, plain and twilled Venetian stair carpets, one hundred thousand yards, and one million yards of carpet bindings, of excellent quality, per annum, and employed seventy men.

The celebrated Eagle Brewery of M. Vassar & Co., was also erected at Poughkeepsie. Twelve years after it covered thirty-five thousand square feet of ground, and made annually twenty thousand barrels of ale, beer, and porter, worth $100,000.

The India Rubber Factory at Troy, New York, having been burned about this time, a new company was immediately formed and a new factory was put in operation, in which one hundred and twenty persons were employed, making daily one hundred pairs of shoes, besides garments and other articles.

The first Coinage by steam power in the United States Mint was done on the 23d March, with a new Coining Press designed by Franklin Peale, and a medal was struck in commemoration of the event. An improved milling machine, invented and introduced at the same time into the United States Mint by Mr. Peale, was also carried by steam.[1]

(1) This coining press, which was a very perfect piece of mechanism, was made with a toggle joint, a contrivance which was not claimed by Mr. Peale as altogether new, as coins had been struck in Europe by such machines many years before, and Mr. M.

Similar machines and presses for cutting out blanks or Planchets for coins were, like those above mentioned, constructed under Mr. Peale's direction, by Messrs. Merrick and Agnew of Philadelphia, for the use of the branch mints at Charlotte and Dahlonega, which, with a third at New Orleans, were created by act of Congress in the last year. A Code of Mint Laws was enacted in January of the next year.

PATENTS.—George B. Dexter, Boston, Jan. 6, water-proof silk hats; Isaac Orr, Washington, D. C., Jan. 20, air-tight stoves. [This patent gave rise to several suits at law, in which the originality of Dr. Orr's invention was disputed; after he had, during several years, received considerable sums from its manufacture, an injunction was granted and sustained against infringements.] Edwin Gordon, Hingham, Mass., Feb. 17, cannon for chain shot; Wm. H. Bell, Washington, D. C., May 14, cannon traverse board for pointing cannon. [By an act of Congress of July 4, this patent and another granted to Mr. Bell in the last year, for elevating cannon, were purchased for the United States government for the sum of $20,000.] Isaac Schnaïtmann, Philadelphia, Feb. 20, glasses for spectacles; Samuel Colt, Hartford, Conn., Feb. 25. [This patent of Col. Colt, recently deceased, was for the celebrated revolving fire arms, the idea of which is said to have occurred to him at an early age, and while on a voyage to India at the age of fifteen, a model was made which is still preserved. Having secured patents in the United States and Europe, he formed, about this time, a company at Patterson, N. J., with a capital of $300,000, for the manufacture of pistols and carbines, which proved unsuccessful and failed. In 1848, during the Mexican war, he resumed the manufacture under a contract with the government, at Whitneyville, Conn., and the next year removed to Hartford, where, in 1850, he projected the immense establishment in which the manufacture has since been conducted. He died January 10, 1862.] Benjamin F. Boyden, Boston, March 31, cast-iron hoe; James A. Gray, Richmond, Va., June 11, metallic coffins; Thomas Blanchard, New York, Aug. 1 to 31, nine several patents for ships' blocks and processes connected with their manufacture; Arnold Wilkinson, Providence, R. I., Aug. 31, polishing iron and brass wire for weavers' reeds. [This included the use of steam power in place of the tedious hand process, of preparing wire for reeds, by the successor of Jeptha A. Wilkinson, the inventor of the reed-making machine, and who made other improvements in the business still carried on by Mr. Frederick Miller.] Isaiah Jennings,

W. Baldwin of Philadelphia, had several years before commenced the construction of a coining press on that principle. Steam power was also used at this time at the Royal Mint in London, and its operation was regarded with great curiosity.—*Franklin Journal, vols.* 22 *and* 23.

New York, Sep. 22, two patents (one being a reissue) for lamps for burning his patent composed of alcohol and spirits of turpentine; J. Arnold and G. G. Bishop, Norwalk, Conn., Oct. 20, forming a web of wool, hair, etc., without spinning; Alonzo D. Phillips, Springfield, Mass., Oct. 24, friction matches—being the first American patent for matches, the constituents of which were chalk, phosphorus, glue and brimstone.—William Woodworth, New York, Nov. 15, planing machine —first patented in 1828.

On the 25th February Mr. Adams, from the Congressional Committee on Manufactures, to whom had been referred a resolution of the House
1837 in the last session, instructing them to inquire into the expediency of promoting the Culture and Manufacture of Silk, communicated a full report on the subject. Much of the information was contained in a letter from Mr. Andrew Judson of Connecticut, a late member of Congress, to whom had been delegated the duty of making the necessary inquiries. He stated that it had been found perfectly practicable to raise mulberries and silkworms throughout the whole of the United States. The Morus Multicaulis could be acclimated in the Northern and Middle States, and upon one acre of land would sustain sufficient worms to raise one hundred and twenty-eight pounds of silk, then worth $640. The process of reeling silk had been found an easy acquisition and was adapted to the labor of the young and the aged. The manufacture of silk was as simple as that of cotton or wool, and far less expensive in buildings and machinery. The weaving of silk fabrics on power looms had been successfully attempted—gentlemen's wear, cravats, etc., having been woven of a texture little if any inferior to the foreign. In this respect we were already in advance of the manufacturers of Europe and of India. This country, it was certain, could successfully compete with others in the culture and manufacture of silk. The importance of these branches of economy both in a pecuniary and moral point of view was immense. The six New England States were more or less engaged in the culture and manufacture of silk, and four of them were encouraging the business by legislative bounties, which New York was also about to do. Silk companies existed in all the Eastern and Middle States, and in the Southern States much interest was felt in the subject. It was proposed in Virginia to devote the worn out tobacco lands to the culture of silk, in order to arrest the emigration which was setting westward and threatened to depopulate the state. The Western States were peculiarly adapted to the business, and a number of companies with large capitals were incorporated in Ohio, and under skillful managers. Seventy families in the vicinity of Canton, in

Stark county, were engaged in making silk, and many were beginning in several other counties. It was commenced in Kentucky about a year and a half ago. In Indiana, Illinois, Missouri, and Tennessee, beginnings had been made.

By an act of Congress, approved March 1, the tenth and twelfth clauses—relating to various articles of hardware, japanned, plated and other metallic wares—of the second section of the act of July 14, 1832, were suspended until the close of the next session.

"An act in addition to the act to promote the progress of Science and Useful Arts," dated March 3, enacted that all patents, grants or assignments made previous to the destructiou of the Patent Office on 15th December, should be recorded anew, when the applicant had deposited in the Patent Office a duplicate as near as might be of the original model, drawings and descriptions, etc., verified by oath, and that such records and copies only should be valid evidences of title. The Commissioner was required to obtain duplicates of such of the models destroyed by fire as were most valuable and interesting to the public, for which purpose $100,000 were appropriated, and agents authorized in twenty different towns. An additional examining clerk and temporary clerks were to be appointed, and the commissioner was required to lay before Congress an annual report, embracing a classified list of all patents granted during the preceding year, with the names and residences of patentees, and a list of expired patents and account of expenditures.

On the 15th September a Standing Committee on Patents was instituted by Congress.

The Secretary of the Treasury on the 10th March, issued a circular requesting information in regard to the propriety of establishing a system of Telegraphs in the United States. In reply, Professor Samuel F. B. Morse, of New Haven, communicated an account of his invention of an electro-magnetic telegraph, and of its proposed advantages and probable expense. By its use he "presumed five words could be transmitted in a minute." The result of his numerous experiments was made public in April, and his first caveat for the "American Electro-Magnetic Telegraph" was entered in October. Having petitioned Congress for aid to make a practical test of his invention, $30,000 were afterward granted, and the first line was erected in June, 1844, between Washington and Baltimore.[1]

(1) The Electro-Magnetic Telegraph of Cook was patented in England, in June of this year (1837), and in July, Steinheil put in operation, between Munich and Bogenhausen, his registered electro-magnetic telegraph, producing dots and marks to stand for letters on fillets or ribands of paper, moved forward by clock work.

A report and statistical tables, prepared by John P. Bigelow, Esq., Secretary of the Commonwealth of Massachusetts, from the returns of the assessors in each county, made for the first time under a recent act of the Legislature, for obtaining "statistical information in relation to certain branches of industry within the Commonwealth," exhibits the following general results of manufacturing and mechanical labor during the year ending April 1st, including the fisheries and all vessels built in the five years preceding, viz.:

Total value of Manufactures $91,765,215 (or averaging the shipbuilding) $86,282,616, whole number of hands employed 117,352; capital invested $54,851,643. The principal branches were boots and shoes, of which the value was $14,642,520; manufactures of cotton $17,409,001; of woolen goods $10,399,807; of leather, including morocco, $3,254,416; whale, cod and mackerel fishing $7,592,290; vessels built in five years $6,853,248. The manufacture of cotton goods (cloth), exclusive of printing, employed mills 282; spindles 565,031; male hands 4,997; female hands 14,757; capital invested $14,369,719; cotton consumed 37,275,917 pounds; annual product 126,319,221 yards of cloth, worth $13,056,659. The woolen manufacture employed 192 mills and 501 sets of woolen machinery, 3,612 male and 3,485 female hands; capital $5,770,750; and consumed 10,858,988 pounds of wool and 236,475 gallons of sperm oil, producing 11,313,426 yards of cloth valued at $10,399,807. The number of Saxony sheep in the state was 46,985, and of Merinos 200,383, all others 127,246. The total population was 701,331.

In consequence of the excessive importations of foreign merchandise in the last three years, under the Compromise Act, amounting in 1836 to $189,980,035, (an increase of $63,458,703 over those of 1834, the first year of its operation, and averaging for the three years $155,465,703 per annum,) a large amount of capital was driven from manufactures to seek investment in agriculture and in western lands. The revenue from customs and from the sale of the public domain had enabled the government at the commencement of the year 1835, to announce the total extinguishment of the public debt; and at the close of the ensuing year left in the Treasury, from the same sources, a surplus of over forty millions of dollars, the greater portion of which was derived from the Land Offices. A removal of the deposits was determined upon by the government, and twenty-eight millions of the surplus revenue was deposited in the state banks. It was liberally loaned to merchants and land-jobbers whose operations tended to swell the receipts. The circulation and discounts of the banks had also, in the last three years, increased over fifty per cent. in consequence of the spirit of speculation, and the abuse, and of credit was but feebly checked by the "specie circular" of the government requiring the value of public lands to be paid in coin. A commercial revulsion, such as the country had seldom witnessed, resulted from these and other causes. It commenced on the 10th May, by the suspension of the New York banks, a measure which soon became general throughout the Union. A decline of over forty-eight millions in the value of the imports—which still amounted to nearly one hundred and forty-one millions, or twenty-three and a half millions in excess of the exports—and of more than twelve and a half millions in the revenue from customs, soon compelled the National Treasury to borrow money. The financial troubles which ensued were not alleviated for several years, notwithstanding various general and local measures of relief, including a Bankrupt Law which obliterated many millions of indebtedness. Numerous factories, particularly in New England, were compelled entirely to suspend business to the great distress of their operatives, and the government was at length compelled to return to a system of higher duties and of protection to domestic industry.

Reports, partial or complete, were made this year of several State Geological Surveys, leading to better knowledge of the natural resources of the country, viz. : of Maine by Dr. C. T. Jackson; of Connecticut by Prof. C. U. Shepard; of Delaware by Prof. J. C. Booth; of Ohio by Dr. Hildreth, Professors Locke and Briggs, and Mr. J. W. Foster; and of Indiana by Dr. D. D. Owen.

Experiments in Smelting Iron with Anthracite Coal were begun this year, and successfully accomplished, it is said, by Baughman, Ginteau & Co., of Mauch Chunk, Pennsylvania.

The consumption of Anthracite Coal in the United States, or the trade in it, amounted this year to 881,026 tons, an increase of 1,735 per cent. in ten years.

The quantity of Sole Leather inspected in New York this year was 665,000 sides, an increase of 150 per cent. in ten years.

Salt to the amount of 2,161,288 bushels was inspected in the State of New York.

The number of Vessels built in the United States during this year was 949, and their tonnage was 122,987,022.

On the 28th May the American packet ship Toronto, of 630 tons, was towed out of the Thames against the tide at the rate of four and a half knots an hour, by the experimental steamboat "Francis B. Ogden," built by Captain John Ericsson, now of New York, and fitted with the patent propelling apparatus of his invention, which has since been so extensively adopted in ocean steamships. Captain R. F. Stockton of the United States Navy, who witnessed the performance, ordered two iron steamboats to be built upon the same principle for the United

States, whither Mr. Ericsson removed at his invitation in 1839, and built the propeller Princeton, for the government, to test the value of the new mode of propulsion.[1]

In Massachusetts seventy-six furnaces were in operation for casting iron, and produced articles to the value of $1,205,840. The sand for moulds was nearly all obtained out of New England.

The manufacture of Machinists' Tools was commenced at Nashua, New Hampshire, by John H. Gage, whose establishment was probably the first in the United States devoted exclusively to that business, which is still, with other branches, conducted on a large scale by Gage, Warner & Whitney.

One of the most complete Wire Manufactories in the country was that of Townsend, Beard & Co., at Fallstown, Beaver county, Pennsylvania, which supplied the valley of the Mississippi with wire. The place contained, in addition to sawing, flour, oil, paper and woolen mills, sash, chair and other factories, a Bucket factory which made thirty thousand buckets annually. Wickersham's Wire Works at Pittsburg, also worked up about six hundred tons of Juniata iron yearly.

Pressed Glass Tumblers and other drinking vessels were first made at this time, the process of making pressed glass being an American invention.

Covered Coat Buttons were extensively manufactured for Mr. Samuel Williston, by J. and J. Hayden, at Haydenville, in Hampshire county, Massachusetts. The factory employed about two hundred girls, and produced daily upward of one thousand gross, from the most simple kinds to the most elegant satin figured buttons. The Williston metallic flexible shank button, patented in 1831, passed through fifteen different hands in the process, the several operations being performed by ingenious machinery invented by the proprietors, who also made iron or pea-jacket buttons by automatic machinery.

There were at this date four Cotton Mills in North Carolina, viz. : at Greensborough, Mocksville, Haw river and Cane Creek. Two or three spinning factories of one hundred to two hundred spindles, each carried by animal power, were in operation in Illinois, producing cotton yarn successfully from material grown in the state. Much cloth was also

(1) The Ogden was named after F. B. Ogden, Esq., for many years American Consul at Liverpool, who had been connected with the first steam navigation on the western rivers and on the ocean; eminent for his attainments in mechanical science, which enabled him to understand and appreciate the merits of Mr. Ericsson's invention, though disregarded and opposed by British engineers and the British Admiralty. Mr. Ogden joined the inventor in constructing the boat, and among other services originated the idea of right angular cramps in marine engines.—*See Atlantic Monthly for July*, 1862.

made in the families of emigrants from states south of Ohio, who employed the cotton produced in the country. Companies had been incorporated in that state within four or five years, for various manufacturing purposes, some of which had commenced operations.

Charters were granted in New York State to the following companies, viz: to the Penn-Yan Manufacturing Company, for twenty-one years, for manufacturing cotton and woolen goods and India Rubber water-proof cloth, or either of them separately—capital $200,000; the Ulster Cotton and Woolen Manufacturing Company, with a capital of $300,000, to be located at the Great Falls of Esopus, in Saugerties; to the Rossie Galena Company and the Rossie Lead Manufacturing Company, each with a capital of $24,000, for raising and separating lead from the "Coal Hill Mine," near the village of Russia, in St. Lawrence county. This rich vein of lead ore opened in 1835, in the azoic gneissoid rocks of St. Lawrence county, was three to four feet wide, and the solid ore averaged ten inches wide. It was worked by the two companies in sections, but with little knowledge of mining operations; the ore being smelted by Moss & Knapp for twenty-five dollars per ton of lead obtained. It was abandoned in 1839 on account of foreign competition, after about 3,250,691 lbs. of lead, worth $241,000, had been sold; but mining was resumed in 1852 by the Northern Lead Company. The West Carthage Iron and Lead Company, in the town of Champion, in Jefferson county, was also incorporated about the same time, with a capital of $200,000, to manufacture iron and lead.[1]

The Troy Academy was revived by an act of the Legislature, and incorporated with the Rensselaer Institute; the latter to be denominated the "Department of Experimental Science," the other the "Department of Classical Literature."

PATENTS.—During this and the three years preceding upward of one hundred patents were granted for improvements in cooking stoves, exclusive of cooking grates, ranges and other stoves. Allen Pollock, Boston, patented March 3, a register and air-box for grates, etc.; Elijah Jaquith, Brattleboro, Vt., March 11, Heber Chase, M. D., Philadelphia, June 10, R. Salisbury, Providence, R. I., Nov. 4, and J. Hungerfield, Dover, N. H., Dec. 26, each a patent for truss for hernia; Henry A. Wells, J. James and R. W. Peck, Brooklyn, N. Y., April 20, forming hat bodies (of wool); Thomas Blanchard, New York, June 14, and H. A. Wells and R. W. Peck, Sept. 22, batting or web for hat bodies (of fur). [Mr. Wells, the inventor of the process now in general use for forming the bodies of fur hats, by depositing the material directly upon a hollow, perforated cone, revolving in connection with an exhausting

(1) Whitney's Metallic Wealth of United States.

fan, obtained the first idea while experimenting in 1833 with Blanchard's machine above named, in which he was interested, and which, though unsuccessful, probably contained the germ of the valuable mechanism now in universal use. Mr. Wells went to England to introduce the patents here named, and found a Mr. Williams endeavoring to supersede the use of the bow in making hats by means of similar machinery, which failed; and in November, 1844, the former filed his caveat for the improved process in the United States Patent Office.]—John W. Cochran, New York, April 29, Daniel Leavitt, Cabottsville, Mass., April 29, and Curtis Parkhurst, Lawrenceville, Pa., Sept. 25, each a patent for many chambered fire arms. In 1836 Cochran's rifles were finished at a factory in Springfield, at the rate of eight per week. Cyrus Alger, Boston, May 30, cast-iron cannon; John Hatfield, Still-water, N. Y., June 3, dipping loco-foco matches; Charles Goodyear, New York, June 17, divesting caoutchouc of its adhesive properties; Stephen C. Smith, New York, Dec. 7, manufacture of India Rubber. [The patent of Mr. Goodyear was the first granted to him in that branch, and that of Mr. Smith was the first American patent for making India rubber boots, shoes, and overshoes, by simply giving them a thin coating of the gum. Mr. Goodyear the next year obtained a patent for making them wholly of that material.]—John B. Ogden, New Jersey, and John Ericsson, subject of the king of Sweden, July 19, sounding instrument for ascertaining the depth of water, etc.; William Hobbs, Springfield, Mass. Dec. 20., secret safety locks; N. J. Wyeth, Cambridge, Mass., Dec. 1, preparing ice for shipping.

The financial difficulties which overtook the country early in the last year, and led to a universal suspension of the banks, as a consequence of previous inordinate importations, injudicious speculation, and

1838 a redundancy of paper currency, was still further increased by a general failure in the grain crops of 1837 and 1838, which raised the price of flour to $10.25 per barrel, and caused a considerable amount to be imported, thereby adding to the drain of specie. But little relief was experienced by the partial resumption of the banks in the early part of this year, the reduction in the amount of imports, and the return of a good wheat-harvest in the present year. The agriculture of the country received an increased amount of capital, skill, and fostering legislation; but manufacturing enterprises were generally suspended, by the glut of foreign goods and the pecuniary embarrassments of this period.

The Silk Culture, which, for several years, had received an increasing amount of attention, was the subject of a Congressional report by the Committee on Agriculture, on April 20. Bounties continued to be paid in different states for raw silk. On April 2, the Legislature of Pennsylvania passed an act to promote the culture of silk, giving premiums of twenty cents a pound for cocoons, and fifty cents for reeled silk, produced in the state, until the year 1843. Toward the close of the year, the silk business, which had already felt the speculative impulse of the times, received a sudden increase, manifested by a rise in the price of mulberry-trees, especially of the multicaulis kind, the price of which rose to forty, fifty, and seventy-five cents, and soon after to between one and two dollars apiece. The culture, importation, and sale of trees chiefly characterized the silk husbandry of the country at this time; and much less attention was bestowed upon the production of raw or manufactured silk. The fictitious value given to mulberry-trees during the next year or two by the prevalent enthusiasm was not of long continuance; and the healthy development of the silk culture received a sudden check by the depression which is sure, sooner or later, to follow an unwholesome stimulation. All manufactured silks were at this time admitted duty-free, except sewings, which paid a duty of twenty-eight per cent., that enabled the American producer to compete with the foreign article in our own markets. Nearly all the raw silk produced in the country was manufactured into sewing-silk, and experienced silk-growers deemed it useless to attempt to promote its culture by a duty on raw silk, with an additional duty on sewings, or a like duty upon all silk manufactures imported. This protection was not afforded until the business had received an almost fatal check by the revulsion in the mulberry culture which followed, causing its almost entire abandonment and destruction of the nurseries. On December 11, a Convention of silk-growers was held in Baltimore, at which about two hundred delegates assembled, who elected Judge Comstock, of Connecticut, president. Resolutions were adopted to form a National Silk-Society (which was organized the next day), and to issue an address to the people of the United States on the culture of silk. They also recommended the Piedmontese reel as the best in use; that cultivators of the mulberry should give attention to the production of silk; that auxiliary silk-societies be formed in the several states; and that another convention be held in Washington in December, 1839. Much practical information was given by members of the convention. Specimens of silk ribbons and galloons manufactured in three weeks from the tree, and woven at the rate of three hundred yards a day, by a young woman, after only three months instruction, upon a loom recently invented in Massachusetts, and certified by a silk-merchant of thirty years experience to be as good as he ever saw, were exhibited to the convention. The National Silk-Society resolved the next day to establish a national silk-journal, devoted to the advancement of the silk cause in the United States, the first number of which was issued in January following.

The value of domestic manufactures exported this year was $8,397,078; of which American cotton goods constituted a value of $3,758,000, or upward of forty-four per cent.

The Howe Pin Manufacturing Company, at Birmingham, Conn., commenced this year the manufacture of "solid-headed pins," under a recent patent obtained by J. J. Howe. The article proved more economical to the consumer by saving the waste and inconvenience occasioned by the slipping down of the spun-head previously in use, while the cost of production was from one-fourth to one-third less, weight for weight, than before, on account of the saving in time, weight of metal employed, etc.

A joint Resolution of the two houses of Congress directed a gold medal to be presented to the son of James Ramsey, of Virginia, as a public acknowledgment of the services of his father in first successfully applying steam to the propulsion of vessels.

An improvement was made in the electro-magnetic machine by Dr. Page, formerly of the Patent Office, by which currents were generated sufficiently powerful to decompose water.

The manufacture of gold spectacles and gold and silver thimbles was commenced at Long Meadow, Mass., by Dimond Chandler, whose successor still carries on the manufacture.

Patents.—Among the most important patents issued this year are the following: to Erastus B. Bigelow, Mass., for an improvement in the loom for weaving knotted counterpanes; to David A. Morton, Groton, N. Y., for an improvement in the mode of attaching springs to carriages; to John Ericsson, New York, for an improvement in propelling steam vessels; to A. D. Ditmars, Chester County, Penn., for a mode of preserving grass for hay by excluding it from the air in bins lined with sheet-lead; to Isaac Sanderson, Milton, Mass., for a discovery in the manufacture of brown paper from a new material called sand-grass; to David Bruce, jr., Bordentown, N. J., for machines for casting and smoothing printing-type; to George C. Lobdell, Wilmington, Del., for an improvement in the mode of making cast-iron car-wheels; to Joseph Harrison, jr., Philadelphia, for an improvement in railroad cars, carriages, and axles; to Frederick Tudor, Boston, Mass., for an improved mode of packing and storing ice; to John Howard Kyan, of Great Britain (by special act of Congress, much censured at the time), a patent for preserving vegetable substances, especially timber, from decay, known as the Kyanizing process; to Nathaniel Bosworth, Philadelphia, for an improvement in the manner of constructing steam-engines; to Charles Goodyear, Roxbury, Mass., for an improvement in manufacturing gum-elastic shoes; to A. A. Hayes, Boston, for a process of extracting tannin from astringent barks; to Cyrus Alger, Boston, for an improvement in the manufacture of ploughs of cast-iron; to Thomas and James Keane, Haverstraw, N. Y., for an improved mode of constructing metal bench-vices; to Walter R. Johnson, Philadelphia, for an improvement in the art of increasing the strength of wrought-iron and steel; to Col. Stephen H. Long, U. S. A., for a suspension and brace bridge; to Elisha K. Root, Collinsville, Conn., for a machine for punching and forming the eyes of axes, hatchets, etc.; to Stephen Ustick, Philadelphia, for an improved brick-press.

The closing year of this decade presents few events of importance in our industrial history. The Silk bill commanded a large share of public

1839 attention; but there were symptoms that the speculation in mulberry trees had reached its height, and would be followed by a reaction. Many who purchased trees in the autumn of the last year in the expectation that, for every thousand dollars invested, they would realize fifty thousand by the sale of the increased buds, were disappointed in their calculations. Morus multicaulis trees were offered in great abundance at "three cents per tree, healthy and well branched;" and a writer ventured to predict that their value in the autumn of 1840 would not exceed three dollars per cart-load. Mr. Physic, of Germantown, Pa., had four hundred thousand mulberry trees growing, and one million of silk-worms, which number he expected soon to increase to fifty millions. His cocoonery was the largest in the world. The "Atlantic Silk Company," Nantucket, capital $400,000; the "Valentine Silk Company," Providence; the Poughkeepsie Silk Company; and the Northampton Silk Company, capital $80,000,—had all sunk their capital and had ceased operations.

The establishment in July of this year of the *Merchant's Magazine*, by the late Freeman Hunt, Esq., deserves to be noted, as an event having an important influence in shaping the commercial and industrial history of the country. The work, through the judgment, enterprize, and integrity of its editors and publishers, and the ability of its contributors, became a popular and authentic exponent of the principles of sound mercantile policy, and a comprehensive record of the leading facts which have marked our material progress during nearly a quarter of a century. It is now, in fact, an almost indispensable appendage to the counting-rooms of the merchant and manufacturer, both in America and in Europe.

Among the developments of the railroad enterprise of this period at home and abroad is the interesting fact, that Messrs. Baldwin, Vail and

Hufty, of Philadelphia, received this year applications from railroad companies in England for a supply of locomotives from their establishment.

An important improvement in the manufacture of Caoutchouc was patented in February, by Mr. Charles Goodyear, of New York. Under the name of vulcanized India rubber he introduced an article in which caoutchouc was combined with sulphur, whereby it is enabled to retain its elasticity at all temperatures, and to withstand any heat short of the vulcanizing point, and any or all known solvents. By its means an abundant natural product, of little value before, has become of great importance in manufactures and the arts. Thousands of operatives are furnished profitable employment; and the lives of great numbers exposed to cold and dampness are, by its uses as clothing, annually saved. It is also constantly found to answer as an excellent substitute for substances the supply of which is becoming inadequate, such as whalebone, tortoise-shell, ivory, etc. At the present time the manufacture of vulcanized rubber in this country embraces clothing of all descriptions, boots and shoes, car-springs, belting and steam-packing for machinery, balls and toys for children, combs, and whalebone, and a great variety of goods made of the hard rubber or rubber ivory.[1]

On the 17th of September, Matthew Carey, of Philadelphia, departed this life, in the eightieth year of his age; and by his decease the system

(1) Caoutchouc or India rubber first made its appearance in this country some forty years ago, in the shape of overshoes. In 1823 there were five hundred pairs of shoes imported into the Boston market, and in 1825 Mr. Thomas C. Wales, of Boston, who was soon after awarded the soubriquet, which he still maintains, of being "*the* rubber-shoe man," first introduced to the public the original Para rubber overshoe in its rough, unfinished state, as made by the Indians of that country. This Para shoe had the entire market of the United States, without competition, from 1825 to the time when the first "Goodyear Patent-shoe" was manufactured in Providence; and even after that, the sales of the "old-fashioned rubbers," as they were called, continued to increase. Mr. Wales, though agent for both, advised the importers to send out lasts to the Indian shoemakers, and by this means so improved the shape of the imported shoe that it would eventually have driven the only patent shoe then known out of market. In the year 1830 or 1831 Mr. Charles Goodyear was passing the depot of the Roxbury Company in New York, and stopped to look at a life-preserver. On examining the tubes by which they were inflated, it occurred to him that he could improve their construction. Some months after this he presented a specimen of his improved tube to the agent of the company, with a view of disposing of it to them. The agent, pleased with his success, advised him to turn his attention to an improved mode of manufacturing rubber. From that time Mr. Goodyear devoted his whole time and attention to this subject. Unsuccessful for years, he persevered, against the advice of his relatives and intimate friends, under the most distressing and embarrassing pecuniary circumstances, till at last, when almost compelled to abandon his experiments, he succeeded in vulcanizing India rubber,—a result which has given him a world-wide celebrity.—*Leading Pursuits*, by E. T. Freedley.

of protection to home industry lost one of its most able and indefatigable advocates. For years he had fought the battle of the American manufacturer almost single-handed, and it was not until after his decease that his countrymen fully appreciated the wisdom of his political philosophy and the ardor and sincerity of his philanthropy.

PATENTS.—Among the most important patents issued this year are the following: to Charles Goodyear, assignee of Nathaniel Hayward, Woburn, Mass., for improvements in the manner of preparing caoutchouc or India rubber; to Moncure Robinson, Philadelphia, for a chair having a shoulder on one side only, for railroads; to William C. Grimes, York, Penn., for a smut machine; to William W. Wiswell, Portland, Me., for cutting coats without back, side, or lapel seams; to Cadwalader Evans, Pittsburg, Penn., for improvements in steam-boilers, and apparatus to prevent explosions thereof; to Stephen Vail, Speedwell Iron Works, N. J., for an improved jack-screw; to William Whittemore, jr., West Cambridge, Mass., for an improvement in the roller-gin for ginning cotton; to Jacob D. Custer, Norristown, Penn., for reversing the motion of steam-engines; to Noble Jerome, Bristol, Conn., for an improvement in clocks; to Joseph Priestly Peters, New York, for a machine for counting pills; to Eliphalet Nott, Schenectady, N. Y., for improvements in Nott's coal-stove; to James Banta, Utica, N. Y., for a machine for packing flour; to Samuel Colt, Conn., for improvements in fire-arms; to Isaac McCord, Harrisburg, Penn., for wire tiller-ropes; to Conrad Liebrich, Philadelphia, for an improved double-catch bolt-lock; to Thomas Shriver, Cumberland, Md., for improvements in coaches and other carriages, extending the perches beyond the jack-bars and axles; to Henry Crum, Clarkstown, N. Y., for a machine for turning in the heads of wooden screws and rivets; to Herman Haupt, York, Penn., for a truss for a bridge; to Thomas Raeny, Philadelphia, for an improved spark-arrester; to Frederick R. Dimpfel, New York City, for a blowing apparatus for furnaces; to Isaiah Jennings, same place, for a new combination of ingredients for burning in lamps; to George S. Griggs, Roxbury, Mass., for a self-acting brake for railroad cars.

CHAPTER VI.

THE MANUFACTURES OF THE UNITED STATES.

1840—1860.

WE are now approaching a period when the manufacturing industry of the country, established upon a solid and permanent foundation, had attained such wonderful expansion that it is no longer possible to trace its progress in detailed statements or isolated facts. In spite of temporary checks and adverse legislation, the Anglo-Saxon steadily widened the circle of his enterprises, until the sound of his hammers rung throughout the whole extent of the populated portion of the republic; and the chronicler of his achievements, bewildered by the multiplicity of details, and abashed at the magnitude of the task, gladly takes refuge behind the imposing, though not always reliable, computations of the decennial census-takers.

Turning to the census of 1840 for information as to the state of Manufactures at that date, we are astonished as well as embarrassed by the meagreness of details. Even of the leading branches in some instances only the capital is given, in others only the product; and we confess we do not know by what rule in arithmetic or mensuration any one could have calculated from official data that the capital invested in manufactures at that date was $267,726,579.

AGGREGATE OF THE STATISTICS OF MANUFACTURES IN THE UNITED STATES, ON THE FIRST OF JUNE, 1840.

	No. of Establ'm'ts.	Capital Invested.	Hands Employed.	Value Produced.
Bricks and lime			22,807	$9,736,945
Carriages and wagons		$5,551,632	21,994	10,897,887
Cotton	1,240	51,102,359	72,119	46,350,453
Chocolate				79,900
Confectionery				1,143,965
Cordage	388	2,465,577	4,464	4,078,306
Hardware and cutlery			5,492	6,451,967
Drugs, medicines, paints, dyes, etc		4,507,675	1,848	4,812,726

	No. of Establ'm'ts.	Capital Invested.	Hands Employed.	Value Produced.
Earthenware	659	551,431	1,612	1,104,825
Flax		208,087	1,628	322,205
Fire-arms			1,744	
Furniture		6,989,971	18,003	7,555,405
Granite			3,734	2,442,950
Glass	115	2,084,100	3,236	2,890,293
Hats, caps, bonnets		4,485,300	20,176	10,180,847
Iron, cast	804	20,432,131	30,497	286,903 tons.
" bar	795			197,233 "
Machinery			13,001	10,980,581
Metals, precious			1,556	4,734,960
" various			6,677	9,779,442
Mills, flour	4,364	65,858,470	60,788	7,404,562 bbls.
" grist	23,661			76,545,246
" saw	31,650			
" oil	843			
Musical instruments		734,370	908	923,924
Leather—				
Tanneries	8,229	15,650,929	26,018	33,134,403
Other factories, including saddleries	17,136	12,881,262		
Liquors, distilled	10,306	9,147,368	12,223	41,402,627 galls.
" fermented	406			23,267,730 "
Paper	426	4,745,239	4,726	6,153,092
Powder	137	875,875	496	8,977,348 lbs.
Printing and	1,552	5,873,815	11,523	7,016,094
Binding	447			
Ships and vessels			767	119,814
Silk		274,374	15,905	6,545,503
" mixed		4,368,991		
Soap and candles		2,757,273	5,641	
Sugar refineries	43			3,250,700
Tobacco		3,437,191	8,384	5,819,568
Wool		15,765,124	21,342	20,696,999

It appears that the production of Cotton Goods was then, as now, the leading branch of pure manufactures, giving employment to over seventy-two thousand persons, and requiring a capital of over fifty-one millions of dollars. In a comparison with careful estimates made by a convention of manufacturers, of the extent of the Cotton manufacture in twelve States, in 1831, the number of factories had increased from 795 to 1,240; the number of spindles from 1,246,503 to 2,284,631; and the value of the manufacture from twenty-six to upward of forty-six millions, or in the ratio of one hundred and thirty per cent. Of the aggregate production of Cotton goods, upward of thirty and one half millions in value was returned by the New England States, upward of twelve millions by the five Middle States, nearly two millions by the Southern, and the balance by the Western States. The number of printing, dyeing, and bleaching establishments reported was one hundred and twenty-nine, and the quantity of printed cottons made in thirty-six print-works in three New England and four Middle States, which were the only ones having print-works, was ascertained to exceed a hundred million yards annually, valued at $11,667,512, or about eleven and a half cents a yard. The increase in the total value of printed cottons was upward of three hundred per cent. More than one half the amount was produced in Massachusetts and Rhode Island. The Dye and Print-Works of the Merrimac and Hamilton Mills at Lowell, together turned out weekly upward of a quarter million yards of goods of their own manufacture, dyed or printed in madder colors, of a price and quality that rivalled the foreign. So skilful were the manufacturers in imitating new foreign designs, and so rapid in executing them, that the importers of choice styles were not unfrequently undersold in a few days by the domestic commission houses.[1] By the employment of the best foreign and native skill, systematic economy, and tact in every branch of the business, aided by a moderately protective tariff, the difficulties attending the introduction of calico printing had been in a great measure overcome. The Manchester Print-Works, commenced in 1839, has been among the most conspicuous and successful in the use of scientific and labor-saving devices, and has contributed largely to the manufacturing enterprise of that city. Equal skill in other departments, but chiefly the introduction of the power-loom and other mechanical improvements, had, within a quarter of a century from the introduction of that machine, raised the cotton manufacture of the United States to the rank it now holds, as the first among American industries, in respect to the amount of capital, the number of hands employed, and value of product. Our dependence on foreign manufacturers was still shown by the annual importation, on an average of the nineteen years preceding 1840, of upward of ten millions' worth of Cotton goods of all kinds, in consequence of which many of the New England factories were about to close, and upward of thirty large cotton-mills at Lowell, running each from six to sixteen thousand spindles, were only

(1) On the 1st of February, 1840, a new pattern of mousseline de laines arrived from France at New York, and was offered by the importer at fourteen cents per yard by the case. The agent of a Rhode Island calico-printing establishment forwarded a piece of the new style of goods to Providence the day after their arrival; and in sixteen days he had the same style of goods, and of equal fabric, in New York, selling at ten cents per yard. The manufacturer had but twelve days to engrave the new pattern on a copper cylinder, from which the engraving was raised on a steel cylinder, then hardened and made ready for impression; the compound of ingredients for colors discovered by chemical experiments; the cloth printed, dried, and cased for market.

able to continue by several times reducing the wages of the operatives, until Congress should act upon the tariff, which, under the compromise act, had now nearly reached the uniform rate of twenty per cent.

In the manufacture of Woolens less progress had been made, but the capital invested exceeded fifteen millions of dollars, employing over twenty-one thousand persons, and yielding a product valued at $20,696,999. Of the value returned, nearly thirteen millions was the product of the six New England States, and about one half that amount was returned by the Middle States. The principal producers of Woolens were the State of Massachusetts, in which the value manufactured exceeded seven millions of dollars annually, New York, which produced about half that value, Connecticut, Pennsylvania, and Vermont. Although the tariff had been modified in 1828, with a view to increased protection to the Woolen interests, which, as the manufacturers claimed, then represented a capital of fifty millions of dollars, and to have increased tenfold since 1815, yet the ad valorem duties, and the mode of valuation established in that and subsequent acts, both for Woolen manufactures and for Wool, had in a great measure defeated the intention of those measures. Notwithstanding great improvements in machinery, as the most effective means of competing with foreign manufacturers, which had reduced the cost of making Woolen cloths, in some of the best conducted mills, more than fifty per cent., many establishments had been compelled to suspend operations. But few successful attempts had yet been made to produce the finer qualities of cloth, although many companies had been incorporated within twenty years for the manufacture of broadcloths. The domestic manufacture of blankets and shawls had reduced the importations of these articles. The power-loom had been successfully adapted by American ingenuity to the manufacture of all kinds of hosiery, which was thereby greatly reduced in price. A like reduction had been made in the importation of foreign carpets, as well as in the cost of the domestic article, which was becoming nearly adequate to the demand. A principal agency in this reduction was the use of improved machinery, and especially of the power-loom, which had been recently, for the first time, adapted to the weaving of ingrain carpeting by the genius of E. B. Bigelow of Massachusetts, by whom it was soon after extended to the production of Brussels carpets and all kinds of looped and velvet pile fabrics. We still continued, however, to import annually upward of ten million dollars' worth of Woolen manufactures.

A regularly organized Silk factory on a small scale had been put in operation by I. W. Gill, Esq., at Mount Pleasant, Ohio, under the superintendence of an experienced English manufacturer, who spun and wove from native silk, velvets worth four to six dollars a yard, hatters'.plush, dress silks, flowered vestings, handkerchiefs, and other fabrics. About the same time, an establishment at Baltimore employed fifteen or twenty Jacquard looms in making silk and worsted vestings, velvets, dress, and other silks. But the chief products of the Silk manufacture consisted of sewing silk, fringes, tassels, gimps, coach lace, and other trimmings. In the manufacture of coach lace, of which there were several factories in the country, Mr. Bigelow had recently substituted for the tedious hand-loom process, the curious automatic machinery from which he subsequently developed the Brussels and Tapestry carpet loom already mentioned. The annual value of silk manufactures imported was very heavy, amounting on an average of the twenty years preceding 1841 to about eight and three quarter millions of dollars; and for the year 1839, including raw silk and one half the value of silk and worsted, to nearly twenty-three millions.

The Iron manufacture constituted one of the great industries of the country, which, though temporarily depressed at this time, in common with most branches of trade and commerce, showed a gratifying increase in the past ten years. The greatly augmented production and reduced cost of Iron making in England within the last thirty-five years, chiefly caused by the more general use of cheap mineral fuel, of the hot blast, and improved machinery, created a powerful competition with the domestic manufacturers, with whom the cost of labor and the interest on capital was so much greater. A prompt adoption of all new and approved processes and mechanical devices, culminating in the recent successful use of anthracite in smelting and puddling, and the application of skill, economy, and enterprise scarcely inferior to that of their rivals, had alone enabled the iron makers to sustain themselves against adverse markets and combinations for their ruin. Many had perished, however, in the effort. The rapid increase of the means of internal communication, bringing into closer connection with the iron interests the vast depositories of fossil fuel and of ore, as well as with the consumers of iron, and the numerous collateral interests with which it is naturally allied, and the large demand for Railroad Iron, enabled them to enlarge, multiply, and perfect their establishments, even through a period of unexampled financial embarrassments from which the country had not yet emerged. The official returns showed a satisfactory increase in the last ten years, and also in the next few years a severe check to this important industry. The number of Iron Furnaces returned in 1840 from twenty-five States was eight hundred and four, whereof nearly one half were in the two States of Pennsylvania and New York. They produced two hundred and eighty-six thousand nine hundred and three tons of cast-iron; of which amount about one fourth is supposed to be made into forms, such as hollow ware, machinery, plough and stove castings, etc., and the remainder into wrought-iron; of which the total quantity returned by seven hundred and ninety-five bloomeries, forges, and rolling mills, was one hundred and ninety-seven thousand two hundred and thirty-three tons. The value of the weight of castings alone, estimated at the market price ($80 per ton), would have amounted to five and three quarter millions of dollars. The remainder of the cast-iron, converted into the quantity of wrought-iron returned, would, at $85 per ton, have been worth sixteen and three quarter millions. If to these sums be added one quarter of a million for converting five thousand five hundred and fifteen tons of pig-iron, imported in that year, into forms, at an average of $50 per ton, the total value of the iron made in the United States in 1840 was upward of twenty-two and three quarter millions of dollars. Including miners, the entire business employed upward of thirty thousand persons, and a capital of nearly twenty and one half millions of dollars. The quantity of iron officially reported, which was estimated by a convention of manufacturers to be sixty thousand tons less than the amount actually made, was nevertheless an increase of seventy-five per cent. upon the estimated product in 1830. Pennsylvania was the largest producer of iron, containing two hundred and thirteen furnaces, which reported ninety-eight thousand three hundred and ninety-five tons of cast-iron made; and one hundred and sixty-nine bloomaries, forges, and rolling mills, making eighty-seven thousand two hundred and forty-four tons. The number of iron-works erected in that State within the ten years preceding the 1st January, 1840, was one hundred and twenty-three—of which five were blast furnaces for using mineral coal, seventy-two charcoal blast furnaces, and forty-six bloomeries, rolling-mills, and forges. Twelve others, including three anthracite blast furnaces, were erected during the year, in which also six iron-works in that State failed, or changed hands, by reason of the depression of the trade.

The country was already supplied, by domestic manufacturers, with the common qualities of steel for all the coarser kinds of agricultural and mechanical implements, such as ploughshares, shovels, scythes, mill and crosscut saws—a single manufacturer of saws in Philadelphia using up one and a half tons every working day in the year. Common English blister-steel was altogether excluded by American competition, which had considerably reduced the price within twelve years. Steel had been made at Pittsburg and in New York, from Juniata iron and that of the Ancram and Salisbury mines, in New York and Connecticut, that would bear comparison, for the finer articles of hardware, with the celebrated hoop L or Danamera steel from England, where alone it was made by reason of the monopoly of the raw material. The want of blister-steel of the first quality, from which sheer-steel and cast-steel are made, and the want of suitable clay for crucibles, had hitherto prevented any competition with Great Britain in the production of the superior qualities of steel for the finer edge-tools and cutlery.

The whole demand of the country for Leather was supplied by domestic tanneries, of which eight thousand two hundred and twenty-nine, returned in 1840, employed twenty-six thousand and eighteen persons, and turned out between seven and eight million sides of leather, valued, with the product of all other manufactories, at $33,134,403. Within a period of twenty years the principal seat of the sole leather manufacture had been transferred from the neighboring Middle States, which had produced oak-tanned leather exclusively, and from Massachusetts, Connecticut, and Vermont, where hemlock bark had been chiefly used, to the hemlock region of the Catskill mountains, in New York, which at this date produced more than one third of all the sole leather made in the Union, and a far larger amount of upper leather also than any other State. The tannery of Zadoc Pratt was probably the largest in the world. The city of New York had already become the largest emporium of foreign hides in the world. Numerous chemical and mechanical improvements had been made in the art of tanning, whereby both the quantity and the quality of leather made from a given weight of hides, was improved. There were manufactories of Saddlery, Boots, Shoes, and Trunks, etc., in every town of any importance; the number of such establishments amounting to seventeen thousand one hundred and thirty-six. The largest amount of capital, and the greatest aggregate production of leather, and manufactures thereof, was prodŭced in Massachusetts, where the product reached the value of ten and a half millions annually.

Of Hats and Caps enough were made for home consumption, and a surplus was left for exportation. Of upward of ten millions' worth made, nearly one and a half million consisted of straw hats and bonnets. Although the valuable machinery used at the present time in the fabrication of fur hat bodies was not yet matured, the selling price of hats was twenty-five to fifty per cent. less than it was ten years before. New York and New Jersey, then as now, produced the largest values of silk and wool hats and caps, and nearly one half of the whole product, while Massachusetts manufactured the largest value of straw hats and bonnets.

The American Flint Glass rivalled in solidity and elegance that of foreign countries. The Glass manufacture altogether, including window glass, glass bottles, etc., employed three thousand two hundred and thirty-six persons in eighty-one glasshouses, and thirty-four glass cutting establishments, in which were produced a value of nearly three million dollars. New Jersey and Pennsylvania were the largest producers. The manufacture of flint glass, which from 1824 to 1836 had rapidly increased, and in 1842 employed seventeen furnaces, had gradually declined with the reduction of the duty, and consequently of the price, under the Compromise Act. The materials consumed were almost wholly domestic and of large value.

Of Soaps and Candles, the American manufacturers, beside supplying the home market, had, including spermaceti candles, over a million dollars' worth to export. They produced nearly fifty million pounds of soap, eighteen million pounds of tallow candles, and three million pounds of spermaceti and wax candles. Massachusetts produced one fourth of the whole quantity of soap returned, and the greater part of the spermaceti candles made.

The quantity of Salt made in nineteen States was six million one hundred and seventy-nine thousand one hundred and seventy-four bushels, employing a capital of $6,998,045, the greater part of it in New York, which produced two million eight hundred and sixty-seven thousand eight hundred and eighty-four bushels.

Domestic Hardware, which a few years before could, with difficulty, be sold without foreign labels, was now firmly established in popular favor. At an establishment in the State of New York, fifty tons of Horseshoes were turned out daily and sold, ready for use, at five cents per pound. The value of Hardware and Cutlery made annually, was nearly six and a half million dollars. American Axes were acknowledged to be of unrivalled excellence. The machines for making Cut and Wrought Nails and Spikes and Wood Screws, had effected a great reduction in the price of those articles, and soon rendered the country independent of importations. The value of Machinery made annually, was nearly eleven millions of dollars, of which the State of New York produced more than one fourth, and Pennsylvania and Massachusetts together upward of one third. In certain important branches of manufacture, machines and processes were employed to facilitate production and reduce the cost, which were wholly unknown in other countries. The Stocking Power-loom, already mentioned, was in use here long before it had been introduced in England. By its aid, a girl, receiving two dollars and fifty cents per week, could knit a piece twenty-eight inches in width and one inch long in a minute, and make twenty pairs of drawers in a day, while by the hand-loom two pairs were a full day's work. Pins were made to the value of about $100,000 annually, by machinery, with a rapidity still more astonishing, and were fastened in papers by a process unknown in England. Being made with solid heads, or all of one piece, they were superior in quality to the imported article. The price of Hooks and Eyes, which thirty years previously was one dollar and fifty cents per gross, had been reduced to fifteen and twenty cents for the same quantity. At one establishment in New Britain, Conn., eighty to one hundred thousand pairs per diem were made and plated by a galvanic battery on the cold silver process. In 1845, upward of half a million gross of Hooks and Eyes, valued at $111,600 were made in the State, and six factories turned out two hundred thousand packs of pins, worth $170,000. The value of gilt, metal, lasting, and other buttons of all kinds annually made, was about one and a half million dollars. In the manufacture of Brass Clocks, of course, our countrymen had no rivals. The manufacturers of Connecticut alone turned out over a million dollars' worth per annum; and were just beginning to export them to England, where they sold at first at an advance of a thousand per cent. on cost.[1]

But while the Clock-makers, Hardware manufacturers' and others, were extending their enterprises and opening new markets for their products, the financial condition of the country was far from prosperous. Money was steadily flowing to England and other foreign countries; credit at home and abroad was nearly annihilated; labor was depreciated, and the products of farm products were nearly fifty per cent. less than had been obtained but a few years before. Cotton had fallen to seven cents a pound; pork and beef to eight dollars a barrel;

(1) "For the last three years," says a correspondent of the *Rochester Democrat* residing at Hartford, "we have been gradually pushing our *notes of time* into foreign countries; and such has been our success that within a few hours' ride of this city one thousand clocks are finished daily, and it is a fair estimate to put down five hundred thousand clocks as being manufactured in this State last year. This year the number will be still increased, as John Bull is so slow in his movements that there is no hope of reform until he has plenty of Yankee monitors. These we are now sending him by every ship that clears from our seaports. In 1841, a few clocks were exported there as an experiment. They were seized by the customhouse in Liverpool on the ground that they were undervalued. The invoice-price is one dollar and fifty cents, and the duties twenty per cent. They, however, were soon released, the owner having accompanied them and satisfied the authorities that they could be made at a profit even thus low. Mr. Sperry, of the firm of Sperry & Shaw, was the gentleman who took out the article. He lost no time, after getting possession of his clocks, in finding an auction-house. They were made of brass-works cut by machinery out of brass plates, and a neat mahogany case enclosed the time-piece. They were a fair eight-day clock, but wholly unknown in England. The first invoice sold for four to five pounds sterling, or about twenty dollars each. Since that time every packet carries out an invoice of the article; and forty thousand clocks have been sold there by this one firm, —Sperry & Shaw. Others are now in the business, and the north of Europe has become our customers. India, too, is looked to as a mart for these wares. Several lots have been forwarded to the ports of China."

wheat to one dollar and twenty-five cents a bushel; and hams, lard, and butter to from six to seven and one half cents a pound. Farmers and planters were unable to pay their debts, and sheriffs' sales were universal, where stay laws had not been enacted to protect the debtor from his creditor. The imports for consumption, which, in 1833, amounted to eighty-eight millions, and within three years rose to one hundred and sixty-eight millions of dollars, declined again, in the three years ending in 1842, to eighty-eight millions. The consumption of imports *per capita* rose from $6.25 in 1833 to $10.93 in 1842, had fallen in 1842 to four dollars and eighty-seven cents, and the next year to four dollars twenty cents. Excessive inflation of the paper currency, and a spirit of reckless speculation were a consequence of the enormous importations. The bank circulation of the country, following the fluctuations in imports, rose from eighty millions in 1833 to one hundred and forty-nine millions in 1837; but on the reduction of imports, fell, in 1842, to less than eighty-four millions. Banks were, consequently, in a state of suspension, and the Federal Government was driven to the use of an irredeemable paper currency, and even with that found itself so totally unable to meet the demands upon it, that the President himself was unable to obtain his salary at the Treasury, and was forced to seek accommodation from the neighboring brokers. In this emergency, Congress, notwithstanding the compromise previously alluded to, passed the Tariff Act of 1842, which largely diminished the list of free goods and established an average charge of thirty-three per cent. upon those dutiable. The passage of this Tariff recognizing protection to American industry, was followed by effects which an able writer on Political Economy has styled, "almost magical."[1] "How wonderful," he says, "were the effects of the tariff of 1842, will be seen upon a perusal of the following brief statement of facts: In 1842, the quantity of Iron produced in the country but little exceeded two hundred thousand tons; by 1846, it had grown to an amount exceeding eight hundred thousand tons. In 1842, the coal sent to market was but one million two hundred and fifty thousand tons; in 1847, it exceeded three millions. The Cotton and Woolen manufactures, and manufactures of every kind, indeed, grew with great rapidity; and thus was made everywhere a demand for food, cotton, wool, tobacco, and all other products of the field, the consequences of which were seen in the fact that prices everywhere rose; that money became everywhere abundant; that farmers and property-holders generally were enabled to pay off their mortgages; that sheriffs' sales almost ceased; and that the rich ceased to be made richer at the expense of those who were poor."

(1) Henry C. Carey.

A succinct recital of the circumstances which attended the passage of this famous Tariff Act, and those subsequent thereto to the present time, is given in the following—

HISTORY OF TARIFFS FROM 1842 TO 1862.

The operation of the Compromise Tariff Act went on by biennial reductions until 1841. During those years, however, great changes overtook the commercial world, and the finances of the government were powerfully affected by them. One effect of the passage of the Tariff of 1828 had been to diminish the import of goods, and to induce, as a consequence, a larger importation of specie. This circumstance gave greater strength to the Banking movement, at a time when the harvests of Europe being abundant, money was then cheap, and credits liberal. These circumstances initiated a season of speculation, which was fostered by the war that had sprung up between the government and the United States Bank. The government, on removing the deposits, placed them with State banks, with the reiterated injunction to "loan liberally to merchants." The numberless circumstances that combined to bring about the revulsion of 1837, and the suspension of the banks, by cutting short the importation of goods, ruined the government revenue, and reduced it to the issue of Treasury notes to meet current expenses. The large imports of the year ending with 1836, had, on the extinguishment of the public debt, caused a large surplus revenue to accumulate, which had, to the extent of twenty-eight millions, been divided among the States. The revulsion now compelled a return to the Tariff for means of revenue. The compromise bill had, however, guaranteed, that after 1842, twenty per cent. should be a maximum duty, except in case of war. It was not thought advisable to violate that Compromise, but the twenty per cent. tax was laid upon a large portion of the articles that had been made free by the Compromise act. This did not meet the requirement, since in that year the value of free articles imported fell from thirty-six to thirty millions, while those dutiable increased less than eight millions. This did not, however, prevent Congress from passing a law to distribute the proceeds of the public sales pro rata among the several States. The law was to become inoperative if the compromise limit of twenty per cent. duties should be infringed. The Tariff, therefore, became a question again in the following year. The wants of the government were made the basis of a new movement, similar to that of the Harrisburg Convention, and a "home league" was formed, October 15, 1841, with the object of restoring the high rates. The proceedings of the "home league" were endorsed by Mr. Clay and the other friends of the "American policy." The President, in his annual Message, December, 1841, called attention to the necessary revision of the Tariff, advising a moderate increase, and a change of the home-valuation principle. The debate upon this passage of the message again opened up the whole question of protection. The financial distress of the Federal government made more revenue urgent, and the distress of the manufacturers was urged as a reason why those duties should be high. While urging high duties, however, *to supply the government revenues, it was proposed to repeal that sec-*

tion of the Land-distribution act, which, by its operation, brought the land revenues back into the Federal treasury upon the violation of the Compromise act.

In the Senate, Messrs. Calhoun, Bagby, Benton, and Woodbury, contended with Messrs. Clay, Evans, and others; and in the House the debate was very general. Mr. Clay declared the government wants to be the paramount necessity, and appealed to the patriotism of all parties to supply them. Mr Calhoun objected to the proposed Tariff that it was worse than that of 1828 The average rate was, indeed, ten per cent. less, but the substitution of cash duties for bonds or long credit, the substitution of specific for ad valorem rates on articles that had fallen in value, the home valuation of goods, the arbitrary mode of collecting, and the fact that it went into operation immediately on its passage, all tended to enhance its injurious features. He said: "I shall not dwell on the fact that it openly violates the Compromise act, and the pledges given by its author, and by Governor Davis, of Massachusetts, that if the South would adhere to the compromise while it was operating favorably for the manufacturers, they would stand by it when it came to operate favorably for the South. I dwell not on those double breaches of plighted faith, although they are of a serious character, and likely to exercise a very pernicious influence over our future legislation, by preventing amicable adjustments of questions that may hereafter threaten the peace of the country." The Bill was passed, with a clause repealing the clause of the land law which suspended the distribution of the public lands, making the distribution unconditional. For this it was vetoed, August, 1842, by John Tyler.

The debates were full, but with comparatively little excitement, and since the want of revenue was so apparent, the bill became a law, without the obnoxious clause: Messrs. Buchanan and Wright voting in favor of it for revenue reasons, but under protest. The law went immediately into operation. Among the changes that it introduced were the payment of duties in cash on the home-valuation, by which the Collector of the port where any description of goods should be imported, was to cause to be ascertained the actual value of the article in the principal markets of the country where it was exported, and at the time of export. To this value should be added costs and charges, including commissions, and the aggregate to be the value on which the duties are charged. All goods of wool imported in an unfinished state, shall be valued as if entirely finished at the place of export. The appraisers, collectors, and naval officers, were to have power to examine parties under oath in relation to values. These were some of the provisions that were considered very onerous. The Tariff went into operation at a time of great general depression in the commercial world, and, consequently, in a revenue point of view, it was not so successful as had been hoped. It did not, however, fail to revive the tariff issue at the general elections. The breach of the Compromise was charged, but the passage was denied as a party measure. The average charge upon dutiable goods under it was thirty-three per cent., and it yielded an annual average of twenty-six million dollars. The change of administration was, in 1846, followed by the Mexican War, and views in respect of the tariff policy were again changed. The new administration proposed three important measures in relation to the duties. The first, to abandon the protective theory in favor of a revenue theory; that is, to reduce the rates of duty, to levy them ad valorem only, to make the rates uniform, and to make them payable in cash; the Warehouse system, to facilitate the carrying trade; and the Independent Treasury, by which the cash duties were to be collected in gold and silver only. The message of the President, December, 1841, remarked upon the importance of revenue rather than protection, and advised a reduction of existing rates as necessary to an increase of revenue. The Secretary of the Treasury made an elaborate report of the same tenor, recommending a revenue tariff, in opposition to a protective tariff, or the adjustment of the imports to such a point as would collect the largest revenue without checking the importation, or, in other words, the course of trade. Such a bill was introduced from the Committee of Ways and Means, by Mr. M'Kay, April 14, 1846. It made eight schedules, in one of which all liquors were charged seventy-five per cent. ad valorem; and all other goods, under their respective schedules, thirty per cent., twenty-five per cent., twenty per cent., fifteen per cent., ten per cent., five per cent., ad valorem, and the remainder free. It was estimated that these duties would give an average of twenty-four per cent. on the dutiable imports, and greatly increase the sum of the duties by admitting a larger trade. This bill was accompanied by the "Warehousing act," which provided for the payment of duties in cash, and that goods may be deposited in the public stores, subject to the order of the owner, for one year, upon the payment of duties; that goods in bond may be transported to any other port of entry, and other provisions tending to facilitate the operations of commerce. These bills again opened up the Tariff discussion. But the former discussions had exhausted argument, pro and con, and there could be little more said on the subject. Mr. Collamer defended the protective principle because "it was necessary to national independence," and the Tariff of 1842, "because it gave revenue enough;" and he denounced the abandonment, as intended in this bill, of protection as a principle of national government. Mr. Rathbone opposed the new bill as "not likely to give sufficient revenue." The debate was very general, but the tariff passed the House, July 3, by a vote of one hundred and fourteen to ninety-five, to go into operation December 1, 1846. The operation of the Tariff was extremely simple, all articles not free being charged with ad volorem duties. The Warehouse system was organized, as also the Independent Treasury system, and the course of trade soon adapted itself to the new regulation of specie payments. The Tariff operated ten years and seven months, viz., from the 1st of December, 1846, to the 1st of July, 1857, and in accordance with the estimates, it averaged twenty-four and one-half per cent. on the dutiable imports. The average duties under the Tariff of 1842 had been twenty-six million dollars per annum. The average of the Tariff of 1846 was forty-six million dollars per annum during its operation. It is to be borne in mind, however, that the effect of the gold discoveries, by imparting great activity to trade in general, promoted larger aggregate exports from the country, which, since it had become a gold-exporting country, could receive its pay only in those goods which were charged with duty. The same influence had also caused a rise in the value of commodities, and, of course, a larger yield to ad valorem duties operating upon those high values.

The same causes which had imparted such activity to the import trade, had given animation to manufactures of all descriptions; and, while the government treasury was overflowing, the general prosperity was apparently sound. The large revenue yielded by the Tariff was in excess of the expenditures, and a considerable accumulation of gold took place in the Treasury vaults. This was not quite in accordance with the sub-treasury law, which contemplated an amount of revenue no greater than the expenditure, so that gold should pass through the Treasury without stopping, thus keeping the specie currency active. The accumulation was felt to be an inconvenience, and the government sought to reduce it by the purchase of its outstanding stock at high premiums; but a permanent remedy was proposed in a reduction of the rates of duty upon all imported goods.

President Pierce, in his message of December, 1856, called attention to the annual report of Mr. Guthrie, Secretary of Treasury, in relation to the necessity of reducing the duties. The report set forth the large revenues in excess of the wants of the government, and argued that as all duties are a tax upon the people, they should be reduced when no longer required for the public service. It advised the placing of all materials that enter into manufactures, such as are free in Great Britain, upon the free list, and also salt, as a necessity for Western provision packers. A Tariff bill was, in accordance with these recommendations, reported in the House, January 14, and engaged discussion. Mr. Durfee, of Rhode Island, advocated free materials, but wished to discriminate in favor of American manufactures. There was but little general interest manifested in the country in respect to the proposed changes. The manufacturers of the East seemed more disposed to favor the free importation of raw materials, than to increase the tax upon the imported goods. The merchants of New York petitioned for the removal of the duties on sugar. The debate in the House went on until January, when it became more general upon the bill reported by the Committee of Ways and Means. Mr. Stanton, of Ohio, said it was very evident that the revenue must be reduced, but that the bill offered was a manufacturers' bill, intended to favor the wool-manufacturers of the East at the expense of the wool-growers of the West. Mr. Washburne, of Illinois, wanted lead protected. Mr. De Witt, of Massachusetts, favored the reduction of revenue by freeing raw materials. In the Senate, Mr. Adams, of Mississippi, proposed making railroad iron free. In the House, Messrs. Smith and Garnett, of Virginia, favored free trade. Mr. Letcher proposed a reduction of twenty per cent. on the tariff of 1846. Mr. Campbell, of Ohio, offered a substitute for the bill, of which the general features were nearly the same as those of the Committee of Ways and Means. This finally passed, one hundred and ten to eighty-four. Mr. Stanton, of Ohio, denounced it as passed by "fraudulent combination of those who favored the protection of hemp, of sugar, iron, and the woollen manufacturers of Massachusetts. It was a blow at the wool-grower." In the Senate, Mr. Hunter substituted a new bill, with large reductions. This was opposed by Mr. Brodhead, of Pennsylvania, who favored the House bills. Mr. Wilson, of Massachusetts, opposed it, because he said the object was to reduce the revenue, and these reductions would increase it by encouraging importation. Mr. Collamer, of Vermont, took the same view of it. Mr. Pugh, of Ohio, opposed both; he said "the wool-manufacturers seek to ruin the wool-growers." Mr. Toombs favored larger reductions. Mr. Butler, of South Carolina, wanted the Tariff abolished altogether. Mr. Toucey, of Connecticut, wanted the revenue diminished by adding largely to the free list. Mr. Hunter's bill finally passed, with an amendment by Mr. Douglas, that wool under twenty cents, foreign valuation, should be free. A Committee of conference finally reported Mr. Hunter's bill, with the free list of Mr. Campbell's. This passed the House, one hundred and twenty-four to seventy-one, March 3d, to go into operation July 1st, 1857.

The effect of the Tariff was to check importation in the spring, and to cause a great accumulation of merchandise in bond, to be released after July 1st. The important reduction from one hundred per cent. to thirty per cent. on spirits, caused a large quantity to arrive, and the failure of the Louisiana sugar crop in that year, added very greatly to the effect of the reduction of the duty upon sugar, from thirty to twenty-four per cent. The elements of revulsion began to manifest themselves with the operations of the Tariff, in the first months of which the goods in warehouse were put upon the market. The money-pressure that followed came in aid of the designs of the projector of the tariff, in reducing the revenue, which fell from $63,875,905 in the last year of the tariff of 1846, to $41,780,621 in 1858. This diminution of the customs, added to that of the land sales under the reaction of speculation, carried the revenue far below the wants of the government. This result once more brought with it the necessity for a revision of the Tariff in order to restore the revenue. The circumstances that attended the session of 1860–61 were such as enabled the passage of the bill reported by the Committee of Ways and Means, with little debate or investigation. The Act restored the highest protective character of the Tariff, replacing the ad valorem with complicated specific duties, and the bill went into operation at such short notice as caused it to operate upon goods ordered under the old tariff. This Act was followed by another change in August of the same year, and by still another in February, 1862. [See Appendix.]

Within the decade of which we are writing, 5,941 inventions were patented in the United States, and among them two of the most important of the present century, viz.: the Sewing Machine and the Magnetic Telegraph.

The first American patent for a Sewing Machine of which we have any record, was one granted to John J. Greenough, of Washington City, February 21, 1842. This machine made what is called the through-and-through or shoemaker's stitch. The needle was pointed at both ends, with the eye in the centre, and was drawn through the cloth one way and then the other by a pair of pincers. We are not aware that any machines, except the model, were ever constructed. In the succeeding year, March 4, 1843, Benjamin W. Bean, of New York, patented a machine for making the running or basting stitch. The cloth was corrugated and a long needle thrust through the fold, and then, the stitch being straightened, was held together somewhat as it is in basting by hand. In the same year George R. Corlies, of Greenwich, N. Y., patented a machine similar to Greenough's; but the first complete Sewing Machine designed and adapted to general purposes, was that patented September 10, 1846, by Elias Howe, Jr., of Cambridge, Massachusetts. One of the principal features of this machine is the combination of a grooved needle, having an eye near its point, and vibrating in the direction of its length, with a side pointed shuttle for effecting a locked stitch, and forming with the threads, one on each side of the cloth, a firm and lasting seam. The main action of the machine consists in the interlocking of the loop, made by the thread carried in the point of the needle through the cloth, with another thread passed through the loop by means of a shuttle entering and leaving it at every stitch. The thread attachment to this shuttle remains in the loop, and secures the stitch as the needle is withdrawn, to be ready to make the next one, and at the same time the cloth is carried forward just the length of the stitch by what is called the feed motion. Wonderfully successful as this machine has been, no prophetic eye then foresaw its glorious future, and no capitalist was willing at that time to risk money in an enterprise so Utopian as manufacturing Sewing Machines appeared to be. Disappointed in finding encouragement at home, the patentee sought it in England, but he was met by a skepticism even more obdurate and discouraging than that of his countrymen, and he returned home in a sailing vessel, paying for his passage by manual labor, and arrived literally penniless.

Since the date of Mr. Howe's patent about 500 improvements upon the Sewing Machine have been patented, some of them, to which we shall elsewhere advert, of hardly less importance than the original invention. Large manufactories have been erected that are now furnishing machines at the rate of more than a hundred a day, and are yet unable to supply the demand. In 1860 the census returns show an aggregate of 111,263 machines made in that year in twelve States, of which the value was $4,247,820. In the manufacture of clothing, caps, shirts, boots and shoes, this little machine has effected almost a revolution, and the amount saved by its use in these branches alone is estimated to exceed sixteen millions of dollars annually. The business, however, is yet in its infancy, and the past results, wonderful as they are, furnish scarcely a criterion by which we can judge of its future.

The other grand invention which we have mentioned as having its origin between 1840 and 1850, perhaps properly belongs to the preceding decade. We believe that it is established that Samuel Finley Breeze Morse conceived and originated a practical plan of Telegraphic communication as early as the autumn of 1832, but it was not until 1844 that the first line of Telegraph in the United States was completed. This was the line between Baltimore and Washington, for which Congress, in March, 1843, had appropriated $30,000, to enable Professor Morse to test his system of Electro Magnetic Telegraphs. The history of this application is another record of persevering effort amidst many discouragements. As early as the autumn of 1838 Mr. Morse was in Washington exhibiting his invention to Congressional committees; but though the results were manifest, the idea seemed too impracticable to justify the appropriation of money, and the session closed without a report in its favor. The inventor then visited England and France to endeavor to secure the patronage of European governments, but in England he was refused letters-patent, and in France he received only a useless *brevet d'invention,* and no exclusive privilege in any other country. He returned home to struggle again for several years with scanty means, and though his efforts were unremitted during the session of 1842–3, he retired on the last night of the session without a hope of success; and we may imagine how greatly he was astonished to hear on the morning of March 4, 1843, that at the midnight hour Congress had appropriated the sum above mentioned to test the practical value of his invention by establishing a line between Baltimore and Washington. The results are before the world. In the sixteen years intervening between 1844 and 1860, it is estimated that 50,000 miles of telegraphic wires were put in operation in the United States alone, and since that time the number has been largely increased by the completion of the line from St. Louis to San Francisco, which was opened Oct. 25, 1861, and thence to Oregon. In Great Britain and Ireland there are about 40,000 miles in operation; in Germany 35,000 miles; in France 26,000; in Russia 12,900; in Italy 6,600; and in Switzerland 2,000 miles.

The two inventions just mentioned are conspicuous illustrations of the practical tendency of the American mind. The Sewing Machine embodied, in a simple and efficient manner, the results of remarkable mechanical ingenuity directed to a specific, practical end. It supplied not only our national industry but that of the world, both in the household and the factory, with an engine which was a needed supplement to a long train of previous inventions and discoveries in mechanical and chemical science, by means of which the production of the raw materials of certain ultimate manufactures had been vastly augmented. Its introduction revolutionized those manufactures, and at the same time, enlarged the field and increased the rewards of female labor, in fitting accordance with the demands of the hour. The Electro Magnetic Telegraph, in like manner, appropriated to the service of mankind the accumulated scientific knowledge of one of the most potent, though subtle agencies of nature, at a time when commercial intercourse between cities and States was everywhere receiving a vast impulse by means of railroads and steamboats, and the quickened intellect of the age demanded a speedier interchange of ideas. This tendency to practical invention had been fostered from the foundation of the government, by the patent system of the United States. It received additional encouragement under the general act of 1836 and by that of 1837, which increased the force of the office, and provided for the diffusion of information on the subject, by the publication of an annual report. An act of March 3, 1839, also provided for the collection of agricultural statistics, and another in August, 1842, granted the right to patent designs which materially contributed to improve the beauty as well as the profit of many branches of domestic manufacture, especially in metallic and textile materials. Under these acts, which gave additional scope and security to inventive talent, though still falling short of a perfect system, the Patent Office, in several of its departments, was reorganized and its business increased. Notwithstanding the rejection of a large proportion of the applications, under the system of examinations established in 1836, so rapid was the increase of applications that additional examining and clerical force was provided by Congress in May, 1848. Of the total number of patents issued from 1790 to January, 1849, amounting to 16,208, about two fifths belonged to the following four important classes: To Agriculture, which provides food for man and beast, and a portion of the raw materials for manufactures, 1,966, or 12.03 per cent. of the whole was devoted; and to the manufacture of Fibrous and Textile substances, including machines for preparing fibres of wool, cotton, silk, fur, paper, etc., for the production of clothing and household fabrics, 1,579, or 8.74 per cent. of the whole belonged. Calorific processes and articles, comprising lamps, fireplaces, stoves, grates, furnaces, etc., for giving heat and light for the comfort and manifold uses of daily life, embraced 1,479, or 9.12 per cent. of all patented inventions; and 1,384 patents, or 8.54 per cent. of the whole, belonged to the class of Metallurgy, and the manufacture of metals and instruments therefrom, which supplied the tools and implements of industry. During the latter part of the ten years now under review, however, the development of the metallic and mineral resources of the country, and particularly of the gold discoveries in California, and the coal and iron mines of other States, had caused the Metallurgic and Calorific classes of inventions to predominate over the Agricultural and Textile kinds.

The following are among the patented inventions of this period, which, from their novelty or practical utility may be presumed to have added to the productive capacities of the nation, in the several departments to which they relate:

I. Among the inventions relating to *Agriculture*, patented early in this decade, that deserve to be mentioned specially, is the Grain Drill, which may be said to have revolutionized the system of grain planting in America. The first successful machine of this description of which we have any record was invented by a practical farmer of Chester county, in Pennsylvania, Moses Pennock, of Kennett Square, who is also accredited with having been the inventor of the Revolving Horse Rake, of which the identical model, in all important respects, may now be seen in almost every hay-field in this country and in Europe. He, however, left the drill in a rude form, and the agriculturists of America are indebted for the improvements that have been made upon it and its present perfection to his ingenious son, Samuel Pennock, now residing on the old homestead, which his ancestors obtained by grant direct from William Penn. Patented in 1841, this invention was regarded with incredulity by those whom it was especially designed to benefit, and it was only after repeated experiments and the lapse of years that its value was recognized and acknowledged. In 1853, it received the first and highest premium awarded to Grain Drills by the Commissioners of the World's Fair, held in the city of New York, and shortly afterward, the British Government incorporated drawings and specifications of it in a Report on Agricultural Improvements. It is asserted that repeated experiments have demonstrated that by the use of this drill a saving of fifteen to twenty-five per cent. may be made in seed, with an increase of yield of six to eight bushels per acre over the old broadcast method of sowing.[1]

(1) The following interesting account of the origin of this invention and its improvements, and the amusing incidents attending its introduction, was furnished the author by the inventor, Samuel Pennock.

"In the year 1836 or 1837, my father, Moses Pennock, resolved to make a machine with which to plant wheat, believing from the nature of the case that wheat so planted would stand the winter better and be more *certain* of making a crop than the then usual method of broadcast sowing. In the above year a rude machine was made with which he planted his wheat. The result being entirely satisfactory, he continued to use it for two or three years, when he invited me, at the expiration of my term of apprenticeship, to come home and see if it could not be improved upon so as to adapt it to general purposes of seeding.

"In 1839 I commenced operations, using the machine in the field during the seeding seasons, both spring and autumn, making such alterations and improvements as the various circumstances suggested.

"In March, 1841, a patent was granted

Among the agricultural inventions of value patented in this decade may be mentioned machinery for hewing plough beams, patented in 1840

for such improvements as were deemed important.

"In the autumn of this year, as I was one day using the machine in a neighboring field, one of the depositing tubes struck a rock and tore it off. I was in a dilemma, several miles from home, or from any shop where the machine could be repaired. On examining more closely I found that it could be repaired by driving the drag bar into its socket, and securing it temporarily by a *wooden pin*. In about fifteen minutes I was on my way rejoicing, but asking myself whether the depositing tubes could not be so attached to the drag bar that upon a similar accident occurring the damage could be repaired without serious cost or delay. In the course of a day or two another rock was struck by the same tube or tooth. This time no damage was done other than to break the wooden pin before mentioned, which in five minutes was replaced. This second accident settled the matter in my mind. I ordered a new machine, with the teeth so attached that on coming in contact with rocks, roots, or other fast substances, a small wooden pin was broken, thereby relieving the machine from any serious damage; and as a few pins could always be carried along, the broken one could be replaced in about *two* minutes and all be right again.

"About this time, a farmer *somewhere* in southeastern Pennsylvania, who, I am sorry to say, was a Quaker, engaged me to drill in his wheat, assuring me that he had nine acres, which statement was afterward confirmed by his son. When the job was done and to be settled for, the field dwindled down to eight acres, I being loser of a half a dollar by the old man's falsehood. By this circumstance I conceived the idea of an arrangement by which the field could be measured by the machine as it was planting the grain, and in a short time I had an instrument attached to the drill, now known as the *agrometer*, which did its part so well that even Quakers never dared to make a mistake in measuring their fields.

"The drill was so entirely new to a large majority of farmers, that hundreds rejected it as '*a humbug*,' declaring that 'I can sow wheat with my hand far better than it can be done by any machine.' It was interesting to listen to the numerous criticisms made and improvements suggested by different farmers; some 'didn't like that ugly *ridge* left by the drill between the rows,' others objected to drilling in *rows*, as it left too much waste land, etc., etc.

"The introduction of the drill, therefore, was for several years an uphill work; none but the most enterprising would consent even to try it. Charles Noble, M. D., of Philadelphia, bought one of the first and sent it to his farm in New Castle county, Delaware, where he made some very interesting experiments. Measuring off several acres, drilling and sowing broadcast alternately, he drilled one and a quarter bushels of seed, and sowed broadcast two bushels of seed to the acre. After harvesting the crop, the result varied from four to seven bushels per acre increase in favor of the drill, exclusive of a saving of three pecks of seed per acre. A number of experiments of this kind were tried in different parts of the county, and all with results equally in favor of the drilling system. So slow, however, were a majority of the farmers to buy drills, that we offered to give them a drill for the increased yield on fifty (50) acres by drilling, over broadcast sowing. Only one farmer accepted this proposal, and by his own report, made after threshing, he gained by the experiment more than seven (7) bushels per acre, which gave three hundred and fifty bushels of wheat for one drill.

"This experiment produced quite an excitement in the neighborhood, where a large number of drills were sold during the next few years.

"About the years 1845 and 1846 several different patterns of what are known as slide drills, were introduced. This style of drill works very imperfectly, except on smooth, *level* land."

by Draper Ruggles, Joel Nourse, and John C. Mason, as the assignees of E. G. Matthews, who, during the same year, imported from Scotland the first subsoil plough, and made valuable improvements in the cast-iron and other ploughs, of which they became extensive manufacturers at Worcester, Massachusetts. In the following year, improvements in the plough were patented by Prouty and Mears, of Boston, who also became celebrated manufacturers. A Mowing and Reaping Machine was patented, in 1842, by J. Read, of Illinois; and another, of which twenty thousand have since been manufactured by a single establishment in the space of about four years, was patented by William P. Ketchum, in 1844. The second patent for the celebrated McCormick Mower and Reaper was issued the next year, and that of Obed Hussey was surrendered and reissued in two patents in 1847. F. McCarthy, of Florida, made improvements in the Saw Gin, adapting it for cleaning both green and black seed cotton, for which he received patents in 1840. Some improvements were made in the mode of baling cotton, the great southern staple, particularly by the application of steam to that process, which was the subject of a patent to P. B. Tyler, of Philadelphia, in 1845, and by others subsequently. The Endless-chain Horse Power was patented, in 1841, by A. and A. F. Wheeler, administrators of W. E. Wheeler, of Albany, New York, who were probably the first builders of them.

II. *In Metallurgy*, several valuable improvements were introduced, among which was a new Pin Making Machine, in 1841, by J. J. Howe, of Derby, Connecticut, which was capable of turning out daily twenty-seven thousand pins, headed, pointed, and ready for silvering, by simply supplying the material at one part of the machine. A machine for sticking pins in paper was, the same year, patented by Samuel Slocum, of Poughkeepsie, New York, and previously of Rhode Island, who, in 1835, had secured in England a patent for machinery for making solid-headed pins, with which, in 1838, a large manufactory was started at Poughkeepsie by Slocum, Gillison & Co., which ten years later was sold out to the American Pin Company, of Waterbury, Connecticut, whither the machinery was removed. In 1843, before which time, under the former tariff, American solid-headed pins had almost superseded the foreign, Mr. Howe also patented a machine for papering pins, and for some years the Waterbury and Howe Pin Companies had obtained almost a monopoly of the manufacture. For the production of wood screws of brass and iron by machinery, carried on, in 1842, by two large companies, at Providence, Rhode Island, where it was first established, and by some in two or three other States, to an extent that was fast arresting importation, Cullen Whipple, of Providence, in

1842, patented a new machine for cutting the threads, and, in 1845, a Self-adjusting Screw Finisher, of much value to the trade. Four patents were granted, in 1846, to Thomas J. Harvey, of New York, for threading and heading wood screws, and two, in 1848, to John Crum, assignor to Henry L. Pierson, of Ramapo Works, New York. Before the close of this decade, the American manufacturers obtained exclusive control of the market, the Providence companies supplying over eighty per cent. of the whole; a single company having, for some years past, turned out about ten thousand gross daily.

Improved file-cutting machinery was patented, in 1845, by Solomon Whipple, of Rhode Island, and, in 1847, by Richard Walker, of New Hampshire, the latter said to be capable of making six or eight common files per hour, and so easily operated that a five horse-power engine would drive at least fifty machines. Portable machinery for planing iron was the subject of a patent granted to Alfred C. Jones, in 1847; and an improved machine for that use, exhibited, in 1849, at the American Institute Fair, in New York, by G. B. Harston, of that city, was estimated to save annually two millions of dollars in files alone, which had been previously used for polishing surfaces of iron. An improvement in the machine for making Horseshoes, Chain-links, etc., was patented, in 1843, by Henry Burden, of Troy, who was also the inventor of a machine for making spikes and rolling puddler's balls. In 1844, patents were granted to Linus Yale, of Springfield, for an improvement in Door Locks, and to Robert Newell, of New York, in 1843 and 1844, for improvements on his Permutation and other Locks. In 1848, patents were granted to the Collins Company, of Connecticut, as the assignees of E. K. Root, for machinery for dressing Axes, to Jordan L. Mott, of New York, for a process of Chilling Iron Castings, and to George F. Muntz, of Birmingham, England, for a Composition Sheathing Metal, being the well known combination of lead with copper and zinc, which bears his name.

III. In the manufacture of *Fibrous* and *Textile Substances*, several valuable inventions were patented. Among these were several of the early inventions of Erastus B. Bigelow, of Massachusetts, which have had a marked influence on several branches of textile art in this country and in Europe. The Power-Loom, for weaving figured counterpanes, etc., was patented in 1840; that for weaving plaids, in 1845, in which year the inventor obtained three other patents for loom temples, speeder-fliers, etc. In 1846, he patented the two and three ply ingrain carpet power-loom, and in the ensuing year, the Brussels and tapestry carpet loom, inventions which have built up not only the first power factory, but some of the most complete and extensive establishments in the country at Lowell, Thompsonville, Tariffville, and Humphreysville, Connecticut, and others in Great Britain, enriching the inventor and his licensees, at the same time reducing the price of carpetings full twenty per cent., and nearly suspending their importation by introducing a radical change in the manufacture at home and abroad. William Sherwood, of Connecticut, also patented, in 1846, an improvement on carpet power-looms, and John Perrins, of Philadelphia, an improvement in the Jacquard Frame for weaving figured fabrics. The self-acting mule, for spinning cotton and other fabrics, received some valuable improvements at the hands of William Mason, of Taunton, by whom they were patented in 1846. It was during the same year that the first patent was granted to Elias Howe, Jr., of Cambridgeport, Massachusetts, for the Sewing Machine already noticed, which was the fifth one recorded, and was followed in 1849, by five other patents for Sewing Machines; and those by 597 others, up to the close of 1863. John Ames, of Springfield, Massachusetts, received, in 1840, a patent for making, ruling, and cutting paper at one operation. In October of the same year, Reuben Daniels, of Woodstock, Vermont, was granted a patent for a machine for reducing worn-out cloths, silk, and other materials to the fibrous state, so as to be manufactured into cloth. Two other patents were issued in that year to Thomas Williams or Williamson, of Newport, Rhode Island, then resident in England; the one for machinery for the manufacture of stuffs in which the fibres of various materials were united by adhesive mixtures, and another for machinery for making felt cloths without spinning or weaving. This invention appears to have been a limited application to the manufacture of felt cloths of machinery previously patented and operated in England, for the production of webbing for hats, by the use of a carding machine, for preparing the materials of pervious cones and exhausting fans, as previously suggested by Blanchard, for forming the web which was afterward dipped in an agglutinating fluid. The American patent did not include its application to the making of hat bodies, which was successfully carried out by H. A. Wells, who took out his first patent for improvement in the machinery by which nearly all hat bodies are now made, in April, 1846. It was assigned to H. A. Burr, and others, in New York, who received additional patents in 1847, and subsequent years. Joseph Whitworth, of Manchester, England, received, in 1848, an American patent for Knitting Machinery, for which object ten others were recorded during the previous nine years. Mr. Sands Olcott, of New Hope, Pennsylvania, in 1840, was granted two patents for preparing the fibres of unrotted Flax for carding and spinning in the manner of cotton, by automatic machinery. He was able to supply a material at eight cents a pound, which was an early approximation to the cottonized flax and fibrillia, now prepared for the same purpose by various mechanical and chemical means. He afterward attracted considerable attention to the subject of spinning flax by machinery, by delivering lectures upon his improvements, which were suspended by his death.

IV. *In Chemical Processes and Manufactures* some important improvements were made, particularly in the treatment of Caoutchouc, and Gutta Percha, and of Sugar Cane, etc. In the former branch, C. B. Arnold and Edward Rogers, as the assignees of Edwin M. Chaffee, of Massachusetts, in 1841, patented a mode of manufacturing balls of Caoutchouc; in 1845, Nelson Goodyear, for combining fibrous substances with gum in forming India Rubber fabrics with a firm body, and smooth surface, like leather; H. H. Day, in connection with Tyre and Helm, of New Jersey, and James Bogardus, of New York, for a machine for cutting India Rubber threads for the production of Shirred goods. C. F. Durant, of New Jersey, in 1848, received a patent for dissolving and softening Gutta Percha and India Rubber in chloroform, and H. H. Day another for preparing Gutta Percha fabrics in imitation of patent leather. Henry Bewley, of Ireland, May 23, of that year, received a patent for making flexible syringes, etc., of Gutta Percha. On the same day with the last, American letters patent were granted to Charles Hancock, Richard Archibald Brooman, and to Charles Keene, severally, for improvements in the manufacture of Gutta Percha, which at that time was attracting much attention, and in that year was first manufactured in the United States. The first related to the manufacture of bands or belting; the second to a mode of moulding, stamping, or embossing; and the last to a combination of Gutta Percha and India Rubber, for making shoes, all of which had been patented in England. A new process of making and refining sugar, which dispensed with the use of clay in refining, and reduced the time two thirds, and increased the quantity and quality of the sugar, was patented in 1843, by Professor Mapes of New York, who also patented a new evaporating pan and filter. In 1845, J. F. Lapice, of France, as the assignee of Charles Louis Derosne, Francis Duplessis, of New Orleans, and others, patented improvements which advanced the sugar interests of the Southern States. Other patents were received in 1846 by N. Rellieux, of New Orleans, by G. Michiels, of Guadaloupe, and by Alfred Stillman, of New York, the last for an improved sugar pan, and in the subsequent years others were issued for the same purpose, to foreign and American citizens.

The compound, or oxyhydrogen blowpipe, so valuable to the analytical chemist and the manufacturer of artificial gems, was the subject of a patent by Professor Hare, the inventor, in 1845. In the same year a patent was granted to Isaac Tyson, Jr., of Baltimore, for the manufacture of Chromate of Potash. Two patents were issued, in 1847, to R. A. Tilghman, an American then residing in England, for subjects of much scientific and practical interest; the one for a mode of decomposing alkaline salts by the action of steam at a high temperature; the other and earlier one for making Sulphate and Muriate of Potash from feld-spar. Martin Kalbfleisch, of Bushwick, New York, received a patent for an improvement in the manufacture of Prussiate of Potash and Soda. An improvement in Calico Printing was patented the same year, by Bennett Woodcroft, of England, who has since been at the head of the Patent Office in that country. The separation of Lard Oil from the solid constituent of fat, by pressure, and also a mode of purifying oils, were patented in 1844, and have proved valuable.

V. In *Calorifics* a large number of patents were issued in the ten years preceding 1850, particularly for stoves, grates, ranges, furnaces, lamps, etc., and in designs for their ornamentation. A combined Caldron and Furnace for the use of agriculturists, was patented in 1840, by Jordan L. Mott, of Mott Haven, New York, whose name often occurs, in earlier and later years, as an improver of stoves, grates, ranges, and other castings. Among other improvements in this line may be named those of Gardner Chilson, of Boston, in 1840, for Bakers' Furnaces, and in 1845 and 1848, for Hot Air Furnaces, and other improvements by the same manufacturer; a mode of warming buildings by converting hollow walls into flues, by John A. Stewart, of Philadelphia, in 1840; a stove for heating rooms, by J. H. B. Latrobe, of Baltimore, in 1846, which is much used in some parts of the country; a self-acting Register for stoves, by Washburn Race, of Seneca Falls, New York, in 1846; improvements in Cooking Ranges, by Moses Pond, of Boston, in 1845 and 1846; and another, in 1846, by J. P. Hayes, of that city, and by other persons. Numerous improvements in parlor and cooking stoves, grates, etc., by R. D. Granger, of Auburn, New York, in 1841, and subsequent years, and by many others. The patents for new designs in patterns for stoves, grates, fenders, etc., by the principal manufacturers, were exceedingly numerous. In ventilators or chimney caps, improvements were patented by Frederick Emerson, by J. P. Hayes, of Boston, and others, in 1847 and 1848. Many improvements in the construction and designing of lamps for burning lard oil, camphene, and other chemical mixtures then coming into use, were made by Dyott and Cornelius, of Philadelphia, Jennings and Rust, of New York, and others.

VI. Navigation and maritime improvements received several valuable additions, in the Metallic Life and other boats, patented by Joseph Francis, of New York, in 1841 and 1845; and the portable India Rubber boat patented by H. H. Day, in 1846; in the numerous modifications of screw, spiral, and other propellers, and in the mode of applying them to ships, including an improved form of propeller, by Eleazer Beard, of Maine, in 1841; a screw propeller, by John Ericsson, in 1845; a mode of elevating and depressing propellers, by R. F. Loper, in the same year, and in the manufacture of ships' sails, by James Maull, of Philadelphia. In 1849, a patent was granted to Abraham Lincoln, of Springfield, Illinois, late President of the United States, for an apparatus for buoying vessels, designed to be placed on each side of the hull of steamboats, or other vessels, and inflated somewhat as a bellows, to float them over sand bars, snags, and other obstructions.

VII. Civil Engineering, and Architecture, received many useful auxiliaries in patent machines and inventions made available in the rapid extension of the railroad and canal system, and the improvement of the river navigation of the country, and in the improvement of wood and iron working machinery. Adapted to the former class of works were numerous machines for excavating and removing earth, extracting trees, stumps, and snags, breaking stones, boring and blasting rocks, excavating and dredging canals, docks, and natural water-courses, etc. A combined canal and railroad was patented in 1845, and a portable coffer dam, in the following year, by S. S Walley, of Charlestown, Massachusetts. An improvement in the mode of anchoring suspension bridges by placing the anchor under the pier, was patented by John A. Roebling, of Pittsburg, Pennsylvania, to whom another patent was granted in 1847, for apparatus for passing suspension wires across rivers, etc. Horace V Russ, of New York, patented, in 1848, the substratum for pavements which bears his name, and a compound break-joint Railroad Rail was the same year patented by B. A. Latrobe, of Baltimore. Machinery forascending and descending inclined planes was the subject of a patent, in 1847, by Geo. H. Sellers, of Philadelphia.

VIII. In land conveyances, comprising carriages, cars, and other vehicles, and the parts thereof, the major part of the improvements patented related to railroad cars, car wheels, brakes, springs, etc. In 1841, Charles Davenport and Alfred Bridges, of Cambridgeport, Massachusetts, patented improvements in the construction of railroad carriages, as did also P. & W. C. Allison, of Philadelphia, in the axles of cars. For a mode of ascending and descending inclined planes by locomotives, which then attracted much attention, a patent was obtained by Ezra Coleman, of Philadelphia, in 1845. Improvements in cast-iron car wheels were patented by Asa Whitney, of Philadelphia, whose method of annealing and cooling them in pits has been very successful; by Anson Atwood, of Troy, New York, in 1847, whose corrugated cast-iron wheels are well known to railroad men; by Isaac Van Kuran, of Rochester, New York, in 1849, and by others. Fowler M. Ray, of New York, in 1848, patented the Metallic India Rubber and Pneumatic Car Spring, which was extensively manufactured for him by the New England Car Company, although W. C. Fuller, of England, had previously obtained patents for the same in both countries, and under his patent they were manufactured by H. H. Day & Company.

IX. In the class of *Hydraulics* were embraced many novelties and some valuable improvements, in water-wheels, pumps, rams, presses, fire engines, etc. John Houpt, of Alabama, in 1841, patented an improved hydrostatic or hydraulic Cotton Press; and a portable Steam Pump, by William Boardman, Jr., in 1847. J. A. Lettellier, of Paris, took out an American patent, in 1848, for an improvement on the Archimedan screw for raising water, which had been previously patented in France. Manoah Alden, of Ralston, Pennsylvania, in 1848, patented the Fan-blower for furnaces, which has proved of much value in the iron manufacture.

X. In Grinding Mills and Mill Gearing, etc., many improvements, valuable to the agricultural classes, were patented, especially in small portable mills to be worked by hand or horse-power, in machines for separating garlic, smut, etc., from grain, and in horse-power for driving threshing machines, straw cutters, etc. An improved Sugar Mill was patented, in 1846, by Alfred Stillman, of New York, and one for grinding grain, paint, drugs, etc., by Wm. Broughton, of London, in the same year. A machine for balancing and finishing Burr Millstones was patented by E. Morrison, of Utica, New York, in 1849.

XI. In Lumber, and the tools and machinery for working it, invention was stimulated by the abundance and cheapness of materials and by the great success attending some earlier improvements in this branch. Two patents were granted, in 1840, to John H. Stevens, of New York; one as the assignee of Chauncey E. Warner, the inventor, for turning wooden boxes, and the other, in which he was the assignee of Elisha Fitzgerald, for cutting splints for friction matches, which was the subject of another patent in the same year by N. T. Winans and Thaddeus Hyatt, of New York. T. I. Wells, of New York city, in 1841, patented a machine for cutting Dovetails and Tenons, in which year a valuable practical patent was recorded by George Page, of Baltimore, for a portable circular saw-mill. Many other useful applications and improvements of circular and other saws were made by adapting them to the sawing of veneerings of greater thinness than before, shingles, clapboards, staves, spokes, and other irregular forms previously cut by hand, or with much greater expenditure of time, labor, and material. These included several modifications of the machine for turning irregular frames by Thomas Blanchard, who received, in 1849, a second extension of his patent; and in the same year he was granted a new one for machinery for bending wood, which was re-issued in 1851. Among these modifications was one by Warren Hale and Allen Goodman, of Dana, Massachusetts, for a lathe adapted for turning Piano legs and similar articles, patented in 1845. In 1848, Mr. Goodman, as the assignee of Wm. Gibbs, of Prescott, also received a patent for planing irregular forms, and another for self-acting machinery for turning such shapes to any desired pattern from blocks of timber. The patent of the Woodworth Planing machine was, by act of Congress, extended, in 1845, for seven years from December, 1849, and has since expired without renewal. A machine for making barrels was patented in 1845 by William Trapp, Jr., of Dryden, New York. A machine for punching and pointing wooden shoe pegs was patented, in 1848, by H. P. Wescott, of Seneca Falls, New York.

XII. *Leather*, including tanning and dressing, the manufacture of boots, shoes, saddlery, harness, etc. In this department of industry many labor-saving improvements were patented, and included, in 1840, two patents by Samuel Sheldon, of Cincinnati, for pricking leather preparatory to stitching; one by John H. Dupont and Theodore Hyatt, of New York, for gum elastic gores for gaiter boots; a method of whitening leather by Prof. Jas. C. Booth, of Philadelphia; for methods of splitting leather by Alpha Richardson, of Boston, in 1841, and by I. P. Fairlamb, of Wilmington, Delaware, in 1848. Among numerous patents for the handling and tanning of hides, mostly designed to hasten the tanning process, was one granted, in 1846, to A. H. Beschorman, of New York, for a foreign invention, which consisted in passing the hides stretched together in an endless belt or apron over a series of rollers, one half of them within and the other half without the vat, for the successive purposes of washing, liming, vatting, tanning, stuffing, or dribbing, etc. Lewis C. England, of Tioga county, New York, in 1847, received a patent for an improvement in tanning called paddle wheel handlers, for stirring the stock in the liquors, and designed to dispense with manual labor in handling altogether. Subsequent mechanical improvements by the same inventor, have rendered the labor of two men sufficient to do the yard work of a tannery working *in* and *out* one hundred and fifty hides per diem, and have brought his system into very extensive use in New England and the Middle States. In the year last named, Simon C. Shive, of Pennsylvania, patented a machine for draughting, cutting and blocking boot patterns, which has been found of considerable practical advantage. In the following year, Joel Robinson, of Methuen, Massachusetts, patented a shoe pegging machine, containing several novel features, and which performed automatically the several processes of punching the holes, inserting and driving the peg with great accuracy.

XIII. In Household Furniture and machines and instruments for domestic purposes, numerous patents were granted, and if few of them were of a conspicuous character, their aggregate influence upon the domestic economy and comfort of the nation, and even their value as articles of manufacture, is not to be measured by their apparent insignificance as inventions. Some have been the foundation of respectable fortunes.

XIV. In the Polite, Fine, and Ornamental Arts there were many minor, and some very valuable improvements patented. The Piano forte received modifications and improvements which were patented by Jonas Chickering, of Boston, in 1840, and in 1843 by Newhall, the Gilberts, Draper, and others of same place, by Senior of New York, Gray of Albany, Schomacker, of Philadelphia, and others. Obed. M. Coleman, of Philadelphia, patented the Aeolian attachment to the piano in 1844, which was the subject of another patent by C. Hirst, of New Orleans, in the following year. Moses Coburn, in 1847, patented a method of combining metallic reeds with piano fortes. In free reed instruments the principal improvements in this period were made by Jeremiah Carhart, of Buffalo, New York, who, in 1846, patented improvements in the bellows for seraphines, and otherwise contributed to the present perfection of the Melodeon. Seraphines were patented by Luther Tracy, of Concord, New Hampshire, in 1848. The printing-press was improved in 1840 by Stephen P. Ruggles, of Boston, and in 1842 by Richard M. Hoe, of New York, who patented in that year improvements in single and double cylinder presses, the latter containing all known improvements, with some new ones, whereby six thousand impressions hourly could be obtained. Subsequent improvements, patented by Hoe in 1845 and 1847, including the first successful attachment of the type to the cylinder and improvements in inking apparatus, increased the capacity of the four cylinder press with revolving type to ten thousand impressions per hour, from which it has been since raised to fifteen thousand and twenty thousand hourly from the ten cylinder lightning press. Useful modifications of the printing-press were also patented in 1844 by Seth Adams, of Boston, whose hand-press for fine work is still used, and in 1846 by Isaiah Adams, of Boston, and by A. B. Tyler, of New York. Several improvements in casting type were patented by the Messrs. Bruce, of New York, and others. Improvements in taking and finishing Daguerreotype pictures were patented in 1846 by F. Langenheim, of Philadelphia, as the assignee of J. B. Isenring, of Switzerland, and by W. A. Pratt, of Alexandria, Virginia, and in 1849, by John A. Whipple, of Boston.

XV. In Surgical and Medical Instruments, etc., the most valuable improvements were those made in dental surgery, especially in the composition and manufacture of artificial teeth, including a mode of obtaining casts from teeth and gums, patented by Daniel T. Evans, of Philadelphia, in 1840; the improvements of B. F. Palmer, now of Philadelphia, in the manufacture of Artificial legs, patented in 1846 and 1849; improvements in surgical apparatus for fractured ankles, by George Yerger, of Philadelphia, in 1849; and finally, that which may be regarded as the crowning surgical invention of the age, namely, the alleviation of pain during surgical operations by the inhalation of the vapor of sulphuric ether, patented in 1846 by Charles T. Jackson, of Boston, and William T. G. Morton, his assignee.

Under the tariff of 1842, which was in operation from June, 1843, to June, 1847, a rapid revival and extension of domestic manufactures, which at the date of its passage were generally depressed, was once more perceptible. Although frequent changes in the revenue system, and especially the fluctuations incident to the ad valorem valuation previously in use, were almost as unfavorable to the manufacturer as the most injurious competition, yet capital and labor speedily accommodated themselves to the change, and activity took the place of general inertia. Cotton and woolen mills were again put in operation, new ones were built and old ones were enlarged. Furnaces, forges, and rolling-mills rekindled their fires and were everywhere multiplied, and were yet unable to supply the demand for iron. Railroads and other internal improvements were pushed with unprecedented vigor. Emigration flowed in from abroad, and instead of swelling the volume of agricultural products, for which a sale could only be found in foreign markets at prices which barely paid the freight and charges, found abundant employment at remunerative and greatly increased wages in the mining and industrial establishments of the country, creating a home market for the farmer at his own door. Invention was stimulated, and by new processes and instruments added much to the productive forces of the country. The production of Iron, which, in 1842, when many of the furnaces were closed, had fallen to less than 230,000 tons annually, was estimated by the Secretary of the Treasury in 1846 at 765,000 tons, having trebled in three years. In 1847 it was supposed to have reached 800,000 tons, and although in the next year, with another change in the financial policy of the government, the production became stationary, and in the next fell off to 650,000 tons, yet Pennsylvania alone, at the close of the decade, produced as much iron as France, more than Russia and Sweden together, and more than all Germany united. Within those ten years the cost of its production had been reduced nearly fifty per cent., and the price of many articles of iron manufacture, as cut nails, had been reduced in nearly equal proportion. Yet such was the activity of all branches of industry, and the increased power of consumption, that at the period of maximum production the domestic supply was insufficient, and upward of 50,000 tons of pig and bar-iron were imported from abroad, exclusive of wrought-iron chains, hardware, cutlery, steel, etc., which swelled the amount to nearly 100,000 tons.

The production and consumption of mineral Coal, which is the pabulum of so many forms of industry, was increased from 1,312,000 tons of domestic Anthracite, and 55,000 tons of foreign coal in 1843 to 3,200,000 tons of Anthracite and 148,000 tons of foreign coal in 1847, the greatly increased home supply being yet inadequate to the demand. The consumption of cotton by Northern manufacturers increased from about 325,000 bales in 1843 to 531,000 bales in 1848; while the cotton producing States, which manufactured but little in the former year, consumed in the last year about 75,000 bales, an increase of eighty-six per cent., while the value of foreign cotton manufactures, which the country was able to purchase in the same time, was nearly doubled. The consumption of domestic and foreign wool in home manufactures was augmented in the same time from fifty-five and a half million to eighty-one and a quarter million pounds, while the value of woollens imported was duplicated in like manner. In addition to the amount of capital invested in these and other manufactures throughout the country, large amounts were expended in increasing the machinery of transporting for inland and maritime trade. The total number of vessels built in the United States in 1842 numbered 1,021, of the aggregate tonnage of 129,084 tons. In 1848 the whole number built was 1,851, and their total tonnage was 318,075 tons, an increase of one hundred and forty-five per cent. in six years. In the steamboat and lake tonnage of the Western and Northwestern States the advance was equally apparent. Thus the lake tonnage, which from 1834 to 1841 had only risen from 28,521 tons to 56,252 tons, reached, in 1846, 106,836, and in 1848, 166,400 tons. The steamboat tonnage of the Western rivers,

29

amounting, in 1842, to 126,278 tons, was almost doubled in the next four years; reaching, in 1846, two hundred and forty-nine thousand and fifty-five tons.

In Railroad enterprise the progress was equally conspicuous, and was only exceeded by that of Great Britain, in which, during a portion of these years, railroad extension amounted to a mania. The total length of railroads in operation in the United States in 1840 was 2,380 miles, constructed (in the previous thirteen years) at a total cost of $69,700,000. In 1847 the entire length of railways in operation was 4,249 miles, and the cost of the same amounted to $123,500,000. At the close of 1849 there were in operation in the United States more than 7,000 miles of railroad, and the cost of construction exceeded $200,000,000. The number of miles built in the last five years was 3,309, of which 1,200 miles were constructed in 1849, and the total length of railroads in the United States was more than one third of the entire length of such roads in Europe and America. Notwithstanding the large amounts of capital thus annually invested in railroads, steamboats, and other improvements, bringing the producer and the consumer into closer proximity and thus advancing the interests of both, even the planting and farming States may be said to have rapidly increased and diversified their industry by introducing and extending their manufactures.

In most of the Southern States manufacturing villages were springing up, and cotton yarn and coarse cotton goods, as well as cut nails and some other wares made in the South, found a ready market in Northern cities. Tennessee, Alabama, Georgia, and South Carolina contained ninety-two cotton-mills, running 136,220 spindles, and consuming 6,000 bales of cotton. The whole number of cotton-mills south of Mason and Dixon's line in 1849 was said to be upward of two hundred and fifty, and their total consumption of cotton 150,000 bales. The Western States in like manner were rapidly extending their manufactures of machinery, iron wares, furniture for the cotton and sugar growing States and the distant West, as well as that of cottons, woollens, bagging, soap and candles, lard and linseed oils, starch, white lead, buckets, tubs, brooms, and other small manufactures to a vast aggregate amount.

Of the progress of the older manufacturing States during a portion of this period some indication is furnished by the state censuses of Massachusetts and New York—the two leading producers—taken in 1845. The aggregate amount of capital invested in manufactures in Massachusetts, as returned by the National census of 1840, was $41,774,446. As reported by the Secretary of the Commonwealth in 1845 it was $59,145,767, an increase of upward of forty-one per cent. in five years. The whole number of hands employed was 152,766, and the value of the product, exclusive of all agricultural products, except wool, flour, and raw silk, was upward of one hundred millions of dollars. The leading articles of production were, boots and shoes, $14,799,140; cotton goods of all kinds, including bleaching and coloring, of which more than one quarter was in calicoes, $19,089,266; woollen goods of all kinds, $8,877,478; whale fishing, $10,371,167; leather, $3,836,657; iron and nails made in rolling, slitting, and nail mills, $2,738,300; machinery, $2,022,648; oil and sperm candles, $3,613,796; paper, $1,750,273; and straw bonnets, hats, and braid, $1,649,496.

In New York the value of the product of twenty separate branches of manufacture returned by 14,965 establishments during the same year, was in total $68,969,713, whereof the products of flour and grist mills amounted to $22,794,474; of saw-mills to $7,577,154; of iron-works to $8,402,586; of tanneries to $6,585,006; of woollen factories (4,916,998 yards) to $4,281,257; of cotton factories (31,234,633 yards) to $2,877,500; of distilleries $4,222,154; of dyeing and printing establishments to $2,086,986; of oil mills to $1,695,025; of carding mills to $1,678,320; of fulling-mills to $1,660,881; and of breweries to $1,313,273. The other branches, as those of glass, rope, chain cable, oil-cloth, and paper, each yielded less than one million of dollars in value.

The manufacturing enterprise of New York was promoted by a general law of the State, enacted in February, 1848, to "authorize the promotion of corporations for manufacturing, mining, mechanical, or chemical purposes," and during the next seven years that State advanced to the foremost rank in the Union in the extent and value of her manufactures.

The legislature of Pennsylvania, in April of the following year, also enacted a general manufacturing law to encourage manufacturing operations in the commonwealth. The laws of the two States agreed, among other things, in making the stockholders severally and individually liable to the amount of stock held by them in the company so incorporated.

This prosperous condition of the national industry, notwithstanding its inherent vitality and resilience under depressing influences, suffered in many departments a serious check by the change of tariff in 1846, and at the close of these ten years, many branches of manufacture, in consequence of heavy importations from abroad, were prostrated from inability to find a market and accumulated stocks on hand.

CHAPTER VII.

THE MANUFACTURES OF THE UNITED STATES.

1850–1863.

An English writer has observed that the history of British Manufactures furnishes abundant ground for astonishment; but that of American Manufactures is much more marvellous.

In 1850, the Federal Government for the first time attempted to ascertain, with an approach to accuracy, the exact development of the Productive industry of the country, not counting any establishment that did not produce five hundred dollars per year; and the astounding fact was revealed that the capital invested in Manufactures exceeded five hundred and fifty millions of dollars, and that the annual product had reached *ten hundred and nineteen millions of dollars.* Eighty-six per cent. of this vast amount was made in fifteen States, leaving to the other twenty-one States and Territories only fourteen per cent. of the total production. New York held the first position as a seat of manufactures, having made twenty-three per cent. of the whole; Massachusetts and Pennsylvania were next in rank, having made fifteen per cent.; Connecticut, five per cent.; New Jersey, four per cent.; Maryland and Virginia, three per cent.; Rhode Island, New Hampshire, Missouri, Maine, and Kentucky, over two per cent. each. Only one manufacturing interest at that time produced over one hundred millions of dollars annually, viz., flour and meal. Three—viz., boots and shoes, cotton, and lumber—amounted to over fifty millions of dollars; while clothing, machinery, leather, and woolens, filled the complement of the third class, producing between twenty-five and fifty millions of dollars. The manufactures were distributed generally among the various States,—none we believe confined exclusively to any one,—though Massachusetts made eighty-five per cent. of the bonnets and straw goods, forty-six per cent. of the boots and shoes, and one-third of the cottons; Connecticut made one-third of the hardware, including guns, and forty per cent. of the India-rubber goods; Pennsylvania produced eighty per cent. of the coal, one-half the hosiery, one-third of the iron, and two-thirds of the perfumery; Delaware produced one-fourth of the gunpowder; Rhode Island, forty per cent. of the calicoes; Vermont, the same proportion of the scales; North Carolina, ninety per cent. of the turpentine; Ohio, sixty per cent. of the lard-oil; Missouri, three-fourths of the castor-oil; and Wisconsin, one-half the lead. The following table, published in 1858 by the Superintendent of the Census, though manifestly imperfect and erroneous in some of its details, is the best exhibit that we have of the number of establishments, capital invested, number of hands employed, and value of products,—in fact a—

General Summary of Manufactures in the United States during the Year ending June 1, 1850.

Manufactures.	No. of Establishments.	Capital.	Cost of raw material.	Male hands.	Female hands.	Value of Product.
Agricultural implements	1,333	$3,564,202	$2,445,765	7,211	9	$6,842,611
Artificial flowers	23	44,100	52,785	62	372	146,120
Asheries	569	485,760	812,190	1,020	4	1,401,533
Bagging, rope, and cordage	417	3,341,506	5,612,247	5,258	799	8,002,893
Baking	2,027	3,390,824	8,367,370	6,351	376	13,294,229
Baskets	67	38,975	40,410	190	13	147,400
Blacksmiths	10,373	5,884,149	5,111,388	24,983	19	16,048,536
Bleachers and dyers	16	563,600	323,924	519	46	686,830
Blocks and pumps	203	339,690	250,088	774	9	878,021
Bonnets, straw, braid, etc	68	336,350	932,674	303	3,468	1,687,248
Book-binders and blank-books,	235	1,063,700	1,560,330	1,778	1,690	3,225,678
Boots and shoes	11,305	12,924,919	23,848,374	72,305	32,949	53,967,408
Boxes, band and fancy	82	136,240	187,796	303	415	434,104
Boxes, packing	206	355,156	500,470	878	13	1,053,741
Brass-foundries	148	1,585,090	2,112,592	1,666	12	3,625,618
Breweries	431	4,072,380	3,055,266	2,336	11	5,728,568
Bricks	1,603	4,367,912	1,474,023	16,726	619	6,610,731
Bricks, fire	4	14,450	2,165	28	......	12,009
Britannia and plated ware	91	592,150	760,978	1,120	156	1,535,765
Brooms	303	314,985	528,842	1,174	10	940,766
Brushes	146	710,800	638,359	1,500	905	1,573,579
Burr mill-stones	9	34,100	25,825	55	......	55,000
Buttons	59	393,000	324,837	467	621	964,359
Cabinet ware	4,242	7,303,356	6,089,546	20,997	1,013	17,663,054
Calico-printers	42	3,922,800	10,462,044	3,351	729	13,680,805
Card machines	31	213,850	267,220	146	14	393,823
Cards, playing	4	147,000	105,260	66	155	176,800
Carpenters and builders	2,790	3,289,308	7,011,930	15,276	6	16,886,819
Carpets	116	3,852,981	3,075,592	3,881	2,305	5,402,634
Carpet-weaving	16	8,396	22,416	37	......	36,025
Cars, railroad	41	896,015	1,393,676	1,554	......	2,493,558
Chandlers	487	4,145,400	7,006,767	2,660	156	10,199,780
Chemicals	170	2,335,715	3,235,380	1,335	54	4,979,630
Clocks	23	499,800	456,834	777	23	1,181,500
Clothiers and tailors	4,278	12,509,161	25,730,258	35,051	61,500	48,311,709
Coaches and carriages	1,822	4,973,707	3,955,689	13,982	58	11,073,630

Manufactures.	No. of Establishments.	Capital.	Cost of raw material.	Male hands.	Female hands.	Value of Product.
Cloth-dressers	30	20,275	39,879	36		55,160
Coal-mining	510	8,317,501	246,414	15,112	6	7,173,750
Coffee and spices	48	438,662	843,254	305	12	1,240,614
Combs	151	633,637	843,482	1,426	362	1,615,850
Confectioners	383	1,035,551	1,691,824	1,388	345	3,040,671
Coopers	2,902	2,383,040	2,644,582	11,900	16	7,126,317
Copper and brass	175	2,850,981	3,062,661	2,388	2	4,942,901
Cork-cutters	11	41,750	53,653	79	2	126,890
Cottons	1,074	76,032,578	37,778,064	32,295	62,661	65,501,687
Cottons and woolens, mixed	103	1,711,720	2,321,986	2,667	1,901	3,693,731
Cutlery and edge tools	401	2,321,895	1,439,462	4,247	28	3,813,241
Daguerreotypists	74	89,925	99,789	141	17	250,267
Distilleries	968	5,409,334	10,543,201	3,985	23	15,770,240
Distilleries, rectifying	38	357,300	658,452	80		791,030
Die-sinkers	2	400	550	3		3,000
Dyers	46	331,950	754,379	434	26	1,086,795
Engravers	112	172,065	130,714	433	47	566,005
Earthenware	30	57,325	17,103	139		100,556
Envelopes	2	10,500	17,180	6	36	45,000
Fire-engines	16	152,700	116,267	248		296,230
Fisheries	1,407	8,962,403	71,517	20,814	424	10,056,163
Flax-dressers and spinners	4	135,700	186,000	160	102	301,808
Flour and grist-mills	11,891	54,415,581	113,036,698	23,260	50	136,056,736
Fringe, gimp, and tassels	38	244,350	233,680	205	681	583,000
Furriers	49	1,116,800	643,170	648	430	1,598,695
Gas	30	6,674,000	503,074	950	2	1,921,746
Gas fixtures	20	104,250	130,969	241		293,725
Gas meters	2	70,000	42,760	92		114,000
Glass	94	3,402,350	1,556,833	5,571	97	4,641,676
Glass-cutters	8	176,600	71,133	174		165,950
Gloves	110	181,200	322,837	329	1,609	708,184
Glue	47	519,950	371,616	378	13	652,405
Gold-beaters	20	62,500	216,380	107	57	336,065
Gold	1,015	1,814,012	57,711	4,804	80	9,551,853
Guns	317	577,509	269,673	1,547		1,173,014
Hardware	340	3,539,025	3,015,688	6,149	881	6,957,770
Hats and caps	1,048	4,427,798	7,100,028	6,974	8,226	14,319,864
Hosiery	85	544,735	415,113	835	1,490	1,028,102
India-rubber goods	34	1,455,700	1,608,728	1,010	1,558	3,024,335
Ink	14	116,650	72,673	49	4	213,648
Ink and lamp-black	3	16,500	29,318	13		62,024
Iron forges	375	8,517,011	5,338,505	7,698	77	9,002,705
Iron foundries	1,319	14,722,749	8,534,024	18,938	31	20,111,517
Iron furnaces	404	16,648,360	7,538,118	20,847	207	13,491,898
Iron manufactures	99	603,800	596,864	1,079	3	1,425,343
Iron mining	197	923,775	65,651	2,192	3	1,217,803
Iron rolling	65	5,214,700	4,353,150	3,800	20	6,936,081
Japanners	9	69,200	48,440	108	14	127,250
Lamps	26	486,300	490,862	918	20	1,060,022
Lamp-black	5	41,250	20,925	23	1	42,250
Lead pipe	10	272,250	678,330	71		797,166
Lead	156	603,196	1,532,585	737	16	2,150,068
Leather-belting	4	26,000	78,035	15	3	105,500
Legs, artificial	3	2,700	1,400	15		14,300
Lithographers	11	76,600	49,650	104	58	136,000
Lime	761	1,124,072	1,106,775	2,834	4	2,286,242
Locomotives	3	445,000	320,440	802		680,000
Looking-glass and picture frames	108	445,240	544,980	884	79	1,252,746

Manufactures.	No. of Establishments.	Capital.	Cost of raw material.	Male hands.	Female hands.	Value of Products.
Loom furnishers	3	$10,000	$4,954	8	35	$15,400
Loom harness	3	4,600	3,296	6	25	9,712
Loom pickers	2	31,000	25,100	20	......	35,500
Lumber-sawing & planing,	17,895	40,038,427	27,593,529	51,766	452	58,520,966
Machinists & millwrights	1,062	19,225,918	11,367,728	27,834	58	27,998,344
Malt	11	271,800	363,660	73	......	471,035
Matches, friction	60	109,140	137,514	481	540	427,823
Mathematical instruments,	90	326,550	165,666	624	40	703,750
Medicines, drugs, & dyes	143	1,427,375	1,657,886	693	134	3,508,465
Military goods	2	203,000	102,900	74	130	183,600
Milliners	532	660,193	1,496,866	181	3,688	2,761,989
Mill-stones	23	81,835	61,791	87	......	164,870
Mineral water and pop	64	228,650	313,631	570	19	760,480
Morocco cases	5	13,500	14,705	26	10	31,200
Morocco dressers	116	1,387,750	2,286,995	1,796	171	3,861,895
Musical instruments	204	1,545,935	698,168	2,307	24	2,580,715
Nails	87	4,428,498	4,438,976	5,227	4	7,662,144
Oil, lard	41	362,950	1,271,602	182	11	1,617,669
Oil, linseed	168	896,650	1,477,645	477	2	1,948,934
Oil, whale	50	2,791,000	6,492,876	492	52	7,839,980
Oil cloths	56	640,700	829,706	648	2	1,256,994
Paints	4	13,000	5,509	22	......	77,000
Paper	443	7,260,864	5,555,929	3,835	2,950	10,187,177
Patent leather	20	192,100	886,495	687	150	1,368,300
Percussion caps	2	5,000	15,350	9	3	30,000
Perfumes and fancy soap	30	197,550	163,826	125	63	355,350
Pickles and preserves	6	103,000	257,895	125	86	366,100
Pins	4	164,800	137,890	58	207	297,550
Plaster, gypsum	140	410,440	239,063	381	......	428,914
Plumbers	124	646,225	1,297,119	1,037	3	2,343,607
Pork and beef, packing	185	3,482,500	9,451,096	3,267	9	11,981,642
Potteries	484	777,544	275,083	2,246	43	1,466,068
Powder	54	1,179,223	860,997	576	3	1,590,332
Printers, lithographic and copper-plate	26	148,500	59,558	241	134	247,200
Printers and publishers	673	5,862,715	4,964,225	6,989	1,279	11,586,549
Pumps	30	86,370	55,493	148	......	166,919
Pyrotechnists	3	8,500	5,200	18	24	20,900
Red lead	2	20,000	21,130	8	......	27,000
Regalias	6	8,000	36,800	13	70	62,500
Rice mills	4	210,000	1,209,000	200	......	1,462,000
Saddles and harness	3,515	3,969,379	4,427,006	12,598	360	9,935,474
Sails	183	266,380	880,414	838	10	1,654,503
Salt and salt-refining	340	2,640,860	1,051,419	2,699	87	2,177,945
Sash and blinds	433	1,066,355	859,827	2,448	49	2,277,061
Scales and beams, weighers	22	184,000	130,267	402	......	359,505
Sewing-silk	27	428,350	848,945	295	554	1,209,426
Silverware	583	3,828,170	4,920,619	4,873	389	9,401,765
Shingles	520	823,940	406,932	2,127	......	985,957
Ship-building and boats	892	5,182,309	7,286,401	12,623	6	16,595,683
Shoe-pegs	24	35,750	13,238	111	15	73,918
Shot	5	245,500	760,421	69	4	988,550
Slates	6	50,000	13,174	109	......	46,700
Slate-pencils	3	4,600	1,800	19	20	15,000
Spice mills	9	64,300	204,244	55	......	248,405
Starch	146	692,675	799,459	686	8	1,261,468
Stationers	8	113,000	207,775	99	126	332,900
Staves and blocks	99	164,153	190,141	428	......	438,794
Steel furnaces	5	52,300	133,420	40	......	172,080

Manufactures.	No. of Establishments.	Capital.	Cost of raw material.	Male hands.	Female hands.	Value of Products.
Steel works	2	$32,500	$37,740	11	......	$53,400
Stone and marble	1,144	4,032,182	2,475,760	9,996	5	8,180,115
Stoves and ranges	230	3,179,475	2,913,943	4,227	......	6,124,748
Sugar refiners	23	2,669,000	7,662,685	1,644	12	9,898,800
Surgical instruments	37	101,450	80,987	189	111	259,400
Suspenders	5	20,800	75,300	35	327	171,000
Tanners and curriers	6,528	20,602,945	22,865,253	22,451	124	37,702,333
Tin and sheet-iron works	2,280	4,129,587	4,305,389	7,365	28	8,933,188
Thread	5	66,100	31,400	42	57	73,400
Tobacconists	1,418	5,008,295	7,341,728	12,261	1,975	13,491,147
Trunks and carpet-bags	116	356,660	765,816	1,056	264	1,558,388
Turners	440	663,615	407,043	1,624	27	1,374,449
Turners, bone and horn	5	3,500	4,280	24	......	13,800
Turners, iron	7	17,800	16,907	52	......	57,000
Turners, ivory	7	30,900	56,880	147	......	111,880
Turpentine	856	1,663,692	1,494,318	3,390	68	2,855,557
Type & stereotype found's,	42	513,700	298,922	775	224	913,200
Umbrellas	80	761,760	1,399,607	814	1,762	2,505,622
Upholsterers	155	565,685	983,961	804	708	1,790,683
Wall paper	6	49,500	52,335	91	2	107,040
Weavers	153	126,290	234,480	377	155	310,109
Whalebone	11	85,100	285,865	199	1	412,000
Wheelwrights	4,226	3,146,211	1,886,551	11,542	7	6,827,451
Whips and canes	70	198,895	237,643	519	532	575,271
White lead	51	3,124,800	3,541,072	1,508	......	5,242,213
White and locksmiths	82	144,082	110,155	413	2	355,137
Wire and wire-workers	83	537,725	534,548	658	18	1,033,249
Whiting	6	31,150	33,000	27	......	76,700
Wool cleaners and pullers,	3	5,000	27,125	11	......	36,900
Woodenware	197	530,165	436,676	1,328	32	1,138,078
Wool carders	630	739,925	1,251,550	1,071	22	1,739,476
Woolens, carding & fulling,	1,817	26,071,542	24,912,455	29,919	14,976	39,828,557
Aggregate, including sundry miscellaneous manufactures not above enumerated	123,025	$533,245,351	$555,123,822	731,137	225,922	$1,019,106,616

Vast as this production is, we find, ten years later, an increase of more than eighty-six per cent. The total value of the manufactures of the United States for the year ending June 1, 1860, as already ascertained in part and carefully estimated for the remainder, will reach an aggregate value of *nineteen hundred millions of dollars;* and if to this amount was added the very large amount of mechanical productions below the annual value of five hundred dollars,—of which no official cognizance is taken,—the result would indeed be one of startling magnitude.

To produce this large aggregate it is stated that one million one hundred thousand men and two hundred and eighty-five thousand women were furnished employment, or in all one million three hundred and eighty-five thousand persons. Each of these on an average maintained two and a half other individuals, making the whole number of persons supported by manufactures four millions eight hundred and forty-seven thousand five hundred, or nearly one-sixth of the whole population. This was exclusive of the number engaged in the production of many of the raw materials and of food for the manufacturers; in the distribution of their products, such as merchants, clerks, draymen, mariners, the employees of railroads, expresses, and steamboats; of capitalists, various artistic and professional classes, as well as carpenters, bricklayers, painters, and the members of other mechanical trades not classed as manufacturers. It is safe to assume, then, that one-third of the whole population is supported, directly and indirectly, by manufacturing industry. These general facts, therefore, plainly indicate that, in point of productive value and far-reaching industrial influences alone, our manufactures are entitled to a front rank among the great interests of the country.

MANUFACTURES IN 1860.

It is a gratifying fact, shown by the official statistics, that while our older communities have greatly extended their manufactures, the younger and more purely agricultural States, and even the newest Territories, have also made rapid progress. Nor has this department of American industry been cultivated at the expense of any other. There is much reason to believe that it affords the safest guarantee of the permanency and success of every other branch. Evidence bearing upon this point is found in the manufacture of agricultural machines and implements, which is one of the branches that shows the largest increase in the period under review. There is little doubt that the province of manufactures and invention in this case has been rather to create than to follow the demand. The promptness of Americans to adopt labor-saving appliances, and the vast areas devoted to grain and other staples in the United States, have developed the mechanics of agriculture to an extent and perfection elsewhere unequalled. The adoption of machinery to the extent now common in farm and plantation labor furnishes the best assurance that the development of agriculture or manufactures to their utmost can never again justify the old charge of antagonism between them in regard to labor, or injuriously affect either by materially modifying its cost or supply.

Agricultural Implements.—The total value of agricultural implements made in 1860 was $17,802,514, being an increase of 160.1 per cent. upon the total value of the same branch in 1850, when it amounted to the sum of $6,842,611. In New England, where this branch of manufactures is less extensive than formerly, the total value was less than two millions, the increase being only about sixteen per cent. In the Middle States, this manufacture increased at the rate of 134 per cent., and amounted in value to upward of five and three quarter millions of dollars, of which the State of New York produced upward of one and a quarter millions in three hundred and thirty-three establishments. In the Western States the increase was quite extraordinary, their product amounting to $8,707,194, or nearly one half of the total value made in the Union. The increment in this section alone was nearly equal to the total value manufactured in the United States in 1850, and was in the ratio of 352.5 per cent. The States of Ohio and Illinois together produced a greater value than any other two States of the Union, the increase in them being 405.5 and 212.2 per cent. respectively. A single county in Ohio (Stark) from fifteen factories turned out a value of $904,480, of which $399,000 was the value of mowers and reapers made by one establishment; while another establishment in Chicago made 4,131 reapers and mowers, worth $414,000. The value reported from the Southern States was a little over one million, exclusive of cotton-gins, an increase of nearly thirty per cent., though several States decreased their production of agricultural implements.

If to the foregoing be added the sum of $2,191,629 as the value of shovels, spades, forks, hoes, and scythes, made chiefly in New England and the Middle States, and $1,152,315 as the value of cotton-gins, made principally in the Southern States, we have an aggregate of $20,831,904 as the annual value of implements and machinery manufactured for the agricultural classes, exclusive of wagons, carts, wheelbarrows, and various articles of hardware, cutlery, etc., not included in the branches enumerated.

Iron and its Manufactures.—The amount of Iron Ore mined in the United States in 1860 was 3,218,275 tons, valued at $2,182,667, an increased value of seventy-nine per cent. in ten years. Ninety-seven bloomary forges made 51,290 tons of blooms, valued at $2,623,178, an average of $51.14 per ton; upward of one half being the product of fifty-seven forges in Pennsylvania.

The quantity of Pig-Iron made in two hundred and eighty-six furnaces, from 2,309,975 tons of ore, was 987,559 tons, valued at $20,870,120, or $21.13 per ton; showing an increase in the total value of fifty-four per cent. over the product in 1850. This branch of the iron manufacture employed a capital of upward of twenty-four and three quarter millions, and nearly sixteen thousand persons. Of the total product, four of the Middle States returned more than fourteen and a half millions in value, and Pennsylvania alone upward of eleven and a quarter millions, or more than one half of the total yield of pig-iron. The Western States made returns of nearly four and a half millions' worth of pig-iron, of which Ohio produced over two and a half millions' worth, being the second in the Union in the extent of its iron business. In most of the Western States the increase was large, but in all but one of the Southern a decrease was found. In the manufacture of Bar, Sheet, and Railroad Iron, two hundred and fifty-six establishments, employing a capital of nearly twenty millions of dollars, and upward of nineteen thousand hands, produced from 656,803 tons of blooms, pig, and other iron ore, 509,084 tons of iron, worth $31,888,705, which was an increase of about one hundred per cent. Of the total amount, 227,682 tons were bar-iron and 235,107 railway iron ; the balance being boiler and nail, plate, sheet, and other articles, as nails, spikes, rivets, anchors, machinery, etc. The average price was $62.11 per ton. In this, as in other branches of the iron manufacture, Pennsylvania was the largest producer, having made 266,253 tons, valued at upward of fifteen millions of dollars, or one hundred and six per cent. more than in 1850. Ohio was the next in the value of rolled iron, and augmented her manufacture one hundred and seventy-three per cent. ; while Massachusetts, which produced a somewhat greater number of tons, showed an increase of two hundred and seventy-seven per cent. on the product of 1850. Maine, Delaware, all showed a large percentage of increase, while Michigan and Illinois, which returned none in 1850, each produced upward of half a millions' worth. Sixteen wire mills returned a value of upward of one and a half million dollars, and fifty-six iron forging establishments, including twelve anchor works, eleven axle shops, and one iron shafting factory, returned somewhat less than two millions as the value of forged work. Seventeen car wheel factories, chiefly in the Middle States, reported an aggregate of more than two million dollars' worth of car wheels made, Pennsylvania and Delaware producing upward of one half of the whole.

Iron Castings of all kinds were manufactured in fourteen hundred and twelve establishments, to the annual value of $36,132,033, whereof twenty millions was the value of castings of a general character, made by nine hundred and fifty-five establishments, chiefly in the Middle and Western States, and giving employment to upward of fifteen thousand hands. The product of these foundries, more than one half of which was made in the United States, was nearly equal to the total value made in 1850. No less than two hundred and ninety stove and hollow-ware foundries were reported, producing an annual value of $10,700,000. The balance of the product consisted of hot-air furnaces, ranges, etc., car wheels, iron railing, and malleable iron castings, the last branch employing twenty-six foundries, producing a value of $930,800.

The manufacture of Machinery, Steam Engines, etc., exclusive of various kinds of special machinery, employed eleven hundred and seventy-three establishments, with a total capital of thirty-three and a quarter millions of dollars and upward of thirty-seven thousand persons, the product of whose labor was a value of forty-six and a half millions of dollars, an increase of sixty-six and a half per centum. The manufacture of cotton, woollen, paper, and other special machinery, including machinists' tools, engaged two hundred and twenty-six establishments, producing an annual value of five and three quarter millions.

Nineteen Locomotive Shops, built in the year about four hundred and seventy engines, valued at nearly five millions of dollars, more than three fifths of which was the product of six factories in New Jersey and Pennsylvania.

Sewing Machines, of which there were few manufactories in 1850, were made in seventy-four establishments to the number of 111,263, of which the value was four and a quarter millions, the larger part being in Massachusetts, Connecticut, and New York; although they were produced to some extent in twelve States.

Fire-arms to the value of upward of two and a quarter millions were made by two hundred and sixty-nine establishments, nine of which, in the State of Connecticut, turned out more than one half the total value. The Hardware factories numbered four hundred and forty-three, scattered throughout nineteen States. They employed upward of ten thousand hands, and the value of the manufacture was nearly eleven millions, an increase of 56.7 per cent. in ten years. Of the total product, upward of seven and a quarter millions was the value made by two hundred and four establishments in New England, and over three and a quarter by two hundred and nine in the Middle States.

The number of Steel furnaces was thirteen. They manufactured 11,838 tons of steel, valued at $1,778,240, of which sum $1,358,200 was the product of nine furnaces in Pennsylvania, which made 9,890 tons. The total product was tenfold the value made in 1850, and the average value returned was $150 per ton.

The various manufactures of Steel, such as cutlery, axes, and other edge tools, carpenters' and other mechanics' tools, springs, saws, steel wire, etc., together gave employment to three hundred and eighty-two manufactories, upward of five and three quarter millions of capital, and more than seven thousand hands, the value of whose product was upward of nine millions annually. Cutlery, axes, artisans' tools, car and carriage springs, and wire, were principally made in New England, and saws, in New York and Pennsylvania. The value of nails and spikes made by ninety-nine factories, was upward of nine and three quarter millions, an increase of 28.6 per cent. Forty-four nail works in two New England States produced upward of three and one half millions —thirty-eight in four Middle States, nearly four and one half millions; and one in Virginia, nearly one and one quarter millions in value.

The value of bolts, nuts, washers, rivets, etc., made in fifty-four establishments, was upward of two millions; and of scales and balances in twenty-two manufactories upward of $359,000.

Including upward of sixteen millions as the annual value of blacksmithing done, the several branches of the iron manufacture above enumerated make an aggregate annual product of nearly *two hundred and six millions of dollars*, which was exclusive of the value of iron work employed in the manufacture of Agricultural Implements, and in various other ways not included in the foregoing.

This large aggregate of the production and ultimate manufactures of a single raw material, constituting the basis of nearly every other form of productive industry, is at once an indication of marvellous progress in the past, and of almost unlimited possibilities in the future. The average product of blooms and pig-iron made from the ore was nearly seventy-four pounds per capita for each one of the total population, and the value of bar and other rolled iron made, averaged about one dollar each; while the average per capita of the total product of iron and its manufactures, was upward of six and a half dollars each. In view of the wide diffusion, exhaustless abundance, and cheapness of iron ores, coal, and other fuel of the best quality, of water power, and of improved mechanism and processes already in use and being constantly introduced, and of the wide circle of important interests to which it is intimately related, the judicious encouragement of this branch of national industry would appear to be in the highest degree desirable, and the early independence of the country by no means improbable. The rapid development of the iron manufacture in several of the Western States, taken in connexion with the vast deposits of rich ore in Ohio, Western Virginia, Kentucky, Tennessee, Missouri, and the Lake Superior region of Michigan, Illinois, and Wisconsin, is a subject of the profoundest interest to the increasing population of the great grain-growing regions of the West, to whom a market is thus opened at their doors for their surplus crops, now burthened with the cost of transportation thousands of miles to the distant and uncertain markets of Europe. Their lands, whether agricultural or mineral, are at the same time enhanced in value by the establishment in their midst of mines, furnaces, forges, rolling-mills, and foundries, of locomotive and machine shops, and other factories that follow in the track of this great agent of civilization and progress; while the cost of hardware, implements, and machinery, is cheapened, and the number of railroads, bridges, canals, and other improvements increased.

COAL.—With the subject of Iron and its manufactures, that of fossil fuel naturally associates itself. The unequalled wealth, and the rapid development of the coal fields of the United States, as a dynamic element in our industrial progress, affords one of the most striking evidences of our recent advance. The product of all the coal mines of the United States, in 1850, was valued at $7,173,750, which was the yield of five hundred and ten mining establishments in twelve States, of which upward of seventy-three per cent. represented the value of the Anthracite trade of Pennsylvania. In 1860, returns were made by six hundred and twenty-two establishments in sixteen States, which employed upward of thirty-six thousand persons, and produced 6,218,080 tons of bituminous and 8,115,842 tons of anthracite coal, valued at $20,243,637, showing the increase to have been in the ratio of one hundred and eighty-two per cent. over the yield in 1850. The increase of capital devoted to coal mining was in the same time two hundred and fifty-three per centum, the increment alone amounting to upward of twenty-one millions. The average cost of bituminous coal at the mines was $1.34, and of anthracite, $1.46 per ton. All but one thousand tons of the Anthracite and 2,690,786 tons of bituminous coal were returned by Pennsylvania, which contained three hundred and ten mining establishments, and increased its product about one hundred and eighty per cent. Ohio and Illinois ranked next in the value of coal mined.

A similar development took place between 1850 and 1860 in the mining of gold, silver, mercury, copper, lead, zinc, chromium, and other metallic and mineral treasures, which were the repositories of crude materials for an immense and varied industry in the metallurgic and chemical arts. The production of the first two—which, as the mediums of exchange, also became the quickeners of foreign commerce—was principally confined to California, producing a corresponding decrease in the yield of the Atlantic States, and doubtless checking, in some degree, the mining of coal and of the baser metals in the latter region.

PETROLEUM.—An important development of the natural resources of the country, and a valuable addition to its exports, was made in the last two or three years of this decade, by the discovery that certain indications—known to the aboriginal and early European inhabitants of the Western country—of inflammable oil existing upon the head waters of the Alleghany river, in New York and Pennsylvania, and somewhat later, in Ohio and Western Virginia, were but the clue to apparently inexhaustible supplies of native oil, accessible at no great depth throughout an extended belt of country, embracing the bituminous coal measures of several States.

This remarkable substance has long been known and collected from natural oil fountains and borings in Burmah and other parts of Asia. As a product of our own country, it was brought to the notice of the white population as early as the middle of the last century, by the Seneca Indians, who found it upon Oil creek, a branch of the Alleghany, in Venango county, Pennsylvania, and near the head of the Genesee river, in New York, whence it received the names of "Seneca oil" and "Genesee oil." It was used by the natives in their religious ceremonies, and as a medicament for wounds, bruises, etc. For the last named purpose it has long been collected, and sold in small quantities at a high price, and has entered into the composition of several popular lotions for rheumatism, etc. But its existence in any vast amount appears to have been unknown until 1845, when oil was obtained while boring for salt near Tarentum, thirty-five miles above Pittsburgh, on the Alleghany, where two springs continued for some years to yield small quantities, sometimes a barrel a day. Experiments having proved its constituents to be nearly the same as those of oil obtained by the destructive distillation of coal, the Upper Spring and mineral rights were purchased, in 1854, by parties in New York, where companies were also formed to search for oil, and also to attempt its purification by the same process applied to the artificial oils. But little was effected until 1857, when Messrs. Bowditch and Drake, of New Haven, commenced operations at Titusville, on Oil creek. In August, 1859, they reached, by boring, at the depth of seventy-one feet, a fountain, which, with a small pump, yielded four hundred, and, with a larger one, one thousand gallons daily. Before the close of the year 1860, the number of wells and borings was estimated to be about two thousand, of which seventy-four of the larger ones were producing daily, by the aid of pumps, an aggregate of eleven hundred and sixty-five barrels of crude Petroleum, worth, at twenty cents a gallon, about $10,000. Wells were soon after sunk to the depth of five hundred or six hundred feet, and the flow of Petroleum became so profuse that no less than three thousand barrels were obtained in a day from a single well; the less productive ones yielding from fifteen to twenty barrels per diem. In several instances, extraordinary means were found necessary to check and control the flow, which has since been regulated by strong tubing and stopcocks. The quantity sent to market by one railroad from the Pennsylvania oil region increased from three hundred and twenty-five barrels, in 1859, to one hundred and thirty-four thousand nine hundred and twenty-seven barrels in 1861, in which year the whole quantity shipped was nearly half a million barrels. The product has since rapidly increased. Previous to May, 1862, at least twenty-five establishments for refining Petroleum had been built or converted to that use from manufactories of coal oil. The subsequent growth of the Petroleum trade, which has its ramifications in nearly every Western State, including those on the Pacific, is one of the marvels of the century. As an article of export, and as a raw material in a multiplicity of uses in the arts, the abundance of this native hydrocarbon renders it one of the most valuable of the natural resources of the country.

COTTON MANUFACTURES.—Among the great branches of pure manufacture in the United States next to that of Iron in its collective values, that of Cotton Goods holds the first rank, both in respect to the value of the product and the amount of capital employed. Aided by the possession of the raw material as a product of our own soil, and by the enterprise and ingenuity of the people, this industry has grown with a rapidity almost unrivalled. Its annual product in 1860, was about one sixteenth of the aggregate of all branches of industry, including the large items of flour and meal, sawed and planed lumber, the fisheries, coal, and the baser metals. It was an established industry in twenty-nine States of the Union.

The aggregate value of Cotton Goods manufactured in the year ending June 30, 1860, by one thousand and ninety-one establishments was $115,681,774, which was upward of fifty millions of dollars in excess of the value returned in 1850, or an increase of 76.6 per cent. The aggregate capital invested was ninety-eight and a half millions of dollars, and upward of one hundred and twenty thousand persons, of whom more than seventy-five thousand were females, were employed in the business. The number of spindles reported was 5,235,727, and of looms, 126,313. The total weight of cotton consumed was 422,704,975 pounds. The number of yards of sheetings, shirtings, and other cloths made—including 271,857,000 yards of print cloths—was 1,148,252,406. The manufactures, in addition, embraced 47,241,603 pounds of yarn, nearly thirteen million pounds of batting, and a large amount of cotton cordage, seamless bags, quilts, coverlets, table-cloths, netting, etc., etc. The average value of cotton goods, per capita, for the whole population was $3.60, and the average quantity of cloth, per capita, was thirty-six and one fourth yards.

The principal increase took place in the New England and Middle States. In the former, five hundred and seventy establishments produced a value of $79,359,900, an increase of 81.24 per cent.; and three hundred and forty establishments in the Middle States reported a value of $26,534,700, the increase being 79.52 per cent. In the Southern States, the total value of Cotton Goods made by one hundred and fifty-nine establishments was $8,145,067; and twenty-two factories in the Western States reported a value of $1,642,107, an increase in the former of 43.70 and in the latter of twenty-nine per cent. The largest production in any one State was in Massachusetts, where two hundred and seventeen factories reported a value of upward of thirty-eight millions. New Hampshire with forty-four, and Pennsylvania with one hundred and eighty-five establishments, were the next in extent, each having turned out a value of over thirteen and a half millions of dollars, in the rates respectively of 54.59 and 134.80 per cent. increase. Rhode Island, with one hundred and fifty-three establishments, exceeded twelve millions of dollars, an increase of eighty-seven per cent. Illinois, Louisiana, Texas, and Utah, which made no returns in 1850, reported an aggregate of over half a million dollars, chiefly produced in Louisiana.

WOOLLEN MANUFACTURES.—Returns were made, in 1860, from twelve hundred and sixty establishments, producing woollen goods (exclusive of worsted fabrics) to the value of $61,895,217; an increase of about forty-two per cent. in ten years. The sets of machinery employed was about 3,209, and the number of hands 41,360, of whom 16,519 were females. The capital invested was nearly thirty-one millions of dollars. The quantity of wool consumed was 83,608,468 pounds; and of cotton, 15,200,061 pounds; from which were manufactured 124,897,862 yards of cloth, 6,401,206 pounds of yarn, 296,874 pairs of blankets, 616,400 long and square shawls, besides table covers, felted cloths, coverlets, etc. The cloths made included satinets, Kentucky jeans, and other cotton warp fabrics usually classed as woollens; and the total quantity was equivalent to nearly four yards to each person in the United States.

The principal seat of the woollen manufacture is in New England, where three hundred and ninety-eight establishments, many of them of large size, employ upward of 25,000 persons, 1,664 sets of machinery, and an aggregate capital of eighteen and three quarter millions; producing woollens of the value of $40,668,498, or sixty-two per cent.

more than in 1850, and within less than three millions of the total product of all the States in that year. The quantity of cloth made, exclusive of yarn, blankets, shawls, coverlets, etc., was upward of eighty and a quarter million yards. Nearly thirty-five million yards of cloth, and one third of all the yarn made in the Union, was the product of one hundred and thirty-four establishments in Massachusetts, having 821 sets of cards, and making an annual value of $19,655,787—an increase of fifty-three per cent. Rhode Island and Connecticut each produced between six and seven millions' worth of woollens, the increase of the former being one hundred and seventy-six per cent., and in the latter nearly thirty-nine per cent. The Middle States, with 476 mills and 920 sets of cards, produced a total value of $15,905,923, of which upward of eight millions was returned for Pennsylvania, from 483 sets of machinery, and less than five millions, from 324 sets of machinery, in the State of New York. In the former State there was an increase of 45.5 per cent.; but the latter showed a decline in the value of woollens made. The Middle States returned more yarn and shawls than New England, but less than half the quantity of cloth. From the Western States, returns were made of 466 sets of cards, and a total value of upward of three millions; and 149 sets of machinery in the Southern States made a value of nearly two millions of woollens. Two factories, with ten sets of cards, in Oregon and California, produced a value of $235,000.

Wool Carding and Fulling employed seven hundred and twelve establishments, converting five and a quarter million pounds of wool into nearly as many pounds of rolls, valued at $2,403,512.

The woollen manufacture, like that of cotton, is one of vast importance to the whole country, and particularly to the agriculturist, who furnishes the raw material. It derives increased importance from the character of the climate, which renders woollen clothing necessary throughout a large part of the Union during much of the year, and from the fact that the home market is always the most valuable to the producer. Although sheep husbandry was much extended and improved between 1850 and 1860, particularly in Ohio, Texas, California, and other States, the wool clip of the latter year, amounting to sixty and a half million pounds, fell far short of the consumption—which could probably be supplied by our own wool-growers, under a protective system in harmony with the interests of producer and consumer.

Worsted Goods were made by two factories in Connecticut, and one in Massachusetts, employing 110 sets of cards, and making 22,750,000 yards of delaines, cashmeres, etc., valued at $3,701,378.

Linen Goods.—The manufacture of Linen goods has made but little progress in this country. As a household industry, the manufacture of flax is less extensive than formerly, its use having been in a great measure superseded by that of cotton. Three mills in Massachusetts, and seven in New York, together consumed, in 1860, nine hundred and ninety-eight tons of flax and hemp, etc., and turned out linen fabrics of the value of $699,570, of which the Massachusetts mills converted six hundred and ninety-five tons of flax, hemp, and cotton into 6,200,000 yards of crash, toweling, and other fabrics, valued at $515,000, in addition to some twine and shoe thread. The largest establishment was that of the American Linen Company, at Fall River, which ran four thousand spindles and two hundred looms, by steam power, making four million yards of crash, etc.

The production of flax fibre in the United States fell off between 1850 and 1860 in all but two States, but has probably increased since the commencement of the war, which has recalled attention to the various chemical and mechanical methods of adapting the flax stock to the use of automatic machinery, after the manner of cotton. On account of the limited demand, much of the flax fibre grown in the Western States for the sake of the seed, has been thrown away as valueless; but experiments now in progress give encouraging prospects that it will ere long be spun and woven as cheaply as cotton.

Silk.—This material is principally manufactured into sewing silk, twist, silk fringes, coach lace, and other trimmings, and employed altogether in 1860 about one hundred and thirty-nine establishments, producing a total value of upward of six and a half millions of dollars. Including tram, organzine, etc., the value of sewings made by forty-two establishments, in three New England and three Middle States, was three and a half millions, and the quantity made was 409,429 pounds, of which Connecticut made 145,135 pounds. Ladies' dress trimmings, fringes, etc., employed ninety factories, chiefly in the cities of New York and Philadelphia, producing $2,804,392; and six coach lace factories made a value of $89,200. Dress silks, ribbons, and other woven fabrics, were made to a limited extent by one or two establishments.

Carpets.—The manufacture of Carpets was increased in the last ten years about 45.4 per cent. The returns showed a production, by two hundred and thirteen establishments, of upward of thirteen and a quarter million yards, of the total value of $7,857,636; of which Pennsylvania produced $2,710,092, and Massachusetts $2,358,278.

Mens' Clothing.—Including one manufactory of seamless garments in the State of New York, the number of establishments making Ready-made Clothing was 3,794, employing a capital of nearly twenty-five millions, and almost one hundred thousand persons. The value of the manufacture exceeded seventy-three and a half millions, and the increase in ten years was fifty-one and a half per cent. This was exclusive of shirts, collars, and gentlemens' furnishing goods, made in two hundred and nineteen establishments, to the value of $7,218,790—making a total of $80,850,555, as the value of mens' clothing manufactured in 1860. The total value manufactured in the Middle States alone was $50,713,785.

LADIES' CLOTHING, including cloaks and mantillas, corsets and hoop-skirts, etc., employed one hundred and eighty-eight establishments, producing a total value of upward of seven millions annually, of which upward of four and three quarter millions was the value of hoop-skirts made—a branch of the ladies' clothing business which, like that of cloaks and mantillas, has had its principal growth within the last ten years. In this department, as well as in that of mens' clothing, the great agency which has revolutionized the business, is the Sewing-Machine, which has also been mainly introduced and improved within that period. It has created, in a great measure, the wholesale and retail trade in ready-made clothing, previously of very limited aggregate value, though employing a vast number of ill-requited female hands. So extensively is it now used in the manufacture of shirts and collars, that the value of these articles made in the city of Troy, New York, in 1860, amounted to nearly $800,000, approximating in value the product of the numerous and extensive iron foundries which have been a source of wealth to that city.

If, to the foregoing branches of the clothing trade, we add $4,543,284 as the product of nine hundred and forty milliners' establishments, $1,483,154 for millinery goods made, $1,053,600 for artificial flowers, $429,554 for ruches, bonnet-frames, and other miscellaneous millinery goods, $4,499,616 for straw goods, and $760,287 for palm-leaf hats, we have a total value of ladies' clothing, millinery, and straw goods, annually produced, of nearly twenty millions; and of mens' and womens' clothing together, a value exceeding one hundred millions annually.

HOSIERY.—The value of cotton and woollen hosiery made in regular factories—of which there were one hundred and ninety-seven in 1860—was $7,280,606, an increase of 608 per cent., largely due to the introduction of improved knitting machinery.

Including between one and two millions' worth of hemp bagging made, the value of the several textile branches enumerated, namely, cotton, wool, worsted, linen, and silk goods of mens' and womens' clothing and furnishing goods, hosiery, etc., amount to upward of two hundred and ninety-five millions of dollars.

PAPER.—The annual production of Paper in the United States exceeds that of either Great Britain or France, and the total consumption is greater than that of both together. The number of paper-mills returned, from twenty-four States, was five hundred and fifty-five, representing an aggregate capital of $14,052,683, and employing nearly ten thousand persons. They manufactured 131,508,000 pounds of printing paper; 22,268,000 pounds of writing paper; 33,379 tons of wrapping, in addition to colored, and bank-note papers, straw board wall paper, etc.; making a total weight of 253,778,240 pounds, valued at $21,216,802, which was an increase of 108.2 per cent. upon the product of the same branch in 1850. Of the total value, the New England States returned $10,502,069, which was more than the whole Union produced in 1850. The State of Massachusetts reported a value of $6,170,127, and the five Middle States $7,908,437, the State of New York having produced about half as much as Massachusetts. The value of Paper Hangings made, in addition to the foregoing, by twenty-six establishments, in five States, was $2,148,800, of which New York returned upward of one half.

PRINTING.—The increase of printing-presses in the Book and Newspaper manufacture, has been great beyond all precedent, and has exerted a most beneficent influence upon the social, moral, and industrial progress of the country, by multiplying and cheapening the vehicles of instruction, and quickening the intellect of the people. Its effects have been everywhere apparent. Never did an army before possess so much of cultivated intellect, or demand such contributions for its mental food, as that lately marshalled in its country's defence. Many of these reading soldiers formed their intellectual tastes during the ten years embraced in this review. In fact, many divisions of the army carried the printing-press along with them, on which the soldiers who filled most of the clerical offices at the several headquarters, issued publications, and printed the forms of official papers. The press is, indeed, the great prompter of enterprise. It has constantly travelled with the emigrant, to diffuse light and intelligence from the remotest frontiers, where it speedily calls into existence the paper-mill, and all the accessories which it supports in older communities.

The book, job, and newspaper establishments reported from thirty-six States and Territories, in 1860, numbered one thousand six hundred and sixty-six. Their total capital exceeeded nineteen and a half millions, and the value of printing executed was $31,063,898, an increase of 168 per cent. Of the total value, six Middle States produced $20,260,906, and the New England and western sections each about four and a half millions' worth.

Lithographic Printing was executed by fifty-three establishments, to the value of $848,230; and *Engraving* to nearly an equal amount, by one hundred and ninety-one establishments.

Book Binding, and the Blank Book Manufacture, employed two hundred and sixty-nine concerns, producing a total value of $3,729,080, of which upward of two and three quarter millions belonged to the Middle States.

The value of the manufacture of Printing-Presses, of Type Founding, Stereotyping, and Electrotyping, together, amounted to $2,531,320; making the total value of printing, and its allied branches, exclusive of paper making, to exceed thirty-nine millions of dollars.

LEATHER, AND MANUFACTURES THEREOF.—The manufacture of Leather is one of the leading interests of the country. It is one of importance to the farmer and stock raiser, as well as to the foreign commerce of the country, because it consumes all the material supplied by the former, and about four million dollars' worth, annually, of foreign hides and skins. The product of six thousand five hundred and twenty-eight tanning and currying establishments in the United States, in 1850, was valued at $37,702,333. The value of sole and upper leather, manufactured, in 1860, by five thousand and forty establishments, was $67,306,452, exclusive of morocco leather, made to the value of $5,920,773, and of $2,101,250 worth of patent and enamelled leather—which, with $380,272 worth of dressed skins, made a total value of $75,598,747; an increase of over 100 per cent. in ten years. Nearly forty-four millions of the total product was returned from the Middle States, which manufactured the larger part of the morocco and patent leather, and upward of thirty-seven and a half millions' worth of other leather—a value nearly equal to that produced by all the States in 1850. The value of common and morocco leather made in New York alone, exceeded twenty-two millions, and in Pennsylvania amounted to nearly fifteen millions. In New England it fell a little short of nineteen millions.

BOOTS AND SHOES.—The manufacture of Boots and Shoes employs a larger number of persons than any other single branch of American industry, not excepting the cotton manufacture. The total number of hands employed in 1860 was 123,026; of whom 28,514, or nearly one fourth, were females. The amount of capital employed in this branch of manufacture was over twenty-three and a quarter millions; and the value of boots and shoes made in 12,487 establishments, was $91,891,498; an increase of $37,924,098, or upward of seventy per cent. on the value of the same branch in 1850. The value made in New England alone, by 2,439 establishments, employing a capital of nearly eleven millions, and 74,292 persons, was $54,818,148; an increase of eighty-three per cent., and upward of three quarters of a million in excess of the total product in 1850. Of that value, forty-six and a quarter millions was returned by 1,354 establishments in Massachusetts, in which State the increase was in the ratio of 91.8 per cent. In Essex county alone the product was fourteen and a half millions, and Worcester and Plymouth counties produced, respectively, nine and a half and nine and a quarter millions' worth of boots and shoes. The city of Lynn produced a value of four and three quarter millions, and Haverhill four millions in value. The six Middle States contained 5,412 boot and shoe establishments, and produced the value of $22,976,783; an increase of 36.9 per cent. The States of New York and Pennsylvania, respectively produced boots and shoes to the value of $10,925,173 and $8,474,127 ; an increase in the former of 40.5, and in the latter of fifty per cent. The city of Philadelphia alone produced the value of $5,472,587, which was the largest amount manufactured in any one place. The city of New York reported a value of $3,750,000. The manufactures of these two cities embrace a finer quality of boots and shoes; and the annual wholesale and retail sales in New York amount to about twenty millions, and in Philadelphia to fifteen millions. In the Western States, the value of this manufacture amounted to upward of nine and three quarter millions, of which three and a half millions was the product of Ohio; and in the Southern States, to nearly four millions; the Pacific States producing about a quarter million worth annually.

Including Saddlery and Harness, made to the value of $14,169,037; leather Belting and Hose, to the amount of $1,481,750; Trunks and Carpet Bags, worth $2,836; Pocket-Books and Portemonnaies, Cap Fronts, Whips, Buckskin Gloves, etc., the total value of leather and its various manufactures, produced in 1860, was not less than one hundred and eighty-eight millions of dollars. During the recent rebellion, the requirements of the government stimulated the manufacture, especially of saddlery and harness, to a remarkable degree.

Manufactures of Wood.—Exclusive of Ship and Boat Building, which, including masts, spars, blocks, etc., amounted to upward of twelve millions of dollars; of carpenters' work, done to about the same amount; of agricultural machinery, coach, carriage, and car building, and other branches into which wood entered as a principal material; the total value of manufactures of Wood, in 1860, was not far from one hundred and sixty millions of dollars.

Of Cabinet Ware, school, and other furniture, the value manufactured was $25,632,293—an increase of about forty per cent. Of that value the New England States produced about five and three quarter millions; the Middle States upward of eleven; and the Western States three and a quarter millions. This was exclusive of a value of $1,021,700 in veneers made in that year.

The value of Sawed Lumber made was $93,338,606; of Planed Lumber, $11,589,736; of sash, doors, and blinds, $9,589,007; of turning, scroll sawing, mouldings, etc., $2,084,325; of packing and other boxes, $2,971,917; of shingles, laths, etc., $1,665,507; of spokes and felloes, etc., $2,213,849; of wooden ware, $2,108,656; of staves, hoops, shooks, etc., $1,713,743.

Of Carriages and *Coaches*, including childrens', the value made was $27,223,255; and of wagons and carts, $8,703,937; and silver ware to the value of $3,571,654.

Musical Instruments.—Our advance in wealth and refinement is attested by the rapid increase in the manufacture of Piano-fortes, and other musical instruments. The total value of these made, in 1860, by two hundred and twenty-three establishments, in nineteen States, was $6,548,432—an increase of 153.3 per cent. It included 21,797 Pianos, made in one hundred and ten establishments, and valued at $5,260,907; of two hundred and forty-five church Organs, made by twenty manufactories, and valued at $824,750; of 12,643 melodeons and harmoniums, made by forty manufactories, to the value of $646,975; and miscellaneous instruments, as æolians, calliopes, accordeons, dulcimers, violins and violincellos, harps, guitars, banjos, flutes, drums, brass and silver instruments, etc., which employed fifty-three establishments, making a value of $315,800. New York State produced upward of half the total value, and Massachusetts was next in value—the increase in the two being 216 and 110 per cent. respectively.

In the quality of the wood grown in the United States, as well as in the dryness of the climate, the American Piano-forte and organ builders possess advantages over the European manufacturers; and on this and other accounts, many of their instruments are acknowledged to be equal to the best of foreign make, and better adapted to the climate.

Distilled and Malt Liquors, etc.—The manufacture of Distilled Liquors, exclusive of alcohol, employed eleven hundred and ninety-three establishments, with a capital of over eleven and a half millions of dollars, and producing annually a value of $26,768,225—an increase of sixty-nine per cent. Malt Liquors were made by twelve hundred and sixty-nine establishments, having a total capital of upward of fifteen and three quarter millions, with a product valued at $21,310,933. The value of Rectified Spirits, returned by two hundred and thirty-two factories, was $7,994,707; of Alcohol, made by twenty-two manufacturers, $4,168,360; of wine, by thirty-two vintners, $400,791; of bottled liquors, $82,610; and of cordials, $30,900—making the total value of spirituous and other liquors, $60,756,526. More than ninety per cent. of all the spirits made was from materials of domestic production, the larger part of the high wines, whisky, and alcohol, being the product of the grain-growing States, Middle and Western; a much smaller amount of New England rum having been made from imported molasses. The manufacture of malt liquors, though of less magnitude, and far less pernicious in its effects, showed a still larger increase, the ratio being 272 per cent. It derives its materials, also, wholly from agriculture—and its extension, therefore, promises more substantial benefits to the country.

Soap and Candles.—These articles employed six hundred and fourteen establishments, producing an aggregate value of $18,464,574, which was exclusive of $1,145,000 worth of adamantine, and $1,800 worth of wax candles, and of fancy soaps, included with perfumery. The increase was eighty-one per cent. on the product in 1850.

Flour and Meal.—This large industry employed 13,868 establishments, and a capital of eighty-four and a half millions; and the value of the product reached the large sum of $248,580,365—of which $82,783,553 was reported from the Middle States, and $108,307,222 from the Western States. The total increase was upward of one hundred and twelve and a half millions in value, and was in the ratio of eighty-two per cent. The value of Bread and Crackers made for sale was $16,980,012.

Sugar Refining was a branch in which a large increase was apparent, the value having been augmented from $9,898,800 in 1850, to

$42,143,234 in 1860, or at the rate of 325 per cent. The larger part of the product was returned from the Middle States, New York alone having reported a value of upward of twenty-three millions.

TOBACCO AND SNUFF employed six hundred and twenty-six establishments, the value of whose manufactures was $21,820,535; and fourteen hundred and seventy-eight Cigar manufacturers reported a product of $9,068,778.

MARBLE AND STONE WORK was produced by eighteen hundred and six establishments, to the value of $16,244,044 annually.

The following Table exhibits the statistics of those branches of Manufactures which, according to the census returns of 1860, yielded an annual product exceeding a million of dollars.

	No. of Establishments.	Capital Invested.	Hands Employed. Males.	Hands Employed. Females.	Value of Product.
Agricultural Implements	1,982	$11,477,239	14,810	4	$17,487,960
Alcohol	22	897,000	208	......	4,168,360
Bagging	34	505,250	661	126	1,109,628
Blacksmithing	7,504	4,940,756	15,719	1	11,641,243
Bolts, Nuts, Washers	54	1,235,300	1,492	12	2,175,535
Bookbinding and Blank Books	269	1,654,830	2,045	2,732	3,729,080
Boots and Shoes	12,486	23,357,627	94,512	28,514	91,889,298
Boxes, Packing	270	1,057,840	1,595	9	2,516,174
" Paper	110	333,196	511	1,090	1,162,777
Brass and German Silver	11	2,086,000	909	36	2,401,600
Brass Founding	183	1,226,460	1,492	......	2,643,754
Bread and Crackers	1,930	3,909,189	6,176	338	16,980,012
Brick	1,595	7,130,128	20,046	410	10,253,734
Brooms	228	505,713	1,144	40	1,428,194
Brushes	121	913,630	1,675	703	2,096,583
Calico Printing	22	3,397,250	3,330	564	7,748,644
Camphene and Burning Fluid	33	505,400	174	......	2,810,960
Candles, Adamantine	5	695,000	181	34	1,145,000
Carpentering	1,323	3,251,327	8,998	8	12,646,392
Carpets	216	4,721,938	3,912	2,771	7,860,351
Carriages	3,917	14,131,537	27,304	157	26,848,905
Cars and Omnibuses	62	2,953,717	3,172	7	4,302,613
Car Wheels	16	1,223,700	523	......	1,996,350
Chemicals	84	3,276,800	1,467	62	4,705,741
Cigars	1,478	3,035,555	7,266	731	9,068,778
Clocks	22	576,100	935	40	1,187,550
Clothing, Ladies'	188	1,421,650	889	4,850	7,181,039
Clothing, Men's	4,014	27,246,093	41,837	72,963	80,830,555
Coffee and Spices	85	1,002,150	487	23	3,502,181
Coffins	210	605,950	671	17	1,024,953
Combs	66	721,700	800	130	1,314,968
Confectionery	541	1,568,478	1,875	465	5,361,100
Cooperage	2,707	4,353,546	13,741	9	11,343,221
Copper Mining	47	8,525,500	5,111	42	3,361,222
Copper Rolling and Smelting	17	5,005,000	885	......	8,144,128

	No. of Establishments.	Capital Invested.	Hands Employed. Males.	Females.	Value of Product.
Coppersmithing	70	$587,550	592	......	$1,281,262
Cordage	190	2,938,289	2,860	618	7,843,339
Cotton Goods	1,091	98,585,269	46,859	75,169	115,681,774
Cutlery	51	869,800	1,305	33	1,366,225
Dyeing and Bleaching	102	2,321,421	2,755	448	3,967,819
Dye Woods and Dye Stuffs	15	732,950	360	4	1,484,191
Edge Tools and Axes	166	2,146,499	2,869	......	3,243,992
Fire-Arms	239	2,512,781	1,986	70	2,362,681
Flour and Meal	13,868	84,585,004	27,626	56	248,580,365
Furniture, Cabinet, etc.	3,594	13,629,526	25,132	1,974	25,632,293
Furs	95	1,163,600	496	797	3,115,755
Gas Fixtures, Lamps, and Chandeliers	33	1,310,850	1,628	4	2,255,900
Glass	112	6,133,666	8,765	251	8,775,155
Gloves and Mittens	126	594,825	453	976	1,176,795
Glue	62	1,052,900	865	10	1,185,625
Gold and Silver Assaying and Refining	13	755,300	223	51	1,140,070
Gunpowder	58	2,305,700	737	10	3,223,090
Hardware	443	6,707,000	9,458	1,263	10,903,106
Hats and Caps	655	4,154,372	7,521	4,243	16,937,782
Hosiery	197	4,035,510	2,780	6,323	7,280,606
India Rubber Goods	27	3,534,000	1,795	973	5,642,700
Iron, Cast (of all kinds)	1,405	24,368,243	26,940	21	36,638,073
" Forged, Rolled and Wrought.	402	23,343,073	21,962	52	36,537,259
" Pig	286	24,672,824	15,854	73	20,870,120
Jewelry	463	5,180,723	5,363	584	10,415,811
Leather and Skins	5,188	39,025,620	25,858	388	75,698,747
Liquors, Distilled	1,193	11,548,675	5,405	11	26,768,225
" Malt	1,269	15,782,342	6,412	21	21,310,933
Locomotives, etc	19	3,482,592	4,174	......	4,866,900
Looking-Glass & Picture Frames.	199	1,008,383	1,884	12	2,854,132
Lumber, Planed	466	4,138,996	3,715	2	11,589,736
" Sawed	19,699	72,503,894	71,207	671	93,338,606
Machinery, Cotton and Woollen..	192	2,492,088	4,370	443	4,902,704
" Miscellaneous	1,213	34,075,530	36,867	8	47,647,964
Malt	85	2,125,750	589	......	3,228,857
Marble and Stone Work	1,806	8,864,675	15,365	14	16,244,044
Medicines, Extracts and Drugs	173	1,977,385	833	226	3,465,594
Millinery and Dress Making	967	1,379,777	132	4,614	4,543,284
Millinery Goods	35	365,900	111	923	1,483,154
Mineral Water	123	585,860	720	7	1,415,420
Musical Instruments	247	4,621,100	4,741	12	6,959,918
Nails, Cut, Wrought, and Spikes..	99	5,810,250	6,721	157	9,857,223
Oil, Coal	64	2,240,518	922	......	4,254,987
" Other	212	8,088,701	2,121	12	18,075,679
Oil and Enamelled Cloth	41	1,265,700	1,205	23	2,916,416
Paints	45	1,615,300	562	1	2,574,955
Paper	555	14,052,683	6,519	4,392	21,216,802
Paper Hangings	26	1,037,600	1,203	91	2,148,800
Perfumery and Fancy Soaps	33	597,000	261	274	1,222,400
Photographs	249	417,250	580	73	1,090,647
Plaster, and Manufactures of	307	1,023,990	864	2	1,110,854
Pottery and Stone Ware	557	1,341,774	2,836	72	2,463,681
Printing and Publishing	1,666	19,622,318	17,826	2,333	31,063,898
Provisions	352	11,484,896	6,680	799	31,986,433
Rice Cleaning	23	529,700	229	213	1,788,126
Roofing	56	352,300	554	......	1,024,019

	No. of Establishments.	Capital Invested.	Hands Employed. Males.	Hands Employed. Females.	Value of Product.
Saddlery and Harness	3,621	$6,478,184	11,963	322	$14,169,037
Safes, Fire-Proof	36	1,026,800	1,093	......	1,910,079
Sails	133	312,075	641	2	1,328,146
Saleratus	11	275,000	172	6	1,176,000
Salt	408	3,775,915	2,227	37	2,456,972
Sash, Doors, and Blinds	986	5,419,487	7,399	7	9,589,007
Saws	42	770,200	756	3	1,237,063
Scales and Balances	43	744,300	725	......	1,292,560
Sewing Machines	74	1,426,550	2,259	28	4,247,820
Shingles and Lath	665	1,128,470	2,177	19	1,665,507
Ship and Boat Building	614	5,472,815	9,259	1	11,667,661
Shovels, Spades, Forks, Hoes	55	963,300	1,188	1	1,638,876
Silks and Fancy Goods	95	1,262,780	940	1,841	2,992,922
Silk, Sewing and Twist	42	1,675,900	583	1,996	3,596,249
Silver, Manufactures of	106	1,712,050	1,283	61	3,571,654
" Plated & Britannia Ware	128	1,537,540	2,172	327	3,676,460
Soap and Candles	614	6,347,138	3,062	185	18,464,574
Spokes, Hubs, Felloes, etc	215	1,422,700	1,635	......	2,213,849
Springs, Car, Carriage, etc	40	1,264,000	1,009	......	2,117 377
Starch	167	2,051,710	1,063	10	2,823,258
Staves, Hoops, and Shooks	295	897,726	1,787	1	1,711,743
Steel, Manufactures of	17	1,666,000	871	18	1,879,840
Straw Goods	39	1,256,700	801	6,803	4,395,616
Sugar Refining	39	9,087,600	3,484	......	42,143,234
Tin, Copper, and Sheet Iron	3,488	9,079,766	11,156	70	16,718,388
Tobacco and Snuff	626	9,494,405	15,869	2,990	21,820,535
Trunks, Valises, Carpet Bags	151	935,800	1,793	299	2,836,969
Turning, Scroll Sawing	253	988,328	1,667	......	2,084,325
Turpentine, Distilled	596	4,007,258	4,032	135	6,423,379
Type and Stereotype Founding	32	1,113,600	795	312	1,276,570
Umbrellas and Parasols	66	1,038,890	551	1,410	2,948,302
Upholstery	199	740,330	876	551	2,920,188
Varnishes	48	1,080,650	312	3	2,402,790
Veneers	25	507,300	192	2	1,021,700
Wagons and Carts	3,305	4,591,968	9,639	2	8,703,937
Watches and Repairing	94	775,611	710	123	1,524,700
White Lead	36	2,453,147	992	2	5,380,347
Wire	25	629,063	727	62	2,018,133
Wooden Ware	229	1,103,770	1,909	24	2,108,656
Woollen Goods	1,260	30,862,654	24,841	16,519	61,895,217
Worsted Goods	3	3,230,000	1,101	1,277	3,701,378
Total of Manufactures in 1860, including Coal and Copper Mining, and Fisheries, and Miscellaneous branches not above specified	**140,433**	**$1,009,855,175**	**1,040,349**	**270,897**	**$1,885,861,676**

Some of the causes which have contributed to lift this department of American Industry to its present stature have been already incidentally mentioned. Among these are the vast though imperfectly developed natural resources of the country for the production of food and raw materials, particularly cotton, hemp, wood, coal, iron, lead, copper, petroleum, and other metallic and mineral products; in the hydraulic power, and facile communication afforded by its numerous rivers and streams. Allusion has also been made to the cumulative productive power of wealth which, though less operative in this than in many older countries, has not been unfelt in the accumulation and concentration of capital, in manufacturing towns, edifices, machinery, and all the appliances of industry, nearly all of which has been the creation of a single half century.

The substantial basis, however, upon which the national prosperity in this and all other branches of industry has been built, is the free scope given by the political system of the United States to every species of enterprise. This freedom of industry, at least throughout those sections of the Union chiefly employed in manufactures, in securing to labor and capital the profits of their exercise, has been a principal agency in attracting and retaining both, which are ever sensitive to the measure of freedom under which they are employed. Having been perfectly free to seek their most profitable employment, according to the natural law of demand and supply, an increasing diversification and multiplication of pursuits has resulted, and contributed thereby to general and individual prosperity. Labor, on the one hand, has been free from the domination of capital centralized in vast overgrown corporations, and capital has, on the other hand, been exempt from the combinations of labor controlled by guilds and trades' unions, conditions incident to the industrial systems of other countries.

A result of this freedom of industry and of religious opinion in the United States, has been an unexampled flow of labor and capital from the redundant wealth and overstocked labor markets of Europe. The number of the natives of other countries living in the United States in 1850 was 2,240,535, and in 1860, 4,131,866. Although these numbers comprised the representatives of nearly every civilized nation on the globe, by far the larger part were of a class having a community of origin, language, laws, customs, and forms of industry with the Teutonic and Celtic races of the United Kingdom and of Germany, by whom these States were originally peopled, and with whose descendants they have readily blended. They consisted very largely of small farmers, mechanics, and laborers, many of whom have sought homes in the agricultural States and Territories of the West, while a still larger proportion have found a market for their skill and labor in the large commercial cities and manufacturing towns, where they have supplied the drain made by steadily westward migration from the older communities. Trained to industry in the workshops of Europe, as many of these were, and acquainted with the mechanical methods and appliances of their respective countries, they have constantly reinforced the ranks of our manufacturers and mechanics with the manual dexterity.

the artistic skill, the patient toil, and other peculiarities which characterize the systems of elaborate and divided labor in older countries. The total number of alien passengers arriving in the United States by sea in the forty-one and one fourth years ending December 31, 1860, was about 5,062,414, exclusive of many entering from the British Provinces without being enumerated. Of this number, about one half were between the ages of fifteen and thirty years, or in the most productive period of life. The acceleration of this immigration in the last twenty years, and particularly in the last half of it, is shown in the fact that while the number arriving in the ten years preceding June, 1840, was a little over half a million, it amounted in the next ten years to upward of one and a half millions, and in the last ten, ending May 31, 1860, to 2,707,624, most of whom declared their intention to remain. The number of emigrants from Great Britain and Ireland alone, in the forty-six years ending with 1860, was 3,048,206, exclusive of large numbers entering by way of Canada; and the immigration from Germany, in the same time, amounted to nearly one and a half millions. The amount of property in cash brought into the country by these five millions of foreigners, has been estimated at not less than four hundred millions of dollars; but the physical, intellectual, and moral worth of the immigrants was a vastly greater increment to the industrial resources of the nation, a due share of which in cunning of hand, inventive talent, order, and perseverance, has been incorporated with the native skill, energy, and enterprise of the manufacturing population.

As the best safeguard of civil and religious liberty, the readiest means of assimilating the foreign with the native population, of quickening the general intellect, and therefore of promoting enterprise, industry, invention, order, and thrift, by rendering labor intelligent and educated, the system of popular instruction in the United States must be regarded as a prominent element of industrial success. As early as 1642, public education was enjoined by law upon each town in Massachusetts, as a matter "of singular behoof and benefit to any commonwealth." The example was early followed by other governments, and the Articles of Confederation in 1787, as well as the several acts admitting new States into the Union, provided for the appropriation of lands in each township for the use of public schools; which measure has become the settled policy of the United States. Several Western States have set apart whole townships of land for that purpose, and a large number of States have ample funds for the support of schools. The whole amount of lands appropriated by the Federal Government for schools and colleges, down to January 1st, 1854, was nearly fifty-three millions of acres. The total amount expended by the general and local governments for educational purposes, to the present time, has been estimated at not less than five hundred millions of dollars. As a consequence of the liberal support given to education by public and private means, less than one fifth of the total native white population, in 1850, or about one in twenty-two, was unable to read and write—and in New England, only one in every four hundred—while the number of illiterate foreigners was about twice the number of natives. Of native white persons over twenty years of age, the proportion unable to read and write in the United States was 8.28 per cent., or one in twelve—in New England, one in 238—and of foreigners over twenty, one in seven.

Much has been accomplished, also, for the education of the mechanical and various professional classes, whose influence has been felt in the progress of the arts, during the last ten years, in the several means of special instruction established in past years—such as Mechanics' Institutes, Polytechnic Schools, Schools of Mining and Engineering, Schools of Design, Art Exhibitions, Annual Fairs, etc. etc. Prominent among these in direct influence upon the character and progress of American industry, was the international system of

Industrial Exhibitions.

Among the plans which were adopted early in the present decade to stimulate progress in the Arts and Manufactures, the most useful and noteworthy was the attempt to exhibit in one building the works of industry of All Nations. In 1850, his Royal Highness, Prince Albert, as President of the Society of Arts, proposed an exhibition of this kind, in order to give "a true test and living picture of the point of development at which the whole of mankind had arrived in this great task;" and he has the credit of having originated the first and most successful of all these exhibitions—that held in London in 1851.

The building was in itself a miracle of art and beauty. It was constructed chiefly of glass and iron, after a plan submitted by Sir Joseph Paxton, and covered an area of about eighteen acres. Its general form was a parallelogram, 1848 feet long and 478 feet wide, the greatest length running from east to west. There was also a projection on the south side, 936 feet long and 48 feet wide. This area was subdivided into twelve avenues, of various widths, the chief or central passage being seventy-two feet wide and sixty-three feet high. The avenues were formed by rows of hollow cast-iron columns, eight inches in diameter, placed in line, twenty-four feet from each other, and which acted as supports for the building and rain-water drains. There were 294,000 panes of glass used in the building, the bulk being forty-nine inches long by ten inches broad; and the total cost of the structure was £142,000, 7*s.* 6*d.* The Exhibition remained open one hundred and forty-one days; the number of persons who visited it is stated at 1,039,165; and the gross receipts at £423,792, 4*s.* 6*d.* The resources of the United States in raw materials, and articles of food, were tolerably represented; but no accurate idea of the progress in the arts, and development of manufactures, could be obtained from the few specimens which found their way to that exhibition. Our countrymen, however, achieved decided triumphs in several departments. The American Reapers; Bigelow's Carpet Power Looms; Day & Newell's Locks; St. John's Variation Compass and Velocimeter; Herring's Safes; and Dick's Anti-Friction Press had no rivals, and afforded conclusive demonstrations of American superiority in utilitarian inventions.

The brilliant success that attended the London Exhibition, suggested to citizens of New York the idea of having one on American soil; and on the 11th of March, 1852, the Legislature of the State of New York enacted a charter of incorporation for "THE ASSOCIATION FOR THE EXHIBITION OF THE INDUSTRY OF ALL NATIONS." The capital was nominally two hundred thousand dollars, with permission to increase it to three hundred thousand. The stock was not sought for in large sums, and was distributed among more than one hundred and fifty individuals and firms. After some vexatious and damaging delays, the formal opening took place on the 14th of July, 1853, though the building itself was not then completed, and barely half the articles intended for exhibition were in position. In consequence, in part, of the delay in opening, the exhibition was not a commercial success; but its influence upon industry, especially manufacturing industry, was undoubtedly beneficial and wide-spread. A list of the articles exhibited, and the names of the exhibitors, can be found in a folio volume published by G. P. Putnam, and entitled "Progress of Science and Mechanism;" and the prominent or especially noteworthy articles, are referred to in a duodecimo edited by Horace Greeley, of New York, entitled "Art and Industry of the Crystal Palace."

The New York Exhibition was followed by one at Munich, in 1854; at Paris, in 1855; and at Manchester, in 1857. But the most important one of all, was the late English Exhibition held in London, in 1862. It was designed that the Exhibition should consist principally of works produced since 1850; but, in consequence of the distracted state of the country, American art and industry were poorly represented, there being only about seventy exhibitors from the United States, in about twelve of the industrial classes.

Another prominent agency which has contributed to the recent wonderful expansion of American industry, in Massachusetts, is the remarkable activity of mind manifested in inventions and discoveries in the mechanical arts, and in physical science. This may be regarded as the natural fruit of the mental culture and freedom secured by the political and municipal institutions of the country, as well as of the national system of patents, which, in common with that of most other nations, secures to genius the reward of originality or utility in its exercise.

As early as 1857, the number of patents issued to American inventors had grown to exceed those granted by the English office, and the number of applications were greater than those in France; although in both those countries there is no rigid preliminary examination of applications, and nearly all patents applied for are granted. The contrast, however, in this particular, between Russia and America is much more marked. In Russia there were but ninety-seven patents granted in the years 1852–1854, of which fifty-six only were issued to natives of the empire; being an average of about nineteen per annum, in a population of sixty-nine millions. For twelve months ending November, 1857, the patents granted amounted to twenty-four, of which but thirteen were to natives of the country; while in the United States, within the same period, there were over forty-five hundred applications filed, and twenty-nine hundred patents granted. In a single year there were one hundred and sixteen patents issued for improvements upon a single machine—the Sewing Machine.

In analyzing the character and objects of the various inventions that have been patented, we find—as indeed, one would expect from the circumstances of society existing in this country, in consequence of its comparatively recent settlement—that much the largest proportion of them are of a utilitarian and labor-saving character. Of the twenty-nine hundred patents issued in 1857, four hundred and thirty-eight were for agricultural implements and processes, including as such Cotton-gins, Rice-cleaners, and Fertilizers; and of the thirty-seven hundred and ten patents issued in the succeeding year, five hundred and ten were for inventions relating to agricultural implements and processes, of which one hundred and fifty-two were for improvements in Cotton-gins and Presses; one hundred and sixty-four for improvements in the Steam Engine, and one hundred and ninety-eight for improvements in Railroads and Railroad Cars. The unceasing demand has been for agencies that would enable man to extract from the material world the largest amount of the elements of human comfort, with the least expenditure of physical labor; though the genius of our countrymen has not, by any means, been confined exclusively to the invention and improvement of machines and processes of manufacture. Within a few years very many designs and patterns have been patented; and we are encouraged to hope that American artisans will soon be able to compete with those of other and older countries in the production of those pleasing forms, figures, and designs, which adapt and recommend certain kinds of manufactured fabrics to people of cultivated taste.

In measuring the relative rank of the States of this Union by the tape line of the ingenuity of their citizens, we find that New York stands first, Pennsylvania second, Massachusetts third, Ohio fourth, Connecticut fifth, and Illinois sixth. Thus, of the thirty-six hundred and sixty-eight persons who received patents in 1858, nearly one-third, or one thousand and seventy-six, were citizens of New York; four hundred and forty-seven of Pennsylvania; four hundred and thirty-eight of Massachuesetts; three hundred and two of Ohio, and two hundred and eleven of Connecticut. And of forty-four hundred and ninety-one patentees in the succeeding year, twelve hundred and thirty-seven were citizens of New York; five hundred and thirty-two of Pennsylvania; four hundred and ninety-two of Massachuesetts; three hundred and ninety of Ohio; two hundred and fifty-six of Connecticut, and two hundred and six of Illinois. The following table exhibits

THE BUSINESS OF THE PATENT-OFFICE FOR TWENTY-FOUR YEARS ENDING DECEMBER 31 1861.

Years.	Applications filed.	Caveats filed.	Patents issued.	Cash received.	Cash expended.
1837	....	....	435	$29,289.08	$33,506.98
1838	....	....	520	42,123.54	37,402.10
1839	....	....	425	37,260.00	34,543.51
1840	765	228	473	38,056.51	39,020.67
1841	847	312	495	40,413.01	52,666.87
1842	761	291	517	36,505.68	31,241.48
1843	819	315	531	35,315.81	30,776,96
1844	1,045	380	502	42,509.26	36,344.73
1845	1,246	452	502	51,076.14	39,395.65
1846	1,272	448	619	50,264.16	46,158.71
1847	1,531	533	572	63,111.19	41,878.35
1848	1,628	607	660	67,576.69	58,905.84
1849	1,955	595	1,070	80,752.78	77,716.44
1850	2,193	602	995	86,927.05	80,100.95
1851	2,258	760	869	95,738.61	84,916.93
1852	2,639	996	1,020	112,056.34	95,916.91
1853	2,673	901	958	121,527.45	132,869.83
1854	3,324	868	1,902	163,789.84	167,146.32
1855	4,435	906	2,024	216,459.35	179,540.33
1856	4,960	1,024	2,502	192,588.02	199,931.02
1857	4,771	1,010	2,910	196,132.01	211,582.09
1858	5,364	943	3,710	203,716.16	193,193.74
1859	6,225	1,097	4,538	245,942.15	210,278.41
1860	7,653	1,084	4,819	256,352.59	252,820.80
1861	4,643	700	3,340	137,354.44	221,491.91

In view of this wonderful increase in the business of the Patent-office, a late Commissioner was justified in saying the inventive genius of the country, great as have been its efforts and attainments, has manifested none of the languor of exhaustion, nor testified any inclination for repose. Each discovery made, like a fire kindled in a dark place, while enlarging the horizon of science, has laid bare yet other and wider fields to be traversed by its ever-brightening sway.

Reviewing the triumphs of invention and discovery in every department of the arts and sciences for the last three quarters of a century, and in marking their beneficient influences in softening the asperities and exalting the dignity of human labor, there is abundant cause for heartfelt exultation.

We are unable, in this place, to do more than glance at a few of the more important patent improvements made since 1850.

I. Of the instruments and operations relating to Agriculture, which constitute a large proportion of all the patent inventions recorded in the United States, the number was very large, and many of them have proved of incalculable benefit to the rural industry of the nation. Although the patents issued always consist largely of improvements on existing implements, the number of new machines and tools adapted to the various departments of rural economy, particularly mowing, reaping and threshing machines, cultivators, drills, seeding and planting machines, ploughs, and dairy implements, was both numerous and important. It is, however, by the successive improvements and modifications of the several parts of valuable machines, which are the subject of the larger number of patents issued, that they are ultimately brought to that perfection of form and construction which renders them so serviceable as labor-saving instruments. Among these the various machines for reaping, mowing, and securing grain and hay, by horse-power, hold a prominent place; both on account of their wonderful service to Agriculture, and because, as practical inventions, they are almost entirely American, and a product of the last twelve or fifteen years.

Since the Great Exhibition in London, in 1851, when public attention, at home and abroad, was strongly directed to the comparative merits of American and foreign implements, as shown by the public trials in England, improvements have followed in rapid succession, and their manufacture and use has been vastly augmented. The number of American patents for Reaping and Mowing Machinery recorded previous to 1845, when the second patent was issued to C. H. McCormick, of Va., was about thirty, including the original Machine of

Obed Hussey, that of C. H. McCormick, the Combined Reaping, Threshing, and Winnowing Machine of Moore & Haskell, of Michigan, and the Mowing Machine of the late Wm. F. Ketchum, patented in 1844, which was the pioneer implement for that purpose. Unusual interest in this class of machinery was also excited by a grand field trial of Mowers and Reapers, held under the auspices of the New York State Agricultural Society, at Geneva, in 1852, when two premiums were awarded, and by that instituted at Syracuse, N. Y., by the United States Agricultural Society, in July, 1857, when fifteen mowing, nine reaping, and fourteen combined Mowing and Reaping Machines were entered for competition. Previous to the latter year no less than one hundred and seventy-six grain and grass harvesters, and sixty-two mowing machines had been patented in the United States. Since that time the number has steadily increased, amounting to between one and two hundred annually, in some years, including several original machines. Among these were many improvements in the appendages and minor details of construction, which have secured greater cheapness, efficiency, or durability; rendering several of the most approved machines the basis of prosperous manufacture, as well as inestimable blessings to the agricultural communities of this and foreign countries. Without disparagement to many other inventors, who have made valuable improvements, the following may be named as successful in the introduction of Mowers and Reapers, single or combined, and of valuable appurtenances to such machines. Many of the patentees, like Hussey, McCormick, Ketchum, and other early inventors, have recorded numerous modifications of the mechanism ; some of them almost yearly, and some several times in the same year, so great has been the stimulus to improvement, and the demand for good implements in this branch of mechanics. Among the patentees of harvesting machinery in 1850, was John E. Heath, of Warren, Ohio, who also patented a machine for raking and binding grain. In 1851, John H. Manny, of Waddam's Grove, Ill., brought forward a Combined Mower and Harvester, which, though far from being a perfectly constructed instrument, shared with that of W. F. Ketchum, of Buffalo, N. Y., the only two premiums awarded for Mowers at the Geneva trial, in the following year. It was the subject of improvements patented by the inventor in 1852 and 1853, and afterward became the basis of numerous improvements made by Walter A. Wood, of Hoosick Falls, Rensselaer Co., N. Y., who purchased a territorial right in the machine. A Grain and Grass Harvester was patented the same year by Wm. H. Seymour, assignor to Seymour, Morgan & Co., of Brockport, N. Y., who has made many improvements in Mowers and Harvesters. The Automaton

WALTER A. WOOD, Hoosick, N.Y.
THE
AMERICAN
FARMERS'
BENEFACTORS.
JOHN A. PITTS.
Buffalo, N.
SAML. PENNOCK.
Kennett Square Penn.
C. AULTMAN, CANTON, OHIO.
E. BALL, CANTON, OHIO.
Engd. by H.B. Hall

Reaper of Jearum Atkins, of Chelsea, Illinois, since extensively manufactured at Dayton, Ohio, was patented the same year. In 1853, Philo, Sylla, and Augustus Adams, of Elgin, Ill., patented an improvement in Grass and Grain Harvesters, provided with platforms and seats for a raker and two binders, and a box to receive the sheaves, etc. And Thomas D. Burrall, of Geneva, N. Y., the same year made an improvement in Reaping Machines by making an additional apron or platform, with gearing, to convert a rear discharge into a side discharge of the grain. This Convertible Reaper took the first premium at the Geneva trial in the preceding year, and a diploma was awarded the inventor at Syracuse, in 1857, for a Mowing Machine, distinguished for its simplicity and solidity of construction. In 1853 and 1854, additional improvements were made in Grain and Grass Harvesters by John H. Manny, of Rockford; and by Howard & Ketchum, of Buffalo; and in Mowing Machines, by M. Hallenbeck and Alanson Gale, of Albany, N. Y. Of more than fifty patents for improvements in Harvesting Machinery, granted in 1855, the Illinois Harvester of Jonathan Haines, of Pekin, Ill., said to be capable of harvesting twenty acres per diem, that of John E. Newcomb, of Whitehall, N. Y., and the Combined Mowers and Harvesters of Dietz & Dunham, of Raritan, N. Y., and of Wm. H. Hovey, of Springfield, Mass., and others, have each acquired a reputation. Among numerous improvements in Mowers and Reapers, patented in 1856, were the well-known Mowing Machines of E. Ball, and of C. Aultman & Lewis Miller, of Canton, Ohio; both assigned to Ball, Aultman & Miller, manufacturers of that place. In 1859, the latter patent was divided, and reissued as six separate patents, and that of Ball was reissued as two. In 1857, the patents for this kind of machinery numbered about one hundred and twenty; among which were five for improvements in Harvesters, issued to Walter A. Wood, of Hoosick Falls. Improvements in Automatic Rakes, for Harvesters, which of late years have attracted much attention, were also patented by two or three persons, in 1856. Among others, in 1857, by John W. Brokan, of Springfield, Ohio, who assigned the patent to Warden, Brokan & Child, to whom were also assigned a patent for a Mowing Machine by Thomas Harding, of that place; and another for a Combined Mower and Reaper, patented by Brokan and Harding conjointly. In 1858, a still larger number of improvements in these machines was patented, and each of the four following years augmented the number of new and successful machines, or of valuable modifications in those already in use. The machines already named, most of which are favorite implements, as well as the older ones of C. H. McCormick, Obed Hussey, W. F. Ketchum, and those of R. S. Allen, of New York city, and others, are each manufactured to the number of many thousands annually. The whole number of Reapers and Mowers made by some ten or twelve leading manufacturers in the four years following 1860, is said to have been about two hundred and fourteen thousand machines.

Of Threshing Machines and Grain Separators, indispensable in large farming operations, which require the Horse-power Reaper, some three hundred and fifty patents had been recorded previous to 1857, including several valuable implements. Among these were the machines of J. A. Pitts, of Buffalo, which received the Gold Medal at the Paris Exhibition, in 1855, Gilbert's Excelsior Machine, Moffat's Improved, Palmer's Rotary, Snyder's, Wagener's, and Zimmerman's Machines for threshing, separating, cleaning, and bagging grain. Allen's Single Horse-power, Hathaway's, and other machines, with many improved machines of later introduction, were patented within the period here reviewed. Instruments for husking and shelling corn have also been greatly multiplied to the benefit of the western farmer. The patented improvements in Ploughs usually outnumber those of any other implement, and, including twenty-eight patents for Hill-side Ploughs, amounted in all, previous to the year 1857, to about five hundred. Some novel and useful modifications of this typical instrument of husbandry, both in form and material, were introduced within the last five years. The Gang Plough, the Sulky Plough, the Shovel Plough, the Plough with revolving or wheel coulter, the Steam Plough, and, the more practicable substitute for the latter, the Rotary Spader, have each occupied the attention of inventors during this time, and with one and two horse Cultivators, Broadcast Seed Sowers and Drills, Iron Rollers, improved Harrows, etc., constitute the great dependence of farmers in the tillage of large farms and plantations. Gang Ploughs were patented by two persons, in 1850, and by several in subsequent years; and, in 1857, three patents were granted for Steam Ploughs, to D. B. Spencer, of Virginia; J. R. Gray, of Wisconsin; and E. Groves, of New York. These were followed by three others, in 1858, in September of which year the Ploughing Machine of J. W. Fawkes, of Pennsylvania, one of the number, was first tested at Centralia, Illinois, with a degree of success and promise not since sustained by it or others in this country. In 1859, four other Steam Ploughs were patented, and many other patents have since been granted for that purpose. A valuable machine for farmers was the portable and inexpensive, but efficient, Hay and Cotton Press, patented in 1854.

II. In the Metallurgic Arts, some useful processes and productions were patented, although, as in other branches, generally the improvements were more numerous than important. James Renton, of Newark, New Jersey, in 1851, patented a deoxydizing apparatus for making wrought-iron direct from the ore by combining a series of flat vertical tubes with a puddling furnace. As an improvement to which, in 1854, he patented the use of a blast or blasts to increase the heat of furnaces for making wrought-iron direct from the ore, which were also the subjects of patents in the latter year byThomas W. Harvey and others, administrators of the Harvey Steel and Iron Company, of New York; and by Bell and Isett, of Tyrone, Pennsylvania; and by George A. Whipple, of Newark, New Jersey, in 1853. In 1852, James McCarty, of Reading, Pennsylvania, patented an apparatus for puddling iron, consisting of a novel form of reverberating furnace. In 1856, Mr. Henry Bessemer, of London, obtained two patents, previously taken out in England—one for his process of making iron and steel by forcing among the particles of molten iron currents of air or gas to keep up the combustion of carbon until it was converted into steel or malleable iron without reheating, and the other for smelting iron ore without ordinary carbonaceous fuel, by underlaying the charge of ore with molten iron, treated as above. These, and additional patents, covering later improvements and machinery whereby iron and steel are now made directly from the ore in vast masses at greatly reduced cost, and also for making car axles and other forgings of cast steel or cast semi-steel, etc., have been again issued to him during the past year (1865). Robert Mushet, of England, also patented in the United States, in 1857, his improved manufacture of malleable iron and steel, by adding to decarbonized cast-iron in the molten state a compound containing iron, carbon, and manganese. In 1857 and 1861, improvements in making malleable cast-iron were patented by Professor A. K. Eaton, of New York, whose method of making steel—practically demonstrated by him at Rochester, five or six years before—was employed at this time by the Damascus Steel Company, and other American works. Chain-making Machines, of ingenious construction, were patented, in 1855, by E. Weissenborn, of New York; wire rope, by John A. Roebling, of Trenton, New Jersey, in 1854; and wire springs for furniture, in 1858, by C. A. and S. W. Young, of Providence, Rhode Island. Bank and other Locks were the subjects of numerous patents by Lewis Yale and other inventors. Four patents were issued in 1852, and the same number in 1856, to Cullen Whipple, assignor to the New England Screw Company, for improvements in machinery for making wood screws. His earlier patent, used by the same company, was reissued in 1850 An improved File Cutting Machine, much used by manufacturers, was patented by Etienne Bernet, of Paris, in 1860. In 1853, David Stuart, of Philadelphia, patented a process of annealing hollow iron ware by coating the inside with a composition of soapstone dust and carbon, and afterward heating them. Machines for planing metals were patented, in 1853, by William W. Sheppard, of Boston; and, in 1859, by Jeremiah Carhart, of New York.

III. The mauufacture of fibrous and textile materials gave rise to numerous patents for improved processes and machinery which have materially contributed to the progress of manufactures. The improvements in Looms were very numerous, and amounted, in the fourteen years, from 1850 to 1863 inclusive, to about two hundred and seventy, including one, in 1854, for operating looms by electricity, patented the previous year in France, by G. Bonelli. Among these, we may refer to the patents for power-looms, in 1850, to Enoch Burt, of Connecticut, who, in the following year and 1853, patented, we believe, the first fancy check power-looms, and to those of Erastus B. Bigelow, William Mason and George Crompton, of Massachusetts, William J. Horstmann and J. J. Hepworth, of Pennsylvania. To the looms for weaving various figured and cut pile fabrics, patented by Samuel and James Eccles, and Barton H. Jenks, of Philadelphia; that of R. W. Sievier, of Manchester, England, patented here in 1854; that of Thomas Cropley, of Roxbury, Massachusetts; of C. G. Gilray, of New York; and, for plain or figured goods, by John Broadbent, of Kentucky.

In carpet looms for ingrain and tapestry carpets there were many improvements by E. B. Bigelow and others, and in the fabric itself improvements were made among others by Thomas Cropley, of Roxbury, Massachusetts, now of Connecticut, whose tapestry steam printed carpets, rugs, etc., felted on a body of India Rubber vulcanized in the process of felting, are said to possess great beauty, durability and cheapness. Improvements were also made by Alex. Smith and by J. G. McNair, both of West Farms, New York, and by many others. Designs for carpet patterns have been the subject of numerous patents in the last few years, especially by the Lowell Manufacturing Co. of Massachusetts, and the Hartford Carpet Co. of New York, as the assignees respectively of Elmer J. Ney and Henry G. Thompson.

In looms for weaving seamless and other bags, improvements were made by Cyrus Baldwin, assignor to the Stark Mills of Manchester, New Hampshire; by Sheldon Northrop of Connecticut; by William Talbot of Maine and S. S. Thomas of Massachusetts, and by Jillson & Sparhawk of Maine, and others. In Flax and Hemp machinery, we had among others, improvements in the dressing and preparation of the fibre, to which the recent scarcity of cotton has given unusual interest as agents in substitution for that material. Among the more important of these were the Hemp Breaking and Dressing Machines of S. A. Clemens of Massachusetts, and of Treat & Randall of Connecticut, and the Chemical process of Peter Claussen of England, in 1851, the Hemp Brake of L. S. Chichester of New York, in 1852 and 1854, machines and processes for Bleaching Flax, by Roth & Lea of Philadelphia, and the Water Rotting process of William Watt, of Glasgow, in the latter year; the Rotary Flax Scutching Machine of W. C. McBride, of New Jersey, previously patented in England, in 1856; the Cylinder Flax and Hemp Dresser of G. F. Schaffer, of New York, in 1861, and eight or ten improvements, in 1862, by G. Sanford and J. E. Mallory, of New York, for breaking, scutching, cleaning, and dressing hemp and flax. An improvement in treating hemp and flax to make them resemble cotton, was patented in the same year by I. P. Comly, of Ohio, and an improvement in flax cleaning and dressing machines, by J. E. Crowell, of Massachusetts. These and other mechanical and chemical devices are now in use, for preparing long and short flax stock as a substitute for cotton, and possess considerable interest in their relation to the problem at present under trial, of assimilating flax, hemp, and other vegetable fibres to the character of cotton, so as to be carded, spun, and woven by automatic machinery at much less cost than formerly. Several valuable improvements were made in Hosiery Looms and Knitting Machinery. The whole number of patents granted for this purpose in the United States up to 1864 was one hundred and twenty-six, of which number one hundred and ten have been issued since 1850 and thirty-six since 1860. The most valuable contribution to this class of textile machinery was that of Timothy Bailey, of Ballston Spa, New York, who was the first to give the world a Power Stocking Loom, having about the year 1852 succeeded in adapting the old knitting frame of Lee to work by power, which was put in operation at Cohoes, and who patented improvements in 1852 and 1854. Patents for Rotary Knitting Machines were taken out in the former year by H. G. Sanford and D. Tainter, both of Worcester, Massachusetts, and others in the following year by Moses Marshall and John Mee, of Lowell. Two other improvements were patented, in 1854, by Henry Burt, assignor to the Newark Patent Hosiery Company, of New Jersey, one being based on an older patent by the same. Improvements were made in that the following year by John Pepper, Jr., and were assigned to the Franklin Mills, Portsmouth, New Hampshire, one of the largest Hosiery Mills at that time in the country, working seven Looms by steam power and sixty by hand. The improvements patented in

1854 and 1855, and subsequent years, by Jonas B. Herrick and Walter Aikin, of Franklin, New Hampshire, covering some novelties in form and construction, but more particularly a needle latch regulator and yarn carrier, capable of adjustment to other machinery, thereby obviating a common defect in them. Another improvement claimed was for a hollow circular needle plate, looped regulator, etc., and the improvements rendered the Aiken machine one of the most valuable and popular of recent invention, being alike adapted to family use as a hand or treadle machine, and to factory purposes as a power-loom. Operated by power it is capable of knitting from ten to sixty thousand loops per minute. An improvement in machines for knitting ribbed fabrics was also patented by Joseph Powell, of Waterbury, Connecticut, during 1854, in which year another was granted to John H. Doolittle, assignor to the American Hosiery Company, of Waterbury, for an improvement to the machine patented in 1851, by Rufus Ellis, of Boston, who obtained another, in 1855, for needles for knitting machines. In addition to two patents for rotary knitting machines in 1856, and one by John Nesmith, of Lowell, Massachusetts, for narrowing and widening the fabric, etc., William Goddard, of New York, took out a patent for manufacturing seamless hosiery or tubular knitted fabrics, and William H. McNary, of Brooklyn, for producing the whole leg and foot by a continuous operation seamless throughout, the mechanism for which was patented in 1860 and 1862. Two patents for knitting machines, with improvements, were recorded in 1858 by Joseph K. and Edward E. Kilbourn of Norfolk, Connecticut, and Pittsfield, Massachusetts, and by others, and James Peatfield of Ipswich, Massachusetts, was granted one for the manufacture of seamless knit gloves, in which the hand, fingers, and thumb were knit separately and afterward knit together by hand. In addition to patents by the proprietors of the Cohoes factories and others in 1858 and 1859, A. J. and D. Goffe, of that place, in the latter year took out a patent for rotary burr presses to circular knitting machines, which was assigned to Downs & Co., of Seneca Falls, New York. In 1860, ribbed knitting machines were the subject of two patents by J. Chantrell, of Bristoll, Connecticut, and one for both plain and ribbed work, using a single presser bar, was issued to Eli Tiffany, of Thompsonville, Connecticut. Among the improvements patented in 1862, was one by J. G. Wilson, assignor to Dixon & Larned, of New York, for knitting seamless stockings, and one by Thomas Langham, of Philadelphia, for producing a circular ribbed fabric by a series of self-acting needles, made to operate a part on the inside and others on the outside. A more recent improvement on rotary round machines by Mr. Leslie, of Brooklyn, admits of narrowing the web at pleasure, which had not been done previously in that kind of machine.

In *Sewing Machines*—a mechanical development of the preceding ten years and altogether of American origin—the progress of invention has been quite extraordinary. In the nineteen years from the date of the first patent in 1842 to 1863, the whole number of patents issued was six hundred and seven, of which only ten were granted previous to 1850. The whole number of applications filed was between eight and nine hundred. Even during the last three years of the period named, in which invention was checked by the war, the number of successful applications was upward of fifty annually.

Without reference to the comparative merits of the different inventions or the specific character of the improvements generally, we shall content ourselves with simply indicating in this place the order in which the most approved machines have been brought forward during the past twelve or fourteen years.

With the exception of an improvement patented in 1849 by Lerow & Blodgett, the first considerable improvement made in the needle and shuttle sewing machine of Elias Howe, Jr.—who gave us, in 1846, the first complete automatic machine for general purposes—was that of Allen B. Wilson, of Pittsfield, Massachusetts, in 1850, in the double pointed shuttle, making a stitch at each backward and forward movement, which was followed by other improvements by him, as the rotating hook and four motion feed in 1851 and 1852. In 1850 a patent was also issued to Bartholomy Thimmonier, of France (assignor to Philip May, of England), in whose behalf, because of a tambouring machine devised in 1820, claims have been made of originating the sewing machine prior to that of Howe. Frederick R. Robinson, of Boston, in the same year, patented a machine adapted to making a variety of stitches, as lock stitch, plain running or basting stitch, cordwainers' stitch, etc., by the use of two needles or hooks, one on each side of the fabric. The short thread used rendered it too slow in operation. In 1851 and 1852, Grover & Baker, of Boston, patented an improvement which has been the basis of a large number of machines, making what is called the double loop, or Grover & Baker stitch, with two threads, which is in some effected by the shuttle, and in others by the rotating hook of Wheeler & Wilson. In the former year, Isaac M. Singer, of New York, was granted a patent for a method of lightening the stitch, and other improvements in the single thread or chain stitch machine. The Singer machine, being adapted to all kinds of work upon leather, upholstering, clothing, etc., has been extensively used. It is characterized by the peculiar feed motion, known as the wheel or continuous feed, and makes the stitch with a straight needle and the shuttle movement of Howe. Of thirty-five patents for improvements in sewing machines granted in 1854, three were to Mr. Singer and one to the late Walter Hunt, of New York, who attempted the construction of a sewing machine some ten years before the date of Howe's patent, but without arriving at practical results.[1] Others were patented by Mr. Singer in 1855, and several—including mechanism for binding hats—in the following year. Improvements were made in 1852 and 1854 by Dr. Otis Avery, of Pennsylvania, and others in 1853 and 1854 by Morey & Johnson, of Massachusetts, and one by William Lyon, of New Jersey, in the latter year. Among the numerous accessories which have contributed to the perfection of sewing machines and its wide range of uses, may be named the guides for binding, patented by O. G. Boynton, of Massachusetts, in 1854; guides for hemming and cording, by H. B. Odiorne, of Philadelphia, and H. W. Dickinson, of Hartford, Connecticut, in 1855; guides for working button-holes, in 1856, by Otis Avery, and sewing guides for hemming, by S. P. Chapin, of New York, in the same year, the last mentioned being one of the most important improvements ever made in sewing machines. In 1856 and subsequent years, some useful modifications of the feed motion and other parts of sewing machines were made by J. E. A. Gibbs, of Virginia, and in 1857, Milton Finkle, of New York, patented improvements in the single thread machine. Gathering or plaiting apparatus as an appendage to sewing machines,

(1) Walter Hunt, who died recently, at the age of 63 years, was noted during a period of more than forty years for the activity of his inventive powers, and his numerous experiments in a wide range of practical art. His earliest patent, we believe, was taken out in connection with W. Haskins, of Martinsburg, New York, for a machine for spinning flax and hemp, which was the nearest approach made up to that time to solve the problem of spinning flax automatically. From that time to 1850, he recorded patents for an alarm for coaches, for a self-supplying twisting machine, knife sharpener, and domestic guard; a globe castor; globe or radiator stove; saw for felling trees; springs for bolts; pantaloon straps, vests, etc.; ice breaker; three patents by himself and his assignees, Augustus T. and George Arrowsmith, for improvement in inkstands, having a float and pad inside to act as stopper, cover, etc.; two in 1848 for a loaded ball and a method of attaching a ball to a wooden cartridge by means of an annular flange and recess on and in the rear of the ball, as in the Minie bullet. Both of the latter were issued in 1850, and assigned to G. Arrowsmith and W. R. Palmer. In the latter year, he patented the Sewing Machine, which had engaged his attention as early as 1834-5, and contained some combinations, as the needle on a vibrating lever, and the shuttle which have been employed in later inventions, although his first machine was laid aside as impracticable. His later inventions were an improved shirt collar in 1856, the original, we believe, of the paper collar so much used at this time; patent heels for boots and shoes, lamps, etc., etc. His enthusiasm as an inventor was only equalled by his self-sacrificing generosity as a friend, and these qualities of hand and heart kept him always in straitened circumstances.

has been the subject of several patents, two of which were granted to G. B. Arnold, of New York, in 1860. Of the same date with these were two other patents by Mr. Arnold, for improvements in the manufacture of Ruffles, or plaited fabrics, as a new article of manufacture, produced both with and without binding or foundation, by the aid of the Sewing Machine, which has been adapted to almost every description of household and factory work heretofore done by hand. By changes in the guide mechanism, the several operations of folding, binding, hemming, cording, felling, braiding, tucking, and working button-holes, eyelets, overseaming, etc., are accomplished, either separately or several of them at once, and the labor of the fingers wonderfully abridged. Machines for working button-holes have been patented by Messrs. Goodes and Miller of Philadelphia, and by D. W. G. Humphreys, of Chelsea, Mass. Guides for sewing welts, were the subject of a patent granted to H. Folsom, of Massachusetts.

IV. In the manufacture of Hats, several improvements were made, principally in mechanism and processes for forming, felting, sizing, and pressing hat bodies—the leading patented improvements being those of L. E. Hopkins, P. Emmons, D. G. Wells, I. H. LaBau, and others of New York; James S. Taylor, of Danbury, L. W. Boynton, of South Coventry, and others in Connecticut; of Andrew Rankin, Isaac Searles, A. B. Taylor, and Seth Boyden, of Newark, New Jersey; of J. Baptiste Laville, of Paris, W. Fuzzard, of Cambridgeport, H. L. Sweet, of Foxboro, and others in Massachusetts.

V. In the manufacture of Paper, the principal improvements related to machinery and processes for preparing paper pulp, and particularly from materials either new or imperfectly utilized before in the paper manufacture. In addition to the valuable improvements made in Europe and America within the current century in paper-making machinery, it has long been the aim of manufacturers of both continents to extract, by cheap mechanical and chemical means, from various refuse and crude vegetable substances, at less cost than from cotton and linen rags, the cellulose or lignin which constitutes a large proportion of vegetable fibre, and is the proximate principle upon which the value of all materials for paper stock mainly depends. In this country, where the paper manufacture has become a prominent industry, exceeding in the annual value of its product that of either France or England, and in the consumption, per capita, both countries together, the subject has within a few years past become one of much interest, because of the increasing price and large consumption of paper, and of the fact that the country has annually imported several million dollars' worth of rags and other paper stock. Although it is possible that the experiments now in progress, under a like stimulus, to produce substitutes for cotton by the mechanical and chemical treatment of flax, hemp, and similar fibres, may at least furnish new sources of paper material in the articles known as cottonized or Claussenized flax and hemp, fibrilia, etc., the attempts to use other materials are nevertheless important. The fibrous materials which within the last ten or twelve years have been most successfully employed as paper stock, are straw, corn husks, and several kinds of wood. The manufacture of paper from Straw has been attempted, with partial success, by different persons in Europe for more than a century past, and has been the subject of several patents in this country since the first was granted to Mr. Magraw, of Pennsylvania, in 1828. White paper, from straw, was first made to any extent at Springfield, Mass., in 1849. In 1853, Messrs. Jean T. Coupier and Marie A. C. Mellier, of Paris, exhibited at the New York Crystal Palace specimens of paper of good quality made entirely of straw, by a process which they patented here the same year, and in 1851 in France, where it was then in practical use. The straw was cut, washed, and boiled in a solution of caustic soda of the strength of 2° to 3° Beaume, in close boilers, at a temperature of 310° F., and afterward bleached with chloride of lime. The inventor, M. Mellier, took out an additional patent in 1857. Improvements on this mode of treating straw for paper were made in, 1858, by Martin Nixon, of the Flat Rock Mills, Manayunk, Penn., which furnished the Philadelphia *Ledger* with the first straw printing paper used by the newspaper press in this country. The improvement consisted in applying the steam in a continuous automatic shower, and also in boiling the straw whole, or uncut, by means of an upward current of steam and a downward current of the alkaline solution. Improvements were also made, in 1859, by Palmer & Howland, of Fort Edward, New York, who patented modifications of the apparatus for making paper pulp, and also in the treatment of straw and other stock, which they boiled under a high pressure in a strong solution of caustic alkali, producing a more perfect disintegration of the fibre and a whiter quality of paper. Patents for the manufacture of paper pulp from straw, grass, etc., were taken out, in 1860, by Eben. Clemo, of Toronto, Canada, by treating with nitric acid and an alkaline solution; and in 1863, by Messrs. Tait & Holbrooke, of Jersey City and New York, by whom the straw was cut and then ground between burr-stones, and afterward treated alternately with caustic alkali, clear water, and acidulous solutions, and finally bleached. By these and other improvements, as the use of rotary boilers, etc., the practical difficulties of reducing straw to pulp have been so far overcome as to warrant the organization of one or more large companies for the manufacture of Straw Paper, which is now extensively used for printing and other purposes.

The manufacture of Paper from Wood, has been attempted at different times in Europe and America. It was the subject of a patent by Messrs. Wooster & Holmes, of Meadville, Penn., in 1830, and of two patents in England in 1853, and another in 1854. In the latter year, Messrs. Watt and Burgess, of London, took out a patent in the United States for a process patented in England the year previous, for making paper from wood shavings, by treating them with caustic alkali, chlorine, or chlorine and oxygen, weak alkali, etc. This patent was reissued, in 1858, by mesne assignment to William F. Ladd, of New York City, and Morris L. Keen, of Royer's Ford, Pa.—to whom it was again reissued in 1863. In the latter year an improved boiler for making paper pulp was also patented by Mr. Keen, which has been of great service in the recent methods of treating wood, flax, hemp, and other fibrous materials. Improvements in preparing wood for paper pulp were also patented, in 1855, by Milton D. Whipple, of Charlestown, Mass., and by Louis Koch, of New York, the former consisting in grinding wooden blocks on the surface of a stone, and the latter in machinery for separating the fibres without destroying them, by means of a series of rollers, etc. An improvement in the treatment of paper stuff, by which the fibres of wood were submitted to the action of sulphurous acid in a liquid or gaseous form, before they were bleached by chlorine, was the subject of a patent, in 1857, by Julius A. Roth, of Philadelphia. In the following year, Charles Marzoni, of New York, and Henry Voelter, of Wurtemburg, each took out patents for reducing wood to pulp by mechanical means—the former using a peculiar stone called "adamantine" in connection with steam and hot water, and the latter a rotary grinder or millstone as the means of abrasion. A. S. Lyman, of New York city, the same year patented a novel mode of separating the fibres of wood, flax, and other fibrous substances, by charging the mass with hot water, steam, compressed air, or other elastic fluid, in a cylinder, and then projecting them into the air, as from a gun, when the sudden expansion of the elastic fluids disrupts the whole mass, which comes down in a shower of flakes. In 1863, Stephen M. Allen, of Woburn, Mass., recorded a patent for the manufacture of paper from wood, in which the wood, cut into suitable lengths, was crushed longitudinally, to preserve the integrity of its fibres, and after being steeped and washed alternately in warm water at different temperatures, was boiled, ground, and bleached. Another method, patented the same year by P. A. Chadbourne, of Williamstown, Mass., produced paper stock from wood by means of reciprocating rasps, files, or scrapers, kept in contact with a rotary log by the agency of springs. George E. Sellers, of Hardin county, Illinois, later in the year took out a patent for preparing woody fibre for paper, by crushing the fibre by pressure vertical to or in the line of the fibre, as on the end of a block. With these and other auxiliary means, there seems to be a reasonable prospect that a cheap, abundant, and unfailing supply of material may be found in the soft white wood of the American linden or basswood, and other species of Tilia, in the poplar, willow, and various resinous trees of the American forest.[1]

The manufacture of Paper from the leaves and husks of Indian corn, which was the subject of a patent by Messrs. Allison & Hawkins, of Burlington, New Jersey, in 1802, and of another by Homer Holland, of Westfield, Mass., in 1838, appears first to have been reduced to practice in Germany, through experiments carried on since 1854. A process patented in Austria, in 1861, was the subject of letters patent granted in the United States, in 1863, to Dr. Aloyse Chevalier Amer De Welsbach, of Vienna. The process, which is said to produce paper of great whiteness, consists in boiling the husks or leaves of maize in an alkaline solution until the fibre is precipitated, when it is dried and carded, to be used in making paper pulp, or as a material for cloth; while the soluble portion, gluten, etc., forms an article of food similar to "oil cake." The husks are said to yield forty per cent. of useful material, of which nineteen per cent. is paper stock, equal to the best linen rags, and costing about four cents a pound. The manufacture under this patent was commenced at Clinton Mills, Steubenville, N. Y. Among the other patents for paper stock were the following: In 1857, for making paper pulp from beets and other refuse, from ivory and from the bark of the root and stalk of the cotton plant; two, in 1858 and 1859, to H. Lowe, of Baltimore, for making paper from reeds; one, in 1858, for making pasteboard and paper from leather shavings, to A. N. Mathieu, of Paris; one, in 1859, to F. De Campoloro, of France, for

(1) In August, 1864, a company of capitalists organized under the name of the American Wood Paper Company, with a capital stock said to amount to ten or fifteen million dollars, commenced to erect, and have since completed and put in operation, at Manayunk, on the Schuylkill near Philadelphia, adjoining the railroad and canal, an establishment which, including the Flat Rock Mills before mentioned, is said to be the most extensive Paper Works in the world. They embrace about ten acres of ground and are capable of producing from twelve to fifteen tons of paper pulp daily. The main building, of stone and brick, one thousand feet long and three hundred and fifty wide, cost $500,000. It is under the management of Messrs. Jessup & Moore, assisted by Mr. Martin Nixon, of the Flat Rock Mills, a descendant of William Rittenhouse, who as early as 1690 erected, near this site, the first Paper-mill in America. A more extended account of these mills will be given in another volume.

making paper from corn cobs; to W. J. Cantelo, of Philadelphia, in 1862, for making paper, cordage, and textile fabrics from different species of Hibiscus; one, in 1863, to Stephen M. Allen, of Massachusetts, for leather paper or "fibrilia leather," made from leather and unrotted ground flax fibre combined, and another for paper for making paper collars; and one, the same year, to Henry Pemberton, of Tarentum, Pa., for paper from sorghum or Chinese sugar-cane. Paper was first successfully made from sorghum fibre, as early as 1859, by Feinour & Nixon, at Manayunk, Pa., where the bagasse or residue, after the syrup was expressed, when heated by Mr. Nixon's patent process for straw paper, and with twenty-five per cent of rope added, made a fair quality of printing paper.

Among other improvements in Paper were those patented by Messrs. McKenzie & Trochsler, of Boston, in 1859, for water marking or stamping indelible designs; a process of waterproofing of paper, by J. Mayrhofer, of New York, and of treating printing and other papers with Glycerine, by James Brown, of London, within the same year; improvements in bank-note and other safety paper, by Henry Hayward, of Chicago, in 1862, and by J. P. Olier, of Paris, in 1863, the latter being made in triplicate layers, the middle one having, if desired, a fugitive color or delible watermark, easily obliterated if tampered with.

Among the improvements in machinery and appliances for Paper-making which were patented, the following may be named, viz.: Paper-cutting machines, in 1854, and other machinery, by Nelson Gavit, of Philadelphia; and in that and the following year, paper-making machinery rolls and driers, by Obadiah Marland, of Boston; three patents, in 1856, to Joseph Kingsland, Jr., of Franklin, N. J., for machinery and processes for grinding paper pulp, and one for paper pulp engines, reissued in 1859; machinery for making, and also for pressing the water from pasteboard, in 1857, by Lewis Koch, of New York; an improvement in the Fourdrinier machine, by James Harper, of East Haven, Conn., in 1862; and in boilers for preparing paper stuff, by Nixon, Keen, and C. S. Buchanan, of Balston Spa, New York, in 1860.

In the Chemical Arts and Manufactures, the principal improvements made in the last fifteen years relate to the various methods of treating hemp, flax, and other fibrous substances as substitutes for cotton in the manufacture of textile fabrics; to the manufacture and purification of coal, lard, and other oils, and petroleum, including Meredith's distillation of coal by hydrogen gas, and the production of new dyes and other products from the residuum or waste matter left after refining the latter article; to the manufacture of paints and pigments from zinc and other minerals; to the manufacture of cane, sorghum, and other sugars and syrups; of soap and candles, friction matches, illuminating gas, and especially in the treatment and uses of Caoutchouc and gutta percha.

VII. In Calorific inventions, including stoves, furnaces, grates, cooking apparatus, lamps, ventilators, the preparation of fuel, etc., there have been numerous improvements since 1850. Of stoves, ranges, grates, etc., there have been endless modifications designed to economize fuel, space, and labor, or answer other ends of domestic economy Among the improvers of these articles, were the following patentees, most of whom have been prominent also as manufacturers, viz.: Gardner Chilson, Moses Pond, J. P. Hayes, G. S. G. Spence, and others in Boston; Anson Atwood, S. Pierce, and James McGregor, Jr., of Troy; R. D. Granger, W. B. & J. G. Treadwell, S. T. Savage, James Easterly, and others in Albany, New York; Washington Race, Seneca Falls; J. L. Mott, Mott Haven, New York, one of the oldest as an improver in this branch,[1] Loftus Wood, J. Jackson, and others in New York City; North, Chase & North, Thomas T. Tasker, Andrew Mayer, Abbott & Lawrence, Leibrant & McDowell, in Philadelphia, and many others.

Among the patented improvements in this class, are comprised

1) Jordan L. Mott, a descendant of one of the first settlers of Long Island, who has been known for upward of a quarter of a century as an inventor and manufacturer, has probably contributed more than any man now living to the early adoption and nearly universal use of Anthracite as a fuel, and also to the beauty and neatness of stoves and all other iron castings of a household kind. His improvements in stoves and grates began almost with the commencement of the Anthracite coal trade—his first patent having been issued, we believe, in 1832—and are borne on the records of the Patent Office in nearly every year from that time until he retired from active business, in 1857. His patents include bars and grates for stoves—parlor, cooking, and other stoves—furnaces, ranges, and fireplaces, of a great variety of patterns; cast-iron columns for buildings; knobs and handles for stoves; eccentric or pivot chairs; a process of chilling castings; bathing tubs; car wheels; flasks for moulding bath tubs; core bar for moulding pipes; combined furnaces and caldron for farm use; rotary chairs, etc. Of these patents, amounting in all to between thirty and forty, he has registered, in a single year, as many as five for different things. His improvements in grates and stoves for burning coal were based upon the laws which govern combustion, and led to the use of nut, pea, and other small sized coal, at a time when the properties of that kind of fuel were little understood, by teaching that the depth of the coal in a grate must be increased with the size of the coal, and the volume of air used in its combustion. He was one of the first to employ the cupola furnace for stoves and other castings for domestic use, and by using remelted iron, introduced a light, smooth, sharp cut, and elegant style of stove plate in place of the rough castings of the blast furnace previously used. By studying the effects of irregular expansion by heat he was able to overcome the tendency to strain and crack by a change in the form of the plates, that is by panelling, curving, or fluting them. At his Works at Mott Haven, some of the lightest castings ever made in proportion to extent of surface, have probably been produced.

the apparatus for drying grain, which, owing to the heavy movements of the grain crops of the West, has been in great demand; also, the devices for cooking and heating by gas, and the still more recent contrivances for supplying Petroleum and its products as generators of light and heat for domestic purposes, and numerous improvements in apparatus for burning gas, kerosene, patent burning fluid, and the various liquid hydrocarbons. The influence exerted upon the latter class of inventions by the introduction of Petroleum, is seen in the fact that from March 1, 1862, to December 30, 1863, the number of applications for patents for Lamps specially designed for burning it, numbered six hundred and twenty-three, while in the three years previous to March, 1861, the number was only one hundred and ninety-three. The machinery for breaking, washing, screening, and otherwise preparing coal for market was also much improved in the same time.

VII. The great activity of every form of productive industry, of travel and transportation in this country, has stimulated improvements in the construction of Boilers, and Steam and Gas and Air Engines, and other appendages, whether for stationary, locomotive, or marine use. The higher cost of coal in the United States has led to modifications of steam boilers, whereby they have been rendered, if not more durable, at least more economical of fuel than English boilers. By an improvement in 1855, a further saving of fuel was made by the consumption of the combustible gases, commonly called smoke. Many of these improvements have been made within the last ten or fifteen years, as well as the introduction of spring gauges, for determining the pressure of steam in locomotive and other boilers; and of upward of forty different kinds of these in use, all but two or three, which have also been improved here, are of American invention. Among the principal improvers in the Steam-engine and its appurtenances, since 1850, may be mentioned the following: John Ericsson, of New York, O. M. Stillman, of Connecticut, S. Wilcox, Jr., of Rhode Island, Philander Shaw & S. H. Roper, of Boston, and others, in Caloric engines; J. C. F. Salomon, Cincinnati, Carbonic Acid and Gas engines; William Mt. Storm, of Troy, New York, Compressed Air or Gas engine; Loper & Nystrom, of Philadelphia, W. Kennish, Jr., of New York, and others, in Marine engines; M. W. Baldwin, of Philadelphia, Ross Winans, Baltimore, and others, in Locomotives; Jacob Perkins, London, Joseph Harrison, Jr., of Philadelphia, and George H. Corliss, of Rhode Island, and others, in Boilers; R. Montgomery, New York (Corrugated) and other Boilers; Horatio Allen, D. G. Wells, F. E. Sickles, New York, Cut-off Valves; Edward Ashcroft, Boston, Pressure Gauges; G. Weissenborn, New York, Filtering Apparatus to prevent boiler explosions, and expedients for the same purpose by Joseph Harrison, Jr., Norman Wiard, of New York, and others; William Baxter, Newark, N. J., Hydro Steam-engine; Paul Stillman, New York, Gas engine; Joseph Echols, Georgia, Water Gauges; Professor M. Vergnes, of New York, Electro Magnetic engines. The Steam Pump or Fire engine is also an American invention of the same period, although it was attempted many years ago by Mr. Ericsson, who designed the Braithwaite engine now used in England. It was first successfully introduced at Cincinnati, in 1852, the constructors being A. & B. Latta, and the engineer, Miles Greenwood, of that city, where the first paid fire department was organized, the same year, through the exertions of the latter gentleman. The Steam Fire Engine has been since improved by Neafie & Levy, of Philadelphia, the Amoskeag Manufacturing Co., of New Hampshire, and others.

VIII. In the manufacture of Leather and its ultimate products, which are interests of great magnitude in the United States, several valuable improvements have been made within the last fifteen years. Several of these relate to methods of extracting the tannin from bark, and to other processes and appliances for quick tanning. Among these more expeditious modes may be mentioned the systems of L. C. England, of Williamsburg and Oswego, N. Y., embracing both handling and liquor making apparatus, patented in 1847, 1850, 1855, 1858, and 1859; the tanning process of Professor A. K. Eaton, of Rochester, N. Y., patented 1852, and involving use of sulphate of potash with the tanning liquids; that of Roswell Enos, of Woodstock, Ill., in 1854, and of Otis B. Wattles, of Waddington, N. Y., in 1855, for tanning compounds; the method of Abraham Steers, of Medina, N. Y., in 1856, for the manufacture of leather and extracts of bark, whereby it was claimed that sole leather could be perfectly tanned in four days, with a great saving of material; the patents of Samuel W. Pingree, of Methuen, Mass., and of E. A. Eliason, of Georgetown, D. C., in the same year, and that of H. G. Johnson, of Cleveland, Ohio, in 1858, have each attracted considerable attention. The latest invention of this kind, and one that gives promise of revolutionizing the leather manufacture, by reason of its great expedition and economy of capital and of material, is that of William H. Towers, of Boston, for which a patent was obtained in December, 1865. By this process, it is said, sheep and goat skins can be tanned in thirty minutes, calf skins in five days, and the heaviest sole leather in thirty days, while the product is deemed superior to that made by other methods.

Many improvements have also been patented in bark mills, in leather rolling, splitting, skinning, and cutting machines, in shoe pegs, heels, tips, etc., and in machinery for sewing, pegging, crimping, etc. Among these may be named Beardsley's Patent Bark Mill, Safford's Rolling and Splitting Machines, and Safford's and Chase's Skiving Machines; Stratton's, Hill's, Knox & Ditchburn's Sole Pressing and Cutting Machines; Baldwin's, Stewart's, and other Shoe Pegs; Bates', McKay's, and other Stitching Machines, and Gallahues', Greenough's, Sturtevant's, Vittum's, and other Pegging Machines; Mitchell's Patent Metallic Tips; Dinsmore's Metallic Heels, and those of W. Hunt, S. Oliver, and others; Lewis's Patent Boot Trees; various improvements in Lasts; McClallan's Wooden Sole Boots and Shoes and Brogans.

IX. In the class of Household Furniture and Domestic Implements, the new articles and the improvements upon old ones patented, are too numerous to be specified, embracing every description of machine, utensil, and contrivance which could add to domestic comfort and economy.

In this wide range of invention were embraced the more important articles of furniture, such as spring sofas, and other beds and bedsteads, refrigerators, washing and wringing machines, etc., in which many improvements have been made, and also such articles as cans and jars for preserving fruits, with the methods of sealing and opening them; brooms and brushes, carpet fasteners, stretchers and sweepers, clothes dryers and clamps, window shades and fixtures.

X. In the department of the Polite, Fine, and Ornamental Arts, the improvements patented in the last few years, though valuable in the aggregate, present few remarkable features. Considerable progress was made in Photography, Engraving, the founding, setting, and distributing of Type, Color printing, Bookbinding, and in Musical Instruments and notations, etc. Modifications and improvements of Hand, Power, Lithographic, and other Printing-presses were patented by several old improvers, as Danforth, Adams, Hoe, and others more recent, as Jeptha A. Wilkinson, Moses S. Beach, S. P. Ruggles, Jedediah Morse, W. H. Mitchell, F. O. Degener, G. P. Gordon, F. L. Bailey, and William Bullock, assignor to George W. Taylor, of Newark, N. J. The Automatic Paper Feeder and Power-press of the last mentioned, patented in 1858, and since improved, gives promise of becoming one of the most effective machines in use. It occupies far less space than the ordinary rotary press, and prints on both sides of a continuous sheet, fed by machinery, and cuts off and piles in regular heaps, without manual aid, newspaper sheets the size of the *Philadelphia Inquirer*, at the rate of eighteen thousand to twenty thousand single impressions hourly, requiring the aid of only one pressman and two assistants.

Type-setting, or composing and distributing machines, single or combined, which will probably soon banish the composing stick, were patented by Victor Beaumont, J. J. Koenig, W. W. Houston, W. H. Mitchell, Timothy Alden, F. W. Gilmer, C. W. Felt, and others. Of these, Mitchell's, which has been several years in operation in large printing establishments in New York; Alden's, which combines both operations with remarkable performance, distributing type altogether automatically, and the machines of Mr. Felt, of Salem, are probably the most noted. For the use of newspaper publishers, very useful machines for printing the address of subscribers have been patented, among others, by H. Moeser, Edward P. Day, S. D. Carpenter, and James Lord, and one by R. W. Wright, in 1865, for feeding up, cutting, and pasting directions on newspapers. Polygraphic Copying Presses, patented by N. Ames and others, were useful inventions of this period.

XI. Although, during the long period of profound peace previous to 1861, many improvements and inventions in the manufacture of Fire-arms and heavy ordnance were made, the number since that year, in consequence of the war, has vastly augmented. The whole number of patents recorded for cannon, projectiles, ammunition, small arms, cartridges, tents, and other implements of war, including machines and processes for their manufacture, previous to 1857, did not exceed three hundred. In the four years, from 1860 to 1863, respectively, the number of applications filed were, in 1860, one hundred and thirty-nine; in 1861, three hundred and sixty-six; in 1862, four hundred and fifty-three; and in 1863, three hundred and twenty-two. In the manufacture of Cannon, the improvements actually patented in those years severally were, seven, thirty, forty-three, and thirty-nine, of which number forty were for loading at the breech. The number of small arms patented in the same years, was forty-seven, forty-four, seventy-two, and eighty-one, respectively, and one hundred and ten of the whole number were for breech-loading arms. Many of the projectors of improvements did not realize their expectations, but the names of Colt, Sharp, Whitney, Allen, Maynard, Spencer, Berdan, and others, became, by their inventions, well known to the public, and Rifles have been invented that can be loaded and fired by practiced hands thirty times in a minute. In the construction and manufacture of Cannon and heavy ordnance, many improvements were patented, of which the most important were those of Parrott, Rodman, Wiard, and Ames.

In the late war, the Parrott rifled guns and projectiles, both in the land and naval service, performed a conspicuous part, nearly three thousand of these guns, ranging in calibre from three to ten inches, and in weight of ball from ten to three hundred pounds, having been ordered by the Government, and made at the West Point Foundry. The first gun on this principle, the essential feature of which is the re-inforcing or strengthening the breech of a cast-iron gun by shrinking upon it a wrought-iron jacket or band, having a definite strength and position proportioned to the size of a gun, was made in 1860, and patented in October, 1861. During that year Mr. Parrott also received two patents for projectiles for Rifled Cannon, which were designed as an accompaniment of the guns, to the neglect in using which he in great part ascribes the bursting of several of the large Parrott guns at Fort Fisher, by the premature explosion of shells within the guns. Later, in the same year, he took out another for an improved mode of applying fuses to shells, whereby they became either time or percussion fuses. These projectiles have been successfully used of the weight of six hundred pounds. An additional patent for an improvement in hooped ordnance, was granted Mr. Parrott in 1862, by which time he began to construct, in the same way, rifled cannon of eight inch calibre, or two hundred pounders, which were mounted at Yorktown, and commended themselves to the approbation of American and foreign artillerists by their performance, as those of less calibre had done before. Two ten inch three hundred pounders, afterward constructed, were disabled from the cause above named, but of other sizes, as thirty pounders and upward, and of the projectiles, the value was abundantly tested in the bombardments of Forts Sumter, Macon, Pulaski, and the shelling of Charleston, where they were chiefly used as siege guns, often at a distance of four thousand yards and upward. Parrott rifled guns of large calibre are used upon United States naval vessels, being able to throw projectiles with greater accuracy and to a greater distance than smooth bore guns. To prevent the bursting of shells within the bore, by friction of the powder within them, on the discharge of the gun, Mr. Parrott successfully adopted the plan of coating the interior walls of the shell with a lacker or varnish of rosin, tallow, and brown soap melted together.

The Rodman gun, while having in some respects a peculiar form, is chiefly distinguished for the mode of manufacture proposed by Lieutenant Rodman, while superintending the casting of eight inch cannon for the United States Government at the Fort Pitt Foundry, in 1845, and, after satisfactory tests, adopted by the War Department, in the casting of all heavy ordnance. It consists in making the casting around a hollow core or core-barrel, as it is termed, into which is introduced a copious stream of cold water, while the outside is kept heated, until the mass of metal is cooled from the interior. This mode of cooling is thought to possess two advantages over the old one of casting solid and then boring out; first, in reversing the strain on the metal, making it less liable to burst; and, secondly, in giving greater hardness to the internal surface of the gun, making it less liable to abrasion by the friction of the projectile, and the action of the gases generated by the burning powder. It has been deemed the only effective way of making cast-iron guns of large calibre.

The gun of Rear-Admiral Dahlgren is distinguished principally by its exterior form. To obviate the contraction consequent on cooling a solid casting of large size from the outside, his castings were made considerably larger than required when finished, and, after cooling, were annealed and turned down to the proper size and shape. The Dahlgren and Rodman guns were generally smooth bore, though some large ones were rifled. Heavy cast-iron rifled ordnance, however, made by any of these modes, has by no means proved a success, the ordinary tests of the proving ground falling short of that to which guns are subjected by rapid and continued firing in battle, where many of them have burst, with disastrous and mortifying results.

The Steel Rifled Cannon is altogether a product of the late war. It was invented and patented by Mr. Norman Wiard, of the Trenton Wiard Ordnance Works, whose contributions in guns, and materials of war manufactured by him, amounted to four and a half millions of dollars, and the cost of experiments on guns to four hundred thousand dollars of his own means, directly expended. Long and favorably known throughout the western country before the war as an intelligent and practical machinist, he at the very commencement of the war turned his engineering abilities and experience as a manufacturer to the service of his country, in the invention and construction of ordnance and other materials of war. As early as May, 1861, he contracted with General D. E. Sickles to furnish three batteries of steel rifled guns for the Excelsior Brigade, which, with the carriages, implements, stores, etc., were completed, inspected, and ready for service on the 4th of July. They were the first steel guns ever made in the United States, and were from original designs by Mr. Wiard, who endeavored to discover and avoid the causes of frequent failure in heavy ordnance. He succeeded in producing guns unrivalled in precision and range, if not also in their powers of endurance. The carriages for these guns were also of new design by the manufacturer, and were the first ever built expressly adapted for rifled cannon, being constructed to give the gun its utmost range without a special adjustment of the carriage. The superiority of these guns as field artillery will not probably be questioned. Mr. Wiard soon after began to construct heavy steel rifled guns for the navy. The blocks of steel from which some of these were made in 1861, weighed eight thousand pounds each, being the largest masses of steel, it is believed, ever made up to that time. Although the steel was of superior quality, and the strength of the guns fourfold that of cast-iron cannon of the same calibre, three of them, made from Government patterns, afterward exploded on the ninth round, after rapid firing in cold weather. Mr. Wiard's metallurgic experience at once suggested the cause, and the remedy, which was a very simple one, to counteract the effects of unequal expansion, but his proposal was not entertained by the Ordnance Department, and his offer to construct new guns designed to obviate the effects of rapid firing upon all heavy ordnance met with the same fate. Having, by a series of costly experiments, satisfied himself of the correctness of his theory, which had long employed his research in connection with steam boiler explosions, Mr. Wiard has given to the world, in different forms of publications, the result of his investigations, which may be profitably studied by scientific and practical men, in relation to this important and still mooted question. In 1862, Mr. Wiard supplied, of his own manufacture, the entire armament, guns, ordnance stores, and equipments of the expedition commanded by General Burnside, to whose entire satisfaction it was fitted out. About the same time he was commissioned to finish a large number of seven and a half inch one hundred and fifty pounder rifled guns, of the Dahlgren pattern, from blocks cast at West Point and Pittsburg, weighing twenty-three thousand pounds each, in the rough. But the order was suspended by the bursting of most of them in remarkable confirmation of his repeated predictions and representations to the Government, as to the defective principle on which, in common with other large guns, they were constructed. This defect in the system of making heavy ordnance as well as the remedy Mr. Wiard claims to have been the first to discover, and he complains that either from interested motives or an undue attachment to effete methods with great detriment to the public service, he has not been permitted to bring into practical use a better plan. By arrangement with the Secretary of the Navy, a large navy gun was constructed in 1864, at a cost of eighty thousand dollars, which has ever since been awaiting at the Works in Trenton, an order for its trial, while the Government is selling for old iron, at a hundredth part of their cost, the old guns and substituting none in their place. In view of the general failure of heavy ordnance, and of Mr. Wiard's large experience and great facilities for manufacturing both rifled and smooth bore guns of the largest size, it might have been expected, that his best and most practical proposals for turning to account the vast amount of the best material accumulated in the Government arsenals and navy yards as worthless guns, would have been accorded a measure of the patronage so long and liberally bestowed upon other patentees.

The Wrought-iron Gun, invented and patented by Horatio Ames, of Falls Village, Conn., in May, 1864, is the latest invention of the kind; and although but few of these have been manufactured as yet, they are said to have successfully withstood every test that has been applied to them. In the opinion of a Board appointed to test one of seven inch calibre, they "possess to a degree never before equalled by any cannon of equal weight offered to our service the essential qualities of lateral and longitudinal strength and great powers of endurance under heavy charges; that they are not liable to burst explosively, and without warning, even when fired under very high charges, and that they are well adapted to the wants of the service generally, but especially whenever long ranges and high velocities are required."

XII. In the class of Medical and Surgical Instruments, many novelties and some useful improvements have been introduced under letters patent within the last twelve or fifteen years, particularly in the departments of Mechanical Dentistry, and in surgical appliances for treating bodily injuries and deformities, as in Artificial Limbs and Eyes, Splints, Crutches, Trusses, etc. The recent war has furnished melancholy occasion and scope for the exercise of ingenuity, both of an interested and benevolent character, in relieving the numerous forms of human suffering induced by its casualties, although but a small portion of the fruits are seen upon the records of the Patent Office. Under the stimulus thus given, patents are still daily multiplied for devices tending to the relief of those permanently disabled by the war. Hospital Beds and Bedsteads, Ambulances, Litters, Stretchers, Hospital Knapsacks, Medicine Panniers, Medicine Chests, Field Companions, Instrument Cases, Tourniquets, Fracture Apparatus, Bandages, Plasters, and other mechanical appliances and dressings, Coffins and Burial Cases, formed but a part of the numerous articles invented, improved, or modified, to adapt them to the peculiar exigencies of the service. A valuable improvement has been made in the manufacture of many articles in this class by the employment of vulcanized or hard Rubber, and Gutta Percha, as materials for the handles of instruments, for Syringes, Splints, etc., and as a base for Artificial Teeth, Obturator Plates, etc., etc.

In the class of Anæsthetics, several important discoveries have been made, of which probably the most valuable is that of the Nitrous Oxide Gas, because of its safety, and freedom from the disagreeable sensations that attend the administration of chloroform and ether. The discovery of its anæsthetic properties was made accidentally, in 1844, by Dr.

Wells, of New Haven, who was led to investigate the subject from the fact that a young man, who had been injured at a public exhibition while under its influence, denied that he was at all hurt. Experiments were made in the extraction of teeth, but it was not until recently, through the agency of Dr. Colton, of New York, that its real value became fully known. More than ten thousand patients have had teeth extracted since 1863 under its influence, without pain, and several capital operations in surgery have been performed—among others, one for the removal of cancer, in which the insensibility was continued for fifteen minutes, with entire success.

XIII. The manufacture of Wearing Apparel, and articles for the Toilet, as branches of trade, have been immensely increased since 1850, and have undergone many changes in form and direction, as well by the introduction of new materials and new articles, as by reason of the many instruments and devices, small and great, for saving labor, and adapting the products to the comfort, convenience, and tastes of the community.

The manufacture of Combs, whether made of metal, horn, shell, ivory, wood, or hard rubber, now so extensively employed, has been greatly improved by new machinery for shaping, pressing, sizing, cutting the teeth, and finishing generally, by automatic processes, and with remarkable precision and rapidity. For making Buttons of every material and style, as well as Button-holes and Eyelets, Studs, Links, Buckles, Clasps, Hooks and Eyes, Suspenders, and other fastenings of garments, many improvements have been patented, chiefly by citizens of Connecticut and Massachusetts. In the making-up, of every description, the Sewing Machine has effected quite a revolution, particularly in the production of Shirts, Shirt Fronts and Collars, Ladies' Collars and Cuffs, Hoop Skirts, and under garments of all kinds, Linen Coats, Blouses, children's wear, which, with nearly every other article of wearing apparel, are now chiefly made by these machines. The manufacturers of one Sewing Machine, elsewhere referred to, which is probably the most extensively used for this purpose, have sold no less than two hundred thousand machines, each of which is estimated, by the proprietors of shirt front and collar manufactories employing from thirty to seventy-five machines each, to save the labor of ten persons. Counting their wages at five dollars a week, the annual saving effected by the machines, made under a single patent, would amount to one hundred millions of dollars.

The highly original and fertile mind which gave the world the first crude conception of this Sewing Machine, also furnished the germ of another American invention, which has already laid the foundation of a large and growing trade. We allude to the Paper Shirt Collar, invented by the late Walter Hunt, of New York, and patented by him July 25th, 1854. The fabric of which this inexpensive and popular article was made, was composed of two pieces of white paper, with one of thin muslin between them, pressed together, and subsequently polished by enamelling or burnishing. As a new article of manufacture, however, the Paper Collar business first became a successful enterprise in the hands of W. E. Lockwood, of Philadelphia, to whom the reissued patents were assigned. About the year 1858, he commenced the manufacture in Philadelphia by steam power, and soon after applied the same method to the production of Ladies' Collars and Cuffs, for which he took out letters patent in 1859. In February, 1863, John F. Schuyler patented an improved apparatus for bending and folding Paper Collars, and assigned the same to Mr. Lockwood, who has since patented other improvements in the machinery. In April and June, 1863, Solomon S. Gray, of Boston, was granted patents for an article now extensively manufactured and sold as Gray's Patent Moulded Collars, for which the fine white paper is cut out of a flat strip of paper and then struck up with dies, or pressed into the desired form—an operation originally effected by a single moulding machine, but now better accomplished by several operations. The inventor has received some eight patents on collars and machines, in this country and in Europe, whither the agents have been sent with American machines and workmen, to establish manufactories in England, France, and Belgium. In addition to those already mentioned, the following, among others, have taken out patents for machinery for making Paper Collars, etc., namely: Henry Howson, of Philadelphia, Thos. McSpedon, Emil Vossnack, and D. M. Smyth, of New York City, and S. Sheperd and Ammi George, of Nashua, N. H.; while Charles Spofford and Valentine Fogerty, of Boston, have received patents for converting the ends of paper collars into an artificial Neck Tie; James H. Hoffman, of New York, for Turned-down Enamelled Paper Collars; G. F. Bigelow, of Chicago, for Collars of the same description, made of one or two pieces of enamelled card-board; Charles K. Brown, of Troy, New York, for strengthening the Button-holes, and other parts subject to strain, by pieces of muslin; G. K. Snow, of Watertown, Mass., for a Paper Collar Packing Envelope, and also for Dies for Cutting Paper Collars; Paul C. Shaw, of Marlboro, Mass., for Paper Collar made with an imitation of a Cravat printed or formed on it. The manufacture of Paper Collars and Cuffs, etc., under different patents, now employs over thirty establishments, in which the hands are principally young females, who make each about eighteen hundred collars per day by machinery. In April, 1863, Julius A. Pease, of New York city, obtained a patent for a Shirt Collar made of Caoutchouc, or India-rubber; and another, in June of the same year, for a Collar made by covering a metal frame with water-proof enamelled cloth or other material.[1] The American Steel Collar was patented in April, 1864; and in September, 1865, two patents were granted to Louis Billon, of Brooklyn, New York, for Metallic Collars and Metallic Shirt Bosoms.

Seamless Felt Wearing Apparel was the subject of a patent issued to Samuel M. Perkins, of Springfield, Pa., in 1853; and other patents for Seamless garments have since been obtained.

The improvements made in the manufacture of Boots and Shoes within a few years past, by the introduction of machinery, have been sufficiently numerous and important to mark an era in the history of the trade, and have probably not been surpassed in their aggregate value by those in any other branch of manufactures. In this, as in every other department of the clothing trade, the principal agency has been the Sewing Machine, operated by steam power. That and other labor-saving machines for cutting out the soles, heels, and uppers, for pegging, burnishing, and other operations, are now driven by the exhaustless energy of steam, whereby the entire system of manufacture has been imperceptibly but effectually revolutionized. Their use has silently brought about a transfer of the work from small shops to large factories, several stories high, in which all parts of the manufacture are carried on under the same roof, each floor being devoted to a separate portion of the work, which is conducted in a manner similar to the factory system of other countries, and of our large cotton centres. In pegged work, which forms the bulk of the manufacture, every operation, except fitting the shoe to the last, even to the polishing and cutting the pegs from the inside, is done by machinery, and the pegging machine has been so perfected as to cut the pegs from a strip of wood, punch the holes, and drive the pegs at a single operation. A machine will peg a ladies' shoe in seven seconds after the work is placed in the machine. It will average one thousand pairs of such shoes a day, and from four hundred to five hundred pairs of shoes with double rows of pegs in the same time. Though usually of wood, hard rubber has also been used for making shoe pegs, and more recently raw hide, which is said to render the pegged shoe very elastic. But as the cost of stitching and binding the uppers of boots and shoes of the better quality is

(1) The same inventor has recently patented a process for making Hats from paper pulp, and a company is being organized in Boston for their manufacture. It is stated that good, durable hats, of various colors, and water-proof, can be made for five cents each. A machine will make six hundred a day.

greater than that of bottoming, but little economy was found in the use of machinery for the latter purpose until the introduction of Sewing Machines. Several machines have been designed or found to be adapted to stitching leather. It is reported that a large company is about being organized in Boston for the manufacture of a Shoe Sewing Machine that will sew a shoe in about twelve seconds. A manufacturer, in October, 1865, sewed on one of these machines ten thousand nine hundred and twenty-five pairs, an average of four hundred and twenty pairs per day, and another stitched eight thousand nine hundred and twenty-eight pairs. Not only are shoes quickly and cheaply made by machinery, but they are better made than by hand. It has been attested that army shoes made by machinery lasted eight months, while hand made shoes did not last more than a month. The soles of the former were sowed with dozens of rows, and were necessarily much more durable. Sewed shoes could now be sold at the same price as pegged, if the same quality of leather were used.

Among inventions of a miscellaneous character, we have had, since 1850, improved machines for manufacturing raw hide and other whips ; for cutting corks ; for splitting horn and shell, and the manufacture of articles from the same ; machines for making paper bags and paper boxes ; for attaching hooks and eyes and pins to cards and papers ; for manufacturing slate pencils ; for making sand paper ; for leathering tacks ; for making cigars. Patents have been filed for exploding and other harpoons ; for processes for making artificial ice ; for annunciators for hotels ; electro-magnetic annunciators for houses ; for forming screw necks and stoppers for glass bottles, jars, etc. ; for aquaria ; for attaching letter boxes to lamp posts ; for magnetic and other alarm bells, and for various descriptions of burglars' alarms, alarm clocks, and sash balances, alarm prisons, etc. ; for fire escapes, bottle fastenings, billiard tables, balls, cushions, etc.; animal traps, fish traps, and machines for recording and counting the votes or yeas and nays in Legislative assemblies, etc.

Of all these, probably the most ingenious and astonishing are the machines invented by Chauncy O. Crosby, of New Haven, for making Fish-hooks and Sewing Needles, which convert the raw wire into the finished article at the rate of one hundred and fifty per minute—a feat never before accomplished in this or any other country.

Indeed, the fertility of American genius, at once speculative and practical in its operations, has left no field of inventive enterprise uncultivated. Following closely the lead of scientific research, with every new development of the laws of the physical world, and every unfolding of the treasures in the vast storehouse of nature's material resources, the inventive American stands ready to supplement the weakness of the corporeal man with the powerful combinations of his mind. Thus the material elements and occult forces of nature are all subdued to the service of man, and through the energy of his brain and the cunning of his hand, as displayed not less in the broad field of its manufactures, than in every other form of national art and industry, the American has contributed to the intellectual, moral, and physical improvement and happiness of mankind.

We have thus endeavored to trace the growth of American mauufactures and invention from their infancy, through the stages of a development unparalleled in the history of any other nation. In the liberty of unrestricted exercise; in the breadth of the field to be cultivated; in the fertility and elasticity of resources, mental and material, as well as in the magnitude of the accomplished results, these great elements of national prosperity now hold a position in few respects inferior, and in most superior, to that attained among any other people. The progress of the country in population, and in its commercial, social, and intellectual condition, within the short period covered by this review, has indeed been marvellous. But the growth of its productive industry, particularly of its manufactures and the evolution of the inventive genius of the country, which has received prominent notice in the foregoing pages, has been still more rapid and astonishing since its emergence from the colonial condition. In recording the leading phenomena of this progress, we have sought to do little more than marshall the facts in their consecutive order and dependent relations, without seeking in disputed principles or theories of political philosophy for the secret of its advance or retardation. The potent causes of the industrial prosperity of these States we apprehend lie near the surface, and are to be found in the freedom of American Institutions generally, in the abundance of the natural resources of the country, and a blending in the composite national character of the best practical elements of the several nationalities represented by its population, and less than in most other countries to the fostering care of the Government, although in a moderate degree the latter cause has not been wanting in the legislation of the federal and local assemblies. Our pages, however, reflect but imperfectly the variety and extent of an industry, the wonderful activity of which has been felt in every department of the national life, and has made its impression upon the social and industrial economy of the world.

In the three fourths of a century that have passed since the United States became one in the family of nations, extraordinary discoveries have been made in physical and mechanical science. These discoveries have been speedily applied to the practical uses of mankind. In this work American genius and energy, though checked by the retarding influences of three foreign and domestic wars, has performed its full share. They have subordinated the tireless energy of Steam to more extensive and varied uses than any other people, including the grand triumph of ocean navigation. They have taught the nations of the earth how to control the subtle energy of the lightning's flash, and from remotest distances to exchange from the pulsating fingers of the electro-magnet currents of thought and intelligence almost as quickly as they are conceived. Even while we write, American genius and perseverance in schemes of practical utility—after having furnished the world with many of its most effective instruments, reticulated the country with lines of Telegraph, and given a wider practical scope to telegraphy, in the fire and police alarm, in the announcement of approaching storms, and in other ways—is busy in consummating the most signal triumph at present anticipated, that of forging the ocean clasp which will belt the whole earth with a girdle more potent and sensational than the fabled cestus of the poets.

In the art of modifying the curious native properties of Caoutchouc and Gutta Percha, and of moulding their plastic elements into a thousand forms of beauty and utility, whether hard or soft, smooth or corrugated, rigid or elastic, American ingenuity and patient experiment have never been excelled, and the whole world participates in the benefits.

Petroleum, as a natural product, has been known, and to some extent utilized, for centuries in other parts of the world. It was reserved, however, for American enterprise to show that there exists, at various depths and in widely distant places, almost exhaustless reservoirs of a substance which, either in its crude state or elaborated by the technical chemist, has within a very short period become one of extensive commercial importance in the arts, as a lubricator, a generator of light and heat, and a source of new and beautiful dyes. It has thus become one of the most valuable and productive of material resources.

The extent and variety of American Mechanical skill are very imperfectly seen in such prominent inventions as the Power, Carpet and Stocking looms; in the Rotary Power Printing-press; the Automatic Type Setter and Distributor; in the Steam Fire Engines; in the Mowing, Reaping, and Threshing machines; the Sewing Machine, with all its various applications by hand or steam power, and the other prominent inventions noticed in the foregoing pages. The multitude of minor improvements, often unrecorded and unregarded by the public eye, which go to make up the aggregate of the mechanical forces of the nation, and to swell the amount of its production, are an important element in the general prosperity, but are too numerous or elusive to arrest even the eyes of the annalist. Since our labors were begun the progress of the nation in its productive capacities and its mechanical inventions has been going on with an accelerated speed, baffling every effort to follow its protean changes. Notwithstanding the fact that a terrible civil war has projected its baleful shadow across the shining pathway of the nation—diverting from the arts of peace much of the strength and genius of the people—the inventive talents of the country have suffered little more than a temporary check, and are now more active than ever before. It will ever remain as a monument of the patriotism, enterprise, and skill of American manufacturers, inventors, and artisans, that the equipment of the vast land and naval armaments of the loyal States, and the enormous consumption of the war in materials and supplies of every kind, were mainly supplied from the workshops of the country. The prompt conversion of its manufacturing establishments in many instances to new uses, according to the demand of the hour, and their speedy restoration since the war to their former purposes, show the flexibility of American industry, as the prosperous emergence of the manufacturing classes from the great contest shows its vitality, and affords the strongest assurance of its permanence and future grandeur.

INDEX

TO

REPRESENTATIVE MANUFACTURERS.

Hon. Nathan Appleton, Boston, Mass.

THIS eminent Merchant and Manufacturer was born in New Ipswich, New Hampshire, in 1779. He entered Dartmouth College in 1794, but left before graduating, to engage in a mercantile business in Boston, with his brother Samuel, establishing the firm of S. & N. Appleton, which for many years occupied a leading position among the firms of that commercial city.

His attention and means were early directed to fostering the growth of domestic manufactures, and he was one of the original proprietors of the Waltham Cotton Manufactory, elsewhere alluded to, where the Power-Loom was first put in operation in this country, in 1815. The success of this establishment, more than any thing else, gave an impetus to the manufacture of cotton goods, and led to the purchase of the site of Lowell, and the erection of the Hamilton Company's Mills, and other large manufactories. His connection with the early manufactories of the country have been already so frequently alluded to in this volume, that more need not be said on the subject in this place.

In 1830, he was elected to Congress as a Representative of the district of Lowell, and again in 1842, where he discharged his duties satisfactorily to his constituents, and with advantage to the nation.

He died July 14th, 1861, bequeathing to his relatives a large fortune and an honorable name.

Samuel Batchelder, Boston.

The life of this venerable Manufacturer covers the whole period of our national history since the adoption of the Federal Constitution. He was born in the town of Jaffrey, New Hampshire, in 1784; but his youth was passed in New Ipswich, in the same State, whither his parents removed within a few weeks after his birth. In early life he evinced decidedly literary tastes, contributing to the "Portfolio," then a leading periodical published in Philadelphia, and this habit of extensive reading has been preserved, notwithstanding the distractions incident to an active business career; and lately he has given to the world a small but excellent Treatise on the History of the Cotton Manufacture in the United States.

His connection with Cotton manufacturing dates from 1808, when he became interested in a factory at New Ipswich, elsewhere referred to in this volume, and which was the second established in the State of New Hampshire. The first mill built in the State was in 1804, with less than five hundred spindles; and it is said that its proprietors felt a degree of hostility against those who erected a second mill, with about the same number of spindles, from apprehension that they would "overdo the business." The erection of these mills attracted to the place a number of Yorkshire weavers and Scotch manufacturers, whom Mr. Batchelder employed in the manufacture of checks and tickings, and other articles, by hand-looms. He continued in this business until 1825, when Mr. Nathan Appleton, and other capitalists interested in Lowell, induced him to remove thither and superintend the erection of the Hamilton Manufacturing Company's Mills, which, from the foundation to their final completion, were built under his supervision. He remained in Lowell until 1831, when he removed to Saco, Maine, to undertake the erection of a Cotton Mill for the York Manufacturing Company, and superintend its operations. Under his management this Company became very successful. Three additional mills were built, and the capital increased to a million of dollars. In 1846, Mr. Batchelder removed to Cambridge, Massachusetts, where he has ever since resided, and of which city he was elected Representative in the Legislature of Massachusetts.

Within this period of time Mr. Batchelder contributed to the Cotton manufacturing interest several important inventions. In 1833 or 1834 he invented and applied the first stop motion to the Drawing Frame, which was afterward patented in England, where it has since been in general use, as well as in this country. In 1835 he invented the steam cylinders and connections, now almost universally used in dressing frames for drying yarns. But probably his greatest invention was the Dynamometer, for ascertaining the power for driving machinery, and first used in the York Mills in 1837. This machine was awarded medals by Fairs and Institutes in this country, and described in scientific journals in Scotland and Germany, where it was pronounced preferable to any known apparatus for ascertaining the power actually used in driving machinery.

Mr. Batchelder, though he has attained the patriarchal age of eighty-two, is still discharging the duties of Treasurer of the York Mills at Saco, and the Everett Mills at Lawrence. Few men at his age equal him in mental and physical activity, and none can present a brighter record of those moral qualities that adorn manhood.

Richard Borden and Jefferson Borden,

Who are called the "Fathers of Fall River," are natives of that town, which has grown during their lifetime, and largely by their enterprise, from a mere hamlet to become a great manufacturing city. They are sons of Thomas Borden, a farmer and a miller, and in their youth they aided him in these pursuits. Fall River, on which the town of the same name is located, is a remarkable stream, having a descent of one hundred and thirty feet in less than half a mile, and for the greater part of its length is confined between high granite banks. The water power, therefore, has nearly all to be occupied between these banks, and the wheels upon which it is brought to act are placed directly in the bed of the river. It is also a characteristic of this river that while it affords an almost uniform and constant supply of water it is never subject to excess, and therefore no injury or inconvenience has ever been experienced from so peculiar a location of the mills. Nearly all the water power and the real estate on which the principal manufactories are now located were owned by the Borden family since the beginning of the last century. The site on which the Fall River Manufactory was erected, in 1815, was originally a mill site, inherited by Thomas Borden from his father, Richard Borden, and the same course of descent applies to the real estate and water power on which was erected the Fall River Iron-works in 1821, the Annawan Manufactory in 1825, the American Print Works in 1834, and the Metacomet Mill in 1846. All of these are now large and prosperous corporations, and owe their success in no small degree to the sagacious management of Richard and Jefferson Borden, who were copartners in the original purchase and supervised their establishment.

Richard Borden was born April 12th, 1795, and has been more especially identified with the Fall River Iron-works Company, of which he is now Treasurer. The success of this Company, which has now a capital of a million of dollars, has been the foundation of their prosperity in furnishing the original capital which has enabled the brothers to extend their enterprises until they have attained gigantic proportions.

Jefferson Borden was born February 28th, 1801, and has directed his attention especially to the manufacture of Textile Fabrics. He is now Treasurer of the American Print Works, organized in 1834, which has a capacity for printing fifteen thousand pieces per week of forty-five yards each, or thirty-five million one hundred thousand yards annually. Its capital is $500,000. *See Manufactures of Fall River, Vol. III.*

Eleuthere Irenee Du Pont, Wilmington, Del.,

Was the founder of the immense Works distinguished as the "Brandywine Powder Works," near Wilmington, Delaware. He was a native of France, and emigrated to the United States in the fall of 1799, landing at Newport, Rhode Island, on January 1st, 1800. Having noticed the poor quality of the Gunpowder then being made in America, he resolved to engage in its manufacture, of which he had some knowledge, having been a pupil of the celebrated French chemist Lavoisier, who had charge of the "Bureau de Poudres et Salpetres," under the French Government.

After some time spent in selecting a location, Mr. Du Pont established himself on the Brandywine creek, about four miles above the town of Wilmington, in the State of Delaware, where he prosecuted the business with such success, that at the time of his decease, at the United States Hotel, in Philadelphia, in 1834, his establishment was the most extensive of its kind in this country, as it now is probably in the world.

Since the decease of the founder, the business has been managed by his sons and grandsons, who maintain the old firm-style of E. I. Du Pont de Nemours & Co. The Works of the firm comprise five complete manufactories, four of them on the Brandywine, and one in Luzerne county, Pennsylvania, where Blasting Powder, for colliers' use, is largely made.

The original Works, on the Brandywine, commenced operations in 1802, and have a capacity for producing five thousand pounds of Sporting Powder per day.

The middle, or Hagley Works, commenced in 1812, comprise two complete sets of Works, in one enclosure, under a fall of twenty-two feet—so arranged, that both can work on the same description of powder; or, if required, one set can manufacture one kind of Powder and the other set another kind. The two combined having a capacity of twenty-five thousand pounds of Blasting Powder per day.

The lower Works, commenced in 1846, are under a fall of twelve feet, and have a capacity of five thousand pounds of Sporting Powder per day.

The Saltpetre Refinery, with Laboratory attached, is two hundred and fifty-eight feet by ninety-six feet, with ample appliances for supplying all the nitre required for the fabrication of Powder, and also considerable quantities for the market, for such purposes as require an article chemically pure. In proximity to the Refinery are large warehouses for the storage of saltpetre.

The Charring Houses for the preparation of Charcoal, three in number, are capable of furnishing all the coal required for the mills, the wood being stored and seasoned in extensive buildings adjacent.

The firm have two shipping points, one on the river Delaware, with magazines, and a wharf at which large vessels can lay; the other on the Christiana creek, with ample wharfage for coasters, and for landing coal, wood, etc.

A Passenger Railway has been established between the city of Wilmington and the property of the Messrs. Du Pont.

Attached to the Powder Works are extensive Machine and Millwright Shops, where all repairs are made, and most of the machinery is built; also a Saw-mill, Planing Mill, Carpenter and Blacksmith Shops, and capacious buildings for the manufacture of wooden and metallic kegs and barrels, and of powder canisters.

Railroad tracks are laid through the Powder Works, and the bulk of the transportation of the Powder, in the various stages of its manufacture, is done on cars drawn by horses or mules, of which the firm have about eighty.

Besides the Powder-mills, the firm own over two thousand acres of land, that stretches for a distance of three miles on both sides of the stream; and on this property there are three Woollen Mills, a Cotton-mill, a Merchants' and Grist Mill, and a population of nearly four thousand persons. The farms attached to the Works are in a high state of cultivation, and the roads are all macadamized for ease of transportation. The buildings on the estate are mostly of stone, and very substantial, and the machinery is of the best and most costly character.

The high reputation so long maintained for the Brandywine Powder is due to the care bestowed on its manufacture and to the constant personal supervision of the owners. The consumption of saltpetre, the principal ingredient in the manufacture, has been in a single year, including the Luzerne County Mills, over *seven millions of pounds*, the bulk of which was imported from Calcutta. The machinery in operation for the manufacture of Gunpowder, is driven by three steam-engines and forty-seven water-wheels, the greater part of which are Turbines.

The manufacture embraces all descriptions of Powder, viz.: Mammoth, Cannon, Mortar, Musket, and Rifle, for Army and Navy ordnance service; Diamond-grain, Eagle, and the various grades of Canister and Sporting Powders; Shipping, Blasting, Mining, and Fuse Powders.

The production of the mills is principally consumed in the United States, the firm having agencies and magazines at all the most important points, with a principal depot for the Pacific States at San Francisco, and agencies in South America, and in the East and West Indies.

To illustrate the progress which has been made in the manufacture of Powder in the United States, it is only necessary to recall the fact that during the Crimean war, the Allies, to enable them to prosecute the siege of Sebastopol, were obliged to procure large supplies of Gunpowder in the United States (one half of which was furnished by the Brandywine Powder Mills), and that the American Powder compared favorably with the best they could procure in Europe. Notwithstanding the immense consumption of Powder during the war for the suppression of the Rebellion, the United States were enabled to procure ample supplies at home for all their wants without importing a pound of Powder, and without interfering with the current demand of the country for Sporting, Blasting, and Mining Powder; which is the more remarkable, from the fact that at the outbreak of the Rebellion all the stocks of Powder in the Southern States were lost by seizure.

Thomas N. Dale, New York,

The founder and President of the Dale Manufacturing Company, at Paterson, New Jersey, the proprietors of the largest Silk manufactory in the United States, is a native of Massachusetts. He commenced his business career as a clerk in a country store, and passed through all the gradations of mercantile experience until he became the head of a large importing house in the city of New York. As a bookkeeper he is said to be one of the most accomplished in that great commercial mart, and the system with which the accounts of the business that he is now engaged in are kept is certainly a model of minuteness, accuracy, and completeness.

Mr. Dale, we believe, was the first to make the sale of Clothiers' and Tailors' Trimmings a specialty, and the firm of Thomas N. Dale & Co., in New York, with their branch houses in Paris, Philadelphia, and Cincinnati, maintain the leading position in this department. The importation of Sewing and other Silks was naturally an important adjunct of this business, and was extensively prosecuted for many years; but when the change of Tariff favored the home production, Mr. Dale, in association with his partners, embarked in the manufacture, at Paterson, New Jersey, and so successfully that he was induced to erect a large and splendid factory, which will be more particularly described in another place. (*See Manufactures of Paterson, Vol. III.*) It is believed that the Sewing Silks manufactured there are quite equal in quality to the imported, and it is proposed to extend the production to include braids, bindings, linings, and other varieties of woven Silks.

Mr. Dale has always manifested a patriotic sympathy with the manufacturing interests of the country, and has been especially zealous in securing protection to the industry of the numerous class whose labor and skill are their principal capital. Realizing the harmony and identity of interests which exist between large and small manufacturers, whose united efforts support and sustain some of the largest cities of Europe, he has aimed to make the manufacture of small wares a prominent and leading branch of American industry. As there is no one item of consumption that drains this country of its precious metals so rapidly as the importation of Silks, those who are instrumental in establishing the manufacture here, even of the elementary or least costly kinds, deserve the support, encouragement, and regard of the American people.

Edward Harris, Woonsocket, R. I.,

Whose name for many years has been identified with highest grade of American Cassimeres, was born in the State of Rhode Island, near Lime Rock, October 3, 1801. Within a few years after his birth his parents removed to Dutchess county, New York, where they remained until 1818, when they again removed to Ashtabula county, Ohio. His youth and early manhood were spent in those hardy labors incident to agricultural pursuits, and in teaching school, and not until after he had attained his majority was he in any wise connected with manufacturing, in which he has since achieved a most distinguished success. In 1823, he returned to the place of his nativity, and entered the counting-house of his uncle, William Harris, then a prominent manufacturer of cotton goods. Here he remained thirteen months, when he obtained a clerkship in a large mill in the vicinity, known as the "Albion," of which he was subsequently manager or superintendent. In these and incidental pursuits his life passed until he had attained his thirtieth year, when having accumulated $2,500, and received a loan from his father of $1,000, he purchased a small woollen mill having one set of machinery, situated in Woonsocket, on the banks of the Blackstone river, and embarked in the manufacture of Satinets. Here he became associated with Edward Seagraves, and for a short period with Willard B. Johnson ; but his first experience was so discouraging that, in consequence of a great decline in wool and woollen goods, he found his capital reduced to a single thousand dollars, and he returned to the Albion Mill as its superintendent, though retaining his interest in the Satinet manufactory, which was managed by his partner. In the subsequent year a great advance took place in the class of goods manufactured at his mill, and his profits were $5,000, which may be said to be the foundation of a fortune that is now princely. These details, that might be called trivial in the history of a manufacturer less eminent, are of value because encouraging to those who are struggling with difficulties and aspiring to success.

In 1837, the partnership with Mr. Seagraves was dissolved, and since then Mr. Harris has had no partner, though it has been his practice to reward fidelity and long service with an interest in the profits of the concern. In the year 1836, he built a new stone mill, five stories high, which is distinguished as Mill No. 2, the original factory, or mill No. 1, being still operated by him, and now contains two sets of machinery and thirteen looms. About this time he engaged in the manufacture of what was called "Merino Cassimeres," with cotton warps and wool filling, finely finished, which, in their day, were quite popular, but which were soon superseded by the more substantial all wool figured or Fancy Cassimeres, first made in these mills in December, 1842.

In 1844, the large brick factory on the west side of the street, fifty by one hundred feet, five stories high, was erected, and in the subsequent year he built No. 4, which is six stories in height, and to which additions have since been made. Both of these factories are propelled by the same power, which is transmitted by means of shafting under the pavement, and they are connected by a bridge that extends from the upper stories across the street. These four mills are now known as the "Old Works," and contain an equivalent of thirty-three sets of cards, one hundred and forty-six looms, fifty-four spinning jacks, with eleven thousand spindles, about thirty gigs, ten shearing machines, forty fulling hammers, and produce an average of twelve thousand yards of the best quality of Cassimeres each week. Adjacent to mill No. 4 is also a cotton factory, with seven thousand spindles, and employed in making sheetings and Domet flannels.

In 1860, Mr. Harris laid the foundations of what will undoubtedly be the most complete and superb woollen manufactory in the United States. It is built of brick, in the form of an L, and if extended in one line, its length would be four hundred and forty-two feet, its width sixty feet, and five stories in height. The aggregate floor superficies is one hundred and fifty thousand square feet. There is in the engine house one Corliss engine of one hundred and seventy-five horse-power, and an immense water-wheel twenty-eight feet in breast and forty feet in diameter, constructed without a central shaft, being supported by gudgeons. The foundations, as well as the whole structure, are of the most substantial character, and the walls of the first story, which is fifteen feet high, are three feet in thickness and faced with granite. This mill now contains eight self-operating mules, of three hundred and thirty-six spindles each, which were imported from Europe, and when completely furnished will have thirty-five sets of forty-eight inch cards, one hundred and forty broad looms, equal to two hundred and eighty narrow, forty fulling hammers and other equivalent machinery, of the most approved construction. Connected with this mill is a brick Dye-house, surmounted with ventilators and a Boiler and Engine House, and in the immediate vicinity on the estate is a Foundry, a Blind and Sash manufactory, boarding houses for operatives, and forty tenement houses. The monthly wages paid to those employed in the various factories now exceeds $25,000, and when the new mill is in full operation this will be largely increased.

One distinguishing characteristic of Mr. Harris's mind, is its just appreciation of the practical, or preference for substance to show. This is apparent alike in his buildings, his machinery, and his manufactured fabrics. It is a trait that was developed early, for his Satinets and Merino Cassimeres were in their day, as his Fancy Cassimeres are now, the most substantial of their class. His instructions to those in his employ have always been to make the best goods possible, without regard to cost. It is generally supposed that Mr. Harris has monopolized secrets in dyeing fast colors, and processes of manufacturing not known to others; but this may be classed among doubtful rumors. Care, attention, time, are the levers with which he achieves success. Five and six weeks are invariably taken to convert the raw material into cloth, and two and three weeks are consumed in finishing the fabric after it leaves the loom. Probably no woollen factory has so large a proportion of double and twist spindles as these mills. Every yard of cloth undergoes careful inspection, and the organs of smell and feeling as well as of sight are employed to detect defects. Many thousands of pieces of cloth are annually sold in the markets as "Harris's Cassimeres" that never were in his mills, and though he makes from two hundred and fifty to three hundred different styles, and it is always possible for accidents to occur in large establishments, through the negligence of subordinates, it is safe to assert that no imperfect goods are ever knowingly sent to the warehouses.

Another mental characteristic of Mr. Harris is his originality, manifested especially in frequent innovations upon the established customs of trade. When his fabrics were sold through commission houses, a highly respectable and responsible merchant in New York solicited the exclusive agency for that city. Consent was given, but only on condition that the merchant would agree, in writing, to place all notes received for the sale of Harris's goods in a separate package, and hold them as a special deposit, not to be used without his consent first obtained, under penalty of punishment in the "State's Prison," and, further stipulating, that no notes of those who held or dealt in slaves should be deposited in that package. In 1855, Mr. Harris opened a warehouse in the city of New York for the sale of his fabrics, and though it was then customary for manufacturers and their agents to allow a credit of eight months, he announced six months as his limit, with an allowance of two and a half per cent., and when others adopted his rule, he reduced his credit to four months, with an allowance of five per cent.; consequently his Bills-Receivable, maturing two months in advance of others, were generally paid, an advantage that those who suffered in the commercial crisis of 1857 will best appreciate. But when the late Rebellion commenced, and others declined all credits, demanding cash invariably, he reversed his former practice, and allowed a credit of three months, believing that the system of short credits thus established, could be maintained ever afterward through force of custom, even if the old rule of long credits should again become general.

As a man, Mr. Harris is no less estimable than he is sagacious as a manufacturer. Radical in his opinions on questions involving public and national morality, he has not hesitated to sacrifice his pecuniary interests whenever they conflicted with his conscientious convictions of duty. As a Senator and politician he has always co-operated with those actuated by sympathy with humanity, and though a millionaire, he has never allowed the fascination of acquisition to canker or check the genial impulses of a naturally kind heart. Among his numerous charities is the munificent gift to the town of Woonsocket of a block of buildings, worth perhaps $75,000, for the establishment of a Free Library and Lyceum. But the subject, too comprehensive for these pages, is reluctantly transferred to others, who, we trust, will prepare a suitable memoir of one who deservedly ranks among the foremost of American Manufacturers.

Joseph Harrison, Jr., Philadelphia,

Whose successful enterprise, at home and abroad, has made his name a familiar one to the manufacturers of two continents, was born in the district of Northern Liberties, now a part of the city of Philadelphia, in 1810; and at the age of fifteen was an indentured apprentice to the art of machine-making—a trade that he had himself selected. A foreman at twenty, in the shop in which he served his time, he commenced life at twenty-one with a fair knowledge of his craft, correct, industrious habits, but with little chance, apparently, or expectation, of special preferment, except in the routine of his calling.

Employed in several prominent machine shops, and as foreman for Garrett & Eastwick, he, in 1837, became associated in partnership with these gentlemen for the manufacture of Locomotive Engines. This firm, soon changed to Eastwick & Harrison, were the originators of several important improvements, that have contributed to the present perfection of the American Locomotive. In their hands, the eight-wheel engine, with four driving and four truck wheels, was first brought into a practicable shape. It is now almost exclusively used in this country for passenger trains, and is obtaining a sure and steady reputation in Europe. The present modes of equalizing the weight on the driving wheels, indispensable to this engine, were patented by Joseph Harrison, Jr., the subject of this notice, in 1839, and are now applied by all the manufacturers of Locomotive Engines in this country. In 1841, a Locomotive called the *"Gowan & Marx,"* weighing but little over eleven tons, was designed and built by this firm, for the Philadelphia and Reading Railroad. The performance of this engine, in drawing one hundred and one loaded coal cars over that road, attracted great attention at the time, as being then without a parallel in the history of railroad transportation. Locomotives, designed and built by Eastwick & Harrison, for the Beaver Meadow, Hazleton and Sugar Loaf Railroads, burned anthracite coal successfully as early as 1835 and 1836, and in a regular freight business over these roads surmounted higher grades than had ever been practically overcome in this country or in Europe.

In 1840, Colonel Melnikoff and Colonel Kraft, two eminent Engineers, were sent to this country by the Russian Government, to examine and report upon the American Railway System, with the view of its adoption in that Empire. The reputation already acquired by Messrs. Eastwick & Harrison in their profession, attracted their attention, and induced these gentlemen on their return to Russia to propose that Mr. Harrison should be sent for, to undertake the construction of the Locomotives and rolling stock for the St. Petersburg and Moscow Railway, a road more than four hundred miles long, then about being commenced under the direction of an eminent American, Major George W. Whistler, who had been called to Russia in 1842, as Consulting Engineer of the Railway Department of that Government. In the Spring of 1843, Mr. Harrison embarked for Europe, and in December of that year, he, in association with his partner in

Eng^d by John Sartain, Phila

Joseph Harrison Jr.

Philadelphia, Mr. Eastwick, and Thomas Winans of Baltimore, concluded a contract with the Russian Government, amounting to three millions of dollars, to be completed in five years. It was a condition that this work was all to be done at St. Petersburg, by Russian mechanics, or such as could be found on the spot.

With workmen entirely unacquainted with the work to be done, and without knowing the language, or the peculiar manner of doing business in a foreign land, Messrs. Harrison, Winans & Eastwick, the new firm established in St. Petersburg, set about the difficult, and to almost every one but themselves, the impossible task of complying with the terms of their contract.

Commencing the business in the straightforward manner they had pursued at home, they asked only not to be hindered, and so well were their plans arranged and carried out, that all the work contracted for was completed, to the entire satisfaction of the Russian Government, and paid for, more than one year before the term of the contract had expired. During the progress of this work, other orders, amounting to nearly two millions of dollars, were added to the original amount, including the completion of the great cast-iron bridge over the river Neva, at St. Petersburg, the largest and most costly structure of the kind in existence, to finish which one year was added to the original term.

Before the close of the first contract, a second one was made for a period of twelve years, for maintaining the Locomotives and rolling stock of the St. Petersburg and Moscow Railway—the parties to the contract being Joseph Harrison, Jr., Thomas Winans, and William L. Winans. This second contract was carried on and finished to the satisfaction of both parties thereto, in 1862. During that year, a contract was concluded with a French company for maintaining the rolling stock of the St. Petersburg and Moscow Railway. This company commenced their work with the machinery in such perfect order as was not perhaps to be found on any railroad of similar length in the world. From this perfection, with all the workshops, tools, and other arrangements ready to their hands, which their predecessors had been twelve years in bringing to completeness, the rolling stock of the road was so much run down in three years as to compel an abrupt termination of the contract by the Government, and a new contract was made, in 1865, with Mr. Thomas Winans and William L. Winans, who were then in Europe, for another term of eight years. It will be thus seen that American reputation in railway mechanical engineering, first began in Philadelphia by Mr. Harrison and his partner, in their intercourse with Colonel Melnikoff and Colonel Kraft, has since maintained itself in Russia against all comers, and has now no competitor.

In 1847, the Emperor Nicholas, accompanied by his son, the present Emperor; the Grand Duke Constantine, his second son; Prince Paskevitch, Viceroy of Poland, with all the high officers of the Government, visited the Alexandroffsky Head Mechanical Works of the St. Petersburg and Moscow Railway, where the work for the road was being done. After spending many hours in a minute examination of every part of the establishment, the Emperor, shaking hands at parting with the American contractors, expressed the greatest satisfaction at what had been shown and explained to him. As an additional mark of his approval, his Majesty sent to each of our countrymen composing the firm, most beautiful diamond rings, of a present value of not less than three thousand dollars each. On the occasion of the opening of the Neva bridge, in the autumn of 1850, then just completed, the Emperor Nicholas, as a further mark of esteem, conferred upon Mr. Harrison the ribbon of the order of St. Anne, with a massive gold medal attached thereto. On one side of the medal is a portrait of his Majesty, and on the obverse, the motto in the Russian language, "For zeal."

In 1852, Mr. Harrison returned to Philadelphia, and set about employing the large means, which had rewarded his enterprise, for the adornment of his native city. He erected numerous and costly buildings, and established the most extensive and probably the first private Gallery of Art in Philadelphia. Though twelve years of the last twenty of his life have been passed abroad, it is evident he has not lost affection for the place of his birth, or forgotten the obligations of a public-spirited citizen.

Early in his engineering life, Mr. Harrison's attention was directed to a means of improving steam generation—more particularly with a view of making the use of this powerful agent less dangerous and liable to explosion. The result of his efforts in this direction is now before the public in the Harrison Steam Boiler—now largely coming into use—which will be noticed more at length in a subsequent volume. The first boiler made on his improved principle was put in operation at Messrs. William Sellers & Co.'s Works, in Philadelphia, in 1859, and supplied steam for their entire establishment for several months in the summer of that year. Mr. Harrison's first patent from the United States is dated October 4th, 1859, though improvements on the original idea have since been the subject of several patents in this country and in Europe. At the International Exhibition held in London in 1862, the highest class Medal was awarded to this Boiler, "for originality of design, and general merit." He is now pursuing, with the zeal and perseverance of his earlier life, the highly important object of making steam generation safe from its present destructiveness to life and property; and, though aiming directly at a complete revolution in the form and material of the present system, he does not fear failure, while success will place him among the benefactors of his race.

Lemuel Pomeroy, Pittsfield, Massachusetts,

A pioneer in the Woollen manufacture in this country, was born in Southampton, Massachusetts, in 1778, and died at Pittsfield, August, 1849. He has been more than once referred to in this volume among the early manufacturers, and nothing more need be added, except a brief synopsis of his life and character.

With but a common school education, he left his father's house at seventeen, with the principles of honesty and piety instilled into his mind and heart, by his worthy parents, as his only capital, to carve his own way through life. Making his home in Pittsfield, Massachusetts, in 1809 he started a Gun factory there, in which he manufactured arms for the United States. For thirty-seven years he continued this business, without ever having a jar with Government, or a word of dissatisfaction.

In 1812, at the beginning of the war, when every thing was uncertain, and when the business in this country was new, he began to manufacture Woollen goods, one of the earliest in the country who engaged in this enterprise. We have before us a copy of the Act passed February 18, 1814, incorporating the Pittsfield Woollen and Cotton Factory, which was probably the pioneer manufactory in Berkshire county, since become distinguished for its numerous and extensive manufactories of Woollen Cloth. This Act constituted Lemuel Pomeroy, Joseph Merrick, Ebenezer Center, Samuel D. Colt, David Campbell, and others a corporation, limiting their ownership of real estate to $30,000, and of personal estate to $100,000; and at the first meeting of the corporators it was voted that the stock consist of one hundred and thirty shares of $1,000 each. His sons, Theodore and Robert Pomeroy, continue the business established by their father in 1812, and probably there is no instance in the annals of American manufactures where one establishment has remained in one family without change for so long a period.

"Mr. Pomeroy," says the Rev. John Todd, who knew him well, "was a gentleman of the old school, and in manner few are or can be more courteous, affable, or agreeable—a politeness not learned in the French school, but which sprang fresh from an expanded and warm heart. In hospitality, at his own house, he was indeed princely. The number who have received a fascinating and warm welcome there, and have shared in a hospitality the most bountiful, is very great indeed, from every part of the land.

"In his business engagements he was honest, liberal, and prompt—universally beloved by all in his employment. He was a most public-spirited citizen, and wielded an influence almost unbounded among his fellow-citizens."[1]

Hon. James Y. Smith, Providence, Rhode Island,

Is a prominent representative of those manufacturers of Rhode Island whose sterling integrity has elevated the standard of commercial ethics, and whose intelligent enterprise has made that little commonwealth, in proportion to its population, the wealthiest in the Union.

Governor Smith was born in the town of Groton, Connecticut, September 15, 1809; beginning his business career in a country store. At the age of seventeen he removed to the city of Providence, of which he has ever since remained a resident, filling many prominent positions of honor and responsibility, and establishing an enviable reputation for unblemished integrity and unflinching patriotism.

From 1826 to 1830 he was engaged in the lumber business with

(1) As illustrative of the growth of the Woollen manufacture, in Berkshire county, since the establishment of Pomeroy's Pioneer Manufactory, we append the following list of Mills in 1864.

NAME.	TOWN.	SETS OF CARDS.	PRODUCT.
L. Pomeroy's Sons	Pittsfield	10	Cloths and woollen cassimores.
Pontoosuc Manufacturing Company	"	8	Balmoral skirts.
Taconic Mills	"	8	Union cassimeres.
Pittsfield Woollen Company	"	6	Fancy cassimeres.
S. N. & C. Russell	"	4	Fancy cassimeres and skirts.
J. V. Barker & Brothers	"	10	Fancy cassimeres.
D. & H. Stearns	"	8	Union cassimeres.
Peck & Kilbourn	"	1	Flannels and balmoral skirts.
W. J. Hawkins & Co	"	1	Flannels and balmoral skirts.
Barker & Tillotson	"	1	Cassimeres.
Berkshire Woollen Company	Great Barrington	12	Fancy cassimeres.
Lee Woollen Company, Elizur, DeWitt & Wellington Smith	Lee	9	Fancy cassimeres.
Glendale Woollen Co., J. Z. & C. Goodrich	Glendale	10	Army cloths and Union cass's.
Barker & Co	Hancock	3	Satinets and balmoral skirts.
William Taylor	"	2	Wool yarn.
— Birmingham	Dalton	1	Balmoral skirts.
Plunkett Woollen Company (3 mills)	Hinsdale	12	Broadcloths, Union cass. and satinets.
F. W. Hinsdale & Brother	"	4	Union cloths.
Dean & LaMonte	South Adams	6	Fancy cassimeres.
Blackinton & Phillips	"	6	Fancy cassimeres.
Briggs & Brother	North Adams	2	Union cassimeres and meltons.
S. W. Brayton & Co	"	4	Satinets and Union cassimeres.
Tyler & Bliss	"	8	Fancy cassimores and tweeds.
S. W. Blackinton & Son	"	10	Do. do.
Perry & Penniman	"	2	Union cassimeres.

James Aborn, becoming his partner during the latter year, and continuing interested with him until 1843. Rhode Island had been the early cradle of the Cotton manufacture, and its growing proportions had already absorbed the attention of the leading minds, and monopolized most of the capital of his adopted city, when, in 1838, James Y. Smith began the manufacture of Cottons at Willimantic, Connecticut, and Woonsocket, Rhode Island ; at a later time we find him interested in several mills at Scituate, and purchasing the well-known Providence Steam Mill. Since then his investments in Cotton manufacturing have steadily increased, and his earlier enterprises have grown into prominent notice, employing hundreds of looms, and including the various operations of dyeing and printing, thus adapting his fabrics for the most extended sale. He had early recognized the principle that adverse fluctuations were least felt by those manufacturers who fitted their fabrics for distribution among the largest number of consumers. At the present time, a Company bearing his name is erecting a large steam mill in Elmwood, adjoining the city of Providence.

His eminently practical mind had been deeply impressed with the great national importance of rendering our country independent of foreign supplies of Flax fabrics, and his attention was directed to means of preparing, for textile purposes, the vast quantity of flax straw which our western farmers regarded as worthless, though economists estimated its marketable value at $15,000,000 to $20,000,000 annually. He sought to develop this neglected mine of wealth, believing it would become an important element in our domestic exchanges, crowding our railroads with freight, and opening to thousands a new field of industry.

After examining the schemes and contrivances of a multitude of inventors, who always found him an intelligent listener and a sympathizing friend, he finally adopted the processes of Roth and Lee, by which the straw, in either the unretted or retted condition, is deprived of the boon and shive by an ingenious scutching apparatus, partly the invention of Governor Smith ; and subsequently, by a safe and speedy chemical treatment, in from one to two hours the fibre is finished, perfectly bleached, glossy and clean, of greatly improved fineness, without being impaired in strength, enabling the manufacturer to subject it to continuous textile operations.

The great facility of the Cotton manufacture has consisted in its being subject to a series of consecutive operations, each promptly carrying forward the material until the cloth was produced by the loom, whilst hitherto Flax fibre has always been spun in the unbleached condition, a large percentage of gum or waste being twisted into the yarn, only to be removed subsequently by bleaching in the yarn or in the piece.

More even and perfect yarns and goods could be fabricated from fibre already clean than by the old mode, which necessarily impoverished both yarn and cloth.

Attempts to remedy this defect in the manufacture of Linen have occupied the attention of the European world for upward of one hundred and fifty years. Berthollet preceded Claussen; both failed from the want of some efficient dechlorinating agent, without which their fibre soon became worthless from the continued action of the bleaching salts. The subsequent discovery of "Roth's Antichlorine" solved this problem by one of the most beautiful chemical formulas, arresting the action of the chloride of lime at any stage of the process, and leaving the fibre perfectly free from its influence thereafter.

The facility thus secured for placing before manufacturers Flax fibres on an equality with Cotton left nothing more to be desired than the practical experience on a large scale of this preparation of Flax, and to achieve this result, Governor Smith commenced, in 1862, the erection, at Delaware, Ohio, of a large mill for the scutching of flax straw, which is now in successful operation, turning out fibre in the unbleached state from the waste straw of the flax fields, suitable for bagging or bale rope, into which it has been converted on the spot. Preparations have been made for extending the Works, with the view of manufacturing the better class of flax fabrics from bleached fibre, and ere long the great question of making the waste of our flax fields available for the purposes of domestic economy will be brought to a triumphant conclusion.

As early as 1843 he was elected to the Legislature, serving through several subsequent years. In 1855, he was nominated for the Mayorality of Providence in opposition to both the regular nominees of the Whig and Democratic parties, and was elected by a large majority over both his opponents, was subsequently re-elected, and declined the nomination for a third term. In 1861, he received the nomination of the Republican party for the office of Governor, but that party was then in the minority. In 1863, he was again their candidate, and carried the State by a large majority. He was elected for two consecutive terms, and during his administration witnessed the close of the war, the successful prosecution of which he had aided with all his energies; averting the draft from Rhode Island by supplying the quota of his State in advance of every call. In his official station he was a warm and efficient supporter of the general Government; and as a citizen, contributed largely of his means in aid of the various efforts for the welfare of the soldiers and their families.

As a merchant and manufacturer Mr. Smith has long been noted for his promptness in meeting the market, in making his operations independent of transient speculation, and looking rather to his general average returns than to temporary fluctuations. No man is more distinguished for simplicity of character, kindness of heart, and unostentatious benevolence. Throughout a long and successful career his benefactions have been numerous and large, springing from the dictates of a generous and kindly heart; and for twenty-five years his good name has been identified with most of the public charities, and nearly every enterprise of a public character which has been projected in the State of Rhode Island.

Orray Taft, Providence, Rhode Island,

Another representative man of the merchants and manufacturers of Rhode Island, was born in the eastern part of the town of Uxbridge, Mass., April 9, 1793. His early education was received at the common schools of his native town, which in those days were held only during the winter months, while in the summer he labored on his father's farm, and there developed a strong and robust physical constitution, which enabled him to endure without injury the severe labors of his business life.

His active mind was not content, however, with the dull routine of a New England farm, and soon after attaining his majority, in the fall of 1815, he sailed for Savannah, Georgia, and there engaged in mercantile pursuits, shipping cotton to the mills in Rhode Island. He remained in business in Savannah until 1829, at first associated with the brothers Sibley, afterward with Edward Padelford, who in 1833 succeeded to the business of the old firm of Taft & Padelford, and established the well-known house of Padelford & Fay, which continued in existence until the breaking out of the Rebellion.

On leaving Savannah, Mr. Taft removed to Providence, Rhode Island, and there established himself in the Cotton business, that he might the more successfully pursue it in the very centre of the manufacturing interest of Rhode Island, and in close proximity to the then rapidly developing industry of the Blackstone valley. At that time, Providence was the great source of supply for the manufactories, not only in its vicinity, but for more than fifty miles around, and its merchants were all more or less closely connected with the manufacturing interests. Prosperity attended the first years of his residence in Providence, and in 1834 he began to make investments in manufacturing property, purchasing an interest in the mills at Albion, which he retained until 1844, but which, owing to causes beyond his control, did not prove so profitable as he anticipated.

About this time, the rapidly increasing business of the country drew the attention of the merchants of Providence to the necessity of more speedy and convenient communication with the mills, and a railroad from Providence to Worcester was decided upon. Associating with other merchants and manufacturers in its management, Mr. Taft labored zealously for its accomplishment, and as its President, from 1848 to 1854, devoted almost his entire attention to the business of the corporation, and by his great energy and resolute action carried the Company successfully through the trials of its infancy, and left it in a position to materially aid in the development of the manufacturing interests of New England.

Retiring from the Presidency of the Railroad when he had placed it in a prosperous condition, he turned his attention to manufacturing, and, in 1853, associated with other merchants in Providence, under the name of the "Wauregan Mills," commenced on the Quinebaug river, in Plainfield, Connecticut, the erection of a large mill for spinning Cotton, the immediate charge of the construction being entrusted to Mr. Amos D. Lockwood, who has since that time erected some of the finest mills in the country. Mr. Taft was one of the corporators, and President of the Company from its incorporation until 1858, when the business firm which he had founded were elected the financial agents of the Company, and its operations came more directly under his personal supervision. In the fall of 1858, the Company decided to still further extend its facilities by adding to the then existing building another of equal size, making a mill five hundred and six feet long, forty-nine feet wide, and containing twenty-five thousand spindles and five hundred and fifty looms. The addition was completed in less than one year from the time of its commencement, and for the five years from 1860 to 1864 inclusive, probably no mill in the country had a more profitable business, its profits amounting to more than one hundred and sixty per cent. on its capital of half a million dollars. At the present time (1866) the Company is still further extending its business by the erection of another mill of the same size, making the number of spindles fifty thousand and the looms about eleven hundred. The combined length of the two mills, were they placed in a line, would be more than a thousand feet.

As a man of business Mr. Taft was prominent among his commercial associates for his high-toned sense of honor and his unswerving integrity, commanding the respect and esteem of all who knew him. Strictly conscientious in all his dealings, he required the same rectitude of purpose in others; and while he despised the petty tricks by which too often, at the present day, the creditor is defrauded, yet to the honest debtor, however unfortunate, he was always ready to lend a helping hand. He was a firm friend to those with whom he was associated for nearly forty years, and among them were some of the most prominent names in the manufacturing history of Rhode Island. Though he sought no political honors, but delighted rather in the reputation of being a useful citizen, he was ever active in the promotion of all public enterprises whose aim seemed to promise some substantial benefit, whether to the city, the State, or the nation; and in all of the many positions of honor and of trust which he held, he showed the same soundness of judgment, untiring energy, and high sense of honor that distinguished his commercial operations.

At the full, ripe age of more than threescore years and ten, on the 27th of January, 1865, after a long and painful illness, Mr. Taft passed away, leaving to his children a parting injunction that briefly expressed the leading motto of his own life, in which an honorable name was valued more than worldly accumulations.

INDEX

TO

AMERICAN INVENTORS.

BLANCHARD, Thomas, of Boston, the inventor of Blanchard's Lathe for turning irregular forms, was born in Sutton, Worcester county, Massachusetts, June 24, 1788. His brother was engaged in manufacturing Tacks by hand, and young Blanchard, before he was eighteen years of age, attempted to invent a machine for making them, in which, after six years' experiments, he succeeded so effectively that by placing in the hopper the iron to be worked, and applying the motive power, five hundred Tacks were made per minute, with better finished heads and points than ever had been made by hand. For this machine he secured a patent, and sold the right of manufacturing to a Company for $5,000. His next attempt was to construct a lathe to turn Musket Barrels, with a uniform external finish from end to end, by the combination of one single, self-directing operation. Notwithstanding about three inches of the barrel at the breech is partly cylindrical and partly with flat sides, both of them were cut by this machine, which ingeniously changed to a vibrating motion as it approached the breech. The superintendent of the Springfield Armory heard of this invention, and he contracted with Mr. Blanchard for one of his machines. When it was in operation, one of the workmen remarked that his own work of grinding the barrels was done away with. Another, employed on the wooden stocks, which were then all made by hand, said that Blanchard could not spoil his job, as he could not make a machine to turn a gun stock. Blanchard answered that he was not sure but he would think about it, and as he was driving home through the town of Brimfield the idea of his lathe for turning irregular forms suddenly struck him. In his emotion he shouted out, "I have got it, I have got it!" The principle of this machine is that forms are turned by a pattern, the exact shape of the object to be produced, which in every part of it is successively brought in contact with a small friction wheel; this wheel precisely regulates the motion of chisels arranged upon a cutting wheel acting upon the rough block, so that as the friction wheel successively traverses every portion of the rotating pattern, the cutting wheel pares off the superabundant wood from end to end of the block, leaving a precise resemblance of the model. This remarkable machine, with modifications and improvements, is in use in the national armories as well as in England, and in various forms is applied to many operations in making musket stocks, such as cutting in the cavity for the lock, barrel, ramrod, butt plates, and mountings; comprising, with the turning of the stock and barrel, no less than thirteen different machines. Besides gun stocks, it is also applied to a great variety of objects, such as busts, shoe lasts, handles, spikes, etc., etc.

Mr. Blanchard received no less than twenty-four patents, including one for bending ship timber, but we believe that even up to the time of his decease, a year or two since, at an advanced age, he had not realized any considerable or adequate reward for his valuable inventions.

BIGELOW, Erastus B., of Boston, one of the most eminent of American inventors, and the founder of the manufacturing town of Clinton, was born in West Boylston, Worcester county, Massachusetts, in the year 1814. His father was a man of limited means, and the son was early inured to toil. He worked for a time on a farm and in a cotton-mill, but before he was eighteen years of age he had invented a hand loom for weaving Suspender Webbing, a machine for making "Piping Cord," and had written and published a book on Stenography, or short hand writing. His first important invention, however, was a power-loom for weaving Counterpanes or Marseilles Quilts, before woven by hand, in which he was entirely successful; but in consequence of the failure of the firm who undertook to make it available, he realized nothing from this invention. This was followed by a power-loom for weaving Coach Lace, which may be said to have been the first of his inventions that brought him prominently into notice, as a number of capitalists united with him and his brother, Horatio N. Bigelow, for the purpose of building and running these looms, and formed the association known as the "Clinton Company."

The next task to which Mr. Bigelow applied himself was to invent a power-loom to weave Ingrain or Kidderminster Carpet. In this he also succeeded, triumphing over all difficulties; producing a loom, first put in operation in the Lowell Carpet Works, that would weave with ease from twenty-five to twenty-seven yards per day, whereas the hand loom production never exceeded eight yards in a day. His latest and probably greatest invention was a power-loom for weaving Brussels Tapestry and Velvet Tapestry Carpets. Specimens of Brussels Carpet woven on this loom were exhibited in England at the Great Exhibition in 1851, and attracted much attention.

Nothing short of actual inspection can give any just idea of the wonderful capacities and lifelike action of this machine. Some one attempting a description of it says:

"Wires three feet or more in length are here inserted and withdrawn with a precision and quickness which no manual dexterity ever attained. Let us watch the operation. First mark that intruding knife or wedge, which, as it rises, separates from its companions the wire next to be taken, and guides the pusher, which shoves it along toward the pincers. The pincers now walk up, grasp the wire, and draw it entirely out. While this is doing, another set of nippers, hanging down like two human hands, come forward, descend, and catch the wire at the moment when the drawing pincers drop their prey. No sooner have they seized the wire than they retreat to their original position, beneath which a small angular trough has just arrived. The fingers relax, and the wire drops into the trough, which immediately returns. Last of all, a triangular pusher, rushing through the trough, sends the rod into the open shed. Note, also, the double action of the withdrawing pincers, which, while they attend to their own special mission, perform also sergeant's duty by constantly bringing into line the straggling wires. Those bird-like three-fingered claws, which dart back and forth with such rapidity, are busy in plaiting the selvedge, and their work is perfect. These too are 'contrived a double debt to pay,' for whenever their thread breaks they instantly stop the loom."

The town of Clinton, in Worcester county, Massachusetts, owes its growth and manufacturing importance principally to these inventions of Mr. Bigelow. The Coach Lace Works now owned by Messrs. Horstmann & Sons, of Philadelphia; the Lancaster Quilt Company, which turns out seventy thousand Counterpanes annually; the Bigelow Carpet Company, which produces one hundred and fifty thousand yards of the finest Brussels Carpets annually, are all the outgrowth and offspring of his genius.

Mr. Bigelow is still in the prime of intellectual vigor, and though now absent in Europe, his native country may yet confidently rely upon him for some new and important device in labor-saving machinery.

BALL, Ephraim, and Cornelius Aultman, of Canton, Ohio, belong to a class of the world's benefactors who have made two blades of grass grow where but one grew before. Both are self-made men, and by their invention of machines adapted to the wants of agriculturists have built up manufacturing establishments that are among the largest and most important in the West.

Ephraim Ball, the inventor of the famous Ohio Reaper and Mower, was born in Stark county, Ohio, in 1812, and passed his youth amid hardships and privations, without the advantages of even an ordinary common school education. Compelled, when not more than fourteen years of age, to seek his own subsistence, he attained the age of manhood with only a knowledge of the ruder parts of the art of a house-carpenter. Having married early in life, he became surrounded by the cares of a family, for whose support, in 1840, he directed all his mental and physical energies to the starting of a foundry for making Plough castings, and a shop for Stocking Ploughs. "Should he now contemplate," says a brief memoir furnished us by one familiar with the facts, "an establishment for casting ocean steamers in one piece the work would look scarcely more formidable. With no previous knowledge of the business—having never seen liquid iron but once in his life—yet obliged not only to plan but to execute all the work himself, he became in turn carpenter, stone cutter, mason, pattern maker, plough stocker, painter, salesman, purchaser, financier, and bookkeeper to the establishment. With hands and brain earnestly employed, and all his hopes centered on success, difficulties, competition, and opposition only solidified his resolution. No wonder that in such a mental gymnasium mind grew rapidly, manners improved, intelligence, skill, judgment, and influence increased. It was a success. Ploughs were made and sold known as 'Ball's *Blue* Ploughs.' A partnership was now formed which has made a name and influence the world over. Cornelius Aultman and Lewis Miller, names well-known on the Patent Office records and throughout the West, became the partners of Mr. Ball, and in 1851 the little shop at Greentown was abandoned, and the (afterward) great firm of Ball, Aultman & Co. appeared at Canton, Ohio, on the Pittsburgh, Fort Wayne, and Chicago Railroad. Here genius had a wider range, and here, in 1854, the West was first cheered by the sight of "The Ohio Mower," a machine with double driving wheels and a flexible finger-bar. The loss of all their shops and tools in the same year by fire deferred the full, practical development of the machine until 1856, when Mr. Ball took out letters patent for his improvement. From that time forward business increased rapidly and improvements followed in quick succession. The "Buckeye" machine was brought out in 1858, after the dissolution of the firm, which took place early in that year. In the hands of his former partners, C. Aultman & Co., this, which also belongs to the family of two wheeled machines, has attained a wonderful success, probably equal to that of the parent machine, as many as seven thousand having been made by them in 1865.

In 1856, Ball, Aultman & Co., made five hundred Ohio Mowers, and it is not known that any other machines with double drivers were made, but, for the sake of comparison, the whole number made may be put at six hundred. The number of machines with single driving wheels made in that year was not far from twelve thousand, or in the proportion of twenty to one. In 1865, of one hundred and twenty thousand machines made, considerably over one half are believed to have been double drivers. That all, or even a majority of these, were Balls' Machines, is not claimed, yet there is little doubt that the success and popularity of his machine contributed greatly to the change in the relative numbers of each class, and to the preponderance of the double drivers.

In 1858, the firm of Ball, Aultman & Co. was dissolved, and each of the original partners proceeded to erect or fit up establishments which are now among the largest of their class in the West, and which will be more particularly described in another place.—*See Manufactures of Canton, Vol. III.*

BORDEN, GAIL, of New York, formerly of Galveston, Texas, is an eminent inventor, who has extended his explorations into fields comparatively untrod by others. His name came prominently before the public by his invention, in 1850, of a Meat Biscuit, containing in the smallest possible bulk all the nutritive properties of the beef or other meat used in its manufacture. The means by which he accomplished this consisted in combining a concentrated extract of meat with the finest flour, and thoroughly desiccating the mixture. Beef, freshly slaughtered, was boiled for a protracted time in a quantity of water, and, after the careful removal of all fat, the broth, separated from the meat, was evaporated by steam heat to a uniform density. This extract, resembling syrup, was then kneaded with the best flour, cut into biscuits, which were subjected to moderate heat in an oven, and then ground into a powder for convenience in packing and use.

The Meat Biscuit received the careful study of many eminent scientific men in this country and in Europe. Professor Playfair, after a prolonged examination, pronounced it an excellent article, retaining unimpaired the nutritive properties of its constituents. Dr. Solly used even more laudatory language. The report, accompanying the award of a Council medal at the Great Exhibition in London in 1851, says: "A more simple, economical, and efficient form of portable concentrated food than the American Meat Biscuit has never been brought before the public."

Mr. Borden, however, entertained the idea that the extract might be perfectly preserved without the agency of the flour used in desiccation, and, after experiments for several years, in which he has been assisted by Mr. J. H. Currie, and Mr. S. L. Goodale, he perfected a process by which the pure broth, previously alluded to, is reduced to a solid form.

The extract, as at present made, is a nut-brown substance of the consistence of *caoutchouc*, readily dissolved in hot water, forming a broth possessing the flavor of delicately roasted meat. The points in the process, which the inventor considers are of cardinal importance, are, 1st. Care in the selection of the beef. 2d. Great promptness in commencing the treatment after slaughter. 3d. Immediate and thorough exhaustion of the meat.

By the use of the vacuum pan the liquid extract is evaporated at a low degree of temperature. A product which is so useful wherever an easily portable aliment is desired, has met with marked favor. Physicians employ it in the sick-room, as a ready means of making beef tea of definite strength, so that they can now prescribe this supporting agent with as much certainty of having a good article made as they have in regard to their ordinary drug prescriptions. The value of this extract in long journeys, by land or sea, is obvious, and its general use by explorers and tourists is not a matter of conjecture. As a means of so perfectly preserving the beef of the great producing districts of the West and Southwest, that the expense of transportation to the consuming cities is reduced to a minimum, this process becomes of national importance, and deservedly takes high rank among the valuable inventions of the century.

While prosecuting his investigations in regard to the preservation of Meat, Mr. Borden became convinced that Milk could, by some process, be materially reduced in bulk, and preserved for any desirable length of time.

Several preparations of milk had already been presented by scientific men to the public of France, England, and America, but the disproportion between their price and that of new milk prevented their general introduction and use. Moreover, many of these preparations contained foreign substances, designed to resemble those solid constituents of milk of which they had been deprived in the process of manufacture, but these artificial substitutes fell far short of the caseine, oil, and salts of new milk in nutritive value. The successful method adopted by Mr. Borden, after a long series of experiments upon a large scale, was substantially as follows: The milk is brought by the dairyman immediately after milking to the factory, where it is subjected to a heating process preparatory to its evaporation in *vacuo*. It is then strained and drawn into the vacuum pan, and reduced to its required density by the abstraction of about seventy-five per cent. of the water. That which is to be carried at once to the city is called plain condensed milk, and resembles a very tenacious syrup. That which is to be placed in cans is mixed intimately in the process with the best white sugar and hermetically sealed. This is known as Preserved Milk, and will keep in perfect order for a great length of time, readily dissolving in water after the lapse of years. This vacuum process, which had never before been carried out, obviates many practical difficulties that had discouraged those who had previously endeavored to condense or solidify milk. The high appreciation in which this article is held by physicians led to its immediate introduction into families in our large cities, and prepared the way for its very general use on voyages. During our late civil war, Mr. Borden's Milk was very extensively employed in the Army and Navy, and the concurrent testimony of soldiers and officers, of those who used it as a luxury and of those who used it in the hospitals, is of the most highly commendatory character.

Several manufactories of this Condensed Milk are now in operation in various parts of the country, the first having been located in Litchfield county, Connecticut. In 1860, more extensive Works were erected on the Harlem Road, Dutchess Co., New York, where three vacuum pans are employed, capable of working five thousand gallons of milk per day. The next important factory is at Brewsters, Southeast, Putnam Co., with a large vacuum pan in which five thousand gallons of milk can be condensed in a day. Mr. Borden is also connected with a factory of a capacity of two thousand gallons, at Livermore Falls, Maine, and one of the same size at Elgin, Kane Co., on the Fox river, Illinois. Connected with the latter is a factory for the manufacture of the Extract of Beef.

Simultaneously with his experiments in the Condensation of Milk, Mr. Borden undertook the preparation of a decoction of Coffee in such a manner as to preserve the fine aroma of the roasted berry. The extract prepared by him contains condensed milk and pure sugar, and is easily soluble in hot water.

He also patented a process for the preservation of the juices of fruits, as apples, currants, and grapes, by which they may be reduced to one seventh of their original bulk, and are not then subjected to fermentation unless dissolved in water. The date of this patent is 22d of July, 1862.

The great success which has crowned the studies of Mr. Borden in the preservation of Food, may be attributed to the fact that he was one of the first to appreciate the importance of taking measures to prevent incipient decomposition or fermentation.

The full developments of the principles adopted by him in the manufacture of these new articles of commerce, has enabled him to preserve in their freshness and richness the most valuable nutritive liquids, and in such a perfect manner as to cause tourists and explorers to consider them among the indispensable necessaries of their journeys, rather than mere luxuries. The value of these products is so highly appreciated that they are being very extensively employed for culinary purposes in families and hotels.

ERICSSON, John, of New York, whose name, during the late Rebellion, became a household word with the American people, by his valuable contributions of engineering skill, was born in the Province of Wermeland, Sweden, in 1803. The son of a mining proprietor, his earliest impressions of machinery were derived from the engines and apparatus for working mines. While yet a mere boy of eleven, he attracted the attention of the celebrated Count Platen, and was appointed a cadet in the Swedish Engineer Corps. In 1820, he entered the army as an ensign, and was soon promoted to a lieutenantcy. In 1826, he obtained leave of absence for a visit to England, with a view of introducing his invention of a flame engine, which he had exhibited in a machine of about ten horse-power. This engine did not realize his expectations, and involved expenditures which induced him to resign his commission in the army and devote himself to mechanics. Numerous inventions followed, among which may be mentioned the steam boiler on the principle of artificial draft, for the introduction of which he joined the established mechanical house of John Braithwaite. After having been applied to numerous boilers for manufacturing purposes, in London, with success, effecting a great saving of fuel, and dispensing with the huge smoke-stacks, this invention was applied to railway locomotion on the Liverpool and Manchester Railway, in the fall of 1829. The principle of artificial draft which characterized this engine is yet retained in all locomotives; but a different mode of producing it was soon after accidentally discovered, and the original inventor derived no benefit from it.

In 1833, he reduced to practice his long-cherished project of a Caloric Engine, and submitted the result to the scientific world in London. The invention excited very general interest, and lectures were delivered in explanation of it by eminent scientific men in England; but the high temperature so affected its working parts, that the machine, as at first constructed, was not available for practical purposes. More recently, he has succeeded in improving upon the original idea, and has produced engines with cylinders varying from six to thirty-six inches in diameter, that are now applied successfully in pumping, printing, turning light machinery of various kinds, and working telegraphic instruments and sewing machines. Several hundred of these are now in practical operation, but the extent of power attainable by this process has not, we believe, even yet been fully ascertained.

In 1839, Mr. Ericsson came to the United States, and was employed under the direction of the Navy Department in the construction of the United States ship-of-war, "Princeton," which was the first steamship ever built with the propelling machinery under the water-line and out of the reach of shot. This vessel was distinguished for numerous mechanical novelties besides the propeller, among which were a direct acting engine of great simplicity, the sliding telescope chimney, and gun carriages with machinery for checking the recoil of the gun.

Mr. Ericsson's list of inventions are so numerous that if set forth in detail they would of themselves fill up a volume. At the great World's Fair in London, in 1851, he exhibited an instrument for measuring distances at sea; a hydrostatic gauge for measuring the volume of fluids under pressure; a reciprocating fluid metre for measuring the quantity of water which passes through pipes during definite periods; an alarm barometer; a pyrometer, intended as a standard measure of temperature, from the freezing point of water up to the melting point of iron; a rotary fluid meter, the principle of which is the measurement of fluids by the velocity with which they pass through apertures of definite dimensions; and a sea lead, contrived for taking soundings at sea without rounding the vessel to the wind, and independently of the length of the lead line. His recent inventions, especially the new form of iron-clad war vessels, known as the Monitors, are so familiar to intelligent readers that they need not any other elucidation than is given them elsewhere in this work.

Mr. Ericsson is now a resident of New York, and a most indefatigable worker. It is no uncommon circumstance for him to pass sixteen hours a day at his table in the execution of detailed mechanical drawings, which he throws off with remarkable facility.

HOWE, Elias, Jr., the author of one of the great inventions of modern times, was born in Spencer, Massachusetts, in 1819. His father was a farmer and a miller, and young Howe aided him in these pursuits, attending school in the winter, until he was seventeen years old, when he was apprenticed to learn the art of the machinist. When he had attained his majority he married, and not long after he conceived the idea of making a machine that would sew, at which he diligently labored in all spare hours after the day's labor. At one time, while in Lowell, he earned but fifty cents a day, and when his wages were increased to sixty-two and a half cents he states that he felt about as well pleased as he has ever felt since. For five years he experimented on the various movements of the machine, and on the 10th of September, 1846, while residing at Cambridgeport, he obtained his first patent

NORMAN WIARD, NEW YORK.
AMERICAN
INVENTORS
AND
REPRESENTATIVE
MANUFACTURERS.
ELIAS HOWE JR. BRIDGEPORT, CONN.
ALLEN B. WILSON, BRIDGEPORT, CONN.
GAIL BORDEN, NEW YORK CITY.
WILLIAM H. TOWERS, BOSTON, MASS.

for the first practical Sewing Machine. "Singularly enough," says an English chronicler, "his fellow-countrymen did not at once see the merit of his invention, and its introduction to the public was first made in England. Shortly after his patent was obtained he sent over a machine to this country, and disposed of the English patent to Mr. Thomas, for, we believe, £200! Mr. Howe himself visited this country soon after the arrival of his machine, and superintended its adaptation to the work required to be done by Mr. Thomas—staymaking. Beyond the £200, we do not see that poor Howe did any good for himself over here; for in 1849 he returned again to America, so poorly off that he was obliged to work his way home before the mast."

On his return to the United States he became involved in a number of expensive lawsuits to establish the validity of his patent, and it was not until 1853 that he granted his first license. Thenceforward, however, fortune began to smile upon him, and in 1855 he had repurchased all the patents he had sold during his season of adversity. He now receives a royalty upon every Sewing Machine manufactured in the United States, and his income from this source cannot be less than $250,000 a year, a large prize for an humble mechanic to win, but yet incomparably trifling compared with the benefit conferred upon the world by the gift of his labor-saving machine.

In 1863 he organized a Company, of which he is now President, and erected a large Sewing manufactory at Bridgeport, Connecticut. *See Manufactures of Bridgeport, Vol. III.*

HOE, RICHARD M., of New York, the inventor of the celebrated Type Revolving Printing-press, was born in the city of New York, September 12th, 1812. His father, an English machinist, came to the United States in 1805, and in 1825 commenced the manufacture of Printing-presses. In this business he was succeeded by his son, Richard, in 1832, who, in association with his brothers, has continued it to the present time, and established the largest manufactory of Printing-presses in this country.

In July, 1847, he received a patent for the Cylinder Press with which his name is identified. It was the first successful type revolving press, and is now used in all the large daily newspaper printing offices, both in England and in this country, where a large number of impressions are required to be thrown off in a few hours. It consists of a horizontal cylinder, fifty-four to sixty-six inches in diameter, on which the types are laid, and of four to ten printing cylinders, which are arranged around the front, and tangential to it. The type cylinder and the printing cylinder are connected by gearing in such a manner that their velocity at the circumference is exactly the same. Each printing cylinder is cut longitudinally, and the fingers project through the slit to take hold of the paper, and relinquish it at the proper moment. Underneath the type cylinders are the inking fountains and the distributing rollers, and between the printing cylinders are the inking rollers. In the operation of the machine the feeding is done by hand, the fingers of the machine closing upon the paper at the right moment, so that one sheet may be drawn in at each revolution of the type cylinder. The sheet thus seized is made to roll around the printing cylinder, and, by revolving in contact with the type cylinder, receives the impression of the types. The fingers then open, and the sheet is carried by tapes to a fly which lays it on a receiving table.

The distribution of the ink is attained by a very ingenious arrangement. The portion of the surface of the large cylinder which is not covered with the form (about two-thirds) is used as an inking table, and contact with the printing cylinder is prevented by the fact of the surface of the table being lower than that of the form of type. The ink is taken from the fountain and distributed on rollers, the last of which deposits it on the inking table, and recedes out of reach to let the form pass. The inking rollers between the printing cylinders, have a similar motion to and from the axis of the large cylinder, coming in contact with the table at each revolution, getting inked, and depositing the ink on the form of type immediately afterward.

The types are placed on a curved bed between column rules tapering toward the centre in such a degree that, if produced, each face of the rule would pass at a distance of half the width of a column on the on the opposite side of the axis of the cylinder. Thus, the sides of the two column rules which press the same column of types are parallel. The rules are held in the form by cross-headed projections entering the bed, and types and rules are pressed together by screws in the sides and ends of the form—thus the types are held by friction. The types in the centre of each column are the only ones perpendicular to the paper when printing. The press stands high, with platforms for the feeders, one above the other, and presents to the eye considerable intricacy and complication. The rate of speed is thirty to thirty-three impressions for each cylinder per minute, or from eighteen thousand to nineteen thousand for a ten cylinder press per hour. The press is capable of modification so as to give double the number of impressions, if necessary.

The *London Times* is printed on a Hoe cylinder, and many of the other leading journals in Europe, where over fifty of these presses have been sold.

LOBDELL, George G., Wilmington, Delaware — a distinguished inventor of Railroad Car Wheels and Tires, of which he is the oldest, and one of the most extensive manufacturers in the country.

The manufacture of Wheels for cars and locomotives is one of great responsibility and delicacy, involving not only the pecuniary interests of railroad companies, but the safety of the travelling public. As a host of ingenious men have attempted to invent a perfect wheel, and failed, those who have succeeded are entitled to a prominent place among meritorious inventors, and are entitled to a favorable consideration from those having the control of the railroad interests of the country. Mr. Lobdell was the first who succeeded in producing a reliable plate wheel —the Bush and Lobdell Wheel; one that entirely superseded the spoke wheel formerly used, thereby saving to railroad companies millions of dollars, and adding greatly to the safety of travel.

Recently he has patented a new form of Single Plate Wheel, for which important advantages are claimed. The object sought to be obtained by this invention is a means of strengthening the rim and flange, which is accomplished by casting a rib on the inside and opposite to the flange, by which that part of the tread which is especially subject to wear can be made thinner, thereby effecting a more durable chill. The mass of gray metal opposite to the flange so strengthens it that breakage is scarcely possible. These Wheels are guaranteed to be equal to any double plate wheel made, and are adapted to any service required on a railroad.

Mr. Lobdell is also the inventor of an improved Hollow Chilled Tire, that is of a form which is not objectionable on account of unequal chilling of the different parts. These Tires are used largely on Southern railroads and under freight engines, and are believed to be more durable than wrought Tires. A set of Tires made by Bush & Lobdell have been in constant use on the Richmond and Petersburg, and Richmond and Danville Railroads, of Virginia, from 1851 to June, 1866—a period of fifteen years—and are not worn out.

Mr. Lobdell's Works, at Wilmington, comprise two foundries—one for Car and Machine Castings of all kinds, and the other for Car Wheels and Tires exclusively. The former has two cupolas, in which thirty-five tons of iron can be melted in a day; while the latter has three cupolas, in which one hundred tons of iron can be melted every ten hours, and has a capacity for producing two hundred and fifty Wheels per day. The Wheels made in this establishment are not cooled in furnaces, but are gradually and equally cooled by being covered up in hot, dry sand, in which they remain until all danger of contracting from the unequal cooling of the different parts is passed. The Works also contain all the boring mills and lathes necessary for fitting one hundred wheels per day, and this machinery can be increased to any desired extent.

Mr. Lobdell has been in the business in which he is now engaged since 1833, having served a regular apprenticeship with Jonathan Bonney, Esq., a practical founder of great experience. He has made the manufacture of Railroad Wheels a special study, and is now, it is said, the oldest established Car Wheel manufacturer in the United States.

MOTT, JORDAN L., whose name appears on the records of the Patent Office more frequently than any other, generally in connection with improvements in Stoves, was born October, 1798. His ancestors, both paternal and maternal, came from England and settled on Long Island as early as 1637.

Mr. Mott is entitled to very great credit for the successful introduction of anthracite coal. In 1820 but three hundred and sixty-five tons of this coal were mined, and even then it was deemed almost impossible to make a fire with it. The late Professor Hare, of Philadelphia, once said it would be as useless for fuel as paving stones, on account of the difficulty of ignition. Mr. Mott concluded that the difficulty consisted in using too large lumps, and reasoned that as it was necessary to use small wood to make a quick and lively fire, a like result might be produced with small coal. His experiments led to the theory, that to obtain the best results from anthracite coal, the depth of the stratum of coal on the grate bars must be governed by the size of the lumps, and the amount or volume of air used in its combustion—that for domestic purposes, small nut sized coal only could be made available, and that in small fire chambers.

In close stoves or furnaces with ordinary draft, whether for domestic use or for generating steam for mechanical purposes, the depth of coal upon the grate bars should be: for pea size, about three to three and one half inches; for nut size, from four to six inches; for egg size, from seven to eight inches—increasing the depth for larger lumps of coal. With this depth, the gaseous product is carbonic acid, and the result the best combustion.

With a less depth on the grate to a like amount of air, the coal *cools out*, leaving the grate covered with unburnt coal, the outside burnt to a cinder, the inside unaffected by combustion. With an increased quantity of coal, the carbonic acid gas, in passing through the enlarged upper increased depth, takes up more carbon, and is converted into carbonic oxyd gas, which burns with a renewed supply of oxygen, as

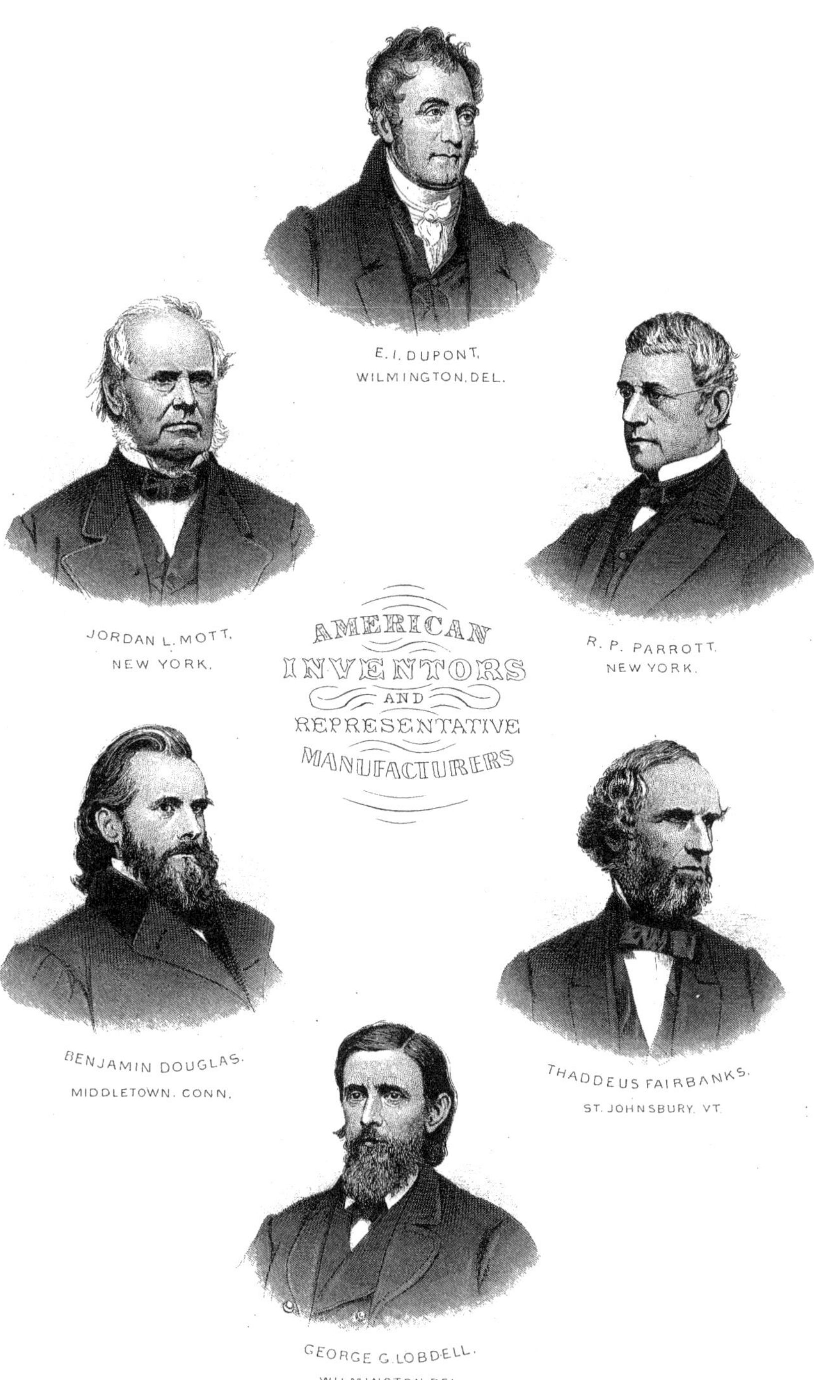

Engd by R. Whitechurch Phila.

witnessed in the blue flame on the top of a steamer's smoke pipe, when using too great a quantity of coal, and wastes a large amount of heat. All intelligent engineers know the importance of a thin, clean fire.

Mr. Mott invented a stove to burn small coal, expressly designed for the great mass of the community, but found great difficulty in persuading people to adopt it. He had also to contend with the prejudice of founders, as they would not manufacture from his patterns, and he was compelled to manufacture for himself, or abandon the invention. At that period, the dealers of the State of New York, and of all New England, resorted to the blast furnaces of New Jersey and Pennsylvania for their stove plates, under the universally erroneous idea that stove plates must be made directly from the ore; that plates made at a second melting would break. For a brief period, Mr. Mott procured his plates as others did, but when the blast furnace men advanced their prices, Mr. Mott resolved to erect a cupola furnace for the manufacture of his stove. He believed that the cause of cupola plates breaking was due partly to inferior metal, such as country founders used in making ploughshares and road scrapers; but more to the flat form of plate, which would not yield to the strain of expansion. Heat a flat plate of glass unequally, and the strain will cause it to break; bend or curve that plate, and heat will merely quicken the curve. So with iron. Mr. Mott made his plate patterns "from edge to edge longer than a straight line," by panelling, curving, fluting, or other device. A month's trial with half a dozen stoves of his own make, with fire of every possible description, convinced him that his reasoning was correct, and that the coarse, rough, heavy plates of the blast furnace would soon give place to the beautiful, smooth, light plate of the cupola. His operations gained the attention of iron men, and before the close of the year cupola furnaces began to be erected, and soon spread over the cities and villages of the Union.

No branch of manufacture has so much improved within the United States as that of fine light castings, since Mr. Mott erected his first cupola, then the only one expressly devoted to making stove castings.

The area of the moulding floor of his first workshop was less than sixteen hundred feet, while the moulding floor of his present Works at Mott Haven, Westchester county, New York, exceeds forty thousand feet. At these Works, bathing tubs six feet long, including flanges, two feet wide, and twenty-two inches deep, have been cast, weighing, without feet, less than one hundred and sixty pounds; believed to be, for extent of surface, the lightest casting ever made in Europe or America.

Before the invention of the stove for burning small or refuse coal, an immense heap of refuse, from the several yards on the Schuylkill, had accumulated at what is now known as West Philadelphia. This mass of refuse coal was purchased in 1835 by Mr. Mott, who had it screened and shipped to the city of New York. This was the first movement that gave value to the small sizes of coal. In that year he patented a stove with the following claim, viz.: "forming the exterior or shell of furnaces, or fireplaces for stoves of various kinds, the bodies of gas retorts and other apparatus, which are to be exposed to great alternations of temperature by the combination of separate rings, rims, or frames of metal, by which means any difference of expansion in the respective parts may take place without the danger of breaking."

Mr. Mott's first foundry was located about one mile below Tarrytown, on the banks of the Hudson. It was the first landing above Sunnyside, the residence of Washington Irving, and in compliment to him, the village was called Irving, and the foundry "The Irving Iron Foundry;" but on account of difficulty in obtaining title, Mr. Mott removed his Works to Morrisania, adjoining the Harlem Bridge, being the nearest point to any part of the city of New York below 132d street, and the only point toward which city improvements could approach. To this place the lot owners and inhabitants have, in compliment to Mr. Mott, given the name of "Mott Haven." At the time of his purchase, about three thousand five hundred acres of land belonged to the cousins of one family. His deed was the first conveyance to any person outside of the family subsequent to 1668, the date of the purchase of the original manor by their ancestors. For several years there were but thirteen tax-payers on the assessment roll for this manor. Since 1846, Mr. Mott has purchased for himself, or as agent for others, about four hundred acres of these lands, on which, at this time, dwell a population of over twelve thousand, mostly families owning or occupying small parcels. Besides "The J. L. Mott Iron-works;" the Montaux Iron and Steel Works, manufacturing steel directly from the ore, by a process invented by Joseph Yates; also the American Danamora Iron-works, and others, are located at Mott Haven.

PITTS, John A., Buffalo, New York, born in Augusta, Kennebec county, Maine, and died in Buffalo, New York, in July, 1859. He was the twin brother of the late Hiram A. Pitts, who died in Chicago, Illinois, in 1860, and when children they were so near alike in personal appearance that their mother was compelled to mark one to distinguish him from the other. Both brothers were naturally ingenious and inventive, and acted in co-operation in all their inventions. One of Mr. Pitts' first inventions was the Endless Chain or Tread Horse-power, which has been considerably modified by others, since the expiration of the patent, but very little improved. The Endless Chain Pump, which is now in general use throughout the country, was also his invention. His attention was subsequently directed to improvements in Agricultural Machines, of which his most important invention was a combined Thresher and Cleaner, commonly called, and widely known, as Pitts' Threshing Machine. For a more particular account of the Works in Buffalo, where these machines are manufactured, now under the management of James Brayley, Esq., see *Vol. III., Manufactures of Buffalo.*

ROEBLING, John A., Trenton, New Jersey. This eminent engineer and pioneer manufacturer of Wire Rope was born in Prussia, in 1806, and educated in that country as a civil engineer. When twenty-one years of age he entered the Prussian service, and served for four years as an assistant in the construction of military roads. In the year 1831, he emigrated with one of his brothers to the United States, with a view of farming, which occupation he pursued for a few years in Butler county, in the State of Pennsylvania. In 1835, he resumed his profession, and was employed on various works in Ohio and Pennsylvania. In the year 1842, he made a proposition to the Canal Board of Pennsylvania to substitute Wire Ropes in place of Hemp Ropes on the inclined planes of the Alleghany Portage Railroad, which in those days connected the eastern and western divisions of the Pennsylvania canal. The annual expense of hemp ropes on those planes was about $20,000. This experiment succeeded, and from that time Mr. Roebling's Wire Ropes have gradually been introduced on all the Inclines, Collieries, and other works throughout the country.

In the year 1850, Mr. Roebling removed from Pennsylvania to New Jersey, and erected extensive Works near Trenton, which are now of a sufficient capacity to manufacture two thousand tons of Wire Rope annually. This process commences with the iron in the bar or bloom, which is rolled down into rods, then drawn into wire and laid into rope.

The subject of *Suspension Bridges* was one of Mr. Roebling's favorite studies in the early period of his professional career. He therefore took a lively and prominent interest in this matter when the question of bridging our numerous rivers began to be discussed. In the year 1844, he contracted with the city of Pittsburg to erect a Wire Suspension Aqueduct over the Alleghany river, in place of the old wooden superstructure. This was a novelty in civil engineering. After its successful completion he contracted with the Monongahela Bridge Co. for rebuilding their bridge in accordance with a plan that he originated.

Four more Suspension Aqueducts, on the Delaware and Hudson canal, in the State of New York, were next erected.

In 1852, Mr. Roebling commenced operations on the Niagara river, and laid the anchorage of the Railroad Suspension Bridge, which connects the Great Western line in Canada West with the New York Central. The lower floor of this work was opened for common travel in 1854. In March, 1855, the upper floor was opened for the passage of trains, and these have continued uninterruptedly ever since. The complete success of the bridge over the Niagara settled the question of the practicability of railroad Suspension Bridges.

A Suspension Bridge of one thousand two hundred and twenty-four feet in a single span, over the Kentucky river, on the Kentucky Central Railroad, was his next enterprise, which, however, when half completed, was stopped by the failure of the Company that undertook the construction of this portion of the road. This work will be resumed and completed at no distant day.

In 1856, Mr. Roebling laid the extensive foundations for the towers of the Covington and Cincinnati Suspension Bridge over the Ohio river. This work was interrupted in 1857, but resumed in 1863, and will be completed in 1867. This will be the largest Suspension Bridge in the world, and no doubt the best built and most substantial. Its cost will be one and a half million of dollars. During the years of 1858, 1859, and 1860, the fine Wire Suspension Bridge over the Alleghany river, at Pittsburg, was erected under Mr. Roebling's superintendence. The Cincinnati Bridge is the tenth public work of this description which he has planned and executed in this country.

TOWERS, William H., Boston, Mass., one of the most versatile and prolific inventors of the present age, was born in Pickaway county, Ohio, in 1826. Though not a New Englander by birth, he belongs to the class who have given a distinctive character to the inhabitants of that section from the fertility of their inventive genius, applied especially to the improvement of articles in common household or personal use. With one or two exceptions, his name appears upon the records of the Patent Office more frequently than any other, generally in connection, it is true, with improvements in small articles; but among his inventions are some that form the basis of large and prosperous manufacturing companies. His first patent was for an improved apparatus for giving rest to the arm in writing; his second for a hot-air register, containing the means of moistening the heated air to suit the occupants of a room; his third for an improved horseshoe, with flanges to fasten it to the hoof without the aid of nails. He also invented a machine for opening oysters, and a creeper to prevent slipping on ice, by which many serious accidents have no doubt been averted.

In 1860, he directed his attention to the improvement of Brooms, and, by distributing among the corn strips of cane or reed, succeeded in producing a much more durable Broom than any heretofore made, and which has become a favorite one with housekeepers, especially in New England, where these Brooms are made in large quantities by the "New England Broom Company."

In 1862, he conceived that the ordinary Dressing Pin would be improved by making a slight spherical or oval enlargement near its centre, by which, without interfering with its facility of penetration, it would remain in its place, and not be subject to being easily or accidentally detached. On further experiment he found that the same object could be obtained by substituting two slight nicks near the point. He disposed of his patent to a number of capitalists in Boston, who have organized a Company known as "The Union Pin Manufacturing Company," who are now producing Pins that compare favorably with the best Pins made in England. They run about twenty machines, each of which makes one hundred and sixty-five Pins per minute.

In the same year he patented a combined Cork and Corkscrew, the latter consisting of a wire passed through the cork from its top to the bottom, and bent at the ends, affording a ready means of drawing the cork without other aid. Among his numerous inventions of recent date is an apparatus for Heating Rooms by Gas, and consists simply of a sheet-iron drum cone, that can be suspended over an ordinary gas burner. By means of this invention travellers may carry their stoves in their trunks, and, if generally adopted, hotel keepers will find their gas bills unaccountably increased, and their profits from fires in rooms considerably diminished.

But, probably, the most important invention which he has made is a new process of Tanning Skins by means of Alcohol. This has been alluded to elsewhere in this volume, and, if the evidence of tanners and eye-witnesses is to be believed, it is destined to effect a revolution in the American system of Tanning. As good sole leather, it is said, can be made by this process in less than thirty days, as by the methods ordinarily practiced in four months. Calf skins of the best quality can be made in from ten to fifteen days. Sweated hides can be tanned into leather equally pliable with that obtained from limed hides, and the loss in weight consequent upon the liming process is by this means saved. The paraphernalia of tanyards is simplified, and less capital will be required to conduct the business. His latest experiments have been directed to producing from raw hide a substitute for hard Rubber, and applicable to all the purposes—combs, jewelry, etc.—for which Rubber is now used.

Mr. Towers possesses that peculiar idiosyncrasy of mental constitution which can scarcely look upon an article, however familiar, without perceiving a means by which it can be improved, and it would be hazardous to assert, while he is living, that any trade or manufacture is established or safe from innovation.

WILSON, Allen B., who is entitled to the credit of having been among the first to discern the value and future triumphs of the Sewing Machine, and also of having made the most important improvements on the original machine, was born at Willett, Courtland county, New York. His first patent bears date November 12th, 1850, and is the fifteenth on the Patent Office records for an improved Sewing Machine. Adopting the lock-stitch of Howe as the one most economical of thread and best adapted for general use, and to which he has ever since adhered, Mr. Wilson's first aim was to make the stitch with less expense of time and power than the original required. This he effected by the use of a double pointed shuttle, making, in combination with the needle, a stitch at each forward and backward movement of the shuttle, instead of one at each throw of the shuttle, as in Howe's machine. He also patented an improvement in the mechanism for holding and feeding the cloth to the needle, and thus regulating the length of stitch, an arrangement which has since been extensively adopted by the manufacturers of Sewing Machines.

On the 12th of August, 1851, Mr. Wilson—who then resided at Watertown, Connecticut—secured a patent for an improvement which, in simplicity, ingenuity, and effectiveness, has seldom been surpassed, and is one of the most valuable ever made in the Sewing Machine. This was for the "rotating hook," which remarkable contrivance was designed to supersede the shuttle, and to make the lock-stitch with greater rapidity, neatness, and economy of power. It also dispenses with the dirt and loss of time in oiling the lubricated slide which guides the shuttle. With some additional combinations, known as the "four motion feed," patented in the following year, the rotating hook, which is cut out of a solid steel rod by ingenious machinery and attached to the main shaft of the machine, in its revolution seizes the loop of thread in the needle the moment it passes through the cloth, opens it out, and carries it around the bobbin, so that the thread is then passed through the loop of the stitch; this is then drawn up with the thread in the needle, so that the two are looped together about half way through the cloth, forming the strongest possible seam, showing the stitching exactly even upon both sides, with no threads above the surface to wear off and allow the seam to rip. It is hardly possible that any mechanical operation can be conceived that is more simple and effective than this invention. Mr. Wilson's claims as inventor of the feed improvements have been fully sustained by the courts, and perpetual injunctions granted in five different suits against infringers of his patent. Although the rotating hook, which is a characteristic feature of the Wheeler & Wilson machines, makes only the lock-stitch, it is claimed that it does it by the fewest possible movements, and at a very trifling expense can be adapted to make the chain stitch as well.

Having thus successfully improved the Sewing Machine, Mr. Wilson was fortunate in entering into a business partnership with Mr. Nathaniel Wheeler, a practical manufacturer, with whom he commenced building the machines, chiefly by hand power, in a small shop at Watertown. The machines thenceforward bore their joint names, and by their success have carried them throughout the civilized world.

The first Wheeler & Wilson Sewing Machine was completed early in 1851, and was sold for $125. This machine, after earning many times its cost for its purchaser, has recently found its way back to the magnificent warerooms of the manufacturers, on Broadway, in New York city, where it is now on exhibition as a curiosity. The firm made at first from eight to ten machines a week, and when the demand increased more rapidly than their facilities for manufacturing could supply, they removed to Bridgeport, and fitted up a manufactory which is now the largest of its kind in the world.

For some years, Mr. Wilson, though still a part proprietor of this manufactory, has had no active share in its management, and has resided in Waterbury, Connecticut, where he has engaged in enterprises of various kinds.

WOOD, Walter A., Hoosick Falls, New York — an extensive manufacturer of Agricultural Implements, and a prominent inventor, who, since 1852, has received upward of thirty patents, principally for improvements in Mowers and Reapers.

In 1850, when Mr. Wood became connected with the manufacture, there was but one Mowing Machine that could be called really successful, although the practicability of mowing by machinery had been established earlier by the inventive genius of the late Obed Hussey. In 1851, not more than three or four hundred machines were sold annually, while in 1865, the whole number of Mowers and Reapers manufactured was but little short of one hundred thousand. The remarkable increase in this branch of manufactures is further shown in the fact, that in 1853 the whole number of machines made by Mr. Wood was two hundred and seventy, while in 1865 nearly seven thousand five hundred were produced in his establishment, giving employment to four hundred and fifty men, and returning an annual value of one million of dollars.

The Works of Mr. Wood at Hoosick Falls comprise a main manufactory two hundred and fifty feet by forty-four, four stories in height; a Foundry, two hundred by fifty feet; a Blacksmith shop, forty-four by eighty; a Repair and Pattern Shop, Office and Warehouse. He has manufactured at the establishment, since 1852, over fifty thousand Mowers and Reapers, and has a capacity for making twelve thousand annually.

Mr. Wood was the first to introduce into Europe, successfully, the Mowing of Grass by Machinery. In 1856, he sent, by the hands of a competent agent, fifty of his machines, which were at once sold, and operated satisfactorily. In the subsequent year he sent out two hundred and fifty machines, and his exportation of Mowers and Reapers to Great Britain and the Continent has since then been about one thousand annually. This prosperous and increasing foreign trade established by him, now amounts to about one half of the total European trade in these machines, the English manufacturers supplying the balance.

Unlike several, whose names have become widely known by dexterously availing themselves of improvements originated by others, Mr. Wood has given indubitable evidence of genius as an inventor as well as enterprise as a manufacturer. *See ante, page* 484.

APPENDIX.

Alphabetical Arrangement of the Tariffs of the United States, For the Years 1842, 1846, 1857, and 1862.

[Revised by Henry Hay, Esq., of the Philadelphia Custom-House.]

	1842.	1846. per ct.	1857. per ct.	1862.
Accordions	per cent. 30	20	15	per cent. 30
Acetic acid	" 20	20	4	" 25
Acid, benzoic	" 20	20	4	" 10
" boracic	" 5	20	4	lb. 5 c.
" citric, white or yellow	" 20	20	4	lb. 10 c.
" muriatic	" 20	20	4	per cent. 10
" nitric, or nitric fort.	" 20	20	15	" 10
" oxalic	" 20	20	4	lb. 4 c.
" pyroligneous	" 20	20	4	per cent. 10
" tartaric, in crystals or powder	" 20	20	4	lb. 20 c.
" sulphuric, or oil of vitriol	lb. 1 ct	10	4	lb. 1 c.
Acids, all kinds of, used for chemical and manufacturing purposes	per cent. 20	20	15	(not otherwise provided for, free.)
Acids, used for medicinal purposes, or in the fine arts, not otherwise provided for	" 20	20	4	per cent. 10
Acorns	" 20	20	15	" 10
Adhesive plaster, salve	" 30	30	24	" 40
Adzes	" 30	30	24	" 35
Ale, in bottles	gal. 20 cts	30	24	per gal. 30
" otherwise than in bottles	" 15 cts	30	24	" 20
Alkanet root	per cent. 20	20	15	per cent. 20
Almonds	lb. 3 cts	40	30	lb. 4 cts.
" shelled	" 3 cts	40	30	" 6 cts.
" paste and oil of	" 9 cts	30	24	per cent. 50
Aloes	free,	20	4	lb. 6 cts.
Alspice, oil of	per cent. 30	30	24	per cent. 50
Alum	lb. 1½ cts	20	15	100 lbs. 60 cts.
Ammonia	per cent. 20	20	8	per cent. 20
" sal	" 20	10	8	" 20
" salts	" 20	10	8	" 20
" carb	" 20	20	8	" 20
Ammoniac, crude	" 20	20	15	" 20
" refined	" 20	20	15	" 20
" bole	" 20	20	15	" 50
Ammunition, except gunpowder and musket balls	" 30	30	24	
Animals for breed	free,	free,	free,	(alive, free.)
Antimony, crude	free,	20	8	per cent. 10
Any goods, wares or merchandise of the growth, produce, or manufacture of the United States, or				

	1842.	1846. per ct.	1857. per ct.	1862.
of its fisheries, upon which no drawback, bounty, or allowance has been paid	free,	free,	free,	free.
Apparel, wearing and other personal baggage in actual use	free,	free,	free,	free.
Aqua fortis	per cent. 20	20	4	per cent. 10
Argol	free,	5	free,	lb. 6 cts.
Arms, fire	per cent. 30	30	24	per cent. 35
" side	" 30	30	24	" 35
Arrack	gal. 60 cts	100	30	gal. 75 c. to $1.05
Arrow root	per cent. 20	20	15	per cent. 20
Arsenic, all	" 20	15	4	" 20
Articles of the growth, produce or manufacture of the U. States, or its territories, brought back in the same condition as when exported, and on which no drawback was allowed	free,	free,	free,	free.
Articles, all, composed wholly or chiefly in quantity, of gold, silver, pearl, and precious stones, not otherwise specified	per cent. 20	30	24	per cent. 35 (crude, free.)
Articles not in a crude state, used in dyeing or tanning, not otherwise provided for	" 20	20	4	per cent. 20
Articles, all, not free, and not subject to any other rate of duty, raw,	" 20	20	15	" 10
Do. do. manufactured	" 20	20	15	" 20
Articles manufactured from copper, or of which copper is the material of chief value, not otherwise specified	" 30	30	24	" 35
Articles worn by men, women, or children, of whatever materials composed, made up in whole or in part by hand, not otherwise provided for	" 30	30	24	" 35
Artificial feathers	" 25	30	24	" 40
Augurs	" 30	30	24	" 35
Awls	" 30	30	24	" 35
Axes	" 30	30	24	" 35
Bacon	lb. 3 cts	20	15	lb. 2 cts.
Baggage, personal, in actual use	free,	free,	free	free.
Bags, bead, made in part by hand,	per cent. 25	30	24	per cent. 35
" grass	" 25	30	24	" 35
" gunny	sq. yd. 5 cts	20	15	" 25

	1842.	1846. per ct.	1857. per ct.	1862.
Bags, woolen	per cent. 40	30	24	p. ct. 30 & lb. 18 c.
" worsted	" 40	25	19	per cent. 35
" flax and hemp	" 25	20	15	" 35
" carpet, woolen	" 30	30	24	" 35
" silk	" 30	25	19	" 40
Balls, billiard	" 20	30	24	" 35
" wash	" 30	30	24	per. ct. 30 & lb. 2 c.
Balsam, copaiva	" 25	30	24	lb. 20 cts.
" of Tolu	" 25	30	24	" 30 cts.
" medicinal	" 25	30	24	per cent. 30
" all kinds of cosmetic	" 25	30	24	" 50
Barege, wool, colored	" 30	30	24	(See Woolens.)
" wool, gray	"	30	24	
" worsted, or silk and cotton,	" 30	25	19	per cent. 35
Bark of cork trees, unmanufactured	free,	15	4	" 30
" Peruvian	free,	15	free,	" 20
" all not specially mentioned	free,	20	8	" 10
Barley	bush. 20 cts	20	15	bush. 15 cts.
" pearl or hulled	lb. 2 cts	20	15	lb. 1ct.
Baskets, wood	per cent. 30	30	24	per cent. 35
" osier	" 25	30	24	" 35
" palm-leaf	" 25	30	24	" 35
" straw	" 25	30	24	" 35
" grass or whalebone	" 25	30	24	" 35
Battledores	" 25	30	24	" 35
Bay water, or bay rum	" 25	30	24	gal. 50 cts.
Beans, tonkay	" 20	20	15	per cent. 20
" vanilla	" 20	20	15	lb. $3.
" all other not specially mentioned	" 20	20	15	per cent. 10
Bed feathers	" 25	25	19	" 30
" ticking, linen	" 25	20	15	(See Flax.)
" " cotton	" 30	25	24	(See Cotton.)
" caps	" 30	30	24	per cent. 35
" screws	" 30	30	24	lb. 1¾ cts.
" sides, as carpeting	" 30	30	24	(See Mats.)
" spreads, or covers, of the scraps of printed calicoes, sewed,	" 30	25	24	
Beef	lb. 2 cts	20	15	lb. 1 ct
Beer, in bottles	gal. 20 cts	30	24	gal. 30 cts
" otherwise than in bottles	gal. 15 cts	30	24	gal. 20 cts.
Beeswax	per cent. 15	20	15	per cent. 20
Bell cranks	" 30	30	24	" 35
" levers	" 30	30	24	" 35
" pulls	" 30	30	24	" 35
" metal, manufactured	" 30	30	24	" 35
Bellows	" 35	30	24	" 35

	1842.	1846. per ct.	1857. per ct.	1862.
Bellows' pipes	" 30	30	24	per cent. 35
Bells, of bell-metal, fit only to be re-manufactured	free,	5	free,	free.
Belts, sword leather	per cent. 35	30	24	per cent. 35
Berries, used for dyeing, all exclusively, in a crude state	free,	5	free,	free.
Berries, not otherwise provided for,	per cent. 20	20	15	per cent. 10
Bichromate of potash	" 20	20	15	lb. 3 cts.
Binding, carpet, if worsted	" 30	25	19	per cent. 35
" cotton	" 30	25	24	" 35
" woolen	" 30	30	24	" 35
" worsted	" 30	25	19	" 35
" silk	" 30	25	19	" 40
" leather	" 30	30	24	" 35
" linen	" 30	20	15	" 35
" quality	" 30	25	19	" 35
Birds	" 20	20	free,	free.
Bismuth	" 20	20	free,	free.
" oxide of	" 20	20	15	per cent. 20
Bitts, carpenters'	" 30	30	24	" 35
Bitumen	" 15	20	4	lb. 3 cts.
Blacking	" 20	20	15	per cent. 30
Black, lamp	" 20	20	15	" 20
" lead pots	" 20	30	24	" 35
" lead powder	" 20	20	15	ton, $10.00
Bladders	" 20	20	15	per cent. 20
Blankets, all	75 c. pc. 15; ov. 75 c. " 25	20	15	Of wool not over 28c. p. lb., 6c. p. lb., p. ct. 15; over 28 and not over 40c., 6c. p. lb., p. ct. 30; over 40c. p. lb. 12c. p. lb., p. ct. 25.
Blankets of mohair or goats' hair,	per cent. 20	20	15	per cent. 35
Bleaching powders	lb. 1 ct	10	4	100 lbs. 30 cts.
Boards, planed	per cent. 30	20	15	per cent. 20
" rough	" 20	20	15	" 20
Bobbin, cotton	" 30	25	24	" 35
" wire, covered with cotton	lb. 8 cts	30	24	" 35
Bodkins, all	per cent. 20	30	24	per cent. 35
Bolting-cloths	" 20	25	free,	free.
Bolts, composition	" 30	30	24	per cent. 35
Bone, black	" 20	20	free,	free.
" alphabets	" 20	30	24	per cent. 35
" chessmen	" 20	30	24	" 35

	1842.	1846. per ct.	1857. per ct.	1862.
Bone, whale, rosettes..................	" 20	30	24	per cent. 35
" tip and bones..................	p. ct. 5 & 20	20	4	" 10
" whale, other manufact'res of	per cent. 20	30	24	" 35
" " not of the American fisheries	" 12½	20	15	" 10
" manufactures of..............	" 20	30	24	" 35
Bonnets, Leghorn....................	" 35	30	24	" 40
" all..............	" 35	30	24	" 40
Bonnet wire, covered with silk.....	lb. 12 cts	30	24	" 35
" " " " cotton,	" 8 cts	30	24	" 35
Books, blank.......................	" 20 cts	20	15	per cent. 20
" periodicals, and other works in the course of printing and republication in the U. S............	lb. 20 & 30c.	20	8	" 20
Books, printed magazines, pamphlets, periodicals, and illustrated newspapers, bound or unbound, not otherwise provided for......	per cent. 8	10	8	" 20
Books of engravings, bound or unbound	" 20	10	8	" 20
Books and instruments, professional, of persons arriving in the U. S.........................	free,	free,	free,	free.
Books, specially imported for the use of schools, etc................	free,	free,	free,	free.
Boots	pair $1.25	30	24	per cent. 35
" laced, silk, or satin, for children..........................	" 25 c	30	24	" 35
" and bootees, of leather.......	" $1.25	30	24	" 35
" rubber............................	per cent. 30	30	24	" 35
Bootees, for women or men, silk...	pair 75 c	30	24	" 35
Borax, or tincal.........................	" 25	25	4	lb. 5 cts.
" refined........................		25	19	lb. 10 cts.
Botany, specimens of..................	free,	free,	free,	free.
Bottles, apothecaries'................	$1.75 *a* $2.25	30	24	per cent. 30
Bottles, black glass....................		30	24	" 30
" perfumery and fancy.......	gross $2.50	30	24	" 35
" containing wine or other articles	gross $3.00	40	30	" 50
Bougies................................	per cent. 30	30	24	" 35
Boxes, gold or silver..................	" 30	30	24	" 35
" musical..........................	" 30	20	15	" 30
" japanned dressing...........	" 25	30	24	" 40
" cedar, granadilla, ebony, rose, and satin............	" 30	40	30	" 35
" all other wood................	" 30	30	24	" 35
" sand, of tin.....................	" 30	30	24	" 35

	1842.	1846. per ct.	1857. per ct.	1862.
Boxes, shell, not otherwise enumerated	per cent. 25	30	24	per cent. 35
" if paper only, not japanned	" 25	30	24	" 35
" snuff, paper	" 25	30	24	" 35
" fancy, not otherwise specified	" 25	30	24	" 35
Brace bitts	" 30	30	24	" 35
Bracelets, gold or set	" 20	30	24	" 25
" gilt	" 25	30	24	" 35
" hair	" 25	30	24	" 35
Brackets	" 30	30	24	" 35
Brads	lb. 5 cts	30	24	M. 2 cts.
Braids, cotton	per cent. 30	25	24	per cent. 25
" in ornaments, for head-dresses	" 30	30	24	" 35
" hair, not made up for head-dresses	" 30	30	24	" 35
" hair, made up for head-dresses	" 25	30	24	" 35
" straw, for making bonnets or hats	" 30	30	24	" 30
Brandy	gal. $1.00	100	30	gal. $1.50 to $2.10
Brass, manufactures of, not otherwise enumerated	per cent. 30	30	24	per cent. 35
" in plates or sheets	" 30	30	24	" 35
" in bars	free,	5	free,	" 15
" in pigs	free,	5	free,	" 15
" old, only fit to be remanufactured	free,	5	free,	" 15
" wire	per cent. 25	30	24	" 35
" rolled	" 30	30	24	" 35
" battery	lb. 12½ cts	30	24	" 35
" studs	per cent. 30	30	24	" 35
" screws	lb. 30 cts	30	24	" 35
Braziers' rods, of 3-16 to 10-16 of an inch diameter	lb. 2½ cts	30	24	
Bricks	per cent. 25	20	15	" 20
Bridles	" 30	30	24	" 35
Brimstone, crude	" 20	15	4	per ton $3.00
" rolled	" 25	20	15	" $6.00
Bristles	lb. 1 ct	5	4	lb. 10 cts.
Bristol stones	per cent. 20	10	4	per cent. 10
" boards	lb. 12½ cts	30	24	" 35
" " perforated	lb. 12½ cts	30	24	" 35
Britannia ware	per cent. 30	30	24	" 35
Bronze casts	" 30	30	24	" 35
" all manufactures of	" 30	30	24	" 35

	1842.	1846. per ct.	1857. per ct.	1862.
Bronze metal in leaf	per cent. 30	20	15	per cent. 10
" powder	" 20	20	15	" 20
" pale, yellow, white, and red	" 30	20	15	" 20
" liquid, gold, or bronze color	" 20	20	15	" 10
Brooms, all kinds	" 30	30	24	" 35
Brushes of all kinds	" 30	30	24	" 35
Buckram	" 25	20	15	" 30
Bugles, glass, if cut	" 25	40	30	" 35
" glass, if not cut	" 25	30	24	" 30
Building-stones	" 10	10	8	" 20
Bullets	lb. 4 cts	20	15	" 35
Bullrushes	per cent. 20	20	15	" 10
Bullion	free,	free,	free,	free.
Bunting	per cent. 30	25	19	per cent. 35
Burgundy pitch	" 20	25	19	" 20
Burlaps	" 25	20	15	(See Linens.)
Burr stones, unbound	free,	10	free,	free.
" bound up	per cent. 20	10	15	per cent. 20
Busts, lead	lb. 4 cts	30	24	" 35
Butter	lb. 5 cts	20	15	lb. 4 cts.
Button moulds, of whatever material	per cent. 25	25	19	per cent. 30
Buttons, metal, all kinds of	" 30	25	19	" 30
" all other	" 25	25	19	" 30
" with links	" 25	25	19	" 30
Cabinet wares	" 30	30	24	" 35
Cables, tarred	lb. 5 cts	25	19	lb. $2\frac{3}{4}$ cts.
" manilla, untarred	lb. $4\frac{1}{2}$ cts	25	19	lb. $2\frac{1}{4}$ cts.
" iron or chain, or parts of	lb. $2\frac{1}{2}$ cts	30	24	lb. 2 cts.
Calomel, and all other mercurial preparations	per cent. 25	25	19	per cent. 30
Camel's hair	" 10	10	8	(See Wool.)
" pencils, in quill	" 20	30	24	per cent. 35
" " other	" 20	30	24	" 35
Cameos	" 7	10	4	" 5
" set	" 7	30	24	" 25
Camomile flowers	" 20	20	15	" 20
Camphor, refined	lb. 20 cts	40	30	lb. 40 cts.
" crude	lb. 5 cts	25	8	lb. 30 cts.
Canary seed	per cent. 20	free,	15	bush. $1 00
Candles, tallow	lb. 4 cts	20	15	lb. $2\frac{1}{2}$ cts.
" wax or sperm	lb. 8 cts	20	15	lb. 8 cts.
" other	lb. 8 cts	20	15	lb. $2\frac{1}{2}$ and 5 cts.
Candlesticks, alabaster	various,	40	30	per cent. 35
" glass-cut	lb. 45 cts	40	30	" 35

	1842.	1846. per ct.	1857. per ct.	1862.
Candlesticks, spa	various,	40	30	per cent. 35
" all other	"	30	24	" 35
Candy, sugar	lb. 6 cts	30	24	lb. 6 and 10 cts.
Canes, walking, finished or not	per cent. 30	30	24	per cent. 35
Cannon, brass or iron	" 30	30	24	" 35
Canvas, for floor-cloth or wearing-apparel, linen	" 25	20	15	(See Flax.)
Caoutchouc gums	free,	10	4	per cent. 10
Cap wire, covered with silk	lb. 12 cts	30	24	as wire, & 5 cts. p. lb. addition'l
" " cotton thread	lb. 8 cts	30	24	
Caps of chip, lace, leather, cotton, silk, linen, etc	p. ct. 30 *a* 50	30	24	(chip,) p. ct. 40 (cotton,) p.ct. 35
Caps, gloves, leggins, mitts, socks, stockings, wove-shirts and drawers, and all similar articles made in frames, and worn by men, women, or children, and not otherwise provided for	per cent. 30.	20&30.	15&24	per cent. 35
Caps, lace, sewed or not	p. ct. 20 *a* 40	30	24	" 35
Capsules	per cent. 20	30	24	" 40
Carbines or carabines	" 30	30	24	" 35
Carbonate of magnesia	" 20	30	24	lb. 6 cts.
" sal, or brinal of soda	" 20	20	8	lb. ½ ct.
" of ammonia	" 20	20	8	per cent. 20
" of iron	" 20	20	15	" 20
Carboys	each 30 cts	30	24	" 30
Carbuncles	per cent. 10	10	4	" 5
Card cases, of whatever material composed	" 30	30	24	" 35
Cards, playing	pack 25 cts	30	24	pk. 15 and 25 cts.
Carmine, water color	per cent. 20	30	24	per cent. 35
" a liquid dye	" 20		15	" 20
Carpets, Aubusson, Wilton, Saxony, Axminster, Tournay or tapestry velvet, Brussels Jacquard, and medallion	sq. yd. 65 cts	30	24	Under $1.25 p. s. yd. 45 c. p. yd; over, 55 c. p. s. yd.
Carpets, Brussels and Brussels tapestry	yd. 55 cts	30	24	p. sq. yd. 28 cts.
Carpets, treble ingrain, Venetian,	sq. yd. 30 cts	30	24	" 6 cts.
" hemp	per cent. 30	20	15	" 20 cts.
" jute	" 30	20	19	" 20 cts.
" druggets and bockings	sq. yd. 14 cts	25	19	" 20 cts.
" all other	" 30	30	24	various.
" matting	" 25	25	19	per cent. 30
" binding	" 30	25	19	" 35
Carriages of all descriptions, and parts thereof	" 30	30	24	" 35

	1842.	1846. per ct.	1857. per ct.	1862.
Carriage springs	per cent. 30	30	24	per cent. 35
Carvers	" 30	30	24	" 35
Cashmere, borders of wool	" 40	30	24	lb. 18 cts. & p.ct. 30
" of Thibet	" 20	25	19	per cent. 35
" cloth	" 40	30	24	(See Wool.)
" gown patterns, wool being a component material	" 40	30	24	lb. 18 cts. & p.ct. 30
Cashmere gowns, made	" 40	30	24	" "
" shawls, Thibet	" 40	30	24	per cent. 35
" " wool being a component part	" 40	30	24	lb. 18 cts. & p.ct. 35
Casks, empty	" 30	30	24	per cent. 35
Cassia, Chinese, Calcutta and Sumatra	lb. 5 cts	40	4	lb. 15 cts.
Cassia, buds	per cent. 20	20	4	lb. 20 cts.
Cassimere, woolen	" 40	30	24	(See Wool.)
" cotton, wool being a component part, chief value	" 40	30	24	(See Wool.)
Castings, iron, even if with wrought-iron rings, hoops, handles, etc	lb. 1 & 1½ cts	30	24	per cent. 35
Castor beans	per cent. 20	20	free,	bush. 30 cts.
" oil	gal. 40 cts	20	15	gal. 50 cts.
Castors, brass, iron or wood	per cent. 30	30	24	per cent. 35
" or cruets, silver	" 30	30	24	" 35
" " plated	" 30	30	24	" 35
" " wood	" 30	30	24	" 35
Castor glasses, not in the frames or cruets, cut	gross $2.50	40	30	" 35
Castor glasses, not in the frames or cruets, not cut	" $4.00	30	24	" 30
Catgut	per cent. 15	20	15	" 30
Catsup	" 30	30	24	" 40
Caustic	" 20	30	24	" 20
Cement, Roman	" 20	20	15	" 20
Chafing dishes	" 30	30	24	" 35
Chains, all	lb. 2½ & 4 cts	30	24	Chain cables, lb. 2c.; chain curbs, gilt, p. ct. 35; chains, ½ in. or over in diam. lb. 1¾ cts.; under ½ in. & not under ¼, 2¼ cts.; under ¼ in. & not under No. 9 wire, 3 cts.; under No. 9, 30 p. ct.; coated with zinc, etc., 2½ c. per lb.; of other metal than iron, 35 p. ct.
Chairs, sitting	per cent. 30	30	24	per cent. 35
Chalk, red	" 20	20	4	" 10
" red, pencils	" 25	30	24	" 30

	1842.	1846. per ct.	1857. per ct.	1862.
Chalk, French	per cent. 20	20	4	per cent. 10
" white	free,	5		ton, $4.00.
Chambray gauze, cotton, as cotton,	per cent. 30	25	24	(as cotton.)
" if wool is a component part	" 40	30	24	(See Silk.)
" of silk only	lb. $2.50	25	19	per cent. 40
Chandeliers, brass	per cent. 30	30	24	" 35
" glass, cut	lb. 45 cts	40	30	" 35
Charts	free,	10	free,	" 20
" books	per cent. 20	10	8	" 20
Checks, cotton	" 40	25	24	(as cotton.)
" princess, wool	" 40	30	24	(See Wool.)
" " worsted	" 40	25	19	lb. 2 cts. & p. ct. 30
" linen	" 25	20	15	as Linens.
Cheese	lb. 9 cts	30	24	lb. 4 cts.
Chemical preparations, not otherwise enumerated	per cent. 20	30	24	per cent. 20
Chenille, cords or trimming of, cotton	" 30	30	24	" 35
Chessmen, bone, ivory, rice or wood	" 30	30	24	" 35
Chicory root	free,	free,	free,	lb. 2 cts.
" ground	per cent. 20	20	15	lb. 3 cts.
China ware	" 30	30	24	per cent, 35; ornamented, 40.
" root	" 20	20	15	per cent. 20
Chip hats or bonnets	" 35	30	24	" 40
Chisels, all	" 30	30	24	" 35
Chloride of lime	lb. 1 ct	10	4	100 lbs. 30 cts.
Chocolate	lb. 4 cts	20	15	lb. 7 cts.
Chromate of potash	per cent. 20	20	15	lb. 3 cts.
" lead	lb. 4 cts	20	15	per cent. 25
Chromic, yellow	per cent. 20	20	15	" 25
" acid	" 20	20	15	" 15
Chronometers and parts	" 20	10	8	" 10
Cinchona, Peruvian	free,	15	free,	" 20
Cinnabar	" 20	25	15	" 20
Cinnamon	lb. 25 cts	30	4	lb. 25 cts.
Citron, in its natural state	free,	20	8	per cent. 10
" preserved	per cent. 25	40	30	" 35
Clasps, all	" 30	30	24	" 35
Clay, ground or prepared	" 20	20	15	" 20
" unwrought	free,	5	4	ton, $5.00
Clayed sugar, white	lb. 4 cts	30	24	lb. 4 cts.
Cloaks, of wool	per cent. 50	30	24	(See Wool.)
Clocks	" 25	30	24	per cent. 35
Cloth, India rubber	" 30	30	24	" 35

	1842.	1846. per ct.	1857. per ct.	1862.
Cloth, woolen	per cent. 40	30	24	(See Wool.)
" oil, 50 cts or less	yd. 35 cts	30	24	per cent. 30
" " over 50 cts	" 35 cts	30	24	" 35
" hemp	per cent. 20	20	15	" 25
Clothing, ready-made	" 50	30	24	" 35
" of wool	" 50	30	24	lb. 18 c. & p. c. 30
Cloves	lb. 8 cts	40	4	lb. 15 cts.
Coaches, or parts thereof	per cent. 30	30	24	per cent. 35
Coach furniture of all descriptions,	" 30	30	24	" 35
Coal, bituminous	ton, $1.75	30	24	ton $1.10 (28 bus.)
" other	" $1.75	30	24	" 60 cts.
Coal-hods	per cent. 30	30	24	per cent. 35
Coatings, mohair or goats' hair	" 20	25	19	" 35
Cobalt	" 20	20	15	" 20
Cochineal	free,	10	4	free.
Cocks	per cent. 30	30	24	per cent. 35
Cocoa	lb. 1 ct	10	4	lb. 3 cts.
" shells	per cent. 20	10	4	lb. 2 cts.
Cocoa-nuts, West Indies	free,	20	4	free.
Codfish, dry	cwt. $1.00	20	15	lb. ½ ct.
Coffee, when imported in American vessels from the place of its growth	free,	free,	free,	lb. 5 cts.
Coffee, the growth or production of the possessions of the Netherlands, imported from the Netherlands	free,	free,	free,	lb. 5 cts.
Coffee, all other	per cent. 20	20	15	lb. 5 cts.
Coffee-mills	" 30	30	24	per cent. 35
Coins, cabinets of	free,	free,	free,	free.
Coke	bush. 5 cts	30	24	per cent. 30
Cold cream	per cent. 25	30	24	" 50
Cologne water	" 25	30	24	" 50
Colors, water	" 25	30	24	" 35
Combs	" 25	30	24	" 35
Comforters, made of wool	" 40	30	24	(See Wool.)
Comfits, preserved in sugar, brandy, or molasses	" 25	40	30	" 35
Commode handles	" 30	30	24	" 35
" knobs	" 30	30	24	" 35
Compasses	" 30	30	24	" 35
Composition of glass or paste, set,	" 20	30	24	" 35
" " " not set,	" 10	10	8	" 10
Coney wool	" 25	10	8	
Confectionary, all, not otherwise provided for	" 25	30	24	lb. 10 cts.
Copperas	lb. 2 cts	20	15	lb. ½ ct.

	1842.	1846. per ct.	1857. per ct.	1862.
Copper bottoms	per cent. 30	20	15	per cent. 30
Copper, braziers'	" 30	20	15	" 30
Copper plates and sheets, other	lb. 2 cts	30	24	
Copper, for the use of the mint	free,	free,	free,	free.
" in pigs, bars	free,	5	free,	lb. 2 cts.
" old, fit only to be re-manufactured	free,	5	free,	lb. $1\frac{1}{2}$ cts.
" manufactures of, not otherwise specified	per cent. 30	30	24	per cent. 35
" ore	free,	free,	free,	per cent. 5
" rods, bolts, spikes & nails,	lb. 4 cts	20	15	" 30
Copper, sheathing for ships, when 14 inches wide and 48 inches long, and weighing from 14 to 34 ozs. per square foot	free,	free,	free,	lb. 2 cts.
Copper, sulphate of	lb. 2 cts	20	15	per cent. 20
Coral	per cent. 20	20	15	free.
" cut or manufactured	" 20	30	24	per cent. 30
Cordage, tarred	lb. 5 cts	25	19	lb. $2\frac{3}{4}$ cts.
" untarred	lb. $4\frac{1}{2}$ cts	25	19	lb. $3\frac{1}{2}$ cts.
" manilla	lb. $4\frac{1}{2}$ cts	25	19	lb. $2\frac{1}{4}$ cts.
Cordials, all kinds	gal. 60 cts	100	30	gal. 75 cts.
Cork, manufactures of	per cent. 25	30	24	per cent. 35
Corks	" 30	30	24	" 50
Cork-tree, bark of, unmanufactur'd	free,	15	4	" 30
Corn, Indian, or maize	bush. 10 cts	20	15	bush. 10 cts.
" meal		20	15	per cent. 10
Corsets	per cent. 50	30	24	" 35
Cosmetics	" 25	30	24	" 50
Cotton	lb. 3 cts	free,	free,	lb. $\frac{1}{2}$ ct.
Cotton, unbleach'd, 100 thr'ds sq. in. or less, and over 5 oz. p. yd.	per cent. 30	25	24	sq. yd. $1\frac{1}{4}$ cts.
100@140 thr'ds, not 5 oz.	" 30	25	24	" $2\frac{1}{2}$ cts.
140@200 thr'ds, "	" 30	25	24	" $3\frac{3}{4}$ cts.
over 200 thr'ds, "	" 30	25	24	" 5 cts.
" bleached, 100 thr'ds sq. in. or less, and over 5 oz.	" 30	25	24	" $1\frac{3}{4}$ cts.
100@140 thr'ds, not 5 oz.	" 30	25	24	" 3 cts.
140@200 thr'ds, "	" 30	25	24	" $4\frac{1}{4}$ cts.
over 200 thr'ds, "	" 30	25	24	" $5\frac{1}{2}$ cts.
" colored, 100 thr'ds sq. inch or less, and over 5 oz.	" 30	25	24	s.y. $2\frac{1}{2}$ c. & p.ct. 10
100@140 thr'ds, not 5 oz.	" 30	25	24	" $3\frac{1}{2}$ c. " 10
140@200 thr'ds, "	" 30	25	24	" $4\frac{1}{2}$ c. " 10
over 200 thr'ds, "	" 30	25	24	" $5\frac{1}{2}$ c. " 10
" other plain woven, costing over 16 cts. sq. yd.	" 30	25	24	" 30

	1842.	1846. per ct.	1857. per ct.	1862.
Cotton, all manufactures of, not otherwise enumerated	per cent. 30	25	24	per cent. 35
Cotton bagging, 10 cts. lb. or less,	sq. yd. 4 cts	25	15	lb. $2\frac{1}{4}$ cts.
" " over 10 cts. lb.	" 4 cts	25	15	lb. 3 cts.
" braces, or suspenders	per cent. 30	30	24	per cent. 35
" caps, gloves, leggins, mitts, socks, stockings, wove-shirts, and drawers	" 30	20.	15&24	" 35
Cotton embroidery, or floss	" 25	25	24	" 35
" hosiery, unbleached	" 30	20	15	" 35
" lace, including bobbinet	" 20	25	24	" 25
" laces, insertings, trimmings and braids	" 30	25	24	" 25
" spool and other thread	" 30	25	24	" 40
" twist, yarn, and thread, all other on spools or otherwise	" 30	25	24	" 40
Counters	" 20	30	24	" 35
Court-plaster	" 30	30	24	" 35
Cranks, mill, of wrought iron	lb. 4 cts	30	24	lb. $1\frac{3}{4}$ cts.
Crapes, silk	lb. $2.50	25	19	per cent. 40
Crash, 30 cts. or less	per cent. 25	20	15	" 35
" over 30 cts.	" 25	20	15	" 35
Cravats	" 50	30	24	per cent. 35 & 40
Crayons	" 25	30	24	" 30
Crayon pencils	" 25	30	24	" 30
Cream of tartar	free,	20	4	lb. 10 cts.
Crockery	per cent. 30	30	24	per cent. 35
Crucibles, all	p. ct. 20 & 30	30	24	" 30
Cubebs	" 20	20	15	lb. 10 cts.
Cudbear	" 10	10	4	per cent. 10
Cupboard turns	" 30	30	24	" 35
Currants	lb. 3 cts	40	8	lb. 5 cts.
Curtain rings	per cent. 30	30	24	per cent. 35
Cutch	" 10	10	free,	" 10
Cutlasses	" 30	30	24	" 35
Cutlery, all kinds	" 30	30	24	" 35
Daggers and dirks	" 30	30	24	" 35
Dates	lb. 1 ct	40	8	lb. 2 cts.
Decanters, cut	lb. 25 to 45 c	40	30	per cent. 35
" plain	lb. 14 cts	30	24	" 30
Delaines, gray	per cent. 40	30	24	" 30
" colored	" 40	30	24	p. c. 30 & s. y. 2c. val. above 40c. per s. y. 35 p. ct.
Demijohns	ea. 15 to 50c	30	24	per cent. 35
Dentifrice	" 20	30	24	" 50

	1842.	1846. per ct.	1857. per ct.	1862.
Diamonds	"	7½	10	4	" 5
" set	" 7½	30	24	" 25
" glaziers	" 25	15	12	" 10
Diaper, linen	" 25	20	15	(See Linens.)
" "	" 25	20	15	"
Diapers, cotton	" 30	25	24	(See Cotton.)
Dice, ivory or bone	" 20	30	24	per cent. 35
Dimities and dimity muslin	" 30	25	24	(See Cotton.)
Distilled vinegar, medicinal	gal. 8 cts	30	24	per cent. 40
Dolls, of every description	per cent. 30	30	24	" 35
Down, all kinds	" 25	25	19	" 30
Drawer-knobs of any material	" 30	30	24	" 35
" " entirely of cut-glass	lb. 45 cts	40	30	" 35
" " " plain do.	per cent. 25	30	24	" 30
Drawers, Guernsey, wool or worsted	" 30	30	24	(See Wool.)
Drawers, knit, without needle-work	" 30	30	24	" 35
Drawers, silk, wove	" 40	30	24	" 35
" cotton, wove	" 30	20.15&24		" 30
Drawing-knives	" 30	30	24	" 35
" pencils	" 25	30	24	gross, $1.00.
Drawings	" 20	20	8	per cent. 20
Drillings, linen	" 25	20	15	
" if cotton be a component material, subject to the regulations respecting cotton cloths	" 30	25	19	" 35
Drugs, dyeing, not otherwise enumerated	" 20	20	4	" 20
" dyeing or tanning, in a crude state	free,	20	free,	free.
" medicinal, not otherwise enumerated, in a crude state,	per cent. 20	20	15	per cent. 20
Dutch metal, in leaf	" 25	20	15	" 10
Dyeing articles, crude	" 20	20	free,	free.
Dyeing drugs, and materials for composing dyes, crude, not otherwise enumerated	" 20	20	free,	free.
Earth, in oil	lb. 1½ cts	30	24	100 lbs. 1½
" brown, red, blue, yellow, dry, as ochre	lb. 1 ct	30	15	100 lbs. 50 cts.
Earthenware	per cent. 30	30	24	per cent. 20 & 35
Ebony, manufact'res of, or of which it is the material of chief value,	" 30	40	30	" 35
Elastic garters	" 30	30	24	" 35

	1842.	1846. per ct.	1857. per ct.	1862.
Embroideries, all in gold or silver, fine, or half fine, or other metal,	per cent. 20	30	24	per cent. 35
Embroidery, if done by hand	" 30	30	24	" 35
Emeralds	" 7	10	4	" 5
Emery	free,	20	8	lb. 1 ct.
" cloth, cotton	per cent. 30	25	24	" 35
Emetic, tartar, medicinal	" 20	30	24	lb. 15 cts.
Engravings, books of, bound or not,	" 20	10	8	per cent. 20
Epaulettes, all	p.ct.25 & 30.	25&30	24	" 35
" gold	free.			
Epsom salts	per cent. 20	20	15	lb. 1 ct.
Essence, all	" 25	30	24	from 25 c. per lb. to $2 per oz. and others 50 p. ct.
Etchings or engravings	" 20	10	8	per cent. 20
Ether	per cent. 20	20	15	" 20
" sulphuric	" 20	20	15	" 20
Extract of belladonna	" 25	30	24	" 40
" Campeachy wood	" 20	20	4	" 10
" cicuta	" 25	30	24	" 40
" colocynth	" 25	30	24	" 40
" elaterium	" 25	30	24	" 40
" gentian	" 25	30	24	" 40
" hyosciamus	" 25	30	24	" 40
" indigo	" 20	20	4	" 10
" logwood	" 20	20	4	" 10
" madder	" 20	20	4	" 10
" nux vomica	" 25	30	24	" 40
" opium	" 25	30	24	" 40
" rhatania	" 25	30	24	" 40
" rhubarb	" 25	30	24	" 40
" stramonium	" 25	30	24	" 40
Extracts and decoctions of dye-woods, not otherwise provided for	" 20	20	4	" 10
Extracts, all other	" 25	30	24	" 40
Fans, all	" 25	30	24	" 35
Fastenings, shutter or other, of copper, iron, steel, brass, gilt, plated or japanned	" 30	30	24	" 35
Feathers, ornamental	" 25	30	24	" 40
" for beds	" 25	25	19	" 30
" vultures', for dusters	" 25	30	24	" 40
Fiddles	" 30	20	15	" 30
Fifes, bone, ivory, or wood	" 30	20	15	" 30
Figs	lb. 2 cts	40	8	lb. 5 cts.

	1842.	1846. per ct.	1857. per ct.	1862.
Figures, alabaster	per cent. 30	40	30	per cent. 10
" other	" 30	30	24	" 10
Filberts	lb. 1 ct	30	24	lb. 2 cts.
Files	per cent. 30	30	24	p. ct. 35 & lb. 2 c.
Filtering-stones	" 20	30	24	per cent. 20
" unmanufactured	" 20	20	15	" 10
Fire-crackers	" 20	30	24	box, 50 cts.
" irons or screens	" 30	30	24	per cent. 35
Fish, in oil	" 20	40	30	" 30
" mackerel		20	15	bbl. $2.00
" " pickled	bbl. $1.50	20	15	"
" salmon, pickled	" $2.00	20	15	" $3.00
" other " in bbls	" $1.00	20	15	" $1.50
" glue, called isinglass	per cent. 20	20	15	per cent. 30
" hooks	" 30	30	24	" 35
" sauce	" 30	30	24	" 35
" skins, raw	" 20	20	15	" 20
" skin cases	" 20	30	24	" 35
Fisheries of the U. States and their territories, all products of	free,	free,	free,	free.
Fishing-nets	lb. 7 cts	20	15	per cent. 35
Fishing-lines, silk	lb. 6 cts	30	24	" 40
Flageolets, wood, bone, or ivory	per cent. 30	20	15	per cent. 30
Flannels, except cotton	s. y. 14c.&40	25	19	p. ct. 30, valued at 30 c. p. sq.yd.
Flasks, or bottles, that come in gin cases	gross $3.00	30	24	per cent. 30
Flasks, powder, brass, copper, japanned or horn	per cent. 30	30	24	" 35
Flat-irons	lb. $2\frac{1}{2}$ cts	30	24	lb. $1\frac{1}{4}$ cts.
Flats, for making hats or bonnets,	per cent. 35	30	24	" 30
Flax, unmanufactured	ton $20	15	free,	ton $15.
" all manufactures of, or of which flax is a component part, not otherwise specified	per cent. 25	20	15	per cent. 30 to 35
Flax seed	" 5	20	15	bush. 16 cts.
Flies, Spanish, or cantharides	free,	20	15	lb. 50 cts.
Flints	free,	5	4	per cent. 10
Flints, ground	free,	20	4	" 10
Floss silk, and other similar silks purified from the gum	per cent. 25	25	19	" 30
Flour of wheat	112 lbs. 70 c	20	15	" 20
" other grain	per cent. 20	20	15	" 20
Flour, sulphur	free,	20	15	" 20
Flowers, artificial	per cent. 25	30	24	per cent. 40
Flowers, all, not otherwise provided for	" 20	20	15	" 10

	1842.	1846. per ct.	1857. per ct.	1862.
Flutes of wood, ivory, or bone.....	per cent. 30	20	15	per cent. 30
Foil, copper..............................	" 30	30	24	" 35
" silver	" 20	20	24	" 35
Foil, tin	" 2½	15	12	" 30
Forks, all	" 30	30	24	" 35
Fossils	free,	free,	free,	" 10
Frames, or sticks for umbrellas or parasols	per cent. 30	30	24	" 35
" plated cruet	" 30	30	24	" 35
" quadrant.........................	" 30	30	24	" 35
" silver cruet....................	" 30	30	24	" 35
Frankincense, a gum	" 25	20	15	" 20
Fringes, cotton..........................	" 30	25	24	" 35
" merino	" 30	25	19	" 35
Frosts, glass	" 30	20	15	" 20
Fruits, preserved in brandy or sugar	" 25	40	30	" 35
" preserved in their own juice	" 20	20	15	" 20
" pickled............................	" 20	30	24	" 35
" green, ripe, or dried.......	free,	40, 30&20	8	" 10
Frying-pans	per cent. 30	30	24	" 35
Fullers' boards	lb. 12½	30	24	" 35
" earth................................	free,	10	8	ton $3.
Furniture, coach and harness.......	per cent. 30	30	24	per cent. 35
" brass, copper, iron, or steel, not coach or harness.......	" 30	30	24	" 35
Furniture, household, not otherwise specified........................	" 30	30	24	" 35
Fur, dressed, all on the skin........	" 25	20	15	" 15
" hats or caps of......................	" 35	30	24	" 35
" hat bodies or felts.................	" 25	30	24	" 35
" muffs or tippets, or other manufactures not specified.......	" 35	30	24	" 35
Furs, hatters, dressed, not on the skin	" 25	10	8	" 20
Furs, undressed, all kinds of, on the skin	" 5	10	8	" 10
Galloons, gold and silver, fine or half-fine	" 30	30	24	" 35
Galls, nut	free,	5	4	free.
Gamboge, crude or refined............	per cent. 15	20	15	per cent. 10
Game bags, leather or twine........	" 30	30	24	" 35
Garden seeds, not otherwise specified	free,	free,	free,	" 30

	1842.	1846. per ct.	1857. per ct.	1862.
Garters, India-rubber, with clasps and of wire	per cent. 30	30	24	per cent. 35
Gelatine	" 30	30	24	" 35
Gems	" 7	10	4	" 5
Gems, set	per cent. 30	30	24	" 25
German silver, manufactured or not	" 30	30	24	" 35
Gilt fancy wares, jewelry, wire, etc.	" 25	30	24	" 35
Gimlets	" 30	30	24	" 35
Gimps, cotton	" 30	30	24	" 35
" silk	lb. $2.50	25	19	" 40
" thread, linen	per cent. 30	20	15	" 35
" wire being a component part, of chief value	" 30	30	24	" 35
Gin	gal. 60@90c	100	30	gal. $1.00 to $1.40
Ginger, green, ripe, or dried	lb. 2 cts	40	15	lb. 5 cts.
" ground	lb. 4 cts	30	24	lb. 8 cts.
" preserved or pickled	per cent. 25	40	15	per cent. 40
Ginseng	" 20	20	15	" 20
Glass, all articles not specified	" 30	30	24	" 30
" crown, plate, polished, or other window—				
not over 10×15	2 to 12 cts. pr. sq. ft.	20	15	sq. ft. 3 cts.
" 16×24		20	15	" 5 cts.
" 24×30		20	15	" 8 cts.
over 1½ lb. per sq. ft. on exc.		20	15	" 8 cts.
" apothecaries' vials, 16 oz.	gross $2.25	30	24	per cent. 30
" bottles, black	various,	30	24	" 30
" broken		20	free,	free.
" buttons, cut, entirely of	lb. 35 cts	25	19	per cent. 30
" colored	per cent. 30	30	24	" 35
" cut, engraved, colored, etc.		40	30	" 35
" disks, optical	lb. 45 cts	30	24	" 10
" green, pocket bottles	various,	30	24	" 30
" looking, plates, silvered	"	30	24	sq. ft. 4 to 60 cts.
" manufactures of, all vessels or wares, of cut glass	lb. 25 *a* 45 cts	40	30	per cent. 35
" manufactures of, all others not specially mentioned	per cent. 25	30	24	" 30
" of antimony	" 30	30	15	" 20
" paintings on	" 30	30	24	" 35
" pressed, plain or mould, not cut, colored or engraved	lb. 10 *a* 14 cts	30	24	" 30
" rough plate, cylinder,				
not over 10×15	lb. 2 to 6 cts.	20	15	sq. ft. ¾ ct.
" 16×24		20	15	" 1 ct.
" 24×30		20	15	" 1½ ct.

	1842.	1846. per ct.	1857. per ct.	1862.
Glass, rough plate, cylinder, not over 24×30, and not over 1 lb. per sq. ft...		20	15	sq. ft. 2 cts.
over 1 lb. per sq. ft. pays an additional duty on the excess at the same rates.				
Glasses, hour	per cent. 25	30	24	per cent. 35
Glauber salts	" 20	20	15	lb. ½ ct.
Glaziers' diamonds	" 25	15	12	per cent. 10
Globes	" 30	30	24	" 35
Gloves	doz. 50 cts. to $1.50 &p.ct. 30	20&30	24	per cent. 35 to 40
" hair	per cent. 25	30	19	per cent. 30
Glue, all	lb. 5 cts	20	15	" 20
Goats' skins, raw	per cent. 5	10	4	" 10
" " tanned	doz. $1.00	20	15	" 25
Gold, all articles composed of	per cent. 30	30	24	" 35
Gold leaf	" 20	15	12	500 leaves, $1.50
" beaters' brine	" 20	20	15	free.
" " moulds	" 10	10	8	per cent. 10
" " skins	" 10	10	8	" 10
" dust	free,	free,	free,	free.
" embroideries	per cent. 30	30	24	per cent. 35
" muriate of	" 25	20	15	" 20
" oxide of	" 25	20	15	" 20
" paper, in sheets, strips, or other forms	lb. 12½ cts	30	24	" 35
" shell for painting	" 20	30	24	" 35
" size	" 20	20	15	" 20
" studs	" 20	30	24	" 25
Grapes, not dried	" 20	30	8	" 20
Grass bags	sq. yd. 5 cts	30	24	" 35
" flats, braids, or plaits	per cent. 35	30	24	" 30
" hats or bonnets	" 35	30	24	" 40
" Sisal	ton $25	25	19	ton $15.
Grease	per cent. 10	10	8	per cent. 10
Green turtle	" 20	20	15	" 20
Gridirons	" 30	30	24	" 35
Grindstones	free,	5	4	" 20
" unfinished	free,	5	4	" 10
Gunny bags	sq. yd. 5 cts	20	15	" 25
Guano	free,	free,	free,	free.
" imitation of	free,	20	free,	free.
Guitars	per cent. 30	20	15	per cent. 30
Guitar strings, gut	" 15	20	15	" 30
Gum Benzoin, or Benjamin	" 15	30	8	lb. 10 cts.

	1842.	1846. per ct.	1857. per ct.	1862.
Gum copal	per cent. 15	10	8	lb. 10 cts.
" elastic articles	" 30	30	24	per cent. 35
" Senegal, Arabic, and Tragacanth	free,	10	8	" 10
" all, and all other resinous substances not specified, in a crude state	per cent. 15	20	8&15	" 20
Gum, substitute, burnt flour and starch	" 15	10	8	per cent. 20
Gums, medicinal, in a crude state,	" 15	20	15	" 20
Gun locks	" 30	30	24	" 35
Gunpowder	lb. 8 cts	20	15	less than 20 cts. 6 cts. p. lb.; over 20 cts. 6 cts. per lb. & 20 per ct.
Guns (except muskets and rifles),	per cent. 30	30	24	per cent. 35
Guts, sheeps', salted	" 20	20	15	" 20
Gutta percha, unmanufactured		20	4	" 10
Gypsum, or plaster of Paris	free,	free,	free,	free.
Hair, Angora goats', raw, 18 cts. or less	lb. 1 ct	20	15	per cent. 5
" do. do. over 18 cts.,	lb. 1 ct	20	15	lb. 3 cts.
" all manufactures of goats' or mohair	per cent. 20	25	19	per cent. 30
" bracelets, chains, ringlets, and curls	" 25	30	24	" 35
" braids, for the head	" 25	30	24	" 35
" cloth	" 25	25	19	" 30
" curled, for beds	" 20	20	15	" 20
" for head-dresses	" 25	30	24	" 35
" gloves	" 25	25	19	" 30
" nets	" 25	30	24	" 40
" pencils	" 20	30	24	" 35
" pins	" 30	30	24	" 35
" powder, not perfumed	" 20	30	24	" 50
" powder, perfumed, all others not specified	" 20	30	24	" 50
" seating	" 25	25	19	" 30
" unmanufactured	" 10	10	8	per cent. 30
" human, uncleaned	" 10	10	8	" 20
Hames, wood	" 35	30	24	per cent. 35
Hammers, not blacksmiths'	" 30	30	24	" 35
Hams, bacon	lb. 3 cts	20	15	lb. 2 cts.
Handles for chests	per cent. 30	30	24	per cent. 35
Hangings, paper	" 35	20	15	" 35
Hare skins, undressed	" 5	10	8	" 10

	1842.	1846. per ct.	1857. per ct.	1862.
Hare skins, dressed	per cent. 20	20	15	" 15
Harlaem oil	" 20	30	24	" 50
Harness	" 35	30	24	" 35
" furniture	" 35	30	various	" 35
Harps and harpsichords	" 30	20	15	" 30
Hartshorn	" 20	20	15	" 40
Hatchets	" 30	30	24	" 35
Hat felts, or bodies, of wool, not put in form or trimmed	each 18 cts	20	15	per cent. 25
Hat bodies, cotton	per cent. 30	30	24	" 35
Hats, Leghorn	" 35	30	24	" 40
" of chip, straw, or grass	" 35	30	24	" 40
" of wool	each 18 cts	20	15	" 30
" all other	per cent. 35	30	24	" 40
Hautboys	" 30	20	15	" 30
Haversacks, of leather	" 35	30	24	" 35
Hayknives	" 30	30	24	" 35
Head-dresses, ornaments for	" 30	30	24	" 35
Hemlock	" 20	20	15	" 20
Hemp, all manufactures of, not otherwise specified	" 20	20	15	per cent. 30 to 35
Hemp, a component part	" 20	20	15	per cent. 35
" Manilla	ton $25	25	19	ton, $25.
" seed	per cent. 20	10	8	lb. ½ ct.
" unmanufactured	ton $40	30	24	ton $40.
Henbane	per cent. 25	20	15	per cent. 20
Herrings	bbl. $1.50	20	15	bbl. $1.
Hides, raw and salted	per cent. 5	5	4	per cent. 10
" tanned	" 20	20	15	" 35
Hobby-horses	" 30	30	24	" 35
Hods	" 30	30	24	" 35
Hoes	" 30	30	24	" 35
Hollow-ware, tinned	lb. 2½ cts	30	24	lb. 3 cts.
Hones	" 20	20	15	per cent. 20
Honey	" 20	30	24	gal. 15 cts.
Hooks, all	" 30	30	24	per cent. 35
Hooks and eyes	" 30	30	24	" 35
Hops	" 20	20	15	lb. 5 cts.
Horn combs	" 20	30	24	per cent. 35
" plates for lanterns	" 20	30	24	" 35
" tips	" 5	5	4	" 10
Horns	" 5	5	4	" 10
Household furniture	" 30	30	24	" 35
" " of cedar, granadilla, ebony, mahogany, rose, and satin wood	" 30	40	30	" 35
Hydrometers, of glass	" 25	30	24	" 35

	1842.	1846. per ct.	1857. per ct.	1862.
Ice	free,	20	free,	free.
Imitation of precious stones	per cent. 7	10	8	per cent. 5
Implements of trade of persons arriving in the United States	free,	free,	free,	free.
India grass	ton $25	25	19	ton, $25.
" rubber, unmanufactured	free,	10	4	per cent. 10
India rubber, boots and shoes	per cent. 30	30	24	per cent. 35
" " other manufactures of India rubber	" 30	30	24	" 35
" " milk of	free,	10	4	" 20
" " suspenders	" 30	30	24	" 35
" " webbing	" 30	30	24	" 35
Indian meal	112 lbs. 20 c	20	15	" 10
Indigo	lb. 5 cts	10	4	free.
Ink	per cent. 25	30	24	per cent. 35
Ink-powder	" 25	30	24	" 35
Ink-stands, glass cut	various,	40	30	" 35
" all other	"	30	24	" 35
Instruments, philosophical	"	30	24	" 40
" " specially imported	free,	free,	free,	free.
Inventions, model of	free,	free,	free,	free.
Iodine	per cent. 20	20	15	lb. 50 cts.
" salts of	" 20	20	15	per cent. 20
Ipecac, or ipecacuanha	" 20	20	15	lb. 50 cts.
Iridium	" 20	20	15	free.
Iron, anchors	lb. 2½ cts	30	24	lb. 2 cts.
" anvils	lb. 2½ cts	30	24	lb. 2¼ cts.
" axles	lb. 4 cts	30	24	lb. 2½ cts.
" malleable iron in castings	lb. 4 cts	30	24	lb. 2 cts.
" band, hoop, and slit rods, all other	lb. 2½ cts	30	24	ton $25.
" bars, flat—1@7 in. wide, and ¼@2 in. thick (not less than 20 per cent.)	ton $25	30	24	ton $17.
" bars, round, ½@4 in. diam. do.	" 25	30	24	" $17.
" " square, ½@4 in. sq're do.	" 25	30	24	" $17.
" bed screws and wrought hinges	per cent. 30	30	24	lb. 1¾ cts.
" blacksmith hamm. & sledges,	lb. 2½ cts	30	24	lb. 2½ cts.
" boiler plates	lb. 2½ cts	30	24	ton $25.
" cables, chains, and parts	lb. 4 cts	30	24	lb. 2 cts.
" cast-iron vessels, sads, tailors' & hatters', stoves, and stove-plates	lb. 1½ cts	30	24	lb. 1¼ cts.
" cast-iron pipe, steam, gas and water	lb. 1½ cts	30	24	lb. ¾ ct.

	1842.	1846. per ct.	1857. per ct.	1862.
Iron, cast-iron butts and hinges...	lb. 2½ cts	30	24	lb. 2 cts.
" castings, all other................	lb. 1 ct	30	24	per cent. 30
" chains, trace, halter & fence of rod over ½ in...............	lb. 4 cts	30	24	lb. 1¾ cts.
" do. do. ¼@½ in..............	lb. 4 cts	30	24	lb. 2¼ cts.
" do. do. No. 9@¼ in.........	lb. 4 cts	30	24	lb. 3 cts.
" do. do. less than No. 9....	lb. 4 cts	30	24	per cent. 30
" cut tacks, brads, and sprigs, not over 16 oz. per M......	M. 5 cts	30	24	M. 2 cts.
" do. do. over 16 oz. per M.	M. 5 cts	30	24	lb. 2 cts.
" galvanized or zinc-coated....	per cent. 30	30	24	lb. 2½ cts.
" hollow-ware, glazed or tinned	lb. 2½ cts	30	24	lb. 3 cts.
" liquor..............................	per cent. 30	20	15	per cent. 10
" nails and spikes, cut..........	lb. 3 cts	30	24	lb. 1¼ cts.
" nails, spikes, rivets, and bolts, wrought..............	lb. 4 cts	30	24	lb. 2¼ cts.
" nails, horseshoe.................	lb. 4 cts	30	24	lb. 4½ cts.
" other, rolled and hammered,	ton $25	30	24	
" pig (not less than 20 per ct.)	ton $9	30	24	ton $6.
" railroad, not over 6 in. high (not less than 20 p. c.)...	ton $25	30	24	ton $13.50.
" sheet, smooth or polished...	lb. 2½ cts	30	24	lb. 2½ cts.
" sheet, all other not thinner than No. 20 wire	lb. 2½ cts	30	24	ton $23.
" sheet, No. 20@25	lb. 2½ cts	30	24	ton $29.
" " thinner than No. 25...	lb. 2½ cts	30	24	ton $35.
" slabs, blooms, loops, and more wrought than pig, and less than bars.........	ton $17	30	24	ton $17.
" taggers' iron........................	per cent. 5	30	24	per cent. 10
" wood screws, 2 in. or less....	lb. 12 cts	30	24	lb. 9½ cts.
" " " over 2 in.......	lb. 12 cts	30	24	lb. 6½ cts.
" " " wash'd or plat.	per cent. 30	30	24	
" wrought for mill, mill-cranks, ships, locomotives, steam-engines, or parts, not less than 25 lbs	lb. 4 cts	30	24	lb. 1¾ cts.
" wrought railroad chairs, nuts, & punched washers,	lb. 2½ cts	30	24	ton $30.
" wrought tubes, steam, gas, and water........................	lb. 5 cts	30	24	lb. 2¼ cts.
" all other manufactures	per cent. 30	30	24	per cent. 35
Isinglass..................................	" 20	30	24	" 30
Ivory..	free,	5	free,	" 10
" black..................................	lb. ¾ ct	20	free,	" 20
" manufactures of................	per cent. 20	30	24	" 35
" nuts..................................	free,	5	free,	" 10

	1842.	1846. per ct.	1857. per ct.	1862.
Ivory, vegetable, manufactures of.	per cent. 20	30	24	per cent. 35
Jacks for piano-fortes	" 30	20	24	" 35
" clothiers'	" 30	30	24	" 35
Jalap	" 20	20	15	lb. 50 cts.
Japanned wares, of all kinds	" 30	30	24	per cent. 40
Jellies, and all similar preparations	" 30	30	24	" 35
Jerk-beef	lb. 2 cts	20	15	lb. 1 ct.
Jet, real or composition	per cent. 20	30	24	per cent. 35
Jewelry	" 20	30	24	" 25
" false, so called	" 25	30	24	" 25
Juniper berries	" 20	20	15	" 10
" plants	" 20	free,	free,	" 30
Junk, old	free,	free,	free,	free.
Jute	ton $25	25	19	ton $15.
" carpeting	per cent. 30	25	15	sq. yd. 6 cts.
" butts	" 25	20	15	ton $6.
Kaleidoscopes	" 30	30	24	per cent. 35
Kerseys	" 40	30	24	under $1 per sq. yd. lb. 18 c. & 30 p. ct.; over, lb. 18 cts. & 35 p. ct.
Kerseymere	" 40	30	24	
Kettles, brass, in nests	" 30	30	24	per cent. 35
" cast-iron	lb. 1½ cts	30	24	lb. 1¼ cts.; copper 35 per ct.
Keys, watch, of gold or silver	per cent. 20	30	24	per cent. 25
" all other, of iron, brass, copper, gold, or silver	" 30	30	24	" 35
Kirschenwasser	gal. 60 cts	100	30	gal. 75 c. to $1.05.
Knitting-needles	per cent. 20	20	15	per cent. 25
Knives, all, of iron, steel, copper, brass, pewter, lead, or tin	" 30	30	24	" 35
Knobs, brass, gilt, plated, or washed, iron, steel, copper, or brass	" 30	30	24	" 35
Knobs, cut-glass	lb. 45 cts	40	30	" 35
" glass, not cut	lb. 12 cts	30	24	" 30
" " with brass, iron, steel, or composition shanks	" 30	30	24	" 35
Knockers	" 30	30	24	" 35
Kreosote	" 30	30	24	" 40
Labels, decanter or other, gilt or plated	" 30	30	24	" 35
Labels, decanter or other, gold or silver	" 30	30	24	" 35

	1842.	1846. per ct.	1857. per ct.	1862.
Labels, printed	per cent. 30	30	24	per cent. 20
Lac dye	free,	5	4	free.
" sulphur	free,	20	4	free.
Lace, all kinds of, made into wearing apparel	per cent. 30	30	24	per cent. 35
Lace, bobbinet	" 20	25	24	" 25
" bobbinet veils, cotton	" 30	30	24	" 35
" coach, worsted	" 35	25	19	p. ct. 35; silk, 40
" shawls, if sewed	" 30	30	24	per cent. 35
" caps, pelerines, chemisettes, handkerchiefs, collars and capes, vails, cotton	" 40	30	24	" 35
Laced boots or bootees	pair 25 to $1.25	30	24	" 35
Laces, all thread	per cent. 15	20	15	" 30
" gold and silver	" 15	30	24	" 35
Lacets, or lacings, silk	" 30	25	19	p. ct. 40; cotton, 35
Lacquered ware	" 30	30	24	per cent. 40
Ladles, iron, tin, Britannia, brass, copper, or gilt	" 30	30	24	" 35
Lake, (water colors)	" 20	30	24	" 35
" drop, do	" 20	30	24	" 35
" paints	" 20	30	24	" 25
Lampblack	" 20	20	15	" 20
Lamp hooks or pulleys, brass, copper, iron, or wood	" 30	30	24	" 35
Lamps, brass, copper, tin, or plain glass	" 30	30	24	" 35
Lamps, cut-glass	lb. 45 cts	40	30	" 35
" with glass chimneys	per cent. 30	30	24	" 35
Lancet cases	" 35	30	24	" 35
Lancets	" 30	30	24	" 35
Lanterns, japanned, tin, gilt, plated, brass, pewter, or copper	" 30	30	24	" 35
Lasting, in strips, for buttons, shoes, or bootees	" 5	5	4	" 10
Latches, iron, brass, steel, gilt, plated, washed, or copper	" 30	30	24	" 35
Lath	" 20	20	15	" 20
Laudanum	" 20	30	24	" 40
Lavender, dry, flower of	" 20	20	15	" 20
" flower	" 20	20	15	" 20
" water	" 25	30	24	" 50
Lead, all manufactures of, not otherwise specified	" 30	30	24	" 35
" black	" 20	20	15	ton $10.
" busts	" 30	30	24	per cent. 35
" combs	lb. 4 cts	30	24	" 35

	1842.	1846. per ct.	1857. per ct.	1862.
Lead, in bars	lb. 3 cts	20	15	lb. 1½ cts.
" in pigs	lb. 3 cts	20	15	lb. 1½ cts.
" in sheets	lb. 4 cts	20	15	lb. 2¼ cts.
" nitrate of	per cent. 20	20	15	lb. 3 cts.
" old	lb. 1½ cts	20	15	lb. 1 ct.
" ore	lb. 4 cts	20	15	lb. 1 ct.
" pencils	per cent. 25	30	24	gross $1.
" pipes	lb. 4 cts	20	15	lb. 2¼ cts.
" pots, black	per cent. 20	30	24	per cent. 35
" powder of black	" 20	20	15	ton $10.
" scrap	lb. 1½ cts	20	15	lb. 1 ct.
" shot	lb. 4 cts	20	15	lb. 2¼ cts.
" sugar of	lb. 4 cts	20	15	lb. 4 cts.
" toys	lb. 4 cts	30	24	per cent. 35
" white	lb. 4 cts	20	15	100 lbs. $2.40.
Leather & all manufactures where leather is chief value	per cent. 35	30	24	per cent. 35
" bracelets, elastic	" 35	30	24	" 35
" garters, elastic	" 35	30	24	" 35
" calf, tanned	lb. 8 cts	20	15	" 30
" patent	lb. 8 cts	20	19	" 35
" sole	lb. 6 cts	20	15	" 35
" upper	lb. 8 cts	20	15	" 25
Leaves for dyeing, in a crude state,	free,	20	free,	free.
" boucho	per cent. 20	20	4	lb. 10 cts.
" medicinal, in a crude state,	" 20	20	15	per cent. 20
" other, not otherwise provided for	" 20	20	15	"
Leeches	free,	20	free,	free.
Lees, wine, liquid	free,	20	15	per cent. 20
Leghorn, and all hats or bonnets of straw, chip, or grass	per cent. 35	30	24	" 40
Leghorn flats, braids, crowns, or plaits	" 35	30	24	" 30
Lemons, in bulk or in boxes, barrels, or casks	" 20	20	8	" 20
" juice	" 20	10	8	" 10
" peel	" 20	20	15	" 10
Lime	" 20	10	8	" 10
" acetate of	" 20	10	8	" 20
Limes	" 20	20	8	" 20
" juice	" 20	10	8	" 10
Linen bags	" 25	20	15	" 35
" canvas, black	" 25	20	15	" 35
" mitts	" 25	20	24	" 35
" tape	" 25	20	15	" 35

	1842.	1846. per ct.	1857. per ct.	1862.
Linens, bleached or unbleached...	per cent. 25	20	15	p. ct. 30 for 30 cts. or under per sq. yd.
" all manufactures of, not otherwise specified......	" 25	20	15	
Lines, fishing	lb. 6 cts	30	24	per cent. 35
" worsted	per cent. 30	25	19	" 35
Linseed	" 5	10	free,	bush. 16 cts.
Linseed cakes or meal	" 20	20	15	per cent. 20
Linsey-woolsey	" 40	30	24	lb. 18 cts. & p. ct. 30
Lint	" 20	20	15	" 35
Liquor, iron	" 20	20	15	" 10
" purple	" 20	20	15	" 20
" red	" 25	20	15	" 20
" tin	" 20	20	15	" 20
" cases	" 30	30	24	" 35
Liquorice paste or juice	" 25	20	15	lb. 5 cts.
" root	" 20	20	15	lb. 1 ct.
Litharge	lb. 4 cts	20	15	lb. 2¼ cts.
Lithographic stones	per cent. 20	20	15	per cent. 20
Loadstones	" 30	20	15	" 20
Lotions, all cosmetic	" 25	30	24	" 50
Lozenges, all medicinal	" 20	30	24	" 50
Locks, all	" 30	30	24	" 35
Looking-glasses, plates or frames,	" 30	30	24	" 35
Lunar caustic	" 20	30	24	" 40
Lye, soda	" 20	20	15	" 20
Maccaroni	" 30	30	24	" 35
Mace	lb. 50 cts	40	4	lb. 30 cts.
Machinery, models of, and other inventions	free,	free,	free,	free.
Machinery for the manufacture of flax and linen goods	per cent. 30	30	8	free.
Madder	free,	5	free,	free.
Madder root	free,	5	free,	free.
Magic lanterns	per cent. 30	30	24	per cent. 35
Magnesia	" 20	30	24	lb. 12 cts.
" carbonate of	" 20	30	24	lb. 6 cts.
" sulphate of	" 20	20	15	lb. 1 ct.
Mahogany, unmanufactured	" 15	20	8	free.
Mallets, wood	" 30	30	24	per cent. 35
Malt	" 20	20	15	" 20
Manganese	" 20	20	15	" 10
Mangoes	" 20	20	15	" 10
Mangroves, or shells of	" 20	20	15	" 20
Manilla grass	ton $25	25	19	ton $25
Manna	per cent. 20	20	15	lb. 25 cts.
Mantillas, silk	" 30	30	24	per cent. 40

	1842.	1846. per ct.	1857. per ct.	1862.
Mantles	per cent. 30	30	24	per cent. 40
Manufactured tobacco	lb. 10 cts	40	30	lb. 35 cts.
Maps	per cent. 20	10	free,	per cent. 20
Marble busts, as statuary	" 30	30	free,	" 10
" manufactures of	" 30	30	24	per cent. 50
" table-tops	" 30	30	24	" 50
" unmanufactured	" 25	20	15	cubic ft. 40 cts.
Marbles, toy, baked or stone	" 30	30	24	per cent. 35
Marrow	" 10	10	8	" 10
Mastic, crude	" 15	20	8	lb. 50 cts.
" refined	" 20	20	8	lb. 50 cts.
Mathematical instruments for colleges and schools	free,	free,	free,	free.
Mathematical instruments	per cent. 30	30	24	per cent. 35
Matches for pocket lights	" 20	20&30	15&24	" 35
Mats, cocoa-nut	" 25	25	15	" 30
" oil or floor-cloth, dish or table	" 30	30	24	" 35
" sheepskin	" 30	30	24	" 35
" table, tow, straw, or flag	" 25	25	19	" 35
Matting, cocoa-nut	" 25	25	15	" 30
" all floor of flags, or grass,	" 25	25	19	" 30
Mattresses, hair or moss, linen tick	" 20	20	15	" 25
Meats, prepared	" 25	40	30	" 35
Medals and other antiquities	free,	free,	free,	free.
Medicinal preparations, not otherwise specified	per cent. 20	30	24	" 40
Medicinal drugs, roots, and leaves, in a crude state, not otherwise specified	" 20	20	15	" 20
Metal, plated	" 30	30	24	" 35
Metallic pens	" 25	30	24	" 35
" slates, paper or tin	" 25	25	19	" 35
Metals, unmanufactured, not otherwise provided for	" 30	20	15	" 20
Mercury or quicksilver	" 5	20	15	" 10
" all preparations of	" 25	25	19	" 20
Merino cloth, entirely of combed wool	" 40	25	19	" 35
" cloth, wool	" 40	30	24	lb. 18 cts. & 30 or 35 per cent.
" fringe, worsted	" 30	25	19	" 35
" shawls, of wool	" 40	30	24	lb. 18 cts. & 30 or 35 per cent.
" " body worsted or combed wool	" 40	25	19	" 35

	1842.	1846. per ct.	1857. per ct.	1862.
Merino shawls, border woolen fringe, sewed on	per cent. 40	30	24	per cent. 35
" trimmings, worsted	" 30	25	19	" 35
Manilla hemp	ton $25	25	19	ton, $25.
Mica	per cent. 20	20	15	per cent. 30
Millinery of all kinds	" 40	30	24	" 35
Mill saws	each $1	30	24	ft. 12½ to 20 cts.
Mills, coffee	per cent. 30	30	24	" 35
Miniature cases, ivory	" 30	30	24	" 35
Miniatures	free,	free,	free,	" 10
Mineral and bituminous substances in a crude state, not otherwise provided for	per cent. 30	20	15	per cent. 20
Mock pearls	" 20	10	8	" 35
Modelling, specially imported	free,	free,	free,	free.
Modelling, not specially imported,	per cent. 30	30	24	per cent. 35
Models of invention, not for use	free,	free,	free,	free.
Molasses	lb. 4½ mills	30	24	gal. 6 cts.
" concentrated	lb. 4½ cts	30	24	lb. 2 cts.
Mops	per cent. 30	30	24	per cent. 35
Morocco skins	doz. $1.50	20	15	" 25
Morphine, acetate, sulphate, or crystals of	per cent. 25	30	24	oz. $2.
Mortars, brass or composition	" 30	30	24	p.ct. 35; marble, 50
Moss, Iceland	" 20	20	15	per cent. 10
" for beds	" 10	20	15	" 20
Mosaics, real, not set	" 7	10	4	" 5
" " set	" 20	30	24	" 25
Moulds, button	" 25	25	19	" 30
Mouse traps, wood or wire	" 30	30	24	" 35
Muffs, of fur	" 35	30	24	" 35
Muriate of barytes, or strontian	" 20	20	15	" 20
" gold	" 20	20	15	" 20
Music, in sheets or bound	" 25	10	4	20
Musical instruments	" 30	20	15	" 30
" instrument strings of gut,	" 15	20	15	" 30
" " " part of metal	" 15	30	24	" 35
Mushrooms, prepared	" 30	40	30	" 35
Musk	" 20	30	24	" 50
Musket barrels	" 30	30	24	" 35
" bayonets	" 30	30	24	" 35
" bullets	lb. 4 cts	20	15	" 35
" rods or stocks	per cent. 30	30	24	" 35
Muskets	stand $1.50	30	24	" 35
Myrrh, gum, crude	per cent. 15	20	15	" 20
" refined	" 20	20	15	" 20

	1842.	1846. per ct.	1857. per ct.	1862.
Nails, cut	lb. 3 cts	30	24	lb. $1\frac{1}{4}$ cts.
" wrought-iron	lb. 4 cts	30	24	lb. $2\frac{1}{4}$ cts.
Nankeen shoes or slippers	pair 25 cts	30	24	per cent. 35
Needles, all kinds	per cent. 20	20	15	" 25
" crotchet	" 30	30	24	" 35
Nests, birds'	" 20	20	15	" 20
Nets, fishing	lb. 7 cts	30	24	" 35
Nickel	free,	5	4	" 10
Nippers	per cent. 30	30	24	" 35
Nitrate of barytes	" 20	20	15	" 20
" iron	" 20	20	15	" 20
" lead	" 20	20	15	lb. 3 cts.
" silver or lunar caustic	" 20	30	24	per cent. 20
" strontium	" 20	20	15	" 20
" tin	" 20	20	15	" 20
Noyeau	gal. 60	100	30	gal. 75
Nut-galls	free,	5	4	free.
Nutmegs	lb. 30 cts	40	4	lb. 30 cts.
Nuts for dyeing, crude	free,	5	free,	free.
" all not specially mentioned,	lb. 1 ct	30	24	lb. 2 cts.
Nux vomica	free,	10	8	free.
Oakum and junk	free,	free,	free,	free.
Oatmeal	per cent. 20	20	15	per cent. 10
Oats	bush. 10 cts	20	15	bush. 10 cts.
Ochre, dry	lb. 1 ct	30	15	100 lbs. 50 cts.
" in oil	lb. $1\frac{1}{2}$ cts	30	15	" $1.50.
Ochres, all, or ochery earths, when dry	lb. 1 ct	30	15	" 50 cts.
Ochres, all, or ochery earths, in oil,	lb. $1\frac{1}{2}$ cts	30	15	" $1.50.
Odors or perfumes	per cent. 25	30	24	per cent. 50
Oil cakes	" 20	20	15	" 20
" cloth	yd. 35 cts	30	24	" 35
" fish, and all productions of American fisheries	free,	free,	free,	free.
" Harlæm	per cent. 20	30	24	per cent. 50
" hemp-seed	gal. 25 cts	20	15	gal. 23 cts.
" kerosene and other coal	per cent. 20	20	15	" 20 cts.
" linseed	gal. 25 cts	20	15	" 23 cts.
" olive, in casks	" 20 cts	30	24	" 25 cts.
" rape-seed	" 25 cts	20	15	" 23 cts.
" spermaceti, of foreign fishing.	" 25 cts	20	15	per cent. 20
Oil of cocoa-nuts	per cent. 20	10	4	" 10
" neats' foot	" 20	20	15	" 20
" palm	free,	10	4	" 10
" palm bean	free,	10	4	" 10
Olives	per cent. 30	30	24	" 30

	1842.	1846. per ct.	1857. per ct.	1862.
Onions	per cent. 20	20	15	per cent. 10
Opium	lb. 75 cts	20	15	lb. $2.
" extract of	per cent. 25	30	24	per cent. 40
Orange bitters	" 20	30	24	" 50
" crystals	" 20	20	15	" 20
" flowers	" 20	20	15	" 10
" flower water	" 20	30	24	" 50
" issue peas	" 20	30	24	" 40
" peel	" 20	20	15	" 10
Oranges	" 20	20	8	" 20
Ore, specimens of	free,	20	15	" 10
Organs	per cent. 30	20	15	" 30
Ornaments, gilt wood, gold paper, or for ladies' head-dresses, silk,	" 30	30	24	" 35
Ornaments, not for head-dresses, of metal	" 30	30	24	" 35
Orpiment	" 15	10	8	" 20
Orris-root	" 20	20	15	" 20
Osiers for baskets	" 20	20	15	" 30
Ostrich plumes and feathers	" 25	30	24	" 40
Oxymuriate of lime	" 20	20	15	" 20
" or chlorate of potasse,	" 20	20	15	lb. 6 cts.
Oysters	" 20	20	15	free.
Pack-thread	lb. 6 cts	30	24	per cent. 35
Paddy	per cent. 20	20	15	lb. ¾ ct.
Paintings on glass	" 30	30	24	per cent. 10
" porcelain	" 30	30	24	" 10
Paints, carmine	" 20	30	24	" 35
" dry or ground in oil, not otherwise provided for,	per cent. 20	20	15	" 25
" Spanish brown, dry	lb. 1 ct	20	15	100 lb. 50 cts.
" " " in oil	lb. 1½ cts	20	15	" $1.50.
" terra umbra	per cent. 20	20	15	lb. 50 cts.
" water colors	" 20	30	24	per cent. 35
" white lead	lb. 4 cts	20	15	lb. 2¼ cts.
Painters' colors	per cent. 20	20	15	per cent. 25
Palm-leaf hats or baskets	p.c. 25 & 35	30	24	40 and 35 per ct.
" leaves, unmanufactured	free,	10	free,	free.
Pannel saws	per cent. 30	30	24	per cent. 35
Paper, for screens or fireboards	" 35	20	15	" 35
" hangings	" 35	20	15	" 35
" all other, and all manufactures of	various,	30	24	" 35
Parasols, silk	per cent. 30	30	24	" 35
Parasol sticks or frames	" 30	30	24	" 35
Parchment	" 25	30	24	" 30

	1842.	1846. per ct.	1857. per ct.	1862.
Paris white, dry	lb. 1 ct.	20	15	100 lbs. 60 cts.
" " ground	lb. 1½ cts	20	15	" $1.50.
Parts of stills of copper	per cent. 30	30	24	per cent. 35
Paste almond	" 25	30	24	" 50
" imitation of precious stones,	" 7	10	8	" 35
" perfumed	" 25	30	24	" 50
" work that is set	" 25	30	24	" 30
Pastel or woad	lb. 1 ct.	10	4	free.
Paving-stones	per cent. 25	20	15	per cent. 10
Pearl, mother of	free,	5	4	free.
Pearls, all	" 7	10	4	per cent. 5
" composition	" 25	30	24	" 30
" mock	" 7	10	8	" 35
" set	" 25	30	24	" 25
Peanuts	lb. 1 ct.	20	15	" 10
Peas	per cent. 20	20	15	" 10
Pelts, salted	" 5	5	4	" 10
Pencils, black lead, camels' hair, or red chalk	" 25	30	24	gross $1 & p.ct.35
" slate	" 20	20	15	per cent. 40
Pencil cases, gold, silver, gilt, or plated	" 25	30	24	" 35
Penknives	" 30	30	24	" 35
Pens, metallic	" 25	30	24	gross 10 cts.
" quill	" 25	30	24	per cent. 30
Pepper, black or white	lb. 5 cts	30	4	lb. 12 & 15 cts.
" Cayenne, Chili, or African,	lb. 10 cts	30	4	lb. 12 & 15 cts.
Percussion caps	per cent. 30	30	15	per cent. 30
Perfumed soap for shaving	" 30	30	24	per ct. 30 & lb. 2 c.
Perfumery vials and bottles	various,	30	24	per cent. 30
Perfumes	per cent. 25	30	24	" 50
Personal and household effects, not merchandize, of citizens of the U. S., dying abroad	free,	free,	free,	free.
Peruvian bark	free,	15	free,	per cent. 20
Petticoats, ready-made, cotton	per cent. 50	30	24	" 35
Pewter, manufactures of, not enumerated	" 30	30	24	" 35
Pewter, old, fit only to be re-manufactured	free,	5	4	lb. 1 ct.
Phosphate of lime	per cent. 20	20	15	per cent. 20
" of soda	" 20	20	15	" 20
Phosphorus	" 20	20	15	" 20
Phosphorus lights, in glass bottles, with paper cases	" 20	30	24	" 35
Phosphuret of lime	" 20	20	15	" 20
Piano-fortes	" 30	20	15	" 30

	1842.	1846. per ct.	1857. per ct.	1862.
Piano-forte ferrules	per cent. 30	30	24	per cent. 35
Pickles	" 30	30	24	" 35
Pimento	lb. 5 cts	40	4	lb. 12 cts.
Pincers	per cent. 30	30	24	per cent. 35
Pincushions, cotton	" 30	25	24	" 35
" silk	" 30	25	19	" 40
Pine-apples	free,	20	8	free.
Pin or needle-cases, all	per cent. 30	30	24	per cent. 35
Pins	lb. 20 cts	30	24	" 35
Pins, silver, iron, or pound	lb. 20 cts	30	24	" 35
Pipes, clay and wood	per cent. 30	30	24	" 35
Pistols	" 30	30	24	" 35
Pitch	" 25	20	15	" 20
" Burgundy	" 20	25	19	" 20
Plaster busts, casts, statues	free,	30	free,	" 10
" court, on silk or on cambric	per cent. 30	30	24	" 35
" of Paris, unground	free,	free,	free,	free.
" " ground	" 20	20	15	per cent. 20
" " calcined	" 20	20	15	" 20
" ornaments	" 30	30	24	" 35
Plane irons	" 30	30	24	" 35
Planes	" 30	30	24	" 35
Planks, wrought or rough	" 20	20	15	" 20
Plants	free,	free,	free,	" 30
Plated wares of all kinds	per cent. 30	30	24	" 35
Plate, silver	" 30	30	24	" 35
Platina, unmanufactured	free,	free,	free,	free.
" manufactures of	per cent. 20	30	24	per cent. 35
" retorts	" 20	30	24	free.
Playing-cards	pack 25 cts	30	24	pack 15 & 25 cts.
Ploughs	per cent. 30	30	24	per cent. 35
" plane	lb. 1 ct	30	24	" 35
Plumbago	per cent. 20	20	15	ton $10.
Plumes, ornamental	" 25	30	24	" 40
Plums	" 25	30	8	lb. 5 cts.
Plush, hair	" 20	25	19	per cent. 30
" mohair or goats' hair	" 20	25	19	" 35
" or shag, worsted	" 30	25	19	" 35
" wool	" 40	30	24	lb. 18 cts. & p.ct. 25
Pocket-books, leather	" 35	30	24	per cent. 35
" paper	" 30	30	24	" 35
Pocket-bottles, green glass	gross $3	30	24	" 30
Polishing-stones	free,	10	8	free.
Pomatum	per cent. 30	30	24	per cent. 50
Pomegranates	" 20	20	8	" 10
Poppy heads	" 20	20	15	" 20
" oil	" 20	20	15	" 50

	1842.	1846. per ct.	1857. per ct.	1862.
Poppy seed	" 20	free,	free,	" 20
Porcelain	" 30	30	24	p. ct. 35 & 40
" glass	" 30	30	24	per cent. 35
" slates	" 25	25	19	" 35
Pork	lb. 2 cts	20	15	lb. 1 ct.
Porphyry	per cent. 20	30	24	per cent. 35
Portable desks	" 30	30	24	" 35
Porter, in bottles	gal. 20 cts	30	24	gal. 30 cts.
" otherwise	" 15 cts	30	24	" 20 cts.
Potasse, prussiate of	per cent. 20	20	15	lb. 5 cts.
Potassium	" 20	20	15	lb. 15 ct.
Potatoes	bush. 10 cts	30	24	bush. 25 cts.
Pots, black lead	per cent. 30	30	24	per cent. 35
" blue	" 30	30	24	" 35
" cast-iron	lb. $1\frac{1}{2}$ cts	30	24	lb. $1\frac{1}{4}$ cts.
" melting, earthen	per cent. 30	30	24	per cent. 20
Poultry, or game, prepared	" 25	40	30	" 35
Pounce	" 20	20	15	" 20
Powder, black lead	" 25	20	15	ton $10.
" blue	" 25	20	15	per cent. 20
" of brass	" 25	20	15	" 20
" puffs	" 20	30	24	" 35
" subtil, for the skin	" 25	30	24	" 50
Powders and pastes	" 25	30	24	" 50
Precious stones, glass, imitation of, set	" 25	30	24	" 30
" " of all kinds, not set	" 7	10	4	" 5
" " other imitations of,	" 7	10	8	"
set	" 25	30	24	" 35
Prepared clay	" 30	20	15	" 20
" vegetables, meats, poultry and game	" 25	40	30	" 35
Preserves in molasses and all others	" 25	40	30	" 35
Pressing-boards	lb. $12\frac{1}{2}$ cts	30	24	" 35
Prints or engravings	" 20	10	8	" 20
Prisms, cut-glass	lb. 45 cts	30	30	" 35
Professional books of persons arriving in the U. S	free,	free,	free,	free.
Protractors, ivory-mounted	per cent. 30	30	24	per cent. 35
Prunella	" 30	25	19	" 35
" for shoes, bootees, and buttons	" 5	5	4	" 10
Prunes	lb. 3 cts	40	8	lb. 5 cts.
Prussian blue	per cent. 20	20	4	per cent. 25
Pullies, iron, brass, copper or wood	" 30	30	24	" 35

	1842.	1846. per ct.	1857. per ct.	1862.
Pumice	free,	10	8	free.
Pumpkins	free,	20	15	per cent. 10
Purple, brown	per cent. 25	20	15	" 25
" tin liquor	" 25	20	15	" 20
Putty	lb. 1½ cts	20	15	lb. 1½ cts.
Quadrants and sextants	per cent. 30	30	24	per cent. 35
Quill baskets	" 25	30	24	" 30
Quills	" 15	20	15	" 30
Quiltings, or bed-quilts, cotton	" 30	25	24	" 35
Quicksilver	" 5	20	15	" 10
Quinine	" 20	20	15	" 45
" sulphate of	oz. 40 cts	20	15	" 45
Rags, of any kind, except wool	lb. ¼ ct	5	free,	free.
Raisins, boxes or jars	lb. 3 cts	40	8	lb. 5 cts.
" other	lb. 2 cts	40	8	lb. 5 cts.
Rakes, iron, steel, or wood	per cent. 30	30	24	per cent. 35
Rape of grapes	" 20	20	15	" 20
" seed	" 20	10	8	lb. 1 ct.
Rasps	" 30	30	24	35 p.ct. & lb. 2 cts.
Rattans, unmanufactured	free,	10	free,	free.
" manufactured	per cent. 20	20	24	per cent. 25
Rattles, wood, ivory, coral, or with bells	" 30	30	24	" 35
Ravens duck, hemp or flax	sq. yd. 7 cts	20	15	" 30
Razors	per cent. 30	30	24	" 35
Razor cases	" 30	30	24	" 35
" strops, wood	" 30	30	24	" 35
Reaping hooks, iron or steel	" 30	30	24	" 35
Red chromate of potash	" 25	20	15	lb. 3 cts.
" lead, ground in oil	lb. 4 cts	20	15	100 lbs. $2.40.
" precipitate	per cent. 25	20	15	per cent. 20
" Venetian, dry	lb. 1 ct	30	15	" 25
" " ground in oil	lb. 1½ cts	30	15	" 25
" wood and red sanders' wood	free,	5	free,	free.
" wool, or fur for hatters	free,	10	8	per cent. 10
Reeds, unmanufactured	free,	10	free,	free.
" manufactured	per cent. 20	30	24	per cent. 25
" weavers'	" 30	30	24	" 35
Reindeer skins, dressed	various,	20	15	" 20
" " undressed	"	5	4	" 10
" " tanned	"	20	15	" 25
" tongues	per cent. 25	20	15	" 20
Reps, natural silk and cotton	" 30	25	19	" 35
" silk	lb. $2.50	25	19	(See Silk.)
Resin	per cent. 15	20	8	per cent. 20

	1842.	1846. per ct.	1857 per ct.	1862.
Resin, of jalap	per cent. 15	20	8	per cent. 20
" nux vomica	" 15	20	8	" 40
Rhodium	" 15	20	8	" 40
Rhubarb	free,	20	15	lb. 50 cts.
Rice	per cent. 20	20	15	lb. 1½ cts.
Rifles	each $2.50	30	24	per cent. 35
Rings, all metal	per cent. 30	30	24	" 35
Rivets, brass, iron, and steel	" 30	30	24	" 35
Rochelle salts	" 20	20	15	lb. 15 cts.
Rods and eyes, for stairs	" 30	30	24	per cent. 35
Roman cement	" 20	20	15	" 20
" vitriol	lb. 4 cts	20	15	" 20
Rope, made of hides cut in strips,	per cent. 20	20	15	" 20
" or cordage of cocoanut shells	lb. 4½ cts	25	19	lb. 3½ cts.
Roots, all not otherwise enumerated	free,	free,	free,	per cent. 30
" arrow	per cent. 20	20	15	" 20
" madder	free,	5	free,	free.
" medicinal, other, crude	per cent. 20	20	15	per cent. 20
Rose leaves	" 25	20	15	lb. 50 cts.
" water	" 25	30	24	per cent. 50
Rosin	" 15	20	8	" 20
Rotten stone	free,	10	8	free.
Rouge	per cent. 20	30	24	per cent. 50
Rubies	" 7	10	4	" 5
" set	" 25	30	24	" 25
Rugs, for bed-coverings, cotton	" 30	25	24	" 35
" all other	" 40	30	24	" 35
Rules, all	" 30	30	24	" 35
Rum	gal. 60@90c.	100	30	(See Gin.)
" bay, or bay water	per cent. 20	30	24	gal. 50 cts.
" cherry	gal. 60	100	30	gal. 75 cts.
Rye	bush. 15 cts	20	15	bush. 15 cts.
" flour	per cent. 20	20	15	per cent. 10
Sabres	" 30	30	24	" 35
Saddle hooks	" 30	30	24	" 35
Saddle trees	" 30	30	24	" 35
Saddlery, all not otherwise specified	" 30	30	24	" 35
" silver-plated, brass, or steel	" 30	30	24	" 35
" tinned, japanned, or common	" 20	20	15	" 35
Saddles	" 30	30	24	" 35
Saffron	free,	20	15	" 10
" cake	per cent. 20	20	15	" 10

	1842.	1846. per ct.	1857. per ct.	1862.
Sago	per cent. 20	20	15	lb. 1½ cts.
Sail duck	sq. yd. 7 cts	20	15	per cent. 30
Sal ammoniac	per cent. 20	10	8	" 20
" diuretic	" 20	20	15	" 20
Salmon, preserved	bbl. $2	30	24	" 35
" pickled	per cent. 20	20	30	bbl. $3.
Salt, bulk	bush. 8 cts	20	15	100 lbs. 18 cts.
" otherwise	" 8 cts	20	15	" 24 cts.
Salted skivers, roans or pelts	per cent. 5	5	4	per cent. 10
Saltpetre, partially refined	lb. ¼ ct	10	8	lb. 3 cts.
" refined	lb. 2 cts	10	8	lb. 3 cts.
" crude	free,	5	4	lb. 2 cts.
Salts, chemical, all	per cent. 20	20	15	per cent. 20
Sardines, in salt	" 20	20	15	bbl. $1.50.
" and all fish in oil	" 20	40	30	per cent. 30
Sarsaparilla	free,	20	15	" 20
Sashes, silk	lb. $2.50	30	24	" 35
Sassafras	per cent. 20	20	15	" 20
Saucepans, metal	" 30	30	24	" 35
Sauces, all kinds	" 30	30	24	" 35
Sausages	" 25	30	30	" 35
Saws, cross-cut	each $1	30	24	lin. ft. 8 cts.
" mill-pit and drag	each $1	30	24	" 12½ to 20 c.
Saw sets	per cent. 30	30	24	per cent. 35
Scagliola tables or slabs	" 30	40	30	" 35
Scales	" 30	30	24	" 35
Scarfs, cotton	" 30	30	24	" 35
" wool	" 40	30	24	lb. 18 cts. & p. c. 35
Scissors	" 30	30	24	per cent. 35
Scoop-nets	lb. 7 cts	30	24	" 35
Scrapers	per cent. 30	30	24	" 35
Sea-weed, and all other vegetable substances used for beds or mattresses	" 20	20	15	" 20
Seeds, garden	free,	free,	free,	" 30
" all others not specified	free,	free,	free,	various.
Segars, worth $5 per M.	lb. 40 cts	40	30	lb. 35 cts.
" " $5–$10 per M.	lb. 40 cts	40	30	lb. 60 cts.
" " $10–$20 "	lb. 40 cts	40	30	p. c. 10 & M. 80 cts.
" " $20 "	lb. 40 cts	40	30	p. c. 10 & M. $1.
" paper	lb. 15 cts	40	30	as other segars.
Seltzer water	per cent. 20	30	24	per cent. 30
Senna	" 20	20	15	" 20
Sextants	" 30	30	24	" 35
Shades, lace, sewed	lb. $2.50	30	24	" 35
Shaving-soap	per cent. 30	30	24	p. c. 30 & lb. 2 cts.
Shawls, wool	" 40	30	24	p. ct. 35 & lb. 18 c.

	1842.	1846. per ct.	1857. per ct.	1862.
Shawls, other	p.ct. 20 & 30	30	24	per cent. 35
Shears	per cent. 30	30	24	" 35
Sheathing-metal, patent, composed in part of copper	free,	free,	free,	lb. 3 cts.
Sheathing-paper	lb. 15 cts	20	15	per cent. 10
Sheets, willow	per cent. 30	30	24	" 30
Sheetings, linen, hemp, or Russia, brown or white	" 25	20	15	" 30
Shellac	free,	5	4	lb. 10 cts.
Shell, baskets	per cent. 25	30	24	per cent. 35
" boxes, not otherwise enumerated	" 20	30	24	" 35
" turtle or tortoise	" 5	5	4	free.
Shells, all other	" 20	5	4	free.
Shingles	" 20	30	24	per cent. 35
Shoe-binding, silk	" 30	25	19	" 40
" " woolen	" 30	30	24	p.ct. 30 & lb. 18 c.
" thread	" 30	20	15	per cent. 35
Shoes or slippers for children	pair 15 cts	30	24	" 35
" " for grown persons, of silk	" 30 cts	30	24	" 35
" " of leather, for men	" 30 cts	30	24	" 35
" " of prunella, stuff, or other materials, except silk, for women	" 25 cts	30	24	" 35
Shoes, *i. e.* double-soled pumps and welts, women's leather	" 25 cts	30	24	" 35
Shot bags and belts	per cent. 35	30	24	" 35
Shovels	" 30	30	24	" 35
Shrubs	free,	free,	free,	" 30
Shuttlecocks and battledores	per cent. 30	30	24	" 35
Sickles, iron, steel	" 30	30	24	" 35
Side-arms	" 30	30	24	" 35
Silk and cotton-vesting	" 30	25	19	" 35
" and worsted valencias, toilenets or crape de Lyons	lb. $2.50	25	19	" 35
" and worsted shawls, hemmed,	per cent. 30	30	24	" 35
" " manufactures of	" 30	25	19	" 40
" aprons, collars, cuffs, chemisettes, turbans, mantillas, and pellerines	lb. $2.50	30	24	" 35
" bobbin or braids	per cent. 30	25	19	" 40
" caps, if entirely of silk	lb. $2.50	30	24	" 35
" cords	lb. $2.50	25	19	" 40
" curls	lb. $2.50	30	24	" 35

	1842.	1846. per ct.	1857. per ct.	1862.
Silk floss and other similar, purified from the gum	per cent. 25	30	19	per cent. 30
" frizettes	" 30	30	24	" 35
" garters, with wire and clasps,	" 30	30	24	" 35
" gloves	lb. $2.50	30	24	" 35
" hat-bands	lb. $2.50	25	19	" 40
" hats or bonnets for women	each $1	30	24	" 40
" hose	per cent. 40	30	24	" 35
" " sewed	" 40	30	24	" 35
" lace	lb. $2.50	25	19	" 40
" manufactures with gold or silver, or other metal	per cent. 30	30	24	" 35
" mitts	lb. $2.50	30	24	" 35
" " sewed	lb. $2.50	30	24	" 35
" not more advanced in manufacture than singles, or tram	lb. 50 cts.	15	12	" 25
" ornaments, oil cloth, suspenders, stocks	per cent. 30	30	24	p. c. 35 ; oil cl. 40
" sewing, all	lb. $2	30	24	per cent. 40
" " raw	lb. 50 cts	15	free,	" 40
" tassels	lb. $2.50	25	19	" 40
" watch-chains or ribbons	lb. $2.50	25	19	" 35
" webbing	per cent. 30	25	19	" 45
" all other articles	" 30	30	24	" 35
Silks, at $1 per yard or less	lb. $2.50	25	19	" 40
" over $1 per yard	lb. $2.50	25	19	" 40
Silver, all manufactures of, not otherwise specified	per cent. 30	30	24	" 35
" bullion and coin	free,	free,	free,	free.
" German, in sheets	per cent. 30	30	24	per cent. 35
" " manufactures of,	" 30	30	24	" 35
" plated metal, in sheets or other form	" 30	30	24	" 35
Syrup of sugar-cane	lb. 2½ cts	30	24	lb. 2 cts.
Skates, under 20 cts	per cent. 30	30	24	pair 8 cts.
" over "	" 30	30	24	per cent. 35
Skeletons	" 30	20	15	" 20
Skins, calf and seal, tanned and dressed	doz. $5	20	15	" 30
" for saddlers, etc	lb. 8 cts	20	15	" 20
" glazed, as patent-leather	per cent. 35	20	19	" 35
" goat and sheep, tanned and not dressed	doz. $1	20	15	" 25
" goat or morocco, tanned and dressed	doz. $2.50	20	15	" 25

	1842.	1846. per ct.	1857. per ct.	1862.
Skins, kid and lamb, tanned and not dressed	doz. 75 cts	20	15	per cent. 25
" kid, tanned and dressed	" $1	20	15	" 25
" of all kinds in the hair, dried, raw, or unmanufactured	per cent. 5	5	4	" 25
" pickled, in casks	" 20	5	4	" 10
" sheep, tanned or dressed	doz. $2	20	15	" 25
" with wool	" $1	20	15	" 15
" tanned and dressed, otherwise than in colors, viz.: fawn, kid, and lamb, known as chamois	" $1	20	15	" 25
Skivers, pickled	per cent. 20	5	4	" 10
" tanned	doz. $2	20	15	" 25
Slates of all kinds	per cent. 25	25	19	" 40
Sledges	lb. 2½ cts	30	4	lb. 2½ cts.
Smalts	per cent. 20	20	15	per cent. 20
Snails	" 20	20	15	" 10
Snuff	lb. 12 cts	40	30	lb. 35 cts.
Snuffers	per cent. 30	30	24	per cent. 35
Soap, all	lb. 4 cts	30	24	lb. 2 cts. & 30 & 35 per cent.
Soda, ash	per cent. 5	10	4	lb. ½ ct.
" preparations or manufactures of	" 20	20	15	
Soles, felt or cork	" 30	30	24	per cent. 35
Spars	" 30	20	15	" 20
Spa, or Spaware	" 30	40	30	" 35
Specimens, anatomical preparations	" 30	30	24	" 35
Spectacle cases, all	" 30	30	24	" 35
" glasses, not set	gross $2	30	24	" 35
" " pebble, not set.	" $2	30	24	" 35
Spectacles, all	per cent. 30	30	24	" 35
Spelter, in pigs, bars, or plates	free,	5	4	lb. 1¼ cts.
" in sheets	" 20	15	12	lb. 2 cts.
" manufactures of	" 20	30	24	per cent. 35
Spokes	" 30	30	24	" 35
Spokeshaves	" 30	30	24	" 35
Sponges	" 20	20	8	" 20
Spoons, all	" 30	30	24	" 35
Spurs	" 30	30	15&24	" 35
Spy-glasses	" 30	30	24	" 35
Starch	lb. 2 cts	20	15	p. c. 20 & lb. ½ ct.
Statues and specimens of statuary	free,	free,	free,	per cent. 10
Staves, all	per cent. 20	20	15	" 25

	1842.	1846. per ct.	1857. per ct.	1862.
Steel in ingots, bars, sheets, or wire over ¼ in. diam., valued 7 cts. or less	cwt. $2.50	15&20	15	lb. 1¾ cts.
Do. do. valued 7@11 cts	" $2.50	20	15	lb. 2½ cts.
Steel, any form not provided for	" $2.50	20	15	per cent. 25
" wire, No. 16@¼ in. in diam.	lb. 5 cts	20	15	lb. 2 cts. & p.ct. 20
" " less than No. 16	lb. 8 cts	20	15	lb. 2½ cts. & p.ct. 20
" all manufactures of	per cent. 30	30	24	per cent. 35
Stereotype plates	" 25	20	15	" 25
Still-worms	" 30	30	24	" 35
" bottoms	" 30	30	24	" 25
Stomach pumps	" 30	30	24	" 35
Stone, Armenian	" 20	20	15	" 10
" ware, common	" 30	30	24	" 20
Stones, Bristol	" 20	10	15	" 10
" mill, fit for use	" 20	10	15	" 20
" not merchantable, ballast.	" 20	20	15	" 10
" oil	" 20	20	15	" 20
Straw baskets	" 25	30	24	" 35
" carpets and carpeting	" 25	25	24	" 35
" for hats, in natural state	" 30	20	15	" 10
Stretchers for umbrellas and parasols	" 12½	30	24	" 35
Strings, bow, if gut	" 15	20	15	" 30
" hatters', if gut	" 15	20	15	" 30
" of musical instruments, if gut	" 15	20	15	" 30
Strychnine	" 20	30	24	" 30
Succory, ground	" 20	20	15	lb. 3 cts.
Sugar, raw	lb. 2½ cts	30	24	lb. 2½ to 3½ cts.
" refined, loaf, lump, crushed, pulverized	lb. 6 cts	30	24	lb. 4 cts.
" refined, tinctured or colored	lb. 6 cts	30	24	lb. 10 cts.
" syrup, concentrated molasses and melado	lb. 2½ cts	30	24	lb. 2 cts.
" white or clayed	lb. 4 cts	30	24	lb. 4 cts.
" moulds, hooped or not	per cent. 30	30	24	per cent. 35
Sulphuric ether	" 20	20	15	" 20
Sumac	free,	5	4	" 10
Surgeons' instruments, all	per cent. 30	30	24	" 35
Suspenders, all	" 35	30	24	" 35
Swans, down of	" 25	25	19	" 30
Sweatmeats or comfits, all	" 25	40	30	" 35
Sword-knots, gold and silver, fine and half-fine	" 30	30	24	" 35
" lace	" 30	30	24	" 35
" silk or worsted	" 30	25	19	" 35

	1842.	1846. per ct.	1857. per ct.	1862.
Table-tops, scagliola	per cent. 30	40	30	per cent. 35
Tallow	lb. 1 ct	10	8	lb. 1 ct.
" candles	lb. 4 cts	20	15	lb. 2½ cts.
Tamarinds	per cent. 20	20	8	per cent. 10
" preserved	" 25	40	30	" 35
Tamboreens	" 25	20	15	" 20
Tannin, medicinal	" 30	30	24	" 35
Tapers, paper, with cotton wick	" 30	30	24	" 35
" stearine	" 30	20	15	lb. 5 cts.
" spermaceti or wax	" 30	20	15	lb. 8 cts.
Tapioca	" 25	20	15	per cent. 20
Tar, Barbadoes, crude	" 15	20	15	" 20
" coal	" 15	20	15	" 20
Tarpaulings	" 20	20	15	" 20
Tartrate of antimony, or tart. emetic	" 20	20	15	b. 15 cts.
Teas, all kinds, from beyond Cape of Good Hope	free,	free,	free,	per cent. 20
Teas, other	per cent. 20	20	15	" 20
Telescopes	" 30	30	24	" 35
Thibet, cashmere of	" 30	25	19	" 35
" shawls, real or goats' hair,	" 40	30	24	" 35
" " of wool	" 40	30	24	lb. 18 c. & p. ct. 35
" " body cotton	" 30	30	24	per cent. 35
Thimbles, all	" 30	30	24	" 35
Thread, escutcheons	" 30	30	24	" 35
" pack	lb. 6 cts	30	24	" 35
Tiles, marble	per cent. 30	30	24	" 35
" paving and roofing	" 25	20	15	" 20
" encaustic	" 25	20	15	" 35
Timber, hewn or sawed	" 20	20	15	" 20
Time-pieces	" 25	30	24	" 35
Tin, all manufactures of	" 30	30	24	" 35
" banca	lb. 1 ct	5	free,	" 15
" block	lb. 1 ct	5	free,	" 15
" boxes	per cent. 30	30	24	" 30
" crystals of	" 30	20	15	" 30
" foil	lb. 2½ cts	15	12	" 30
" granulated	lb. 2½ cts	20	15	" 20
" in bars	lb. 1 ct	5	free,	" 15
" in pigs	lb. 1 ct	5	free,	" 15
" in plates	lb. 2½ cts	15	8	" 25
" " galvanized	lb. 2½ cts	15	8	lb. 2½ cts.
" in sheets	lb. 2½ cts	15	8	per cent. 25
" liquor	per cent. 20	20	15	" 20
" muriate of	" 20	20	15	" 30
" oxide of	" 20	20	15	" 30

	1842.	1846. per ct.	1857. per ct.	1862.
Tinctures, bark, and other medicinal	per cent. 30	30	24	per cent. 40
" odoriferous	" 25	30	24	" 50
Tippets, if classed as millinery	" 30	30	24	" 35
Tobacco, manufactured	lb. 10 cts	40	30	lb. 35 cts.
" leaves, or unmanufactured	per cent. 20	30	24	per cent. 25
Toilet glasses	" 30	30	24	" 35
Tongues, neats, smoked	" 20	20	15	" 20
" reindeer	" 20	20	15	" 20
" sounds	" 20	20	15	" 20
Tonqua beans	" 20	20	15	" 20
Tools and implements of trade in use by persons arriving in the United States	free,	free,	free,	free.
Tooth brushes or powders	per cent. 30	30	24	35 and 50 per ct.
" picks, all	" 30	30	24	p.ct. 35; quills,30
Toys, of every description	" 30	30	24	per cent. 35
Trays and waiters, all	" 30	30	24	p.c. 35; japan'd 40
Treacle, molasses	lb. 4½ mills	30	24	gal. 6 cts.
Trees	free,	free,	free,	per cent. 30
Trusses	per cent. 30	30	24	" 35
Tubes, cast	" 30	30	24	" 35
" wrought	" 30	30	24	" 35
Turpentine, spirits of	gal. 10 cts	20	15	gal. 15 cts.
Turtle, green	per cent. 20	20	15	per cent. 20
Twine	lb. 6 cts	30	24	" 35
Types, metal	per cent. 25	20	15	" 25
" new	" 25	20	15	" 25
" old	" 25	20	15	free.
Umber		20	15	lb. ½ ct.
Umbrellas	per cent. 30	30	24	per cent. 35
Umbrella furniture	" 30	30	24	" 35
Vanilla, beans	" 20	20	15	lb. $3.
" plants of	free,	free,	free,	per cent. 30
Varnishes, of all kinds	per cent. 20	20	15	p. c. 20 & gal. 50 c.
Vases, porcelain	" 30	30	24	per cent. 40
Vegetables, prepared	" 20	40	30	" 35
" used in dyeing, crude,	free,	5	free,	free.
" not otherwise provided for	" 20	20	15	" 10
Veils, lace, cotton, or silk	" 50	30	24	" 35
Vellum	" 25	30	24	" 35
Velvet binding, cotton	" 30	25	24	" 35
" " silk	lb. $2.50	25	19	" 40

	1842.	1846. per ct.	1857. per ct.	1862.
Velvet cotton	per cent. 30	20	24	per cent. 30
" silk	doz. $2.50	25	19	" 35
Verdigris	per cent. 20	20	15	lb. 6 cts.
Vermicelli	" 30	30	24	per cent. 35
Vermillion	" 20	20	15	" 25
Vessels, cast-iron, not otherwise specified	lb. 1½ cts	30	24	lb. 1¼ cts.
" copper	per cent. 30	30	24	per cent. 35
Vestings, cotton	" 30	25	24	
Vests	" 50	30	24	" 30
Vinegar	gal. 8 cts	30	24	gal. 6 cts.
Violins	per cent. 30	20	15	per cent. 30
Violin strings, gut	" 15	20	15	30 and 35 p. ct.
Vitriol, blue	lb. 4 cts.	20	15	" 20
" green	lb. 2 cts	20	15	lb. ½ ct.
" oil of	lb. 1 ct	10	4	lb. 1 ct.
" white	per cent. 20	20	15	per cent. 20
Wadding paper	" 30	30	24	" 35
Wafers	" 25	30	24	" 35
Wagon boxes	lb. 1½ cts	30	24	" 30
Waiters, all	per cent. 30	30	24	" 35
Walking-sticks or canes	" 30	30	24	" 35
Washes	" 25	30	24	" 50
Waste or shoddy	" 10	5	4	" 20
Watch crystals, when not set	gross $2	30	24	" 35
Watches	per cent. 7½	10	8	" 20
Watch materials and parts of watches	" 7½	10	4	" 20
Water wheels, of iron	lb. 1½ cts	30	24	" 30
" colors	per cent. 20	30	24	" 35
Wax beads	" 25	30	24	" 30
" bees', bleached or unbleach'd	" 15	20	15	" 10
" sealing	" 25	30	24	" 35
" shoemakers'	" 15	20	15	" 20
Webbing, India-rubber	" 30	30	24	" 35
Wedgewood ware	" 30	30	24	" 35
Weld	free,	5	4	free.
Wet blue	per cent. 20	20	15	per cent. 25
Whalebone, of foreign fishing	" 12½	20	15	" 20
" of American fishing	free,	free,	free,	free.
Wheat	bush. 25 cts	20	15	bush. 20 cts.
" flour	112 lbs. 70 c	20	15	per cent. 20
Whetstones	per cent. 20	20	15	" 20
Whips	" 35	30	24	" 35
Whisky, all	gal. 60 cts	100	30	(see Gin.)
Whiting	lb. 1 ct	20	15	dry, lb. ½ c.; oil, 1½

	1842.	1846. per ct.	1857. per ct.	1862.
Wick cotton or wick yarns, as cotton yarn	per cent. 30	25	24	per cent. 35
Wigs	" 25	30	24	" 35
Willows	" 25	20	15	" 20
Wines, all	gal. 6@60 c.	40	30	" 50
Wire, brass	per cent. 25	30	24	" 35
" all other	lb. 5@11 cts.	30	24	" 35
Wood, bar	free,	5	free,	free.
" Brazil	free,	5	free,	free.
" Brazilletto	free,	5	free,	free.
" camwood	free,	5	free,	free.
" chessmen	per cent. 30	30	24	per cent. 35
" dye, all in sticks	free,	5	free,	free.
" ebony and granadilla	per cent. 20	20	8	free.
" fire	" 20	30	24	per cent. 20
" lignum vitæ	" 30	30	8	free.
" log	free,	5	free,	free.
" Nicaragua	free,	5	free,	free.
" Pernambuco	free,	5	free	free.
" red	free,	5	free,	free.
" rose, satin, cedar, mahogany, and all cabinet	per cent. 15	20	8	free.
" sandals, in sticks, dust, or powder	free,	5	free,	free.
" unmanufactured, of any kind not enumerated	per cent. 20	30	24	per cent. 20
" all manufactures of, not otherwise specified	" 30	30	24	" 35
Wool, all manufactures of	" 40	30	24	p.ct. 30 & lb. 18 c.
" and hair of alpaca, goat, other like animals unmanufactured—value, less than 18 cts.	7c. or less per cent. 5	30	free,	per cent. 5
Do. do. at 18 cts.	lb. 3c. & p.c. 30	30	free,	" 5
Do. do. 18@24 cts	" "	30	24	lb. 3 cts.
Do. do. over 24 cts	" "	30	24	lb. 9 cts.
Wool, belts for paper	per cent. 25	30	24	per cent. 30
" blankets for printers	" 25	30	24	" 30
" clothing, ready made, all kinds	" 50	30	24	lb. 18 c. & p. ct. 30
" cloths, shawls, and all manufactures	" 40	30	24	lb. 18 c. & p. c. 30
" delaines, cashmeres, barege, gray	" 40	30	24	s. yd. 2c. & p. c. 30
" hats	each 18 cts.	20	15	per cent. 30
" on the skin	lb. 3c. & p.c. 30	20	15	" 15
Woolen bags	per cent. 40	30	24	lb. 18 c. & p. c. 30
" cassimere	" 40	30	24	lb. 18 c. & p. c. 30

	1842.	1846. per ct.	1857 per ct.	1862.
Woolen stockings, bindings, mitts, gloves, floor-cloth or hosiery.....	per cent. 30	30	24	per cent. 35
Woolen and worsted yarn,				
Finer than No. 14................	" 30	30	19	lb. 12 c. & p. c. 30
Value 50 cts. or less, and not finer than No. 14..............	" 30	30	19	per cent. 30
Value 50 cts. and not over $1,	" 30	30	19	lb. 12 c. & p. c. 20
" over $1..................	" 30	30	19	lb. 12 c. & p. c. 30
Worms for stills......................	" 30	30	24	per cent. 35
Wormwood, oil of	" 30	30	24	" 50
Worsted stuff, all piece goods......	" 30	25	19	" 35
" and silk shawls...........	" 30	30	24	" 35
" " " hemmed,	" 30	30	24	" 35
" " manufactures of	" 30	25	19	" 35
" all manufactures of.......	" 30	25	19	
Yams....................................		20	15	" 10
Yarns, coir		20	15	lb. $1\frac{1}{2}$ cts.
" hemp............................		20	15	lb. 5 cts.
Zinc, nails................................	per cent. 30	30	24	per cent. 35
" in pigs, or unwrought.........	free,	5	4	lb. $1\frac{1}{4}$ cts.
" in sheets.........................	" 10	15	12	lb. 2 cts.
" oxide of..........................	" 20	20	15	lb. $1\frac{3}{4}$ cts.
" manufactures of................	" 30	30	24	per cent. 35

WOOLEN GOODS PRODUCED IN THE UNITED STATES DURING THE YEAR ENDING JUNE 1, 1860.

[This valuable Table was prepared from official returns, and has never before been published.]

States.	No. of Estab-'me'ts.	Capital Invested.	Pounds of Wool used.	Pounds of Cot'n used in Satinets.	Cost of Raw Materials.	No. of Hands Employed. Male.	Fem.	Annual Cost of Labor.	Value of Product. 1850.	1860.	Per Cent. Incr'e.	Yards of Woolen Cloth.	Pounds of Yarn.	Pounds of Rolls.	Pairs of Blankets.	No. of Shawls.
Maine	63	$984,600	2,619,891	82,500	$1,091,272	593	555	$279,392	$1,022,929	$1,835,138	79.4	2,509,100	17,100	192,111	96,680	
New Hampshire	68	1,441,850	3,903,204	89,000	1,636,598	866	672	422,870	2,139,967	2,633,310	23.5	5,782,641	341,630	69,700	44,400	
Vermont	51	1,749,850	4,092,510	279,500	1,681,825	901	1,178	414,228	1,820,769	2,961,137	62.63	3,975,882	3,000	39,548		
Massachusetts	138	8,978,153	33,535,197	4,855,370	12,442,525	7,624	5,280	3,020,650	12,781,514	19,665,487	53.85	34,399,348	2,160,071	17,300	57,207	157,000
Rhode Island	57	3,168,500	6,832,600	3,056,200	4,070,224	2,593	1,636	1,069,176	2,504,700	6,915,205	176.8	19,343,600	112,800	....	....	100,000
Connecticut	84	2,491,000	7,179,819	1,472,503	4,043,124	2,308	1,459	949,020	4,974,959	6,840,220	37.49	14,301,043				
Total, N. Eng. States	461	$18,813,953	58,163,221	9,835,078	$24,965,568	14,885	10,780	$6,155,336	$25,244,838	$40,850,497	61.81	80,311,614	2,634,601	318,659	198,287	257,000
New York	195	3,211,255	7,738,884	193,683	3,564,911	2,588	1,719	1,014,803	7,605,774	6,049,017	Dec.	7,951,679	....	280,000	6,000	230,000
Pennsylvania	309	4,395,410	7,309,494	4,337,000	4,488,805	3,804	2,355	1,425,540	5,792,566	8,279,218	42.9	23,405,469	2,988,650	176,255	42,347	110,200
New Jersey	35	583,400	1,175,800	239,500	548,678	532	303	203,126	1,020,941	1,085,104	....	1,754,575	179,600	....	8,325	19,200
Maryland	30	321,200	....	....	269,355	254	133	88,008	319,240	612,092	91.7	1,153,857	16,000	7,800	515	
Delaware	6	118,000	147,500	100,000	78,807	79	38	27,888	249,510	156,635	Dec.	427,200	35,000	7,500	250	
Total, Middle States	575	$8,629,265	16,371,278	4,870,183	$8,950,496	7,257	4,548	$2,759,375	$14,988,031	$16,182,066	8.0	34,692,780	3,219,850	471,525	57,437	359,400
Ohio	163	774,560	1,602,751	....	637,533	638	207	210,756	1,513,978	1,036,467	Dec.	1,078,266	234,805	406,350	5,760	
Indiana	120	526,441	1,333,696	....	458,099	506	100	171,240	528,700	801,621	51.6	680,355	153,525	389,686	5,910	
Illinois	50	263,350	576,600	....	193,002	181	35	59,596	370,870	295,480	Dec.	176,960	71,200	252,300	1,525	
Michigan	30	133,400	308,700	....	117,295	103	54	38,856	192,043	203,566	....	172,723	16,100	136,000	140	
Wisconsin	26	118,300	356,000	....	115,149	92	31	31,560	60,105	214,790	259.0	285,000	12,500	89,000		
Iowa	28	107,980	320,700	....	109,756	121	24	30,706	112,454	184,013	63.6	133,315	25,400	144,500	910	
Missouri	97	246,085	941,714	....	283,615	186	19	54,576	358,427	458,644	27.9	358,000	4,300	719,200	370	
Kentucky	118	512,595	2,218,050	170,700	730,935	614	87	144,456	803,507	1,164,761	44.9	2,230,246	7,925	761,950	885	
Total, Western States incl'ng one in Minn.	633	$2,683,481	7,658,811	170,700	2,645,634	2,442	557	$741,806	$3,940,084	$4,357,842	10.6	5,114,865	525,755	2,899,586	15,500	
Virginia	108	523,570	1,476,520	10,000	496,194	457	115	123,660	826,746	859,749	....	1,007,714	21,000	329,210	1,500	
North Carolina	28	252,900	594,390	....	180,641	137	140	64,680	71,470	331,133	363.0	639,000	....	82,000		
South Carolina	10	60,800	303,800	....	75,920	50	55	13,440	15,100	100,062	562.0	300,000	....	49,175		
Georgia	30	263,400	1,088,530	142,500	286,767	192	217	68,592	....	500,261	....	1,435,060	....	79,000		
Alabama	16	151,500	348,635	5,000	115,570	109	103	37,596	21,800	234,949	977.0	613,410	....	84,000		
Louisiana	1	75,000	69,150	....	31,300	40	20	6,720	....	45,200	....	48,800				
Texas	10	73,600	171,150	18,000	50,230	51	7	12,120	22.000	75.796	244.0	94,976	....	86.250		
Mississippi	10	90,500	328,997	75,600	143,459	215	36	25,728	31,670	188,357	494.0	569,203	....	58,000	150	
Arkansas	11	33,000	125,500	....	36,240	22	5	5,340	8,800	45,476	416 0	....	....	125,000		
Tennessee	70	88,300	470,665	....	165,258	100	10	21,720	111,225	227,872	104.0	18,000	....	460,000		
Total, South'n States	294	$1,612,570	4,977,337	251,000	$1,581,579	1,373	708	$379,596	$1,108,811	$2,608,855	135.0	4,726,103	21,000	1,352,635	1,650	
Aggregate, incl'ing 4 mills, Pacific States	1,967	$31,900,939	88,804,319	15,200,061	$38,234,532	25,926	16,618	$10,087,773	$45,281,764	$64,243,260	41.3	124,897,862	6,401,206	5,061,405	314,874	616,400

COTTON GOODS MANUFACTURED IN THE UNITED STATES DURING THE YEAR ENDING JUNE 1, 1860.

(This valuable Table was prepared expressly for this work from Official Returns, and has never before been published.)

States.	No. of Estab.	Capital Invested.	Pounds of Cotton used.	Value of Raw Material.	No. of Spindles	Looms.	No. of Hands. Male.	No. of Hands. Fem.	Annual Cost of Labor.	Value of Product in 1850.	Value in 1860.	Incr. per ct.	Yards of Cott'n Cloths	Pounds of Cott'n Y'rn & Thread.	Pounds of Batting.	Yards of Print Cloths.
Maine,	19	$6,018,325	23,733,165	$3,319,335	281,056	6,877	1,828	4,936	$1,368,888	$2,630,616	$6,235,623	140.8	60,377,000	481,823	200,000	3,000,000
New Hampshire.	44	12,586,880	51,002,324	7,128,196	636,788	17,336	3,829	9,001	2,888,604	8,861,749	13,699,994	50.4	151,713,609	221,000	290,000	25,621,750
Vermont	8	271,200	1,447,250	181,030	17,600	362	157	222	78,468	280,300	357,450	27.5	4,030,000	576,000	95,000	2,100,000
Massachusetts ...	217	33,704,674	134,012,759	17,224,592	1,673,498	42,779	13,691	24,760	7,798,476	21,394,401	38,004,255	77.58	415,291,438	3,776,340	3,200,000	76,691,280
Rhode Island	153	10,052,200	41,614,797	5,799,223	814,554	17,315	6,353	7,724	2,847,804	6,495,972	12,151,191	87.05	147,652,300	5,072,114	306,240	79,734,837
Connecticut	129	6,627,000	31,891,011	4,028,406	435,466	8,675	4,028	4,974	1,743,480	4,122,952	8,911,387	116.14	78,161,000	2,282,250	1,557,000	24,539,515
Tot'l, N. E. States.	570	$69,260,279	283,701,306	$37,680,782	3,858,962	93,344	29,886	51,617	$16,725,720	$43,785,990	$79,359,900	81.24	857,225,347	12,409,527	5,648,240	211,687,382
New York	79	$5,366,579	23,945,627	$3,030,216	348,584	7,885	3,017	4,552	$1,380,252	5,019,323	6,611,528	31.72	68,157,121	1,715,480	2,466,466	40,144,418
Pennsylvania	185	9,208,440	37,496,203	7,396,888	476,979	12,994	6,431	8,580	2,774,460	5,812,126	13,673,439	135.25	114,395,986	9,739,181	2,072,500	14,025,200
New Jersey	44	1,316,550	9,094,649	1,242,610	123,548	1,567	982	1,490	459,892	1,289,648	2,952,688	121.20	12,593,610	4,121,742	678,050	6,000,000
Delaware	11	582,500	3,403,000	570,102	38,974	986	520	589	220,224	538,439	941,703	74.89	12,220,000	603,128	300,000	....
Maryland	20	2,254,500	12,880,119	1,698,413	51,835	1,670	1,093	1,594	576,780	2,021,396	2,973,877	42.16	20,356,031	33,120	182,000	....
Dist. of Col'mbia.	1	45,000	294,117	47,403	2,560	83	70	25	19,800	100,000	74,400	decr.	980,000	....	....	....
Tot'l, Midd. St'tes.	340	$18,773,569	87,113,715	$13,985,632	1,042,480	25,185	12,113	16,830	$5,431,408	$14,780,932	$27,227,635	84.2	228,702,748	16,212,651	5,699,016	60,169,618
Ohio	8	$265,000	3,192,500	$374,100	19,664	540	372	466	$151,164	$594,204	723,500	21.7	4,100,000	1,300,000	932,000	....
Indiana	2	251,000	1,813,944	229,925	11,000	375	177	190	84,888	86,660	344,350	......	3,800,303	....	166,600	....
Illinois	3	4,700	95,000	11,930	....	......	10	1	2,640	....	18,987	......	....	....	94,700	....
Missouri	2	169,000	990,000	110,000	5,000	80	85	85	30,600	142,900	230,000	......	1,000,000	500,000	90,000	....
Kentucky	6	244,000	1,826,000	214,755	8,192	76	130	116	41,280	445,639	315,270	decr.	71,350	1,439,600	298,000	....
Utah	1	6,000	12,000	6,000	70		4	3	3,420	....	10,000	......	....	10,000	....	....
Tot'l, West. St'tes.	22	$939,700	7,929,444	$946,710	43,926	1,071	778	861	$313,992	$1,269,403	$1,642,107	29.	8,971,653	3,249,600	1,581,000	
Arkansas	2	$37,000	187,500	$11,600	....	......	14	11	$4,428	17,360	23,000	......	100,000	....	....	....
Tennessee	30	965,000	4,072,710	384,548	29,850	243	323	576	139,180	508,481	698,122	37.29	1,981,400	2,801,968	14,400	....
Virginia	16	1,367,543	7,544,297	811,187	49,440	2,160	694	747	260,856	1,446,109	1,489,971	......	11,064,557	908,184	25,000	....
North Carolina	39	1,112,750	5,540,738	601,364	41,884	761	446	1,290	185,220	985,411	1,005,567	......	4,605,072	3,451,485	....	....
South Carolina	17	801,825	3,978,061	431,525	30,890	525	343	549	123,300	842,440	713,050	decr.	5,866,018	1,000,708	....	....
Georgia	33	2,126,103	13,907,904	1,466,375	85,186	2,041	1,131	1,682	415,332	1,395,056	2,371,207	69.97	17,850,034	4,594,480	....	....
Florida	1	30,000	200,000	23,600	1,600	20	40	25	7,872	49,920	40,000	decr.	149,000	120,000	....	....
Alabama	14	1,316,000	5,246,800	617,633	35,740	623	543	769	198,408	398,585	1,040,147	160.96	7,610,668	1,647,000	....	....
Louisiana	2	1,[illegible]00,000	1,995,700	226,600	6,725	150	220	140	49,440	....	466,500	......	2,376,000	550,000	....	....
Mississippi	4	230,000	698,800	79,800	6,344	90	106	109	36,264	22,000	176,328	......	1,130,509	196,000	....	....
Texas	1	450,000	588,000	64,140	2,700	100	130		15,600	....	80,695	......	719,400	....	....	....
Tot'l, South. St'tes	159	$9,436,221	43,960,510	$4,718,372	290,359	6,713	3,989	5,898	$1,435,900	$5,665,362	$8,104,587	43.	53,352,658	15,369,82[illegible]	39,400	
Aggregate	1,091	$98,409,769	422,704,975	$57,331,496	5,235,727	126,313	46,766	75,206	$23,907,020	$65,501,687	$116,334,229	77.6	1,148,252,406	47,241,603	12,967,956	271,857,000

INDEX TO VOL. II.

www.ingramcontent.com/pod-product-compliance
Lightning Source LLC
LaVergne TN
LVHW021105110826
845150LV00001B/173